D -
D1917149

ATLANTIC STUDIES ON SOCIETY IN CHANGE

NO. 134

Editor-in-Chief, Ignác Romsics
Founder, Béla K. Király

HUNGARY UNDER SOVIET DOMINATION

1944–1989

György Gyarmati
and
Tibor Valuch

Translated by Sean Lambert
Copyedited by Matthew Suff
Typeset by Andrea T. Kulcsár

Social Science Monographs, Boulder, Colorado
Atlantic Research and Publications, Inc.
Highland Lakes, New Jersey

Distributed by Columbia University Press, New York
2009

EAST EUROPEAN MONOGRAPHS, NO DCCXXXIX

The publication of this volume was made possible by grants from
The National Cultural Fund
and the Hungarian Institute of International Affairs

Nemzeti Kulturális Alap

Magyar Külügyi Intézet
Hungarian Institute of International Affairs

All rights reserved, which include the right to reproduce this book or portions thereof in any form whatsoever, without the written permission of the publisher.

Copyright © 2009
by Atlantic Research and Publications, Inc.

ISBN 978-0-88033-637-6
Library of Congress Catalog Card Number 2008936735

Printed in Hungary

Table of Contents

Preface to the Series

The present volume is a component of a series that is intended to present a comprehensive survey of the history of East Central Europe.

The books in this series deal with peoples whose homelands lie between the Germans to the west, the Russians, Ukrainians and Belorussians to the east, the Baltic Sea to the north and the Mediterranean and Adriatic Seas to the south. They constitute a particular civilization, one that is at once an integral part of Europe, yet substantially different from the West. The area is characterized by a rich diversity of languages, religions and governments. The study of this complex area demands a multidisciplinary approach, and, accordingly, our contributors to the series represent several academic disciplines. They have been drawn from universities and other scholarly institutions in the United States and Western Europe, as well as East and East Central Europe.

The editor-in-chief is responsible for ensuring the comprehensiveness, cohesion, internal balance and scholarly quality of the series that he has launched. He cheerfully accepts these responsibilities and intends this work to be neither justification nor condemnation of the policies, attitudes and activities of any person involved. At the same time, because the contributors represent so many different disciplines, interpretations, and schools of thought, our policy in this, as in the past and future volumes, is to present their contributions without major modifications.

The authors of this volume are distinguished historians. György Gyarmati is holder of a candidate's degree in historical sciences, chief director of the State Security Services Historical

Archives. His primary research area is Hungarian political and social history in the second half of the 20th century. Tibor Valuch is DsC. historian, senior researcher at the Institute for the History of the 1956 Hungarian Revolution. His main research area is twentieth-century Hungarian social and cultural history.

Budapest, March 15, 2009

Ignác Romsics
Editor-in-Chief

I. THE RECONSTRUCTION OF STATEHOOD AND THE PROVISIONAL PERIOD

1. Antecedents: A Fragmented Country

The guns fell silent on Europe's World War II battlefields in May 1945. Combat had ended in Hungary, the Third Reich's neighbor to the east, just three weeks previously. In order to understand Hungary's post-World War II fate, one must consider a few prior events that had a significant impact on later developments. These precursors took place primarily in the spring and autumn of 1944.

Forces from Nazi Germany invaded Hungary, which had been fighting in alliance with the Third Reich, on March 19, 1944. Hitler ordered the invasion after discovering that the Hungarian government under the leadership of Prime Minister Miklós Kállay had sought contacts with the Western powers, above all Great Britain, following Germany's decisive defeats at El-Alamein and Stalingrad. Berlin thus came to view its already reluctant Hungarian ally as politically unreliable, undermining the Wehrmacht's strategic position in southeastern Europe, particularly in the light of the situation in Italy and the effectiveness of the Tito-led resistance in Yugoslavia. Following Germany's invasion, Hungary and Regent Miklós Horthy, who had served as the country's head of state for 25 years, lost nearly all of what remained of their previously limited capacity for sovereign action. The aforementioned might require some explanation. The government of Prime Minister Döme Sztójay, who had served as Hungary's ambassador to Berlin prior to the German invasion, was inclined to provide Hitler with unconditional support. Miklós Horthy, however, was operating under the assumption that the Axis powers would lose the war, and believed that his continuing influence over Hungary's General Staff, which had sworn loyalty to him, offered some scope for action. Moreover, there remained an informal political coalition around Horthy that, like the regent, maintained hope that Allied (British) troops would reach the country via Croatia from Italy ahead of Red Army troops advancing from the southeast. Anglo-American wartime propaganda, which was aimed primarily at deceiving the Germans, nourished this hope. The doctrinaire anti-Bolshevism of interwar Hungarian public opinion also contributed to this groundless "waiting for the West" even in the midst of an increasingly obvious transformation in the balance of power and the situation on the front. With the once-distant Soviet specter drawing relentlessly near, a segment of both Hungary's political elite and society at large clung ever more tenaciously to this desperate hope.

The Western Allies had attempted through covert diplomatic and intelligence channels to persuade Miklós Horthy to establish contact with the Soviets. It was only after Romania changed sides in August 1944, however, that Hungary's political leadership realized that the "division of labor" among the Allied powers that had begun the process of crushing the Third Reich would bring the Soviet Red Army to the eastern part of the European continent. The regent finally sent a covert delegation to the Soviet Union under the leadership of Hungary's former military attaché to Moscow, General Gábor Faragho, at the end of September 1944. On October 11, the Hungarian delegation concluded a preliminary armistice agreement, which Horthy wanted to invoke as soon as possible. This was the regent's objective when he announced in a radio address on October 15, 1944, that Hungary had dropped out of the war. Horthy had originally planned to make the announcement somewhat later, around October 20, since arrangements for it had to be made before the very eyes of Hungary's newly reinforced German occupiers. Horthy's decision to bring the date forward was based on both Soviet pressure and secret intelligence that Arrow Cross leader Ferenc Szálasi, whom the Germans had come to support, was organizing a far-right putsch.

The fact that Horthy had been compelled to make the announcement earlier than originally planned played a role in Hungary's failure to drop out of the Axis alliance. However, the disloyalty of a portion of the military leadership, which continued to believe in Germany's "ultimate victory," was also a major factor contributing to the fiasco. Many of those officers who remained loyal to Regent Horthy, who also bore the title of commander-in-chief, interpreted the October 15 proclamation as a mere political declaration of intent, having received no clear military orders in this regard.

Hungary's attempt to drop out of the war collapsed before it even got off the ground. The Germans kidnapped Horthy's son, the threat to whose life they used to blackmail the regent into retracting the announced armistice, abdicating and handing leadership over the country to Ferenc Szálasi. The latter used a hastily assembled faction of Parliament to invest himself with the title of "national leader," which concentrated the powers of prime minister, head of state and commander-in-chief in his hands. As Hungary's unqualified leader, Szálasi proclaimed undying loyalty towards Nazi Germany. Beyond military defeat, Szálasi's continued support of the Germans also foreshadowed Hungary's legal classification as a vanquished power at the end of the war.

British Prime Minister Winston S. Churchill was also in Moscow conducting negotiations in the middle of October 1944. During his negotiations at the Kremlin, Churchill, disregarding the formal appurtenances of diplomatic concord, reached the so-called percentage agreement with Soviet leader Joseph Stalin, the tacit division of Europe into spheres of interest by means of which the Soviet Union would receive priority in determining the post-war political reorganization of east-central and southeastern Europe. Moreover, the Soviets were able to further boost their share of influence over Hungary as a result of the increased military effort and losses that would be required to subdue the country under the leadership of the staunch German ally Szálasi. As Soviet Minister of Foreign Affairs Vyacheslav Molotov wrote in his memoirs,

“I participated actively in the formation of the first Hungarian government… I established it, and rather quickly.”[1] This statement was not a mere reflection of Molotov’s heightened self-awareness as a policy-maker.

The failure of Hungary’s attempt to leave the Axis powers produced very unique circumstances with regard to the country’s political reconstruction at the end of the war, as well as, for a time, territories of extremely diverse “status.” The agreement signed in Moscow required Hungary to withdraw its state authority to the borders of the country defined in the 1920 Treaty of Trianon. As a consequence, several frontier regions, most of which contained a Hungarian majority, entered a transitional period in which they were legally “ownerless.” In addition to suffering the ordeals associated with the passing front, many people living in these territories, particularly Transylvania and southern Hungary, fell victim to nationalist-inspired anti-Hungarian atrocities. More than 100,000 people from these areas sought refuge within Hungary’s Trianon borders.[2]

Soviet forces had already penetrated deeply into the eastern half of Trianon-demarcated Hungary when the Arrow Cross regime came to power. By the time that Ferenc Szálasi had formed his own government and decreed “total mobilization” in support of Germany, he only exercised control over that part of Hungary lying to the west of the River Danube. In the meantime, the Red Army had reached the River Tisza and had vanguard units within 90 kilometers of Budapest. The evacuation of Hungary’s state administration from Budapest began at the beginning of November, which prompted a significant portion of the city’s civilian population to flee as well. At the same time, Hitler ordered that Hungary’s capital city be held at all costs. Retreating German and Hungarian troops destroyed strategically important roads and railways and blew up Danube bridges. In Budapest, both regular troops and Arrow Cross paramilitary units attempted to eradicate as many as possible of those Jews who had escaped deportation earlier in the year.[3]

While Szálasi's military and government administration established itself in Hungary's westernmost city of Sopron (and its environs), an increasing number of the country's citizens resided in a "no-man's-land" lacking any kind of state administration. Meanwhile, there existed no valid base of authority within the country to negotiate essential issues, such as the execution of the armistice agreement, with Soviet leaders representing the Allied powers. The political power vacuum that emerged following Miklós Horthy's downfall impelled Moscow to place increased emphasis on the role of Hungarian communist émigrés, many of whom had spent decades living in Soviet exile. In 1944, these émigrés had produced several documents outlining their various concepts regarding the planned political transformation of Hungary. Most of these initially envisioned an immediate communist takeover following the return of the Communist Party's leaders from exile, although subsequent variations gradually reduced their focus to winning the sympathy of a broader segment of society. Contemporary communist jargon referred to this as being of a "people's front" character, with the aforementioned Churchill–Stalin meeting having played an important role in promoting movement in this direction. The Kremlin's preferred communist predominance in the domain of east-central and southeastern Europe's political reconstruction was distinctly palpable in Poland and Bulgaria. The Anglo-American Allies repeatedly protested at the preponderance of communist power in these countries. Stalin was still somewhat receptive to the objections of his allies, and thus compelled Hungarian émigré Communist leaders in Moscow to devise a more moderate program, one that might work within the framework of a coalition government. Stalin thought that propagation of such a program might also help to win the support of citizens living in those parts of Hungary still under Szálasi's control and perhaps even prompt some units of the military to disavow the country's Arrow Cross national leader. Moreover, a more moderate communist platform would be less likely to alienate those living behind the front in eastern Hungary and would make collaboration with other Hungarian parties involved in political reorganization possible.

Hungary's former statehood ceased to exist during the autumn and winter of 1944. The Arrow Cross regime that had come to power under the auspices of Germany's military-diplomatic administration of occupation could hardly be characterized as constitutional. At the same time, there existed no other forum of power to represent Hungary's constitutional statehood. Moreover, not only did the "revisionist Hungary" whose borders had been expanded in several stages around the beginning of World War II fall apart at this time, but the so-called "mutilated Hungary" established via the Treaty of Trianon in 1920 disintegrated as well. Tens of thousands of employees of Hungary's state administration flooded the roads in flight before the advancing "Soviet horde," along with retreating German and Hungarian military forces and hundreds of thousands of civilians. Many Hungarians fled from the regions of Upper Hungary, Sub-Carpathia, Transylvania and southern Hungary, which had become virtual no-man's-lands where they were exposed to the threat of atrocity and aggression as a result of a stipulation contained in the preliminary cease-fire prescribing the return of Hungary's borders to their pre-1938 position. Almost all of the war-ravaged country lay in ruins. Those on the roads towards the west were just as fearful that stragglers from the German army would deprive them of their horses and wagons as they were that marauding Soviet soldiers would plunder their remaining personal possessions or seize them for so-called *málenkij robot* ("a little work")—forced labor in the Soviet Union that could last for many years. During these months, Hungary was more a historical-geographical concept than an existing social-political entity.

2. Debrecen: The First Phase of the Provisional National Government

Communist leaders arriving in Hungary began to reorganize their party behind the advancing front in November 1944 under the name Hungarian Communist Party (HCP), first in Szeged, a city lying along the River Tisza near the southern border of the country, and in the agricultural regions of eastern Hungary known as the Stormy Corner (Viharsarok). In accordance with Moscow's expectations, these Communist leaders sought the collaboration of Horthy-era opposition party representatives in establishing an institution representing Hungary's new statehood. The most radical element of the preliminary Communist Party program, which at Moscow's insistence had been moderated to include the preservation of private property and multi-party democracy, was the radical transformation of Hungary's previous system of land ownership. The parties that were to play a significant role in Hungarian political affairs over the coming years, such as the Independent Smallholders' Party (IShP), the Social Democratic Party (SDP), the National Peasant Party (NPP) and the Civil Democratic Party (CDP), all reconstituted themselves in these same locations during the month of November 1944, largely without their previous leaders. These parties had all operated in opposition for various lengths of time during the Horthy era until their prohibition following the German occupation of Hungary.

At the beginning, the aforementioned parties organized behind the front using "anybody who happened to be around." At the beginning of December, representatives of these parties, along with communist delegates who had arrived from Moscow, jointly founded the Hungarian National Independence Front, which established contact with the leaders of the anti-fascist Great Power coalition. This political forum requested that it be allowed to establish institutions of state power representing "the other Hungary" to stand in opposition to the Szálasi regime. After the multi-party front received permission from the Great Powers to establish such institutions, two members of the Hungarian Communist Party leadership, Ernő Gerő and Imre Nagy, flew back to Moscow, where they engaged in consultations with members of Miklós Horthy's September cease-fire delegation and, in just two or three days, finalized the planned pace and stipulations of Hungary's new statehood after receiving instructions from Kremlin leaders. Gerő and Nagy decided to include four members of the aforementioned Horthy cease-fire delegation in the soon-to-be-formed Provisional National Government, while Stalin insisted that only two HCP members be appointed to the initial cabinet. The composition of the Provisional National Government was designed, on the one hand, to serve as a message to those living under the Szálasi regime, as well as the military's officer corps, that the "Horthyites" would have nothing to fear if they repudiated the Arrow Cross and switched allegiance to the multi-party front. On the other hand, Moscow intended the arrangement to serve as a demonstration to the Anglo-American Great Powers that, contrary to the situation in Poland and Bulgaria, there were no plans for a communist-dominated system change in Hungary.

Practical preparations for the establishment of the Provisional National Assembly began in December 1944. Rapidly organized people's assemblies in the Soviet-occupied region of eastern Hungary delegated representatives to the future Parliament through public acclamation. Due to a lack of vehicles and the danger of travel in the occupied territories, Soviet military vehicles were used to transport nominated delegates to Debrecen, the largest city in eastern Hungary, where the Provisional National Assembly was established on December 21. Around 35 percent of the Assembly's 230 delegates belonged to the Hungarian Communist Party, whereas the party's own estimates placed the total number of Communists in Hungary at 3,000, or not even 0.1 percent of the country's population. Social Democrats and Smallholders each accounted for a further 25 percent of the Assembly's delegates, while the remaining 15 percent of the body was composed of National Peasant Party, Civil Democratic Party and independent representatives. Jurist Béla Zsedényi was appointed as president of this truncated Parliament, which, because it included representatives from roughly only half of Hungary, declared itself entitled to pass only resolutions, not laws.

In accordance with a preliminary agreement made in Moscow, General Miklós Béla Dálnoki was named as president of the Provisional National Government formed at the same time as the Provisional National Assembly. General Dálnoki, who had served as the director of Miklós Horthy's military bureau and, later, as commanding general of the Hungarian First Army, defected with part of his staff to the Soviets at the time of Hungary's unsuccessful attempt to drop out of the war. In addition to Dálnoki, three other members of the Moscow cease-fire delegation, notable non-Communist Party independents from the *ancien régime*, were appointed to the cabinet. (One of the three was Géza Teleki, the son of former Prime Minister Pál Teleki, who had committed suicide when Hungary entered World War II.) In accordance with Stalin's instructions, the Communist Party had only two official ministers in the government, Minister of Agriculture Imre Nagy and Minister of Commerce József Gábor. However, nominally independent Minister of Social Welfare Erik Molnár had earlier been a member of the then-illegal Communist Party, while National Peasant Party Minister of the Interior Ferenc Erdei secretly joined the Hungarian Communist Party around the time of his appointment to the cabinet. (This was not a rare phenomenon during these years, when HCP members who functioned officially within the ranks of another party were referred to as crypto-communists.) Two members of the reorganizing Social Democratic Party and two members of the Independent Smallholders' Party also received positions in the government, although only IShP Minister of Foreign Affairs János Gyöngyösi retained his post throughout the so-called provisional period. The Soviet guardian overseeing the birth of Hungary's new statehood instituted a provisional Hungarian government whose composition included both a sufficient number of its protégés and enough *de facto* and nominal non-Communist Party members to appease Anglo-American fears of communist hegemony.

The Provisional National Assembly regarded itself as a repository of Hungary's new statehood, to be instituted as part of the country's radical system change, although at the outset the mere fact of its establishment was considered to be of primary importance. The Assembly was actually no more than a virtual (and truncated) parliament, which held a total of only two sessions before Christmas and was not subsequently reconvened for more than nine months, until September 1945. The Assembly did, however, take the significant steps of putting an end to Hungary's legal interregnum and authorizing the Provisional National Government to sign the cease-fire agreement with representatives of the Great Powers on January 20, 1945. Although military operations dragged on in the Transdanubian half of Hungary until April 1945 and the Szálasi government continued to function in exile from Austria until the end of March, Hungary's involvement in the war ended with the signing of this armistice agreement. In fact, the Provisional National Government declared war on Germany amid a total lack of constitutionality on December 28, 1944, and thus Hungary closed the war as a *de jure* belligerent, although organization and deployment of Hungarian forces pursuant to the cease-fire agreement never did take place. (The Presidential Council abrogated the formal state of war between Germany and Hungary only ten years later, via statutory decree 9/1955.)

The cease-fire agreement signed in Moscow circumscribed Hungary's state sovereignty in its establishment, as in other defeated countries, of the Allied Control Commission to oversee compliance with the stipulations of the armistice. As a result of competition between the Allied powers, Allied Control Commission legations from the power whose military forces had occupied a given country often attempted to play a dominant role in the affairs of that country. Since Hungary had fallen within the Red Army's sphere of operations, Lieutenant General Kliment E. Voroshilov was appointed as chairman of the Allied Control Commission in the country, serving as the leader of the body until being replaced by his deputy, General Vladimir P. Sviridov, during the spring of 1946. Allied Control Commission advisor Georgij M. Pushkin, who subsequently served as the Soviet Union's ambassador to Hungary, also exercised a significant influence over the Commission's operations.

The Soviet leadership of the Allied Control Commission in Hungary was free to make its own decisions regarding the scope of its authority to oversee implementation of the cease-fire agreement. It is for this reason that on several occasions over the subsequent months Voroshilov was able to prevent the Provisional National

Assembly from reconvening to address critical unresolved legal issues. The list of concerns over which the Soviet leadership of the Allied Control Commission claimed authority is long indeed: the foundation and operation of political parties, the launching of newspapers, government dismissals and appointments, the nomination of county administrative leaders, the foreign travel of Hungarian citizens, including that of the country's reconstituted diplomatic corps, and the way in which Hungary conducted its interstate relations. The National Supreme Council established to temporarily exercise the authority of head of state also came into being as a constitutionally ambiguous product of political considerations. In sum, although Hungary was formally in the process of establishing a multi-party parliamentary system, from the very outset this nominal transformation occurred under circumstances of sharply circumscribed statehood and impaired domestic and foreign political sovereignty.

The reorganization of Hungary's state administration at the end of World War II was similarly fraught with contradiction. One of the Provisional National Government's first enactments, ratified at the beginning of January 1945, was to essentially revive Hungary's former institutional structure. For a period of several months, however, there were no competent government institutions functioning in the eastern half of Hungary, where local state administration had collapsed in the wake of the front as it rolled westward across the country beginning in the autumn of 1944. This situation endured for a varying length of time even following the establishment of the Provisional National Government. With German and Soviet requisitions and depredations having largely crippled Hungary's transport and communications systems, functioning central executive agencies were severely limited in their scope of authority. Dissemination of government directives was thus extremely slow and haphazard. This vacuum in the exercise of state administration and authority inevitably compelled communities to engage in autonomous local organization in order to ensure their basic daily subsistence. At the local level, there were three domains that at the time required urgent community-based social cooperation and organization: public health, work and provision. These public efforts included mass burials, disposal of animal carcasses, delousing, medical treatment and care for women who had become pregnant or infected with venereal diseases after being raped by Soviet soldiers, and provision of scarce commodities such as matches, paraffin oil and salt, as well as fulfillment of Soviet military requisitions and mandates, such as the repair of bridges and roads and the provision of food. The need to satisfy these imperatives was the main factor prompting the establishment of these variously named local or national committees during the period of interregnum in the discharge of state authority and information. With state authority having disintegrated at its higher levels, these committees were initially compelled to conduct both administrative and executive duties, as well as to being forced to perform *ad hoc* legislative and judicial functions.

With the aforementioned government decree having stipulated the revival of Hungary's former state administrative structure and the national committees already functioning at the grass-roots level, the building up of Hungary's institutions of state authority had by the spring of 1945 become a synthesis of diverse processes. The claim to authority that the national committees had acquired through their "virtue of necessity" had to be revoked if the traditional organizational structure of Hungarian state administration was to be reestablished. It was precisely in these national committees that the Communists discerned the embodiment of the desired "popular and democratic" character of Hungary's transformation. The Communists thus emphasized the political importance of the committees, even as they strove to paralyze them since the Communist Party did not have full control over their operations. Because the Communists were the first to recognize that the foci of local authority would become the nucleus of Hungary's reconstituted state administration, they preceded others in placing their more competent party cadres in "traditional" administrative positions.

The announced establishment of Hungary's new statehood, based on the country's former state administrative structure, produced both a general dissonance between words and deeds and numerous everyday problems. The most conspicuous of these was a minimization of state activities and the attendant reduction of the "democratic" transformation of Hungary's institutions of state administration to mere politically motivated personnel changes. A so-called verification process, in which a committee was established to "examine the *conduct* of civil servants subsequent to the date September 1, 1939, to determine whether it was inimical to the interest of the Hungarian people," underpinned these changes. This retroactive examination of prior conduct rather than concrete activity implicitly opened the door for subjective verdicts. Another factor contributing to the subjectivity of this process was the fact that the verification committees were composed of delegates from political parties that wanted to have as many of their cadres as possible in positions of state administration. As a result, a remarkably paradoxical commonality of interests arose between those conducting the verifications and those being verified. Civil servants who felt that they needed support in order to obtain the verification required to retain their jobs were often eager to join one of the functioning political parties, which were happy to accommodate such "verification seekers" as a means of increasing their base of support. This created a situation in which the members of various parties sitting on the committees engaged in tacit deals of the "you assent to the verification of the former Horthyite in our party and I will assent to the verification of the former Arrow Cross sympathizer in yours" type. This politically motivated "human trade" was widespread in the spring and summer of 1945. This process was applied to an expanding number of state administrative offices as time went on, with both allied and rival parties carefully monitoring one another's relative strength within the ranks of the country's state administration all the way down to its lower echelons. Little by little, these "coalition-equilibrium" criteria were extended to support staff and office assistants at state institutions, and even local council midwives, gravediggers and furnace stokers.

The only substantial modification of Hungary's institutional executive power structure that took place at this time was the disbanding of the Hungarian Royal Gendarmerie and the establishment of a unified Hungarian State Police in its place. The effective strength of this new police force was set at 30,000, the combined size of Hungary's two previous law enforcement organizations in 1944, although this number had risen to 47,000 by the end of the year. The Communist Party dominated this new police force from the outset. The Communists controlled just a relative majority of around 40 percent of Hungary's ever-mutating state administrative apparatus in 1945–1946, although they held a majority of its leading positions from the beginning. The overrepresentation of the HCP was even greater in the so-called Political Security Division, which served as a virtual Communist political police. Serving as the head of this division was Gábor Péter, who had operated as an illegal Communist agent for the Soviet secret services since the 1930s. One of Péter's deputies was a Hungarian communist émigré who had become a colonel in the NKVD and worked in the Political Security Division on "service assignment" until the spring of 1947. The function of this police division was just as much to act as a Communist auxiliary force in the evolving domestic political power struggle as it was to perform practical duties related to the prosecution of war criminals.

3. Budapest: The Second Phase of the Provisional National Government

The front had passed over Hungary's western border by the middle of April 1945. It was at this time that the Provisional National Government moved from its initial headquarters in the city of Debrecen in eastern Hungary to Budapest, which lay in ruins following an intense month-and-a-half-long siege. This is also when Hungary began to assess the devastation suffered during the war. Approximately 440,000 provincial Jews had been deported to concentration camps by the autumn of 1944, more than six times the number of men taken prisoner by the Soviets on the front. Those subject to persecution and internment in Hungary following Ferenc Szálasi's rise to power in October 1944 can be divided into three main groups. In cooperation with the Germans, the Arrow Cross regime's "party service" had set its sights on the roughly 250,000 Jews remaining in Budapest, confining them to ghettos, executing them along the banks of the Danube and deporting them to Germany. The Red Army and its special SMERSH units had taken nearly 300,000 people prisoner as they pushed through Hungary from the east and southeast between October 1944 and the end of March 1945. Approximately one third of these captives were civilians destined for Soviet labor camps. A further 250,000 Hungarian citizens were deported to the east between the conclusion of military hostilities and the end of 1945. Most of the latter were Hungarians who had fled to the territory of the collapsing Third Reich before the approaching front, in compliance with the Szálasi regime's evacuation order. Some 300,000 of the nearly one million Hungarians who fled westward were taken captive in the parts of Austria and Germany occupied by the Anglo-American Allies. Most of these 300,000 captives, both soldiers and civilians, had returned home by the summer of 1947. Only 150,000 of the approximately 600,000 Hungarians deported to the Soviet Union had returned by this time. A further total of around 250,000 Hungarians had returned from the Soviet Union by the end of the "officially registered" releases in 1951, while another 10,000 finally made their way home over the following five years. The majority of the latter contingent were released from the Gulag prison camp network following Stalin's death in 1953. Addition of all the numbers of returning Hungarian captives suggests that nearly one third of those deported to the Gulag camps died or disappeared in the Soviet Union, most of them without a trace.

In addition to the above, further coercive measures induced a modern-day migration of peoples in the region of Europe including Hungary following the end of the war. Nearly 200,000 "Swabians" were forced to leave Hungary as part of the general expulsion of Central and Eastern European Germans sanctioned in the Potsdam decrees. Around 70,000 Hungarians and an equal number of Slovaks "switched countries" pursuant to an agreement on population exchange, concluded under political pressure between the Hungarian and Czechoslovak governments at the beginning of 1946. (A further 40,000 Hungarians either fled or were unilaterally expelled from Slovakia to Hungary.) Some 300,000 Hungarians moved or fled to Hungary from various European states, including neighboring countries, during the immediate post-war period. A portion of these was composed of those people who had sought refuge following the anti-Hungarian massacres perpetrated by Romanians in eastern Transylvania in the autumn of 1944 and by Yugoslavs in southern Hungary at the turn of 1944–1945. Approximately 200,000 non-prisoners of war returned to Hungary from refuge in the West, while an equal number chose to remain abroad permanently. In material terms, approximately 40 percent of Hungary's national wealth was destroyed during the war, including a staggering 60 percent of the country's roads, railways, bridges and road and rail vehicles.

Armed conflict continued to rage in the western half of Hungary when the Provisional National Government launched its most far-reaching socio-economic and political program, land reform, in the eastern half of the country. Hungary was still an agrarian state at the time of World War II, with the majority of the country's population deriving its subsistence from agricultural activities. Hungary's traditional preponderance of large estates, most of which were in the hands of the Church and the nobility, continued to represent the country's most significant source of potential socio-political conflict during the interwar period. Just a little over than 1,000 families with benefices of more than 575 hectares owned nearly one third of Hungary's agricultural land, while 1.2 million dwarf holdings of 0.575 to 2.875 hectares accounted for a total of only 10 percent of the country's arable land, and the more than 200,000 smallholders with between 2.875 and 5.75 hectares of land owned an even smaller percentage than that.[4] In other words, although 85 percent of Hungary's landowners were either dwarf holders or smallholders, they owned a total of less then one fifth of the country's agricultural land. Moreover, there were an additional three million Hungarians who derived their subsistence from agriculture although they owned no land whatsoever.[5]

Diagram 1:
Size structure of land ownership, 1935, 1946 and 1949 (cadastral hold)
[1 cadastral hold = 0.57 hectares]

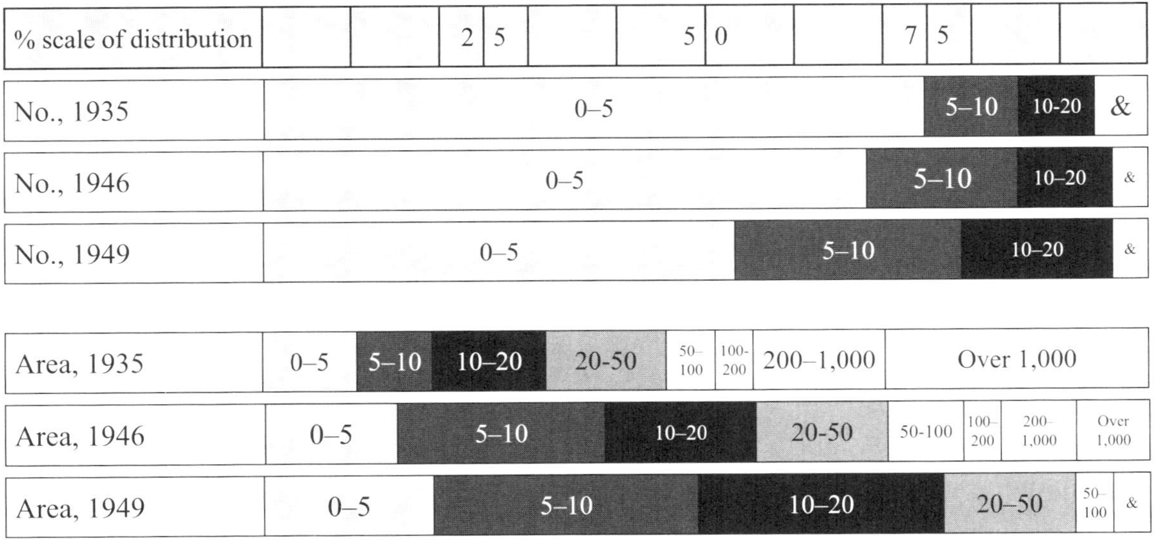

& = all higher size categories together (20–50, 50–100, 100–200, 200–1,000, over 1,000), which in number amount to a fraction of 1%, which cannot be shown for technical reasons, but amount to a sizeable proportion in aggregate area, as the lower group of lines shows.

The parties gathered in a pro-reform coalition at the end of the war all agreed on the importance of seizing the opportunity to eliminate Hungary's traditional ecclesiastical and secular large-estate structure of land ownership. There were, however, differences in the viewpoints of the various parties with regard to the magnitude and means of land reform. The Independent Smallholders' Party placed emphasis on the establishment of so-called medium-sized peasant holdings that would be capable of market-oriented production, while the National Peasant Party and the Hungarian Communist Party advocated distributing smaller portions of land to many more people. The IShP land distribution concept can be considered to have been more rational from an economic standpoint, while that of the NPP and the HCP would have produced a more radical socio-political change to Hungary's agrarian structure. It was, however, the viewpoint of a third, completely external, entity that was to determine the outcome of the debate between the parties: the Soviet president of the Allied Commission. General Voroshilov believed that the war might be brought to an end sooner if Hungarian soldiers fighting for the Germans learned that land awaited them if they returned home, behind the front lines. Soviet airplanes dropped several million leaflets regarding the impending land reform throughout Transdanubia in the hope of triggering mass desertions from Hungarian military units. Although the Soviet front propaganda proved to be far from effective, it did decide the outcome of the land reform dispute between Hungary's political parties. The Provisional National Government's land reform decree was eventually based on the more radical HCP-NPP concept. The Communists also hoped that the fact that HCP Minister of Agriculture Imre Nagy would oversee the political-administrative tasks related to the redistribution of land would provide their party with a boost in popularity.

Some 75,500 large estates were confiscated or appropriated, with the promise of later compensation, as a prerequisite to the planned land redistribution program. (The estates of prominent members of the Arrow Cross and Hungary's far-right movement, as well as those of landowners found to have committed war crimes, were subject to confiscation.) A total of only 3.22 million hectares, or just under 60 percent, of the land thus acquired was redistributed to the people, while 28 percent of it (mostly woodland) was designated as state or cooperative property. Cities and communities used the remaining fraction of this land for common pastures and housing. Around 640,000 people received land as part of the redistribution program, two thirds of whom had been landless agricultural workers, dwarf holders and smallholders. The average size of the distributed plots was 2.875 hectares, thus greatly increasing the number of people classified as smallholders. This land redistribution nevertheless failed to meet demand. Nearly half of Hungary's eligible agrarian poor, several hundreds of thousands of agricultural workers and dwarf holders, received no land at all as part of the reform program. The only way of resolving this inadequacy would have been to appropriate a larger portion of market-producing medium-sized peasant holdings, which would not only have placed Hungary's food supply in jeopardy, but would have turned the landowning peasantry against the new system as well. A more extensive program of land reform would have thus been both economically and politically counterproductive.

Both the nearly half a million new landowners and the one million long-time peasant smallholders experienced considerable difficulty in cultivating their newly acquired or existing land. Agricultural implements confiscated from the large estates were insufficient in number to provide for the needs of Hungary's new landowners, a deficiency that was again exacerbated by the failure to redistribute all of the seized implements. War damage to peasant farms served to aggravate this situation. Literally one third to one half of Hungary's peacetime stock of draft animals would have been required for the production of bread grain on peasant farms, whose number had now increased by one quarter (whereas only 45 percent of Hungary's stock of cattle and 36 percent of the country's stock of horses remained following the wave of military requisitions). Indicative of the state of peasant agriculture at this time was the fact that there was one horse for only every six farms following the passing of the front, compared to one for every other farm before the war.

The government that was distributing land with one hand was forced to almost immediately begin levying contributions with the other, apparently failing to calculate the catastrophic reduction in the production capacity of Hungary's agricultural sector in the formulation of its tax and "compulsory delivery" decrees. Village farmers learned in the spring of 1945 that the government had decided to raise their taxes by one third compared to the previous year in order to help to cover the cost of reconstruction. Soon thereafter, at the time of that year's harvest, a new tax category related to Hungary's defeat in the war was introduced, the "reparations contribution." Those who had owned land prior to the redistribution were subjected to a vastly elevated "vae victis!" tax, which stipulated that "double the sum of last year's contribution be remitted immediately in the form of tax for the first half of the current year, in view of the fact that this year's tax contribution is expected to be four times higher than that of last year."[6] During the second half of 1945, the government began to back its increasingly frequent tax impositions with threats of repossession, auctioning and internment, indicating that a progressive rise in interest on overdue payments had generated a burdensome increase in the arrears of insolvent peasants. In order to compensate for losses due to inflation and to increase its own stocks of food, the government also began to collect taxes in both cash and kind.

The reconstruction of Hungary's affairs of state accelerated following the Provisional National Government's move to Budapest. First, representatives from Budapest were included in the Provisional National Assembly; then, at the beginning of the summer, delegates from the Transdanubian region of western Hungary were appointed to the Assembly through expedited procedures referred to as elections. The establishment of new public offices and reorganized state institutions proceeded at the same bustling pace as efforts to clear rubble and to repair the transport infrastructure and production facilities. Many of the newly appointed staff at these public offices were incompetent political appointees. Popular tribunals began the process of bringing those considered to be war criminals to justice with equally great intensity. Those who during the wartime years had not compromised themselves to the degree necessary to merit prosecution in court, but whose relationship to the former regime qualified them as *persona non grata* in the new system, were placed in increasingly crowded internment camps.

Most of the *ancien régime*'s political proponents, the military General Staff and a broad segment of the state administration, had fled at the end of the war and did not return to Hungary. The landowners who remained in the country were subjected to confiscation of their wealth even if they were the target of no other official proceedings. Moreover, the former public and official functions of the landowning class were tightly connected to the vanished ethos of "gentlemanly Hungary," and thus it was not only for political reasons that this class was not included in the reorganization of the country's sociologically transformed institutional system. (This social stratum's mistrust and rejection of what it understandably regarded from its own perspective as a slipshod new regime that had no respect for the "sanctity of private property" also played a role in its exclusion from the process of rebuilding Hungary's institutions of state.) In any event, the features and characteristics of Hungarian public life had undergone a truly rapid and drastic change by the end of the summer of 1945. The effort of Hungary's newly emerged or reactivated parties to extend their activities to every corner of the country, naturally in competition with one another, was an enormous factor in this transformation. A literally continual succession of well-attended popular assemblies, party recruitment campaigns and promotional events took place throughout the country. There was, however, a very pragmatic reason for the popularity of these events: people hoped to cross paths with somebody who could provide them with at least a small piece of information regarding family members or relatives who had disappeared during the wartime tempest. The practically endless list of names published under the title

"Who Knows Something about this Person?" in local newspapers bears testament to this quest for information regarding vanished kinsfolk.

Great Power politics also played a role in the politicization of everyday public life in Hungary during this period. Although the Anglo-American powers acknowledged the Soviet-sponsored formation of Hungary's new statehood, they were reluctant to recognize the country's Provisional National Government. Citing the Yalta Conference Agreement, the Anglo-American Allies predicated recognition of the new Hungary on the establishment of a truly democratically elected parliament and government. This condition coincided the most closely with the ambitions of recently returned Hungarian émigré communists, who by the end of the summer had come to believe that the Hungarian Communist Party had taken a significant lead in the months-long inter-party competition for popularity and new recruits. When in the middle of August Allied Control Commission Chairman Kliment Voroshilov pressed Provisional National Government leader Miklós Béla Dálnoki to hold parliamentary elections, he did so not only to satisfy the Anglo-American Allies, but to exploit the perceived popular superiority of the Mátyás Rákosi-led Hungarian Communist Party as well. Rákosi was so confident in his party's strength that he asserted at an electoral assembly in late September that, in alliance with the Social Democrats, "a captivating victory of the workers' parties looms on the horizon." Another HCP leader, ideological and cultural chairman József Révai, predicted that that the Communists and the Social Democrats would together win 70 percent of the votes in the impending elections.

The Provisional National Assembly, which had only existed on paper since its initial two-day session in December 1944, had to be reconvened in order to provide the legal foundations for parliamentary elections. The Assembly's Budapest session began during the first week of September, when it passed several previous government decrees into law by oral vote. The Assembly also ratified an expedited election law, although it was the only case in which the body observed traditional codification procedures—proposal, general and detailed debate and adoption. The new election law excluded several social categories from those to whom the right to vote had been extended, a logical extension of anti-fascist provisions that had already been implemented during the period. Conversely, this legislation eliminated previous restrictions regarding wealth, education and gender, inscribing into Hungarian law a universal, egalitarian and secret ballot. The electoral system established as part of the legislation was based not on individual candidates, but on district party lists, with surplus votes to be applied towards supplementary mandates drawn from national party lists.

There were several characteristics unique to the subsequent electoral campaign. One of them was the fact that it was enough to voice rejection of the interwar *ancien régime* with mere rhetorical flourishes, since it was evident to everybody that the outcome of the war had produced its permanent extinction. It was well known that the coalition imperative of the provisional period would persist, thus mitigating the degree of campaign enmity between the naturally competing, although still interdependent, parties. The Independent Smallholders' Party advocated establishing the socio-political structure of "popular-democratic Hungary" on civil parliamentary foundations rooted in a fortified class of landed farmers. Even in communist rhetoric, emphasis of these same watchwords merely reflected an exhortation to bring about radical change. With regard to what the Hungarian Communist Party viewed as its primary social base, the industrial workforce, the party naturally advocated the intensive industrialization of what was still an agrarian country. The HCP nevertheless attempted to win votes within Hungary's large agrarian population by claiming primary responsibility for the rapid and radical land redistribution that had just been implemented.

Contemporary Hungarian public opinion expected the parties to express a position regarding the country's international status and peace prospects, particularly with regard to the permanent settlement of its post-war borders. Campaign speakers attempted to avoid the latter issue, with the Communist and National Peasant

Parties particularly inclined to substitute the expulsion of a portion of Hungary's German population as a foreign policy theme. There was also agreement among the parties that gaining the favor of the Great Powers would be to Hungary's practical benefit, although there was a divergence in the emphasis that they placed on achieving this objective. The Communists placed esteem for the Soviet Union and its "liberating Red Army" in the forefront, while the other parties hoped to secure a "just peace" for Hungary by gaining the support of all the victorious Allied powers in equal measure.

Municipal elections held in Budapest and its environs on October 7, 1945, represented a kind of preliminary measure of party strength in advance of the impending National Assembly elections. Communities on the outskirts of Budapest, most of which had become contiguous with the capital city, although they continued to maintain their autonomy, were included in these elections due to the fact that 60 percent of Hungary's industrial workers were concentrated in the greater urban agglomeration. The Communists and Social Democrats stood a particularly good chance of winning votes cast in this so-called *red zone*. This prospect materialized partially when the joint "workers' unity front" of the HCP and the SDP received the most votes in the working-class settlements outside Budapest, such as Csepel, Kispest, Pesterzsébet, Pestszentimre and Soroksár. The Independent Smallholders' Party, however, swept many districts of Budapest, particularly those on the Buda side of the Danube, such as the Castle, Víziváros, Rózsadomb, Hűvösvölgy, Lágymányos and Kelenföld, where they won over 70 percent of the vote. In all, the IShP won an absolute majority of 50.5 percent of the vote in Budapest, 8 percent more than the workers' parties. It was evident from a tally of the variously colored ballots that female voters had dictated the outcome of the elections: whereas men had voted in nearly equal number for the IShP and the HCP, 53 percent of women voted for the Smallholders, while only 40 percent voted for the Communists.

The results of the National Assembly elections held on November 4, 1945, confirmed the hopes and fears associated with those held in greater Budapest less than a month earlier, expectations that opinion polls had forecast with great accuracy: a solid and absolute victory for the Independent Smallholders' Party. For the distribution of seats in the Hungarian legislature between 1944 and 1949, see the diagram on page 95.

These National Assembly elections represented a turning point in the history of Hungary's post-war political system in several regards. Since the consequences of the vote will be examined in the next chapter, only a few observations regarding the elections will be made here. The first one concerns the number of parties permitted to participate in the ballot. Although several new parties had begun to organize following the "Debrecen period," the Soviet leadership of the Allied Control Commission granted only one of them—the civil-leftist Hungarian Radical Party (HRP)—a license to operate officially. This factor also played a role in the transformation of the Independent Smallholders' Party (57 percent) into a so-called *umbrella party*, a qualifier retained to this day. In addition to the IShP's primary base of support reflected in the party's name, the Smallholders attracted the votes of those from practically every segment of society who were skeptical of the parties viewed as having the closest ties to the Soviets. Not only the Communists (17 percent) and the Social Democrats (17 percent) belonged to the latter category. The National Peasant Party (7 percent) was from its beginning commonly considered to be the Communists' agrarian "branch party." The minute size of Hungary's urban bourgeoisie, much of which had either not survived the war or emigrated, is duly reflected in the fact that two parties of contrasting character—the left-liberal Hungarian Radical Party and the more conservative Civil Democratic Party—together received less than 2 percent of the vote in the National Assembly elections.

Secondly, seen from another perspective, one might conclude that the party structure permitted by the Allied Control Commission was not an accurate reflection of Hungary's contemporary body politic. As a result of the Soviet Union's more direct influence over the party formation process, only a limited multi-party system emerged in Hungary following World War II. The victorious Great Powers, however, collectively supported the introduction of such a system following the war, whereas the Declaration on Liberated Europe envisioned the formation of a broad anti-fascist government coalition. In Hungary, the latter resulted in the government coalition winning almost all of the seats (97 percent) in Parliament. There was no significant opposition in Parliament, since no such opposition had even been permitted to organize. The election results suggested that nearly "the entire country was pro-government." Thirdly, a unique demographic as well as socio-political characteristic of the elections was the multiple increase in the number of female voters, while several hundred thousand male voters were unable to participate in the elections because they were sitting in Allied prison camps throughout Europe.

And finally, an observation derived from a brief look at the entire continent of Europe. In those countries liberated by the Anglo-American Allies, such as France and Italy, the Communist and/or Social Democratic Parties won a majority in the immediate post-war elections, while Hungary was the only country in Soviet-dominated Central and Eastern Europe in which a party representing a civil parliamentary system gained an absolute majority in these elections.

Notes

1 Lajos Izsák and Miklós Kun, *Moszkvának jelentjük... Titkos dokumentumok, 1944–48* [We Report to Moscow... Secret Documents, 1944–48] (Budapest, 1994), p. 288.

2 Ignác Romsics, *Az 1947-es párizsi békeszerződés* [The 1947 Paris Peace Treaty] (Budapest, 2006), pp. 75–85, and Enikő A. Sajti, *Impériumváltások, revízió, kisebbség. Magyarok a Délvidéken, 1918–1947* [Exchanging Empires, Revision, Minority. Hungarians in Southern Region, 1918–1947] (Budapest, 2004), pp. 319–340.

3 Mária Ormos, *Magyarország a két világháború korszakában, 1914–1945* [Hungary in the Era of the Two World Wars, 1914–1945] (Debrecen, 1998), p. 178.

4 Sándor Szakács, *A népi demokratikus agrárfejlődés kezdetei Magyarországon, 1945–1948* [The Beginning of People's Democratic Agrarian Development in Hungary, 1945–1948] (Budapest, 1971), p. 8.

5 The land area of Hungary is approximately the same as that of the US state of Indiana.

6 János Botos, György Gyarmati, Mihály Korom and Tibor Zinner, *Magyar hétköznapok Rákosi Mátyás két emigrációja között* [Everyday Life in Hungary between Mátyás Rákosi's Two Periods of Emigration] (Budapest, 1988), p. 46.

II. THE PERIOD OF POWER DUALISM

1. Rivalry within the Coalition

The histories of modern democracies generally devote more space to election years. Election periods are eventful, with the emergence of new or transformed party organizations, the analysis of the campaign and subsequent voting results, the description of governments and their initial "course-changing" measures, and so on, all requiring increased attention. The history of Hungary's elections in the five years following the end of World War II departs considerably from this rule. This is due partially to the fact that general elections were held in Hungary every other year during this period, and thus no Hungarian Parliament completed its traditional four-year cycle, and partially to the radical changes in the domestic political environment that took place in the country during non-election years. Parliamentary elections held in 1947 and 1949 essentially served to sanctify the political transformations that had taken place during the intervening years. The year 1946 and the first half of 1947 represented such periods of transformation, as will be discussed below. The most significant aspect of these periods was the successful effort of the Independent Smallholders' Party's coalition partners and *de facto* rivals to prevent that party from exploiting its political supremacy.

Nominations to state and cabinet offices corresponded largely to the results of the 1945 National Assembly elections, the first expression of public volition providing the new system with social legitimacy. Ferenc Nagy of the Independent Smallholders' Party was appointed as speaker of the National Assembly, while Reformed clergyman Zoltán Tildy, also of the IShP, was appointed as prime minister. Cabinet nominations were not, by contrast, always based on the outcome of the elections. The aforementioned Yalta Conference agreement, for example, stipulated the maintenance of coalition government, and thus the IShP was not able to govern alone, in spite of having an absolute majority of seats in the National Assembly. It was the personal intervention of Allied Control Commission President Kliment Voroshilov, however, that partially served to prevent the IShP from attaining all its desired cabinet positions. Conflict regarding the formation of the government centered on the post of minister of the interior, an office responsible for the direction of the police and public administration, which the Independent Smallholders' Party relinquished to the Hungarian Communist Party under Soviet pressure. (Imre Nagy, the former HCP "minister of land distribution," was appointed to the post.) The other cabinet office exercising control over an armed force, that of minister of defense, was at the time considered to be much less important, since the Hungarian military operated under the immediate supervision of the Allied Control Commission in the period prior to the conclusion of the peace treaties. Had the Ministry of the Interior, however, not been under the direction of the Communists, it would have been much more difficult to secure the direct influence and intensive collaboration of "Soviet advisors."

Negotiations regarding the distribution of the other cabinet posts were much less contentious, with the Independent Smallholders' Party eventually gaining a total of nine portfolios, the same number as the other coalition parties combined. However, just one month later, the Hungarian Communist Party managed to alter this parity to its own benefit and to the detriment of its coalition partners. A so-called Economic Supreme Council was established to coordinate Hungary's production capacity with efforts to repair war damage and fulfill post-war reparations obligations. The HCP member Zoltán Vas, another returned Moscow émigré, was appointed as general secretary of this body, furnishing him with a broad overview of the economy and authority over a matter that fell under the competency of all the economic cabinet posts. Through its control over the Economic Supreme Council, the HCP managed to gain a decisive influence over the functions of the Hungarian economy. At the same time, it was possible for the Communists to publicly castigate ministries under the control of other parties for the fitful pace of reconstruction and disruptions in the supply of staple commodities. This notably took place during the winter of 1945–1946, when catastrophic shortages, particularly in the cities, triggered the outbreak of a succession of hunger-fueled strike movements. (We will consider the broader ramifications of this later.)

Following its consideration and adoption of the new government program, the National Assembly formed following the 1945 general elections turned its attention towards another urgent issue related to Hungary's socio-political transformation—determining the country's form of government. The Habsburg dynasty, the last to rule Hungary, had been deposed more than a quarter of a century earlier, in 1921. Restoration of Hungary's previous kingdom-without-a-king, while just an anachronism from a domestic political standpoint, would have had more serious repercussions abroad, where it would hardly have served to improve the country's standing and prestige. (Revival of the idea of Habsburg restoration would have just given rise to even more international complications. Furthermore, it would have been unrealistic to establish a "Hungarian king" after having abolished ranks of nobility and destroyed the economic foundations of the noble landowning class through radical land reform. There are no historical sources indicating that any attempt to restore the monarchy in any form ever occurred in Hungary during the post-World War II period.) Parliament's left-wing parties (the Hungarian Communist Party, the Social Democratic Party and the National Peasant Party) explicitly supported proclamation of a republic as Hungary's form of government. At the outset, representatives from the Independent Smallholders' Party espoused differing opinions in this regard, although, following an internal debate, the party's pro-monarchy minority deferred to its pro-republic majority "in the country's foreign political interest." The IShP, however, remained even thereafter more restrained in its public support of the republican form of government in deference to the beliefs of a portion of the party's extremely diverse electoral base. The initial reluctance of IShP representatives to support the proclamation of a republic dissipated after they received behind-the-scenes guarantees that, in addition to retaining the prime minister's seat, the party's nominee would stand unopposed for the office of president. Subsequently, the only significant force to maintain support for restoration of the monarchy was Hungary's Catholic episcopate, whose primary spokesman was the newly appointed Archbishop of Esztergom József Mindszenty. Although the Catholic bishops wielded no formal political authority, they did maintain a significant influence over public opinion. Not even Mindszenty, however, openly espoused an anti-republican stance, initially attempting to delay discussion of Hungary's future form of government, and then, after failing to have the issue removed from the agenda, proposing that the question be put to a national referendum. Although such a referendum was never held, a national opinion poll conducted in January 1946 indicated that 68 percent of Hungary's urban population and 64 percent of the country's rural population favored institution of a republican form of government, while only 21 percent and 25 percent, respectively, favored restoring the monarchy. (Nearly 3 percent of those polled endorsed "dictatorship" as the country's form of government, while some 7 percent of those questioned declined to voice any opinion.)[1]

On February 1, 1946, the National Assembly ratified legislation establishing the republic as Hungary's form of government. The adopted law contained stipulations regarding the organizational and functional structure of the democratic republic, thus serving as a sort of "mini-constitution." The Assembly elected Zoltán Tildy, the previous prime minister, to serve as president of the republic, while fellow Independent Smallholders' Party representative Ferenc Nagy became the new prime minister and Catholic cleric Béla Varga, also of the IShP, replaced Nagy as speaker of the National Assembly. The IShP thus held the most important political offices in Hungary. The first significant change to the cabinet took place one month later, when the Hungarian Communist Party appointed László Rajk to the post of minister of the interior in place of Imre Nagy, who had proven too conciliatory for their purposes.

In terms of Hungary's reconstituted statehood, the parliamentary elections resulted in the establishment of a legitimate legislative process and government. Recognition from the Anglo-American Allies and exchange of ambassadors followed soon thereafter. There were, however, further consequences stemming from the significant shift in the balance of power in the National Assembly following the elections of November 1945. Intense competition had taken place between the parties for positions within Hungary's political institutions during the so-called provisional period prior to the elections. As referred to earlier, the parties had vied ardently even for offices that, from a political standpoint, could have been considered minor. The so-called workers' parties (the Hungarian Communist Party and the Social Democratic Party) predominated in these struggles not only in the earlier Provisional National Government, but in the majority of lower-level local council and executive institutions as well. These institutions functioned outside the radar screen of the Allied Control Commission's Western missions, whereas Soviet military commanders operating on the ground were able to provide strong, yet largely inconspicuous, support for new cadres from these so-called workers' parties. By the end of 1945, these parties were thus able to acquire a significant majority of the most important positions throughout most of Hungary's state administrative hierarchy.

Diagram 2:

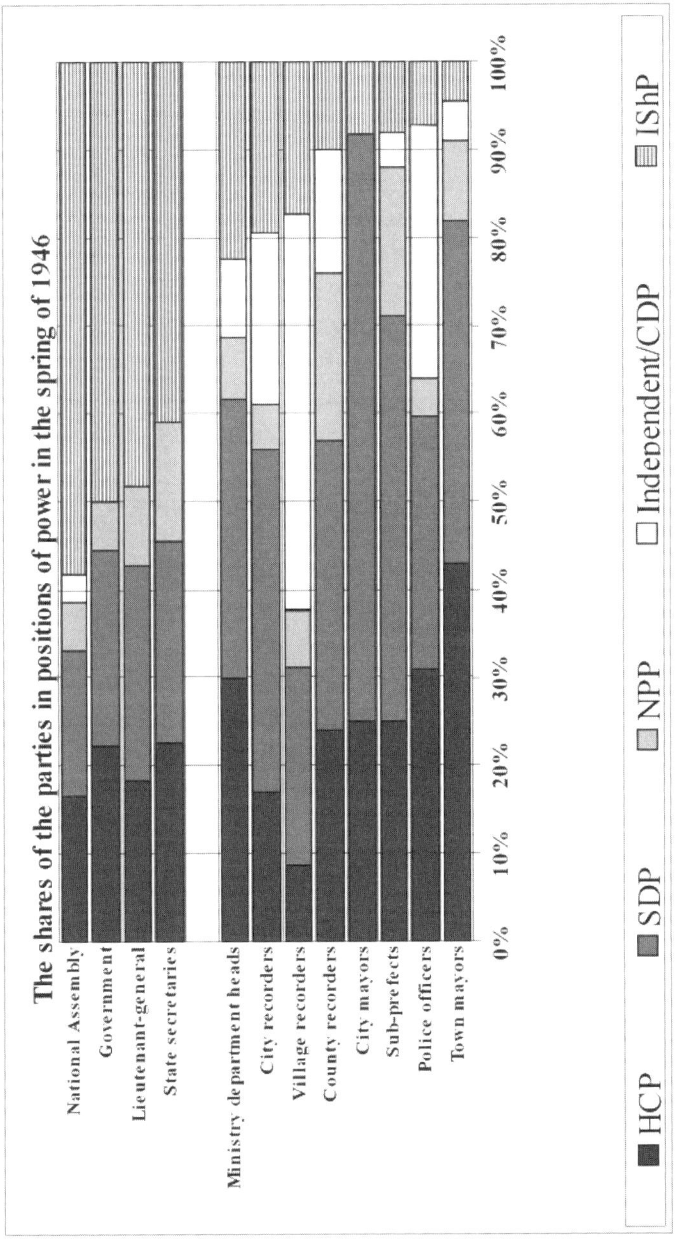
The shares of the parties in positions of power in the spring of 1946
National Assembly
Government
Lieutenant-general
State secretaries
Ministry department heads
City recorders
Village recorders
County recorders
City mayors
Sub-prefects
Police officers
Town mayors
0%
10%
20%
30%
40%
50%
60%
70%
80%
90%
100%
HCP
SDP
NPP
Independent/CDP
IShP

The redistribution of key political positions among the parties following the elections was accomplished in proportion with the voting results in appointments to the office of county lord lieutenant (the government's local county representative). A substantial majority of senior ministry officials, county magistrates and deputy lord lieutenants, and most of the leaders of the country's major public institutions were members of the left-wing parties. While the Independent Smallholders' Party did hold a legislative majority, it commanded only insignificant representation at the local level, precisely where the agrarian party's base of support was located. This kind of "power dualism" does not necessarily trigger functional difficulties in more established democracies. However, in what István Bibó, Hungary's most profound post-war political thinker, aptly termed the country's "trial democracy," this dualism resulted in a protracted political crisis in spite of the fact that the contending parties were governing together in a *pro forma* coalition and that the question lying at the root of the conflict between them had stemmed from the quest to establish a consistent system of republican institutions in the new Hungary.

In the meantime, courts were reestablished and, along with so-called popular tribunals founded to prosecute war criminals, had begun to function. (The Allied Great Power missions countersigned the chief verdicts of the popular tribunals.) With the issue of the country's form of government having been resolved, the only thing left to be done before all three branches of political power functioned in accordance with Hungary's constitutional renewal was the legitimization through elections of the lower levels of the executive branch, the local councils. This condition had, in fact, been partially satisfied, with municipal elections having already been held, as previously mentioned, in Budapest and its surrounding communities prior to the National Assembly elections.

The political duality existing within the branches of political power and the ambition of the Independent Smallholders' Party to strengthen its mandate in local government elections led to a collapse of the governing coalition. The three parties that had finished behind the IShP during the National Assembly elections, despite nevertheless having attained an inordinate share of legislative power, established a formal alliance called the Left-Wing Bloc in the spring of 1946. Thereafter the so-called bloc parties, the Hungarian Communist Party, the Social Democratic Party and the National Peasant Party, as well as the now "solitary" Independent Smallholders' Party, all attempted to expose to their own benefit the political incongruities that pervaded the institutional system following the elections. The IShP continued to press for the proportional distribution of political offices and the earliest possible calling of local council elections. The bloc parties, on the other hand, utilized a diverse array of parliamentary and extra-parliamentary tactics aimed at preventing the IShP from gaining further political ground. Among these tactics were the following: breaking up the IShP, or, as HCP General Secretary Mátyás Rákosi put it during an internal speech, "reducing it to its constituent elements," curtailing Parliament's legislative capacity and enhancing that of *government by decree*, through the so-called authorization law, strengthening the role of the *inter-party consultations* as part of the latter effort, exploiting the easily aroused public outrage of Hungarian society to produce *popular verdicts*, and, finally, modification of previous civil service verification procedures to include another counter-selective political element: the *B-list*. These tactics will be analyzed in order.

At the time of the formation of the Left-Wing Bloc in February and March 1946, the parties constituting the bloc began trumpeting the slogan "Out of the Coalition with the Enemies of the People!" Bloc parties subsequently demanded that the Independent Smallholders' Party expel 60 of its parliamentary representatives from the party, claiming that they were not fit to serve in the National Assembly of a democratic Hungary. (The number of IShP representatives to be ousted was based on calculations that a 60-deputy reduction in the IShP's parliamentary faction, combined with the allegiance of approximately two dozen left-wing partisans that had been planted in the IShP itself, would yield a National Assembly majority for the Left-Wing Bloc.) The IShP elected to partially comply with the

Left-Wing Bloc's demand, with the 20 representatives thus expelled or otherwise compelled to withdraw from the IShP subsequently forming the Hungarian Freedom Party (HFP) under the leadership of Dezső Sulyok. The HFP formally functioned in opposition, although the new party largely continued to vote with the IShP in Parliament. Although the Left-Wing Bloc did thus manage to decrease the size of the IShP's parliamentary majority, it did not succeed in reducing that party "to its constituent elements."

The increasing importance of the *inter-party consultations* and heightened role of *government by decree* must be interpreted together as interrelated processes. The inter-party consultations served as a forum for political coordination in which all coalition parties received an equal number of representatives. The bloc parties routinely blocked any Independent Smallholders' Party initiatives put forward at these consultations, and thus most of the resolutions that emerged from the meetings appeared publicly to be manifestations of coalition consensus. Most of the decisions that emerged from the inter-party consultations—again at the insistence of the left-wing parties—subsequently took form in a series of government decrees by way of the authority law. The latter law authorized the government to draft legislation addressing urgent and extraordinary war-related situations that otherwise would have fallen under the authority of the National Assembly. This administrative construction is reflected clearly in the published minutes of the inter-party consultations and meetings of the cabinet. A reading of the minutes from both bodies shows that most major decisions were made at the inter-party consultations, which the Left-Wing Bloc had come to dominate, while the government's role was reduced to making minor codifications or adjustments at most.[2] This construction did not contradict the formal criteria regarding the exercise of democratic authority. However, its focus on government by decree and reduction of the role of Parliament made it possible to ignore the majority principle. The establishment of the previously mentioned Supreme Economic Council as the "peak ministry" directing the reconstruction program and reparations production also served the interests of the Hungarian Communist Party.

The issues of the *people's verdicts* and the *B-list* were also connected to the coalition conflict of 1946. After realizing that voting for local councils would probably produce an even bigger Independent Smallholders' Party majority than previous elections had done, Hungarian Communist Party leaders attempted to prevent the elections from being held. One of the means by which the Communists sought to forestall the elections was the organization of the so-called people's verdicts, which were ostensibly aimed at removing reactionary elements from Hungary's public administration. The wave of several hundred HCP-inspired popular assemblies that swept across Hungary during the spring months of 1946 were designed to demonstrate that, with reference to the IShP, "While you have a majority in Parliament, we have a majority in the streets." The HCP mobilized its supporters for these heated assemblies, which often resulted in violent and aggressive acts such as assaults on community houses and municipal offices. The HCP-engineered assaults on public venues and institutions of this type were designed to undermine the security of local public life. HCP General Secretary Mátyás Rákosi supported the use of such methods, and encouraged these demonstrations of power, until these "people's verdicts" began to degenerate into frequently uncontrollable rampages, often with anti-Semitic overtones, and even several pogroms, some of which included lynchings.

These people's verdicts took place together with a series of measures beginning in May 1946 that were aimed at purifying the ranks of the civil service, known collectively as the *B-list.* In addition to considerations of political counter-selection, formulation of the B-lists was based on valid economic grounds: namely, the fact that Hungary's public administration had grown substantially as a result of the country's "revisionist" wartime territorial expansion, and was consequently too large for the devastated and reparations-burdened post-war national economy to support. The selection committees dominated by the bloc parties, however, focused at least as much attention on purging politically undesirable Independent Smallholders' Party sympathizers from the state payrolls as they did on reducing government expenditures through the planned dismissal of approximately 100,000 civil service employees. Hungarian Communist Party Minister of the Interior László Rajk furthermore ordered that civil servants who had been the target of people's verdicts be automatically included on the B-lists. The aforementioned measure not only served to prevent the IShP from applying the principle of proportional representation, but actually further curtailed the IShP's acquired minority representation in local and regional administration. The minister of the interior replaced those thus expelled from the civil service with "democratic cadres" who had finished hastily established crash courses in public administration.[3]

2. The Dream of Society: Consolidated Poverty

Life in Hungary following World War II was difficult enough even without the government and coalition crises that afflicted the country in 1946. According to surveys of supplies conducted in the months following the first harvest after the passing of the front, Hungary's stock of bread grain was half of that needed to meet minimal demand, while that of meat was 20 percent, that of milk 30 percent, that of eggs 40 percent and that of sugar less than 10 percent. These shortages of basic provisions resulted in the emergence of intense barter-based commerce between villages and cities, referred to as "bundling," as well as a boom in black market trade. Such commerce occurred in a more organized form when the management of workshops and factories approached village officials regarding the trade of their products for needed provisions. One such barter-based transaction between a mine and a village at the end of 1945 took place according to the following "price list":

100 kg of first-class heating coal =	14 kg flour
	40 kg barley
	40 kg ground corn
	30 kg potatoes
	26 kg beans, peas or lentils
	3 kg poppy seeds
	1.5 kg live pork
	1.5 kg poultry
	0.75 kg fat
	1 liter cooking oil

Barter exchange values for industrial products and agrarian goods proved to be a more stable basis for trade than Hungary's currency, the pengő, following the onset of runaway inflation at the beginning of the year. Moreover, the multitude of urban employees, most of whom subsisted on weekly wages, were not able to participate in such "bundling" commerce. The following anecdote regarding a secondary school teacher illustrates the dizzying pace of inflation in Hungary at the time: on the way to school on payday morning, the teacher stoically calculated that he could purchase a single egg with his weekly salary; however, by the time that he reached the market with his case full of bills he found out that his weekly pay could buy him only a yolk.

In retrospect, the tone of newsreels and propaganda films from the period of renewal in 1945–1946 can seem pathetically contrived. However, they were, in fact, not as exaggerated and artificial as one might think. Both the subsistence crisis and the lack of official initiative hampered the intensity and results of reconstruction efforts. The nameless millions who labored strenuously to resurrect the country from its post-war ruins seemed to truly believe—or want to believe—the slogan "The country is yours; you are building it for yourself!" Hungarians seemed to be working with this motivation in mind, at least until the above slogan became one of the official mottos of the Hungarian Communist Party Congress in the autumn of 1946. The zeal with which so many Hungarians worked at great personal sacrifice to create more humane living conditions as quickly as possible can only be explained in this way. Circumstances changed in this regard, however, with the onset of the so-called inflationary period in the summer of 1946 and once again with the introduction of the forint as Hungary's legal tender on August 1, 1946. Industrial wage data from the phase of the post-war renewal and reconstruction period lasting until the August 1946 currency reform serve to corroborate contemporary accounts of "a society crippled in body and soul."

Diagram 3:

The changes of salary of the industrial workers as a monthly average

August 1945 – July 1946

(August 1938 = 100 %)

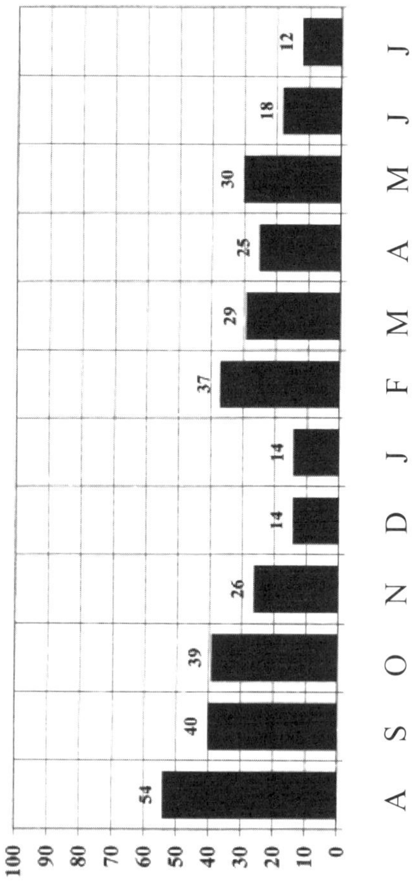

The previously mentioned shortages together with the low wage levels shown in the chart reflect the magnitude of economic hardship that prevailed in Hungary following World War II, particularly among city dwellers. In an opinion poll conducted in the agglomeration of greater Budapest asking workers to rate their present standard of living on a scale of 0 to 100, with 0 representing that of January 1945 and 100 that of "peacetime," one quarter of male workers and one third of female workers reported scores of under 10, while 58 percent of males and 60 percent of females reported scores of under 33. While the above chart merely registered a broad statistical average, the results of the poll reveal that women were even more pessimistic than men regarding their economic circumstances. This is probably due to the fact that the privations of the post-war period weighed more heavily upon women, who bore primary responsibility for putting food on the table and otherwise managing the household. Food distributions took place periodically at factories and other places of employment in order to raise the morale of workers, although the press publicity that attended these events failed to report that the value of these allocations at inflation-valorized prices was deducted from their weekly pay. Unbearable economic hardship and attempts to neutralize it through official propaganda together served to trigger a wave of strikes among industrial workers during the winter of 1945–1946.

The data in the chart also indicate that what were referred to as wages again vanished into thin air during the summer of 1946 following a brief period of improvement that spring. In another opinion poll taken at this time, a substantial majority of respondents answered "yes" to the question "Do you consider 50 percent of the standard of living recorded during the final pre-war year to be sufficient for the beginning of the stabilization period?" Within the prevailing circumstances of acute scarcity and economic hardship, for most Hungarians the prospect of attaining 50 percent of their pre-war standard of living represented the relative "security" of consolidated poverty. Those participating in the above poll did not suspect that attainment of 50 percent of the pre-war standard of living in terms of average wages was an implicit part of official economic stabilization propaganda.

By the time of the forint's introduction on August 1, 1946, the pengő had already ceased to bear a practical market value. The pengő's exchange rate was intelligible only mathematically at 4.6×10^{29} to the forint. (That is, one new forint was worth 460,000,000,000,000,000,000,000,000,000 pengő.) The valorization of the forint was consequently calculated against the pengő at its 1938 market value. Another factor in the timing of the introduction of the forint was the return to Hungary of most of the National Bank of Hungary's gold, currency and bond reserves, which the Szálasi regime had removed to the Third Reich in December 1944. The US State Department ordered that the US army allow these somewhat-plundered reserves to be returned to Hungary from Germany in the summer of 1946. The "gold train" that arrived home in August contained 30,000 kilograms of gold ingots and coins, which were of sufficient value to provide backing for the newly introduced currency.

The objective of establishing wages at 50 percent of their pre-war average did not by any means imply that all employment categories would receive the equivalent of half their pre-war pay. This figure was merely a composite average, which was applied unevenly towards various groups of workers and employees depending on their status in the new system. The wages of unskilled and semi-skilled industrial workers were indeed set at the proclaimed level of 50 percent, while those for skilled labor, which was in sharp demand during the period of post-war reconstruction, were set at an even higher rate. The overall wage rates of these three so-called workers' categories approached 60 percent of their pre-war levels with the inclusion of various supplementary benefits provided to employees at state-owned workshops and industrial units. The inclusive target of 50 percent was met by setting the salaries of more highly qualified civil service employees at hardly one third of their pre-war level. The salaries of civil servants classified in the higher wage categories during the pre-war period were set at around one quarter of their 1938 level, while those of civil servants formerly classified in the lower wage categories were set at 30–40 percent of their 1938 level. Teachers' salaries were set at just over 20 percent of their 1938 level.

There was an additional dimension to this program of wage adjustment as well. The average *per capita* wage of factory workers before the war was 220 pengő, or just under three quarters that of the 294-pengő average *per capita* wage of employees in Hungary's pre-war state administration. This ratio underwent a reversal following the economic stabilization, when the average 312-forint wage of a state administrator was just over two thirds that of the average 466-forint wage of a factory worker. Thus, in addition to a general decline and leveling of wages, the economic stabilization entailed "pro-worker" positive discrimination to the detriment of "elbow-sleeved, suspender-wearing" state officials. Pensions decreased by a similar average of nearly 60 percent as well. Furthermore, a succession of decrees issued in the autumn of 1946 curtailed the number of those eligible for pension benefits. The true motive for this measure becomes evident only through an examination of political background material, which reveals that those who had "served the counterrevolutionary system" over the previous decades were deemed unworthy to receive state pensions.

Profits derived from the exchange of the essentially valueless former currency were just enough to pay off the state budget deficit. The government attempted to maintain budgetary equilibrium partially through introduction of the new wage scale. The dismissal of nearly 100,000 state employees by means of the previously mentioned B-lists produced considerable savings on the expenditure side of the budget. This was true even if one considers the fact that the number of people who remained on Hungary's state payroll in 1946 (approximately 185,000) was more than 50 percent higher than that recorded during the final year before the war (approximately 120,000).[4] The reduction in state expenditures stemming from the "stabilization" of wages and pensions was nevertheless considerable. Whereas payment of pensions and civil service wages had consumed nearly one half (48 percent) of Hungary's state budget in 1938, these payments accounted for just over one quarter (26 percent) of the state expenditures in 1946. Budget resources disengaged in this way were not, however, sufficient to defray Hungary's reparations quota and related expenditures, among them the increasing cost of providing for the subsistence of occupation forces.

The difference was generated through the aforementioned budget-trimming measures as well as modifications to the tax system and the imposition of an ever-broadening range of government price controls, which were again aimed chiefly at the agrarian sector. Although it took months for the forint to become readily available throughout Hungary, particularly in the countryside, following its introduction on August 1, farmers (agricultural producers) received notices from the state revenue office almost immediately following that date calling upon them to promptly pay all due taxes and arrears in the new currency. Following the introduction of the forint, the government ceased, due to uncontrolled inflation, to require that agricultural producers settle their tax obligations in kind.

Hungary's agrarian community took even more profound umbrage at the fact that the stabilization price control ratios had dictated a reduction of roughly 50 percent in the costs of agricultural products and labor. The price of wheat of 40 forints per 100 kilograms established as the base of comparison was 58 percent of the nominal forint–pengő valorization, while the assessed value of corn calculated against this same standard showed a 33 percent decline and that of potatoes a 39 percent decline. The average price of industrial goods, on the other hand, was 30 percent higher than its conversion value. In practical terms, this meant that those engaged in agriculture (would have) had to produce and sell at least double the amount of produce in exchange for the same pre-stabilization amount of industrial commodities. This imprudent reduction in the real exchange value of agricultural products made it extremely difficult for Hungary's more prosperous agricultural producers to make economic progress, frequently threatening even the minimal profitability of their operations. For smallholding peasants and farmers, including those who had received land pursuant to the land reform hardly more than a year earlier, the exchange values defined in the stabilization program made meeting even the basic conditions of their subsistence impossible.

Exchange value of various industrial and agricultural commodities following the 1946 currency reform

Industrial commodity	Exchange value in wheat in 1938	Exchange value in wheat in 1946	"Loss" calculated as percentage
1,000 bricks	140 kg	600 kg	428%
100 kg of iron bar	150 kg	420 kg	280%
Single blade plow	400 kg	850 kg	212%
1 pair of boots	100 kg	300 kg	300%
1 grain sack	8 kg	40 kg	500%

According to government propaganda, those Hungarians attempting to derive a livelihood from agriculture would have to contend with a devaluation of "only" 50 percent in stabilization price ratios for the rest of the year 1946. During the early autumn of that year, farmers vented their dissatisfaction with the government's stabilization initiative during a succession of protest assemblies, some of which began to assume the character of incipient "peasant rebellions." The Independent Smallholders' Party press and, even more so, the National Peasant Party press repeatedly called attention to the anomaly of the gap between the relative prices of agricultural and industrial goods. Moreover, in September 1946 the leaders of the Independent Smallholders' Party and President Péter Veres of the National Peasant Party jointly organized a large-scale farmers' demonstration in Budapest after having been accused of presiding over the continual subversion of the peasantry from the comfort of their urban villas. The price ratios between industrial and agricultural commodities were modified somewhat following this demonstration. Discussion of this general and compulsory restriction related to Hungary's war reparations paves the way for an examination of the country's post-war peace process, which had entered its decisive phase at this same time.

3. Preparing the Post-War Peace and the Peace Treaty

Most of the primary stipulations contained in Hungary's post-war peace treaty were based on those of the armistice agreement discussed in Chapter One. Although the country's lack of sovereignty made it impossible for Hungary to conduct its foreign affairs independently following World War II, the country's post-war government did adopt various positions with regard to questions of foreign policy. This diversity of opinion was partially a product of the composition of the governing coalition. Although all the parties in Hungary's coalition government were compelled to recognize and accept the fact of the country's subordination to the Great Powers, they did so with various distinctions. The Hungarian Communist Party naturally attempted to influence Hungary's foreign policy in accordance with Soviet ambitions and expectations. (The latter was connected closely to the fact that without Moscow's active support, the HCP could have hardly managed to attain a degree of political power far exceeding the party's popular approval.) The Independent Smallholders' Party, above all IShP Prime Minister Ferenc Nagy, on the other hand, maintained diplomatic contacts with the American and British legations in Budapest, which repeatedly raised the ire of the Soviets. The Social Democratic Party also made overtures towards London through their contacts inside the British Labour Party, especially after recognizing that they could not compete with the Communists for Moscow's patronage.

The posture of the various political parties that reorganized—or were permitted to reorganize—in Hungary following World

War II with regard to foreign policy issues first diverged around the question of the post-war expulsion of the country's ethnically German population. This divergence was, however, based much more on considerations pertaining to domestic politics and party sociology than it was on issues of foreign policy. The Hungarian Communist Party uniformly supported the expulsion of the Germans, commonly referred to as "Swabians." Certain National Peasant Party representatives, notably Imre Kovács and Ferenc Erdei (the latter as minister of the interior), surpassed even the Communists in the radicalism of their calls for the expulsion of Hungarian citizens of German nationality. The Independent Smallholders' Party, on the other hand, along with the Social Democratic Party, was much more reserved on this issue, rejecting the concept of "collective guilt" proclaimed in the Potsdam Agreements. The IShP and the SDP embraced the notion of personal, legally demonstrable liability, shunning that of ethnically and linguistically based collective discrimination. The vast majority of Germans who had settled in Hungary over the preceding 200 years had undergone cultural assimilation, merging organically into agrarian society with their well-tended farms, particularly in certain regions of Transdanubia. The IShP, above all, (would have) considered these rural Germans to be part of its electoral base. Within Hungary's more industrialized districts, especially cities, there were many skilled laborers and craftsmen of German nationality, most of whom formed part of the SDP's base of support.

Government decrees issued in December 1945 prescribed the expulsion of the majority of Hungary's ethnic Germans in spite of the divergent standpoints of the coalition parties on this issue. Beyond the motive of complying with the Potsdam provisions of the victorious Great Powers, there were three other factors underpinning this decision. The first was the need to create housing for the hundreds of thousands of refugees who, as mentioned in the previous chapter, had fled either from the approaching front or from territories lying outside Hungary's pre-1938 borders. The second was the need to disengage more land for redistribution through confiscation of the larger, and for the most part better-equipped, "Swabian" farmsteads. The third factor was related in part to the population exchange that took place between Czechoslovakia and Hungary, which will be discussed below.

In addition to the conflicting positions of the Hungarian political parties during the post-war period, the "status" of various European countries, particularly that of neighboring states, at the close of World War II dictated the divergent aspect of Hungary's foreign policy measures at this time. Following the war, many Hungarians viewed Yugoslavia not only as a militarily potent subsidiary victor, but as a proto-communist state as well. (Until 1948, the Hungarian Communist Party press portrayed Tito's Yugoslavia as a model state in which the process of forming a "people's democracy" had already made exemplary progress. This propaganda was a manifestation not of contemporary Hungarian political opinion, but of the domestic political aspirations of the HCP leadership.) The establishment of constructive neighborly relations with Yugoslavia was also to Hungary's fundamental benefit in the light of the fact that approximately a quarter of a million Hungarians remained in the South Slav state after the war.

Hungary's relations with its neighbor to the north, Czechoslovakia, were more turbulent from the very beginning. Czech leader Edvard Beneš won Stalin's support by relinquishing Sub-Carpathia to the Soviet Union and signing a secret agreement to provide the Soviets with raw materials (uranium) that had become of strategic importance following the end of the war. The quasi-reconstitution of the interwar Czechoslovak state thus made possible and indeed necessitated the reclassification of Germany's wartime ally of Slovakia, a vanquished enemy state, as a subsidiary victor. The policy of reconstituting Czechoslovakia as a "purely Slav state" entailed the proclamation of the collective responsibility of its German and Hungarian minorities for the country's wartime collapse, and the subsequent expulsion of these minorities on these grounds. Czechoslovakia managed to win Moscow's endorsement for this plan even though the Potsdam Agreement had stipulated only the expulsion of ethnic Germans from Czechoslovakia (as well as Poland and Hungary). Contrary to the Soviets, the Anglo-American Allies did not offer approval for the prospective expulsion of Slovakia's Hungarian minority. However, Prague was able to exert such an intense degree of diplomatic pressure on the Hungarian government through its representation, as a subsidiary victor, on Hungary's Allied Control Commission that the cabinet of Independent Smallholders' Party Prime Minister Ferenc Nagy felt compelled to sign the population exchange agreement on February 27, 1946. According to this agreement, the government of Czechoslovakia had the right to expel the same number of Hungarians from Slovakia as that of Hungary's Slovak minority who agreed to resettle voluntarily in Slovakia.

After the signing of the population exchange agreement, Czechoslovak recruitment committees launched a six-month propaganda campaign aimed at convincing as many members of Hungary's Slovak minority as possible to relocate to Slovakia. A total of 73,000 Slovaks ultimately volunteered to take part in the population exchange, just a fraction of the number of Hungarians living in Czechoslovakia, by then without the rights of citizenship as a result of the 1945 Beneš decrees. Czechoslovak leaders therefore appealed to the victorious Great Powers to have the unilateral expulsion of a further 200,000 members of Slovakia's Hungarian minority included among the provisions of the post-war peace treaty. However, as a result of renewed Anglo-American opposition to this proposal, Prague initiated a program of administrative Slovakization, offering to reinstate the Czechoslovak citizenship of those Hungarians who agreed to declare themselves Slovaks, and, furthermore, in the autumn of 1946, deported thousands of Hungarians to the districts of western Bohemia and Moravia from which the Sudeten Germans had been expelled. (Post-war Czechoslovakia's fetish with the creation of an ethnically homogeneous, exclusively Slav nation state was institutionalized in other forms as well. Jewish Holocaust survivors from Prague and the Sudetenland, who had assimilated culturally with surrounding Germans, were divested of their Czechoslovak citizenship as "Germans," while those from Slovakia, who had assimilated culturally with surrounding Hungarians, were stripped of their citizenship as "Hungarians." Many of the Jews thus affected were only released from internment camps, sometimes the very same ones in which they had been held prior to their deportation to German concentration camps, in the wake of intense international protest.)

The victorious Great Powers, while increasingly at loggerheads with each other, sponsored another of their Czechoslovak ally's aspirations as well, acceding to the annexation of three villages on the Hungarian side of the Danube—Dunacsún, Horvátjárfalu and Oroszvár—and their immediate environs to Czechoslovakia as a means of providing a border buffer to what was still considered to be the "Slovak capital city" of Bratislava (Pozsony). Moreover, the Czechoslovak government continued to demand that it be granted the authority to unilaterally expel 200,000 Hungarians from Slovakia. The Hungarian Territorial and Political Committee taking part in preparatory negotiations prior to the Paris Peace Conference spent almost the entire month of September 1946 discussing the issue of these unilateral expulsions, submitting a "people with the land" counterproposal calling for the approximately 4,000 km^2 of territory in southern Slovakia in which Hungarians made up over 75 percent of the population to be incorporated into Hungary. (Enactment of such a measure would have increased the land area of Hungary by 4 percent and decreased that of Czechoslovakia by 3 percent.) More than 150,000 Hungarians lived in the strip of southern Slovakia defined in the Committee's initiative, which would have thus resolved the status of three quarters of the 200,000 Hungarians targeted for unilateral expulsion in the Czechoslovak proposal. The Hungarian counterproposal also advocated taking in Hungarians living outside the defined territory.[5] Both the Czechoslovak and Soviet peace delegations rejected this plan. The issue of what to do with the Hungarians left in Czechoslovakia after the population exchange was subsequently removed from the agenda of the preparatory negotiations with the proviso that the matter be resolved within the framework of bilateral talks. Although this condition was later included among the stipulations of the peace treaty, the question was never resolved as specified. With the Czechoslovak government having remained completely unreceptive to the notion of any border adjustment, it continued to pursue a policy of discrimination towards those Hungarians who had not been subjected to unilateral expulsion, offering to reinstate their Czechoslovak citizenship only if they agreed to officially declare themselves Slovaks.

Hungary adopted a different stance *vis-à-vis* Romania in the course of preliminary peace treaty negotiations from the one that it took up towards Czechoslovakia and Yugoslavia. This was based on two considerations: first, paragraph 19 of the Romanian armistice agreement stipulated that the Great Powers "agree that Transylvania, or the larger part thereof, should be returned to Romania on the condition that this is upheld in the peace settlement"; second, Romania, like Hungary, was classified as a subsidiary defeated power. These factors prompted Hungarian diplomats to estimate that it might be possible for Hungary to retain at least a small portion of the half of Transylvania that the Romanian armistice agreement had "left hanging in the air." Subsequently uncovered historical sources have confirmed what people at the time could have only surmised based on uncertain and incomplete evidence—that during the war, the Anglo-American Allies contemplated the notion of making certain modifications to the territorial stipulations contained in the Treaty of Trianon, including the possibility of establishing an autonomous, or even independent, Transylvania. Documents from the Soviet Ministry of Foreign Affairs indicate that similar alternatives surfaced in Moscow at the same time, although the Soviet diplomats and political figures who played an active role in the post-war peace process rejected these options.[6]

The Hungarian Ministry of Foreign Affairs' peace preparation division devised several proposals with regard to a smaller part of Transylvania, exploring the possibility of reducing the number of Hungarians left under Romanian dominion through bilateral population exchanges of various dimensions. The Hungarian government eventually elected to incorporate two of these many proposals into its negotiating platform: a "Greater Partium" plan applying to approximately 22,000 km^2 of territory, and a "Smaller Partium" plan applying to approximately 12,000 km^2 of territory, which would have increased the size of Hungary by 12 percent and decreased that of Romania by 5 percent. The prospect of a minor adjustment of Hungary's border with Romania received a boost in the middle of April 1946, when, during talks with a Hungarian government delegation in Moscow, Soviet officials voiced no objection to the idea of Hungarian representatives submitting the "Smaller Partium" proposal for consideration at the preliminary negotiations for the Paris Peace Conference set to take place that summer.

Hungary's post-war political leaders slowly arrived at the bitter conclusion that their hope for at least a partial "revision" of the country's Trianon borders had been an illusion. As it turned out, the Great Powers had intentionally built some ambiguity regarding Transylvania's future territorial affiliation into the previously cited paragraph of Romania's armistice agreement as a means of fostering competition between the rival Antonescu and Horthy governments for the much-coveted historical region, whose potential acquisition would manifestly require withdrawing from the Axis alliance and siding with the Allies. Whereas Romania succeeded in making this turnabout, Hungary, as mentioned in Chapter One, failed in its attempt to pull out of the Axis and conclude a separate peace with the Allied powers, and thus, for Moscow at least, the motive of enticing Hungary to switch its military allegiance through the prospect of retaining territory in Transylvania had lost its relevance. Although the Kremlin did subsequently consent to Hungary's submission of the "Smaller Partium" proposal during the preliminary peace conference negotiations, members of the Hungarian Territorial and Political Committee participating in the talks could not have been aware that deputy Ministry of Foreign Affairs and State Department officials from the victorious Great Powers had decided during a conference being held in London at the same time that the land area of 104,000 km^2, most of it located in the historical region of Transylvania, annexed from Hungary to Romania via the Treaty of Trianon in 1920, would revert in its entirety to Romania. Both Stalin and Molotov already knew of this decision when they deceptively permitted the Hungarian delegation to advance the "Smaller Partium" proposal in Paris. The territorial dispute between the two subsidiary vanquished powers entailed another, more significant, Great Power aspect, namely that any "concession" on Stalin's behalf with regard to Transylvania would have signaled a withdrawal of confidence from Prime Minister Petru Groza's left-wing government in Bucharest, which the Soviet leader himself had placed in power against the objections of the Anglo-American Allies and whose recognition as a wartime co-belligerent Molotov repeatedly advocated during meetings of the Council of Foreign Ministers.[7]

Hungary's efforts to secure territorial concessions in Transylvania during the preliminary peace negotiations held in Paris during the summer of 1946 were thus doomed to total failure. The Hungarian delegation participating in the talks did launch a last-ditch initiative to secure territorial concessions in the region, withdrawing its summarily rejected "Smaller Partium" proposal in favor of a modified plan calling for a reduced, 4,000-km^2, strip of land along the Romanian side of the pre-war border to be included in post-war Hungary. The latter proposal would have moved the pre-war frontier just 20 kilometers to the east, thus placing predominantly Hungarian-inhabited cities, such as Arad, Nagyszalonta, Nagyvárad, Nagykároly and Szatmárnémeti, in Hungary and reducing Romania's land area by 1.7 percent. Soviet Deputy Minister of Foreign Affairs Andrey Vyshinskiy continued, however, to support Romania's position on this matter, while in the interests of unanimity the other Great Powers declined to reconsider the issue that had already been discussed and apparently settled several times previously. This is how nearly two million Hungarians again wound up living as a minority in Romania after World War II.

Only minor rhetorical and editorial changes were made to the text of the peace treaty following the closure of the preparatory peace negotiations in October 1946 and their signing in Paris on February 10, 1947. The military provisions of the Paris Peace Treaty stipulated that the size of Hungary's army be limited to 65,000 troops and called for the future release of Hungarian prisoners of war, although without specifying a time frame for their repatriation. The provisions furthermore prescribed a 90-day deadline for the withdrawal of Allied military forces from Hungary, although they permitted the Soviet Union to keep troops in the country in order to secure supply lines to its occupation zone in Austria.

The economic provisions of the Paris Peace Treaty stipulated that Hungary pay war reparations of 200 million dollars to the Soviet Union and a combined 100 million dollars to Yugoslavia and Czechoslovakia, specifying that these indemnities be paid primarily in machinery, transport infrastructure and vehicles, and grain. Hungary's 300 million dollars in reparations constituted roughly one third of the country's gross national income of approximately one billion dollars calculated for the years 1938–1939 and 1943–1944. Divided by the eight-year term of reparations payments defined in the treaty, reparations nominally represented no less than just under 4 percent of Hungary's gross national income for the years cited. (Calculated otherwise, Hungary's war reparations payments imposed a burden of 33 dollars per citizen, or an annual 4.1 dollars per citizen over the eight-year duration of payments.) The true cost of reparations was actually much higher when viewed within the economic context of post-war Hungary, where the war had consumed some 40 percent of the country's estimated 1944 gross national assets, while gross national income remained at just around 50–65 percent of that recorded during the final year of peace for many subsequent years. These factors resulted in an immediate "doubling" of the magnitude of reparations in relation to production capacity. Hungary's reparations burden was again doubled as a result of wartime inflation having weakened the Hungarian currency's exchange rate against the dollar from five pengő to the dollar in 1938 to ten pengő to the dollar after the war. Another factor undermining Hungary's solvency at this time was the Soviet Union's claim to the trade surplus that the country had accrued towards the Third Reich during the war, which at 280 million dollars amounted to nearly the total value of its war reparations. The paradoxical situation thus arose in which many Hungarian companies were compelled from the spring of 1945 to dismantle and send to the Soviet Union machinery and equipment that (would have) constituted part of Hungary's reparations payments. Another circumstance weighing on Hungary's economy following World War II was the country's obligation to supply the Allied Control Commission and Soviet occupation forces, which numbered 1.5 million in 1945 and 500,000 beginning in the summer of 1946, with provisions without compensation. The Red Army furthermore confiscated, in violation of international military prescripts, supplies that retreating German forces had left in Hungary. All of these factors combined served to quintuple the magnitude of Hungary's reparations payments in real terms as compared to their nominal sum, to 20–25 percent of gross national income and 30–45 percent of budget expenditure during the years 1945–1948. (This value decreased somewhat as a result of reconstruction yields.)

In order to gain a comprehensive understanding of Hungary's war reparations burden, it is necessary to jump ahead a little in the chronological order of events. As a form of political compensation for the impending fusion of the Hungarian Communist Party and the Social Democratic Party, Soviet Minister of Foreign Affairs Vyacheslav Molotov announced during the summer of 1948 that Moscow had cancelled half of Hungary's remaining reparations debt of approximately 130 million dollars towards the Soviet Union. It should be noted, however, that Hungary, although it had nominally remitted only 70 million dollars of its 200-million-dollar reparations obligation towards the Soviet Union by mid-1948, had in fact already paid more than the stipulated sum if the vastly undervalued exchange rates at which the transactions occurred are taken into consideration. By the time that the Soviet government declared an end to war reparations in January 1953, Hungary's total remittance of 131 million dollars in goods to the Soviet Union represented, along with the conversion of its trade assets with Germany into trade liabilities, an "overpayment" of 150 percent.

4. Destroying the Majority Party

Until the second half of 1946, the Hungarian Communist Party attempted to reduce the power of the Independent Smallholders' Party primarily through political means, including occasional recourse to the support of the Allied Control Commission's Soviet leadership. Evidence of an approaching intensification of the conflict among Hungary's coalition parties was palpable almost immediately following the several-month period of domestic political restraint that had prevailed at the time of the preliminary negotiations for the Paris Peace Conference. In the middle of September, the Independent Smallholders' Party parliamentary representatives, along with those from the Hungarian Freedom Party that had earlier split from the IShP, rejected a motion filed by HCP Minister of the Interior László Rajk, who, according to Hungarian parliamentary convention, should have thus submitted his resignation. However, the IShP Political Committee itself immediately proposed that Rajk nevertheless retain his post, a political gambit to which the HCP responded at its Third Party Congress just a week later, when it proclaimed its "Out of the Coalition with the Enemies of the People!" program aimed unequivocally at the IShP.

The Hungarian Communist Party subsequently unleashed a torrent of press and parliamentary attacks against the Independent Smallholders' Party in which they alleged that the latter party had exhibited a lack of resolve in the "struggle against reaction" and even harbored, or at least tolerated, reactionary elements within its ranks. In the second half of October, the parties constituting the Left-Wing Bloc issued a joint memorandum in which they demanded that the IShP subject itself to a process of self-purification. IShP leaders responded to these attacks by putting their political objectives and grievances on parade. The fact that party leaders could not reach accommodation even at the inter-party consultations, the primary forum for dialog between the parties, demonstrates the degree to which relations between the coalition parties had deteriorated. Moreover, the parties failed to resolve their differences in spite of the fact that the consultations in question had lasted for an extraordinarily long period of time.[8] Most, but not all, of the circumstances and events surrounding the political wrangling described above were reflected in the press polemics of the period. Notable among the unpublicized episodes was an HCP backstage proposal according to which the HCP would, after a year and a half of obstruction, consent to the calling of local council elections on the condition that the Parliament relinquish its right to nominate town clerks—key figures in Hungary's local public administration who would thenceforth serve in the capacity of state civil servant, a status over which the minister of the interior exercised the authority of appointment. Adoption of this initiative would have enabled the HCP to "override" the results of the local council elections through its capacity to determine the appointment of high-ranking officials in the thousands of agrarian communities where the party commanded only minimal support. However, IShP Prime Minister Ferenc Nagy rejected this proposal, which Minister of the Interior László Rajk had mediated on behalf of the Communists, resolving instead to delay calling local council elections until after the ratification of the peace treaty and the withdrawal of Soviet troops.[9]

The internal conflict that beset Hungary's governing coalition during the autumn of 1946 apparently stemmed from two interrelated factors. The first of these was the fact that public opinion had turned against the government as a result of the essentially final peace treaty provisions stipulating the withdrawal of Hungary's borders, with the one minor exception alluded to earlier in this chapter, to their pre-1938 location and the imposition of war reparations. (The fact that no Hungarian government could have educed more favorable peace treaty conditions following Hungary's wartime conduct is another matter.) It was for this reason that the coalition parties, otherwise in conflict with each other, unanimously agreed not to publicize the stipulations of the peace treaty in their definitive form until after the treaty had been signed.[10] The second factor lying at the root of the coalition infighting was the fact that both the Hungarian Communist Party and the Independent Smallholders' Party had begun positioning themselves for the post-treaty period. With the Cold War still in its "incubation period,"[11] the HCP was concerned that its position would weaken if the party's Soviet sponsor were forced, along with its army, to leave Hungary following the expiration of the Allied Control Commission's mandate, while the IShP—together in all likelihood with a majority of the population—maintained the contrasting hope that restitution of the country's sovereignty would make it possible to forestall the aspiration of the Communists to attain absolute political power and to continue forging the socio-economic order of the new republic.

Events did not turn out this way. As a consequence of the deepening stalemate between the Great Powers, the Hungarian Communist Party was able to continue what Mátyás Rákosi had described as reducing the Independent Smallholders' Party "to its constituent elements," now resorting to both parliamentary and extra-parliamentary measures to attain this objective. In December 1946, the HCP-controlled Military Political Section of the Ministry of Defense arrested a dozen people, including a former military officer, a dismissed civil servant and several lower-echelon IShP activists. Subsequent, physically abusive, interrogations conducted under the authority of the recently reorganized State Protection Department (known in its Hungarian-language acronymic form as ÁVO) were aimed at coercing the detainees to confess that they had been engaged in the plotting of a "conspiracy against the republic" with the complicity of IShP leaders and parliamentary representatives. In January 1947 the Gábor Péter-led political police took several IShP representatives into custody as a result of the confessions extracted during these interrogations. After the Hungarian Communist Party press launched an intense smear campaign, as vehement as it was untrue, in which it charged that the IShP representatives had been part of the so-called "conspiracy against the republic," a parliamentary majority voted to suspend the immunity of the implicated representatives in order to clarify the matter. Again invoking information obtained during the coerced confessions, proponents of the conspiracy indictment subsequently had IShP National Deputy General Secretary Vince Vörös arrested, and publicly accused the IShP General Secretary Béla Kovács of having been "connected" to the plot as well.

The Independent Smallholders' Party majority in Parliament dug in its heels at this point. What IShP representatives had previously suspected had by then become obvious: the aforementioned sequence of events represented nothing less than a "show trial aimed at crushing the Independent Smallholders' Party."[12] IShP General Secretary Béla Kovács became the focus of Hungarian Communist Party intrigues and open attacks beginning in February 1947. Soviet Ambassador A. Pushkin intervened on behalf of the HCP, requesting Prime Minister Ferenc Nagy that Kovács be handed over for questioning, although the National Assembly rejected a motion to suspend the IShP general secretary's parliamentary immunity. From the middle of February, the Communists instigated a daily succession of heated negotiations aimed at compelling Kovács to nevertheless submit himself to questioning at the hands of the political police. Eventually the sides arrived at a compromise agreement by which Kovács would, while retaining his parliamentary immunity, turn himself in voluntarily to ÁVO headquarters for a maximum of two days of interrogation, on the condition that Hungarian police authorities not be permitted to take him into custody. This is precisely what took place, at least until the second day of questioning on February 25, when Soviet military intelligence authorities seized Kovács and carried him off to the Soviet occupation zone in Austria. The IShP general secretary was held captive at the Soviet military intelligence general headquarters in Baden bei Wien until the autumn of 1951, when he was taken to the Soviet Union and, without trial, sentenced to 25 years of forced labor. (Kovács was permitted to return to Hungary in 1955, was released from detention in 1956 and died in 1959. The Supreme Military Prosecutor's Office of the Soviet Union rehabilitated Kovács in 1989.[13])

Although the Soviet seizure of the general secretary of the leading government party shocked and appalled many Hungarians, the broader public continued to be soberly skeptical of the "conspiracy" and the complicity of the Independent Smallholders' Party therein. A series of trials took place in Hungary during the spring and summer of 1947 whose purpose, along with the attendant coverage in the Communist press, was to demonstrate the involvement of IShP representatives and party activists in the alleged plot. By the end of the sequence of seven consecutive trials, a total of 258 of those charged during the hearings had been convicted, while a further 120 people were confined to internment camps for years without indictment. The composite results of opinion polls conducted within every stratum of Hungarian society at the time indicated that 70–75 percent of people doubted that the so-called conspiracy represented a threat to the republic, while 20–25 percent of people found this threat to be credible. The results of the polls suggest that most Hungarians discerned the inherent contradiction contained in the Hungarian Communist Party's fraudulent conspiracy campaign: namely, that it would not be in the interests of the strongest political party in the country, in this case the IShP, to plot against its own power. There was, however, one aspect of the anti-IShP Communist intrigue that was based in truth: the calculation that—particularly after the publication of the time frame for the signing of the peace treaty—the majority of Hungary's population wanted the Soviet army to leave the country, just as a quarter of a century earlier, in 1920, the majority of Hungarians had wanted Serb and Romanian forces occupying various parts of Hungary under Entente auspices to leave the country. This expectation became one of the primary topics of everyday conversation in Hungary, from the coffeehouse table to the dinner table. Or as they say, if proclaiming the desire for the Soviet army to leave Hungary had been deemed an anti-state activity, "half the country could have been taken into custody."

The closing act of the conspiracy drama had, however, not yet begun. In the middle of May 1947, Independent Smallholders' Party Prime Minister Ferenc Nagy went on vacation to Switzerland, where IShP officials notified him that the government had received information from the Soviet agencies that had interrogated IShP General Secretary Béla Kovács indicating that he, as prime minister, had also been aware of the conspiracy. Prime Minister Nagy indicated immediately that he would return to Hungary as soon as possible, although it seemed as if there were some factions in Budapest that did not expect him to do so: during a telephone conversation with Hungarian Communist Party General Secretary Mátyás Rákosi, who was filling in for Nagy in his absence, the HCP leader told the prime minister that the Soviet allegations could not simply be dismissed as mere fabrications. Prime Minister Nagy was then urged to wait in Bern for a minister who had been dispatched to Switzerland to apprise him of the situation. A witness's account of a telephone conversation between HCP Deputy General Secretary Mihály Farkas and Prime Minister Nagy testifies to the deceitful character of the affair:

> I just happened to be in Mihály Farkas's office when a telephone call was put through from Switzerland... I heard that he was speaking to Prime Minister Ferenc Nagy. Farkas remarked casually:
> "Feri [the diminutive form of the prime minister's given name], unfortunately your name has come up in connection with the conspiracy. The prosecutor would like to have a talk with you, so please come home quickly and straighten the matter out."
> I was horrified, and when Farkas put down the telephone I commented:
> "He's going to slip out of our grasp—he's not going to come home."
> "This is precisely what we want to happen."
> Farkas then began to talk about something else.[14]

Subsequent communications from Budapest therefore no longer urged Prime Minister Nagy to return to Hungary, but to submit his resignation as soon as possible. Moreover, the continual stream of messages dispatched to Nagy in Switzerland began to warn the prime minister that he could encounter trouble as he passed through the

Soviet occupation zone in Austria on his way home. Finally, telephone negotiations between Budapest and the Hungarian Embassy in Bern yielded an agreement by which Ferenc Nagy would submit his letter of resignation to a government representative if the latter brought with him from Budapest the prime minister's youngest son, then five years old. Although this exchange took place only on June 2, the Hungarian Press Agency MTI announced Nagy's resignation as a *fait accompli* already on May 29. Under sharp and persistent Soviet pressure, President Zoltán Tildy on May 31 appointed Independent Smallholders' Party cabinet member Lajos Dinnyés, a puppet of the Communists, to succeed Nagy as prime minister.

Three days later, Independent Smallholders' Party Speaker of the National Assembly Béla Varga fled Hungary after learning that a warrant had been issued for his arrest. The new, by then commonly referred to as "left-wing," IShP leadership unburdened itself of another 50 party representatives through expulsions and persuasion. Thereafter, only those IShP representatives were permitted to continue serving, both at the national and local level, who were acceptable to the Communists or who, in fact, were already collaborating with them. It is, however, worth noting that a dozen representatives withdrew from both the Social Democratic Party and the National Peasant Party at around the same time, because they did not want to be accessories, as members of Left-Wing Bloc parties, to the Hungarian Communist Party's illegitimate campaign to subvert the IShP. Among the representatives who withdrew from the bloc parties, former Social Democratic Party member Károly Peyer and former National Peasant Party member Imre Kovács soon thereafter left the country. Some two dozen accredited Hungarian diplomats, including ambassadors Aladár Szegedy-Maszák (Washington), Pál Auer (Paris), István Kertész (Rome) and Ferenc Gordon (Bern), submitted their resignations in order to protest at the politically motivated witch hunt taking place at home. Over the subsequent months, those political exiles mentioned over previous paragraphs, former Prime Minister Ferenc Nagy among them, assumed leading roles in the organization of

Hungarian émigré affairs in the West, establishing the Hungarian National Committee, which enjoyed particular support from the United States until the suppression of the Hungarian Revolution of 1956. This support, along with the establishment of Radio Free Europe, helped to provide for the livelihood of émigrés for shorter and longer periods of time as well.[15]

5. Multiply Hijacked Elections

Records of the secret political police that became accessible in 1990 have contributed extensively to the understanding and repudiation of the alleged post-war conspiracy against the republic and the involvement of the Independent Smallholders' Party in the fabricated plot. The chief of the political police, Gábor Péter, ordered that the IShP's primary party organizations and officeholders be put under surveillance beginning at the time of the November 1945 National Assembly elections. Agents kept Péter abreast of the daily movements and activities, sometimes even the following day's agenda, of the prime minister, the president and certain IShP ministers. Every night, the chief of the political police compiled the most important intelligence gathered during the day in a report, which he had waiting on Mátyás Rákosi's desk the next morning. (Rákosi took a particular interest in these intelligence reports in advance of inter-party consultations so that he could find out beforehand what the IShP was intending to propose during the meetings.) This intelligence would have produced evidence of any collaboration of IShP officials with the "conspirators"—had such evidence existed. Writing his memoirs two decades later, Rákosi continued to lament this deficiency, complaining that his political police had not provided him with enough ammunition to inflict a decisive defeat upon his political foes.

The Independent Smallholders' Party still had more representatives in Hungary's National Assembly than all the other parliamentary parties combined, even after the slander campaign against it had been going on for 20 months. Although the four-year parliamentary cycle was not even half over, Hungarian Communist Party leaders, citing a fundamental change in the country's political dynamics, managed to persuade the president of the republic to call early elections. The franchise law was amended before the elections so as to reduce the number of eligible voters by some half a million as compared to 1945. Moreover, the HCP took steps to encourage the greatest possible number of parties to participate in the elections, figuring that the party's relatively stable electoral base would carry more weight if those of its rival parties were diluted. With a single exception, the leaders of the new parties participating in the early parliamentary elections—István Barankovics of the Democratic People's Party, Zoltán Pfeiffer of the Hungarian Independence Party and István Balogh of the Independent Hungarian Democratic Party—were all former members of the IShP. The leader of the fourth new party, Margit Slachta of the Christian Women's Camp, had been elected to Parliament as a Civil Democratic Party candidate. (One of the stipulations contained in the amended franchise law had prevented former IShP representative Dezső Sulyok, who had founded the Hungarian Freedom Party after leaving the IShP in 1946, from taking part in the early elections.)

The parliamentary elections held in 1947 are commonly known as the "blue-slip elections" in reference to the blue-colored voter's registration card that citizens could use to cast ballots at locations other than that of their legal residence. The Hungarian Communist Party had a large number of these so-called blue slips printed for its own use, dispatching party members furnished with such documents via train, truck and occasionally even bicycle to vote at polling stations in multiple districts. It is difficult to estimate the total number of illicit "blue-slip" votes cast in the 1947 parliamentary elections, although it seems certain that the HCP obtained at least 62,000 extra votes through this method of ballot stuffing, and indeed some researchers suspect that the actual number was at least double that.

Although the abuse of the blue slips was instantly exposed, only later did the 1947 parliamentary elections become known as the "blue-slip" elections. There was, however, another method of electoral fraud employed during the 1947 elections that had an even greater influence on their outcome: namely, the way in which the Hungarian Communist Party utilized its control over public administration and the political police to restrict access to the ballot box, instructing loyal state bureaucrats to obstruct delivery of the certificate authorizing enrollment in electoral registers to citizens whom police informants had deemed "reactionary"—that is, those who presumably did not vote for one of the three parties in the Left-Wing Bloc. Only those who during the inter-war period had not been members of an organization or party qualified as right-wing were eligible to receive this certificate, the so-called registration form. Thus, in the event of insufficient documentary evidence, it was possible for those in relevant positions of the public administration to arbitrarily select whose applications for the electoral registration forms to accept and whose to put on hold pending the receipt of certified "proof." A total of 467,000 potential voters were denied the right to participate in the 1947 parliamentary elections through this method of administrative fraud, although tens of thousands of these essentially disenfranchised citizens did in September 1947 receive *ex post facto* notification of their inclusion on electoral registers. These 467,000 otherwise eligible voters, most of whom would have presumably cast their ballots for non-bloc parties, represented 8.5 percent of Hungary's total electorate, the equivalent of 35 parliamentary mandates. The official results of the 1947 elections are rendered most palpable when taken in comparison to those of the 1945 elections.

**Distribution of the votes
of the 1945 and 1947 parliamentary elections**

Parties	**Votes**				
	1945		1947		Changes
	Numbers	%	Numbers	%	%
HCP	802,122	16.96	1,113,050	22.27	+ 5.31
SDP	823,314	17.40	744,641	14.90	- 2.50
Workers' parties together	*1,625,436*	*34.36*	*1,857,691*	*37.17*	*+ 2.81*
NPP	325,284	6.88	415,465	8.31	+ 1.43
Left-Wing Bloc together	*1,950,720*	*41.24*	*2,273,156*	*45.48*	*+ 4.24*
IShP	2,697,503	57.02	769,763	15.40	- 41.62
Governing parties together	*4,648,223*	*98.26*	*3,042,919*	*60.88*	*- 37.38*
CDP	76,424	1.61	50,294	1.00	- 0.61
HRP	5,762	0.12	84,169	1.68	+ 1.56
DPP*	0	0	820,453	16.41	x
HIP**	0	0	670,547	13.42	x
IHDP***	0	0	260,420	5.21	x
CWC****	0	0	69,536	1.39	x
Opposition parties together	*82,186*	*1.74*	*1,955,419*	*39.12*	*+ 37.38*
All together	**4,730,409**	**100.00**	**4,998,338**	**100.00**	

* Democratic People's Party
** Hungarian Independence Party
*** Independent Hungarian Democratic Party
**** Christian Women's Camp

The biggest loser among the parties participating in the 1947 National Assembly elections was the Independent Smallholders' Party, which got 71.5 percent fewer votes than it had in the 1945 elections, giving the party 15 percent of the total number of votes cast, compared to 57 percent in 1945. The previously mentioned IShP "successor parties" absorbed almost all of the votes that had drifted away from the IShP itself. The IShP and its offshoots consequently received an absolute majority—52 percent—of the vote in the 1947 elections, even though the curtailed franchise, the incomplete structural and organizational development of the newly founded IShP successor parties, and the administrative contraction of the non-bloc electoral base had put these parties at a disadvantage. The majority of Hungary's voting public had thus rejected the incipient Soviet-type political system for a second time. The new parties can be viewed as the "winners" of the 1947 elections especially if one considers the performance of the minor opposition parties from the previous parliamentary cycle, which received more than one third of the vote in 1947 compared to under 2 percent in 1945. The strong showing of these parties again spelled fiasco for Hungarian Communist Party General Secretary Mátyás Rákosi, who, in a report to Moscow before the 1947 elections, had predicted that the former opposition would win a total of no more than 15 percent of the vote.

On the opposite, "left wing" of the political spectrum, the Hungarian Communist Party won 40 percent more votes in the 1947 elections than it had in the 1945 elections, giving the HCP 22 percent of the overall vote, while the Social Democratic Party received 2.5 percent fewer votes in 1947 than it had in 1945, giving the SDP somewhat less than 15 percent of the overall vote. (The two workers' parties thus recorded a composite gain of less than 3 percent of the overall vote in the 1947 parliamentary elections.) The third party in the Left-Wing Bloc, the National Peasant Party, gained 1.5 percent more votes in the 1947 elections than it had in the 1945 elections, giving the NPP 8.3 percent of the overall vote. Having won just 45 percent of the overall vote, the Left-Wing Bloc parties failed to attain their "joint" objective of gaining an absolute majority of seats in the new Parliament. The bloc thus still needed the support of the battered remnant of the Independent Smallholders' Party in order to form a government.

The Left-Wing Bloc parties, however, managed to achieve their coveted absolute majority in Parliament after Hungarian Independence Party leader Zoltán Pfeiffer submitted a petition to the Election Court requesting that the 1947 parliamentary elections be declared invalid and new elections called due to the "blue-slip" voting fraud. Hungarian Communist Party leaders subsequently persuaded their Left-Wing Bloc coalition partners to submit to the Court a joint counter-petition accusing the Hungarian Independence Party of having committed electoral fraud in connection with its collection of so-called recommendation forms required of newly established parties. This joint Left-Wing Bloc petition furthermore called upon the Election Court to annul all of the Zoltán Pfeiffer-led HIP's parliamentary mandates. Fearing another reprimand from Moscow if this initiative failed, Mátyás Rákosi summoned the Communist president of the Election Court, Ákos Major, to his villa, where the HCP leader cautioned him that the Court's decision would determine whether or not Hungary would be "plunged into civil war." Rákosi's illegitimate warning seems to have had its intended effect: the Election Court invalidated all 49 of the HIP's mandates. The National Election Committee subsequently issued its own ruling on this matter, retroactively declaring itself to have been collectively "deceived" with regard to the HIP's allegedly fraudulent collection of the recommendation forms, initiating procedures to dissolve the party, which HCP Minister of the Interior László Rajk immediately implemented. The omission of the HIP's 46 annulled mandates from the total number of those in the National Assembly served to increase the relative proportion of seats won by other parties participating in the 1947 elections, thus giving the Left-Wing Bloc an absolute, 56 percent, majority of parliamentary representatives, even without the support of the Independent Smallholders' Party. Those representatives who wanted no part in the HCP's obvious attempt to gain total political power had already withdrawn from the coalition parties. The shift in the distribution of power in Parliament that resulted from this and the prohibition of the HIP served to increase the HCP's relative majority in the National Assembly to 27 percent, thus giving it predominant control over the legislative process as well. For the distribution of seats in the Hungarian legislature between 1944 and 1949, see the comparative diagram on page 95.

This signaled an end to the period of power dualism that had begun following the 1945 parliamentary elections. During the several months in which the new, condensed (phony) coalition governed the country, the Communists totally dictated the tenor of political life in Hungary, their every move aimed at achieving absolute power. Over the next year and a half, most opposition party leaders—Dezső Sulyok, Zoltán Pfeiffer, István Barankovics and Margit Slachta—were forced to flee the country, further augmenting the ranks of Hungarian political émigrés in the West.

Notes

1 István Feitl, Mrs. Márta Lázár Gellér and János Kende, eds., *Demokratikus köztársaságok Magyarországon* [Democratic Republics in Hungary] (Budapest, 2007), p. 94.

2 Julianna Horváth, Éva Szabó, László Szűcs and Katalin Zalai, *Pártközi értekezletek. Politikai érdekegyeztetés és politikai konfrontáció, 1944–1948* [Inter-Party Consultations. Political Interest Coordination and Political Confrontations] (Budapest, 2003); István G. Vass, ed., *Tildy Zoltán kormányának minisztertanácsi jegyzőkönyvei, 1945. november–1946. február* [Minutes of the Council of Ministers of the Government of Zoltán Tildy, November 1945–February 1946] (Budapest, 2005); László Szűcs, ed., *Nagy Ferenc első kormányának minisztertanácsi jegyzőkönyvei, 1946. február–november*, I–II [Minutes of the Council of Ministers of the First Government of Ferenc Nagy, February–November 1946, vols. I–II] (Budapest, 2003); István G. Vass, ed., *Dinnyés Lajos első kormányának minisztertanácsi jegyzőkönyvei, 1947. június–szeptember* [Minutes

of the Council of Ministers of the First Government of Lajos Dinnyés, June–September 1947] (Budapest, 2005).

3 György Gyarmati, "Harc a közigazgatás birtoklásáért az 1946. évi hatalmi dualizmus időszakában" [The Struggle for Control of State Administration during the Period of Power Dualism in 1946], *Századok* 3 (1996): 497–570.

4 More precisely: Hungary's strictly defined civil service apparatus following the B-list dismissals in 1946 numbered 128,000 employees, compared to 75,000 in 1938. However, in budgetary terms, those working for major state-operated services, such as the Hungarian State Railway and the Hungarian Post Office, were counted as civil servants as well.

5 Ignác Romsics, *Az 1947-es párizsi békeszerződés* [The 1947 Paris Peace Treaty] (Budapest, 2006), pp. 212–223.

6 Ignác Romsics, ed., *Amerikai béketervek a háború utáni Magyarországról. Az Egyesült Államok Külügyminisztériumának titkos iratai, 1942–1944* [American Peace Plans with Regard to Post-War Hungary. Secret Documents of the US State Department. 1942–1944] (Gödöllő, 1992), and Tofik Iszlamov, "Erdély a szovjet külpolitikában, a második világháború alatt" [Transylvania in Soviet Foreign Affairs during the Second World War], *Múltunk* 1–2 (1994): 17–50.

7 For a description of the meetings of this body, see Mihály Fülöp, *A befejezetlen béke. A Külügyminiszterek Tanácsa és a magyar békeszerződés* [The Unfinished Peace. The Council of Foreign Ministers and the Hungarian Peace Treaty] (Budapest, no year specified).

8 The document communiqué also contains the Left-Wing Bloc's aforementioned letter and the IShP's response. In Horváth, Szabó, Szűcs and Zalai, *Pártközi értekezletek. Politikai érdekegyeztetés és politikai konfrontáció, 1944–1948*, pp. 292–326.

9 Ferenc Nagy, *Küzdelem a vasfüggöny mögött*, I [Struggle behind the Iron Curtain], vol. 1 (Budapest, 1990), pp. 340–341.

10 Romsics, *Az 1947-es párizsi békeszerződés*, p. 226.

11 See Ferenc Fischer, *A megosztott világ, 1941–1991* [A Divided World, 1941–1991] (Budapest and Pécs, 2001), pp. 61–86.

12 István Csicsery-Rónay, Géza Cserenyei and Mária Palasik, *Koncepciós per a Független Kisgazdapárt szétzúzására* [Show Trial to Crush the Independent Smallholders' Party] (Budapest, 1998). See

the second volume of the above-cited memoirs of Ferenc Nagy for more information.

13 Mária Palasik, *Kovács Béla, 1908–1959* [Béla Kovács, 1908–1959] (Budapest, 2002).

14 Lajos Halas, *Az R[endező] Gárdától a Munkásőrségig* [From the O[rganizing] Guard to the Workers' Militia] (Budapest, 1986), pp. 126–127.

15 Gyula Borbándi, *A magyar emigráció életrajza* [Memoir of the Hungarian Diaspora] (Budapest, 1989).

III. BUILDING THE STALINIST POLITICAL SYSTEM, 1947–1950

The one-year interval between Ferenc Nagy's emigration and the foundation of the Hungarian Workers' Party (June 1947–June 1948) was referred to at the time as "the year of transition." The Hungarian Communist Party dictatorship either destroyed or marginalized its coalition partners in precisely the same way as it did its parliamentary opposition: viewed from the perspective of a competitive multi-party system, it had no adversaries left in the political ring. The dictatorship itself had come to believe that there remained little, if any, substantial impediment to its unrestricted exercise of political power. The triumphant conceit implied in the notion of the "year of transition" was rooted in an outlook that had become focused entirely on party politics. However, if one looks beyond the narrow horizon of inter-party struggle, the half a dozen years following World War II appear much more like "years of transition."[1] A succession of fundamental transformations, in fact, took place in Hungary with regard to ownership rights, management of the economy, cultural life in its broadly defined sense and the operation of the country's increasingly pervasive state institutions every year, from the end of the war until the end of 1950. *In other words, two interconnected system changes took place in Hungary between 1945 and 1950.* The true turning point in this dual process took place during the summer of 1948 with the foundation of the Hungarian Workers' Party (HWP). Although certain archetypical elements of the communist *Einrichtungswerk* (preparatory work) were already in place by the time that the HWP was founded, it took another two and a half years for the party to finish building its comprehensive institutional system. (Major transformations continued to occur in each subsequent year until 1956, the end of the period presently under examination, as well. However, these transformations represented mere internal adjustments and rash modifications of the communist dictatorship to its initial archetypes.)

1. Communist "Left Face!" in Foreign and Economic Policy

It is just as difficult to interpret the dual system change that took place in Hungary in the years following World War II by utilizing the criteria of a competitive multi-party system as it is one-sided to explain the events that took place during the period solely in terms of domestic political developments. The communist system change that took place in the second half of 1947 was in large part a product of the *gradually* sharpening antagonism between the Soviet Union and the Anglo-American Great Powers: that is, the beginning of the Cold War.[2] After the din of battle subsided in 1945, Soviet penetration of the region of Europe lying between Stettin and Trieste in the west and the Curzon Line and the Bosphorus in the east represented a possible, although not inevitable, option. The Communist Parties of France and Italy, dominant political forces in those countries in the years following World War II, were squeezed from power following the proclamation of the Truman Doctrine in the spring of 1947. In response, Moscow quickly orchestrated the removal of proponents of civil parliamentarianism throughout its sphere of influence in Eastern Europe. In addition to the deposal of Independent Smallholders' Party Prime Minister Ferenc Nagy described in the previous chapter, Peasant Party leaders Iuliu Maniu of Romania and Nikola Petkov of Bulgaria were removed from office (the former was sentenced to life in prison, the latter executed) and Deputy Prime Minister Stanisław Mikołajczyk of Poland was forced to flee the country, all during the three-month period from the end of May until the beginning of September. During the latter month, the Cominform was founded in Szklarska Poręba, Poland, essentially to coordinate the affairs of the international workers' movement as the successor to the Comintern, which had been dissolved in 1943. The founding statement of this Soviet-dominated international

Communist Party organization called upon member parties to take power in their home countries.

The latter exhortation resounded in Hungarian Communist Party Deputy General Secretary Mihály Farkas's mid-October 1947 briefing to the party apparatus regarding Hungary's post-election domestic political situation in which Farkas said "What's going to happen here and what's right for the Hungarian people is what the Communist Party wants." During the briefing, Farkas referred to reappointed Prime Minister Lajos Dinnyés and what remained of the Independent Smallholders' Party as "lapdogs," also praising the National Peasant Party for having long been subservient towards the Communists. Farkas went on to harshly denounce the HCP's "fraternal" Social Democratic Party, which, according to the deputy general secretary, had failed to keep up with the times. According to Farkas, "the SDP is now just a temporary party, which will unite with the Communist Party in the near future. [...] We live in an age in which all roads lead towards communism."[3] Stalin's new doctrine abandoning the Soviet Union's post-war tactical moderation, formerly referred to as "the king's mirror," thus became tangible in Budapest.

Other developments that took place in Eastern Europe at this time were also symptoms of "the beginning of a new era," although the impressions of those who lived through the period have only coalesced into a broad illustration of history with the passing of time. The countries mentioned above, along with Czechoslovakia, were not permitted to participate in the post-war European reconstruction program, the Marshall Plan. For the Atlantic powers this signaled, among other things, that Moscow intended to incorporate the region that had fallen within its sphere of influence following World War II into its own closed political and economic environment. However, it was not immediately evident even to the leaders of the Communist Parties that were in the process of establishing dictatorships in the countries of the region that the Kremlin was planning to isolate them not only "from the West," but from one another as well. A series of initiatives took shape at the end of World War II aimed at the integration of the small states in Eastern Europe into various forms of consortium (customs unions and federations). Yugoslavia served as the initial standard-bearer for these proposals, while neighboring countries—although the notion of a Hungarian–Romanian coalition also emerged in public at this time—for the most part just expressed their support for the regional integration following the *de jure* reinstatement of their sovereignty with the signing of the peace treaties. Eastern European states viewed such integration not only as a potential source of economic benefit, but as a means of mollifying the historical grievances and ongoing antagonism that existed between them as well.

The integration endeavors of the countries located in the Danube basin appeared to be taking form when in the summer of 1947 Josip Broz Tito and Georgi Dimitrov concluded the Bled agreement, which called for the foundation of a customs union between Yugoslavia and Bulgaria over the short term and the establishment of a political federation comprising the two countries over the longer term. Hungary not only voiced its solidarity with the Yugoslav–Bulgarian initiative, but, during Tito's official visit to Budapest in December 1947, advocated the establishment of a similar customs union with Romania, which might eventually integrate with a future Yugoslav–Bulgarian federation. Although Moscow was well aware of the integration proposals being drawn up in Eastern Europe and provided its preliminary approval for the Bled agreement, Stalinist propaganda, which had previously been permissive in this regard, ordered a sudden halt to these initiatives in January 1948, characterizing the incipient integration process as a distorted fantasy. Yugoslavia's aspiration to achieve a greater degree of sovereignty as manifested in these regional integration schemes was partially responsible for triggering the internal "little Cold War" between Moscow and Belgrade that lasted until Stalin's death in 1953. This conflict had a decisive impact on both (military) investment and politics in Hungary. The next phase in the practical application of the antithetical "two-world" doctrine was the foundation of the Council for Mutual Economic Assistance

(Comecon) in January 1949. Although the official objective of this organization was to coordinate the development of socialist planned economies in Europe, in practice its activities were confined to overseeing the conclusion of agreements on goods exchange between the Soviet Union and its other member countries, whose Communist Parties continued to pursue autarkic economic policies largely in isolation from one another until the end of the following decade.

Hungary's transition to a planned economy began following the August 1947 parliamentary elections, which had served to solidify the influence of the left-wing parties within the governing coalition. The government had already been compelled to reject participation in the Marshall Plan on July 10 of that year. The Hungarian Communist Party had called for a further radical transformation of Hungary's ownership structure as part of the party's economic development program proclaimed during the previous year's HCP congress. The HCP promised that transition to a planned economy would be to the benefit of Hungary's majority agrarian populace, which had, as previously discussed, considered the stabilization price ratios to have been a direct attack on its economic existence. Published economic development guidelines may have provided some hope of such improvement, although from the very beginning these prescriptions did not correspond to those contained in the genuine plans that the HCP had prepared exclusively for internal use.

Diagram 4:
Investment under the three-year plan

	Plan (million forints)				Fulfillment	
Branches	Published		Actual		Current prices	
		%		%		%
Industry	1,745	26.5	2,129	32.3	3,592	34.7
Agriculture	2,000	30.4	987	15.0	1,842	17.8
Transport	1,676	25.4	1,800	27.3	2,180	21.0
Social and construction (S & C)	1,164	17.7	1,669	25.4	2,744	26.5
Total	6,585	100	6,585	100	10,358	100

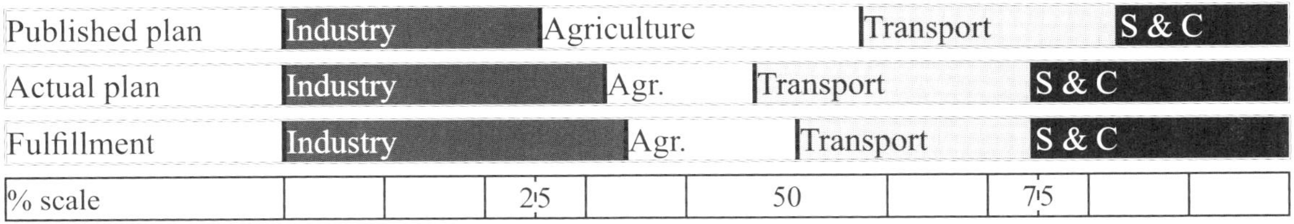

The double-entry bookkeeping that took place even during the planning phase of Hungary's economic transformation indicates that the stability price (dis)proportions had generated such a sharp degree of antagonism that the Hungarian Communist Party decided that it would be wise to propagate counterfeit economic policies that would be acceptable to the peasantry and the remnants of its political parties and accurately reflect the economic weight of Hungary's agrarian sector, while keeping the party's true economic plans inaccessible to the public under the classification "strictly confidential." The HCP was able to keep their genuine program secret because the party's coalition partners not only had no influence over the plans being devised under the auspices of the Economic Supreme Council, but had no right to review them either. While the HCP's public program accorded more government investment to agriculture than to any other sphere of the economy, the party's true economic plans stipulated less than half the publicly stated amount of support for the agrarian sector. The HCP, in fact, implemented these confidential economic policies, relegating agriculture to the bottom of the list in terms of both nominal and proportional state support. In contrast to the official propaganda slogan "flowering agricultural, prosperous peasantry," a comment that HCP leader Mátyás Rákosi made in private regarding the rationale for continuing to appoint Agrarian Party candidates to head the Ministry of Agriculture reflects the party's true stance towards the agricultural sector: "The peasantry won't have any suspicion that they are being increasingly exploited in favor of the city." (Independent Smallholders' Party members Árpád Szabó and István Dobi served as minister of agriculture in 1947–1948, while Ferenc Erdei filled the post from 1949 until 1953. Both Dobi and Erdei had secretly joined the Hungarian Communist Party by the time that they assumed leadership over the Ministry of Agriculture.)

The operation of a centrally planned economy required the acquisition of the means of production and financial goods on the one side, just as it necessitated the regulation of redistribution so as to eliminate consumer market mechanisms on the other. The successive phases of the nationalization process that had begun at the end of 1945 served this purpose. Private energy-related enterprises (mines, power plants) and large companies involved in heavy industry—among them the Csepel Manfréd Weiss Steel and Metal Works, the Rimamurány-Salgótarján Iron Mill, the Győr Carriage and Machine Factory, and the Ganz factory group—were the first to be nationalized. The process continued with the enactment of the bank nationalization law in the autumn of 1947. Half a year later, in the spring of 1948, factories and companies employing more than 100 people were nationalized, although by this time the government had dispensed with even the pretense of legality. On March 25, one month after the emigration of Social Democratic Party Minister of Industrial Affairs Antal Bán, several hundred reliable workers' cadres were summoned to appear at the headquarters of the ironworkers' union, where Hungarian Communist Party State Secretary for Industrial Affairs Imre Karczag told them that they would serve as "worker directors" at their newly nationalized plants and factories. With their letters of commission in hand, these new so-called worker directors were sent to take control of their respective workshops, specifically to seize company ledgers in order to have their remittance rights frozen. (The majority of those appointed to this new position had not previously been acquainted with such economic and banking terms.) As a result of this act, 84 percent of those working in Hungary's industrial and manufacturing sector became employees at state-owned enterprises. The bill sanctioning nationalization of these plants and factories was submitted to Parliament only a month later, in April 1948, and it was passed essentially unopposed. From this point onwards, the concept and functional role of Parliament ceased to be comprehensible in their historical senses.

Diagram 5:

Employees of all the state-owned enterprises
in the rate of employees of industry

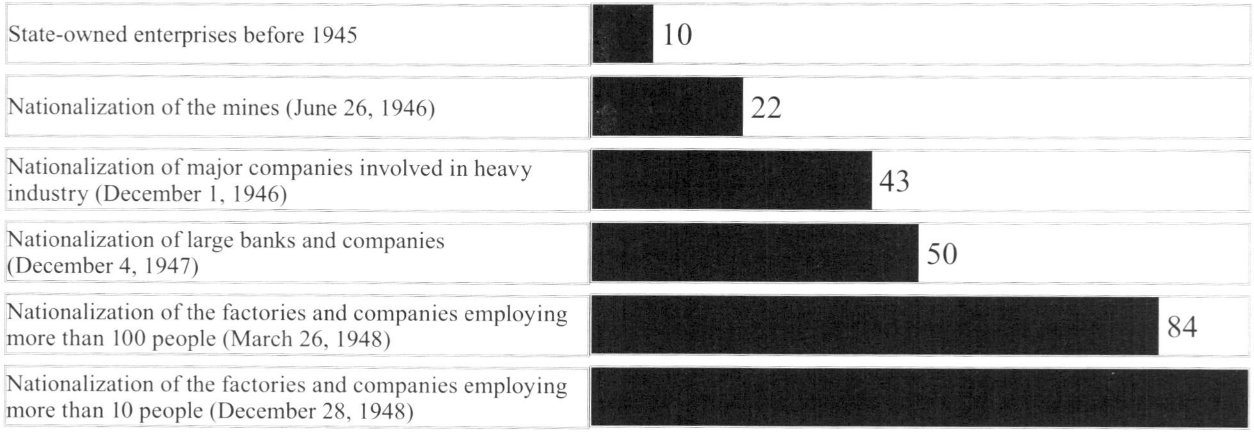

Source: Ernő Csizmadia, *Az MSZMP agrárpolitikája és a magyar mezőgazdaság* [The Agrarian Policy of the HWP and Hungarian Agriculture] (Budapest, 1984), p. 21.

The second important event to take place in March was the commemoration of the hundredth anniversary of the 1848 Hungarian Revolution. More precisely, it was at this time that events connected to the broader "centennial year" were held. The political choreography of this series of celebrations reflected, on the one hand, an attempt of the Hungarian Communist Party to place itself within a historical context, while, on the other hand, demonstrating that the party was the sole authentic guardian and current exponent of the 1848 revolutionary tradition. The HCP presented its reinterpretation of the events of 1848–1849 within this ideological framework. The communists attempted to transform the 1848 uprising into a "people's democratic revolution" and the subsequent War of Independence into a popular insurrection against foreign, Habsburg (connoting German) tyranny. The HCP furthermore endeavored to obscure the dominant political role that members of the nobility such as István Széchenyi, Lajos Batthyány, Bertalan Szemere, Ferenc Deák and László Teleki had played in the 1848 Revolution, highlighting instead the revolutionary activities of commoners such as Sándor Petőfi and Mihály Táncsics. The party proclaimed that the communist-led revolutionary transformation that was taking place in Hungary would serve to accomplish the unachieved objectives of the 1848 Revolution. Lajos Kossuth was the only one of the former revolutionary protagonists to remain an unblemished hero under the communist reinterpretation of the events that took place in Hungary in 1848–1849. Kossuth's name was attached to an award founded in that year (the Kossuth Prize) recognizing outstanding work performance and scientific, academic and artistic achievement. The HCP's chief ideologue, József Révai, directed the politicization of the 1848 Revolution's centennial anniversary. The first and last prescriptions contained in a political catechism that Révai prepared for the occasion summarize the essence of his effort to infuse the centenary celebration of the 1848 Revolution with communist ideology: "1848 must be portrayed as a precursor of Hungarian people's democracy [...] The working class, having already become unified [see below] will unite its interests with the peasantry and they will finish the work started in 1848 together, carrying the country forward towards socialism on a path of people's democracy." It is, however, worth noting that HCP Speaker of the National Assembly Imre Nagy gave a commemorative address that diverged greatly in both content and rhetoric from the HCP's depiction of the Revolution of 1848–1849, expressing genuine reverence for the revolutionary events and heroes from 100 years previously.[4]

2. Communist "Left Face!" in Domestic Politics

The most important political event that occurred in Hungary during the spring of 1948 was the unification of the Social Democratic Party and the Hungarian Communist Party. The six-month process of merging the two parties was carried out through use of the mechanisms of both political organizations and the political police. The SDP had essentially split in two by the beginning of 1948 as a result of months of intense communist pressure—which included both repeated promises and increasingly strident incrimination—on the party to unite with the HCP. SDP General Secretary Árpád Szakasits resorted to his well-tested "I'm not even here" method of resolving the conflict, departing for Moscow with a government delegation while his deputy, György Marosán, remained at home to take care of the shady affair. Marosán, whom many in the SDP had ceased to consider as a true member of the party, did not hesitate to act, declaring at a summarily convened assembly of SDP functionaries—where, according to contemporaries, most of the SDP members failed to be present—that party officials (Anna Kéthly, Antal Bán, Ime Szélig, Ferenc Szeder and three dozen lower-echelon apparatchiks) who had expressed opposition to the merger with the HCP would be divested of their functions. The discharged SDP officials had espoused the "cooperation, but not unification" viewpoint, which local, regional and factory-based party organizations had also advocated in petitions sent to the SDP central secretariat from all over Hungary during the previous two months. Provincial agencies of the State Protection Department

(ÁVO) had begun harassing SDP functionaries operating in their jurisdictions following the onset of this flood of petitions, warning them that they would be wise to quit expressing solidarity with "the right-wing reactionary Kéthly clique." Some of these functionaries were even detained for short periods of time in the hope that a few days behind bars might help them to see the light.

Avid intimidation on the part of the political police appeared to be more persuasive than agitation. By the time that Marosán publicly pronounced the political excommunications described above, the open opposition of the recalcitrant members of the Social Democratic Party had already begun to diminish. On February 22, János Kádár of the Hungarian Communist Party and István Szurdi of the Social Democratic Party signed an inter-party agreement identifying precisely which SDP officials would have to be dismissed from their posts and excluded from the party because they had been deemed unfit for admittance to the unified workers' party. The political police played a role in forming this agreement, whose lists of "*persona non grata*" were based on the organization's "situation reports." The SDP continued to engage in this process of self-destruction at its March party conference and thereafter, dismissing several dozen county deputy lieutenants, mayors, chief notaries and nearly half of the party's parliamentary representatives in accordance with a steady succession of communist wish lists. The process of fusion between the SDP and the HCP, which had already begun with the merger of local, municipal and county SDP organizations with their HCP counterparts, culminated with a three-day "unification congress" beginning on June 12, 1948. Through the purging of tens of thousands of people from the SDP before that date, the communists had ensured that the unified Hungarian Workers' Party (HWP) founded at the congress would conform to "genuinely Marxist" expectations. Árpád Szakasits was appointed as chairman of the HWP, while Mátyás Rákosi became the general secretary of the new party and György Marosán, Mihály Farkas and János Kádár were selected to serve as its deputy general secretaries.

László Rajk and János Kádár offered a concise outline of the projected script for building the Hungarian Communist Party—or rather, to be precise, the Hungarian Workers' Party—dictatorship during joint consultations held in Moscow at the end of May. (As non-Muscovites, the two had been sent on a one-month visit to the Soviet Union to make the acquaintance of Soviet party leaders.) In the course of their Moscow consultations, Rajk and Kádár asserted that the most important task to be completed following the merger of the Social Democratic Party and the Hungarian Communist Party was to establish the new People's Front to replace the moribund Hungarian National Independence Front, citing the nationalization of parochial schools, "the struggle against the main enemy of democracy, the Catholic Church," the reform of public administration, the writing of a new constitution, the suppression of the kulaks and the establishment of agricultural cooperatives as the other essential duties of the new Hungarian Workers' Party.[5] Rajk and Kádár accurately outlined the Hungarian Workers' Party's main objectives during their consultations in Moscow, although their calculation that they could be achieved before the end of the year proved to be way too optimistic. It took several years for the new party to complete them, as we will see later. The new party placed particular emphasis on the collectivization of agriculture on the Soviet model. In August 1948, just two months after the party was founded, HWP General Secretary Mátyás Rákosi proclaimed the launching of its collectivization program, which was to meet with only partial success. This matter will be discussed in detail in the section of the book dealing with the operational mechanism of the 1950s.

The enactment of the law nationalizing parochial schools on June 16, 1948, was obscured in the "shadow" of the Social Democratic Party–Hungarian Communist Party fusion, which had taken place just a few days previously. This is one of the reasons why the details of this issue have been relegated to the side stage of national education policy and more recent Church history references, whereas it was one of the central elements of communist ideology and the political assertion of the atheist worldview. This did not represent a mere separation of Church and state in accordance with the increasingly secularized concepts of state and social organization, but a ruthless suppression of religious faith and, whenever possible, the liquidation of its main institution(s), the Church(es). Although the Hungarian Workers' Party attempted to follow the Soviet model in this instance as well, the party failed to take one fundamental difference between Hungary and the Soviet Union into account. Whereas the Russian Orthodox Church had always operated in subordination to the Russian state as a consequence of so-called Caesaropapism, Hungary with its majority Roman Catholic population was, like most European states, part of Vatican-centered Latin Christendom. Because Hungary was part of this "global Church," the state could act on matters pertaining to Church organizations and operations only in consultation with the Holy See.

Hungary's population by religious affiliation in 1949

Denomination	**No. of adherents**	**Proportion, %**
Roman Catholic	6,240,427	67.8
Greek Catholic (Uniate)	248,355	2.7
Reformed	2,014,707	21.9
Evangelical (Lutheran)	482,152	5.2
Jewish	133,682	1.5
Orthodox	36,010	0.4
Baptist	18,874	0.2
Unitarian	9,447	0.1
Other	7,153	0.1
Not known	1,521	0.0
No religious affiliation	12,291	0.1
Total	**9,204,799**	**100**

Nationalization of parochial schools was not the first step taken in terms of religious and Church policy following World War II. The Churches also resented the 1945 land distribution, at the beginning of which the Holy See's diplomatic representative, Apostolic Nuncio Angelo Rotta, had been expelled from Hungary under Soviet pressure. During the summer of 1946, Minister of the Interior László Rajk had dissolved a succession of Catholic groups and associations, while placing those of the Protestant denominations under review prior to their eventual disbandment, which took place in 1950. An agreement was reached at an inter-party conference in March 1947 that removed religious instruction from its place among the compulsory subjects at schools. (A statutory decree enacted in September 1949 validated this agreement.) The state subsequently nationalized 5,407 parochial elementary schools, 113 parochial secondary schools and almost 100 parochial lyceums during the summer of 1948.

Hungary's Catholic priesthood and episcopate, primarily Archbishop of Esztergom Cardinal József Mindszenty, spoke out against the nationalization of parochial schools. The country's already tightly controlled press portrayed the opposition of the Catholic clergy as "intrigues of clerical reaction," although it either distorted or chose to ignore the extensive degree of social aversion and dissent that had been manifested towards the nationalization of parochial schools throughout the country, even in remote villages. Evidence of the breadth and intensity of this opposition has been preserved in political police "morale reports" remaining from the year 1948.[6] One criminal trial connected to the demonstrations that took place in opposition to the nationalization of parochial schools resulted in a verdict of the death penalty, while most of the population of the village where the protest took place (Pócspetri) became the target of persecution and slander; however, authorities arrived at the conclusion that the most effective method of suppressing social resistance was to get rid of the head of Hungary's Catholic Church.

The Archbishop of Esztergom, Cardinal József Mindszenty, was from the very outset the most uncompromising adversary of the social and political transformation that had been taking place in Hungary since the end of World War II. The archbishop's vociferous anti-communism was part of the reason why he became the primary objective of a "dedicated line" for surveillance of "ecclesiastical reaction" that the political police had established already in October 1945. Cardinal Mindszenty became the target of increasing attacks following the initiation of a communist press campaign on behalf of the nationalization of parochial schools at the beginning of 1948. Mátyás Rákosi not only played a role in this with his frequent public pronouncements, but served as the coordinator and director of the multi-faceted maneuver as well.

Intentionally more overt police surveillance during the autumn of that year, together with the continuing slander campaign, were, in fact, intended to acclimatize the general public to expect that the archbishop's arrest would be the inevitable outcome of the dispute. Mindszenty's secretary had already been placed under arrest and the archbishop's residence searched several times before the archbishop himself was taken into custody during the Christmas of 1948. Mindszenty was brought to trial the following February and subsequently condemned to life in prison for treason and foreign currency trafficking.[7]

Sources recently made accessible reveal another related aspect of the Mindszenty affair. Although Mátyás Rákosi wanted to rid himself of the Archbishop of Esztergom at any cost, even he considered the prospect of his imprisonment to be too risky. Although the forced retirement of Reformed Bishop László Ravasz and the two-year prison sentence imposed upon Lutheran Bishop Lajos Ordass at around this time had suitably alarmed Hungary's minority Protestant community, they were intended also to serve as warnings to Mindszenty. The communist slander campaign and public threats of prosecution were aimed at either prompting Mindszenty to voluntarily leave the country or inducing the Pope to summon the archbishop to Rome for service at the Vatican. Although Hungary had severed its diplomatic relations with the Holy See by this time, Rákosi secretly attempted to effectuate the latter alternative, partly through covert diplomatic channels and partly through the mediation of Church officials whom he had sent to Rome.[8] Just as he had a year and a half earlier in connection to Ferenc Nagy, Rákosi determined that it would be more politically expedient to launch yet another slander campaign against "the criminal prelate on the run from justice" than it would be to have Mindszenty put on trial, especially since his political police had been unable to produce any suitable *corpus delicti* against the archbishop, in spite of Rákosi's increasingly frequent reprimands.[9]

Rákosi made other miscalculations in the course of his battle campaign against Mindszenty as well. The Hungarian Workers' Party leader based the tactics on the faulty premise that the Church could be dealt with in the same way as a political party slated for destruction. It is difficult to determine in retrospect if Rákosi's short-sightedness prevented him from recognizing the strength of the deep social foundations and thousand-year institutional tradition of the Church(es), or if he did recognize this and simply chose to ignore it. The relevant historical sources in Moscow and at the Vatican have not yet been made accessible. The deluge of sources that have been made available for research in Hungary indicates that the mistaken preconceptions of those HWP leaders presiding over the party's handling of the so-called Mindszenty affair probably caused them to fall into their own trap. These leaders would have become the object of national ridicule if following the increasingly hysterical slander campaign that took place during the second half of 1948 they had not brought the steadfast Mindszenty to trial. The flimsy evidence introduced against the archbishop could have hardly been deemed admissible from a legal perspective—it was merely part of the stage settings for the politically motivated show trial.

3. New People's Front, New Elections, New Constitution, New Schools

Although former Social Democratic Party official Árpád Szakasits was appointed to serve as chairman of the Hungarian Workers' Party when it was founded in June 1948, no real authority had been attached to this position. The nomination of Szakasits to the post of HWP chairman nevertheless represented an affront to the vanity and ambition to achieve total power of HWP General Secretary Mátyás Rákosi. As a consequence, Szakasits had hardly settled in his new chairman's office when an even more stately appointment was found for him, although at the cost of another legal and constitutional scandal. One month after the Social Democratic Party–Hungarian Communist Party merger, Hungary's ambassador to Cairo, Viktor Csornoky, was ordered to return to Budapest, where the State Protection Division arrested him on July 30 on suspicion of espionage. Csornoky just happened to be the son-in-law of President Zoltán Tildy, who voluntarily submitted his resignation as a result of his indirect connection to the affair. Parliament unanimously accepted Tildy's resignation, electing Szakasits to succeed him as president of the republic on August 3, 1948. Csornoky was sentenced to death for treason and executed in December 1948.[10] Zoltán Tildy and his wife spent the next eight years living under house arrest.

The period following the "turning point" of 1948 was characterized by two marked processes: the culmination of the concentration of power and the increasing criminalization of public life. The concentration of power was manifested in the cabinet reshuffle that took place at the time of Tildy's replacement as head of state. This reshuffle resulted in the following personnel changes: Hungarian Workers' Party Deputy General Secretary Mihály Farkas replaced National Peasant Party Chairman Péter Veres as minister of defense; another HWP deputy general secretary, János Kádár, was appointed to serve as minister of the interior in place of fellow HWP member László Rajk, who became minister of foreign affairs, a much less powerful cabinet position. The reason for Rajk's transfer from the Ministry of the Interior to the Ministry of Foreign Affairs was not publicly apparent at the time, especially since over previous years he had been viewed as one of the Hungarian Communist Party's key figures for a couple of reasons: first, as an implacable party militant, Rajk had effectively served the cause of building the communist dictatorship, thus earning the nickname "iron-handed minister of the interior" from his contemporaries; second, he, perhaps even more than Rákosi, was the "star" of the Hungarian

Communist Party within the media circumstances of the day, the most emblematic figure among the party's leadership.[11] One of the reasons for Rajk's "demotion" to minister of foreign affairs was the fact that he had come into conflict with Rákosi's other trusted party subordinate, chief of the political police Gábor Péter. The latter had long wanted to increase the autonomy and authority of the political police force. Rákosi believed that the process of strengthening the political police could begin only following the unification of the Social Democratic Party and the Hungarian Communist Party, although he considered the cabinet reshuffle to be the most effective means of resolving the conflict between his key subordinates.

Among the first steps that János Kádár took as minister of the interior was to "upgrade" Gábor Péter's police division, transforming the force into an autonomous and higher-echelon organizational unit within the Ministry. The name of the organization was officially changed from the State Protection Department (or ÁVO in its Hungarian-language acronymic form) to the State Protection Authority (ÁVH) of the Ministry of Interior at this time. The previously separate economic police division and passport authority were then merged into the ÁVH. The most important consequence of the changes to the political police was that Gábor Péter became almost as powerful as the minister of the interior, who was still formally the police chief's superior. In fact, the relative authority of the various ministers and key officeholders depended primarily on whom Rákosi favored or wanted to play off against one another at any given moment.

As newly installed minister of the interior, János Kádár announced in September 1948 that a so-called act of sabotage had been exposed at the Hungarian–American Oil Industry Company, or Magyar–Amerikai Olajipari Részvénytársaság (MAORT). This resulted in the so-called MAORT trial, the first in a succession of so-called economic show trials. Among those taken into custody were the company's president, Paul Ruedemann, and his deputy, George Bannantine, who, as US citizens, gained their release after signing false confessions (and paying a tidy sum of money). Charges were filed only against the company's Hungarian employees. Among the company leaders brought to trial, the recently retired former CEO Simon Papp, an internationally recognized petroleum engineer and geologist, was condemned to death, a sentence that was subsequently commuted to life in prison. (Papp was released from prison in 1955.) Another defendant, Bódog Ábel, was sentenced to ten years in prison, where he died in 1953. The true motive for the trial in which the leaders of MAORT were charged with sabotage and espionage was to bring foreign-owned capital interests under state control without compensation. The state acquired the British-owned Hutter and Lewer chemical company at this same time, again accusing the concern's management of espionage. One year later, around the turn of the year 1949–1950, the ITT-owned Standard Electricity Company (Standard Villamossági Részvénytársaság) was expropriated through a similar miscarriage of justice. A total of 25 people were charged in three separate trials in connection with the latter case. Company CEO Imre Geiger and ministry official Zoltán Radó were condemned to death and executed, while the other defendants were sentenced to between five years and life in prison. (A Chief Public Prosecutor's Office review of the case conducted in the 1950s determined that "the Standard case was based on a sequence of illegalities."[12] The verdicts of the other trials mentioned above were annulled only after 1990.)

Hungary's institutional system was reorganized and subordinated to the party dictatorship in several other areas as well in 1949. In January, the national committees that had been established during the political interregnum at the end of World War II were dissolved. In February, the Public Administration Court that had supervised the lawful exercise of executive power for fifty years was abolished. The National Labor Administration Office that had been formally established in the previous year to conduct the "distribution" of Hungary's labor force in accordance with the needs of the planned economy also began operating at this time. Additionally, the Hungarian Independence People's Front (HIPF, or simply People's Front) was established in place of the

Hungarian National Independence Front founded at the end of 1944. Although the names of the two organizations were similar, their functions were substantially different. In a briefing to the Central Directorate, Mátyás Rákosi defined the primary objective of the new organization as "decreasing the significance of the bourgeois parties and accelerating their demise, their liquidation." László Rajk remarked publicly at the time of the HIPF's foundation that "those who proclaim a program other than the building of socialism are not a constructive government opposition, but the enemies of the Hungarian people."

Among the parties in the languishing opposition, the István Barankovics-led Democratic People's Party and the Margit Slachta-led Christian Women's Camp were disbanded at the beginning of 1949. Because these parties had been dissolved, they could not join the new formation. However, not even the nominally functioning remnants of the coalition parties took a genuine role in the formation of government policy. They sang their swansongs as part of the Hungarian National Independence Front chorus, without any distinct voice. A few members of the former coalition parties who were openly loyal to the Hungarian Workers' Party were permitted to occupy seats in the new National People's Front Council. They thus exercised a formal influence over the composition of the joint list of so-called "People's Front" candidates, who by then stood unopposed in elections. The Hungarian Workers' Party Operative Election Committee, in fact, drew up these lists of joint candidates, which, in order to maintain appearances, were officially published by the People's Front. The political deceit characteristic of the period is reflected clearly in the composition of the HIPF's central leadership, which consisted of Mátyás Rákosi as chairman, László Rajk as general secretary and crypto-communist fellow travelers István Dobi and Ferenc Erdei as vice-chairmen.

The establishment of the new—and in reality false—People's Front did not automatically entail the calling of fresh National Assembly elections. The current Parliament had completed only one third of its four-year mandate. Since, as will be shown, the institutional and organizational process of building the communist dictatorship had by no means been completed, could the legitimization of the "transformations" that had taken place since August 1947 have been the true objective of the elections called for May 15, 1949? Why did the Hungarian Workers' Party leadership feel the need to substantiate its dominance, by then uncontested, through the holding of early, single-list elections? The answer to these questions can be traced to both foreign and domestic political factors. The motive in terms of foreign policy for calling new elections was based on the HWP's compulsion to satisfy Moscow's expectations. The Cominform's official censure of Yugoslavia in the summer of 1948 had included reproof of the Tito-led Communist Party of Yugoslavia for its alleged merger with the country's people's front. The leaders of the HWP wanted to demonstrate to Moscow that this was not the case in Hungary. The primary domestic political motive for holding the early elections was to symbolically cross the Rubicon: the consummation of communist dictatorship in such a way as to maintain an outward appearance of legality. In spite of the fact that the ranks of the National Assembly had been largely purged of opposition, Rákosi continued to worry that only a parliament consisting exclusively of his adherents would adopt "the constitution sanctioning the council and single-party system" without resistance.[13] The modified voting procedure for the 1949 elections—the single-list ballot—seemed to be a suitable way of ensuring that the attempt to legitimize communist authority through ratification of a new constitution would be successful.

Even amid the incessant victory propaganda, the leadership of the Hungarian Workers' Party was aware that its triumph was fraudulent, since the party had not managed to generate genuine social support commensurate in degree with its unquestionable political dominance. On the contrary: the nationalization of parochial schools and the campaign to subvert Mindszenty had engendered increased aversion towards the HWP and sympathy for the party's adversaries. The Archbishop of Esztergom had proclaimed 1947 to be the Year of Mary—also called the Year of the Blessed Virgin—

in Hungary.[14] Devotional pilgrimages held to mark this event sometimes attracted tens of thousands of participants. A total of 4.6 million pilgrims took part in these sacred passages to shrines and other locations throughout Hungary in 1947, in spite of the fact that the political police utilized a diverse array of administrative and organizational tactics to prevent people from reaching the designated pilgrimage sites. Seen from another perspective, a significant majority of Hungary's eligible voters evinced support for their faith and its bishops—among them Mindszenty—at these pastoral assemblies. The archbishop's subsequent arrest and trial aroused further manifestations of solidarity. In addition to intense foreign protest, there was a succession of both Church and secular petition campaigns at the turn of the year 1948–1949, although the communist-controlled domestic press was not permitted to report on these events. Demonstrations resulting in clashes with the police and arrests took place throughout the country.

By holding the new elections, the Hungarian Workers' Party wase attempting to counterbalance the permanent, albeit symbolic, popular "referendum" that had been taking place against it over the previous year. The HWP's election drive was based on both stilted victory propaganda and an equally intensive negative campaign against "ecclesiastical reaction." Another Communist campaign tactic was to engage party activists to persuade members of the local clergy to support the People's Front by publicly denouncing their own superiors and the "reactionary supreme cleric" and soliciting their congregations to participate in the elections. The single-list voting procedure introduced for these elections made an HWP victory inevitable—only the magnitude of the party's victory was at stake. The results of the May parliamentary elections ran true to form: an extraordinary 95 percent of Hungary's eligible voters cast ballots in the election that produced an equal 95 percent majority for the People's Front. This provided the HWP with 71 percent of the representatives in Parliament, precisely the percentage that the HWP leadership had defined in its "election plan" prepared three months earlier. The following table shows the distribution of mandates in

Diagram 6:

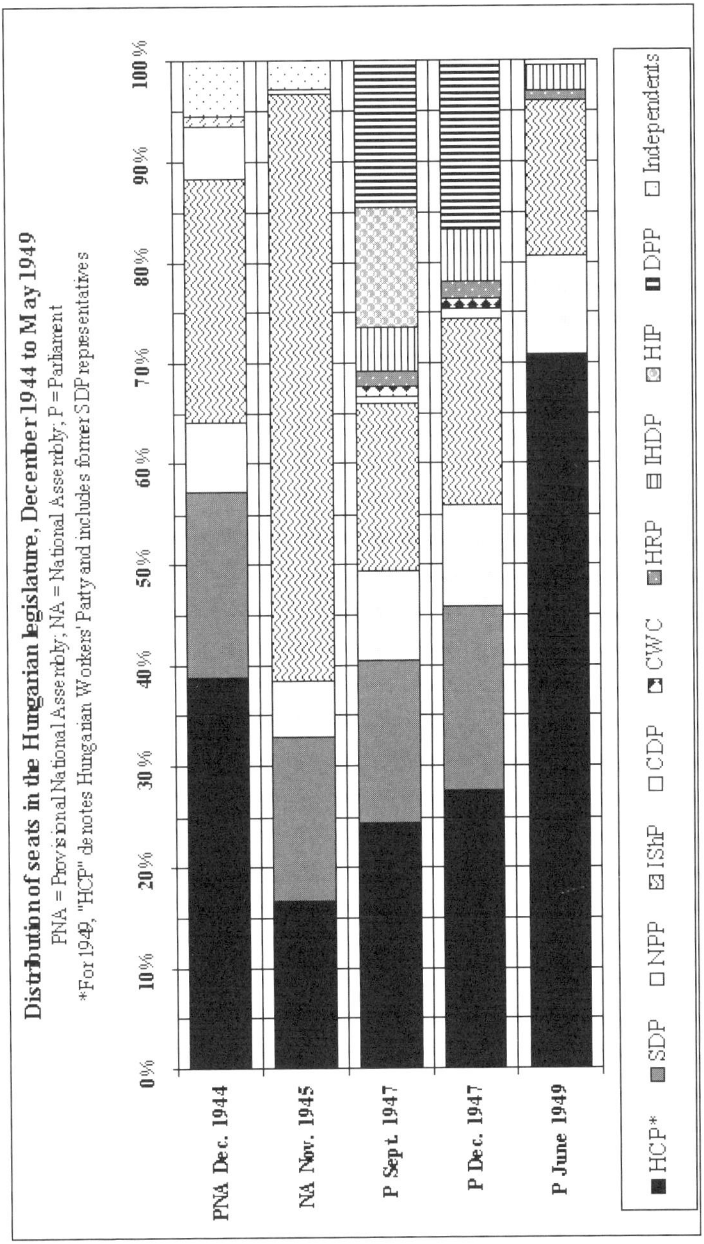
Distribution of seats in the Hungarian legislature, December 1944 to May 1949
PNA = Provisional National Assembly; NA = National Assembly; P = Parliament
*For 1949, "HCP" denotes Hungarian Workers' Party and includes former SDP representatives
0%
10%
20%
30%
40%
50%
60%
70%
80%
90%
100%
PNA Dec. 1944
NA Nov. 1945
P Sept. 1947
P Dec. 1947
P June 1949
HCP*
SDP
NPP
IShP
CDP
CWC
HRP
IHDP
HIP
DPP
Independents

Hungary's National Assembly between 1944 and 1949 according to party affiliation. The data provide a clear demonstration of how the Communist Party managed to gain a dominant foothold in Parliament through the calling of "early" elections every other year and the gradual elimination and integration of other parties.

Rákosi's calculations proved to be correct. On August 18, 1949, the "People's Front" Parliament adopted without significant debate Hungary's new constitution, which came into effect two days later, on August 20. The constitution's preamble declared that Hungary "with the support of the Soviet Union [...] has begun to lay the foundations of socialism as the country proceeds along the path of people's democracy towards socialism." This pronouncement of political principle was appropriately located within the document's preamble. But specification of the single-party system was not mentioned either within the preamble or the main body of the constitution—although it would have been proper in section II, entitled "Social System." The term "party" is not, in fact, used anywhere in the text of the constitution. However, the following phrase appears completely out of context in section VIII of the constitution regarding civil rights and obligations: "... the leading power in state and social activities will be the working class supported by people's democratic unity and *directed by its vanguard*." In contemporary Marxist (Stalinist) jargon, the "vanguard of the working class" was a cliché referring exclusively to the Communist Party—or, to be country-specific, by now the Hungarian Workers' Party. The constitution thus cloaked the HWP's exclusive political authority, which, as cited above, was implied in just one instance, within a shroud of intentional textual obscurity and rhetorical embellishments.[15]

The decision of leading Communist Party ideologists at a conference in Moscow that beginning in 1949 the widely used term "people's democracy" should refer to the notion of proletarian dictatorship could also be classified under the subject of linguistic politics. HWP chief ideologist József Révai, who had espoused a differing opinion in this regard, was forced to exercise ritual self-criticism and recant his previously held viewpoint.

The open declaration at Stalin's insistence of the transformation in the meaning of this term was no less worrying than the unadorned reference to "the single-party system." It was for this reason that the expressions "people's democracy" and "people's democratic" that appeared repeatedly in the constitution were used in the previously cited sections of the document. The constitution was equally obscure with regard to the powers of the various branches of government, striving, as István Bibó put it, to maintain the "appearance" of their Montesquian *Trias Politica*. Its structural arrangement implied that the separation of the legislative, executive and judicial branches of government would be preserved; however, clauses of the document defining the modes of implementing political volition contradict this. The separation of powers specified in the constitution was, in fact, just as fictive as were the stipulated freedoms of assembly, speech and religion.

The constitution did, however, proclaim the predominance of state and cooperative ownership and the utilization of both economic and cultural production within the framework of the "state people's economic plan." The document likewise stipulated the radical restructuring of public administration, subordinating local and regional government to centralized state authority as part of the so-called council management system. (This will be discussed in its proper chronological position later in the text.) The constitution's changes to Hungary's political structure are reflected most clearly in its transformation of the legislative process and bodies of government authorized to participate therein. The new constitution abolished the republican form of government and the office of president of the republic, establishing the Presidential Council of the People's Republic (PCPR) to carry out the functions of the head of state. Although the chairman of this new institution was invested with virtually no authority, the PCPR itself, as a "collective head of state," commanded substantial legislative and executive power. The body was entitled to compose and issue so-called statutory decrees, which the new constitution had declared to be of equal authority to parliamentary legislation. The constitution stipulated that PCPR decrees needed to be introduced only retroactively, during the first session of Parliament following their publication. In practice, this meant that the political decisions of the autocratic ruling party could be passed into law without overseeing of any form. The likewise Communist-dominated National Assembly was not even obliged to place debate of PCPR-initiated laws on its agenda. Moreover, beginning at this time Parliament was convened only once or twice a year—and then only for a few days—in order to provide nominal legal sanction to party aspirations, thus further circumscribing the legislative body's competence and authority. Partially as a result of this, from the adoption of the new constitution in 1949 until 1956, the end of the period presently under examination, 265 PCPR statutory decrees were enacted, while Parliament passed only 62 laws during this time. In a speech given when the new constitution was submitted to the National Assembly, Rákosi already referred in a declarative tone to the "the Presidential Council, which exercises the rights of Parliament."[16]

Another measure taken in connection to the adoption of the new constitution was to replace Hungary's traditional blazon, the so-called Kossuth Coat-of-Arms, with a non-traditional heraldic symbol in which the five-pointed red star connoting communist authority was the dominant graphic element. (This was to entail literal political significance during "the days of the falling stars" during the 1956 Revolution.) In 1950, the date August 20 was declared a holiday celebrating the new Constitution of the People's Republic, superseding the traditional national holiday held on August 20 to commemorate the founder of the Hungarian state, King Saint Stephen.

From the summer of 1949, the Hungarian Workers' Party utilized the fortified dual mandate of the new Parliament and constitution to further build the party dictatorship's institutional system. This is when the People's Economic Council began to operate under the leadership of HWP strongman Ernő Gerő, who had control over the party's economic policy. Furthermore, the National Planning Office was established to replace the abolished Economic Supreme Council.

Diagram 7:
Annual counts of National Assembly acts (Parl.) and Presidential Council decrees (Pres.), 1949 to 1957

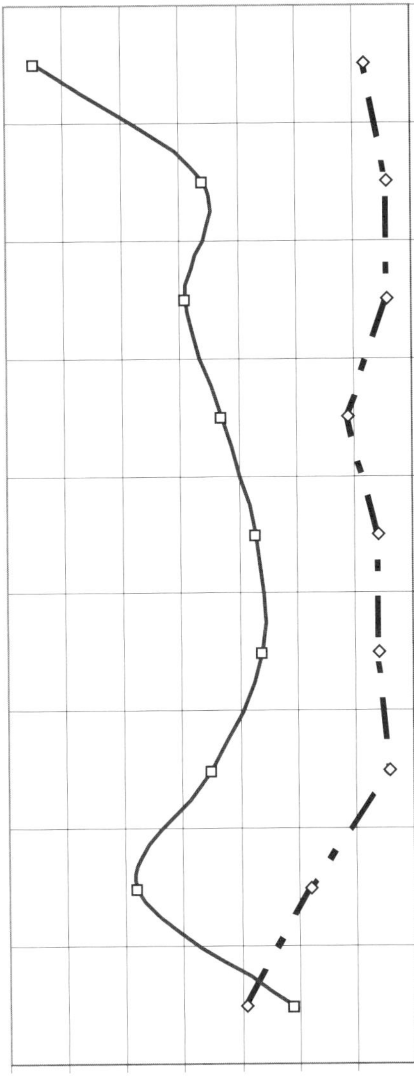

	1949	1950	1951	1952	1953	1954	1955	1956	1957
Parl.	29	18	4	6	6	11	4	4	8
Pres.	21	48	35	26	27	33	39	36	65

Zoltán Vas, who had served as the head of the latter organization, was appointed as leader of the new planning office. The Gerő-led central council determined the main course of the party's economic policies, including those pertaining to the country's Cold War defense industry and military investment, while the Vas-led agency administered the central planning of these policies. The primary initial objective of these newly founded economic organizations was to prepare the developmental and investment program of the five-year economic plan scheduled to start at the beginning of 1950 in place of the operative three-year plan that was slated to be terminated prematurely at the end of 1949.

The subsequent step in the nationalization process was the transfer during the second half of the year of private wholesale companies and small and medium-sized plants and factories employing between 10 and 100 people to state ownership. Trade unions were also nationalized during the course of the year. The unions, which had previously operated as self-governing interest-protection organizations based on trade or trade category, were placed under the authority of the ministerial department deemed to be closest to its labor profile. As a result, both employees and employers essentially became "fellow members" of sector-based state trade unions.

Education, culture and science were included in the process of subordination to direct party leadership as well. Newspapers and periodicals that were deemed unnecessary in terms of disseminating party propaganda were eliminated one after another. Publishing houses, theaters and cinemas were placed under the direct authority of the state, which strictly controlled what books, plays or films would receive *nihil obstat* permission to be published or presented in public. Hungarian Radio—there was still no television in Hungary at this time—was transformed into a mouthpiece for communist agitprop as part of this system of centralized control. The Hungarian Academy of Sciences, which had previously functioned as an autonomous public institution, was reorganized and nationalized in accordance with the Hungarian Workers' Party's ideological aspirations. Over one hundred members of the Academy judged from a Stalinist perspective to be "reactionary" were expelled from the body. Those among the expelled academicians who also taught at universities were subsequently stripped of their chairs, usually within one year.

Among the Presidential Council's initial decrees was one abolishing obligatory religious education in schools and closing 17 out of 22 post-secondary theological institutes, including four university departments, as part of its program of "university reform." At the same time, "educational academies" were established, at which workers were retrained in accelerated courses to serve as public school teachers. The largely autonomous system of people's colleges founded at the end of World War II was dissolved. The National Alliance of People's Colleges (NAPC) had formed around certain secondary and post-secondary educational institutions over the previous years. The pedagogic and social foundations of the NAPC were based precisely on the primarily communist-proclaimed objective of making Hungary's educational system accessible to the greatest number of talented students from poor and disadvantaged backgrounds. The prestige of the people's colleges was reflected in the fact that just a year earlier the leader-coordinator of the national people's college movement, László Kardos, became the youngest person to receive a Kossuth Prize after the award was established in March 1948. The people's colleges were stigmatized and abolished in the summer of 1949 for manifesting essentially the very same characteristics that had previously been considered their virtues. The NAPC could not have been tolerated at a time when "verbalism, dogmatism, conformism and schematism had begun to take control of life."[17]

Along with its ideological-political defects and counterproductive organizational-curricular provisions, the changes carried out in the educational system did produce a noteworthy positive result. The introduction of universal elementary education up to the eighth grade, the extension of compulsory schooling to the age of 16, the sharp increase in the number of trade schools and secondary schools and the expansion of the instructional profile can be considered to have been to the benefit of society in spite of all the educational transformation's intrinsic faults. Connected as it was to the fervent nationalization process, state budget funds were used to finance the education system at all levels. The consequent lack of tuition led to a further increase in the number of students, not only in regular, daytime classes, but in evening and extension courses established for full-time workers as well. During the 1950s, children of parents branded as bourgeois or so-called kulak "class enemies" were only permitted to enroll at universities and certain secondary schools after having passed through an intensive screening process. Those from these stigmatized classes who were determined to continue their studies quickly discovered a method of circumventing the ideologically dictated administrative impediments to their further education: they went to work, usually performing some type of manual labor, for a period of time, after which they could gain admittance to secondary and post-secondary educational institutions as one of the regime's favored "worker cadres."

The political system's "opening of the school doors" was linked to the introduction of Russian language as a compulsory subject and an increased emphasis on the study of ideological topics, such as Marxism in its various thematic aspects and Soviet and Hungarian party (meaning the Communist Party) history, to the detriment of functional, professional and vocational instruction. Since these subjects had, for social and cultural reasons, hardly been part of the Hungarian school curriculum previous to this time, those accorded the task of teaching them were often only two or three lessons ahead of their students in the course syllabus. Counterbalancing this bulk on the other end of the scale was the fact that no one was any longer excluded from the educational system because they were poor—an economic condition that continued to apply to the majority of Hungary's population. At the same time, girls and women were fully integrated into educational institutions of every type at every level. Colleges of education were expanded in order to train a sufficient number of teachers for the new system. University education shifted

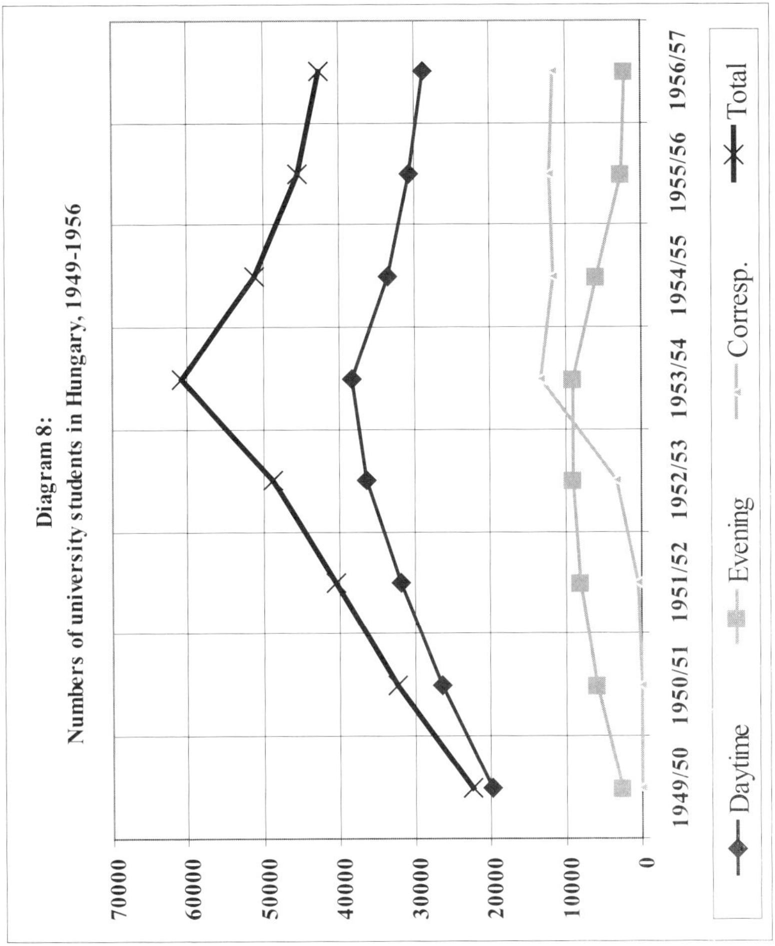

Diagram 8:
Numbers of university students in Hungary, 1949-1956

its focus to the training of engineers and economists to satisfy the needs of the industry-centered planned economy. The instruction of agricultural engineers (agronomists) also began to be consolidated at both the university and college level after an initial period of politically induced disarray in this field.

4. Cold War in the Hungarian Fashion: the Rajk Trial

In 1949, just as in the previous year, the fervent effort to build the party dictatorship entailed political witch hunts and show trials. After weeks of trumpeting the May "People's Front victory" in a display of communist self-promotion, Hungary's increasingly hysterical press shifted its attention to a new scandal that emerged when Minister of the Interior and Hungarian Workers' Party Deputy General Secretary János Kádár announced to the party's Central Directorate on July 11, 1949, the "uncovering of a Trotskyite spy ring." According to Kádár's account, "The investigation and exposure of the enemy under the immediate direction of comrade Rákosi [...] succeeded as the result of two years of persistent work." The expressed time frame is noteworthy, because the primary defendant in the show trial staged on the basis of the alleged spy ring, László Rajk, had as minister of the interior eagerly helped the Hungarian Communist Party to attain its fraudulent electoral victory. Moreover, Rajk had served at the head of one of the People's Front electoral lists just two months before Kádár presented the espionage charges to the party secretariat. The secondary defendant in the eventual show trial, Tibor Szőnyi, had been appointed to head the cadre division at the Hungarian Communist Party headquarters precisely two years earlier. Only such a person who enjoyed the unqualified confidence of party leaders, as Szőnyi did until his arrest, was qualified to fill this post.

The fact that Szőnyi just a year before had committed a nearly unpardonable conspiratorial transgression during the selective merger with the Social Democratic Party, making written notes on an issue of which only a few were apprised and whose documentation represented the pinnacle of indiscretion, is another matter. Namely, Szőnyi had recorded details and analysis not only of chief of the political police Gábor Péter's surveillance of a large number of Social Democratic Party officials, but of the planting of informants in Hungarian Communist Party organizations as well. "In my opinion, the mission of the ÁVO's intelligence operations is not and should not be to monitor party organizations and infiltrate the party. […] To seek information regarding party organizations, and leading party members has a destructive, discipline-loosening and demoralizing effect."[18] The readers of Szőnyi's notes, Mihály Farkas and Mátyás Rákosi, seemed to approve of his apprehension. However, Szőnyi could not have been aware that it was precisely Farkas and Rákosi who had instructed Gábor Péter to prepare an "anti-Trotskyite" Hungarian trial utilizing, in addition to his own intelligence, personal information from Szőnyi's central cadre division. Thus, on the one hand, the cadre division and the ÁVO had cooperated under their own party leadership in the lustration of Social Democrats at the time of the party fusion, while, on the other hand, Szőnyi had infringed upon a matter that, with the knowledge of Rákosi and Farkas, had been made Gábor Péter's special assignment. The ÁVO chief delivered the commissioned, fabrication-filled "Trotskyite espionage" script in September 1948. The key members of the Hungarian Workers' Party State Protection Commission, Mátyás Rákosi, Ernő Gerő, Mihály Farkas and János Kádár, judged Péter's work to be both of poor quality and "not yet opportune," returning it to the "author" for correction. In this original version, the role of primary defendant had been assigned to a former SDP member elected to serve on the HWP Central Directorate, Pál Justus, who, by the time that the show trial actually started, had been relegated to the part of minor co-conspirator. Because Rajk had been transferred from the Ministry of the Interior to the Ministry of Foreign Affairs, Gábor Péter was able to continue his intelligence-gathering activities within the ranks of the HWP, relieved of the burden of official subordination to his inter-party rival, while also drawing into his sights the person who, as mentioned above, had "informed" on him to his superiors. It was hardly a coincidence that on May 16, 1949—the day following the single-list elections—Tibor Szőnyi became the first suspect to be taken into custody as part of the series of arrests that signaled the beginning of the Rajk affair. Gábor Péter then had Szőnyi subjected to ten days of brutal interrogation before extracting from him a confession indicating that his "higher contact" in the alleged conspiracy had been none other than László Rajk. The latter was arrested on May 30.

As compared to the previously mentioned show trials, the Rajk case was different in three respects. First, membership of the autocratic party, even its leadership, did not prevent anyone from being qualified as an enemy. Second, the General Belkin-led Soviet counterintelligence bureau devised the main components of the fabricated charges. The task of obtaining the appropriate confessions was left to Hungarian party and political police officials. Third, the accused, including Rajk, were the victims of a ritual homicide whose genuine target was elsewhere. The original charges were composed according to the script utilized during Stalin's purges of the Soviet party leadership in the 1930s. Soviet "advisors" in Budapest simply updated the central accusation of "Trotskyism" contained in the 1930s scenario to "Titoism."[19] The show trial's true primary defendant *in absentia* was Josip Broz Tito, who had already established a Soviet-type system in Yugoslavia by the summer of 1945, but was unwilling to submit completely to Moscow's dictates, with an emphasis placed on the word "completely." Tito was willing to ally Yugoslavia to the Soviet Union in a close ideological and strategic partnership, but was not prepared to totally relinquish the country's sovereignty. It was for this reason that the Cominform, the mouthpiece for Stalin's hysteria, branded Belgrade's party leadership as nationalist-deviationist in a 1948 decree. However, at this time the so-called Informbiro faction within the Communist Party of Yugoslavia was expected to oust Tito and usher Yugoslavia back into the Moscow-dominated "proletarian-internationalist" camp. After Stalin realized that he could not simply "lift a little finger and Tito will be gone," he attempted to compensate for his failure with a propaganda victory. This was the purpose of the conspiracy dramas, including the Rajk trial, that were staged in the Soviet satellite states in the vicinity of Yugoslavia. (The show trial of Bulgarian party leader Traicho Kostov was organized shortly after Rajk's.)

There was a further, fourth, unique feature of the Rajk trial that has not yet been discussed, because it became a dormant issue during the proceedings. This was none other than Mátyás Rákosi's megalomania, which manifested itself in his attempt to transform the Rajk trial into a "worldwide conspiracy" stretching as far as the United States. In his zeal to extend the scope of the trial, Rákosi managed to come up with an international secret service adventurer named Noel Field, who, after being abducted in Prague and taken to Budapest, was discovered to have operated as a double agent for both the Americans and the Soviets. The Soviet secret services promptly had Field taken to Moscow, where he remained for years "partly" as their own agent. The Soviets thus effectually prevented Rákosi from amalgamating Field into the script of the Rajk trial.[20] Even more crass nonsense could have been squeezed into the proceedings, although this would have been fatefully counterproductive due to Moscow's involvement in the concern. The fact that the Field affair indeed represented a multi-faceted combination game in the sordid intelligence battle between the Great Powers is another issue. The genuine historical documentation of the Field case began only in the past decade, following the end of the Cold War.[21]

János Kádár, who actively collaborated in the effort to get his old chum, László Rajk, to play his assigned role,[22] briefed the Hungarian Workers' Party Central Directorate on "the latest results of the investigation" during the body's September 3, 1949, session. By this time, the charges of "Titoism" had already superseded those of "Trotskyism" contained in earlier versions of the trial script. According to the revised allegations, Rajk and his co-defendants had allied themselves as "imperialist lackeys" with Tito in order to overthrow Hungary's "democratic state order." This was the chief indictment submitted to the people's tribunal three days later, subsequently reemerging as a refrain in the public prosecutor's arraignment: "Not only Rajk and his accomplices are sitting in the dock, but their foreign masters and imperialist abettors as well, in Belgrade and Washington […] Tito and his band, Yugoslavia's leadership clique, act as the intermediary and the chief agent for the commands of foreign imperialists and as the shock troops of imperialism."[23] The prosecutor, the judges, the witnesses and the defense attorneys all recited their dialog from memorized scripts, and thus no significant mishaps occurred during the tragic drama that was broadcast live on the radio from September 16 to September 24. The court issued its verdicts according to the instructions of HWP General Secretary Mátyás Rákosi, who was in Moscow for talks. László Rajk, Tibor Szőnyi and András Szalai were condemned to death and executed. Lazar Brankov and Pál Justus were sentenced to life in prison and Milan Ognjenovich to nine years in prison. In order to make the conspiracy to overthrow the established order of the state seem more plausible, the cases of two—likewise communist—generals implicated in the affair, György Pálffy and Béla Korondy, were transferred to a military court. A few days later, they were also sentenced to death.

Between the grain harvest and the grape harvest of 1949—those sentenced to death in the trial were executed on October 15—a perfidious slander campaign, one even more strident in tone than those that had taken place previously, and a continual, incriminatory press offensive attended every phase of the miscarriage of justice. Hundreds of bogus "letters to the editor" as well as plant collectives and party organizations included in the defamation campaign demanded that "an example be made of the murderers who had betrayed the party," although workers from the latter factories first discovered that they had unanimously aligned themselves with "the vigilance of comrade Rákosi" only from press reports. Mátyás Rákosi did not fail to reciprocate "the unwavering support exhibited among the working people," backing that had given the Hungarian Workers' Party general secretary the strength to make it through the "sleepless nights" that he had to endure during the struggle against "the traitors embedded in the party." Rákosi recapitulated the "lessons to be learned from the eradication of the Rajk gang" during a meeting of Budapest party activists held following the end of the show trial, although before the implementation of the death sentences, on September 30, 1949. It was during this speech that Rákosi proclaimed the program of hysterical vigilance towards everyone and everything. "Vigilance is a matter that concerns not only the Political Committee, not only the Central Directorate or the ÁVH, but our whole party. Let every party organization, functionary and member be vigilant; let all of the working people be vigilant, taking note of even the slightest enemy voice or action. Let it seek and find the hand of the enemy behind every mistake [sic]." This is precisely what happened over subsequent years, although it was first necessary to clear the huge mound of debris stemming from the Rajk affair. Judgments were pronounced against more than 100 other civilians and military officers in 30 associated so-called background trials. Among those found guilty, 15 were sentenced to death and executed, 11 were condemned to life in prison and more than 50 others received sentences of more than five years in prison. Several of these people committed suicide, while others died in the course of brutal interrogations held during the investigative phase of the trials or afterwards in prison. Those against whom it was impossible to concoct even the flimsiest of indictments were interned for an undetermined period of time. During a September 1949 meeting of the Cominform held in Hungary, Yugoslavia was expelled from the organization on the basis of incriminating "evidence" that had emerged during the Rajk trial in Budapest and the Kostov trial in Sofia. For the next decade, Tito served as an oft-chastened enemy and Hungary as the front line in the preparations for a possible war against Yugoslavia.

Compensation for "work well done" in the shadow of the gallows did not go unrewarded. On the day following the executions of those condemned to death during the Rajk trial, Minister of the Interior János Kádár signed a proposal pursuant to which 50 members of the ÁVH, including Gábor Péter and the organization's high command, were decorated on November 1, 1949. Two dozen of those thus honored received promotion for their "outstanding service and determination." The second half of the reward arrived in the form of a Christmas present. The central leadership of the Hungarian Workers' Party spent even the holidays at work. On Christmas Eve the State Protection Committee passed a resolution, which the Political Committee endorsed two days later, that completely separated the State Protection Authority from the Ministry of the Interior, transforming the organization into an autonomously functioning quasi-ministry in its own right. This "supreme resolution" was published as a Council of Ministers' decree on December 28.[24] Grandiose official ceremonies and special publications commemorated Stalin's seventieth birthday in all the countries belonging to the "peace camp" at around this time. Party and government commissions were established to organize and direct these celebrations. Mátyás Rákosi was the leading force behind these efforts, extolling "the successive victories of Hungarian democracy" and presenting the "wise teacher and creative genius of all of progressive humanity" with the birthday present of a Hungary that had undergone an almost complete transformation based on the Soviet model. Official propaganda in all the Cominform member countries used such accolades to laud Stalin during this period.

5. Final Phase in the Building of the Party Dictatorship: Establishment of the Council System

Only the finishing touches remained to be made in the process of Hungary's complete Bolshevization. One of these was to purge the system of those "left-leaning" former Social Democrats who two years previously had cooperated faithfully in the liquidation of their own party. The following allegations were utilized in connection with the series of arrests and trials that began in the spring of 1950 in an attempt to imbue them with the appearance of standard criminal justice procedures: that the accused had served as informants for the Horthy-era police and/or engaged in espionage on behalf of the United Kingdom by way of their connections to the British Labour Party. Courts convicted Chairman of the Presidential Council of the People's Republic Árpád Szakasits, Hungarian Workers' Party Deputy General Secretary György Marosán and National Planning Office Chairman Imre Vajda on these charges, while Minister of Justice István Ries died after being subjected to harsh interrogation while deprived of his medication. More than 200 people were imprisoned and as many more were confined to the Gödöllő or Recsk internment and forced labor camps as a result of the trials of former Social Democrats.

The effort of several years to build the institutions of party dictatorship culminated with the launching of the council system of state administration, likewise based on the Soviet model, in 1950. A Council of Ministers' decree stipulated the transformation of Hungary's territorial-administrative subdivisions as part of the reorganization of state administration, eliminating the so-called truncated counties that had emerged along the country's borders as a result of the Treaty of Trianon. (At the same time, the official name of these administrative units was changed from "castle county" (*vármegye*) to plain "county" (*megye*)). A total of 19 counties were established in place of the former 25, while the largest county in terms of area, Pest-Pilis-Solt-Kiskun County, was divided into two parts. The borders of county administrative subdivisions (*járás*) were subsequently transformed as well, through various territorial transfers and modifications. (We will return to this subject in relation to another matter later in the book.) There were 60 municipalities classified as cities in Hungary at this time. The administrative status of some of these cities was significantly altered in the course of these territorial changes. The former administrative category of municipal city, which was independent of county administration, was eliminated, and, if possible, cities with a significant population of industrial workers were made into the seats of the modified counties. (Besides Budapest, five of the previous 12 municipal cities—Debrecen, Győr, Miskolc, Pécs and Szeged—were reclassified as so-called county cities, which were equal in terms of administrative status to the counties, in 1954.) The administrative boundaries of Budapest were expanded considerably in order to include nearby "satellite cities" and agrarian villages within the city's districts. Many of the municipalities thus incorporated into Budapest had formerly been part of the so-called "red belt" that encompassed the city, with its large factories and affiliated workers' colonies. This expansion of Budapest's peripheral districts led to a transformation in the city's social-vocational composition, increasing its so-called worker–peasant population and diminishing the significance of its "bourgeois elements."[25]

The reshaping of the function and operational mechanism of Hungary's public administration system was even more significant than the changes to its territorial structure described in the previous paragraph. Minister of the Interior János Kádár expounded upon the need for these changes in the preamble of a bill submitted to Parliament in May 1950:

> … [council-based administration] will ensure the solid unity of state power, centralized authority and the assertion of the country's interests; it will ensure that every sphere of state administration will be fully engaged in the implementation of the five-year people's economic plan [launched in January 1950]. The solid unity of the state is manifested in the superior and inferior status of the various councils with regard to one another and the ultimate subordination of them to state power and the supreme organs of state administration: the National Assembly, the Presidential Council of the People's Republic and the Council of Ministers.

Naturally, they were also subordinated to the party organizations structured in a similarly hierarchical way. At the lowest level of the configuration of councils established in place of the traditional system of local government stood the community, town or, in the case of cities, district councils. These were subordinate to regional county or city councils, which were in turn subordinate to county councils. Initially, county councils functioned in theoretical subordination to the government, although the direction and supervision of these councils were transferred to the Ministry of the Interior until 1954.

Conditions related to the "intensifying class struggle" were to be applied to the transformation of administration that took place in the course of building the thoroughly ideology-based party dictatorship. According to a party directive regarding this administrative transformation, "All aspects of the reorganization process should serve as a weapon in the various phases of the political struggle and should thus be formulated in correlation with existing circumstances. Now, for example, attention should be accorded to the period of struggle against the kulaks." The poorer segments of the peasantry were regarded with hardly less suspicion than were the kulaks. The leadership of the Hungarian Workers' Party was generally leery of the "reactionary countryside"—and vice versa! (This will be discussed during the section of the book dealing with the collectivization of agricultural production.) It was for this reason that the HWP considered reining in the county districts to be one of the most important aspects of the functional and territorial reorganization of state administration. The boundaries of the county districts were redrawn in order to "increase the industrial worker composition of the population and [...] make it possible to designate the greatest possible number of worker elements [...] the central government will rely primarily on this unit [the county district], since the objective of centralization is entirely achievable here." The HWP subsequently strengthened the grounds for its emphasis on the importance of the county districts with the justification that they represented the most effective setting for waging the "struggle against the kulaks." The party put (urban) "worker cadres" in charge of county district and even village councils in regions with a predominantly agrarian population. According to another passage of the party guidelines cited above, "if a worker is capable of serving as general manager of a company, then he is also capable of serving as the leader of the [administrative] sections of these [council] organizations." Political dependability was the main criterion for appointment to these positions, in accordance with the dictate that "party cadres must be named to fill key positions." It was for these same reasons that so-called personnel commissioners, known colloquially as "cadre officials," were deployed at the county district level. (Personnel groups or departments performed these functions in the cities and within the county councils.)

Although it was not possible to accomplish all its objectives at once, the Hungarian Workers' Party leadership attempted to assemble its candidate list for the so-called council elections based on the previously outlined considerations. The results of the several rounds of council elections held in the second half of 1950 were no different from those of the single-list National Assembly elections held one year earlier, although they did produce the radical effect of eliminating the organizational and operational order of pre-communist era public administration at the local level as well. At the same time, the opportunity for citizens to genuinely select their own leaders ended with these elections.

From the strict standpoint of administrative history, the 1950 council elections did represent the first local "elections" in Hungary in over a decade, since 1939. Moreover, it was advisable for the expanded number of eligible voters to participate in the elections, even if there were no alternative choices offered, since from this time onwards staying away from the ballot box was viewed as a passive manifestation of anti-government behavior. In terms of broadly defined manpower, the new administrative system produced as a result of the elections held on October 22, 1950, and by-elections held one week later consisted of 220,000 council members. The so-called executive committee was recruited from among the principal municipal, city, county and county district leaders that emerged as the result of these elections. The council secretary and the council president served as the two key figures of these executive committees at every level. The headline articles and reports contained in official party newspapers resounded in unison with news of the 97 percent "people's front victory" and voter turnout in the elections.

The establishment of the council system represented the final step in the creation of the single-party communist dictatorship. The institutional and structural order of the Hungarian model of the party state had been completed and put into operation by the end of 1950. This was the product of a six-year, frequently interconnected, dual system change begun at the turn of the year 1944–1945. With the support of the neighboring Soviet Union, which also held Hungary under military occupation, the Hungarian Communist Party had been able to knock its political rivals out of the political ring, just as it was able to do to its temporary allies. The party utilized the familiar techniques of political power struggle in combination with illegitimate and explicitly unlawful procedural methods to gradually establish a total dictatorship. Total, because it not only took the conventional domains of political life under its complete control, but made every sphere of social organization subject to its sole and exclusive will.

Using a phrase from Imre Madách, one would have subsequently expected "the machine to keep turning, while the creator rests." But it did not happen this way…

Notes

1 Éva Standeisky, Gyula Kozák, Gábor Pataki and János M. Rainer, eds., *A fordulat évei* [The Years of Transition] (Budapest, 1988), and István Feitl, Lajos Izsák and Gábor Székely, *Fordulat a világban és Magyarországon, 1947–1949* [Transition in the World and Hungary] (Budapest, 2000).

2 Ferenc Fischer, *A megosztott világ* [The Divided World] (Budapest and Pécs, 2001), pp. 61–86.

3 Archives of the Politikatörténeti Intézet [Institute of Political History], 274. SZB. F. 243. ö. e.

4 György Gyarmati, *Március hatalma—a hatalom márciusa. Fejezetek március 15. ünneplésének történetéből* [The Power of March—the March of Power. Chapters from the History of March 15 Celebrations] (Budapest, 1998), pp. 98–106.

5 Lajos Izsák and Miklós Kun, *Moszkvának jelentjük... Titkos dokumentumok, 1944–1948* [We Report to Moscow… Secret Documents, 1944–1948] (Budapest, 1994), pp. 263–264.

6 Állambiztonsági Szolgálatok Történeti Levéltára [State Security Services Historical Archives], section 1. 1.2.

7 Margit Balogh, *Mindszenty József, 1892–1975* [József Mindszenty, 1892–1975] (Budapest, 2002).

8 György Gyarmati, "A Mindszenty-ügy diplomáciai rendezésének kudarca" [The Failure of Diplomatic Settlements to the Mindszenty Affair], *Történelmi Szemle* 1–2 (2000): 69–90.

9 Mátyás Rákosi, *Visszaemlékezések, 1945–1960* [Recollections, 1945–1960], vol. 2 (Budapest, 1997), pp. 711–712.

10 The Supreme Court of the Republic of Hungary annulled the verdict against Viktor Csornoky in 1992.

11 Ferenc Donáth, *A Márciusi Fronttól Monorig* [From the March Front to Monor], selected by Tibor Valuch (Budapest, 1992), pp. 286–290.

12 Gábor Baczoni, "Négy törvénysértő per utóélete" [The Repercussions of Four Unlawful Trials], in György Gyarmati, ed., *Államvédelem a Rákosi-korszakban* [State Protection during the Rákosi Era] (Budapest, 2000), p. 333. For more information on these economic show trials, see Lajos Srágli, *A MAORT* [MAORT] (Budapest, 1998), and Klára Katona, "A MAORT Története a fordulatok éveiben Magyarországon" [The History of MAORT during the Years of Transition in Hungary], in György Gyarmati, ed., *Trezor 2. A Történeti Hivatal évkönyve 2000–2001* [Vault 2. Yearbook of the History Office, 2000–2001] (Budapest, 2002), pp. 137–158.

13 István Feitl, "Pártvezetés és országgyűlési választások, 1949–1989" [Party Leadership and Parliamentary Elections, 1949–1989], in György Földes and László Hubai, eds., *Parlamenti választások Magyarországon, 1920–1989* [Parliamentary Elections in Hungary, 1920–1989], 2nd ed. (Budapest, 1990), p. 280.

14 The founder of the Hungarian state, King Stephen, offered guardianship over his kingdom to the Virgin Mary. The cult of Mary that arose as a result of this act was a centuries-old tradition in Hungary.

15 *A Magyar Népköztársaság Alkotmánya* [The Constitution of the People's Republic of Hungary] (Budapest, 1956). It was necessary to expound upon the cited section of the constitution in order to refute the commonly held viewpoint that paragraph three of Hungary's amended 1972 constitution was the first to state that "the Marxist-Leninist party of the working class is the leading power of society." By this time, the "leading power" referred to the Hungarian Socialist Workers' Party (HSWP), which had superseded the Hungarian Workers' Party at the end of 1956. For the text of the 1972 constitution, see *A Magyar Népköztársaság Alkotmánya* [The Constitution of the People's Republic of Hungary] (Budapest, 1972). The official texts of the 1949 and 1972 constitutions are also contained in the following book: Ignác Romsics, ed., *Magyar történeti szöveggyűjtemény,*

1914–1999 [Compilation of Hungarian Historical Texts, 1914–1999] vol. 2 (Budapest, 2000), pp. 13–22, 296–306.

16 *A dolgozó nép alkotmánya. Beszéd az Országgyűlés 1949. augusztus 17-i ülésén* [Constitution of the Working People. Speech during the National Assembly's August 17, 1947, Session]. See Mátyás Rákosi, *Válogatott beszédek és cikkek* [Selected Speeches and Articles] (Budapest, 1955), pp. 328–329.

17 László Kardos, ed., *Sej, a mi lobogónkat fényes szelek fújják... Népi Kollégiumok, 1939–1949* [Ho, Radiant Winds Blow Our Banner... People's Colleges, 1939–1949] (Budapest, 1977), pp. 31–32. See also István Papp, *A népi kollégiumi mozgalom története, 1944-ig* [The History of the People's Colleges Movement until 1944] (Budapest, 2008).

18 Archives of the Political History Institute, fond 274 11/10, ö.e., contained in György Gyarmati, "Kádár János és a Belügyminisztérium Államvédelmi Hatósága" [János Kádár and the Ministry of the Interior's State Protection Authority], in György Gyarmati, ed., *Trezor 1. A Történeti Hivatal Évkönyve* [Vault 1. History Office Yearbook] (Budapest, 1999), pp. 123–124.

19 Tibor Hajdu, "A Rajk-per háttere és fázisai" [The Background and Phases of the Rajk Trial], *Társadalmi Szemle* 11 (1991): 17–36.

20 In Hungarian party and secret service jargon, the word "amalgamate" was used to represent the molding of an array of contrasting facts, incidents and fabrications into an apparently coherent story. Using this method, it would have been possible to devise a much more sensational conspiracy script using biographical details of HWP leaders, those of Ernő Gerő and Mátyás Rákosi for instance, involved in staging Rajk's show trial.

21 Bernd-Rainer Barth and Werner Schweizer, eds., *Der Fall Noel Field. Schlüsselfigur der Schauprozesse in Osteuropa I-II* (Berlin, 2005–2007).

22 János Kádár, among his other functions, was the godfather of László Rajk's son born in 1949.

23 *Rajk László és társai a népbíróság előtt* [László Rajk and His Associates before the People's Court] (Budapest, 1989), p. 213.

24 Contrary to Communist Parties in other Soviet satellite countries, the HWP bridled at the ministerial classification of the political police, because the newly adopted amendments to the constitution required this. Rákosi and his associates later cast aside such scruples,

amending constitutional provisions regarding the structure of government, and the establishment and dissolution of ministries, via Presidential Council decrees.

25 Zoltán Hajdú, *A magyar közigazgatás földrajza* [The Geography of Hungarian Public Administration] (Pécs, 2003).

IV. SYSTEM OF TERROR AND ANARCHY, 1951–1953

The Hungarian Workers' Party began the year 1951 by taking stock of its future tasks. The HWP's Second Party Congress was held at the end of February and the beginning of March of that year. The timing for this assessment was appropriate. The objectives contained in the plan for communist takeover pronounced during the party congress in 1948, which culminated in the building of the council-based system of state administration, seemed to have been realized. The fact that the party leadership was a full year late in achieving the aims outlined in its "preliminary calendar" was another matter. Originally the party had intended to complete the comprehensive reorganization of state administration by the time of its launching of the first five-year economic planning cycle, which occurred at the beginning of 1950. Two protracted issues upset this plan: preparations for József Mindszenty's show trial during the second half of 1948, which caused a delay of half a year, and the judicial murder of László Rajk and his associates, which preoccupied Rákosi between the spring and the autumn of 1948. This caused a postponement in the party dictatorship's integration of further institutions into its system, in spite of Rákosi's renowned capacity for hard work.

1. Cold War Hysteria in the Economy

During his preparations for the party congress, Rákosi concentrated his efforts on laying the groundwork for a new round of political purges. The Hungarian Workers' Party general secretary was planning to decimate what could be referred to as his own fledgling state apparatus. This will be discussed later, because a more powerful wave of hysteria temporarily delayed the implementation of his objective. Stalin summoned the various Communist Party leaders from the satellite states to Moscow at the beginning of January 1951. During the subsequent consultations, the master of the Kremlin ordered the immediate launching of a new armaments program, whose scope and late-1953 deadline for implementation almost all of the Communist Party leaders present deemed to be impracticable. Several of the latter expressed their doubts about the program, an act for which they were reprimanded. Rákosi, on the other hand, courted favor with Stalin in the manner of a teacher's pet, objecting to the fact that "Hungary's development quota was the smallest." Referring to Bulgaria's larger quota, the HWP general secretary later remarked as follows: "Hungary has a bigger population and more industry than the Bulgarians. Mihály Farkas, then the minister of defense, was with me at the time and it was our opinion that the numbers that we had received were small in comparison to those of other countries and that we could accept them."[1]

Upon their return from Moscow and under the supervision of Soviet advisors, the Hungarian Workers' Party began the process of boosting the targets contained in the first five-year plan in order to make it possible to hastily insert the revised objectives into the agenda of the impending party congress. Historical literature refers to this modified 1951 alternative version of the five-year plan as the "raised" or "stepped-up" plan, which primarily affected the benchmarks for the armaments industry and military development. The party congress elevated the resultant directives for development and investment, which were in megalomaniacal disproportion to the country's true attributes and resources, to the status of a resolution the following month. This entailed the less significant "theoretical" consequence of Hungary's violation of the military provisions of the 1947 Paris Peace Treaties. There were, however, more serious repercussions for the non-industrial branches of Hungary's economy, particularly the agricultural sector, due to a commensurate decrease in the proportion of development funds that they received. All of society suffered from the drastic restrictive measures affecting public provision. A subject-by-subject examination of the ambitions articulated at the HWP's "great leap" conference—and their consequences—provides a picture of the general conditions in Hungary at the beginning of the 1950s.

While both the 1949 "preliminary" variation of the plan and the initial five-year plan launched in 1950 stressed the industrial development of the economy, the "stepped-up plan" of 1951 carried this to an even more unrealistic extreme. The Stalinist revision of Cold War arms doctrine was immediately reflected in the policies of the Hungarian Workers' Party leadership: "Political considerations always determine investment, while economic factors play only a secondary role." There was another factor connected to these issues as presented in HWP propaganda. A November 1949 Cominform proclamation deemed neighboring Yugoslavia to be not only an ideological enemy, but the "organizer of attacks aimed at the people's democratic states." This regional "little Cold War" led to the declaration that Hungary "is not a gap, but a bastion in the front line of the peace camp."[2] (In communist phraseology, the expression "peace camp" was used to refer to the Soviet Union, China and Moscow's satellite states.) Although the related propaganda offensive was belligerent in character, the investments themselves were geared primarily at fortifying Hungary's defensive capabilities. Stalin's vision of the outbreak of a third world war—and the accompanying fierce propaganda—demanded and legitimized the primacy of military development.

The prevailing concept that the benchmark of development in the material sphere was the weight (in fact excessive) of industrial production within the national economy can be interpreted within the context of the militant burdens that the situation imposed on Hungary at the time. That is to say that the fanaticism with which the Hungarian Workers' Party leadership attempted to transform Hungary into what a contemporary slogan referred to as "a country of iron and steel" was the common product of ideological and political preconceptions. These notions neglected to take into account a lack of both energy resources and raw materials. Moreover, they depended on self-sufficiency, since all the socialist countries pursued autarkic economic policies, regardless of the existence of Comecon. They were, in fact, forced to do so, since they were isolated from "the other world economy."

The so-called plan-command system was designed to promote the practical application of political will in the economic sphere. The main objective of this system was to replace the rational economic order based on the flow of goods and money and market conditions with a centrally directed mechanism of production and distribution. This was rooted in the premise that the interests of the state and the needs of society could both be measured accurately in a centrally integrated and nationalized economy whose production was geared towards the "mere" fulfillment of specified targets. Commercially based market competition was completely eliminated, while central commands became the production multiplier. Although the planning process did formally include rational components, these were distorted by irrational counter-interests. Itemized, institution-specific, target numbers contained in preliminary framework plans distributed by the National Planning Office to the ministries and their subordinate production units were "turned around" at the company level. These enterprises routinely inflated, with the approval of their superior organizations, the amounts of raw materials, machinery, industrial infrastructure, and so on, needed to reach the prescribed final production targets. This mid-level official compliance was partially the result of ignorance and partially the product of a "self-defense reflex" aimed at deflecting accountability. At the company level, the so-called preliminary plan guideline numbers that again passed through the hierarchy required a reciprocal requisite/final product proportional adjustment. (This was not a question of preliminary estimates based on a budget-profit principle, because there was no true verification of "what and how much" calculations in this hit-and-miss process of "breaking down and adding up" the numbers in the plan, precisely because the market had been eliminated from the equation.) There was another source of uncertainty built into the system that frequently served to augment this ambiguity: by the time that the preliminary plan had filtered through the system, the centralized plans themselves had often changed. To use a musical term, *da capo al fine*—the process resumed from the beginning.

At the same time, a seemingly rational series of measures served to further stimulate the institutionalization of another variation of irrationality. A separate official apparatus was established to oversee performance of every significant task. The year 1951 marked the peak in the foundation of the various so-called industrial sector trusts. The objective of this "profile cleansing" was to prevent companies from producing goods of all kinds in the manner of a "general store," and thereby to create a system in which products (or product groups) of a certain type were turned out at a single location—or just a few locations, at most. The profile manager thus frequently gained an immediate monopoly over a given product and, for the lack of market control, was encouraged to utilize as much material as possible to produce goods that required as little labor input as possible. While this process did not put an end to parallel production, it did thus serve to eliminate the manufacture of goods requiring less material, more complex assembly or greater know-how. Moreover, if a certain product was omitted from the requisites contained in the planning mechanism as a result of these anomalies, its centrally commanded production could resume only two years later, at the very earliest, since annual plans were subject to the legislative process. The politically inspired production mentioned above not only removed the profit motive from the system, but prompted those active in the economy to provide quantity-centered reports detailing production in cubic meters, kilowatts and tonnes. In addition to its programmed wastefulness, the plan-command system resulted, on the one hand, in a heap of unused products and, on the other hand, a lengthy list of goods in short supply. To cite an everyday example: reports on plan fulfillment clearly demonstrate that warehouses were full of heavy, cast-iron chandeliers, which many people did not buy, if for no other reason, because their ceilings, many of which were hastily rebuilt following the war, could not support them. At the same time, the common light switch, which was no more than a few ounces in weight, was constantly one of the leading items on the list of scarce commodities. On the macroeconomic level, the maximally centralized plan-command system was itself responsible for institutionalizing planned economic anarchy.[3] (If it is proper to apply even a touch of irony with regard to the period of vigilance hysteria now under examination, one could say that even the shrewdest of "enemy imperialist vandals"—even if working together as a group—would have had a difficult time devising a more counterproductive economic mechanism. The company-level, microeconomic and labor-organizational deficiencies of this system will be discussed later.)

The table below and the diagram on the next page summarizing the first five-year plan's investment program and its results do not only demonstrate that the amount of resources allocated to the development of industry was almost equal to that earmarked for all other branches of the economy. The interim indicators for the years 1950–1952 reveal even more significantly that the fulfillment rate of under 80 percent recorded at the end of the planning cycle was not the consequence of the scaled-back investment policies of the 1953 "new phase" associated with Prime Minister Imre Nagy to be discussed later in the book. The fulfillment rate of the so-called

The plan directives and fulfillment of the investment structure of the first five-year plan, by plan titles

(billion forints)

Branch	Provisional 1949 plan		Adopted 1950 plan		Enhanced 1951 plan		Fulfillment 1950–52		Fulfillment 1950–54	
		%		%		%		%		%
Heavy industry		–	18.3	36.0	37.5	44.1	17.1	44.1	29.2	43.3
Light industry		–	3.0	5.9	3.5	4.1	1.1	2.8	2.3	3.4
All industry	*17.0*	*48.8*	*21.3*	*41.9*	*41.0*	*48.2*	*18.2*	*46.9*	*31.5*	*46.7*
Agriculture	6.0	16.7	8.0	15.7	11.0	12.9	4.4	11.3	9.3	13.8
Transport	6.0	16.7	7.5	14.7	10.0	11.8	6.0	15.5	8.6	12.8
Social & cultural	6.0	16.7	7.4	14.5	14.0	16.5	5.3	13.7	11.7	17.4
Other	–	–	6.7	13.2	9.0	11.6	4.9	12.6	6.3	9.3
Altogether	**35.0**	**100**	**50.9**	**100**	**85.0**	**100**	**38.8**	**100**	**67.4**	**100**
Total fulfillment by comparison with the 1951 plan directives							45.6%		79.3%	

Diagram 9:

The structure of the 1951 plan (a) and its fulfillment (b) by branches, in %

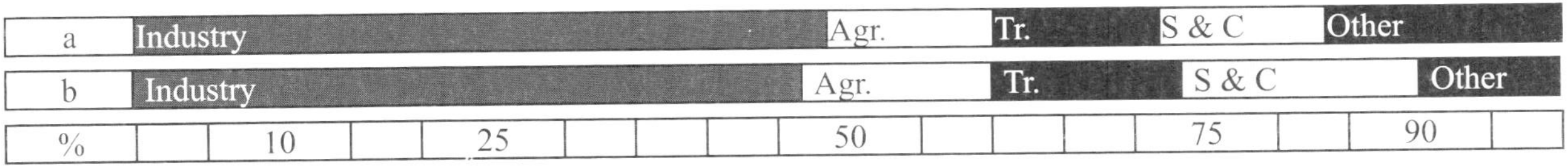

The fulfillment proportions of the branches (b) compared with the 1951 plan (a)

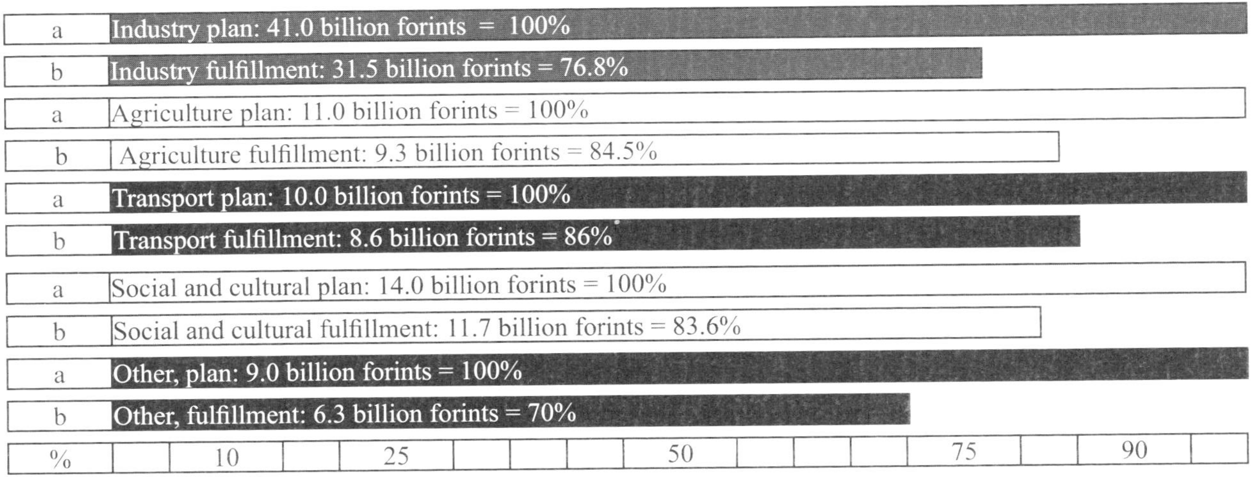

stepped-up targets was only 45 percent even during the radically voluntaristic first three years, whereas the prorated objectives stipulated 65 percent fulfillment. (See the data showing "total fulfillment" on the last line of the table.)

Finding the funds necessary to finance implementation of the targets that focused primarily on heavy industrial and military investment presented a problem from the very beginning. Finance of the initial three-year plan (1947–1949) and beginning of the first five-year plan (1950) were both, in fact, capital-based. During the take-off period of Hungary's plan-command economy, capital input entailed, on the one hand, an ever-expanding range of nationalization and, on the other hand, politically motivated tax, wage and pension measures. Hungary's 1950s heavy industrial and military investments represented an extra burden for all of society, because, in addition to the previously cited reasons, they allocated almost all available resources towards capital-intensive spheres of the economy with the longest period of return. The primary sites of base-material production and their attendant basic infrastructure—mining, coal-powered energy production and pig-iron smelting—consumed investment resources, leaving limited capital for the manufacture of items on the second level of the product vertical, such as machinery and equipment. Among the emblematic budget-consuming industrial enterprises launched during this period were the Stalinváros (now known as Dunaújváros) iron works, the Várpalota thermal power plant, the Komló anthracite-coal plant and the Borsod lignite-coal plant.

2. Collectivization of Agriculture

The decision to pursue a policy of forced industrial investment made emulation of another form of "socialist primary capital accumulation" adapted from the Soviet model all the more important. The essence of this procedure was, in the absence of external resources, to channel gross profit-proceeds stemming from one sector of the economy to another, one that was viewed as preferential from a developmental standpoint. Agriculture was the main casualty of this redistribution process, while the above-mentioned heavy industrial sector was the main beneficiary. Mátyás Rákosi announced immediately after the foundation of the Hungarian Workers' Party, on August 20, 1948, a plan to radically transform Hungary's agricultural system. Rákosi explicitly referred to the Soviet *kolkhoz* system as the model to be adopted in Hungary while speaking about the incorporation of Hungarian peasants into agricultural cooperatives during a November 1948 meeting of the Hungarian Workers' Party Central Directorate. The HWP general secretary made the wildly inaccurate assertion during this speech that the number of private peasant farms had undergone a drastic decline since the 1945 land reform because the peasantry had become convinced of "the superiority of joint cultivation." By the summer of 1949, the number of dwarf holdings of between 0.57 and 2.85 acres had, indeed, decreased by more than 400,000 in the four years since the land reform, which had produced 437,000 new landowners. However, the reason for this sharp drop in the number of private peasant farms was the fact that already in the post-war reconstruction period, Hungary's economic policies, slanted in favor of heavy industry, made it impossible for the majority of new landholders, most of whom were dwarf holders, to stabilize their agricultural operations and livelihoods. As a result, the HWP's economic policy was not able to gain the support of the poorer "worker–peasant strata" for the party even through its program of land reform. The comparative diagram of the size structure of land ownership of 1935, 1946 and 1949 can be seen on page 17.

The incorporation of peasant livelihoods into agricultural cooperatives essentially served to place the operations of the agrarian sector under state supervision and control. Various means were employed in an attempt to achieve this: establishment of organized state authorities to govern the sale of agrarian products; stipulation of obligatory sowing/production prescriptions—comparable to the plan-commands employed in nationalized industry—for private peasant farms; the total elimination, if possible, of the private marketing of agricultural goods by means of the stipulation of mandatory post-harvest deliveries and the creation of state purchasing monopolies. Compulsory partnerships—defined as cooperatives—did, in fact, emerge, as a result of economic necessity and political pressure. However, the objective was the total collectivization of the entire agricultural sector in order to gain control over the greatest possible proportion of its gross proceeds for allocation to industrial investments. This ambition is reflected in a confidential 1949 economic policy directive, according to which "as a very significant source of potential revenue, we must make much more significant use of agriculture in the future."

The majority of the peasantry did not, however, wish to voluntarily relinquish its existential autonomy. Not the tens of thousands who had worked their fingers to the bone in order to eke out a stable livelihood on parcels distributed as part of the 1945 land reform, and especially not the hundreds of thousands—millions including their family members—whose traditional legacy of agricultural proficiency (for indeed they had such) had provided them with a hard-earned subsistence and an accustomed, respectable and, for all its difficulties, satisfying lifestyle. Propaganda characterizing the cooperative form of production as being superior to that of private agriculture proved to be just as ineffective at convincing the majority of farmers to voluntarily join cooperatives as the other main ideological principle that "private peasant agriculture results in the daily reproduction of capitalism" was. In his urging of an acceleration to the collectivization process in 1949, Rákosi urged the Hungarian Workers' Party leadership, as he had in connection with forced industrial development, to assert the primacy of the party's political will: "Every other consideration, including that of the organization of production, must be subordinated to this objective." In this way, ideologically based political voluntarism resulted in the emergence of a system in which irrationality constituted an integral component.

The precept "divide and rule" was coupled with Machiavellianism. An attempt was made to generate an artificial class struggle within the various traditional and genuinely somewhat contentious strata of the peasantry. The more prosperous peasants, those holding more than 14.25 acres of land, were qualified as "a remnant of the exploitive classes" and classified as "kulaks," a term imported from the Soviet Union. The crude propaganda campaign that was waged against the more well-to-do peasants, which rivaled in intensity that targeting "clerical reaction," represented a mere ripple across the waters in the light of the fact that the party's ultimate objective was to effectively eradicate them as a group. Nothing provides a clearer reflection of this than an outburst from Ernő Gerő, the "second man" in the party hierarchy. Speaking with a group of central party leaders, Gerő concluded regretfully that "in our struggle against the kulaks we have no Siberia," where an unbearably harsh climate, augmented with a little taste of the Gulag lifestyle, would finish them off. Rákosi himself, however, did not hold a much more positive view of those classified officially as "allied working peasantry," declaring that "The adequate means of the new farmers and the middle peasantry represent an adversary to the formation of cooperatives [and thus] the peasants must be forced to make a greater sacrifice towards the building of socialism."

The everyday methods of cooperative organization had a much more direct effect on every stratum of the peasantry than the related ideological slogans or economic theory did. One of these methods was a progressive *agricultural development contribution* corresponding to the area of privately owned land. The "agriculture" column of the table shown above detailing the first five-year plan's investment ratios reveals that the total sum of the various fines and penalties, which will be discussed later, imposed on peasants amounted to nearly as much as the targeted budgetary contribution outlined in this sphere as part of the state redistribution program. The so-called *consolidation of land holdings* also had an impact on all those involved in agricultural production. This entailed a concentration of jointly cultivated lands on the more fertile boundaries of the cooperatives in order to increase their efficiency and profitability. Those operating outside the cooperatives were allotted non-contiguous parcels of land on less productive and, for the most part, more remote boundary territories in exchange for privately owned holdings in these locations, thus further encumbering their agricultural livelihoods. Another of these methods was the system of *compulsory deliveries and tax contributions*, which were regularly adjusted (which is to say, of course, that they were increased) to differ from and supersede those announced during the year. The latter burden was impossible to bear, not only for the so-called kulaks, who were also obliged to pay many surtaxes, but for the other strata of the peasantry as well. Tax impositions, with both their impracticable magnitude and their attendant fines for late payment, thus represented a form of economic pressure to join the agricultural cooperatives. "Account-Settling Committees" reinforced with police routinely appeared at the doorways of "debtors" who had been unable to satisfy the levied tax obligations. The tasks of these committees included collection, seizure and auctioning, operations known euphemistically in official jargon as "transferring." The "beneficence" of the labor of these "commandoes" was based on the scope of further "compensation penalties" imposed for "damaging the people's economy."[4] *Internments* stemming from the "sabotage of the planning law exposed through official vigilance" and the compilation of so-called *kulak lists* could also be classified as forms of administrative compulsion of this type. During this process, the number of kulaks to be registered per municipality and country district was specified in a quasi-plan-command, regardless of whether or not there was a sufficient number of farmers living in the jurisdiction of a given authority who owned enough land to qualify for legal inclusion on the kulak list. According to the relevant paragraphs, this affected approximately 4,000 private farms, resulting in almost twice the number of people being registered on the kulak lists in the early 1950s, which entailed numerous further discriminatory measures. (The children of more prosperous farmers—so-called "kulak offspring"—were officially prevented from pursuing their education, beginning at the high school level.)

The forced reorganization of Hungary's agricultural sector at the beginning of the 1950s indeed resulted in significant transformations of the production structure and the sociological characteristics of society. However, the magnitude of these changes was by no means as great as the propaganda of the time claimed it to be. Rákosi wanted the collectivization process to have reached its final stages by the scheduled promulgation of the "stepped-up" plan in 1951. However, heavily encumbered, although defiant, private farmers, and not "socialist agricultural cooperatives," nevertheless continued to produce a major share of Hungary's food. The tables seen on the next page pertaining to these changes in the agricultural sector do not reflect the complexity of the transformations, the peasantry's struggle to "endure" and the countless means of escape. However, the aggregated data do still help us to gain an understanding of the main aspects of the changes to the agricultural sector. The numbers show that the first half-decade of collectivization managed to decrease the number of private peasant farms by only just more than one quarter, with more than a million such farms recorded in 1953, 72 percent of the number recorded in 1949. The number of private agricultural holdings of between 11.4 and 14.25 acres, in fact, increased by 10 percent during the initial years of collectivization. These consisted primarily of plots distributed among families on "kulak holdings" in order to avoid political discrimination and the supplementary tax burdens imposed upon this land-ownership category. An analysis of the data contained in the table also reveals that the number of cooperative members increased by more than double that of the decrease in private peasant farms between 1949 and 1951. This was primarily the result of the fact that, for the lack of a better alternative, many of those agricultural indigents and dwarf holders who did not receive their own holdings as part of the 1945 land reform, in addition to those who had become insolvent during the interim, proved to be receptive to the vehement and often coercive pro-cooperative agitation.

Change in the structure of arable land ownership by types of agricultural holding, in 1949 and 1953
(In 1,000 cadastral hold, and as a percentage of the total arable land)

	1. Private peasant holdings	2. Holdings of peasants classed as kulaks	1 + 2 together	3. Production cooperatives	4. State farm	3 + 4 together	Total arable land
1949	7,731	1,650	9,381	76	113	189	9,570
%	80.8	17.2	98.0	0.8	1.2	2.0	100.0
1950	7,391	1,271	8,662	419	463	882	9,544
%	77.4	13.3	90.7	4.4	4.9	9.3	100.0
1951	6,620	942	7,562	1,253	685	1,938	9,500
%	69.7	9.9	79.6	13.2	7.2	20.4	100.0
1952	6,019	530	6,549	1,795	1,050	2,845	9,394
%	64.0	5.7	69.7	19.1	11.2	30.3	100.0
1953	5,067	449	5,516	2,478	1,300	3,778	9,294
%	54.5	4.8	59.3	26.7	14.0	40.7	100.0

Change in the number of private peasant holdings, production cooperative members, and state farm workers, in 1949 and 1953

	Number of private holdings				5.	6.	7.	8.
	1. 1–10 cadastral *hold*	2. 10–20 cadastral *hold*	3. 20–25 cad. *hold*	4. Over 25 cad. *hold*	1–4 together	No. of production cooperation members	No. of state farm workers	5–7 together
1949	1,122,700	240,300	30,600	47,200	1,440,800	12,900	32,000	1,485,700
%	75.6	16.2	2.0	3.2	97.0	0.9	2.1	100
1950	1,064,200	234,000	33,700	34,000	1,365,900	119,500	91,000	1,576,400
%	67.5	14.8	2.1	2.2	86.6	7.6	5.8	100
1951	1,037,600	224,500	23,400	25,000	1,310,500	260,100	125,000	1,695,600
%	61.2	13.2	1.4	1.5	77.3	15.3	7.4	100
1952	967,000	207,700	17,700	14,000	1,206,400	290,000	181,000	1,677,400
%	57.7	12.4	1.0	0.8	71.9	17.3	10.8	100
1953	870,900	143,800	14,200	10,200	1,039,400	293,600	229,000	1,562,000
%	55.8	9.2	0.9	0.6	66.5	18.8	14.7	100

These years produced two lasting effects. The first was that the security of both the individual and the individual's property, as well as the care with which those who hoped to earn an honest living through agricultural activities, were undermined to the greatest possible degree. The second was that society's traditional hierarchy was turned on its head. This was not a question of the disappearance of the former, partially noble, major landowners—there existed in the villages below and alongside the so-called "noble society" another stratum holding property and prestige. Following the communist takeover, erstwhile agricultural indigents, those lacking both land and status, became the primary beneficiaries of the new system. With their party membership booklets in hand, these people ruled in place of the nobility as neophyte local leaders—council chairmen and secretaries, cooperative presidents, party secretaries and local police chiefs. ("Vagabonds" of similar status were ushered in from elsewhere to follow in their footsteps.) In the transparent smaller communities and villages of which most of rural society was composed, people were slow to acknowledge, in spite of the obvious administrative power's preferences, that former day laborers, servants and hired men were exercising authority over their formerly more prosperous peasant employers. Moreover, the confidence of a significant majority of Hungarians, not only those among the country's agrarian population, in the legality of society and leadership at all levels was severely shaken. Even the weekly and monthly "mood reports" drawn up at the time referred, in their own way, to this change in the disposition of society. According to these accounts, an ever-greater proportion of society had, so to speak, "fallen under the influence of the class enemy's intrigues" or "followed in the wake of the kulaks and clerical reaction." The direct and indirect forms of pressure, together with a continual sequence of intentionally humiliating administrative measures, naturally triggered self-defense reflexes, mimicry and aversion. Under the circumstances, this antipathy was latent and difficult to discern, although nevertheless palpable in spite of the fact that the henchmen of the State Protection Authority (ÁVH) and informants did everything within their power to make "passive resistance" of this type a punishable offense. This resulted in a process of reaction and counter-reaction that served to weave a web of passive solidarity against the outside attempt to seed disunity within agrarian society. This is reflected in the parts of the reports in which official cadres complain to their superiors of the failure to "sharpen the class conflict" in the villages to a degree conforming to the party's expectations. In spite of the shrill exhortations blaring from electronic loudspeakers installed on local council houses and the continual urging of the "agits" (agitation brigades), Hungary's rural community did not "extract the kulaks from itself." Although there were internal squabbles from time to time, village-based agricultural society did display a passive solidarity of interests in the face of the externally inspired efforts to divide it.

The "results" of these efforts are manifested clearly in the fact that during the years presently under examination some 360,000 people, many more than had been guided into the cooperatives, left the agricultural sector, "offering" their land to the state. Hungary's political leadership was initially glad to receive this land, as a means of reaching one of its primary objectives of at least curtailing the amount of private property in the country if its total elimination were to prove impossible. The land acquired in this way was used to increase the area of cooperatives and state farms, although this form of expansion contained the drawback of entailing an attendant boost neither in the size of the labor force nor in inventories. Moreover, the expansion of the area of these collective farms served to increase the magnitude of their compulsory production and delivery quotas. The "dog biting its own tail" phenomenon then began to take effect. Historical research corroborates the collective memory of 1952 as the harshest year of the collectivization process. In spite of the rise in the total area and labor force of the collective farms, their proportion of Hungary's total agricultural production decreased. One of the reasons for the decline in productivity on the collective farms was that an increasingly significant share of their land was composed of uncultivated so-called "territory not subject to land tax," which by that time had come to include one tenth of Hungary's total arable land. A large number of people (more than 100,000) were forced to leave the villages altogether as well, after having concluded that changes made to the "socialist sector of agriculture" had resulted in the preservation of the poverty that Hungary's agrarian indigents had earlier attempted to escape. (The temporary reversal of this trend will be discussed later in the book during an analysis of the "new phase" associated with Prime Minister Imre Nagy.)

Those who had left the agricultural sector contributed significantly to ensuring that the 650,000 new workers required to meet the needs of the stepped-up plan's industrial program would be available. However, this generated another set of seemingly unmanageable problems. Private farms outperformed the collectivized portion of Hungary's agricultural sector in terms of both gross proceeds and productivity. It was therefore impossible to come even close to compensating for the decline in production stemming from the flight of labor from the collectivized sphere of agriculture. The mass of migrants from the agricultural sector, who had previously been self-sufficient in terms of food, subsequently became dependent on the state redistribution system for their alimentary subsistence. This entailed, as the result, the long lines and shortages that had already become a routine fact of life in the cities, prompting the reintroduction of the grocery ticket system in March and April 1951. Other factors evidently played a role in the decision to take the latter measure, because if the reintroduction of food tickets represented what Rákosi himself referred to as a "typical wartime maneuver," then it was hardly credible to claim that "the workers themselves had asked for it." Within the context of daily hardship and privation, the distorting mirror of the latest in a long sequence of official lies could elicit only bitter smiles even from those blessed with a sense of humor. At the same time, it was not possible to publicize the true reason for the shortages, since this was classified as yet another military secret—namely, the fact that within the context of rising Cold War hysteria following the outbreak of the Korean War, the quota of so-called impounded food was doubled. The culprits—more precisely scapegoats—for the artificially created shortages thus had to be uncovered elsewhere. This, however, fell under the jurisdiction of the political police. The ÁVH did not hesitate, providing the party press with information that it used in a several-week-long campaign of exposing the alleged discovery of hidden food. One day black market goods were found in the granary of a "discredited gendarme officer's widow," the next day in the shed of a "kulak's son-in-law" and the following day in the cellar of a "Horthy lackey and former district administrator." The true purpose of the press campaign was clearly to pin the blame for the public provision crisis on "the black marketeering and hoarding class enemy, the kulaks" and "the remnants of Horthyite reaction."

3. The Emergence of the Dictatorship's Structural Contradictions

Social history, in tandem with sociology, refers with requisite academic detachment to the metamorphosis of Hungary's peasantry described in the previous paragraphs as "intra-generational mobility." However, it is difficult to avoid the inclusion of qualifying elements into an otherwise objective, "neutral" narrative of the transformation in the status of those involved in agriculture and those who abandoned the sector. Those who left their land wound up in the cities or working on construction projects related to greenfield industrial investments. There was an overabundance of demand for these people, most of whom, for the lack of relevant skills and qualifications, joined the expanding ranks of "necessity workers." Uprooted from their familiar rural environment, they arrived at their workers' dormitories, night lodgings and, more rarely, rented accommodations on the periphery of urban industrial existence with an acute feeling of uncertainty. Another portion of the large group of Hungarians who left the agricultural sector at this time were compelled to make long trips to work, so-called commuting that entailed no less adversity than that faced by those who had moved to the vicinity of their new places of employment. The many former agriculturalists who rode the "black trains" established for the purpose of transporting people from the countryside to work in the city therefore had to cope with prolonged periods of separation from their families as well as adaptation to a new environment. During these years, infrastructural development was low on the list of priorities; more precisely, the scope of investment in housing and public utilities and provision was not commensurate with Hungary's relatively rapid and extensive industrial expansion. Short-lived political calculations immediately classified former peasants as members of the proletarian dictatorship's primary social base, the working class. The multitude of newly reclassified Hungarians, however, noticed that their economic situation and social stature had not improved one bit as a result of their having been included in the system's, so to speak, privileged faction. On the contrary. The uncertain feeling that these people had of having left one station and not yet arrived at another often produced a disheartening effect, the same one that Theodore Dreiser depicted in his novel *An American Tragedy* with the phrase "a frozen wind blows in no man's land." A more general social consequence of all of this, one that did not pertain exclusively to the peasantry, was the great degree of dictatorship-generated *compulsory mobility* that characterized a large majority of both intra- and inter-generational changes in occupation, residence and lifestyle.

This chapter will begin to recount the various forms of persecution that afflicted hundreds of thousands of Hungarians in the years following those just discussed. (More on this later.) Here one must refer to the traits and accumulated consequences stemming from the dictatorship's structural constraints. In grossly simplified form these were as follows: megalomaniac aspirations that were aimed at the transformation of Hungary's economy and society; the overambitious and domineering "totality" and exaggeratedly short "immediate deadline" with which the party intended to achieve it; "the Word was fulfilled" ideological automatism that rigidly excluded alternatives of any kind; forced experimentation in a country-sized laboratory on people who were both unaware of the redemptive nature of the objective—the mystery of socialism—and totally unacquainted with its essential substance. Finally, "the party, as vanguard" attempted to achieve its ambitions with the help of those who were not prepared (or who had not been prepared) to understand the characteristics of the project to be implemented (socialism or communism). Furthermore, people were not prepared to communicate these characteristics when they become cognizant of them; nor were they ready to conduct the technical management of the various sub-processes of production, let alone their synchronization and logistical harmonization.

Almost every branch of the social sciences and their methodological arsenal could and should be mobilized to individually verify the dozen or so attributes and distinctive features detailed above. However, this book will refrain from doing so. Instead, an anecdote will be used to illustrate why it was that even contemporaries suspected that the building of socialism was doomed to failure in spite of the total engagement of the party dictatorship. According to the anecdote, when construction work foundered, this was because there was either no gravel or not enough water, or the cement was late in arriving, or there was not a shovel available for mixing concrete. On the rare occasions when all of these things were on hand, an assembly of party members was held to mark the occurrence, while non-party members were sent in search of the missing blueprints. But by the time that they had found the plans—and the party assembly had come to an end—the cement had "gone bad," the water had evaporated, and the deadline for redeeming the allotted bricks had expired. Luckily, none of the trucks designated for transport of the bricks was running, and thus they did not deliver the bricks unnecessarily, saving precious diesel fuel. This is mentioned here, as part of the discussion of the peasantry's change of fortune at the beginning of the 1950s, because this was the largest stratum of Hungarian society, and the party leadership hoped to reach the home stretch of their program by making the majority of peasants "system-compatible." The generations-old, simultaneously fixed and flexible, peasant farming regimen was also thrown into disorder for those who remained in the agricultural sector. Those who had been compelled to leave the sector confronted the chaos and "programmed" counterproductive character of socialist investments with the above-described work regimen intact. They were forced to face all that which had accrued from the previously detailed—and unintelligible to the practical mind—planned economic anarchy.

The situation of industrial workers in the 1950s resembled that of those employed in the agricultural sector insofar as diverse forms of economic and administrative pressure were built into the organizational system of production in the various branches of industry. And although industrial development benefited from a redistribution ratio that was many times higher than that of the agricultural sector, this by no means meant that the income and subsistence conditions of industrial workers were commensurately better than those of people trying to earn a living in agriculture. Deficiencies in labor and plant organization were the primary factors circumscribing the objective of utilizing human and mechanical capacity to the maximum degree in this domain. This became the greatest impediment to continual, purposeful production. The party attempted to counterbalance frequent production stoppages through regular month-, quarter- and year-end "spurts" (campaign-style accelerated work), especially since production shortfalls and tardiness were classified as legal infractions whose criminal consequences threatened managers and employees alike. The party attempted to repair frequent short-circuits in the organization of production through the introduction of "work sacrifices." Work campaigns of various types and propaganda crusades engaged in the ritual search for enemies were held one after another.

It was enough for more attentive Hungarians to read the most important party organ, *Szabad Nép*, which the regime had attempted to transform into permanent "obligatory reading," in order to ascertain with weekly or monthly accuracy, based on the topic of the campaign then in progress, which part of the system required emergency traumatological intervention. The work competition movements named after various Soviet "vanguard workers" were examples of this. The most widespread of these movements was the so-called Stakhanovite movement, although the Utkin and other movements were also significant, as were their many Hungarian versions, such as the Csorba, Gazda, Deák, Loy and Röder movements.[5] The "holiday shifts" organized in honor of Soviet or Hungarian Communist Party congresses, the November 7 and April 4 holidays or the birthdays of Stalin or Rákosi served the same purpose. These years might be referred to as the period of campaign socialism.[6] "Work pledges" made on these occasions were aimed essentially at compensating for production shortfalls stemming from chronic material shortages or mere disorganization. The pace of work was frequently accelerated to counterbalance involuntary periods of inactivity. Quota surpluses stemming from these devices had two consequences—praise-accompanied rewards and just the opposite. The political leadership routinely determined better results to have been the result of, so to speak, "relaxed norms" in terms of production specifications. In response to the quota surpluses, the party regularly raised general production targets. The party compelled the nationalized trade unions to accede to these increases, thus depriving these organizations of their interest-coordination function based in collective solidarity.[7]

This, in itself, succeeded in producing among a significant majority of workers a sense of counter-interest with regard to the various Stakhanovite campaigns and work competitions, which, in fact, inspired latent production slowdowns. Ideologically motivated cadre policies made an equally potent contribution to the decline in industrial-technical production. One further example of mutually offsetting cross-affiliations will be mentioned here. Officials at the 1951 party congress declared that there was a need to urgently train 11,000 engineers and 17,000 technicians during the remainder of the five-year plan's cycle.[8] But while this was simply an impracticable resolution, at the same time they announced that an identical number of "conscious and ideologically developed skilled laborers" would be recruited to work in state administration and mid-level executive positions related to the fulfillment of people's economic targets. Worker cadres promoted in this way were deployed in three primary areas—the council system being built at the time, the organization of agricultural cooperatives and the rapidly expanding military officer corps. "Party confidence" based on the decision to recruit state administrators and mid-level executives from among "sufficiently class-conscious" skilled workers steered tens of thousands of the latter towards the above-listed fields, whereas their skills would have been best suited to the implementation of industrial development programs. Incessant vigilance campaigns "exposed" those who continued to practice their trades as unreliable or "harmful elements." Long-time skilled laborers, the majority of them former social democrats, were the primary target of these campaigns. Between 1950 and 1952, there occurred several such crusades, in which skilled workers were revealed to be remnants of so-called "enemy detachments of right-wing social democrats engaging in incitement against peaceful work."

Investments connected to the first five-year plan not only absorbed the large number of unemployed in Hungary following World War II, which peaked at around half a million in 1948, but actually produced a growing shortage of labor. This applied particularly to the aforementioned large-scale investments and to mines. Neither the labor recruitment brigades that circulated regularly throughout the country nor the Labor Reserve Office established to oversee deployment of the labor force managed to satisfy the demand for workers. Managers of major investment projects commonly applied to the latter office, using their contacts within the party in competition with one another to gain the largest possible quota of skilled workers from the ever-more inadequate "supply of people." Two other constructions served to increase the number of those available for work. Firstly, Ernő Gerő, the party leader responsible for overseeing the economy, adopted the Soviet practice of putting inmates in prisons and internment camps to work. With nearly 400,000 court convictions having been pronounced in Hungary between 1950 and 1953 alone, prisoners represented a major supplementary source of labor. The ÁVH provided convict labor "on loan," particularly for work in mines and at military installations and fortifications. Toiling under the supervision of ÁVH units established particularly for this purpose, these prisoners represented an essentially free source of labor.[9] The Recsk internment camp was the most infamous of these sites of convict labor, while modern research indicates that the Csolnok mine was the deadliest. Secondly, those convicted of lesser offenses were sentenced to "corrective-educational work." The deployment of the latter to work at major investment projects suffering most acutely from a shortage of labor enabled skilled workers to remain engaged in industry. The sentences of those condemned to perform such "corrective-educational" work included wage reductions, typically of 20 to 40 percent. The statutory decree pertaining to "criminal protection of the planned economy" that came into effect in 1950 served a similar purpose. According to this decree, it was not only those workers, workers' brigades, enterprises and managers who failed to meet production standards that could be qualified as saboteurs; those engaging in "arbitrary departure" could be so qualified as well. According to sentencing instructions that the Supreme Court issued one year later, arbitrary departure would thenceforth "qualify as a criminal act even in the absence of harmful intent." Thus both the political police and the judiciary constituted an integral part of the dictatorship's "workforce administration."

The all-inclusive centralized authority of the Hungarian Workers' Party leadership defined the wage and consumption circumstances of Hungary's population. Rákosi's slogan "Let us not kill the goose that lays the golden egg" was indeed a euphemistic summons rooted in the previously discussed diagnosis of everyday problems. Resources squandered on the armaments program and its related investments produced an economic situation in which almost all of society struggled with nearly continual privation and difficulty in meeting its everyday needs. Using 1938 as the pre-war base year, as is customary for the purpose of making economic comparisons, the wage level at the time of the introduction of the forint in 1946 was established at 50 percent of that recorded before World War II.

The average wage level in Hungary did not, in fact, reach that of the "labor-exploiting" Horthy era throughout the decade-long period until 1956.

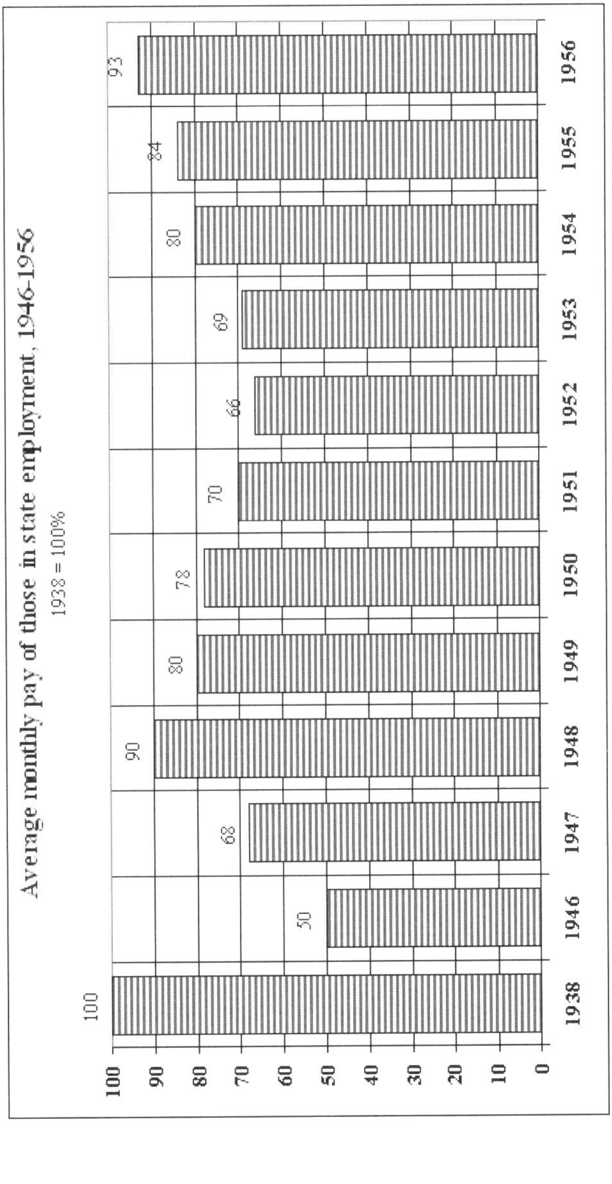

The period presently under examination can be divided into three sub-periods. Wages rose at a relatively rapid rate in the first two years following World War II, reaching 90 percent of the pre-war base by 1948 as a result of reconstruction efforts. However, wage conditions began to deteriorate following the communist takeover, with the average income falling over the next four years in unison with the building of the party dictatorship. This process reached its nadir in 1952, when the average wage level fell to that registered in 1947, at 66 percent of the 1938 base. Wages began to rise again only during the prime ministership of Imre Nagy to be discussed later in the book, although the diagram seen on the next page clearly demonstrates that the average wage level had not even reached that recorded in the base year by the outbreak of the Revolution in 1956. These data provide information regarding the economic circumstances of workers and employees engaged in Hungary's so-called nationalized sector. The standard of living of independent peasant farmers was 80–90 percent of that of workers and employees in the nationalized sector during these years, while that of those working in agricultural cooperatives was 75–80 percent, and that of those working in state farms 65–75 percent. The data for state farm workers are valid only until 1953, when the state increased their pay in order to bring it closer to that of agricultural cooperatives' workers.

One must deduct from these basic wage levels a "special tax" imposed during the Rákosi era, the so-called plan loans and peace loans that the dictatorship initiated for various purposes on several occasions following the start of the first five-year plan. Those classified as workers and employees were expected—or, rather, forced!—to remit an average of one month's salary for this purpose, thus automatically reducing their yearly salaries by around 8 percent. Those employed in intellectual domains or as party cadres made an additional contribution in the name of "ideological self-education," occasionally receiving in their pay envelopes a coupon for newly published editions of the works of Lenin, Stalin and Rákosi, the cost of which had already been deducted from their wages. Centrally directed party propaganda was unwilling to acknowledge any evidence of deteriorating economic circumstances, even when various ministries reported that "the increasing privations of the working classes have undermined faith in the building of socialism." Furthermore, party headquarters ordered that statistical data be regrouped because they had been compiled in a "completely un-party-like" way. These data could not, in fact, have been assembled in such a way as to show an increase in living standards conforming to political expectations. The primary element of the statistical correction was to "sum up" protocol and decoration expenses related to national holidays and party events as a separate item at all levels, from workplaces to ministries. Such occasions as the April 4 military parade, the "beer and sausage" May 1 celebrations, the November 7 commemorations of the Bolshevik Revolution and the series of ceremonies held throughout Hungary in recognition of Mátyás Rákosi's sixtieth birthday were paid for in this way under the pretext that "these were aimed at increasing the welfare of the people." There existed two groups of privileged citizens amid these circumstances of permanent economic hardship: those belonging to the high-level party and ministerial apparatus, who were eligible to do their shopping at "separate shops" established specifically for them, and miners, who received somewhat better provisions at distinct "miners' cafeterias."

4. Institutionalized Chaos in the Administrative System

Establishment of the national system of administrative councils was completed by the end of 1950, when the leaders of the new hierarchy were inaugurated in hundreds of official ceremonies. The 6,500 council presidents and secretaries were the key officeholders within the 220,000-member council system. In February 1951, the Political Committee of the Hungarian Workers' Party issued its initial appraisal of the performance of the new councils and their party cadres. Mátyás Rákosi had the following text inserted into the subsequently formulated draft resolution: "The establishment of the councils resulted in, in addition to the broadening of democracy, however, due to the lack of vigilance, the further penetration of the enemy into the state apparatus." In this case, the term "enemy" referred primarily to the former city, municipal and district clerks who had been elected to serve as council secretaries. Such experienced administrators were elected to serve as council secretaries in approximately 20 percent of the cities and municipalities in Hungary. Although the majority of these clerks first obtained office only after 1945, they were still qualified as class enemies for having, so to speak, served in the former system (as well). (The term "former system" thus applied not only to the Horthy era, but also to the years immediately following World War II.) The party secretary not only voiced his opinion that the permeation of reaction into "the new organs of democratic administration" was intolerable, but, as previously mentioned, had himself led the effort to expose this "new enemy." Rákosi repeated this charge during his general secretary's report delivered during the HWP's Second Party Congress at the end of February, and then, during an April 19 session of the Political Committee, accused Minister of the Interior Sándor Zöld of having been personally responsible for the situation. Zöld, who had himself participated in earlier purges, was well aware of the fate that awaited him. Thus, before the authorities had time to arrest him, he killed his family members (mother, wife and children) and then himself.

Rákosi, who declared Zöld's suicide to be a "betrayal of the party," was therefore compelled to find another high-ranking (and living) scapegoat. His next choice centered on János Kádár, who, as the party official chosen to submit the bill introducing the council-based administration, could be considered to have taken part in the preparation of the new system. Kádár was taken into custody along with Minister of Foreign Affairs Gyula Kállay on April 21. Kádár, Kállay and Zöld had all been among the "national" (that is, not "schooled" in Moscow) leaders of Hungary's communist movement who had been placed under arrest one after another since February 1951. Those taken into custody as part of this purge of national communists included Sándor Haraszti, Ferenc Donáth,

Géza Losonczy and Szilárd Újhelyi. Rákosi and Mihály Farkas claimed that that the aforementioned were "secret agents" who had remained in the Hungarian Workers' Party leadership and/or various important state-administrative posts following the "exposure of the treacherous Rajk." All of them were brought to trial, convicted and sentenced—Sándor Haraszti to death, although the punishment was not carried out, János Kádár to life in prison, Ferenc Donáth, Gyula Kállay and Géza Losonczy each to 15 years in prison and Szilárd Újhelyi to 8 years in prison.[10] This essentially served to remove all those officials from the party leadership who had not attained various key positions in the party state *nomenklatura* as "Muscovites." This miscarriage of justice contained two other unique features: first, contrary to earlier such cases, no protracted slander campaign accompanied the prosecution of those cited above, whose convictions were publicized in short press communiqués similar to that pertaining to the conviction of Kádár, "the anti-Soviet nationalist and guardian of Rajk's counter-revolutionary legacy"; second, all of them survived the madness of these dark years of persecution and were released from prison in 1954.

In the meantime, the process of purging the initially appointed leadership of the new council system came to an end. By the summer of 1951, more than 500 council leaders and 800 other "old" civil servants employed as part of the council system had been dismissed. Party leaders then ordered that 600 further local officials be removed from their positions by the end of the year in order to eradicate to the greatest degree possible the "remnants" not only of the Horthy era, but of the Rajk period as well. New local elections should have been held in at least one third of the municipalities in Hungary as a result of these purges. However, the Hungarian Workers' Party Political Committee resolved this issue with a single stroke, decreeing that new people could be appointed to replace those dismissed without elections, through co-option. The relevant party organs and cadre divisions were thus relieved of the burden of performing the perfunctory act of holding new elections.

The personnel departments and relevant party organs of the municipal, district and county councils had more than enough work to do even without the extra burdens stemming from the purges outlined above. It soon became apparent that not even new cadres whose class background, dependability and party loyalty were beyond reproach were performing their duties as expected. Particularly within the villages, bonds of kinship and acquaintance, the "everybody knows everybody" effect, served to obstruct the struggle against the kulaks, the strict enforcement of compulsory-delivery requirements and the coercion of peasants into agricultural cooperatives. The party thus began to "rotate" these politically unimpeachable council leaders to other municipalities, districts and counties. Personnel units and divisions, the so-called cadre officers, were responsible for the implementation of this practice of so-called *cadre rotation*. However, three factors hampered efforts to introduce a degree of efficiency and stability to the administrative system. First, the rotated council chairmen and secretaries were initially unfamiliar with local conditions; then, after having served six months or a year at their new locations, they were often accused of having become "too deeply connected to village society." Second, the party continually promoted these officials or ushered them away to take administrative courses or study at party schools. Separate "cadre search groups" established to "find a sufficient number of new people's cadres" proved unable to unravel the clump of Gordian knots stemming from the continual movement of officials within the administrative apparatus.

The third factor was of a different character, although it caused no less trouble. A significant portion of the new people's cadres were barely literate. Thus these *homines novi* were forced to deal with numerous, often contradictory, "higher" instructions, whose very reading and comprehension often surpassed their limited intellectual capabilities. For every one or two of these directives that the new cadres managed to decipher, thus enabling them to take the initial steps towards their implementation, another half a dozen remained unread on their desks. Although they frequently worked late into the night, the local cadres often had neither the time nor the energy to complete obligatory daily, weekly and monthly reports. Sooner or later, ÁVH officials became involved in these proceedings, detaining a large number of these local council chairmen and secretaries for neglecting their duties or, if a document or stamp were found lying on their desks at night, for "the handling of confidential information in a manner that might make it accessible to the class enemy."

As demonstrated above, the party's cadre policies in the first half of the 1950s triggered a counter-reaction in its "own base." The councils' administration system degenerated in a functional sense to being no more than the party's "general servant" at the local level. In practical terms, this entailed little more than exacting ransom from their peers. Even if a given council leader was not posted in his home village or district and was thus not compelled to force his own relatives to "sweep out the attic" or to seize their last remaining piglet in compensation for "tax arrears," he knew very well that a colleague from the party apparatus was doing the very same thing with his own parents and kinsfolk. To leave this system of one's own free will was difficult—and risky. The need to expand the labor force to meet the needs of the previously mentioned "stepped-up" plan of 1951 offered a means of escape.

In addition to the previously mentioned recruitment campaigns, the party attempted to moderate the industrial labor shortage through a peculiar redeployment of workers between economic sectors. The People's Economic Council, the Labor Reserve Office and the Ministry of the Interior produced a joint plan aimed at "promotion of employment for those with vocational disabilities and elderly people who would like to work." This plan also stipulated, with regard to state administration, that "elderly or disabled people must be appointed to replace at least 95 percent of able-bodied [administrative officials] under the age of 40 and the latter be engaged in production." This duly undermined the party's cadre policy, providing many council administrators with the opportunity to request "redeployment to production," either because they had had enough of playing the objectionable role of persecutor, or because the arrest of many of their colleagues had served as a warning that it could only be a matter of time before they were detained as well. This resulted in the large-scale exodus of recently appointed (or co-opted) council cadres from the administrative apparatus in 1952.

There were 128,000 people employed in Hungary's state administration following the termination of the B-list process in 1946, as discussed earlier in the book. This number rose to 246,000 in 1952 and 260,000 one year later. However, the increase in the number of those working in the dictatorship's state apparatus had periodically been even higher (much higher, in fact) than the approximately 100 percent rise that had taken place between 1946 and the end of 1952. These fluctuations stemmed from the continual purges and departures of council cadres mentioned in the previous paragraph. The system of cadre management based on ideological parameters practically collapsed at the turn of the year 1952–1953. During a meeting of party secretaries in December 1953, Mátyás Rákosi ordered that between 250 and 300 industrial worker cadres be recruited within one week in order to begin training to prepare them for appointment to the post of council chairman the following March. In doing so, Rákosi's intention was not to seek replacement for another "old, reactionary" faction of the upper-level state administration, but to substitute "people's cadres" of peasant origin with those whom he deemed to be more reliable industrial workers. The Hungarian Workers' Party general secretary intended to place these new cadres at the head of councils located in communities where the organization of agricultural cooperatives had made the least progress. However, the parameters outlined in the belatedly submitted list did not correspond to those prescribed either: "Politically mature, vocationally outstanding large-scale industrial worker cadre with at least an eighth-grade education." Those who had drafted and tendered the list of proposed worker cadres reported that the managers of the large factories from which they had been selected had protested that the loss of those being redeployed to the administrative councils placed their company's capacity to meet production targets in jeopardy. Rákosi consequently made the "Solomonic decision" to immediately transfer 100 "better-performing" incumbent council chairmen to villages in which the collectivization process was behind schedule, while designating the most qualified candidates from the compiled list to become council chairmen after having completed a six-week administrative crash course. The lack of education among those employed in the state apparatus did not diminish with the passage of time. The table below shows the education level of workers in Hungary's state administration as recorded in the year 1954:

Less then 8th Grade	79%
Completed 8th Grade	10%
Completed High School or Higher Elementary School	7%
Completed University or College	4%

No data are available regarding the qualifications of employees at the various levels of Hungary's state administration. One may presume, however, that there was a greater concentration of administrators with a higher degree of education working in ministries, while documents surviving from the period suggest that many of those operating within the municipal and district apparatus struggled with basic literacy. Of course, these officials may have possessed knowledge and skills acquired outside the classroom, regardless of their level of formal education. While equally experienced farmers and herdsmen may have experienced difficulty when operating a welder or a grinding machine, experienced lathe operators may not have been adept at milking cows or reaping hay either. Moreover, all of them felt an equal sense of frustration when, as freshly appointed "people's or worker cadres," they were compelled to function within the confines of strict budgetary constraints. The circle appeared to be closing. The dictatorship's reserve of ideologically suitable, at least minimally educated (heavy) industrial (skilled) worker cadres available to fill even low-level executive posts within the state administration stood on the verge of depletion. Neither did the assignment of the even larger number of those who had been forced to relinquish their land to positions requiring skilled labor serve to substantially improve industrial production. Simply too many people were forced into dysfunctional roles in too short a time. The dictatorship associated with the name of Rákosi had begun to suffer functional breakdowns in an increasing number of areas, stemming from its own defective structure a full half-decade following its seizure of absolute power. Expressed in other, perhaps more explicit, terms: it was not true that "deviations" and "voluntaristic transgressions" were really a common, everyday occurrence, and even less true that Mátyás Rákosi's so-called "cult of personality," which was really nothing more than an accumulation of empty rhetoric and euphemistic disinformation, stood at the root of the problem. Institutionalized irrationality was one of the system's immanent characteristics. During the days of the system's collapse in 1956, István Bibó referred to this institutionalized terror-based anarchy as the "bestial state."

5. The Professional Victim and the Professional Executioner

As tight-fisted as Rákosi and the party leadership were in terms of wages and consumer goods in the early 1950s, they were equally as extravagant when it came to initiating a spate of persecution that kept all of Hungarian society gripped in a state of fear. The institutionalized persecution of the dictatorship, stemming from its aforementioned structural constraints, could afflict anybody at any time. A sufficient analysis of the organic or ideologically contrived groups that existed in Hungary at the time reveals that they were all subject to mass persecution. Former army and gendarme officers, collectively termed lackeys of "Horthy-fascism," formed a separate "caste" even if they did not happen to be interned or under observation: the police utilized members of this group in order to conduct what had become constant mutual surveillance. Within the working class, former social democrats were stigmatized as "class traitors," while long-time communists who had not belonged to one of the minority "Moscow-loyal" circles were branded "factionalists." The political police established distinct "kulak-thrashing units" during the period in which János Kádár served as minister of the interior (1948) in order to put this segment of the peasantry, deemed to be a "class enemy," in its place. There were two additional social and occupational groups whose members were placed under individual observation during the 1950s: the "secular" *intellectuals* with university degrees and *clerics* (priests, monks, nuns and seminarians). There was more than enough room for every single individual belonging to one of these groups in the political police's registration system, which came to include 1.2 million people, or more than 20 percent of Hungary's adult population, established to catalog those under surveillance or otherwise judged to be (internal) enemies.

As a potentially suspicious segment of society, the entire intelligentsia became the subject of preventative surveillance. Keeping tabs on groups working in "fixed" occupations, such as engineers, doctors, teachers, attorneys, judges or institutional researchers working under the auspices of the nationalized Academy of Sciences, was no problem, since they had become fully integrated and status-dependent members of the dictatorship's institutional system. It was a similar case with the declassified individuals such as the philosopher now working as a stock-keeper, the agricultural engineer who had become a night watchman, the former university professor serving as a librarian, or the one-time district notary maintaining railway track beds for a living. So-called "freelance" lawyers were monitored through their professional organizations, while writers and painters were also congregated in trade guilds and their works were published or presented in public via nationalized publishers and commercial enterprises only after having passed through strict censorship. Certain white-collar institutions and professions were implicitly under dual observation, such as the prosecutor's chamber or journalists, whose staff editorial meetings hardly differed in composition from party assemblies. Non-party members had been permitted to work as teachers, at museums and archives and in theater companies, although the ÁVH's dossier of cadres, updated monthly, of people from among these professions became progressively thicker.

Hungary's Churches were the recipient of even harsher treatment than that described above, with the Rákosi system regarding them, above all the Catholic Church, as inherent enemies to be subdued at all costs. From the point of view of the dictatorship's party headquarters, the Mindszenty trial had not produced all the desired results. Although placing its most intransigent leader behind bars had indeed forced the Hungarian Catholic Church to its knees, it had not led to the Church's disintegration. The fact was that Catholics had already become accustomed to kneeling—in prayer. During Cardinal Mindszenty's show trial, Hungary's episcopate received confidential instructions from Pope Pius XII indicating that they should be prepared to undergo martyrdom in the name of their faith and freedom of their Church.[11] The party did not succeed in dividing the Fathers of the Church to the desired degree, and nor was it able to drive a wedge within the lower clergy and its bishops as deeply as intended. With the notable exception of Archbishop of Eger Gyula Czapik, whose singular portrayal in the memoirs of Mátyás Rákosi as an amiable, near-"bosom buddy" represents nothing less than a "denunciation before history," the majority of clerics engaged in various forms of passive resistance. However, within the given circumstances, there was no means of total escape. The party's only concrete claim to success was its forced signing of a so-called pact between the state and the Church on August 30, 1950[12]—more than a year and a half after Cardinal Mindszenty's conviction and compared to Rákosi's original prognosis that he would "eradicate Church reaction" by the end of 1948.

The ÁVH, however, detained approximately 500 monks and nuns from the various religious orders active in Hungary in the weeks preceding the signing of this agreement. Then, on the day following the conclusion of the accord, the minister of the interior hastened to issue a statutory decree dissolving religious orders. At the time of the enactment of this decree, 23 male orders were operating in Hungary, with some 2,600 members, located in 187 monasteries and, until their nationalization, 26 high schools and 5 hospitals. The 40 female orders active in the country at this time had 8,950 members, located in 456 convents and other community institutions. Until their nationalization, these nuns also operated 220 schools of all types and 80 hospitals, orphanages and nursing homes.[13] The property, school buildings and hospitals belonging to the disbanded religious orders were confiscated during the autumn of this year, while a large number of the now vagrant monks were interned. Just 10 percent (284) of them received the "secular grace" of being appointed as diocese priest under the jurisdiction of the various episcopates.

Following the forced signing of the "agreement" with the Catholic Church, an accord that was not codified as a legal enactment during the entire period under discussion, the Hungarian Workers' Party leadership essentially reduced Church policy to a matter for the political police. It was in this context that in 1951 the party launched a new offensive against Hungary's episcopate, which did not support the "peace struggle" with sufficient, so to speak, zeal. The political police had managed to recruit many so-called "peace priests" from among the lower-ranking clergy for this propaganda campaign aimed at exposing "imperialist warmongering." The episcopate had published a statement in which it expressed the importance of world peace and reconciliation, but the Hungarian Workers' Party did not deem it to be sufficiently "combative." The dictatorship trained its sights particularly on the Archbishop of Kalocsa, who was traditionally second in line behind the Archbishop of Esztergom in Hungary's Catholic Church hierarchy. It was quite apparent that the verdict of the newest grandiose show trial, that of Archbishop of Kalocsa József Grősz, who had just three quarters of a year previously countersigned the above mentioned agreement between the state and the Catholic Church, had been prepared earlier than the indictment. The script of the Gábor Péter-led ÁVH for the "proceedings in the case of József Grősz and his accomplices" was dated May 10, 1951, while the Archbishop of Kalocsa was taken into custody only on May 18.[14] The trial produced verdicts just six weeks later, at the end of June: 15 years in prison for József Grősz and between 8 and 14 years in prison for five associates tried along with the Archbishop of Kalocsa.

Four more bishops were placed under house arrest at the beginning of the trial—Bishop of Veszprém Bertalan Badalik, Bishop of Csanád Endre Hamvas, Bishop of Vác József Pétery and Bishop of Székesfehérvár Lajos Shvoy. Appointed to replace these bishops were "peace priests" selected from among office managers and vicars who had shown the ÁVH evidence that that they were prepared to serve two masters. They rendered unto God the things that were that God's and unto the reigning Caesar (the state party) the things that were that Caesar's. Additionally, the so-called State Office for Church Affairs was established the day after the arrest of Bishop Grősz, on May 19, 1951.[15] The legal function of this office was to manage Hungary's denomination-related affairs under the auspices of the Council of Ministers. This provided the party with an organization through which the ÁVH could, under the guise of maintaining official inter-agency contacts, keep the Church(es) under direct everyday supervision through the newly appointed bishops and other informants recruited from among the clergy.

A unique aspect of the show trial of József Grősz was the fact that it engendered more background and auxiliary proceedings than the Mindszenty trial had. A total of 24 such trials produced nearly 250 convictions, including 15 death sentences. However, contrary to the main trial, in which two thirds of the defendants were clerics, the majority of those accused in the auxiliary procedures were "secular reactionaries." The table on the next page shows the number of Catholic clerics imprisoned or interned during the communist period in Hungary.

Clerics arrested and/or interned in Hungary between 1945 and 1989						
	"Rákosi Era" 1945–1956		"Kádár Era" 1957–1989		Total 1945–1989	
	Number	%	Number	%	Number	%
Priests	294	67	145	33	439	100
Monks	177	72	68	28	245	100
Total	471	69	213	31	684	100

These data reveal that more than two thirds of priests and monks imprisoned or interned in Hungary between the end of World War II in 1945 and the fall of communism in 1989 were incarcerated during the broadly defined Rákosi period, while only one third of them were locked up during János Kádár's more than three decades in power.[16] (There were, of course, people imprisoned during both the Rákosi period and the Kádár period, such as the Piarist monk Ödön Lénárd, who spent almost 20 years in prison during the more than four decades of communist dictatorship in Hungary.) During the Rákosi era, the Churches, primarily the Catholic Church, were designated to play the role of the scapegoat to be blamed for all of the system's problems. These institutions and their priests and ministers became the dictatorship's "professional" victims.

The State Protection Authority played the role of professional, institutionalized executioner in this system. The Gábor Péter-led political police, as Péter himself stated in one of his reports to Moscow, served as Rákosi's indispensable *aides-de-camp* in his effort to attain absolute power. Péter subsequently became the commander-in-chief's essential "platoon sergeant" managing the everyday operations of the dictatorship. This direct working relationship between Rákosi and the ÁVH at the beginning of the 1950s did not stem only from the elevation of the political police to quasi-ministerial status. It was also a result of the fact that Péter himself had again become a permanent presence at the meetings of the central party leadership, those of the Political Committee, even though he was not a formal member of this body. Gábor Péter's unofficial authority was also strengthened as a result of the downfall of a succession of ministers of the interior (Rajk, Kádár and Zöld), often as a result of his own intrigues. Péter was, in terms of both rank and political means, more powerful than the interim ministers who succeeded those listed above (Árpád Házi and József Györe).

To this day, historical works dealing with this period portray political power during Rákosi's reign as having been concentrated in the hands of the troika of Rákosi, Ernő Gerő and Mihály Farkas, or the so-called "foursome" comprising the latter as well as József Révai. This analysis is valid only if one considers the party dictatorship's formal institutionalized hierarchy. However, an examination of the period reveals that during the darkest years of the dictatorship from the Rajk trial until the end of 1952, Gábor Péter is a more appropriate fourth member of the "foursome" than Révai. Nobody, with the exception of Rákosi, had more authority than ÁVH officials to make an investigation of anybody at any time or in any place. From the party-controlled economy to culture, from ministries to village pressing houses, from the so-called "provocative" ringing of church bells to the draining of quarry water, the ÁVH had the power to freely establish the "facts of the case" with regard to alleged acts of sabotage, conspiracy, espionage and treason. The ÁVH was structured to perform this task and, playing the role of "the fist of the party," found its daily quota of enemies in all quarters, just as Mátyás Rákosi had instructed the whole country in his previously mentioned summons following the Rajk trial.

There was a unique power-sociological aspect with regard to the ÁVH's authority as well. Gábor Péter's organization naturally looked into all matters that Rákosi or the party leadership deemed to be worthy of investigation. This stemmed from the party dictatorship's institutional-organizational routine and the functional role of the political police. However, the ÁVH also maintained an additional "free capacity" to conduct independent action aimed at preserving—or more precisely disrupting—order among the subjugated population. That is to say that Hungary's political police served not only as the party dictatorship's vigilant sentinels and commandoes, but as an unregulated and unrestrained guerrilla force as well. The ÁVH operated without even tacit "authority" conferred from above. The vigilance hysteria that discerned enemies everywhere and in everyone had by this time become an implicit element of the system, not merely an accessory feature. ÁVH agents themselves may have been the most acutely aware of the fact that anybody could fall from a position of authority into their grasp as a detainee. Members of the political police continually felt compelled to prove their "solid and unshakable party loyalty" through relentlessly brutal treatment of the multitude of presumed "enemies" in order that they the interrogators would not one day join the ranks of the interrogated.

The macrocosm in the microcosm is reflected most clearly in a particular case involving "class struggle- and vigilance-based state protection." A young man murdered a village party leader near the southern border of Hungary. He testified that his motive had been the fact that the official had laid claim to an evicted well-to-do farmer's house, into which he, his six younger siblings and widowed mother had applied to move from their hovel at the edge of the village. The perpetrator immediately turned himself in to the police and admitted to his crime. It was not an everyday case, although it was unambiguous and would have been easily addressed through the courts. It did not, however, happen this way. County political police detectives dispatched to investigate the crime began their probe by placing the village's prosperous vineyard owners under arrest. Interrogators then coerced these "murder-provoking kulaks" to confess that they had drunkenly incited the ill-fated culprit to take revenge against the party official. Three of these "kulaks" were put on trial for this alleged crime. However, the primary defendant maintained throughout the proceedings that he had committed the crime entirely of his own volition, without encouragement, and the court thus acquitted the three accused instigators. Despite this, the political police nevertheless confined them to internment camps for several years. The three men gained their release only with the closing of the camps, not long before the young man convicted of murdering the party official was discharged from prison.

Eviction, relocation and internment were all utilized as means of retribution against society. Removal of "unreliable elements" from the vicinity of Hungary's western and southern borders began after the Cominform issued a resolution in 1949 declaring Yugoslavia to be an enemy. This relocation involved 450 people and their family members. Another series of forced relocations took place within the context of the war hysteria that occurred following the outbreak of the Korean conflict in 1950, when 5,000 Horthy-era senior civil servants, high-ranking military and police officials, landowners, industrialists and their families were expelled from Budapest and provincial industrial centers. (Among these people were Jewish survivors of concentration camps.) Some of these 5,000 people were relocated to hinterland villages, while others were sent to sparsely populated territories in eastern Hungary such as the Nagykunság and the Hortobágy.[17] The latter region contained the largest work camp, where evicted and relocated persons were forced to do agricultural work in exchange for their "state provisions." Another objective of the evictions and relocations was to provide housing for the large number of cadres and ministerial, military, police and ÁVH functionaries who had moved to Budapest and the provincial industrial hubs.

The occupations of the heads of families displaced between May 21 and July 18, 1951 (Total: 5,182)

Ministers and widows	28
State secretaries and widows	34
Generals and widows	272
Army staff officers and widows	1,417
Police staff officers and widows	302
Gendarmerie officers and widows	98
State officials and widows	881
Industrialists and widows	191
Bankers and widows	180
Wholesalers and widows	410
Landowners and widows	310
Directors and widows	387
Store-owners and widows	40
Aristocrats and widows	31
Condemned criminals' dependants	38
Other occupations	563

However, not everybody could be taken away, and soon there were not even any places left to take them. People could, nevertheless, still come to grief in the vicinity of their own homes. If a farmer left ruts in the muddy roads of a village as he passed through by wagon on his way home from his fields, he could be charged with "impairing public traffic routes." If a worker was late for his shift at a factory, he could be accused of having committed the criminal offense of "sabotage jeopardizing the fulfillment of the plan law." The following is an excerpt from the stated grounds for a five-year prison sentence:

> The court established the guilt of the accused in spite of his denials, concluding that execution of the crime of unauthorized border crossing begins when an individual leaves his house with the intention of leaving the country

> in an illicit fashion. Although the accused had not yet left his house [*sic*!], the packing of one portion of his moveable possessions and the consignment to a secure place of the other represented the act of illegal border crossing even though he could not carry through with the physical act, which only his arrest prior to the receipt of his passport [thus indicating that he had carried through with the legal process of applying for a passport!] served to prevent.

During the first half of the 1950s, a total of between 100 and 200 private passports were issued per year.

Irrationality? Folly? A sequence of official lies? Yes! These are precisely what held the system together. The constant vigilance hysteria arising from the enemy-hunting campaigns deprived all of Hungarian society, including party members, of the "presumption of innocence." Any person (or phenomenon) deemed by an organ of state power or one of the 35,000 police informants (or network of individuals) to be an enemy (or enemy manifestation) could immediately be classified as a perpetrator of a punishable offense (or criminal fact) even in a passive, unintended manner. If somebody was deemed to be an enemy on political grounds, not only was this person subjected to prosecution even in the absence of legal evidence, but his family members, work colleagues and friends were also liable to be qualified as "accomplices" for failure either to report or even to recognize the antagonistic character and intent of the individual in question. The political police, to quote the writer Gyula Illyés, served its master, the party leadership, as a "self-motivated watchdog." However, the active participation of numerous additional branches of the socialist state mechanism was indispensable in order for the system of institutionalized terror to work as efficiently as possible.

This is why it is difficult to determine the proportion of judicial verdicts that were rooted in political considerations as compared to those based on genuinely criminal acts or omissions. Punitive measures related to the "struggle against the kulaks" may have pertained to 35,000–40,000 people, according to a precise definition of the target group; however, the broad, idiosyncratic interpretation of the term "kulak" doubled this number, while nearly 400,000 more peasants were convicted of transgressions under the category "public provision crimes" between 1948 and 1953, and police invested with the authority of "petty offense courts" imposed fines and punishments in 850,000 cases between 1951 and 1953 alone. A total of over a million more criminal procedures were initiated with the public prosecutor's office on the basis of various denunciations, informant allegations and preliminary police inquiries between the spring of 1950 and May 1953.

Approximately 650,000 indictments were eventually filed, of which 60 percent resulted in guilty verdicts. This seems to be a large number not only if one intuitively imagines the individual lives of the condemned workers and peasants; it is also very large if one considers the mere fact that the officials involved—police, prosecutors and judges—had to administer around 700 cases per day during the designated time period. (For readers from North America, it is worth keeping in mind the fact that all this took place in a country the size of the US state of Indiana.) This accelerated legal process was feasible if, for example, court hearings in a trial of 13 defendants and their sentencing to a total of 95 years in prison lasted for a total of no more than one hour. Prison routine was also streamlined in this way. Prison guards were instructed to handle those detained in such a way as to not have to "settle accounts with anybody." One prison doctor even informed his patient "I'm not here to cure you, but to make sure that you are able to serve out your sentence."[18]

However, the mechanism began to stall at the prison level as well. Police vans delivered a continual supply of those pronounced guilty in the course of nearly non-stop trials to the prison gates, although fresh shipments were received with increasing reluctance. In the spring of 1952, a public announcement was broadcast in the vicinity of prisons requesting that "all those under the age of 39 who are in possession of a soldier's book and are fit to serve on the staff of penal institutions apply immediately at the nearest council house for such employment." This public recruitment of prison guards did not only suggest that there was a lack of personnel to operate and secure Hungary's overcrowded prisons; since the task of keeping watch over the various categories of enemy elements—"counts, barons, military officers, priests and other fascists," according to one directive—was on the list of politically sensitive positions, it was also an indirect indication that the search for "reliable people's cadres" had failed. This represented yet another breakdown of the system: not only was the stock of working-class "human resources" available to fill the position of council president or council secretary depleted, but the "cadre material" suitable for work as prison guards had also been spent.

The din of a large-scale spring festival obscured the sound of the newest system malfunction during the first week of March 1952, when village council house loudspeakers and, in locales still without electricity, traditional town criers gave the public the following instruction: "With houses tidy and decorated, let everyone prepare in a befitting fashion for the sixtieth birthday of the wise leader and mentor of our people, Stalin's greatest Hungarian pupil, comrade Mátyás Rákosi." The entire population of Hungary was mobilized to celebrate this occasion. Wordsmiths penned a series of panegyrics extolling Rákosi; factory workers held work competitions and prepared miniature models of their plant machinery in honor of the birthday of the Hungarian Workers' Party general secretary; "the working peasantry" expressed its devotion towards "the beloved leader" with homespun woven rugs and an array of folk-art representations of agricultural products. The clergy, more precisely the "peace priests," were not to be excluded from the procession of those eulogizing Rákosi on his sixtieth birthday. According to one such homage, "[not only] with our Church and its congregations… [but] with the entire Hungarian people we express our wish that his [Rákosi's] leadership of the country will bring long years of bountiful results." The author of these lines also pledged that "We will strive to continue serving in such a way that our gratitude and affection for Mátyás Rákosi will not be in word only, but in truth and life as well."[19] A butcher endowed with artistic ambitions chose to commemorate the occasion by making a lard bust of Rákosi, which he displayed in the window of the shop where he worked. This butcher's shop became an undeclared pilgrimage site, where people could view what was quietly considered to be the most accurate representation of the party leader.

After taking a brief respite to recover from the fatigue of participating in the nationwide ceremonies held to mark his sixtieth birthday, Rákosi reciprocated the "affection and gratitude of the Hungarian working people" with a gift of his own, accepting the post of chairman of the Council of Ministers in accordance with a Political Committee proposal calling for the merger of state and party leadership. From August 14, 1952, Mátyás Rákosi served in the dual capacity of party secretary and prime minister, thus formally concentrating all the prerogatives entailed in the leadership of the party state dictatorship in his hands. Meanwhile, the party took measures to ensure that national celebrations would not diminish labor productivity, reclassifying Hungary's most important modern national holiday, the March 15 commemoration of the Revolution of 1848, and the second day of Christmas (December 26), as "normal workdays." At the same time, during their preparation for the 150th anniversary of the birth of Lajos Kossuth, party officials had the group of statues erected on the square in front of the Parliament building in honor of the preeminent nineteenth-century Hungarian leader during the Horthy era "replaced," because it contained representations of "discredited reactionary nobles" in addition to that of a "melancholy" Kossuth. Based on instructions from József Révai, the new composition portrayed Kossuth "beaming with optimism," while the ancillary figures consisted of a revolutionary worker, a people's warrior and a working peasant.

Dark clouds again began to gather in the skies over the countries of the peace camp at the turn of the year 1952–1953, with a new element complementing the stock of vigilance themes. The Soviet Communist Party leadership had staged an anti-Zionist trial (the case of the "Jewish doctors") in response to a recent bomb attack on the Soviet Embassy in Tel Aviv. As a result, the Hungarian Workers' Party decided to place the fight against Zionism on the party agenda. Rákosi held consultations on this issue at a February 19 meeting of the party's Central Directorate during which he asserted that beginning in 1950 former ÁVH leader Gábor Péter, whom the party and government leader had arrested in early January, "was working with the Zionists… but we did not attach enough importance to this fact." (Gábor Péter was one of the few key members of the party dictatorship to fill the same post for an extended period of time, serving as head of the ÁVH for eight years.) Party headquarters requested information regarding the ancestry of high- and mid-level state-administrative cadres. Following his return from a visit to Moscow in January 1953, Ernő Gerő transmitted instructions according to which Zoltán Vas was expelled from the party's Political Committee and appointed to lead a mining facility in Komló, and István Szirmai was dismissed as head of the Hungarian Radio Office and subsequently detained as part of a hastily implemented purge of the party apparatus and the ÁVH, which had also included Gábor Péter's arrest. A total of 18 of the 80 people taken into custody during this vigilance campaign were eventually convicted. Although this campaign produced no death sentences, one person committed suicide prior to his arrest, while two more ended their own lives while in custody and another died during interrogation.

Stalin died on March 5, 1953. Three days later, the Hungarian National Assembly adopted legislation preserving his "immortal memory." During the middle of the month, Parliament amended the electoral law and called new national elections. On March 28 the National Council of the Hungarian Independence People's Front was convened for the first time since its establishment in 1949. In the middle of April, this body issued a summons exhorting the population to support and follow "unanimously the wise leader of our people and the Hungarian Workers' Party, Mátyás Rákosi!" The latter appeared at the top of candidate lists in every electoral district, followed by Ernő Gerő and Mihály Farkas. Party propagandists also took part in the preparations for the elections, publishing the keynote campaign themes in an article entitled "Electoral Preview for the Working People" that appeared in the April–May issue of the HWP ideological periodical *Társadalmi Szemle.* This article portrayed the previous years as an earthly paradise, predicting that "the sky is the limit" in Hungary's further development. Electoral trappings suggested that the impending vote was to be of truly "decisive" importance, with the party even permitting Horthy-era triumphal gates to be reconstructed in the villages to complement the customary socialist banners and adornments. Local electoral committees received candidates at these gates as they arrived to deliver their campaign speeches. From the beginning of March, the party curbed its harassment of the "working peasants" and even the kulaks. During the second half of April, grocery store warehouses and shelves were stocked with an unprecedented amount of food. Many people considered this phenomenon to be a sign of an "immediate easing" following Stalin's death, although it was, in fact, part of centrally planned electoral preparations. The party also took great care to organize a system whereby it was able to regularly apprise officially appointed local canvassers of the names of those who had not yet appeared at the polling station to vote on election day (May 17, 1953). Those who expressed reluctance to cast their ballots were reminded that a list would be compiled of those who had not participated in the elections… The voting results in some electoral districts were nevertheless announced only after Rákosi personally endorsed the "partial results."[20] These efforts proved to be fruitful, with the official final voting results showing, as in 1949, a 98 percent landslide majority for candidates appearing on the People's Front lists.

Mátyás Rákosi was able to proclaim complete victory in his assessment of the elections. However, the "other Hungary" was unable to voice its true opinion in the early 1950s. By this time it had become advisable to discontinue the earlier popular practice of keeping a diary. Those sent to conduct house searches on what had come to be referred to as "the nights of doorbell fright" were often given specific instructions to look for personal compositions, letters and manuscripts. A poem that Gyula Illyés committed to paper in 1951, "A Sentence about Tyranny" nevertheless survived the period, although it was made public only at the time of the Revolution in the autumn of 1956. This poem is included in this chapter as follows because it deals with the period presently under examination, even if this expression of contrasting thought lay at the bottom of the drawer for many years on end:

Gyula Illyés

A SENTENCE ABOUT TYRANNY

Where tyranny exists
that tyranny exists
not only in the barrel of the gun
not only in the cells of a prison

not just in the interrogation block
or the small hours of the clock
the guard's bark and his fists
the tyranny exists

not just in the billowing black fetor
of the closing speech of the prosecutor,
in "the justified use of force"
the prisoners' dull morse

not merely in the cool postscript
of the expected verdict
there's tyranny
not just in the crisp military

order to "Stand!" and the numb
instruction "Fire!", the roll of the drum,
in the last twitch
of the corpse in the ditch

not just in the door half open
and the fearful omen,
the whispered tremor
of the secret rumour

the hand that grips,
the finger before the lips,
tyranny is in place
in the iron mask of the face

in the clench of the jaw
the wordless O
of pain and its echo
and the tears

of silence-breeding fears,
in the surprise
of starting eyes

tyranny supplies
the standing ovation, the loud
hurrahs and chanting of the crowd
at the conference, the songs

of tyranny, the breasts
that tyranny infests,
the loud unflagging
noise of rhythmic clapping,

at the opera, in trumpet cry,
in the uproarious lie
of grandiose statues, of colours,
in galleries,

in the frame and the wash,
in the very brush,
not just in the neat snarl
of the midnight car

as it waits
outside the gates

tyranny permeates
all manners and all states,
its omnipresent eyes more steady
than those of old Nobodaddy,

there's tyranny
in the nursery
in father's advice, in his guile,
in your mother's smile

in the child's answer
to the perfect stranger;

not just in wires with barbs and hooks
not just in rows of books,
but, worse than a barbed wire fence
the slogans devoid of sense

whose tyranny supplies
the long goodbyes;
the words of parting,
the will-you-be-home-soon-darling?

in the street manners, the meetings
and half-hearted greetings,
the handshakes and the alarm
of the weak hand in your palm,

he's there when your loved one's face
turns suddenly to ice
he accompanies you
to tryst or rendezvous

not just in the grilling
but in the cooing and the billing,
in your words of love he'll appear
like a dead fly in your beer

because even in dreams you're not free
of his eternal company,
in the nuptial bed, in your lust
he covers you like dust

because nothing may be caressed
but that which he first blessed,
it is him you cuddle up to
and raise your loving cup to

in your plate, in your glass he flows
in your mouth and through your nose
in frost, fog, out or in
he creeps under your skin

like an open vent through which
you breathe the foul air of the ditch
and it lingers like drains
or a gas leak at the mains

it's tyranny that dogs
your inner monologues,
nothing is your own
once your dreams are known

all is changed or lost,
each star a border post
light-strafed and mined; the stars
are spies at window bars,

the vast tent's every lamp
lights a labour camp,

come fever, come the bell
it's tyranny sounds the knell,

confessor is confession,
he preaches, reads the lesson
he's Church, House and Theatre
the Inquisition;

you blink your eyes, you stare
you see him everywhere;
like sickness or memory
he keeps you company;

trains rattling down the rail
the clatter of the jail;
in the mountains, by the coast
you are his breathing host;

lightning: the sudden noise
of thunder, it's his voice
in the bright electric dart,
the skipping of the heart

in moments of calm,
chains of tedium,
in rain that falls an age,
the star-high prison-cage

in snow that rises and waits
like a cell, and isolates;
your own dog's faithful eyes
wear his look for disguise,

his is the truth, the way
so each succeeding day
is his, each move you make
you do it for his sake;

like water, you both follow
the course set and the hollow
ring is closed; that phiz
you see in the mirror is his

escape is doomed to failure,
you're both prisoner and gaoler;
he has soaked, corroded in,
he's deep beneath your skin

in your kidney, in your fag,
he's in your every rag,
you think: his agile patter
rules both mind and matter

you look, but what you see
is his, illusory,
one match is all it takes
and fire consumes the brake

you having failed to snuff
the head as it broke off;
his watchfulness extends
to factories, fields and friends

and you no longer know or feel
what it is to live, eat meat or bread
to desire or love or spread
your arms wide in appeal;

it is the chain slaves wear
that they themselves prepare;
you eat but it's tyranny
grows fat, his are your progeny

in tyranny's domain
you are the link in the chain,
you stink of him through and through,
the tyranny IS you;

like moles in sunlight we crawl
in pitch darkness, sprawl
and fidget in the closet
as if it were a desert,

because where tyranny obtains
everything is vain,
the song itself though fine
is false in every line,

for he stands over you
at your grave, and tells you who
you were, your every molecule
his to dispose and rule.
(1950)

Translated by George Szirtes

Notes

1 Mátyás Rákosi, *Visszaemlékezések, 1945–1956* [Memories, 1945–1956], vol. II, eds. István Feitl, Mrs. Márta Lázár Gelléri and Levente Sipos (Budapest, 1997), pp. 860–861.

2 Imre Okváth, *Bástya a béke frontján. Magyar haderő és katonapolitika, 1945–1956* [A Bastion on the Peace Front. Hungarian Military Power and Military Policy, 1945–1956] (Budapest, 1988).

3 The following books provide a model of this system based on economic theory: János Kornai, *A hiány* [Shortage] (Budapest, 1980), Section 1, pp. 33–310, and idem, *A szocialista rendszer* [The Socialist System] (Budapest, 1993), Section 2, pp. 65–399. The following case study arrives at the same conclusion: Tibor Kovácsy, "Az utasításos gazdaságról" [On the Command Economy], *Történelmi Szemle* 2 (1981): 191–202.

4 Gyula Erdmann, *Begyűjtés, beszolgáltatás Magyarországon, 1945–1956* [Harvest and Compulsory Delivery to the State in Hungary, 1945–1956] (Gyula, 1992).

5 Iván Pető and Sándor Szakács, *A hazai gazdaság négy évtizedének története, 1945–1985* [Four Decades in the History of the Domestic Economy, 1945–1985], vol. 1 (Budapest, 1985), pp. 177–178.

6 György Gyarmati, "A kampány-szocializmus állama" [The State of Campaign Socialism], in Márta Font and István Kajtár, eds., *A magyar államiság első ezer éve* [The First Thousand Years of Hungarian Statehood] (Pécs, 2000), pp. 239–263.

7 Lajos Sz. Varga, *Szakszervezetek a diktatúrában, 1948–1953* [Trade Unions during the Dictatorship, 1948–1953] (Pécs, 1995).

8 Resolution adopted at the second congress of the HWP. Lajos Izsák, editor-in-chief, *A Magyar Dolgozók Pártja határozatai, 1948–1956* [Resolutions of the Hungarian Workers' Party] (Budapest, 1998), pp. 129–135; Andor Ladányi, *Felsőoktatási politika, 1949–1956* [Higher Education Policy, 1949–1956] (Budapest, 1986), p. 28.

9 György T. Varga, *Adalékok a börtönügy és a rabmunkáltatás történetéhez, 1949–1953* [Supplementary Information on the History of Prison Affairs and Labor, 1949–1953], Vault 2, ed. György Gyarmati (Budapest, 2002), pp. 159–175.

10 György Kövér, *Losonczy Géza, 1917–1957* [Géza Losonczy, 1917–1957] (Budapest, 1988), pp. 209–228.

11 Csaba Szabó, "A katolikus egyház helyzete Magyarországon, 1945–1953" [The Situation of the Catholic Church in Hungary, 1945–1953], in idem, *Egyházügyi hangulatjelentések, 1951–1953* [Church Mood Reports, 1951–1953] (Budapest, 2000), pp. 42–43.

12 Jenő Gergely, *Az 1950-es egyezmény és a szerzetesrendek feloszlatása Magyarországon* [The 1950 Agreement and the Dissolution of the Orders in Hungary] (Budapest, 1950).

13 Historical sources pertaining to religious orders active in Hungary at this time vary significantly with regard to their estimates of the number of religious orders and members operating in the country. This divergence may be the result of the different aims of the various sources of the period. The data used in this book come from the following work: József Gyula Orbán, *Katolikus papok békemozgalma Magyarországon, 1950–1956* [The Catholic Priest Peace Movement in Hungary, 1950–1956] (Budapest, 2001), p. 56.

14 Csaba Szabó, *A Grősz-per előkészíte, 1951* [Preparations for the Grősz Trial, 1951] (Budapest, 2001).

15 Szilvia Köbel, *"Oszd meg és uralkodj!" Az állam és az egyházak politikai, jogi és igazgatási kapcsolatai Magyarországon 1945–1989 között* ["Divide and Conquer!" The Political, Legal and Administrative Relations of the State and the Churches between 1945 and 1989] (Budapest, 2005).

16 Károly Hetényi Varga's two series of publications serve as the starting point for the data shown in the table: Károly Hetényi Varga, *Papi sorsok a horogkereszt és a vörös csillag árnyékában I–IV* [The Fate of Priests in the Shadow of the Swastika and the Red Star I–IV] (Abaliget, 1992–1998), and idem, *Szerzetesek a horogkereszt és a vörös csillag árnyékában I–III* [Monks in the Shadow of the Swastika and the Red Star, I–III] (Abaliget, 1999–2003). The author of these series of books died before he was able to analyze and incorporate into his work a significant portion of the documents that were gradually becoming accessible. The table is the product of an examination of documents related to Church affairs in the Hungarian National Archives and the State Security Services History Archives. The writer of these lines is responsible for any inaccuracies in these data, which are based on research that has not yet been completed and reviewed. Moreover, data regarding Hungary's other religious denominations are not available.

17 László Kiss, *Zárt táborok a Hortobágyon és a Nagykunságban, 1950–1953* [Closed Camps in the Hortobágy and the Nagykunság, 1950–1953] (Budapest, 2005), pp. 13–50; Zsuzsa Hantó and Miklós Füzes, eds., *Kitaszítottak I–III* [The Expelled I–III] (Budapest, 2001–2006); György Gyarmati, "Toll—ecset—pokoljárás. Dietrich Adolf festő polgári életpályája, 1869–1953" [Pen, Brush, Descent into Hell. The Civilian Life of the Painter Adolf Dietrich, 1869–1953], *Duna-Part* (2004) 2: 54–60.

18 Rudolf Pfitzner, "A börtönirodalom pszichológiai jelentősége a lelki sérülések gondozásában" [The Psychological Significance of Prison Literature in the Treatment of Emotional Wounds], in Rudolf Pfitzner, Kamil Kárpáti, Tibor Tollas and Bálint Tóth, eds., *Füveskert, 1954–1995* [Herb Garden, 1954–1995] (Budapest, 1995), pp. 143–147; Géza Kelety, *Szeretetből élni* [Living on Love] (Budapest, 1997).

19 This quote from Albert Bereczky is cited in the following work: László Papp, *Tíz év és ami utána következett, 1945–1963. Adalékok a Magyarországi Református Egyház XX. századi történetéhez* [Ten Years and That Which Followed 1945–1963. Additional Data

Regarding the 20th-Century History of the Hungarian Reformed Church] (Bern, 1992), pp. 92–93.

20 István Feitl, "Pártvezetés és országgyűlési választások, 1949–1988" [Party Leadership and National Assembly Elections, 1949–1988], in György Földes and László Hubai, eds., *Parlamenti választások Magyarországon, 1920–1998* [Parliamentary Elections in Hungary, 1920–1998] (Budapest, 1999), pp. 276–285.

V. DESTALINIZATION AND RESTALINIZATION BETWEEN 1953 AND 1956

1. Imre Nagy's "New Course" and Mátyás Rákosi's "Russian Roulette" Policy

The official results of the parliamentary elections held in the middle of May 1953 were intended to demonstrate that Hungarian society, at least the portion of it that had not been incarcerated and was thus compelled to participate in the balloting, wholly supported the regime. Mátyás Rákosi hastened to Moscow at the end of the month in order to provide Soviet leaders with a personal account of his most recent "success." However, news of Rákosi's "sweeping electoral victory" did not leave a major impression on the Communist Party of the Soviet Union Presidium, which was immersed in the struggle for succession that had broken out following Stalin's death. Instead, according to reports from Soviet Ambassador to Hungary A. Kiselyov and Soviet advisors located at various Hungarian ministries, the Soviets confronted Rákosi with the catastrophic conditions that prevailed in his home country. Had he not heard this criticism from the masters of the Kremlin, the Hungarian Workers' Party leader would have certainly denounced it as a spurious campaign of slander perpetrated by hostile imperialist agents. In addition to the censure, Rákosi was compelled to suffer a demand from Soviet leaders that he vacate one of his two political offices—either that of party leader or that of prime minister. This ultimatum presented Rákosi with yet another conundrum, because he found none of his fellow party leaders to be a suitable choice for either position. The HWP and government leader enumerated for his Soviet interlocutors the flaws and incompetence of randomly cited potential "successors." Rákosi's monologue served to heighten the antipathy that the Soviet leaders felt towards him, although it did succeed in putting an end to the "consultation." After arriving back in Hungary, on June 3, 1953, Rákosi presented the Secretariat of the HWP with an appraisal of his meeting with Soviet leaders, more precisely his subjectively edited version of what had transpired during his trip to Moscow. Based on what Rákosi had elected to tell the members of the Secretariat, the body determined that only minor changes were needed.

After learning that its instructions had not been carried out, the CPSU Presidium summoned a Hungarian Workers' Party delegation consisting of Rákosi, Ernő Gerő, Imre Nagy, András Hegedüs, István Hidas, Béla Szálai, Rudolf Földvári and István Dobi to make a visit to Moscow in the middle of June. (Two members of the so-called "foursome" of inner party leaders, Minister of Defense Mihály Farkas and leading ideological-cultural official József Révai, were thus not among those invited). The CPSU Presidium focused particularly severe attacks on Rákosi during the delegation's visit to Moscow. Although Rákosi had managed to obscure Hungary's catastrophic state in a shroud of triumphal propaganda at home, the Soviets had access to detailed information regarding the true state of affairs, which they utilized in their excoriation of the HWP general secretary: "His adventurism is ruining the country." The CPSU Presidium's pillorying of Rákosi for Hungary's mismanagement also contained a pronounced element of anti-Semitism. The Soviets held Rákosi personally responsible for what they deemed to be a situation in which "Jews oppressed non-Jews in the party." (This might also explain why Révai and Mihály Farkas were not included in the delegation.) The staging of these negotiations was also extraordinary. Following the Soviet party leadership's castigation of Rákosi and his associates, the Hungarian delegation was left alone for two days in order to compose "self-criticism" with regard to the stated criticisms. The "*homo kominternicus*" Ernő Gerő, who had earlier spent a quarter of a century living in Moscow, was the first member of the delegation to recover from the intense barrage of criticism that the Soviets had inflicted upon their Hungarian guests. Gerő formulated a list of the party's catastrophic policies: forced industrialization, the megalomaniacal expansion of the military, coerced agricultural cooperative affiliation, the decline in the standard of living stemming from these measures, chronic shortages, an excessive number of legal sanctions, and the cult of personality surrounding Rákosi. Gerő essentially compiled an inventory of the policies that the Mátyás Rákosi-led party had adopted as "examples to be followed" from the Soviet Union during Stalin's reign.

The Hungarian party delegation finished its assigned "homework" in three days' time, after which it was sent home with instructions to make the compiled list of failures public in the form of an official party resolution. Such direct and meticulous Soviet intervention in Hungarian politics was unprecedented even during the Stalinist era, when Rákosi felt that he knew how to tailor the Hungarian Workers' Party's policies to Moscow's expectations. The most conspicuous peculiarity of the negotiations was, however, the fact that the Soviet leadership did not dismiss Rákosi even after its reprimand of the HWP general secretary, instead urging him in a final warning to engage in a greater degree of "teamwork." Although Rákosi was permitted to retain his post as party general secretary, the latter requisite entailed his resignation as prime minister in favor of "the Hungarian" Imre Nagy.[1] This change in personnel was a reflection of the prevailing balance of power within the CPSU Presidium. (Prime Minister Georgy Malenkov seemed at the time to have more authority than CPSU General Secretary Nikita Khrushchev.) Examined from a historical perspective, this indicates that the Hungarian party was still expected to adjust its policies to the prevalent power dynamics in Moscow even after Stalin's death. In addition to Nagy's appointment as prime minister, the Soviets also insisted that the government be given a greater degree of authority over the affairs of state, which had previously represented one of the exclusive prerogatives of the party. That is to say, the post-Stalinist Soviet party leadership expected to stimulate a significant improvement in the operational mechanism of Hungary's party state system without replacing its primary representative.

Rákosi seemed to draw a lesson from his second harsh upbraiding. The Hungarian Workers' Party general secretary's June 27, 1953, speech to the party's Central Directorate was nearly a verbatim "confession" of those transgressions recorded in the transcripts of the Moscow negotiations. The tenor of Rákosi's speech stood in stark contradiction to the stereotypical flourishes that the general secretary had used during the election campaign just a month and a half previously to describe the party's successes in the building of socialism. "There is hardly an aspect of people's democracy in which our party has not committed grave mistakes… [these] mistakes are such that if we do not make immediate changes, we will be threatened with a crisis of the most serious magnitude." Rákosi went on to enumerate a detailed list of the HWP's flawed measures, identifying the party official who had been in charge of each specific policy domain: Ernő Gerő, economy; Mihály Farkas, military; József Révai, culture. The HWP general secretary did, however, concede that he had been primarily responsible for the party's failure, even wringing from himself the admission that "I led the State Protection Authority. I intervened in its operations, I said who should be arrested, who should be beaten, who should be convicted and what kind of punishment they should receive."[2]

This act of self-criticism was not publicized, not even within the Hungarian Workers' Party itself. Rákosi's admission shocked the members of the Central Directorate, just as the chastening from Soviet party leaders had stunned the general secretary just a few days previously. Since all those present at Rákosi's speech had labored faithfully to implement the discredited policies, it was not difficult to convince the 100-member body that making it public would "undermine the authority of the party and our enemies would use it against us." Not only Rákosi, but also leading and mid-level party functionaries were worried that if the one million members of the HWP were informed of the self-criticism, news of it would surely spread beyond the party into the general population, the consequence of which could be to ignite the smoldering antagonism against them. (It is also noteworthy that the first detailed reports of the 1953 East

German workers' uprising had just began to filter into the country.) This collective fear resulted in a decision to verbally disclose to a strictly screened segment of the party only a whitewashed synopsis of the explicitly critical resolution that the Central Secretariat had adopted with regard to Rákosi's speech.

Imre Nagy was appointed as prime minister in accordance with the explicit and unequivocal wish of Soviet party leaders. In his June 4, 1953, policy speech to the National Assembly, Nagy announced the beginning of a New Course in the building of the socialist system. Nagy stated during the address that, as part of the program, he wanted "to ensure that the Council of Ministers, in cooperation with the legislature, would be invested with full authority to conduct the affairs of state." Through implementation of the New Course, Nagy aimed to emancipate control of the government from the previously omnipotent Hungarian Workers' Party leadership and to remedy the unlawfulness that predominated in this sphere. The program's economic policy also placed emphasis on rational considerations, stipulating that the government "not establish objectives whose attainment lacks the necessary requisites." The new prime minister's address suggested that the megalomaniacal industrial development of the preceding years could be halted, while promising that the repression of the peasantry would be alleviated, the injustices of the compulsory delivery system would be redressed and "the working peasantry would be left to farm in security, be accorded precise and timely information regarding its obligations and be permitted to freely sell its surplus production." Although it is rarely mentioned, Imre Nagy devoted a separate subsection to the New Course's policy *vis-à-vis* Hungary's intelligentsia, which the new prime minister deemed to have been "enveloped in mistrust, whose end result is neglect," whereas "there is a shortage of experienced and qualified intellectuals in almost every sphere of our economic, cultural and scientific life." In place of the earlier "unwarranted purges," Nagy invited and encouraged intellectuals to "utilize the knowledge that they have attained in their fields of specialty to the benefit of the country."[3] Since the text of the new government program was couched in the standard party jargon, it required a great deal of attention to discern its essential reform objectives. However, confidential mood reports from the period indicate that many people had managed to immediately "decode" the novel elements contained in Nagy's inaugural address broadcast over the radio after he was appointed as prime minister.

Imre Nagy's corrective program produced positive changes in everyday life within a short period of time, which served to heighten its creditability. The New Course suspended several major budget-consuming investments, such as the construction of the Budapest subway system's (second) line, and decreased the pace of industrial development. The program also contained measures aimed at increasing production of consumer items in order to better satisfy the basic needs of the population, and reduced tax and delivery obligations imposed upon Hungary's peasants. The Nagy government furthermore adopted a resolution that cancelled the peasantry's tax arrears and penalties for late payment, thus annulling 640,000 legal procedures involving some half a million citizens, most of them private farmers. Peasants were especially grateful for the provision of the New Course requiring the government to specify tax and delivery quotas on agricultural products three years in advance, thus facilitating the management and viability of private agricultural operations. These measures also made it possible to leave the forcibly constituted agricultural cooperatives at the end of the economic year (!) and introduced a moderate liberalization of free-market trade on agricultural products. The Nagy government closed internment and forced labor camps during the autumn, granting amnesty to a large number of prisoners. According to somewhat divergent data contained in various sources, a total of between 44,000 and 47,000 people were released from confinement at this time. Moreover, the Nagy government reduced the number of people under constant police surveillance. Those who had been expelled from their homes for political reasons were not, however, permitted to move back into their former residences, and nor were they allowed to reclaim or seek compensation for confiscated property. The regime was particularly strict in its efforts to prevent expellees from returning to Budapest, as a result of which some 25,000 former residents of the city attempted to earn their livelihoods in nearby towns and villages.

The prices of certain basic consumer goods such as food and clothing were reduced in the week following the inauguration of the Nagy government, which was followed by a universal wage increase at the beginning of 1954. The initial agenda of the new government included measures to alleviate social unrest and improve the population's standard of living. The government also initiated the process of reforming the structure and operations of the state institutional system in 1954. Prime Minister Nagy himself directed the reform of the council system, which he transferred from the Ministry of the Interior's sphere of authority to that of the Council of Ministers. Parliament enacted legislation sanctifying this operational system. Specialist working groups began the task of modifying the preferences contained in Hungary's model of economic and agricultural development at this time as well.[4]

The positively received initiatives and changes described above represented only one aspect of domestic political developments in 1953. Mátyás Rákosi, who continued to serve as the general secretary of the Hungarian Workers' Party, supported only minimal fulfillment of the expectations that had been outlined at the Kremlin. Although the sequence of measures had been designed primarily to avert catastrophe, Rákosi nevertheless objected to what he described as the "excessive independence" of the government and its subordinate bodies. The general secretary utilized his leadership of the HWP to counterbalance the government's policies through his direct control over the party hierarchy operating within state institutions. Just more than a week following the proclamation of the New Course program, around the time of the Budapest HWP Committee's July 11, 1953, party activist meeting, Rákosi learned that Soviet Minister of the Interior Lavrentiy Beria had been arrested. The HWP general secretary regarded this as a positive development, since Beria had been the Soviet party leader who had launched the sharpest and most humiliating attacks against him during his visit to Moscow. Rákosi's mood improved considerably as a result of Beria's downfall, to such a degree that the HWP general secretary showed flashes of his "former self" during the meeting of Budapest party bureaucrats.

Rákosi attempted to trivialize the earlier miscarriages of justice, just as he did the significance of Imre Nagy's announced changes. At the same time, the Hungarian Workers' Party leader satisfied the demands imposed upon the "collective leadership" in Moscow—verbally: speaking continually in the first person plural, he stated that "our party, particularly our party leadership, committed grave mistakes in the course of its work… In the heat of creative labor, we committed even serious errors." Rákosi's stereotypical use of the *pluralis majestatis* was intended to obscure the reprimand that he had received in Moscow and the sections of the "classified" Budapest party resolution citing his personal responsibility for the country's catastrophic condition. The task was no less than to moderate and adjust the targets contained in the central plan, whose fundamental principles nevertheless remained the same, urging "every conscious worker to engage in steadfast labor to fulfill the current plan, to maintain staunch discipline, to intercede with undeviating vigor against those who violate planning discipline." Rákosi similarly emphasized the need for "the entire might of our party and people's democracy to stand behind the agricultural cooperatives… We must continue to proclaim the superiority of cooperative production… thus we summon supporters and members to unite in defense of the agricultural cooperatives." Consistent with this logic, Rákosi took the step of essentially annulling, "in the name of" the party over which he had retained leadership, the government decree abolishing the kulak lists:

> Kulaks will remain kulaks, with or without a list… experiences with the kulaks over recent days have again demonstrated that you can't make a silk purse out of a sow's ear… In short, comrades will understand that the measures that our party is proposing are aimed at the undeviating building of socialism. We will correct the mistakes that

> have been made and continue our building of socialism in such a way as to ensure that the standard of living of our working people and specifically the industrial workforce will continually rise.[5]

The accounts of those present at the meeting also made it seem as if they had received two sets of vastly disparate instructions, which did not prevent them from honoring both with the customary "extended applause." The assembled party functionaries, who were unaware of the significant events that had taken place behind the scenes, could hardly have perceived more than an occasional volley of hail in the midst of a summer storm, followed by a clearing of the skies when the party leader offered his prescription for mitigating the damage. For these people, their "old" boss Rákosi continued to represent the primary political authority, not the neophyte Prime Minister Imre Nagy with his notion that the country's problems could be corrected through governmental measures.

Through his repeated use of the words such as "staunch," "steadfast" and "undeviating," Rákosi was attempting to retroactively legitimize the senselessness built into the system during the previous years, for otherwise he would have been compelled to voice rejection of what was essentially his own Stalinist mechanism. However, since he could not openly defy Moscow, Rákosi did reluctantly acknowledge the changes that had taken place in spite of his conceptual and personal aversion towards them. The Hungarian Workers' Party general secretary believed, not without justification, that the distribution of power within the CPSU Presidium might change to his benefit as a result of the post-Stalin struggle for succession taking place at the time. (Rákosi immediately drew this conclusion from Beria's arrest, although he could not have known that the former Soviet minister of the interior would be shot within half a year.) One might even say that Rákosi was playing "Russian roulette," having concluded that he stood a good chance of surviving his opposition to the "New Course." Figurative language aside, the HWP leader was capable, through his command over the party apparatus, of organizationally counterbalancing, even repelling, the measures that Imre Nagy was attempting to implement through the government administration.

This system, primarily at this juncture, reveals the closed character of the state and party institutional structure's operational mechanism, as well as the way in which the communist dictatorship functioned on an everyday basis. The basic formula for this system was to introduce a dual, essentially parallel, organizational order. From top to bottom, this hierarchy consisted of national (central), county (Budapest), district, city (Budapest districts) and municipal party organizations and administrative authorities, which operated in subordination to one another, increasing in number as the pyramid broadened. There were two unique and noteworthy aspects of this system. First, the so-called specialist apparatus—ministry-controlled administrative, industrial, agricultural, trade and education divisions or officials—was "built into" the lower levels of the council-based executive system. Second, in municipalities, plant and workplace organizations represented the basic level of the party's organizational hierarchy.

The dual, party and administrative, organizational order operated under the control of the Hungarian Workers' Party both in its vertical "pyramidal" hierarchy and in its horizontal nexus.[6] A likewise twofold counter-insurance system at every level and a so-called "sphere of authority" list included among the privileges of higher-level party organizations guaranteed the operation of this hierarchy. The former meant that party executive and legislative organs had permanent authority over state (council) executive agencies functioning at the same level. The personal counter-insurance system further fortified this formalized administrative order: leading party functionaries were members of the state institutional system's executive organs, while those holding key offices in state institutional organs were members of party legislative bodies. Some examples: Mátyás Rákosi was general secretary of the HWP and a member of the Political Committee, as well as a member of each government from 1945 to 1953; Ernő Gerő was a member both of the Political Committee and of the Council of

The organizational-operational structure of the party state institutional system

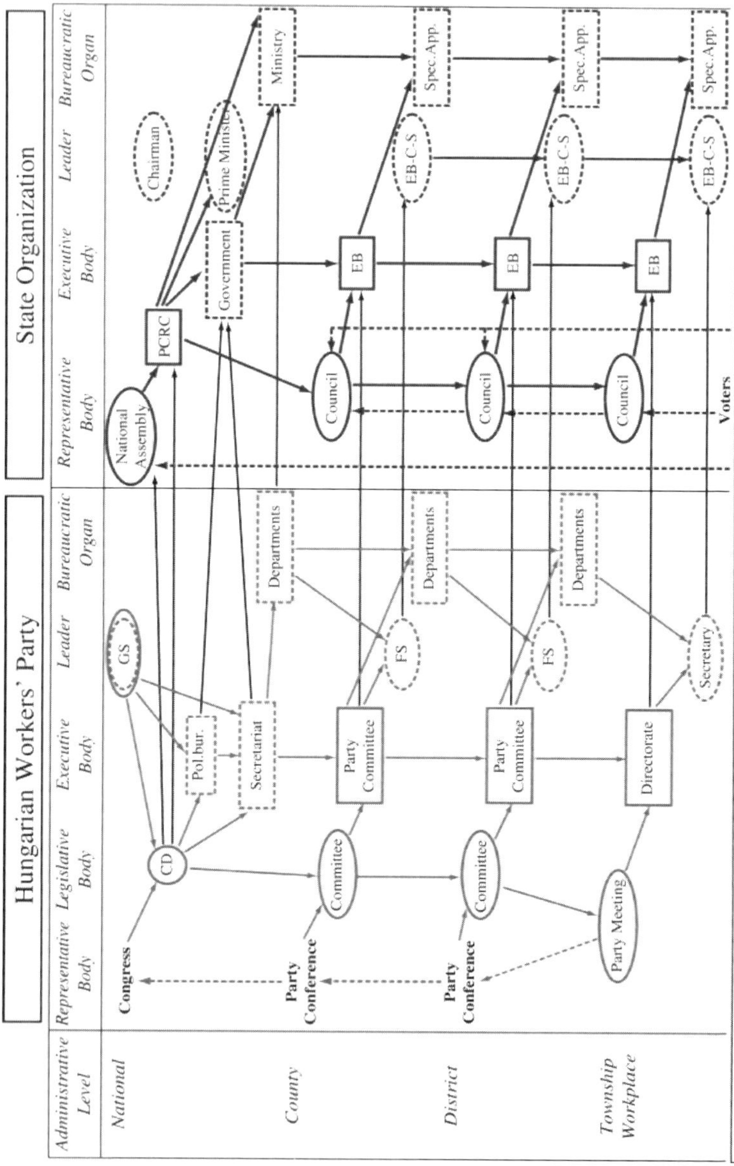

CD – Central Directorate; GS – General Secretary; FS – First Secretary; PCRC – Presidental Council of the People's Rebublic; Chairman – Chairman of the PCRC; Pol. bur. – Politbureau; EB – Executive Bureau; EB–C–S – Executive Bureau–Chairman–Secretary; Spec. App. – Special Apparatus

© József Vonyó

Ministers almost throughout the period 1945–1956; Mihály Farkas, János Kádár, Antal Apró, József Révai, Zoltán Vas, Béla Szalai and, until his arrest, László Rajk held "dual positions" at the highest level for longer or shorter periods of time. At the lower levels, county, municipal or village party secretaries were almost always members of county, municipal or village councils, while county, municipal and village council chairmen and/or secretaries were most often members of county, municipal or village party committees as well. In the case of council administration, local district army, police or State Protection Authority (ÁVH) leaders as well as company directors and agricultural cooperative chairmen were often "appointed" to serve on county councils, municipal councils, and so on.

Another means of securing Hungarian Workers' Party power was the unofficial "sphere of authority" list, which historical and political science literature also refers to as the "*nomenklatura*" or *nomenklatura* system.[7] The "sphere of authority" list pertained to the "election" of functionaries to leading positions; more precisely, it nullified the concept of an "election." Leading party and state positions were, in theory, filled via election. (This did not apply to the leaders of the institutions functioning under the authority of the so-called specialist administration, such as company directors, school principals, tax office and land office managers, and so on, who were always appointed.) The "sphere of authority" list granted party organizations the prerogative to issue preliminary recommendations for formally elected cadres, thus ensuring that the results of the voting would reflect the will of the party. Elections were thus counterfeit almost without exception, while even those rare candidates who had the opportunity to run for office without prior party approval in "pure" elections were stigmatized in their greater or lesser constituencies. This system entailed another common practice: following the frequent personnel changes that took place in this domain, party officials did not even bother to carry through with the sham electoral process outlined above, "co-opting" a new person to replace those who had been dismissed, "promoted" to a higher position, sent to party school or perhaps even arrested, with a simple party resolution. One further aspect of this arrangement should be noted: the organizational by-laws of the HWP required party members to advocate "party" positions and decisions in all instances, even in non-party forums.

In sum, leading cadres from the Hungarian Workers' Party, production or administrative institutional network were present in a dual capacity in almost every forum qualified to make decisions or to issue decrees. This power-sociological synthesis represented the system's "normal" functioning as long as state administration procedures served simply as formal endorsements of party directives, a condition that lasted until July 1953, when government prescriptions transmitted via "New Course" state administrative channels began to occasionally conflict with party commands emanating from Rákosi's Secretariat. Beginning at this time, it became crucial for the HWP general secretary to exploit the party state's organizational-sociological insularity in order to take advantage of his discretionary superiority. However, to use a popular formulation, this same factor resolved Murphy's "boss regulation" dilemma for the cadre administration's several thousand functionaries: rule 1: the boss is always right!; rule 2: if the boss happens not to be right, then rule 1 immediately takes effect! Prime Minister Nagy's program and its associated governmental activities were not intended to question the primacy of the party, but simply to reduce the number of impracticable objectives and judicial murders that had become an implicit part of the system. Rákosi, however, was just as disinclined to consider the iniquities of his reign of terror as he was to moderate his dictatorial zeal and the supremacy of his unquestionable faith.

As absurd as it might seem, Mátyás Rákosi came to represent Hungary's "constitutional order" in the course of the split of control over the system that stemmed from conceptual disagreements commingled with personal ambition. As previously mentioned, paragraph 56 of the 1949 Constitution, which instituted the system of communist dictatorship, while it was a constitutionally slipshod ideological formula, did explicitly state that "the leading force in state and social activity is the vanguard of the working class"—that is, the Hungarian Workers' Party. Rákosi, however, never invoked this "constitutional backing" during his year-and-a-half-long power struggle with Prime Minister Imre Nagy, in spite of the fact that he remained the primary party leader. There were three factors that prevented Rákosi from doing this: firstly, he himself had routinely infringed not only existing laws, but the "party constitution"—the by-laws of the HWP—as well; secondly, it appears that in spite of his guile, the idea of invoking this article of the constitution simply did not occur to him: that is, he rejected the "constitutional primacy" of the party if it served, as in the case of the confidential resolution of June 1953, to encroach upon his own omnipotence;[8] thirdly, and most importantly, retaining his position at the head of the party depended to a much greater degree on the favor of the CPSU Presidium than it did on any kind of constitutional or party norm. *Nota bene*, Nagy, too, called for Moscow's arbitration in all instances in which he wished to "validate" his policies in contrast to those of Rákosi.

This is what happened in December 1953, when Imre Nagy appealed for the Soviet party leadership's support for his policies after a meeting of the Hungarian Workers' Party Central Directorate, held at the end of October to assess the initial measures implemented as part of the "New Course." As a result, Rákosi received another reprimand at a December 1953 Moscow summit, where Soviet leaders identified him as the demonstrable instigator of the opposition, primarily that of the party apparatus, to the government's program. They also informed the HWP leader that the changes that had taken place in June, particularly the failure to implement the government measures taken thereafter, "could have resulted in a downfall."[9] Another indication of the Soviet leadership's positive appraisal of the Nagy government's program was its granting of a loan of 100 million rubles to Hungary in order to help to settle the country's earlier accrued foreign debts, mostly to Western countries. Although this sum represented only half of that requested, the stipulation that repayment of the loan begin only in 1957 also seemed at the time to be favorable.[10]

2. From the Indecisiveness of Decision-Makers to Imre Nagy's Pyrrhic Victory

The discord between the party and the government was reflected in a peculiar way during the Hungarian Workers' Party's Third Congress, held at the end of May 1954, just less than a year after the proclamation of the "New Course." Mátyás Rákosi pronounced the opening speech to the nearly 800 delegates attending the Congress in the form of an HWP Central Directorate report, placing his address within the historical framework of the tenth anniversary of the Communist Party's legal existence (under whatever name it took) in Hungary. Rákosi's speech focused on Hungary's economic development since the end of World War II, particularly since the HWP's First Party Congress in February 1951. The HWP leader inundated his listeners with a deluge of economic data and statistical comparisons, which they could follow only with great difficulty during the course of the several-hours-long address. Rákosi's oration may well have left the audience with the impression that Hungary's post-war economic development had been an unprecedented success—this was precisely the objective of the address. The general secretary's speech naturally either whitewashed or totally ignored the economically catastrophic contradictions and voluntarist errors that the June 1953 resolution and the New Course were intended to rectify.

Rákosi made a remarkably crude attempt to gloss over this awkward issue, closing his economic appraisal of the ten-year period with the assertion that the Hungarian Workers' Party leadership's "resolutions of last June, October and December corrected these problems." According to the general secretary's interpretation, the torrent of economic successes outlined in his speech had made it possible for "the Central Directorate of our party to undertake a new course in the building of socialism in Hungary… in accordance with the new situation."[11] Contextually, Rákosi had made the claim that only a slight correction—"fine-tuning" in modern parlance—was needed to the successes attained under his leadership in order to achieve the total victory of socialism. The logical conclusion of this fraudulent train of thought was that party resolutions adopted in June 1953 and thereafter had "designated the only correct and expedient method of building socialism."[12] In addition to evincing Rákosi's attempt at self-justification, the cited declaration is pertinent for two other reasons: firstly, this rhetorical *salto mortale* marked the first time that the HWP general secretary had offered unambiguous public support for the New Course; secondly, it accentuates the fact that he would continue to act in just the opposite manner, as will be described below.

In his speech, "State Administration and the Duties of the Councils,"[13] Imre Nagy also placed the issue under examination within a ten-year context. If the essence of Rákosi's speech had been lost in jungle of numerical data, the substance of Nagy's address was cloaked in a theoretical discourse citing classic Marxist philosophers. Nagy's speech was centered on two main themes: the authority of state organizations in a communist-controlled proletarian dictatorship, and the integration in the most advantageous way possible of the majority population of non-party members into the party-dominated social system. The latter represented the so-called people's front issue.

Prime Minister Nagy began his speech with a critical assessment of the first theme, contending that deficiencies in the operations of the councils and conceptual ambiguities hampering the building of socialism and undermining the strength of the people's state were paralyzing state administration. Nagy then spent nearly an hour expounding upon the historical foundations of the council system and the "two phases" of people's democracy in Hungary before pronouncing the following judgment: "The party not only led, but often substituted for organs of state authority and administration. This reduced the autonomy, stature and responsibility of organs of state authority and administration, at the same time rendering the party's true political leadership over state and council organizations more difficult." Although the prime minister referred repeatedly to the "internal" defects of state administrative and council organizations, he also voiced the conclusion that the party's excessive authority and stifling omnipotence represented the primary impediment to the functional operation of state administration. On the one hand, in conformance with the classic communist concept of state, Nagy explicitly rejected the "bourgeois" separation of powers. On the other hand, the prime minister cited both the 1949 constitution and the Hungarian Workers' Party Central Directorate's (confidential) June 1953 resolution in an appeal to delegates, specifically HWP leaders, to relinquish the party's omnipotence and invest the state institutional structure with true authority, from the Presidential Council through the government and ministries to the council administrative system at its various levels. Nagy provided dozens of examples to support his contentions that the party's interference in the operations of state and administrative organizations was the primary cause of their paralysis and that the bloated apparatus had become exceedingly clumsy and bureaucratic.

Prime Minister Nagy padded the second theme of his speech, the so-called people's front issue, with both Marxist and classically patriotic rhetorical flourishes, concluding that "Within the context of people's democracy, the people's front represents a broad and comprehensive mass movement, whose backbone is the worker–peasant alliance and which embraces the large majority of the population." This formula was a corrected variation of the preliminary version of Nagy's speech, which referred not to a movement, but to an "organization" in which personal membership was possible. Party leaders had rejected the use of the word "organization" during a Political Committee debate prior to Nagy's speech, expressing their concern that the people's front, which had been established in 1949 to supersede and obviate all other political organizations, might become a viable alternative to the Hungarian Workers' Party.[14] Thus only a revival of the dormant movement was permissible, although Nagy tested the boundaries of this prospect in his various reflections during the finalization of the text of his speech.

The speech that Imre Nagy delivered at the Hungarian Workers' Party's Third Congress contained the same duality as that which he had made upon assuming the post of prime minister one year earlier, utilizing awkward, bureaucratic party jargon in combination with highly opportune proposals aimed at transformation of the communist dictatorship into a functional system. On the one hand, Nagy presented these proposed changes as being, in addition to an unavoidable repair of a breakdown in the system, an organic amelioration of the communist institutional structure that had been introduced just three or four years previously; on the other hand, the prime minister made repeated references to the 1949 Constitution, not only to provide himself with political cover, but also to demonstrate that the functional operation of state organizations was legitimate from a constitutional standpoint. In addition, the prime minister attempted to provide the existing "Moscow practice" with a domestic theoretical foundation of sorts, asserting that there had emerged a tendency to provide government and state administrative organizations with a larger degree of autonomy. Nagy's attempt to base theoretical support for his policies in Moscow's practices was undoubtedly designed to heighten his prime ministerial authority to the detriment of Rákosi, who had shown himself unwilling to voluntarily relinquish his unmitigated hold over power. This was also Nagy's motive for advocating the reactivation of the people's front, which he hoped would serve to expand his own national base of support in opposition to Rákosi's party apparatus, which was at the very least suspicious, if not unequivocally hostile, towards the prime minister's designs.

As a result of lower-level party office and delegate elections held over the previous months, nearly half of those present at the Hungarian Workers' Party's Third Congress were freshly selected "new cadres." If, as a report drawn up at the time indicated, the party's Budapest general conference for election of officials had been characterized by "large-scale passivity, uncertainty, superficial pragmatism and indifference,"[15] then what could such meetings in more remote locations have been like? Delegates at such meetings held outside the capital city could have hardly been better informed or have had a higher level of education than those attending the Budapest conference, who were themselves generally deficient in these areas. However, delegates nevertheless surely discerned by the end of the meeting that the speech of the HWP Central Directorate's reelected general secretary Mátyás Rákosi had placed general emphasis on the claimed achievements, referred to at the time as "victories," of the previous decade, while Imre Nagy focused on the problems that had accumulated over that period. This may have been the source of the type of uncertainty cited above. This was also reflected in the fact that, contrary to established practice, the "party parliament" did not elevate the pronounced assessments of either General Secretary Rákosi or Prime Minister Nagy to the status of resolution, merely declaring that following their hearing and debate the party considered them to be "guiding principles." The few who were more educated in the history of the workers' movement may have speculated that a new "dual authority" was developing within the single-party dictatorship. Those who understood the pragmatic aspect of this issue could have clearly distinguished the entrenched rift that existed within the party leadership.

Two no less important questions were either glossed over or completely ignored during the one-week Hungarian Workers' Party Congress. The first of these was "the elevation of the standard of living of our working people." To have mentioned anything in this regard would have been sanctimonious indeed, since Hungary's standard of living had deteriorated continually compared to even that of the post-war reconstruction period ever since the communists had taken power. The "New Course" measures aimed at improving this situation had, at most, attained the "has not deteriorated further" category in the period of more than half a year since their adoption. The second question was that of redressing, as much as possible, the previously perpetrated miscarriages of justice. Rákosi attempted to postpone any review of the unlawful show trials that had taken place under his leadership, while Nagy, who had been temporarily stripped of his authority at the time of the trials and was thus not personally implicated in the most flagrant judicial injustices, favored a reexamination of the verdicts. Moscow supported Nagy's objective as long as "it would not undermine Rákosi's authority, since this represents the authority of the party as well," as Chairman of the Presidium of the Supreme Soviet Kliment Voroshilov said during another consultation held between Soviet and Hungarian party leaders just two weeks before the HWP's Third Congress.[16] It was for this reason that Imre Nagy's initiatives to review the trials were rather sporadic in nature, while Mátyás Rákosi, as the head of the so-called rehabilitation committee, had control over the selection of those to be discharged from prison and the timing of their release.

János Kádár, Gyula Kállai and the so-called "March Frontists" who had been taken into custody in the spring of 1951 were released from prison without publicity during the summer of 1954. The reason why the release of these people was given priority was that they had been imprisoned following "quiet trials" in the midst of the storm of propaganda surrounding the prosecution of Archbishop of Kalocsa József Grősz. László Rajk was rehabilitated half a year later, at the end of 1954, amid the type of strict secrecy that had become routine by that time. An examination of the role of Rákosi and two other members of the Hungarian Workers' Party's Political Committee, Ernő Gerő and Mihály Farkas, in the 1949 show trial would hardly have been avoidable had Rajk's rehabilitation been made public. The prosecution and imprisonment of the freshly rehabilitated János Kádár helped to defer inquiries into the former minister of the interior's involvement in Rajk's show trial. Following his release, Kádár accepted the party offices offered to him, thus beginning a gradual climb back up the rungs of the HWP hierarchy. With only a few isolated exceptions, those communists and former Social Democratic Party leaders who still remained in prison were released only following the fundamental transformation in Hungary's political climate that took place in the spring of 1956. The rehabilitation process was extended almost exclusively to party functionaries, while the cases of the nearly 25,000 "commoners" imprisoned for the most part on spurious political charges between

1949 and the summer of 1953 were not subjected to review. The blame for the unlawful imprisonments was placed on former ÁVH chief Gábor Péter, who had been arrested in January 1953 and sentenced to life in prison in March 1954. The CPSU Presidium had, incidentally, devised this tactic as well during the aforementioned consultations held in May 1954. Gábor Péter was imprisoned in the name of restoring "socialist legality" following a show trial whose fraudulence rivaled that of those in which the former secret police leader had earlier collaborated. Had Péter been given a fair trial, the identity of those who had exercised true control over the ÁVH, "the fist of the party," may have become apparent. The newspapers published only a two-line report, referred to among journalists as a "minus piece," regarding Péter's imprisonment.

The status of the State Protection Authority also transformed somewhat after 1953, although only to such a degree as to provide a paradigm of the intrinsic limits to change contained in the internally divisive New Course. Numerous measures were taken after Imre Nagy became prime minister, as the "emanation" of the Moscow-inspired Hungarian Workers' Party resolutions that were intended to soften the reign of terror of the previous years. One of these initiatives was to reincorporate the ÁVH into the Ministry of the Interior's organizational structure. At the same time, the department's authority over the council administrative system was withdrawn, thus transforming it into a purely police ministry (while control over local district administration became part of the portfolio of the Secretariat of the Council of Ministers). Ernő Gerő, who had been responsible for the reorganization and "regularization" of the ÁVH, was appointed as minister of the interior. Gerő, acting with his well-known efficiency, declared his tasks to be completed at the end of 1953. Although Gerő formally relinquished his post as minister of the interior in July 1954, he had agreed, following consultations with Prime Minister Imre Nagy early in 1954, to shift the focus of his activities back to the economy in his capacity as deputy president of the Council of Ministers responsible for this domain. László Piros, who had until this time served as deputy minister in charge of the political police, was appointed to succeed Gerő as minister of the interior. However, there remained between Mátyás Rákosi and the ÁVH a common interest in ensuring that they would have to reveal as little as possible regarding their complicity in the large number of judicial miscarriages that had taken place in Hungary over the previous years. Gerő again played a key role in the effort to obscure this connection, concluding that further review of the show trials "would jeopardize the party's leading core in its present form." Due to his personal involvement in the trials, Gerő stood to benefit from the greatest possible cover-up of the illegalities that had taken place, working in solidarity with Rákosi and Piros, the latter of whom was reappointed to the HWP's Political Committee. Although Imre Nagy, to use a tennis term, enjoyed the "service advantage" over Rákosi and his associates, he still had no realistic chance of making significant progress in his attempt to rectify past injustices within the political environment that prevailed at the time. The Kremlin's lukewarm support for Nagy's endeavor further frustrated the prime minister's attempt to conduct a comprehensive review of the show trials.

Those implicated in the judicial abuses that had been carried out on an industrial scale over the previous years engaged in a well-organized and concerted effort to obstruct a thorough review of the unlawful trials and verdicts. The futility of Imre Nagy's attempt to redress the miscarriages of justice, particularly the most flagrant examples thereof, was built into the system. It was, at the same time, outwardly evident that the New Course had not produced the anticipated improvement to the production and efficiency of the economy. The fact that they could not have produced the expected degree of progress in the time available is another matter. The operational and organizational anomalies, including those at the local district and people's economic level, inherent in the radically voluntarist economic policies of the preceding years become obvious only with the launching of the New Course's reform measures. For the first five years after the communist seizure of power, the Hungarian Workers' Party victoriously trumpeted the surpassing of its production targets, while attributing every failure to so-called conspirators and saboteurs, who were referred to the competency of the ÁVH. That is, the deceit surrounding the system's economic policy that had accrued over the previous half decade was exposed as part of Nagy's effort within the context of the New Course to restrain Rákosi's excesses. The HWP general secretary and the party apparatus, on the other hand, attempted to blame Prime Minister Nagy and his New Course for the system's obvious operational flaws and difficulties. The distorted arguments refracted through the political prism of the era, as always, provided grounds for arguments both *pro* and *contra*.

Economic data showed that domestic consumption measured in retail trade rose around 25 percent during the first half of 1954 as compared to the first half of the previous year, thus lifting the everyday standard of living of the "working people" to a significant degree. Rákosi attempted to trump the improving macroeconomic data by claiming that they indicated a decline in productivity. The numbers war continued in reports prepared for the Hungarian Workers' Party's Political Committee. One such report stated that real wages had declined 23 percent from 1950 until the proclamation of the New Course, while another asserted that the level of public provision, transport and healthcare in Budapest, where the majority of Hungary's working class lived, had deteriorated dramatically compared to the level not only of 1950, but of the 1930s as well. Half a year later, a report to the Political Committee complained that "As a result of the New Course, the *per capita* income of the peasantry, particularly the privately farming middle peasantry, is significantly higher than that of the workers."[17] Although there is no way of verifying the accuracy of these data, it is probable that each of these politically motivated interpretations presented only partial truths.[18] The method of recording the underperformance of the five-year plan concluded at the end of 1954 represented a "collective problem." (It was noted in an earlier chapter that production did not even reach 80 percent of the targets defined in the stepped-up plan.) The politicization surrounding the final balance sheet of the planning cycle was rooted in a dispute between those who claimed that the budget deficit had stemmed from Rákosi's megalomaniacal ambitions and those who blamed Imre Nagy's New Course for the shortfall. Rákosi opposed the June 1953 party resolution and the New Course government program even though they were partially a product of the fact that the irrational economic policies of the previous five years had threatened the country's economy with collapse. The party general secretary routinely voiced the conclusion that the increasingly autonomous Nagy government had caused the failure of the first five-year plan. These mutually obstructive conceptions prevented the realistic resolution of practical "what and how many" questions, thus deferring efforts to launch the second five-year plan until 1956. Rákosi announced this delay during his speech at the party congress following preliminary consultations with the Political Committee.

A meeting of the Central Directorate was convened at the beginning of October 1954 in order to discuss the continuing economic problems and the measures to be taken to address them. Due to the announced delay in the launching of the new five-year plan, the 1955 interim economic plan served as the basis for preliminary Political Committee negotiations on this issue. Rákosi, Gerő and Nagy played the key roles during these preliminary talks, although only in individual succession, while the others were away. The prevailing conception among committee members thus tended to change depending on which of these party officials was "leading the chorus." Since Rákosi returned from his summer holiday only during the final phase of the preparatory work and Gerő had taken sick leave, the proposals submitted to the body for adoption were based on Imre Nagy's economic conceptions. During the Central Directorate meeting, both the prime minister and other prominent members of the Directorate endorsed the proposals, calling for an "end to the wrangling." While it appeared that Nagy had succeeded in obtaining the support of the majority of the party's "legitimate," elected body, Rákosi nevertheless managed to convince the Central Directorate to simply approve the proposals, deferring their "refinement" to the status of resolution to the Political Committee. However, since Rákosi had in the meantime gone to Moscow for "medical treatment," Nagy was able to pass the Central Directorate's version of the proposal through the Political Committee in the form of a party resolution on October 22. The prime minister also prompted his own governmental body, the Information Office, to launch an extensive press campaign expressing support for the resolution and the New Course. Nagy initiated this campaign with an article in which he reported information that had previously been detailed only in confidential party resolutions and provided a tightly reasoned description of the period of more than a year and a half of strife that had taken place between the advocates and opponents of the New Course. Moreover, the prime minister published in his October 25 article the first frank public commentary on the previously taboo "bedroom secret" of the show trials: "The June party resolutions will be fulfilled when we release our innocent comrades from prison and give them back to the party, to life and to work. We must and will account for the grave errors that have been made in this domain… The party and the collective leadership have and will have the necessary strength to ensure that the crimes committed in the past will never repeat themselves." At the same time, the prime minister initiated an active personnel policy, reshuffling his cabinet and reorganizing the ministerial support apparatus with the aim of forming "his own team."

The Patriotic People's Front held its founding congress during the subsequent two days, on October 23 and 24. Not long before, during the Hungarian Workers' Party's Third Congress, Imre Nagy had made a speech in which he almost completely stripped his diction of its customary party jargon. The overwhelmingly positive reception of Nagy's uncommonly emotional address suggested that even non-party members might be receptive to the prime minister's espoused "Hungarian path" in the building of socialism. During his speech at the Patriotic People's Front Congress, Nagy stated that "June policy has prevailed, and conjecture of its failure has suffered a shameful defeat."[19] Nagy's biographers have referred to this moment as a "small October victory."[20] After more than a year of effort, the "New Course" appeared to be in the ascendant. Other leading cadres who had previously vacillated between the two camps in the Rákosi–Nagy dispute were then able to support this conclusion as well. Among them was Chief Public Prosecutor Kálmán Czakó, who, contrary to his previous practice, began to send the prime minister reports documenting Rákosi's complicity in the show trials. These documents showed that those participating in the interrogation of defendants indicated repeatedly that they had uncovered no evidence of their involvement in the alleged charges. "When this happened, Gábor Péter and [his deputy] Ernő Szűcs informed their personnel that the party leadership had ordered the arrests and it was the duty of the ÁVH to support this action."[21] All of those familiar with the June 1953 resolution were aware that it was not the person named in the document, Mihály Farkas, who was primarily responsible for devising this formula, but Rákosi himself. However, this fact was only documented on paper at a time when the HWP general secretary's power was seemingly waning.

However, it soon became apparent that the developments in October had been a Pyrrhic victory. Mátyás Rákosi was in Moscow having his "political disease" treated at the Kremlin. The Hungarian Workers' Party general secretary hoped to find in the Soviet capital the antidote to Nagy's political ascendancy, which news arriving from Budapest following his departure seemed to confirm. The court of arbitration for domestic political disputes in Hungary continued to sit in Moscow, where the struggle for succession for Stalin's throne had not yet come to an end. The distribution of power within the CPSU Presidium was shifting at the time, while relations between the superpowers had again become tense after a brief period of détente. Either one of the aforementioned factors would have been enough to trigger a reevaluation of the "New Course" in the Kremlin. It was this combination of circumstances, not anything that had happened in the capital of the satellite state, that produced a situation in which Rákosi, for his purposes, had "arrived at a good time." Within this changed environment, the general secretary's systematic machinations against Imre Nagy became much more effective. Following two months of absence, Rákosi returned to Hungary at the very end of November, having regained the support of the majority of the CPSU Presidium. During meetings of the Hungarian Workers' Party's Political Committee held in December 1954, Rákosi was able to open a front against the prime minister with the tacit approval of his patrons in Moscow, referring to the New Course as a "year and a half full of problems and difficulties" for which Nagy and his "right-wing deviationist" policies were responsible. During the meetings, Rákosi described Nagy's revival of the former people's front organization as "degradation of the proletarian dictatorship," censuring the prime minister for delegating a certain degree of influence within this body to the dissolved former coalition parties. Feeling as if he was firmly in control again, Rákosi specified "dealing strictly" with the government to be one of the party's tasks.

Rákosi subsequently initiated the summoning of the Hungarian Workers' Party leadership to Moscow. During the talks held in January 1955, it was Nagy's turn to face criticism from the members of the CPSU Presidium. Nikita Khrushchev accused Nagy of representing anti-party views, while Soviet Prime Minister Georgy Malenkov characterized Hungary's prime minister as a Bukharinist, or right-wing deviationist. (Malenkov, who offered a degree of support for Nagy, was dismissed from his post one month later.) However, to Rákosi's undisguised disappointment, the Soviet party leadership permitted Nagy to remain in office, although it ordered him to exercise public self-criticism and to correct his identified errors.

Rákosi undoubtedly interpreted his Moscow justification as a sweeping mandate to reassume uncontested political supremacy in Hungary. Following their return to Hungary, the Hungarian Workers' Party general secretary did everything that he could to remove Nagy from power. Two factors played into Rákosi's hands at this time—Nagy's physical infirmity (repeated heart attacks) as well as his "political illness." (This was similar to that from which Rákosi had suffered following the October session of the Central Directorate.) The prime minister was unwilling to accept the "charity" of remaining in office at the expense of his own self-approbation simply in order to "wait out" the time until a possible, and uncertain, change of direction in Moscow—it was most likely that Soviet leaders would one day decide that they had finally had enough of Rákosi. Another reason for Nagy's reluctance was the fact that many of those party leaders who had thrown their support behind the New Course just a few months previously had deserted the prime minister and his reform program once Rákosi appeared to regain his former domination over the political system. In any case, Nagy's genuine physical illness and political obstinacy impelled him to have the New Course declared an official *ad acta* at the HWP Central Directorate's next meeting at the beginning of March 1955. The only reason why Nagy was not dismissed at this time was the fact that he had been scheduled to participate in several events connected to the national commemoration of the tenth anniversary of Hungary's "liberation" on April 4, 1945. However, just ten days later, Rákosi had Nagy expelled from the Political Committee and the Central Directorate and dismissed from his post as prime minister all in the same breath. The appointment of 33-year-old András Hegedüs, who had risen through the Communist Party apparatus following World War II as Ernő Gerő's right-hand man, ensured that Rákosi would again be capable of asserting his unmitigated political will on the country via the government. Gerő's appointment to the position of deputy prime minister (in practice as Hegedüs's superior, not his subordinate) served to reinforce Rákosi's grip on power.

Although ordinary citizens were increasingly uninformed of what was occurring inside the corridors of power, they nevertheless reacted, in their own way, to the changes that were taking place. The suspension or retrenchment of a portion of the planned large investments and the simultaneous moderate liberalization of peasant agricultural activities manifested itself almost immediately in Hungary's employment structure, with the number of unskilled laborers leaving the construction industry in order to return to their village plots (77,000) almost equaling the increase in the number of those engaged in agriculture registered during the New Course (79,000).

3. Rákosi the Restalinizer and the "Jus Murmurandi"

A series of significant international events took place at the time of Imre Nagy's dismissal from the post of prime minister in the spring of 1955. Great Britain, France and the United States formally concluded their ten-year occupation of West Germany on May 5, 1955, thus permitting the Federal Republic of Germany to become a member of NATO on May 9. Just one week later, on May 15, the four Great Powers that had occupied Austria following World War II signed the Austrian State Treaty, which reestablished the country's state sovereignty and declared its neutrality. During these same days, the Soviet Union—in association with its European satellite states—founded its own international military organization, the Warsaw Pact. At the end of May and the beginning of June 1956, First Secretary of the Communist Party of the Soviet Union Nikita Khrushchev and Soviet Premier Nikolai Bulganin led a delegation on a visit to Yugoslavia, where they reestablished party and state relations that had been broken during the Stalin era. Josip Broz Tito was, of course, flattered that "Mohammed went to the mountain," although there was a more important factor behind Khrushchev's Walk to Canossa than mere formal reconciliation. The Soviet leaders, who had adopted an aggressive foreign policy in order to attain their European and broader geopolitical objectives, offered Belgrade the prospect of "strategic partnership," while pledging to honor Yugoslavia's sovereignty. Hungary became a member of the United Nations at the end of this same year, in December 1955.

The same party body that had just half a year previously voted to support Imre Nagy was responsible for implementing the restalinization program during the March 1955 session of the Hungarian Workers' Party Central Directorate. The document known as the "March resolution" came to serve as a symbolic reference to Hungary's restalinization, just as the "June program" had come to represent the objectives of the 1953 New Course. It is worth noting that as a result of elections held at the time of the HWP congress just a year before, 90 percent of lower-level, municipal, district and county party secretaries were "new cadres": that is, they had been serving for just over a year, since 1954. Hardly any of these neophyte party secretaries were included among the HWP's higher leadership, 65 percent of which consisted of officials who had been members of the Central Directorate during the previous congressional cycle, that is, since 1951.[22] These veteran members of the Central Directorate considered the 1955 March resolution to represent a "rehabilitation" of their pre-1953 activities that had been the subject of criticism during the year and a half of the New Course.

Beginning in April 1955, the government of Prime Minister András Hegedüs initiated the process of using its executive powers to suppress the measures associated with the New Course. The authority, or more precisely lack of authority, of the government at this time is reflected in the fact that the new Hegedüs government did not deem it necessary to dismiss any of the ousted prime minister Imre Nagy's cabinet ministers in order to implement a reversal of New Course era policies. Mátyás Rákosi again became the sole point of reference at the center of the political power structure. At the government level, this ensured that every member of the Council of Ministers Presidium (András Hegedüs, Ernő Gerő, Antal Apró, István Hidas and József Mekis) and three ministers (Minister of the Interior László Piros, Minister of Defense István Bata and Minister of Light Industry Béla Szalai) were also members of the Hungarian Workers' Party's highest operative governing body, the Political Committee.[23] This meant that 8 of the 13 members of the Political Committee also served in some government position. It is hardly surprising in the light of the need for HWP officials to adapt to the new situation that Chief Prosecutor Kálmán Czakó, who was not among the group of political insiders mentioned above, hurried to swear an "oath of allegiance" to the once again all-powerful Rákosi, voluntarily providing the HWP leader with a series of reports in which he attempted to vindicate himself for having furnished Imre Nagy with detailed information regarding the judicial murders and rehabilitations. Czakó's efforts, however, managed only to delay his dismissal—which had been scheduled to take place immediately after the inauguration of the Hegedüs government—for a few months, until August 1955.[24]

The fact that even Ernő Gerő, whose dependability was largely beyond question, felt the need to make a gesture signifying his loyalty is even more conspicuous. Gerő went about doing this in his characteristically cunning manner. Following Imre Nagy's second propitious visit to Moscow at the beginning of 1954, Gerő had voiced the defamatory conclusion that "Péter has transformed the State Protection Authority into a vile den of criminals." One year later, in a memo prepared on the day following the Central Directorate resolution reinstating the Stalinist system, Gerő asserted that one of the primary transgressions of the New Course was the fact that it had placed the ÁVH under excessive party supervision, thus transforming the Hungarian Workers' Party into "a veritable forum for the discrediting of state protection organs."[25] This statement was simultaneously a form of veiled self-criticism, since Gerő had served as the minister of the interior in the cabinet that had curtailed the autonomy of the political police, and a declaration of allegiance to the ÁVH.

The new government repealed Imre Nagy's three-year tax and compulsory delivery guarantee, at the same time increasing the magnitude of these obligations. This in itself served to diminish the free-market sale of agricultural products, although other restrictive measures were also imposed to curb such commerce. The rise in compulsory deliveries was extended to agricultural cooperatives, while taxes were increased for private artisans and retailers, both of which groups had grown in number during the New Course era. Harsh compulsory procedures characteristic of the early 1950s were reintroduced with regard to the establishment of new agricultural cooperatives. Moreover, a portion of the industrial investments suspended two years previously were reactivated, a measure that included an immediate 10 percent increase in machine industry production norms. Only one element of the Nagy government's program was implemented at this time, namely the plan to reduce the number of personnel working in the political apparatus by 40,000 in the course of the year 1955.[26] The primary objective of the policies outlined above was to reduce domestic consumption at all levels in order to create the supply of export commodities necessary to decrease Hungary's foreign trade deficit. The latter shortfall had grown to an alarming degree with countries lying outside the "socialist camp," although for political reasons only a narrow segment of the political elite was aware of this fact. The peace loans were reintroduced for the same reason. Taken together with these other measures, this so-called loan, which actually was closer in nature to an indemnity, was more than enough to again elicit nationwide aversion to the existing system, which also failed to achieve its primary objective of producing a significant reduction in both the foreign trade deficit and the government budget deficit. The failure of these policies to improve Hungary's foreign trade and budget balances was such that Rákosi, Gerő and Hegedüs were each compelled to make visits to neighboring "fraternal states" at the beginning of 1954 in order to ask for loans. During their visits to Prague, Warsaw and Moscow, the three Hungarian Workers' Party and government officials claimed that the country's growing budget imbalance was a result of Imre Nagy's "harmful" policies, although they nevertheless returned home empty-handed on each occasion.

Mátyás Rákosi was not content to have Imre Nagy expelled merely from the inner circle of power, gradually divesting the former prime minister of all his even indirect political functions. Nagy was removed from his post as the vice-chairman of the Patriotic People's Front, and stripped of his university professorship and his membership of the Hungarian Academy of Sciences, while his published works, speeches and articles were banned. This arbitrary manifestation of hysterical hatred culminated in Nagy's expulsion from the Hungarian Workers' Party at the beginning of December

1955. These retaliatory measures against Imre Nagy turned out to be counterproductive, serving to increase the degree of popular sympathy for the isolated and likely permanently monitored former prime minister.[27]

The gradual increase in the autonomy of certain newspapers and other publications during the year-and-a-half-long "new course" contributed to Nagy's rise in popularity. Some journalists and writers, who had until 1953 been expected to function as mere party propagandists, either called into question or explicitly rejected the March 1955 Stalinist resurgence. Party resolutions adopted after Rákosi's return to absolute power did not resolve the many problems that afflicted the country, at most sweeping them under the rug. However, the once again omnipotent Rákosi and his bureaucratic entourage not only rejected writings, citing the contradictions and discrepancies contained in their policies, but also labeled them as manifestations of destructive, anti-party deviation, for which their authors were subjected to administrative and party disciplinary procedures. With the Kremlin having helped him to regain absolute power, the Hungarian Workers' Party general secretary felt free to completely disregard the remark that Nikita Khrushchev had made at a consultation of party leaders held in May 1954, when he told the HWP general secretary "Comrade Rákosi… you seem to believe that after shooting Beria, we should shoot criticism as well."[28]

The return of compulsory uniformity in expressed political opinion following the Stalinist restoration in March 1955 entailed two problems: first, both those journalists, authors and editors who had previously published critical writings and those loyalists who had rigidly followed the party leadership's frequently changing "single true path" were members of the Hungarian Workers' Party; second, these journalists and writers came from diverse party backgrounds. Among them were some who prior to 1953 had uncritically acclaimed Rákosi's rule—honored favorites of the regime who did public penance for their previous pen-pushing in support of the Stalinists following the public exposure of the judicial murders; others had been critical of the Rákosi regime during the initial period of Stalinist ascendancy and had only recently been released from prison or had languished as ignored pariahs. It is almost impossible to gauge the degree of political disunity within the journalist-*littérateur* caste that played a functional role in the legitimization of the system. However, the proclivities of this group may be reflected to a certain extent in the fact that the HWP Political Committee managed to compile a list of 34 "loyal" writers at the time of a scandal surrounding the confiscation of the September 1955 issue of *Irodalmi Újság*, while 59 writers, including 29 Kossuth Prize recipients, signed the subsequent Memorandum addressed to the party leadership protesting against "the use of force, unwarranted administrative intervention and imperiousness."[29]

The question of the intelligentsia's political loyalty became a critical political issue due to a combination of factors.[30] At a 1955 meeting of the Hungarian Workers' Party Central Directorate convened to assess the year and a half that had passed since the March transformation, Rákosi offered a more or less improvised elaboration of his prepared report on the status of the "ideological front," asserting that "the comportment of a significant number of writers is worse now than it was at the time of the March resolutions." Minister of the Interior László Piros reiterated the HWP general secretary's assertion, stating that the services of the ÁVH should be employed in order "to eradicate the right-wing and on more than one occasion hostile viewpoints that have emerged on the literary and artistic front."[31] Subsequent speakers cautioned against the utilization of Gábor Péter's successors in the political police force to impart a greater sense of insight to men of letters, while others attempted to transform the "Memorandum affair" into a central political issue exceeding its true significance. In the course of their comments, András Hegedüs, Márton Horváth and Ernő Gerő provided Rákosi with the outlines of a "new conception" according to which recalcitrant writers and journalists had conspired with Imre Nagy to form a *party opposition*. Within just a few days, the continuously operative Gerő had devised a comprehensive and far-reaching plan of action as well. The latter maintained the appearance of "legality" and conformity with party procedure, invoking HWP resolutions that established a variety of retaliatory devices ranging from "consultations" and censure to dismissal from office and expulsion from the party in order to compel those who had signed the Memorandum to recant. The HWP censured Tibor Déry, Zoltán Zelk, László Benjámin, Tamás Aczél, Tibor Méray, Endre Szervánszky, Péter Kuczka and Géza Losonczy, while expelling Sándor Haraszti, Miklós Vásárhelyi and, earlier, Miklós Gimes from the party. The HWP then passed a separate resolution on December 3 revoking Imre Nagy's party membership.

In spite of this series of administrative measures, Rákosi was unable to entirely restore the political conditions that had predominated in Hungary at the beginning of the 1950s. Just as Moscow had mistakenly presumed in 1953 that the process of destalinization could take place in Hungary without removing Rákosi from power, the Hungarian Workers' Party general secretary lacked his earlier support from Stalin, which would have made total restalinization possible in 1955. (To be more precise, he lacked the possibility of alluding to this prospect.) Rákosi supposed, not without reason, that he had gained victory in his duel with Imre Nagy, especially when measured against the fate of Beria and Gábor Péter. However, the HWP general secretary's megalomania and paranoia prevented him from noticing that both as a result of and in spite of the succession struggle that was taking place within the CPSU Presidium, the new Soviet party leadership had taken active foreign policy measures aimed at repositioning itself *vis-à-vis* the United States and its Cold War allies. While Rákosi had previously adapted the political conditions in Hungary to all of the Soviet Union's foreign policy corrections—or escapades—and variations in the roles or distribution of power within the CPSU leadership, it seemed at this time as if "Stalin's best Hungarian pupil" was no longer able to adjust to such changes. That is, Rákosi chose to ignore them, because taken both individually and collectively, the political transformation that had taken place in Moscow had served to counteract the Stalinist reincarnation that the HWP general secretary embodied, thus placing his reclaimed political supremacy in jeopardy. Rákosi's tacit recognition of this fact prompted him to portray those espousing contrasting opinions as enemies to be eliminated.

Through the above-mentioned resolutions and censure, the Rákosi-led Stalinist party leadership transformed the memorandists into a "factious, anti-party platform" exceeding its true political weight and influence. The Hungarian Workers' Party leadership's simultaneous denunciation of Imre Nagy and the critical intelligentsia also served to create a political alliance between these intellectuals and the former prime minister. The party leadership had an array of routine political measures at its disposal to silence and isolate both Nagy and recalcitrant writers and journalists, even without placing them under arrest. HWP resolutions that explicitly declared their collaboration naturally produced a significant degree of political solidarity between the former prime minister and members of the critical intelligentsia, thus creating a genuine party opposition from people who had previously maintained only a loose and sometimes contentious relationship.

The Hungarian Workers' Party leadership's transformation of the Memorandum affair into a central domestic political issue at the end of 1955 entailed many significant consequences, further increasing the number of paradoxical political situations. The declaration in a party resolution of the existence of a party opposition put an end to spurious assertions regarding "party unity" that since the beginning of the new course two and a half years previously had served to conceal the divisiveness that had surfaced within the party. As a result, those standing on the opposite side of the fissure that had opened within the HWP began to act in accordance with the openly declared circumstances. During the winter months of 1955–1956, the Rákosi-led HWP leadership attempted to convince lower-level party organizations of the legality of the actions that they had taken against the internal opposition. This was necessary because doubts had emerged among members of the intelligentsia and party organizations regarding both the validity of the incriminating resolutions and the lawfulness of its retaliatory measures. The HWP leadership had to convince these party members that the "intensifying class struggle" had made it imperative to open up a front against "those who yesterday were still comrades" as well as those who had already suffered the consequences of a similar previous wave of hysteria. There was a third factor that made it necessary for the HWP leadership to convince those subject to party discipline of the legality of its tactics. Rákosi had many personal flaws, but he was not dull-witted. Although he cloaked his offensive against those driven into party opposition in the ideological trappings of the "class struggle" in accordance with the ritual of the system and era, the HWP general secretary was aware that his leadership role was at stake. Although he did not and could not admit this fact, he was likely forced to recognize that, in the words of Simone de Beauvoir, "the power of circumstances" had changed along with the circumstances of power. Although Rákosi never entertained any scruples that would prevent him from sending even his own comrades to the gallows or to prison, he was at this time unable to take such action against those classified as members of the party opposition. This represented a marked difference between the interval of restalinization presently under consideration and the period of "classical" Stalinism prior to 1953.

Criticism of Rákosi and his fellow Hungarian Workers' Party leaders among those forced into opposition became increasingly radical. During this time, Imre Nagy inserted the following passage into an analysis of domestic political circumstances that he had written half a year earlier: "Standing at the head of the party is such an individual who in the opinion even of his own narrow clique is theoretically unqualified and whose thirst for power and leadership ambition are exceeded only by his theoretical confusion."[32] Géza Losonczy, whom the party had rehabilitated following his release from prison, although he had since been censured for his signing of the Memorandum, assailed the condemned party resolution in a speech analyzing the system that he delivered during consultations with the "party court"—the Central Supervisory Committee.

Losonczy's criticism—of the document's lapses, its questioning of the legitimacy of the procedure and its declarations alluding to the "threatening environment" stemming from the "eradication of the party cadres"—provided as precise a diagnosis of the system's flaws as the series of questions addressed to the reigning party leadership:

> On what grounds do they prevent democracy within the party, democracy whose fundamental constituent element is the capacity of party members—all party members—to freely express their opinion with regard to all economic, social, cultural, domestic political, foreign policy and personnel issues? Why have they not held to account those who have suppressed criticism, who have disregarded intra-party democracy? [...] When did our party—whose primary strength should be its truth and justice—acquire the custom of stating falsehoods before the entire Hungarian people? [...] Since when has it been forbidden for communists and the people to mourn their dead? Since when has it been forbidden to express indignity at the torture and murder of communists and honorable people? Why is lamentation of our dead deemed to be "anti-party and anti-people" and why is it not deemed so to persecute communists and honorable people? And following these terrible events, which have been the subject of only limited official public disclosure, who counts as a loyal son of the party and people? He who attempts with all his might to bring those responsible, regardless of their identity and function, to justice, those who take measures to create an environment in which all honorable working people—who make up 99 percent of the country's population—can live "peacefully" and quietly? Or he who does everything possible to prevent problems from being exposed, to ensure that accountability ends at a very minimal level and that legality and order are not truly able to become solidified in the country?[33]

The party leadership paradoxically considered those who had "merely" been categorized as belonging to the internal Hungarian

Workers' Party opposition to be the equivalent of those, principally Imre Nagy, who had been expelled from the party. (Neither did those in opposition make a distinction between those who had remained in the party and those who had been expelled.) Another such ambiguity was the fact that although the new year of 1956 had arrived, there was no official word regarding the launching of the new "five-year" plan that had previously been scheduled to start at that time. (And what is more, the Central Directorate placed the issue of determining the plan's "preliminary target figures" on its agenda amid radically transformed circumstances only six months later.) The party leadership also repeatedly delayed consideration of the rapidly changing international situation, which was exercising a significant impact on Hungary as well. More accurately, it was again only Imre Nagy who had examined these matters in the essays that he wrote during his exclusion from public political life.[34] (It is, of course, questionable whether Nagy would have had the time and energy to write these essays if he had remained in the ring grappling with everyday governing duties as well as Rákosi's opposition.) In some of the dozen and a half analyses written during the second half of 1955, Nagy examined new developments in the field of international relations—the rapprochement between Moscow and Belgrade, the signing of the Austrian State Treaty and the formation of the so-called bloc of "non-aligned states." In his consideration of these themes, Nagy did not fail to observe that Hungary's regional status had undergone a partial transformation, particularly with regard to its relations with Yugoslavia. Mere investigation of this issue was already considered to be controversial, since Rákosi himself represented the main impediment in this regard. In other essays Nagy concentrated on domestic politics, expounding the "correctness" of his viewpoints and criticizing the party leadership's policies. Moreover, Nagy hoped for a time even following his expulsion from the HWP that the series of issues addressed in his essays might be introduced for open discussion at "official party forums." However, under the given circumstances, this hope was illusory, although not necessarily as a result of Nagy's extra-party "incompetence." One of Nagy's contemporaries aptly observed that the primary reason that official party debate was impossible was the fact that "nothing is more dangerous for the dictatorship than doubts propagated by its own followers—than heresy."[35] Imre Nagy became an outright *persona non grata* precisely because he represented intra-party (!) dissent and, in spite of the increasingly hysterical ostracism to which he was subjected, continued to serve as a viable alternative to Rákosi.

In another of the paradoxical occurrences at this time, on June 7, 1955, the Hungarian Workers' Party Political Committee took steps to curtail Cardinal Mindszenty's prison sentence, while only four days later, on June 11, an even more exclusive body of party leaders—the HWP Political Committee Secretariat—adopted a separate resolution regarding "the suppression of clerical reaction."[36] The latter move seemed like an attempt on the part of party leaders to repair a momentary "short circuit," to counterbalance their seemingly conciliatory previous measure. The HWP Political Committee Secretariat's directive stipulated that "suitable administrative actions be taken to suppress reactionary manifestations on the part of the Church." The directive added that "illicit religious ritual and illegally operating monastic orders must be eliminated as quickly as possible." Two days later, on June 13, Minister of the Interior László Piros issued a broad reinterpretation of the party resolution, ordering the ÁVH to urgently increase the intensity of "operative efforts against hostile elements functioning on an ideological plane." As part of this endeavor, Piros emphasized the point that "The party resolution pertaining to the struggle against clerical reaction must be enforced with particular vigor."[37]

Implementation of this order caused a partial breakdown in the operations of the political police. Meanwhile, the sentence of the other imprisoned high Catholic Church official, Archbishop of Kalocsa József Grősz, was also reduced, but there was not a word about his and/or Mindszenty's release from prison. Not until half a year later, at the end of November 1955, did the ÁVH's "clerical reaction" division arrange to have the two archbishops kept under house arrest. An episcopal summer residence located in southern Hungary in the village of Püspökszentlászló was initially outfitted to accommodate both Mindszenty and Grősz, although both were relocated two months later—the Archbishop of Esztergom to a confiscated noble residence in the village of Felsőpetény along the country's northern border and the Archbishop of Kalocsa to the village of Tószeg, near Szolnok, in central Hungary. A report from the "internal reaction" division reveals that arranging for Mindszenty and Grősz to be kept under house arrest took up so much of the ÁVH's resources at this time that the political police was forced to temporarily postpone executing the party resolution's stipulation regarding the liquidation of illegal religious orders. The ÁVH attempted to compensate for this delay by detaining almost all of the Jesuit brothers who were still at liberty. The ÁVH report stated that "18 central and regional leaders were taken into custody," ten of whom were convicted in separate trials that took place in late 1955 and early 1956.[38] A perceptible transformation took place in the ÁVH's anti-clerical operative maneuvers as it conducted the efforts outlined above, shifting its focus from imprisonment at any cost to infiltration of both the active clergy and the entire spectrum of those who had belonged to the monastic orders banned in 1950 with a comprehensive network of informants.

4. The Twentieth Party Congress of the CPSU: the Fragmented Political Playground

Just as the Soviet party leadership's fear of a renewed intensification of Cold War tension had determined the fate of the "new course," another event of international significance that took place in Moscow initiated the decline of Rákosi's year-long Stalinist restoration. During the second half of February 1956, the Communist Party of the Soviet Union held its 20th Party Congress, the first to take place since Stalin's death. For ten full days, the Soviet "party parliament" conducted its work according to established practice. The congress adopted a closing declaration proclaiming the preventability of the Third World War and the post-Stalinist doctrine of peaceful coexistence. An additional closed session with newly appointed party leaders and officials in attendance was held on February 25. During this meeting, CPSU First Secretary Nikita Khrushchev delivered his speech *On the Cult of Personality and Its Consequences,* an appraisal of Stalin's more than 25-year reign of terror that contained calculated allusions to current Soviet domestic politics. Khrushchev's review of the purges and judicial murders that had become an organic part of the system shocked his audience even more than expected. Over the following days and weeks, news of Khrushchev's speech, which was intended to be secret, spread throughout the world in verbatim translation. Reaction to the CPSU first secretary's speech was extremely mixed. Khrushchev's biographer described instances in which the speech was criticized on the grounds that it "delivered a blow not only to Stalin's reputation, but also to that of the entire communist movement." The Soviet party leadership quickly launched a propaganda campaign aimed at stemming the damage resulting from what Khrushchev's biographer depicted as the "serious crisis that it [the speech] provoked within the world communist movement."[39]

Rákosi would have encountered no difficulties had he been compelled only to give an account of that which had been said during the plenary sessions of the CPSU 20th Party Congress. Neither did his typically distorted estimation that the Hungarian Workers' Party had long functioned in accordance with principles outlined at the Moscow congress exceed a level that could be tolerated. Rákosi's dilemma stemmed from the fact that Khrushchev's secret speech had become widely disseminated in Hungary within just a few weeks as well. Moreover, many Hungarians gained access to the genuine text of the CPSU first secretary's address, not merely the abridged and somewhat euphemized synopsis of the speech that had been distributed within the inner HWP party apparatus. The latter arrived via "twin airmail"—partially through the broadcasts of Radio Free Europe and partially through so-called meteorological probes, whose most important load contained not technical instruments, but propaganda material from the West.[40] The increasingly widespread familiarity in Hungary with the authentic text of Khrushchev's speech undermined the credibility of Rákosi's self-justifying version of events, quickly putting the HWP general secretary on the defensive. This was partially a result of the fact that Stalin's incrimination in Moscow represented another "summons" to publicly disclose his true role in the series of judicial murders that had taken place in Hungary, particularly László Rajk's show trial and subsequent execution, for which Rákosi had earlier claimed "credit." Moreover, continuing tension in relations between Hungary and Yugoslavia had also become increasingly awkward for the Soviet party leadership after Tito repeatedly signaled to both Moscow and Budapest through quiet diplomatic channels that he considered Rákosi to be a *persona non grata* for having long voiced public vilification of both him and the Yugoslav Communist Party to a degree that surpassed even Stalin's expectations. Finally, although HWP officials who had survived conviction in the show trials had been released from prison, with reluctance on the part of the authorities, one after another, they had still not been rehabilitated, for want of a relevant party resolution. The keeping of former members of the banned Social Democratic Party behind bars was presumably the result of the ÁVH's alleged discovery of underground SDP organizational activities in 1955. Minister of the Interior László Piros justified the continued repression of former social democrats on the grounds that "the most dangerous and harmful enemies are clerical reaction and right-wing 'soc dems' [social democrats], because they maintain powerful contacts with the masses [*sic*].'"[41]

Rákosi employed his routine "pull and release" strategy to extract himself from the predicament in which Khrushchev's 20th Party Congress speech had placed him. The Hungarian Workers' Party general secretary first began to dispense prevarications mixed with partial confessions to party activists expecting to receive information on the CPSU congress. In a speech to party activists in Eger, Rákosi utilized his previously "copyrighted" formula for deflecting blame, claiming that the former ÁVH leader Gábor Péter had deceived him. Both in Eger and at a subsequent party forum, the HWP general secretary attempted to make this transparent lie more plausible by contending that Rajk had sealed his own fate when he "misled the party" and "was not candid with the party." (That is, when Rákosi's manipulations and coercion from his own comrades who had helped to engineer the trial, above all Mihály Farkas and János Kádár, prompted Rajk to finally confess to the charges.) These allegations regarding Rajk elicited such a great degree of indignation within lower-level party organizations throughout Hungary that, during a May 18 speech to party activists in Budapest, Rákosi felt compelled to acknowledge that he had played the primary role in staging the Rajk trial, claiming repeatedly that he had been "misled." The HWP general secretary immediately attempted, however, to counterbalance his confession with threats to the party apparatus, announcing a comprehensive organizational and territorial restructuring and "rationalization" of Hungary's state and party administration. After issuing this indirect threat to the livelihoods of the party dictatorship's cadres, Rákosi was quick to impart the message that "your fate continues to depend on me." Although, as will soon be described, Rákosi exercised a decreasing influence over events, his proclaimed administrative reorganization effectively impeded the operations of the party- and state-administrative apparatus for a period of several months.

The Hungarian Workers' Party general secretary's attempts to deflect responsibility for the show trials had the most direct impact on the political police. During the spring of 1956, Rákosi publicly contravened the tacit solidarity of interests that had existed between him and the ÁVH for essentially ten years. The emphasis in the previous sentence must be placed on the word "publicly," since within the context of the given system, it was one thing to "expose" Gábor Péter's culpability (as well as that of his company) at internal party forums but it was quite another to transform the ÁVH into a public scapegoat for the miscarriages of justice that the organization had discharged with the "authorization" of the

HWP party leadership. The greater public was not and could not have been aware of the far-reaching incrimination and purges that had taken place within the political police in the meantime. The majority of Hungary's citizens thus had no reason to alter its view of the organization that had served as the feared and despised "fist of the party" and whose operations remained essentially unchanged under the direction of Péter's successor, László Piros. In the light of the hardship and suffering that the ÁVH had caused over the years, it was not without reason that that popular blame for its (pre-1953) crimes and everyday acts of despotism continued to center on Rákosi and the László Piros-led Ministry of the Interior and its political police.

Two consultative political forums, which may be considered as opponents, were established in Budapest following the CPSU 20th Party Congress. One of these groups formed around the Soviet Union's Ambassador to Budapest Yuri Andropov—who had served as Moscow's top diplomat in Hungary since the summer of 1954 and had thus directly experienced events related to the second half of the "new course," Imre Nagy's removal from power and Rákosi's Stalinist restoration and consummation. Beginning in March 1956, even Andropov was compelled to recognize that the situation in Hungary had changed. Those Hungarians with whom the Soviet ambassador held regular consultations, including those related to his official functions, repeatedly voiced their opinion that Mátyás Rákosi's leadership over the Hungarian Workers' Party had become an increasing burden to the party. Those with whom Andropov maintained regular contact were neither party rebels nor active supporters of Imre Nagy and his policies—they were members of the HWP Political Committee. Although Andropov's reports and memoranda consistently refer to Rákosi and his colleagues in the leadership as "our friends," the Soviet ambassador must have observed that even the HWP's hard-line Stalinists were in favor of getting rid of the party's general secretary. In more precise terms, a cunning game of "mutual stalking" had begun to take place. Andropov's Hungarian "conversation partners"—Ernő Gerő, András Hegedüs,

István Kovács, János Kádár and Lajos Ács—attempted to ascertain during their meetings with the Soviet ambassador whether the CPSU leadership stood firm in its support of Rákosi, hoping that Moscow might be prepared to initiate the HWP general secretary's dismissal. However, the Soviet ambassador, seeking cover in his diplomatic status, always attempted to maintain the appearance that HWP leadership decisions belonged strictly to the competency of Hungarian party officials, informing his superiors in Moscow that Political Committee members were engaged in cautious preparations to force Rákosi from office. Although Moscow's continued backing of the HWP general secretary (for want of a better alternative) even after the 20th Party Congress would have made it difficult for Andropov to openly support those who advocated Rákosi's removal, the Soviet ambassador truly identified with the Kremlin position. Andropov's denunciation of the HWP leadership in his reports was based primarily on his contention that it had abandoned Rákosi at a time when the general secretary was advocating more decisive action against party malcontents and had not raised objections when party organizations themselves began to sabotage implementation of HWP resolutions. Severely compromised during the Rajk affair, he was also averse to the procedures launched against Mihály Farkas, who had been made a scapegoat in order to redeem Rákosi. Andropov doubted that they could be implemented in accordance with the CPSU Presidium's expectation, voiced repeatedly for two full years, that in the meantime "the authority of the party and its leadership will strengthen."[42]

The quiet behind-the-scenes wrangling that was taking place between Soviet Ambassador Yuri Andropov and Moscow's party clientele was not made public. One could say that the conspiratorial activity described above was a logical consequence of the prevailing system and the political impulses of those who had operated the dictatorship for the previous decade. However, this explanation does not provide sufficient grounds for an interpretation of the political situation that existed in Hungary beginning in the spring of 1956. The CPSU 20th Party Congress and the publication of Khrushchev's secret speech hampered Rákosi's restalinization scheme to such a degree that he and his fellow party leaders found it increasingly difficult to control and operate, in a mode commensurate with their political education, the political construction that they had created. Within the context of the Rákosi-championed Stalinist operational mechanism, the foundation of a *public* party opposition forum of the type that came into existence in Hungary in March 1956 would not have been possible.

The forum alluded to above was called the Petőfi Kör (Petőfi Circle). This organization, which functioned under the auspices of the Workers' Youth Alliance, was established during the period in which Imre Nagy served as Hungary's prime minister, although its operations were suspended following Nagy's dismissal. The Petőfi Circle was reactivated following the 20th Party Congress of the CPSU, functioning in the role of a "social parliament" in which all present were given an opportunity to voice their opinion. Participants in the frequent meetings of the organization expressed increasingly explicit criticism of the state and party leadership. Eventually, thousands of people began to attend Petőfi Circle events at which questions of current interest, such as economic difficulties, freedom of the press and unresolved issues surrounding the judicial murders, were opened to public debate.[43] The increasingly candid nature of debate at the meetings of the Petőfi Circle made them seem as though they were not taking place in the shadow of a monolithic party dictatorship. There were essentially only two sensitive issues that had not yet been included on the organization's agenda: Hungary's dependence on the Soviet Union and the multi-party political system. The profusion of acknowledgments of unlawful acts that had taken place began attaining a critical mass as a result of the first-hand reports and unrestrained discussion of them that took place following the partial opening of the prison gates. Several of those incriminated in the course of earlier show trials spoke at meetings of the Petőfi Circle, shaking skeletons out of the closet one after another. The newly rehabilitated Szilárd Újhelyi, who had also spent time in prison, made a significant distinction during one of the organization's meetings: "In this instance an entire country and people must be rehabilitated, not just a certain group."[44] Hungarian public opinion had long come to expect a broad and open resolution to what both Rákosi and those within the HWP leadership who wanted to replace him as party general secretary hoped to settle as "an internal party affair" in which any investigation into the unlawful acts that had been committed would be extended only to the cases of selected party members.

All of this was supplemented at the beginning of June by the transformation of a "personal affair" into a political event, when more than 500 notable public figures, both party and non-party, visited Imre Nagy at his home to congratulate him on the occasion of his 60th birthday. The Hungarian Workers' Party leadership publicly condemned this "demonstration," thus according publicity to an event that the party had hoped to keep as quiet as possible. In the meantime, the meetings of the Petőfi Circle became a "free market" of information. Among the periodicals appearing at the time, *Irodalmi Újság*, *Új Hang* and *Szabad Ifjúság* counted as pro-reform publications. (Of course, some of those who wrote for these periodicals had just a couple of years previously attempted to outbid one another in their glorification of Rákosi.) Of the debates held at meetings of the Petőfi Circle, the one that took place on June 27 was the most outspoken: in a broad interpretation of the announced topic of press freedom, participants began to focus on the subject of *freedom* in general. A Soviet secret service communiqué from the period quoted a statement from a person in attendance at the meeting offering a precise self-definition of dissidents from within the system (!): "The young people in the Petőfi Circle are the saviors of the country. Those in the Petőfi Circle are communists, albeit Hungarian communists, who do not want to copy Russian methods. The intellectual revolution that the Petőfi Circle has launched will be continued. If we, members of the Petőfi Circle, represent the March Youth of our day… then Imre Nagy is our Lajos Kossuth."[45] (The March Youth was the name of a group of young radicals active during the Hungarian Revolution of 1848. Lajos Kossuth was the central figure, in both practical and symbolic terms, of the Revolution. Already during his lifetime Kossuth was dubbed the "apostle of Hungarian liberty," and the cult that surrounded his person survived undiminished into the twentieth century.)

During the spring and early summer of 1956, the Petőfi Circle became the main public forum for the expression of public opinion in Hungary. It would nevertheless be foolish to think that such an agora, in itself, would have been enough to dethrone the embodiment of the communist dictatorship, Mátyás Rákosi. This was in spite of the fact that the dismissal of the Hungarian Workers' Party general secretary had by this time become inevitable—only its timing and method remained in question. Rákosi himself was forced to deflect both direct and indirect demands for his resignation at the end of June 1956. Then, on June 28, security forces dispersed a massive workers' demonstration in Poznań, Poland, provoking an incident in which 50 people were killed, 300 wounded and several hundred arrested. Taking inspiration from what had taken place in Poland, the HWP leader planned to take similar steps in Hungary. Two days following the events in Poznań, Rákosi was still able to get the HWP Central Directorate to qualify the activities of Imre Nagy and the Petőfi Circle as "anti-people's democracy and anti-party actions," thus making the continued operations of the organization impossible. At the same time, intentionally or unintentionally leaked information had spread, indicating that the "leader" had instructed the Ministry of the Interior to begin compiling a list of those to be arrested. (Historical research has yet to uncover clear evidence of the existence of the so-called "list of 400" that survives in the memories of people who lived through the period.) In any event, even if Rákosi did make such a plan, he never had the opportunity to implement it. And while Andropov's position as the key figure in the closed "political salon" that had emerged amid the increasingly palpable crisis would have enabled him to play the role of kingmaker, the Soviet ambassador always refrained from doing so. Although Andropov's reports on the situation in Hungary became increasingly pessimistic in tone as Rákosi's position weakened noticeably from

March until the end of May 1956, he did not lift a finger to prevent the outcome of this process from taking place. Finally, the quietly plotting Hungarian party leaders decided to take action aimed at unseating Mátyás Rákosi. To do this, they utilized a tactic that they had learned from the HWP general secretary over a period of ten years, obtaining from the imprisoned former ÁVH leader, Gábor Péter, a written confession regarding the staging of the show trials that implicated not only the current scapegoat, Mihály Farkas, but also, to an even greater degree, Rákosi himself.[46]

The pace of events accelerated following the move to oust Rákosi. Gábor Péter's fateful submission was dated July 10, 1956. The document was quickly translated into Russian and sent to Moscow, which prompted the CPSU Presidium to send one of its members, Anastasiya Mikoyan, to Budapest five days later, on July 15, in order to resolve the Rákosi affair. Following an urgently conducted series of negotiations, Mátyás Rákosi—officially at his own request, although in fact at the initiative of the Soviet party leadership—asked to be relieved from his post as general secretary of the Hungarian Workers' Party on the first day of the HWP Central Directorate session that began on July 18. This proved to be the deposed party leader's final public appearance in Hungary. Following the conclusion of the Central Directorate's session, Rákosi traveled to the Soviet Union, ostensibly for medical treatment. (He never returned—or was never able to return—to Hungary.)

Yugoslavia's Ambassador to Moscow Veljko Mićunović, who held regular consultations with Khrushchev regarding developments in Hungary at this time, recorded the hectic changes that were taking place in the Soviet stance *vis-à-vis* Rákosi. On July 15, the Yugoslav ambassador made the following entry in his diary:

> Khrushchev requested that I notify Comrade Tito of the following. The situation in Hungary is extremely complicated. Suslov returned from Budapest and read his report to the Central Committee Presidium during its meeting. The Russians decided that they are going to strongly support Rákosi! Khrushchev said that they are

> quite aware of what a difficult situation he is in, although they also know that everything that he did was based on orders from Stalin. Rákosi is only as guilty as they are here in Moscow [*sic*!]. Rákosi cannot openly admit this, just as the Russians can't. This is why after listening to Suslov's report they decided that they would support Rákosi! [...] Khrushchev also said that the Hungarians had rehabilitated László Rajk, who had been innocently sent to the executioner. Although I made no comments on this either, it is clearer than day that Rákosi cannot rehabilitate László Rajk and remain the leader of Hungary at the same time. Khrushchev expressed his disapproval with regard to the Hungarians for their having expelled Imre Nagy from the party. He claimed that they hadn't even asked the Russians about this. Nagy should have been kept in the party; he would come in handy now. They have no other choice than to support Rákosi. Khrushchev would like it if Tito would understand what he is doing, because he is afraid that a new conflict could break out between Yugoslavia and the Soviet Union as a result of the Soviet support for Rákosi. Now Mikoyan has traveled there to negotiate with the Hungarian comrades...

One day later, on July 16, Mićunović's diary entry indicated that the Soviet position towards Rákosi had changed:

> Khrushchev began by saying that he would like to inform me of Mikoyan's Budapest negotiations. Everything is turning out much better than they had hoped, because the Hungarian comrades have decided that Rákosi is going to resign. Rákosi also took part in the Budapest consultations and he agreed totally with that decision. Khrushchev also hopes that this represents a decisive step towards a political resolution of Hungary's internal crisis. He asked that I notify Tito of this.[47]

This "sliding together" of the dates makes it obvious that Khrushchev informed Tito via his ambassador of the decision that the "Hungarian comrades" would make following Mikoyan's intervention even before notifying his Budapest vassals, themselves, of their choice. More precisely, the inner Hungarian Workers' Party elite had also come to support Rákosi's dismissal and were simply waiting for permission from the Kremlin to get rid of the politically and morally spent dictator. Moreover, the Hungarian party leadership's act of compromising Rákosi through Gábor Péter removed the "final obstacle" preventing Moscow from fully restoring its geo-strategically important relations with Belgrade. The aspirations of the Hungarian and Soviet party leadership thus fell into accord, rendering negotiations related to appointment of Rákosi's successor the main purpose of Mikoyan's mission to Budapest. These talks did not entail any particular difficulty, since Moscow's preferred choice, Ernő Gerő, readily agreed to become the new leader of the HWP after feigning an obligatory initial reluctance.

It is another question whether those from both inside and outside the Hungarian Workers' Party who advocated change accepted the official justification that Rákosi had resigned due to his "deteriorating health condition," any more than they accepted the selection of the no-less Muscovite Ernő Gerő to succeed him as HWP leader. Gerő's appointment clearly defined the limits of Khrushchev's destalinization policies, demonstrating that the Kremlin continued to tolerate only tested, unconditionally pro-Soviet cadres at the head of the empire's satellite states. Both János Kádár, who was appointed to serve as Gerő's deputy, and György Marosán, who had been released from prison just a few months previously, reemerged as members of the principal HWP leadership following Rákosi's resignation. Ernő Gerő's inauguration as party secretary revealed the continuity that he had assumed with his predecessor. The new HWP leader intimated that a veil would be drawn over the past, proclaiming a *tabula rasa*, although the unburied corpses of the victims of judicial murder cast a shadow over this clean slate. Gerő nevertheless seized the opportunity to launch an immediate attack on the Petőfi Circle, an assault that Prime Minister András Hegedüs, who had remained in his post following Rákosi's resignation, bolstered with his contention that the organization consisted of "right-wing elements gathered around Imre Nagy." Meanwhile, the announcement of new production norms for the construction industry generated a strike mentality in the country. Many Hungarians maintained that the reshuffling that had taken place within the HWP's party leadership was a hoax that had merely moved them "out of the frying pan and into the fire." And not only at home. It is noteworthy that the Soviet ambassador stated in one of his reports that "Comrade Mikoyan's participation in the plenary session ensured" the "success" of the July session of the HWP Central Secretariat—that is, Gerő's supplanting of Rákosi as party leader. Mikoyan's visit to Budapest represented only the first half of his mission. After leaving Hungary, the CPSU Presidium member continued to Belgrade, where he was supposed to convince Tito to accept the personnel changes that had taken place within the leadership of the HWP. However, Mikoyan failed to accomplish this task, because Belgrade maintained throughout the subsequent two months that Gerő's policies would "essentially be a continuation of Rákosi's."[48] In a phenomenon that was typical of the reaction in Hungary to the changes that had taken place within the leadership of the HWP, a great number of Hungarians voluntarily participated—even at the expense of their vacation time—in harvesting activities in 1956 in order to ensure that their families would have enough to eat during the winter.

Politics seemed on the surface to have gone into summer recess in Hungary during the weeks following Mátyás Rákosi's dismissal in July 1956. The US election campaign had not yet reached the home stretch, while athletes were in the final stages of their preparations for the Melbourne Olympics. The nationalization of the Suez Canal caused a moderate diplomatic and press clamor, although British naval forces finally pulled up anchor to sail back to England 12 years before the expiration of the 100-year concession on the waterway. The day following the bloody suppression of the Poznań protests, the French newspaper *Le Monde* launched a regular one-page feature called "Destalinization in Eastern Europe," which only reluctantly included Gerő's replacement of Rákosi as one of its topics. (The autumn months nevertheless substantiated Western press reports: there was no lack of news from this region.) Observant diplomats noticed that lower-level Soviet–Yugoslav relations had become more intensive since the beginning of the year. Khrushchev even dissolved Cominform in order to ensure that this organization would not hinder his efforts to mend relations with Tito. Only intelligence professionals and political analysts unraveled the possible reasons for the increasingly tight cooperation that was taking place between the Soviet Union and Yugoslavia. The steady rise in the number of meetings between high-ranking military officials and experts from the various service branches seemed to exceed those necessary for a post-Stalin consolidation of Soviet–Yugoslav relations. As a matter of fact, Moscow began using its reparations payments from Austria to finance the Škoda Works' quiet arming of Egypt. These weapons were sent via Hungary to ports in Yugoslavia, from which country they were shipped to Cairo, a fact that was not reported in the press.

Hungary's public life then seemed to be on sabbatical as well. The large number of people who were on summer vacation at this time may explain why Ernő Gerő claimed in consultations with an advisor at the Soviet Embassy in Budapest that during his little more than one month as party general secretary, "We have gradually been implementing the resolutions adopted at the Hungarian Workers' Party Central Directorate's July session… and things are proceeding normally in the country." Not even the Soviet ambassador, however, took the latter assertion at face value, stating in a report addressed to the Moscow CPSU Presidium during these days that the Rákosi–Gerő switch had somewhat diminished the "extremely tense domestic political situation… [although this] is still very complicated and merits close attention." Moreover, Andropov openly expressed dissatisfaction with the performance of the Gerő-led HWP leadership, something that he had never done during Rákosi's reign: "They are pursuing a policy of compliance… they make extremely feeble use of power… they have not taken decisive steps to ensure the success of the hard line."[49]

Andropov's analysis was valid insofar as the Hungarian Workers' Party leadership truly did not seem to know what to do without Rákosi. The new HWP leaders were uniformly resolute only in their rejection of the ousted general secretary's request to be permitted to return from Moscow in order to resume participation in Hungarian political life. The last thing that the HWP leadership—or the Hungarian people—needed was for Rákosi to return to Hungary just when they thought that they had got rid of him for good. Neither is there any evidence that HWP leaders made any attempt to rethematize politics. A *sine ira et studio* examination of the resolution entitled "Party Unity for Socialist Democracy" that the HWP Central Directorate adopted on the day following Rákosi's dismissal produces a nearly point-by-point sensation of *déjà vu*: economic policies based on the country's true production capacity and striking the necessary balance between agricultural and industrial development as well as an improvement of conditions of subsistence; guarantees ensuring the sovereignty of state political organs (Parliament, councils) and respect for relevant constitutional provisions; "solidification of socialist legality" through a "vigorous improvement of the operations of state protection organs" and strict compliance with the principle that "guilt cannot be determined based on confession of culpability that lacks other supporting evidence." Taken along with subsequent passages referring to the People's Patriotic Front and the utility of the intelligentsia[50]—specifically the "old intellectuals"—this resolution bears a distinct resemblance to the positions that Imre Nagy advocated in 1953–1954 and for which he was branded a right-wing revisionist and, eventually, an enemy of the party. The resolution contained only one item that diverged from the policies of the excommunicated prime minister—endorsement of the Five Principles of Peaceful Coexistence (*Panchsheel*), which had been published only after Nagy's dismissal.

As has been referred to previously, Hungarians continually concocted jokes and anecdotes referring to the political anomalies in Eastern Europe. The following *bon mot* was among those in circulation at this time:

– What is a revisionist?

– A person who three days earlier voices the same opinion as that declared at the Kremlin and two days earlier does so before they have heard it at the Budapest party headquarters as well.

The Hungarian public regarded the Hungarian Workers' Party Central Directorate resolution with indifference or opposition for two reasons: first, by this time it did not believe even in positions that Imre Nagy had advocated almost word for word just three years previously if they were associated with Ernő Gerő, whom it viewed as Rákosi's alter ego; second, although the HWP leadership had adopted what was essentially the former prime minister's "program," it paradoxically continued to demand that Nagy exercise humiliating public self-criticism before readmitting him to the party. (The wrangling between Nagy and the HWP leadership with regard to his readmission to the party continued until the middle of October, 1956.)

The Ernő Gerő-led Hungarian Workers' Party leadership nevertheless continued to consult the script that Rákosi had left behind, preparing, for example, preliminary studies and operative plans for administrative restructuring that the deposed general secretary had announced that spring just as if nothing had happened in the meantime. As late as the middle of September, second-echelon members of the Secretariat and the Political Committee were busy planning cadre transfers connected to the administrative reorganization in the absence of Ernő Gerő and János Kádár, who were out of the country. Meanwhile, the "class struggle vigilance" that had permeated the system under Rákosi's direction did not seem to be diminishing. One of the many examples of this continued mentality was the HWP leadership's consideration of whether the recently rehabilitated György Aczél, who would play an important role in political affairs over the subsequent decades, was dependable enough to serve as the party secretary of the merged Győr–Vas County, or whether it would be wiser to first send him to the CPSU Political Academy in Moscow for further "development." New party leaders became increasingly less inclined to rule themselves as they jounced down the wheel ruts inherited from the exiled Rákosi.

Making the political police into a scapegoat for the miscarriages of justice and nearly boundless degree of everyday tyranny that characterized the reign of terror was another of Rákosi's legacies. As previously described, the ÁVH was reincorporated into the Ministry of the Interior, where it assumed the role of a Trojan Horse. While the ÁVH was compelled to carry out orders to release many of those unjustly imprisoned during Rákosi's rule, the political police conspired with the public prosecutor's office to ensure that some measure of stigma would be left on the majority of those awaiting rehabilitation. At the same time, the political police took complete control over the Ministry, transforming 9 of its 14 departments into ÁVH "higher units." Moreover, five of the Ministry's seven most powerful officials, including Minister of the Interior László Piros, were high-ranking ÁVH officers. In late 1955 and early 1956, Piros, with authorization from the Hungarian Workers' Party Political Committee, organized this inner circle of ministry leaders into a separate body—the so-called State Protection Council—and began to replace county, municipal and district police chiefs with ÁVH officers. (These positions had not previously belonged to the political police.) This expedited efforts to place "even more reliable" cadres in the aforementioned positions, and progressed so quickly that by June 1956 80 percent of county leaders and 57 percent of municipal district leaders were members of the ÁVH. Thus by the middle of László Piros's mandate, the Ministry of the Interior had essentially been transformed into an ÁVH-controlled State Protection Ministry. (It was for this reason that it was difficult to distinguish the "regular" police from the ÁVH at the time of the 1956 Revolution.)

The Hungarian Workers' Party Political Committee discussed the operations of the State Protection Authority (ÁVH) at almost every one of its meetings following Rákosi's dismissal. Political Committee members gave voice to increasing disapproval and outright condemnation of the "company's" activities, reproach that was also aimed at ÁVH leader and Minister of the Interior László

Piros, who attended committee meetings in his capacity as substitute member of the body. Initially, committee members merely reviewed material decisions related to the issue of rehabilitation, later going so far as to declare in a resolution connected to a proposal sabotaged by Piros that the courts "must deliver verdicts that conform to the truth! [*sic*]" This statement was a clear retroactive assessment of the justice system and the political police that operated under its control. The Political Committee's establishment of an investigative panel to examine the role of the ÁVH in the show trials was an explicit demonstration of the collective mistrust with which it regarded Piros. Most of the panel's report could have hardly surprised Political Committee members, who were already well aware that "high-ranking officers from the Soviet state security apparatus participated in various proceedings" and that many people "were taken into custody by the State Protection Authority based on unverified confessions, conjecture arising from various circumstances or orders from certain members of the party." The report stated that "brutality of such staggering dimensions came to light that it is hard to find words with which to depict them." However, the Political Committee's reception of the report suggests that enumeration of the many atrocities that had taken place was not the body's (only) objective—it also wanted to "strafe" the minister of the interior himself. As a result of the report, the Political Committee initiated proceedings against nearly three dozen people, ten of whom worked directly with Piros in "sensitive" leading positions. The latter were immediately dismissed from their offices, while loyal and competent cadres were appointed to "8–10 key positions" within the ÁVH leadership. When the establishment of the investigative panel was announced, László Piros exclaimed the following among his confidants during a session of the State Protection Council: "We have reached the point where people are all talking at great length about state protection operations. Things are leaking out."[51]

This apparently helped even the public prosecutor's office to see the light. In order to demonstrate that they supported the destalinization process, prosecuting attorneys rejected an increasing amount of investigative material proceeding from the political police on the grounds that it was not suitable evidence for pressing criminal charges. At the same time, the party leadership received an increasing number of complaints from both the national police and the military of past and present ÁVH misconduct. On the one hand, the Hungarian Workers' Party leadership attempted to withdraw from the role of "godfather" directing the ÁVH from the background, acting as if it had not served as the political police's "employer-owner." On the other hand, hitherto allied organizations such as the national police, army and prosecutor's office, recognizing that the ÁVH's position of privilege was weakening, prepared to renounce their comrade-in-arms solidarity with the political police. All of this took place behind closed doors, within the confidential closed circles of the state party system. Amid an erosion of its power and prestige, the party leaders attempted to quietly distance themselves from the political police. From a political perspective, the HWP leadership's hesitation is to a certain degree understandable, since the ÁVH had in essence remained its only "reliable" source of support.

An even greater degree of uncertainty and confusion spread within mid- and lower-level organizations of the Hungarian Workers' Party at this time. This stemmed from the failure of the HWP to issue the long-accustomed "executive decrees" in support of party resolutions during the months in which Ernő Gerő served as general secretary, as well as the reluctance of subordinate party functionaries to act in the absence of leading party officials when the latter were abroad. (György Marosán went to Berlin to "gather information" and then took a vacation in the Thuringian Forest, while Ernő Gerő traveled to the Crimean peninsula and Moscow in order to recover from the rigors associated with his appointment to the post of general secretary, and János Kádár went to Beijing to represent the HWP at the September congress of the Communist Party of China, subsequently meeting up with Gerő in Moscow, from which city they returned to Hungary only during the second week of October.) The disruption of the dictatorship's regular operating procedure returned like a boomerang to strike the entire system that had rigidly suppressed all autonomy and delegated authority. Sensing the impending storm, lower-ranking HWP leaders searched for guidance, but routinely discovered that their superiors were just as uncertain about what to do as they were. Thousands of party cadres were, to quote Jean-Paul Sartre, "condemned to be free," although after nearly a decade of acting solely in accordance with party resolutions and orders from above, they did not know what to do with their sudden "liberty." As the summer of 1956 drew to a close, the more sensitive among these cadres began to grow restless as an intangible feeling of uncertainty gradually permeated the entire ruling order.

Notes

1 György T. Varga, ed., "Jegyzőkönyv a szovjet és a magyar párt- és állami vezetők tárgyalásairól, 1953. június 13–16." [Minutes of the Negotiations between Soviet and Hungarian Party and State Leaders, June 13–16, 1953], *Múltunk* 2–3 (1992): 234–269.

2 The self-critical party resolution recorded these statements as well. See "Az MDP Központi Vezetőségének határozata a párt politikájában elkövetett hibákról és azok kijavításáról" [HWP Central Directorate Resolution on the Mistakes in Party Policy and Their Correction], in Lajos Izsék, ed., *A Magyar Dolgozók Pártjának határozatai, 1948–1956* [Resolutions of the Hungarian Workers' Party, 1948–1956] (Budapest, 1998), pp. 188–206, and Ignác Romsics, ed., *Magyar történeti szöveggyűjtemény, 1914–1999* [Collection of Hungarian Historical Texts], vol. 2 (Budapest, 2000), pp. 69–84.

3 Imre Nagy, *Egy évtized. Válogatott beszédek és írások, 1948–1954* [One Decade: Selected Speeches and Writings, 1948–1954], vol. 2 (Budapest, 1954), pp. 349–376.

4 The prime minister offered a much more detailed description of the contribution of specialists in forming the government program in an earlier conference of fellow agricultural experts held in October 1953. Imre Nagy, "Agrártudósaink és mezőgazdasági szakembereink

feladatai a mezőgazdasági termelés fellendítésében" [The Duties of Our Agronomists and Agricultural Specialists in the Boosting of Agricultural Production], in *ibid.*, pp. 402–428.

5 Mátyás Rákosi, "A Magyar Dolgozók Pártja Központi Vezetősége 1953. júniusi határozatának végrehajtásáért" [For the Implementation of the June 1953 Resolution of the Hungarian Workers' Party Central Directorate]. Speech to Budapest party activists held on July 11, 1953, in Mátyás Rákosi, *Válogatott beszédek és cikkek* [Selected Speeches and Articles] (Budapest, 1955), pp. 564–581.

6 József Vonyó, "A pártállam politikai intézményrendszere Magyarországon" [The Political Institutional System of the Party State in Hungary], in idem, ed., *Az ötvenes évek Magyarországa játékfilmeken* [1950s Hungary in Feature Films] (Pécs, 2004), pp. 7–15 and appendices I–IV. The author would like to thank József Vonyó for permission to use his copyrighted organizational table. See also György T. Varga, "Adalékok és szempontok az MDP hatalmi helyzetéhez" [Additional Data and Considerations Regarding the HWP's Power Status], *Múltunk* 2 (1998): 175–182.

7 György T. Varga and István Szakadát, "Íme, a nómenklatúrák!" [Here Are the Nomenklaturas!], *Társadalmi Szemle* 3 (1992): 73–95; István Szakadát, "A káderforgó. A hatásköri listák elemzése" [The Cadre Catcher. Analysis of "Sphere of Authority" Lists], *Társadalmi Szemle* 8–9 (1992): 97–120; Tibor Huszár, *Az elittől a nómenklatúráig. Az intézményesített káderpolitika kialakulása Magyarországon, 1945–1989* [From the Elite to the Nomenklatura. The Formation of Institutionalized Cadre Policy in Hungary 1945–1989] (Budapest, 2007); György Gyarmati, "A káderrendszer és a rendszer kádere" [The Cadre System and the System's Cadre], *Valóság* 2 (1991): 51–63.

8 The term "cult of personality" derived from the period and still in use today does not fully describe the essence of the "Rákosi phenomenon." The cult of personality is a developing or established system that attempts to portray the "superiority over the common man" and charismatic character of the number one person in every authoritarian regime. Mátyás Rákosi, on the other hand, repeatedly placed himself in a position of singularity above power or social norms of any type—even following his stern reprimand in Moscow in 1953! The Hungarian Workers' Party general secretary did this

even though his authority could be calibrated at only a Lilliputian fraction of Stalin's or that of the Kremlin's post-Stalinist Gullivers.

9 Magdolna Baráth, ed., *Szovjet nagykövetі iratok Magyarországról, 1953–1956. Kiszeljov és Andropov titkos jelentései* [Soviet Ambassadorial Documents Regarding Hungary, 1953–1956. Secret Communiqués from Kiselyov and Andropov] (Budapest, 2002), p. 121.

10 János M. Rainer, *Nagy Imre, 1953–1958. Politikai életrajz II* [Imre Nagy, 1953–1958. Political Biography II] (Budapest, 1999), p. 37.

11 *A Magyar Dolgozók Pártja III. kongresszusának jegyzőkönyve* [The Official Minutes of the Third Congress of the Hungarian Workers' Party] (Budapest, 1954), pp. 45–46.

12 *Ibid.*, pp. 47–48. One can only speculate that it was for this reason—in order to avoid the prospect of confronting himself—that Rákosi neglected to include this address in the 1955 collection of speeches and articles that included dozens of much more particular, vacuous selections. Mátyás Rákosi, *Válogatott beszédek és cikkek. Negyedik, bővített kiadás* [Selected Speeches and Articles. Fourth, Expanded, Version] (Budapest, 1955).

13 Nagy, *Egy évtized. Válogatott beszédek és írások, 1948–1954*, II, pp. 480–575.

14 For more detailed information regarding the formation of Imre Nagy's people's front concept and its reception—and rejection—in the pre-congress Political Committee, see Rainer, *Nagy Imre, 1953–1958. Politikai életrajz II*, pp. 47–49, 56–57.

15 Bálint Szabó, *Az "ötvenes évek"* [The "1950s"] (Budapest, 1986), p. 170.

16 János M. Rainer and Károly Urbán, "'Konzultációk.' Dokumentumok a magyar és a szovjet pártvezetők két moszkvai találkozójáról, 1954–1955-ben" ["Consultations." Documents Regarding the Two Moscow Meetings of Hungarian and Soviet Party Leaders in 1954–1955], *Múltunk* 4 (1992): 138.

17 Rainer, *Nagy Imre, 1953–1958. Politikai életrajz II*, pp. 31–32, p. 73.

18 Rákosi and his supporters from the economic policy party apparatus (István Friss and Béla Szalai) attempted to utilize statistical data to prove that production and productivity had declined in several domains. The implicit bias in their presentation of the data was obviously the fact that every sudden change entails difficulties and "transformational deficit," especially when considering the anarchic

production structure of the previous "campaign socialism" described in earlier chapters.

19 Imre Nagy's speech at the Patriotic People's Front Congress, in Lajos Péter Kovács and József Sipos, *A Nagy Imre vonal* [The Imre Nagy Course] (Budapest, 1989), p. 290.

20 Rainer, *Nagy Imre, 1953–1958. Politikai életrajz II*, pp. 81–95.

21 Ibolya Horváth, Pál Solt *et al.*, *Iratok az igazságszolgáltatás történetéhez* [Documents on the History of the Judicial Administration], vol. 1 (Budapest, 1992), p. 505.

22 Cf. Bálint Szabó, ed., *A szocializmus útján. A népi demokratikus átalakulás és a szocializmus építésének kronológiája, 1944–1980* [On the Path towards Socialism. Chronology of the People's Democratic Transformation and the Building of Socialism, 1944–1980] (Budapest, 1982), pp. 513–516, and idem, *Az "ötvenes évek"*, p. 278.

23 Cf. József Bölöni, *Magyarország kormányai, 1848–1992* [Hungary's Governments, 1848–1992] (Budapest, 1992), pp. 139, 164, and András Nyírő, *Segédkönyv a Politikai Bizottság tanulmányozásához* [Reference Book for the Study of the Political Committee] (Budapest, 1989), p. 18.

24 Rainer, *Nagy Imre, 1953–1958. Politikai életrajz II*, pp. 156–157, and Horváth, Solt *et al.*, eds., *Iratok az igazságszolgáltatás történetéhez*, vol. 1, p. 400.

25 Baráth, ed., *Szovjet nagyköveti iratok Magyarországról, 1953–1956*, p. 139, and Rainer, *Nagy Imre, 1953–1958. Politikai életrajz II*, p. 122.

26 In the period from January to March and in May 1955, the HWP Political Committee repeatedly dealt with the issue of reducing the size of the political apparatus, which had grown by two and a half times since 1949. Hungarian National Archives, HWP-HSWP documents, archive group 276, 53/212–217 and 222 and 229.

27 Imre Nagy's biographer gives consideration to both archival sources regarding the dismissed prime minister's ÁVH surveillance, which was aimed at collecting compromising evidence against him for a possible trial, and to the instances in which this was exposed already at the time in question. Rainer, *Nagy Imre, 1953–1958. Politikai életrajz II*, pp. 157–158, 163–164, 180–181, 207–209.

28 Rainer and Urbán, "'Konzultációk'. Dokumentumok a magyar és a szovjet pártvezetők két moszkvai találkozójáról, 1954–1955-ben," p. 138.

29 Árpád Pünkösti, *Rákosi bukása, száműzetése és halála* [Rákosi's Downfall, Exile and Death] (Budapest, 2001), pp. 320–321. The head of the ÁVH's counter-"internal reaction" department, Sándor Rajnai, estimated in a report drawn up at around this time that there were 1,100 "writers, critics and copy editors" and 2,050 "journalists and publishers" working in Hungary. György Gyarmati and Katalin S. Varga, eds., *A Belügyminisztérium Kollégiumának ülései, 1953–1956* [Meetings of the Ministry of the Interior Council, 1953–1956], vol. 2, compiled by Erzsébet Kajári (Budapest, 2005), p. 598.

30 See the following: János M. Rainer, *Az író helye. Viták a magyar irodalmi sajtóban, 1953–1956* [The Writer's Place. Debates in the Hungarian Literary Press, 1953–1956] (Budapest, 1990); Éva Standeisky, *Gúzsba kötve. A kulturális elit és a hatalom* [Hamstrung. The Cultural Elite and the Political Power] (Budapest, 2005), particularly the chapters entitled "Hitviták. Az írók és az 1953-as 'új szakasz'" [Debates on Faith. Writers and the 1953 New Course], pp. 206–228, and "Déry Tibor és Nagy Imre" [Tibor Déry and Imre Nagy], pp. 351–358; idem, *Írók lázadása. 1956-os írószövetségi jegyzőkönyvek* [The Writers' Rebellion. Minutes of the 1956 Meetings of the Writers' Union] (Budapest, 1990).

31 Minutes of the November 9–12, 1955, session of the HWP Central Directorate (Hungarian National Archives, HWP-HSWP documents, archive group 276, 53/51).

32 Rainer, *Nagy Imre, 1953–1958. Politikai életrajz II*, p. 174. Rainer also analyzed contemporaneous documents included in the collection: Imre Nagy, *A magyar nép védelmében* [In Defense of the Hungarian People], vol. 2 (n.p., 1957), pp. 143–184.

33 Gábor Hanák, ed., "Beszéd a Központi Ellenőrző Bizottság előtt. 1956. február 6" [Speech before the Central Supervisory Committee, February 6, 1956], *Historia* (1990): 27–29. More passages of Losonczy's speech are quoted and given contextual analysis in the following work: György Köver, *Losonczy Géza, 1917–1957* [Géza Losonczy, 1917–1957] (Budapest, 1998), pp. 242–245.

34 Nagy's biographer offered a detailed analysis of these essays, some of which are contained in Nagy, *A magyar nép védelmében*. See Rainer, *Nagy Imre, 1953–1958. Politikai életrajz II*, pp. 143–184.

35 Miklós Molnár, *Egy vereség diadala* [The Triumph of a Defeat] (Paris and New Jersey, 1988), p. 55.

36 The two resolutions are contained in the following work: Margit Balogh and Jenő Gergely, *Állam, egyház, vallásgyakorlás Magyarországon, 1790–2005* [State, Church and the Exercise of Religion in Hungary, 1790–2005] , vol. 2 (Budapest, 2005), pp. 970–975.

37 Gyarmati and Varga, eds., *A Belügyminisztérium Kollégiumának ülései, 1953–1956*, vol. 2, pp. 902–907.

38 *Ibid.*, p. 903. Also see Gábor Bánkuti, *A Rend és a Szerv, 1953–1956. A jezsuita rend "átfogásának" kísérlete* [The Order and the Organ, 1953–1956. The Attempt to "Seize" the Jesuit Order] (Pécs, 2008).

39 For information regarding the reception of Khrushchev's secret speech in the Soviet Union, see Roy Medvegyev, *Hruscsov. Politikai életrajz* [Khrushchev. Political Biography] (Budapest, 1989), pp. 106–129.

40 László Borhi, *Magyarország a hidegháborúban. A Szovjetunió és az Egyesült Államok között, 1945–1956* [Hungary in the Cold War. Between the Soviet Union and the United States, 1945–1956] (Budapest, 2005), pp. 292–293.

41 Gyarmati and Varga, eds., *A Belügyminisztérium Kollégiumának ülései, 1953–1956*, vol. 2, pp. 904 and 910.

42 Aleksandr S. Stikalin, "A szovjet nagykövetség és az MDP-n belüli harc, 1956 tavaszán—kora őszén" [The Soviet Embassy and the Struggle within the HWP between the Spring and Autumn of 1956], *Múltunk* 2 (1998): 23–49, and Baráth, ed., *Szovjet nagyköveti iratok Magyarországról, 1953–1956*, pp. 269–306. In order to protect himself, Rákosi was preparing to expose János Kádár's role in the Rajk affair, although since Rákosi himself later had him imprisoned, Kádár's exposure was made relative in comparison to that of Farkas, who had also served as the HWP general secretary's "accomplice." Andropov, who had strongly objected to the procedures initiated against Farkas, informed Moscow of Rákosi's intention to implicate Kádár without attaching commentary of any sort. *Ibid.*, pp. 277–278.

43 Titles contained in edited volumes regarding meetings of the Petőfi Circle indicate the following to have been the topics of organizational meetings: I. Two Economic Debates; II. Philosophers' Debate; III. Historians' Debate; IV. Partisan Meeting and Press Debate; V. Two

Economic Policy Debates; VI. Educators' Debate; VII. Industrial Designers' Debate—Physicians' Debate. Volumes I–III were published in the *Politikatudományi Füzetek* [Political Sciences Notebooks] (Budapest, 1989–1990), while volumes IV–VII were published by the Institute for the History of the 1956 Revolution, between 1991 and 1993.

44 András B. Hegedűs, "Petőfi Kör—a reformmozgalom fóruma" [Petőfi Circle—The Forum of the Reform Movement], in András B. Hegedűs and János Rainer, eds., *A Petőfi Kör vitái. I* [Debates of the Petőfi Circle, I] (Budapest, 1989), p. 21.

45 Mária Ember pronounced the quoted words outside the June 27 forum of the Petőfi Circle. Mrs. Ember was the wife of leading Petőfi Circle figure András B. Hegedűs and in 1956 served as a reporter for the daily newspaper *Magyar Nemzet*, where she worked with Géza Losonczy, a member of Imre Nagy's inner circle. Although it is not known where Mrs. Ember made this statement, KGB Chairman Ivan Serov quoted it in his July 26, 1956, report to the CPSU Presidium as information derived from the chief Soviet advisor working at Hungary's Ministry of the Interior. In V. Szereda and A. Stikalin, *Hiányzó lapok 1956 történetéből. Dokumentumok a volt SZKP KB levéltárából* [Missing Pages from the History of 1956. Documents from the Former Archives of the CPSU Central Committee] (Budapest, 1993), pp. 69–70. An essentially identical, although stylistically divergent, translation of this quote is contained in the following work: Éva Gál, András B. Hegedűs, György Litván and János M. Rainer, eds., *Jelcin-dosszié. Szovjet dokumentumok 1956-ról* [Yeltsin Dossier. Soviet Documents about 1956] (Budapest, 1993), pp. 29–30.

46 Gábor Péter's submission to the HWP Party Committee (July 10, 1956), in Gábor Koltay and Péter Bródy, eds., *El nem égett dokumentumok* [Unburned Documents] (Budapest, 1990), pp. 13–29.

47 Veljko Mićunović, *Tito követe voltam. Moszkva, 1956–1968* [I Was Tito's Envoy. Moscow, 1956–1968] (Budapest, 1990), pp. 86–88.

48 Yuri Andropov's August 30, 1956, letter to the CPSU Central Committee Presidium, in Gál, Hegedűs, Litván and Rainer, eds., *Jelcin dosszié*, pp. 32, 35–36.

49 See V. Astafyev's memorandum regarding his August 28, 1956, discussion with Ernő Gerő, in Baráth, ed., *Szovjet nagyköveti iratok*

Magyarországról, 1953–1956, p. 340, and Y. Andropov's previously cited August 30, 1956, letter to the CPSU Presidium, in Gál, Hegedűs, Litván and Rainer, eds., *Jelcin-dosszié*, pp. 32–332.

50 "Party Unity for Socialist Democracy." Originally published in the July 23, 1956, issue of the HWP newspaper *Szabad Nép.* Also see Lajos Izsák, editor-in-chief, *A Magyar Dolgozók Pártja határozatai, 1948–1956* [Hungarian Workers' Party Resolutions, 1948–1956] (Budapest, 1998), pp. 439–460.

51 György Gyarmati, "A politikai rendőrség (ÁVH) útja 1956-hoz" [The Path of the Political Police (ÁVH) to 1956], in Imre Okváth, ed., *ÁVH—politika—1956* [ÁVH—Politics—1956] (Budapest, 2007), pp. 69–95.

VI. TORRID COLD WAR AUTUMN. THE REVOLUTION IN HUNGARY, 1956

1. The Reform Aspirations of the Literati and Students

Public life became livelier in September 1956 following the political doldrums of the summer vacation period. The Petőfi Circle resumed its debate evenings on September 19, when it rehabilitated the National Alliance of People's Colleges after the Hungarian Workers' Party's hasty party resolution. This would have been an important development if the aforementioned party resolution had proposed reviving the elite "professional educational system of the former Eötvös College... [and its] positive performance."[1] This, however, did not occur, primarily because the alliance's legion of anti-Stalinist "old boys," many of whom had in the previous decade been ostracized and sometimes even imprisoned, understandably focused on gaining restitution.[2] Similarly, the Hungarian Writers' Union (*Magyar Írók Szövetsége*) voted at its September 17 general assembly to remove from the organization's presidium writers who had compromised themselves irrevocably during the Rákosi era, replacing them with previously disregarded or censured authors in spite of the "prior instructions" contained in the HWP Political Committee's resolution. The dismissal of these presidium members was not surprising in the light of the fact that Mátyás Rákosi had been removed as party general secretary just two months previously. The primary cause of excitement at the Writers' Union general assembly was the fact that several of those present had posed questions regarding Imre Nagy's possible rehabilitation, remarks that elicited explicit approval from the audience, thus transforming the meeting into a veritable demonstration of sympathy for the ousted former prime minister.

Whether the events described above were really so significant as to "leave a mark on history," or simply became magnified in importance retroactively is another question. Do incidents of relatively minor consequence acquire an excessive degree of historical significance when the chronicler engages in a teleological search for the combustible material and "fuses" that set off a later explosion? The specific character of the period and system—in the present case the impact that the process of destalinization that began in the summer of 1956, notably Rákosi's dismissal, exercised on Hungarian society and relations between Budapest and Moscow—was also a factor.

An examination of developments that occurred at this time can be approached from three perspectives. The first is a methodical analysis taking into account the personal experiences of people who lived through the period. János Kornai has produced a model of the contradictions implicit in the process of destalinization, indicating the existence of many discrepancies between theoretical considerations and their practical application.

> The system in its classical form constitutes a coherent whole… Reform destroys the coherence of the classical system, although it is unable to establish a substitute… People begin to ponder the cause of the many negative phenomena. The road to comprehension is a long one. In its first stage, one examines individuals in search of the problem. During this phase Stalin and all the little Stalins are qualified as villains who bear responsibility for every difficulty. In the second stage, not only are certain individuals identified as the source of trouble, but an unwisely chosen political system is as well. Later, not even this provides an explanation. Socialism is a good system, although the form of socialism that has been implemented is defective.[3]

During the autumn of 1956, Hungarian society had begun to move from the first to the second stage of this model.

Two everyday factors supplemented the process described above. The first was the public discourse and disposition that prevailed in Hungary, particularly Budapest, which viewed Ernő Gerő's replacement of Rákosi as the general secretary of the Hungarian Workers' Party as a merely provisional measure. A journal kept in 1956 from the perspective of "the man on the street" repeatedly indicates that almost everybody believed that Gerő's leadership over the party was merely temporary.[4] The second was the so-called "Kucsera effect" referring to the caricature of a party functionary whose incompetence is surpassed only by his arrogance.[5] The effect is compatible with the logic of Kornai's aforementioned model in its attempt to find scapegoats for problems, specifically to identify and excoriate the puppets of Rákosi at the lower levels of the institutional hierarchy. There appears, however, to have been further impulses at work as well in this instance: an advanced variation of "the emperor's new clothes" phenomenon in which the subject smiles at the sovereign, ridicules him and begins to laugh heartily, both at the object of derision and at his own irreverence—at the fact that he dares to laugh at all. Rákosi's deposition and exile, as well as the inability of his underlings who remained in place to come up with a plausible "script" of any sort regarding what was to come next, elicited an amorphous feeling of occasionally euphoric freedom. More and more members of Hungarian society, which had been frightened into mute submission for an entire decade, now found that they could openly broach any issue, even with critical or reproachful intensity, without being subjected to the formerly routine retribution.

Under the circumstances described above, the proper reburial of the more prominent victims of the show trials became imperative, a circumstance that evidently aroused the apprehension of the party leadership. Hungarian Workers' Party officials initially wrangled over the degree of publicity to be afforded the funeral ceremony, and then over whether or not it would be indecorous for the ÁVH to provide security for the event. Eventually they decided to delegate the task of maintaining order at the funeral to the army, although many plainclothes political police officers and informants were also deployed among the crowd. On October 6, the day of martyrs,[6] more than 350,000 people gathered in spite of the gloomy, damp weather to pay their last respects to László Rajk, Tibor Szőnyi, András Szalai and General György Pálffy. Official government and party representatives, such as Antal Apró, Károly Janza, Ferenc Münnich and László Orbán, pronounced flowery *mea culpa* at the funeral, although a eulogy from a survivor of the show trials, Béla Szász, was much more in tune with the sentiments and aspirations of the hundreds of thousands of mourners assembled around the catafalque:

> Fabricated charges and the gallows took László Rajk to an unmarked grave seven years ago, although today his death stands as a warning sign, because when hundreds of thousands of people file past the coffins, they are not only paying final tribute to the victims, but bearing witness to their passionate desire, their uncompromising determination to lay an era to rest, to forever bury tyranny and the moral dead of a shameful day, to render harmless the law of the fist and the Hungarian disciples of the cult of personality.[7]

The decision to include Political Committee doyen Antal Apró—who had been a member of the powerful inner party body when the Hungarian Workers' Party leadership decided to send Rajk and his associates to the gallows in 1949—in the official delegation lacked political discernment and tact. Only the absence of leading party figures was more conspicuous than Apró's "elephant in the living room" appearance at the funeral. János Kádár traveled to China in September to represent the HWP at the Chinese Communist Party congress before beginning a three-week visit to the Soviet Union, while Ernő Gerő went on vacation to the Crimea at this same time. The timing of their trips was not without reason: both of them returned to Budapest on October 7, the day after (!) the reburial of Rajk and his associates.

Reports of the reburial ceremony held at the Kerepesi Cemetery in Budapest speculated that the "silent" demonstration of those in attendance reflected a high degree of public tension. Some subsequent accounts of the event contemplated the following question: why did the upheaval break out not then, but just two weeks later? Among those who were monitoring the seismography of public sentiment at the time, it was not only Pius Zimándi who remarked as follows: "Political unrest is growing; public discontent is going to erupt in some form this autumn. It became evident that the pace of events was accelerating. However, there was probably nobody who could have predicted precisely when and under what circumstances the eruption would take place."[8] The funeral of the most renowned victims of the show trials was, in truth, surrounded by "the sound of silence." During a ceremony held on the evening of October 6 at the Batthyány eternal flame commemorating the aforementioned martyrs of 1849, students from the Loránd Eötvös University Faculty of Arts and the University of Fine Arts in Budapest began to chant the slogan that was to spread quickly throughout the city: "We won't back down, while Stalinism's still around!" (*Nem állunk meg félúton, sztálinizmus pusztuljon!*)[9]

The number of alternative forums and the variety of themes that they addressed continued to expand within this environment. The reason for this was that the post-Rákosi government and party leadership still had not come up with the desired plan to revamp the system. One of the manifestations of public dissatisfaction with this lack of official action to repair the system was the series of writer-reader gatherings that took place following the "rebellious" general assembly of the Writers' Union, after citizens in various cities in Hungary requested that the organization call meetings to examine various issues whose media coverage had been inadequate. At the very outset of an October 16 meeting in the city of Győr, the playwright Gyula Háy told the 1,000-member audience that there were more urgent questions on the evening's agenda than literature, a statement that opened the floodgates for an outpouring of popular opinion on current domestic issues, which included the stationing of Soviet troops in Hungary, the absence of autonomy in domestic and foreign affairs, the neglect of national tradition, amends for the injustices and judicial murders that had been committed during the Rákosi era, including the rehabilitation of Cardinal József Mindszenty, the export of uranium ore to the Soviet Union, and the need to hold new elections.[10] The same thing occurred at Writers' Union meetings held in other cities, although the issues discussed at them varied to some degree: in Debrecen and Kaposvár, for example, agrarian problems represented one of the major items on the agenda. Debate societies and "reform clubs" patterned after Budapest's Petőfi Circle began to form in rapid succession throughout Hungary, primarily in university towns. Such organizations usually named themselves after famous Hungarian progressive patriots: those in Pécs and Győr were also called the Petőfi Circle, while those in Debrecen and Eger took the name Kossuth Circle, that in Veszprém was called Batsányi Circle and that in Kaposvár took the name Zrínyi Circle. By this time, even the local Hungarian Workers' Party committee in Miskolc had begun to refer to the Avas coffee house—the favorite hangout of the city's artists, writers and journalists—as the Pilvax café.[11] In the words of István Bibó, "small circles of freedom" had begun to thematize public life not only in Budapest, but in other larger cities throughout Hungary as well.

The unrest at universities and colleges in Hungary began with the politically infused reform of the country's post-secondary curriculum in which increased emphasis was placed on functional, career-oriented subjects at the expense of Stalinism-imbued Marxist ideology, the Russian language and systematic Cold War military training. Discourse at institutions of higher education in Hungary initially focused on the issues of curricular reform and student welfare, such as dormitory conditions and cafeteria food, before quickly expanding to encompass topical political issues as well. This ferment is reflected in the rapidly evolving succession of student reform programs and student council resolutions that emerged at this time, proposals that almost always made a clear distinction between "internal" institutional reform and "external" desiderata related to domestic politics.[12]

Following the reburial of László Rajk and his associates, Ernő Gerő and János Kádár returned to Budapest from the Soviet Union "for a short visit" before moving on to Belgrade in the middle of October at the head of a large official delegation, which included Prime Minister András Hegedüs. More than a year after the Soviet Union had initiated the process of rapprochement with Yugoslavia, Hungarian Workers' Party leaders felt that they could no longer postpone normalization of bilateral party and state relations with Hungary's southern neighbor, although had they been truly aware of the rising degree of unrest in the country, they may have thought it wiser to further delay their visit. During the short interval of time that they spent in Hungary, the helmsmen of the HWP made only one noteworthy decision, restoring Imre Nagy's party membership in an attempt to satisfy the recalcitrant members and eliminate what they believed to be the source of popular discontent. After resolving this issue, was there any good reason for Hungary's main decision-makers not to go through with their planned visit with Josip Broz Tito?

On October 16, 1956, the day following the departure of the Hungarian party and government delegation for Belgrade, the monolithic red curtain of the Communist Party dictatorship started to tear in Szeged, the largest city in southern Hungary. "On October 16, 1956, we, the students of the Szeged University of Medical Sciences, the Szeged College of Education and the Szeged School of Music Education, founded our own university youth organization, the Unified Alliance of Hungarian University and College Students (known in its Hungarian acronymic form as MEFESZ). Our goal is to restore freedom of thought and to cast off the intellectual yoke that Stalin and Rákosi have placed upon us." And since, according to the announcement, the Communist Party's youth organization (known as DISZ in its Hungarian acronymic form) "has lost the confidence of young people… in the spirit of the 20th Party Congress we have decided to establish a new unified youth organization that is completely unaffiliated with DISZ."[13] According to a monographer examining the question, this "act was close to revolution, since it founded an independent organization in a dictatorship in which nothing could be independent of the party."[14] Although its reference to the 20th Congress of the Communist Party of the Soviet Union clearly indicates that the manifesto had not transcended the bounds of the Communist paradigm, it does fit in the "close to revolution" category when viewed according to Raymond Aron's concept of so-called anti-totalitarian revolution.[15] Two days later, on October 18, MEFESZ published a resolution that tightly linked the desired reform of the system to the restoration of national sovereignty:

1. We adhere to our progressive national traditions:
a. We want to celebrate March 15, October 6 and King Stephen's day [August 20, which had commemorated the 1949 Communist constitution in previous years] in an appropriate manner;
b. Let the midday bells sound on the radio in commemoration of Hunyadi's [János Hunyadi's] world-renowned victory;
c. Let the Kossuth Coat-of-Arms be our national symbol again!
2. Bring those who murdered László Rajk—Mihály Farkas, Mátyás Rákosi and their accomplices—to justice in a public trial!
3. We want true and sincere friendship with the Soviet Union! In the interests of this ambition:
a. Withdraw foreign military forces from Hungarian territory!
b. Return our prisoners of war!
c. National economic policy! Let our commercial life stand upon the principle of equality in every regard![16]

The foundation of a sociopolitical organization such as this was only worthwhile, as the proclamation indicates, if it was "of national magnitude." Therefore several student delegations traveled from Szeged to other universities in Hungary to encourage their peers to support the initiative. The enthusiasm with which these delegations were received is not surprising in the light of the fact that similar unrest prevailed among students at universities and colleges throughout the country—it just happened that those in Szeged were the first to come up with the mode and form of expressing their demands.[17] Within just a few days, between October 19 and 21, students at every university in Hungary—Debrecen, Miskolc,

Budapest, Veszprém, Sopron and Pécs—had issued summons, declarations, demands and proclamations similar in tone and content to that published in Szeged.

The destalinization process progressed elsewhere in the socialist camp as well during the Hungarian Workers' Party leadership's visit to Yugoslavia. On October 18, CPSU General Secretary Nikita Khrushchev made an unscheduled visit to Poland, where the "national communist" Władysław Gomułka had been appointed to serve as the leader of the Polish Communist Party in spite of Moscow's reservations. Following heated negotiations behind closed doors, Soviet and Polish party leaders struck a deal according to which Poland would remain under the control of the Polish United Workers' Party and would continue to honor its obligations as a member of the Eastern Bloc alliance, while in return the Soviets would abide by the principle of inter-state equality. As an initial gesture, the Soviet Union recalled Marshal Konstantin Rokossovskiy, who had served as Poland's minister of defense as "Stalin's unsolicited gift" since the late 1940s.

Although the domestic press and radio (there was still no television in Hungary at that time) offered only significantly belated and ideologically selective reports on the developments in Poland, even this fragmentary information served to accelerate the pace of events. On October 22, there were several initiatives in Hungary to "establish contacts with representatives of Polish youth" and organize mass demonstrations to express solidarity with the changes that had taken place in Poland. Students in all the aforementioned university cities other than Budapest prepared the newest versions of their political demands on this same date, when university departmental and administrative leaders at the University of Szeged conducted negotiations with student representatives, while city council, Hungarian Workers' Party and DISZ officials joined those from the university in Sopron in negotiations that took place at that institution's student parliament. In Miskolc, university students had already concluded an alliance with young workers from the city's factories and begun talks with the local municipal and county leadership. The same situation prevailed at universities and colleges in Budapest, where the physical proximity of these institutions of higher education facilitated communication between students from various departments and dormitories. Lists of student demands in Budapest expanded and changed from assembly to assembly, frequently adopting a more radical tone by the time that earlier versions had been published in university newspapers or distributed in lithographed leaflets. By the time that the Ernő Gerő-led party and government delegation had returned from Belgrade to Budapest on the morning of October 23, convening at a meeting of the HWP Political Committee in order to discuss the visit to Yugoslavia as well as the main domestic developments that had taken place over the previous week, several thousand students had already departed in orderly ranks from the campus of the University of Debrecen towards the city center bearing an *approved, joint manifesto* that they intended to present to state and party leaders at scheduled talks. (Local citizens and factory representatives joined the students as they proceeded towards the inner city of Debrecen at around 11 a.m.)

At this juncture when the unrest in Hungary was on the brink of eruption, it would be worthwhile to examine some of the factors that contributed to the erosion of the system and bore a significant impact on subsequent events. The totally centralized, rigid character of the Communist dictatorship rendered it unable to tolerate or pragmatically manage alternatives of any type. Since, for reasons previously described, the party was no longer able to resort to the use of brute force, its vertical hierarchical structure collapsed. According to a confidential report prepared for Hungarian Workers' Party leaders on October 22, "A portion of the functionaries are incapable. They do not dare venture out among the masses, because they cannot answer their questions."[18] Regime officials were simply unable to cope with the horizontal "base organizational" activity that the foundation of MEFESZ had initiated within the student movement. The national student "network" was established in under a week, producing nearly identical "fragmentary political programs" in the form of summons and manifestos. In another radical change, the "social parliament" of the Petőfi Circle (re)activated in the spring of 1956 represented an increasingly outspoken forum for debate, but no more. The primary objective—Rákosi's removal from power—had been the product of political combinations beyond their control and an awkwardly coordinated joint measure between mutually suspicious party leaders in Budapest and Moscow. The new university and college student movement that emerged in the autumn, on the other hand, managed to establish an alternative political platform with a supporting organizational foundation in just one week. This, of course, profited from the moral capital that the sociopolitical civil courage that had begun to manifest itself in the spring of 1956 had generated, just as it had harnessed the bitterness stemming from the oppression and persecution that had occurred during the previous decade's reign of terror, suing for compensation and "non-material damages" on behalf of the victims.

The following are the 16 points that students from the Budapest Technical University issued on October 22, 1956. They reflect the desiderata that students at universities throughout the country disseminated at this time, diverging only in their compositional form. The "enough is enough" mentality that prevailed in Hungary at this time did not evolve in Budapest and ripple outwards in an ever-greater radius: it emerged uniformly throughout the country at the same time, not only in the capital city and the aforementioned university towns, such as Szeged, Debrecen, Miskolc, Pécs, Veszprém and Sopron, but in the villages and rural areas as well.

1. We demand the immediate evacuation of all Soviet troops, in conformity with the provisions of the Peace Treaty.
2. We demand the election by secret ballot of all Party members from top to bottom, and of new officers for the lower, middle and upper echelons of the Hungarian Workers' Party. These officers shall convene a Party Congress as early as possible in order to elect a Central Committee.
3. A new government must be constituted under the direction of Imre Nagy: all criminal leaders of the Stalin–Rákosi era must be immediately dismissed.

4. We demand a public inquiry into the criminal activities of Mihály Farkas and his accomplices. Mátyás Rákosi, who is the person most responsible for crimes of the recent past as well as for our country's ruin, must be returned to Hungary for trial before a people's tribunal.
5. We demand that general elections by universal, secret ballot be held throughout the country to elect a new National Assembly, with all political parties participating. We demand that the right of workers to strike be recognized.
6. We demand revision and readjustment of Hungarian–Soviet and Hungarian–Yugoslav relations in the domains of politics, economics and cultural affairs, on a basis of complete political and economic equality and of non-interference in the internal affairs of one by the other.
7. We demand the complete reorganization of Hungary's economic life under the direction of specialists. The entire economic system, based on a system of planning, must be reexamined in the light of conditions in Hungary and in the vital interests of the Hungarian people.
8. Our foreign trade agreements and the exact total of reparations that can never be paid must be made public. We demand to be precisely informed of the uranium deposits in our country, on their exploitation and on the concessions to the Russians in this area. We demand that Hungary have the right to sell its uranium freely at world market prices to obtain hard currency.
9. We demand complete revision of the norms operating in industry and an immediate and radical adjustment of salaries in accordance with the just requirements of workers and intellectuals. We demand a minimum living wage for workers.
10. We demand that the system of distribution be organized on a new basis and that agricultural products be utilized in a rational manner. We demand equality of treatment for individual farms.
11. We demand reviews by independent tribunals of all political and economic trials as well as the release and rehabilitation of the

innocent. We demand the immediate repatriation of prisoners of war (from World War II) and of civilian deportees to the Soviet Union, including prisoners sentenced outside Hungary.

12. We demand complete recognition of freedom of opinion and of expression, of freedom of the press and of radio, as well as the creation of a daily newspaper for the MEFESZ organization (Unified Alliance of Hungarian University and College Students).
13. We demand that the statue of Stalin, a symbol of Stalinist tyranny and political oppression, be removed as quickly as possible and be replaced by a monument in memory of the martyred freedom fighters of 1848–1849.
14. We demand the replacement of emblems foreign to the Hungarian people by the old Hungarian Kossuth Coat-of-Arms. We demand new uniforms for the army, which conform to our national traditions. We demand that March 15 be declared a national holiday and October 6 a day of national mourning on which schools will be closed.
15. The students of the Technological University of Budapest declare unanimously their solidarity with the workers and students of Warsaw and Poland in their movement towards national independence.
16. The students of the Technological University of Budapest will organize as rapidly as possible local branches of MEFESZ, and they have decided to convene in Budapest on Saturday, October 27, a Youth Parliament at which all the nation's youth shall be represented by their delegates.[19]

2. The Country Provoked into a Fight for Freedom

The government and party delegation that returned from Yugoslavia on October 23 was confronted with the developments described above, reacting to them in a manner that reflected incomprehension, rigid rejection and panic-stricken confusion. Initially they had the minister of the interior and ÁVH chief László Piros prohibit the planned student demonstration, then an hour and a half later they commanded him to issue an announcement permitting the event. (The two members of the supreme leadership who were most inclined to panic, József Révai and György Marosán, believed that they could deter those planning to take part in the demonstration by "leaking" news that they would issue the order to shoot.) Students were not only incensed that Hungarian Radio officials had refused to broadcast their demands, primarily due to the stipulation that Soviet troops leave the country, but were angry that the high leadership was not willing to meet with them. The attitude of party leaders was as follows: "How did these rag-tag students, after defecting from the legitimate institutional system of the workers' state, come to think of themselves as potential negotiating partners with us, hardened veterans of the workers' movement and the designated leaders of the country?" The Hungarian Workers' Party leadership met continually throughout the day of October 22, although it believed preliminary debate regarding Ernő Gerő's evening radio address on the party and government delegation's visit to Yugoslavia to be more important than any attempt to assuage the domestic unrest that had built up in Hungary.

Amid these circumstances, the student demonstration, which was strikingly disciplined until it reached the common meeting point, became a self-propelled, autonomous mechanism. Students from the Pest side of the capital city assembled at the statue of the Hungarian national poet Sándor Petőfi, while their peers on the Buda side departed from the square in front of the Technical University towards their designated meeting point: the statue of the Polish military commander Józef Bem, who had served as a general in the Hungarian army during the Revolution of 1848–1849. (Hungarians considered both Petőfi and Bem to be heroes of the Revolution, while Bem was also viewed as a symbolic representative of Hungarian–Polish friendship.) The demands made in October 1956, both explicit and implicit, resembled those contained in the "What Does the Hungarian Nation Want?" program issued at the beginning of the 1848 Revolution. Every single point contained in the Technical University's list of 16 demands cited above has an equivalent precursor in the revolutionary program published more than 100 years earlier. Although many people recall the 1956 revolutionary image of the "flag with the hole"—the Hungarian tricolor with the despised "Rákosi Coat-of-Arms" removed from the middle—photographs reveal that most people participating in the October 23 demonstrations carried either old or hastily improvised versions of the Hungarian flag bearing the traditional Kossuth Coat-of-Arms. Well-known actors recited 1848 revolutionary poetry at both the Petőfi and Bem statues in Budapest as well as at similar demonstrations, most of which were held at statues of either Petőfi or Kossuth, in other cities in Hungary such as Debrecen, Szeged, Miskolc and Kaposvár. In the days preceding October 23, duplication of the Kossuth Coat-of-Arms that became ubiquitous during the Revolution resumed as if it had again become the symbol of Hungarian statehood (just as in 1849, 1918 and during the period of the Second Hungarian Republic between 1946 and 1949). The name of the new National Guard that began to organize just a few days later, the *nemzetőrség*, could also trace its historical antecedents to the Hungarian Revolution of 1848.[20]

From the perspective of political symbolism, use of these themes and images not only represented a revival of history, but indicated the emergence of a new social movement demanding more tolerable living and political conditions and greater expression of national self-identity (see points 1, 13 and 14 in the Technical University's list of demands). At the same time, the party state leadership possessed neither a genuine political program nor a significant degree of support within Hungarian society, which had come to view it as anti-national in character. The Moscow-dictated geopolitical circumstances and the Soviet military units stationed in Hungary had come to represent the Hungarian Workers' Party leadership's greatest sources of support.

It is worth noting that the Soviet Special Forces Corps stationed in Hungary had been placed on alert on October 18.[21] During the autumn of 1956, the predominant viewpoint in Hungary was that if there must be communism in the country, then it should be similar to that in Tito's Yugoslavia or Gomułka's Poland. In addition to the "historical friendship" between Hungary and Poland, the latter factor provided the prime motive for the demonstration in solidarity with the events that had taken place in Warsaw.

Imre Nagy was the only person in Hungary whom both the participants in the mass demonstration and the Hungarian Workers' Party leadership regarded as a possible mediator between them, the former because they believed that their demands would be satisfied if he were to become prime minister again, and the latter because they considered him to be capable of preserving the rule of the Communist Party. Although within the given circumstances the positions of the two sides hardly seemed reconcilable, the demands being made at the time essentially remained within the confines of the existing system. As he prepared to resume his active role in politics, Nagy was faced with the following dilemma: whereas many HWP leaders considered both him and his 1953 political program to be unacceptable, many of the points contained in the various lists of demands that were circulating at the time had transcended the boundaries of his envisaged reform of the system. The dizzying speed with which the pace of events accelerated during this period, as well as the incompatibility of the large number of political actors who emerged as the Revolution approached, also worked against Nagy.

The mass demonstration moved from the Bem statue in Buda across the Danube to Kossuth Square in front of the Parliament building on the Pest side of the river. Demonstrators chanted various slogans, including some calling for Imre Nagy's return to power. This prompted the former prime minister to appear on the balcony of the Parliament building overlooking the crowd, where he delivered a spontaneous and awkward speech in which he urged a negotiated resolution of the discord. The fact that Nagy still held no formal office of any kind and thus could not speak or act on behalf of anybody served to compound the ineffectiveness of his speech. The expressed sympathy of the amorphous masses for Imre Nagy did not represent a legitimate mandate, which within the given conditions would have necessarily placed the former prime minister in opposition to the whimpering and rancorous party leadership, a situation that Nagy himself did not desire. The fact that Nagy's own comrades viewed him as an unwanted element when they "expelled" him back into the Hungarian Workers' Party's leading body and appointed him as prime minister provides an indication of the pitfall that lay before him. (This will be discussed later.) At any rate, Nagy's speech on the balcony of the Parliament building did not manage to assuage the explosive unrest in the country. (The party leadership was still busy "revising" Gerő's evening radio address, while Imre Nagy was awaiting a call from the Political Committee and had not yet left for the Parliament, and the multitude of demonstrators on Kossuth Square had not yet heard—could not have yet heard—that the ÁVH had fired into a similar crowd gathered in the city of Debrecen at around 7 p.m. that evening, killing three people, the first mortalities of the Revolution.)[22] The demonstrators dispersed from Kossuth Square following Nagy's speech in three main groups: the first, mostly those who had been marching and demonstrating since the early afternoon, returned home; the second, composed primarily of the more tenacious and those who had joined the demonstration late, went to the headquarters of Hungarian Radio located behind the National Museum, partially because they hoped to force radio officials to accede to their previously rejected demand that the list of 16 points cited above be broadcast over the air and partially because a rumor had spread that "the ÁVH is shooting Hungarians at the radio building"; the third group marched towards the City Park in order to unilaterally fulfill point 13 on the list of demands by removing one of the most hated symbols of the dictatorship—the Stalin statue.

Ernő Gerő became the temporary focus of one thread of the simultaneous events that took place on the evening of October 23 when at 8 p.m. he delivered a live monologue on the radio, which was broadcasting from the Parliament building due to the commotion at the Hungarian Radio headquarters: in this address,

Gerő described the notion that the Hungarian Workers' Party leadership should no longer be able to dictate the course of events in the country as an internal party affair as a nationalist provocation. Gerő's speech served to highlight the sharp contrast between the continual party supervision over radio broadcasts and the non-observance of "the other Hungary." Prior to Gerő's reproachful address, Hungarian Radio had treated listeners to a communiqué regarding the freshly concluded Hungarian–Yugoslav inter-party talks, although it neglected to inform them of the events that had taken place in Budapest that day, including the circulation of the 16-point list of demands. The ÁVH units that had been dispatched to the Hungarian Radio headquarters to subdue the demonstrators who continued to insist that the latter manifesto be read over the radio had by this time resorted to use of their weapons, thus carrying through with the threat that the militant wing of the party leadership (Ernő Gerő, Antal Apró, József Révai, György Marosán and Minister of the Interior László Piros) had issued that afternoon. The general secretary of the HWP consummated all of this later that evening, when for the lack of confidence in the "commitment" of the police and army, he asked the commander of the Soviet armed forces stationed in Hungary to help to "restore order."

Gerő's measure both precluded the possibility of a negotiated settlement of the upheaval and immediately compromised Imre Nagy, whose leadership over the government party leaders were compelled to restore the next morning. Although Nagy refused the Hungarian Workers' Party general secretary's request to sign the statement requesting Soviet military assistance to quell the turmoil, on the morning of October 24 the radio reported the news of Nagy's reappointment as prime minister along with that of the government decree imposing martial law because "fascist, reactionary elements have launched an armed attack against our public buildings and police." It is for this reason that for a time public opinion associated Imre Nagy with the subsequent Soviet intervention. In the 24 hours following their return from Yugoslavia, Gerő and his fellow party leaders essentially managed to transform Hungary's reform movement into a fight for freedom entailing the threat of international conflict. Moreover, they succeeded in manipulating media reports in such a way as to place Imre Nagy under suspicion of "complicity" even before he had been reappointed to the office of prime minister.

This misconception played a role in the refusal of Ferenc Donáth and Géza Losonczy, pro-Nagy reformers who had served time in Rákosi's prisons, to accept their *in absentia* nominations to the truncated Hungarian Workers' Party Central Directorate that had been in session throughout the night of October 23–24. Both Donáth and Losonczy concluded that within the given situation Nagy would serve as nothing more than a decorative handkerchief in the breast pockets of Gerő and his hard-line comrades, and thus declined to play a walk-on role in the affairs of party and state. Thus there continued to be no effective channel of communication or negotiation between the rapidly organizing revolutionary groups and the party leadership representing the *ancien régime*. As a consequence, the events that took place during the Revolution formed a bewildering conglomeration of initiatives and actions. The armed groups established at the beginning of the popular uprising, which were composed primarily of young workers and so-called "Budapest lads," deployed themselves at strategic locations along main roads entering Budapest from the countryside (Móricz Zsigmond Circus, Széna Square, Baross Square and Corvin Alley), thus forming a defensive ring around the inner city. The insurgents engaged in regular armed encounters with Soviet military forces as they moved into Budapest, as well as with ÁVH units, particularly during the first days of the uprising. Until October 25, Hungarian Radio, broadcasting from the Parliament building under the supervision of Gerő and the HWP leadership's confrontational faction, transmitted repeated reports about "fascist counterrevolutionary elements… marauding counterrevolutionary groups… bandits who have infiltrated factories and public buildings… murderers in search of a bloodbath… the movements of counterrevolutionary provocateurs" and the so-called success of operations aimed at suppressing them.

Hungarian Radio also broadcast continuous accounts regarding which armed groups had laid down their arms and "raised the white flag."[23]

Events proceeded correspondingly in Hungary's other major cities, particularly those in which universities were located, although the mode and degree of communication between local revolutionary committees, workers' councils and Hungarian Workers' Party representatives varied from location to location. Their heightened feeling of isolation prompted party officials to display an increasing degree of flexibility in their negotiations with the newly emerged revolutionary organizations, while the latter were also disposed towards compromise, particularly during the initial days of the Revolution, as a result of their own uncertainty and lack of means. Given these conditions, the two sides were able to avoid conflict in most of these places in spite of their mutual mistrust. Local civil society began to materialize in towns and villages only two or three days later, which is not surprising in the light of the fact that radio broadcasts reaching the countryside and both central and local party newspapers carried "official issue" information. Although an occasional railway worker or student returned from Budapest to rural Hungary in the days before October 28 to counterbalance the disinformation that the media had been disseminating, at least within their private environment of family and friends, dismal infrastructural conditions frequently prevented local HWP functionaries from reaching the closest major city or establishing telephone contact with party officials in Budapest in order to acquire accurate information regarding the prevailing state of affairs. Even when they did manage to reach a party superior, they were often advised to simply act as they saw fit amid the given local circumstances.

The situation was very different in Budapest, where the increasingly fractious and crumbling party leadership proved unable to generate any kind of constructive alternative, although its militant wing did manage to provoke further bloody atrocities. On October 24, the Antal Apró-led Military Committee established armed detachments consisting of dependable units of the ÁVH and members of the Partisan Alliance in order to defend Budapest's administrative district and eliminate concentrated armed resistance. The committee deployed the various armed units designated to secure the administrative district in government ministries and adjacent buildings, while Soviet tanks arrived "from outside" to reinforce them. On the morning of October 25, troops from these units exchanged fire with regular army forces on Kossuth Square as a result of a miscommunication, prompting their armed comrades to conclude that the thousands of civilian demonstrators who had gathered on the square located in front of the Parliament building had launched an "attack." This episode, whose precise causes are still unclear, degenerated into a bloody massacre when the unarmed demonstrators were caught in crossfire between the various military units present on the square. Historical research indicates that the incident claimed 60 to 80 dead and nearly 300 wounded.

On the afternoon of October 25, following talks between hastily dispatched CPSU representatives Mikhail Suslov and Anastas Mikoyan and available Hungarian Workers' Party leaders, an announcement was broadcast that János Kádár would replace Ernő Gerő as party general secretary effective immediately, thus validating the widespread opinion that Gerő had been a merely provisional party leader. Minister of the Interior László Piros was dismissed shortly thereafter and replaced by Ferenc Münnich. At the same time, Kádár's appointment as the HWP's new general secretary reflected the millennia-old voluntarist logic of empire versus province: however, instead of Rome, Moscow *locuta, cause finite est* ("Moscow has spoken, the case is closed"). The ousting of Gerő and the minister of the interior-cum-ÁVH chief László Piros following the Kossuth Square massacre provided the insurgents with indirect proof that members of the political police—the ÁVH—were to be regarded as public enemies who derived support from the confrontational faction of the party leadership. Bloody incidents in other parts of the country (Esztergom, Miskolc, Kecskemét and Zalaegerszeg) served to reconfirm this conviction. The most tragic of the latter was the ÁVH fusillade in Mosonmagyaróvár, which inflicted as many casualties as the Kossuth Square massacre. Some of the ousted higher-level party leaders fled to Moscow, while many members of the state and party apparatus from outside Budapest sought refuge at various Soviet military bases or, if they were located in counties along the border, slipped along with ÁVH officers into Czechoslovakia or Romania or across the Soviet border into Sub-Carpathian Ukraine.[24]

October 28 is often cited as a "turning point" in the rapidly evolving, mosaic-like chronicle of the Revolution. It was on this date that the contradictory changes that occurred following Kádár's succession of Gerő became clearly visible. One of the most significant of these transformations was the organization of factory *workers' councils*—an endeavor that had not been among the demands committed to paper prior to the outbreak of the Revolution. The first official reference to the establishment of such councils appeared among the "immediate measures" that the National Council of Trade Unions published in the October 26 issue of the daily newspaper *Népszava* with the endorsement of the Writers' Union. In its news broadcast that very same evening, Hungarian Radio reported the establishment of several workers' councils, such as those at the United Light Bulb factory in Budapest and at major foundries in Ózd and Diósgyőr, while the new János Kádár-led Hungarian Workers' Party leadership hurried to declare that "it considers the election of factory workers' councils to be appropriate." It is one of the bitter ironies of these historic days that the party leadership hoped that the formation of workers' councils would prevent the "harm and destruction of the armed ruffians… [and] defend the working class and the cause of socialism from mercenary elements,"[25] while at the same time, a general strike spread throughout Hungary just as the councils were being formed.

One of the peculiarities of the initial days of the Revolution was that after bringing Imre Nagy back as prime minister in the early morning hours of October 24, the Gerő–Kádár duo continued to call the shots at the head of the fading party autocracy. Exploiting his name and new status as a means of preserving their legitimacy, it appears that Nagy's associates in the party leadership were, in fact, attempting to isolate him, faltering only after the massacre that took place in front of the Parliament building. Some attempted to rescue Nagy from this quarantine, or at least distinguish him from the party leaders. One of Nagy's most devoted followers, Petőfi Circle Secretary Gábor Táncos, provided support for this cause in a radio statement in the name of the organization urging listeners to back the new prime minister. This motive is also reflected in a summons, as concise as it was desperate, that the Revolutionary Committee of the Loránd Eötvös University Faculty of Arts issued at around the same time: "The people of the country do not know that it was *not you* who called in Soviet forces, *not you* who signed the decree imposing martial law… We know this, but that is not enough. Make a statement on the radio without delay! Distinguish yourself from those who have betrayed the people!"[26] As part of the attempt to compromise Nagy, on the early morning of October 26, the Antal Apró-led Military Committee and the dismissed András Hegedüs arranged to have a government communiqué calling for the suppression of the Revolution read on Hungarian Radio without first consulting the new prime minister: "The Ministers' Council [*sic*!] summons the population of Budapest not to go out on the street for the entire day! This is necessary because beginning early this morning, operations will be launched throughout the city aimed at locating the remnants of armed counterrevolutionary groups and restoring order."[27] Nagy became a truly effective prime minister only following this intolerable artifice, preventing the Military Committee from carrying through with its announced plan to eradicate armed revolutionary groups, particularly the one based at Corvin Alley. On the day following the massacre on Kossuth Square, "the news of which spread like wildfire throughout the city," it was simply unacceptable to initiate another "attack that would foreseeably claim a massive number of civilian victims."[28]

Amid the rapid succession of turbulent events, neither the crumbling Hungarian Workers' Party leadership nor the Soviet party envoys who had been dispatched to Hungary realized until October 25 that the Revolution and the increasingly comprehensive and organized "social self-determination" that had emerged in the country could not be brought under control in the same way as the 1953 Berlin uprising or the demonstrations that had taken place in Poznań that summer. (Domestic armed forces—at least those that were still considered to be reliable—were certainly not of sufficient strength to suppress the Revolution, while the intervention of the Soviet military had merely served to fan the flames.) Recognition of the above circumstances increased Prime Minister Nagy's room for maneuver, making it possible for him to seek a political resolution to the crisis. However, it was only two days following the removal of the Gerő–Hegedüs–Piros triad that Nagy truly acquired the authority embodied in the office of the prime minister with the ambiguous support of the continually maneuvering János Kádár and in sharp opposition to Antal Apró, István Kovács and Sándor Nógrádi. Hungarians began to perceive the consequences of Nagy's increasing power in both the tone and the content of news reports beginning on October 28. What by this time had been rechristened Free Kossuth Radio introduced its midday news broadcast with the long-prohibited tolling of noon bells. At 2 p.m. on the afternoon of October 28, the members of Nagy's new government, whose composition still did not reflect the prime minister's political outlook, took their oaths of office. In a radio address delivered early that evening, Prime Minister Nagy categorically rejected the characterization voiced over previous days of the events that had taken place in Hungary since October 23 as a "counterrevolution," defining them as a "national democratic movement that embraces and fuses the entire people into one." In his speech, the prime minister also made reference to the formulation of a government program based upon revolutionary demands, endorsing the "new, democratic forms of self-government" (revolutionary committees and workers' councils) and pledging to revamp the detrimental wage and quota system and recalibrate pensions and family allowances. Nagy also declared that the Kossuth Coat-of-Arms would be reinstated as Hungary's national emblem, while March 15 would again be celebrated as a national holiday. The prime minister concluded his address by proclaiming the dissolution of the ÁVH and announcing the beginning of the withdrawal of Soviet troops from Budapest.[29] By the time of Nagy's speech, around 3,500 inmates had been discharged from various prisons in Hungary, more than one quarter of all prisoners in the country. One third of those released were political convicts. (The release of prisoners continued over subsequent days as well, resulting in the discharge of approximately 10,000 inmates by the end of October, including 3,300 political convicts.)[30]

Nagy accomplished about as much as he possibly could have during the first five days after his reappointment to the office of prime minister, although this was still viewed as inadequate amid the fairly natural "Lord grant me—and as soon as possible" popular impatience that predominated in Hungary at the time. Moreover, very few people were aware of the continual behind-the-scenes criticism and opposition to which Nagy was subjected after becoming prime minister (as historical sources reflecting this constant quibbling have become available only in the last decade). This represents only one side of the issue. The other regards the conditions under which Nagy entered a new orbit and environment after becoming prime minister. The biographer of one of Nagy's closest confidants, Géza Losonczy, raises this question in a general sense with regard to the pro-reform intellectual circles that supported the prime minister: "The communist intellectuals who supported Imre Nagy spent much of the 13 days of Hungary's Revolution of 1956 searching for a suitable role in an initially incomprehensible script that was not actually written by them."[31] Imre Nagy, the central figure in the group picture, did the same thing: he was forced to do so, originally as a result of the fact that he had not (re)assumed his position according to the ritual of the Communist system. In fact, only Nagy, himself, had thought such a scenario possible—even among his closest followers.[32] Just ten months previously, at the end of 1955, Nagy wrote the following in one of his aforementioned political analyses-cum-polemical essays: "A return to new course policies and foundation of the country's economic, political and cultural life on June principles would help to span the ever-burgeoning crisis and prevent a catastrophe. However, it is doubtful that by tomorrow this would bring a solution to the problems—that it is enough to return to the June principles… It is to be feared that if this does not happen, people will lose their confidence in the June path and the Communist Party and reject them, thus we must go back much further in order to remain masters of the situation. As a result of the foolishness and political blindness of Rákosi's state and party leadership, it has become increasingly uncertain where we will be able to stop."[33] Regardless of how accurate Nagy's Cassandra prophesies turned out to be, it is one thing to predict something on paper as a political analyst and quite another to actually face the fact—if his own previously written passages even occurred to him at all—that "the word was made flesh" and take immediate and practical action. (Just think of how the "rollback" and "liberation of captive peoples" theory and propaganda of the Eisenhower administration collapsed in a no less inglorious and rapid manner when it was forced to deal with the "independently launched" Hungarian initiative in October 1956.)[34]

By October 1956 this fundamentally transformed situation had materialized. Within these new circumstances, Nagy was compelled to deal urgently with expectations and challenges of four types: Moscow's tolerance level, the metamorphosis of the Hungarian party and government leadership, the expectations of the revolutionary "base levels" and the crisis in Nagy's personal communist identity. These four factors exercised a mutual influence on one another as they formed the events that would eventually produce a dénouement to the crisis.[35]

1. *Moscow's tolerance level.* The boundaries of Moscow's tolerance, although they can hardly be defined precisely under the conditions that prevailed in the autumn of 1956, seem to have essentially extended to those outlined in the Khrushchev–Gomułka pact. The Nagy government barely managed to convince the Soviet

party leadership in Moscow through the latter's representatives in Hungary (Mikoyan, Suslov and Andropov) to accept a coalition political arrangement based on the "limited multi-party system" that had existed in the country between 1945 and 1947, although this formula differed from the Polish variation not only with regard to political pluralism, but to an even greater extent because Gomułka's "national communism" enjoyed the support of the Polish United Workers' Party, thus ensuring the preservation of Communist rule. The same thing could not be said of the Hungarian Workers' Party in its decomposed form at the end of October 1956.

2. *The metamorphosis of the Hungarian party and government leadership.* This is a manifold issue. Ernő Gerő, László Piros, András Hegedüs, Antal Apró and the Military Committee of which the latter served as leader remained Nagy's intransigent foes until the very end. Their antagonism was not confined to personal aversion, but extended to a "don't negotiate—shoot" confrontation-centered mentality that precluded a political resolution to the conflict. That which Nagy's adversaries represented entailed two outcomes, one worse than the other in political terms: first, the situation whereby the Hungarian army and police would become essentially worthless, forcing them to depend on the similarly crumbling ÁVH, which pitted itself against the urban guerilla tactics of the insurgents, which would have certainly failed to quell the upheaval, although in such a way as to potentially transform the sporadic armed skirmishes that characterized the early days of the Revolution into a full-blown civil war; second, the *ultima ratio regum* of serving as Muscovite walk-ons for an intervention on behalf of the Soviet military.

If the Gerő–Hegedüs–Piros trio that faded into the background around October 25 is eliminated from consideration, then a political-sociological fault line becomes apparent between György Marosán, who vociferously supported the establishment of a military dictatorship, Antal Apró, who although more reserved than the former employed a more tenacious operative routine to organize such a system, Ferenc Münnich, István Kovács and János Kádar on one side, and Imre Nagy and Zoltán Szántó on the other.

It should be noted that the formally dismissed diehard Rákosi supporters Gerő and Hegedüs continued to attend meetings of the Hungarian Workers' Party Political Committee until the very end! In fact, Soviet emissary Anastas Mikoyan, who was also present at the meetings, occasionally cautioned Hegedüs about his militant radicalism.[36] This "five-horse team," including Kádár, prevented Nagy from bringing his sympathizers to power—from organizing his own "cast of players"—just as Gerő and company had done previously, blocking the prime minister's repeated attempts to include Géza Losonczy and Ferenc Donáth in his government. Other Nagy supporters—Budapest Chief of Police Sándor Kopácsi, Sándor Haraszti, József Szilágyi, György Fazekas, Miklós Vásárhelyi, Miklós Gimes, Szilárd Újhelyi and Gábor Tánczos—all occupied the obscure middle ground between the center of power and the base levels. Imre Nagy thus remained a structurally isolated prime minister even after the apparent removal of the compromised pro-Rákosi members of the party leadership from power.

3. *The revolutionary "base levels"* were composed of the following: local "revolutionary committees" and "national councils" based on those that had been established at universities and within the intelligentsia, workers' councils formed at the same time as the former, but separately, and various armed resistance groups, which were distinct from "civil" revolutionary organizations only in Budapest. These base-level organizations differed markedly between the countryside—municipalities and villages—and the city—Budapest and major university towns. In the countryside, most revolutionary committees and national councils assumed local government and administrative duties within just a few days. Some local council officials retained their posts even after the outbreak of the Revolution, attending to daily administrative tasks, particularly those related to public provision, in a unique "people's front" arrangement with the newly established base-level organizations. Most armed police forces operated under the authority of these organizations, either directly or in cooperation with military units stationed in the vicinity. The base-level organizations in the

countryside deployed various combinations of police and military forces to neutralize the deconcentrated units of the ÁVH, placing them under quarantine or protective custody (if their members had not already fled). Since the activities of these base-level organization were focused on "running" the community, their political desiderata were essentially confined to four main issues: withdrawal of Soviet troops from Hungary, disbanding the ÁVH, bringing those responsible for the judicial murders of the previous decade to justice, and the holding of national and local elections as soon as possible.[37] The question of whether to preserve or dissolve agricultural cooperatives represented the main local political theme in villages and rural areas in Hungary at this time. The acquisition or possible elimination of tax sheets (tax books) was another frequent topic of discussion in rural Hungary during the Revolution.

The factory workers' councils replaced the members of company management bodies with their own appointments, although likewise only as a function of local conditions. The councils almost always dismissed the director of the company running a given factory as well as the personnel manager (the cadre officer), although deputy directors and mid-level managers were often elected to serve as council representatives. During this period, the workers' councils used strikes as a political weapon, predicating their return to work on a complete withdrawal of Soviet troops from the territory of Hungary. The issues of wages, production norms and working conditions were also at the top of the hierarchically structured lists of council demands. The workers' councils organized so-called plant guards under their own authority, although they occasionally cooperated with local revolutionary committees in the interests of maintaining public order. In terms of "national politics," the councils extended the demands contained in the manifestos that the intelligentsia and students had published before the Revolution only in their stipulation that they be legally integrated into Hungary's institutional structure. The workers' councils also sought to locate independent sources of provision for workers at the plants and factories in which they operated to serve as a supplement to general public provisions.

The armed revolutionary groups were the most amorphous organizations to form in Hungary during the Revolution. The significant majority of those who joined such groups were semi-skilled or unskilled workers between the ages of 18 and 30 who decided that they had seen enough of the Communist regime's "workers' policies" over the preceding years. There were few university students among the members of the armed resistance groups, while the number of high school students, particularly those from industrial trade schools, was somewhat higher. A significant proportion of the young people active in armed groups came from unsettled family backgrounds, and since schools were closed during the Revolution, they took advantage of the ready availability of weapons to "play soldier for real." The war and partisan films that dominated cinema schedules in the 1950s provided this phenomenon with further impetus. Although their lives were at stake, for these youngsters throwing Molotov cocktails at Soviet tanks or skirmishing with ÁVH or the Hungarian military forces represented an act of roguish bravado. The operational range of these armed revolutionary groups was limited to districts of the city with which they were familiar, where their geographical knowledge and guerilla warfare tactics made it possible for them to take on much larger regular forces. During the final days of October, many of those freshly released from prison joined the ranks of the armed revolutionaries.[38] The size of these groups changed continually, reaching a composite total of between 13,000 and 15,000 members. Their distribution throughout Budapest and the effective communications network that had developed between them by the end of October invested these armed groups with a considerable degree of military potency. Armed revolutionaries regarded the Nagy government with a mixture of aversion and skepticism, primarily because they believed that it would have been the duty of "big time politics" to order the Soviet military to leave Hungary; however, this did not happen.

4. *Imre Nagy's identity crisis.* According to his biographer, Nagy was dumbstruck when at the beginning of his October 23 speech from the balcony of the Parliament building the massive crowd gathered

on Kossuth Square below him booed and hissed when he addressed them as "comrades!" Following his speech, Nagy proceeded to the Hungarian Workers' Party headquarters, where he was forced to cope with not only a profusion of information, but also the antipathy with which his comrades received him. He experienced "confusion, helplessness, total collapse" in "confronting unknown forces" that could not be fathomed, but at most "perceived" through metaphysical impulses.[39] It was hardly a matter of Nagy not knowing how to perform the functions of prime minister: in addition to his previous tenure as head of government, Nagy had held numerous cabinet positions and served as the speaker of Parliament over the years since the end of World War II. However, Nagy was really not suited for the role or status into which he had been thrust: his comrades in positions of power treated him as an irremovable "leper," while the multitudes before Parliament viewed him as a frail and disconcerted old man instead of the savior whom they had coveted. The issue of whether or not he should abandon the hope of reviving the "new course" associated with his first term as prime minister was certainly not among Nagy's greatest concerns at this time, while he also certainly realized that the conclusion derived at a meeting with his confidants that morning—"Polish-style transformation, although no multi-party system"—represented an *ad acta.* Nagy certainly lacked experience—just as every other political leader in the country did—in the use of peaceful political means to pacify and consolidate a country that had been turned on its head (and was the domain of a dictatorial superpower as well). In a metaphorical sense, it was like trying to reconstruct a healthy chicken egg from a rotten and cracked duck egg: nobody had either the means or the know-how to do this.

Under the conditions outlined above, Nagy indeed did everything within his power, struggling with his "political kinsfolk" in isolation from his true political allies. With the existing sociopolitical system collapsing around them, they attempted on the one hand to govern within the confines of the former institutional and ritual order, while on the other hand the institutions and representatives of the new—or at least corrected—sociopolitical order were working at cross purposes. The succession of scholarly publications that appeared around the fiftieth anniversary of the 1956 Hungarian Revolution produced the general result of expanding the previously "Budapest-centric" view of the Revolution to include the "revolution in the provinces."[40] Works dealing with the history of the Revolution in cities, towns and villages in Hungary outside Budapest reveal that in the majority of these locations, representatives of the former local administration and new revolutionary organizations cooperated to form a sociopolitical forum serving as a vehicle for communication between "the old" and "the new." No such joint "negotiating table" emerged at a centralized level in Budapest

The events that took place in Hungary between the spring and autumn of 1956 were in many regards reminiscent of those that occurred in 1848. However, the initial Soviet military intervention on the night of October 23–24 immediately transformed the romantic-heroic Petőfi theater stage into a bloody urban battleground. It is doubtful that elaborate rhetoric of any type would have convinced the highly inflamed armed insurgents and "courageous" Soviet-backed ÁVH forces to seek conciliation. Imre Nagy, had he attempted to intervene directly, would probably have met with the same fate as those caught in the crossfire on Kossuth Square on October 25… He only had to think of the *bon mot* popularly attributed to Ferenc Deák: "If we cannot do that which is desirable, let us do that which is possible." A rational assessment of the situation that prevailed in Hungary during the final week of October 1956 suggests that the latter statement accurately describes the range of options that the Nagy government had at its disposal. Imre Nagy's second tenure as prime minister took place within circumstances that neither he nor anybody else could have foreseen. Whereas the Nagy government's reform ambitions essentially remained within the paradigm of the system, Ernő Gerő's machinations provoked Hungary into an armed uprising, which manifested itself in the emergence of dozens of civil war combat zones in the country, particularly within the city of Budapest. After overcoming his initial paralysis, Nagy attempted to convince hostile party leaders to utilize political means rather than armed force in their efforts to contain the damage that the Revolution had caused. The prime minister succeeded "only" in establishing the possibility of a negotiated political settlement to the conflict in opposition to his saber-rattling comrades.[41]

With the days of militant confrontation behind him, or at least in the hope that they were, Nagy initiated implementation of his "ready-made government program" on October 28. The prime minister hardly had any other alternative than to adopt the point-by-point demands that had emerged at the onset of the Revolution. Although some of these demands transcended the boundaries of his established political program, Nagy could not very well ignore them. The prime minister therefore set about the task of reshuffling his cabinet—for the third time in a week—with the objective of establishing a "government of national unity" that he believed might satisfy the demands of the mutinous country. In this regard, Nagy again found in the course of his separate negotiations with Kádár that it was easier to reach political compromise with Moscow's emissaries, Mikoyan and Suslov, than it was with his own compatriots in the party leadership. It was following talks with the latter on October 30 that the prime minister made a statement on the radio announcing the nullification of the single-party system and the restoration of the multi-party government. Former President and Prime Minister Zoltán Tildy succeeded Nagy at the radio microphone, advocating the elimination of the compulsory delivery system that burdened Hungary's peasantry and the calling for free elections to be held as soon as possible.

Nagy requested some of the former members of the 1945 coalition cabinet to join his national government, while the rapidly reorganizing political parties were permitted to delegate the remaining ministers. It was in this manner that the following people gradually joined Nagy's government: Zoltán Tildy, Béla Kovács and István B. Szabó from the Independent Smallholders' Party, Anna Kéthly, Gyula Kelemen and József Fischer from the Social Democratic Party, and István Bibó and Ferenc Farkas from the Petőfi Party, which had formed as the successor to the National Peasant Party. (The party affiliation of Ferenc Erdei is unclear, since this successor to his former National Peasant Party declined to "acknowledge" him. Neither did the transforming Communist Party declare as one of its own the crypto-communist who was/remained the deputy chairman of the Council of Ministers. The latter was to become the leader of the official delegation that conducted negotiations during the first days of November regarding the withdrawal of Soviet troops from Hungary.) Over subsequent days, the Civil Democratic Party, the Hungarian Radical Party, the Hungarian Independence Party, the Hungarian Freedom Party and the Democratic People's Party were also reconstituted, thus nearly rounding out the assortment of parties that had existed in 1947.

The revival of the multi-party system made it necessary for the Hungarian Workers' Party to take action as well. Following a one-day period of hesitation, János Kádár accepted Zoltán Szántó's assertion that the largely nominal formation of which he had just been appointed as general secretary had become unfit to lead the country during the previous decade of dictatorship. The reestablishment of the Social Democratic Party following the reintroduction of the multi-party system presented the party with a natural competitor, while the so-called party opposition within the Writers' Union was also considering the foundation of a new communist party. For Kádár, there had suddenly emerged too many rivals who were attempting to make hay in the same sociological field. As a consequence of all these factors, the HWP was quickly abolished early on October 31, the day following the restoration of the multi-party system, and the Hungarian Socialist Workers' Party (HSWP) established in its place. The members of the so-called executive committee that organized the HSWP were, in addition to János Kádár and Imre Nagy, Zoltán Szántó, Ferenc Donáth, Sándor Kopácsi, Géza Losonczy and György Lukács. Among the leading officials in this new communist party, János Kádár, Imre Nagy, Géza Losonczy and Pál Maléter became members of the government, the latter as minister of defense. Kádár probably felt no anguish upon learning that he would have to part company with Gerő and Hegedüs as a result of the party reorganization, while Nagy sympathizers had gained considerable overrepresentation within the leadership of the newly formed HSWP. Kádár's founding statement was the only thing more noteworthy than the political-sociological composition of those who had organized the new party: "Those who founded the party have long struggled against the Stalinist tyranny of Rákosi, Gerő and Farkas… In the glorious uprising of our people, communists… have stood firm… the Hungarian Socialist Workers' Party defends our national honor and the independence of our homeland."[42]

It is not known if the October 30 attack on the headquarters of the Hungarian Workers' Party's Budapest organization played a role in Kádár's rapid change of opinion with regard to the proposed establishment of a new communist party, a notion towards which he had initially expressed aversion. The incident began when ÁVH guards posted at the headquarters apprehended some insurgents while they were out on patrol. Other revolutionaries soon arrived to rescue their brothers-in-arms from ÁVH captivity at the headquarters building, where they were met with gunfire. Both the noise of the ensuing clash and the swift channels of communication that had emerged between the various groups of revolutionaries quickly attracted a throng of revolutionaries, who practically laid siege to the party headquarters. Budapest party secretary Imre Mező called both the central party headquarters and the Ministry of Defense to request reinforcements. As the result of a miscommunication, a tank unit that had been dispatched to the headquarters after a significant period of delay inadvertently joined the skirmish on the side of the revolutionaries, firing at the besieged building. This convinced both the ÁVH guards and the party functionaries trapped inside to surrender. Imre Mező was shot dead immediately after stepping out of the headquarters, while others were herded in front of the building and gunned down. Several of the captured ÁVH were lynched and their bodies desecrated. Of those trapped in the party headquarters on October 30, a total of 23 had lost their lives by the end of the day.

Imre Nagy, when he was not participating in meetings of the government or party leadership, regularly received delegations from new revolutionary organizations. Representatives from Budapest revolutionary committees and workers' councils were as eager to meet the prime minister as those from similar organizations located outside the capital city. These consultations were as important for Nagy as they were for the "mediators of the Revolution" from whom the prime minister was able to learn at first hand about what was taking place outside the Parliament building, either in Budapest or other cities and regions of Hungary. The inability to predict the amount of time that it would require for a delegation to reach Budapest from Győr, Miskolc, Kaposvár or other locations in Hungary during the Revolution made these meetings difficult to plan. Beyond their informational value, the talks were also useful to the prime minister with regard to integration of the newly formed organizations into the transformation process. The revolutionary committees and workers' councils, particularly those from the provinces, probably appeared to the prime minister to have quickly established their specific roles and, in spite of the inevitable friction with regard to the scope of authority and competence, to be suitable for incorporation into Hungary's new institutional structure during the period of post-revolutionary normalization.

The pacification and institutional incorporation of the armed revolutionary groups represented a much greater risk factor. Beginning on October 27–28, Budapest Chief of Police Sándor Kopácsi, Pál Maléter and the prime minister himself held talks with delegations from several revolutionary groups, which were very adamant about retaining their "guerilla" status. Kopácsi first came to an agreement with Loránd Eötvös University students who had obtained weapons from the Faculty of Arts revolutionary committee to provide security for the institution's campus and buildings, persuading them to conduct further operations as a lawful unit of the National Guard. The latter organization had begun to form in parallel to the dissolution of the despised ÁVH, deriving its designation *nemzetőrség* from the identically named military reserve force that had operated in Hungary during the 1848 Revolution. A decoding of the force's historical name suggests that it may be viewed as a paramilitary civil defense force.

Major General Béla Király outlined the purpose for establishing the new National Guard at the founding session of the Revolutionary Armed Forces Committee on October 31:

> The national democratic Revolution triumphed without united central leadership. However, this triumph can only be preserved if the Revolution's victorious young people, university students, young workers, combat units, our currently forming factory guards and our army and police... protect under united leadership the achievements of the Revolution from the danger of attempted restoration or attacks from reactionary elements.

This circumlocution suggests that there was friction between various related ministries regarding command and authority. Király's clarification that "every armed unit that does not belong to the army or police on this day" would be integrated into the National Guard seems to have been an attempt to resolve this discord, although such forces could have been placed under the authority of the aforementioned organizations. Béla Király believed that potential conflict regarding direction and supervision could be averted by placing the National Guard under the direct authority of the prime minister and the Revolutionary Armed Forces Committee that he had established.[43] This, however, served to institutionalize the establishment of separate law enforcement and paramilitary organizations under the jurisdiction of the prime minister, as Hungary's administrative structure took on an increasing pluralistic character.[44] According to statistics from the Budapest Police Headquarters, more than 18,000 National Guard membership cards were issued in Budapest by November 3, while this many again were presumably issued throughout the rest of Hungary as well. Units of this "civilian" National Guard were established in over half of the communities in Hungary, although only half of them, at best, had access to weaponry. It is for this reason that most of these National Guard forces based in locations outside Budapest operated in cooperation with local police, army and border guard units.

As a function of his office, Imre Nagy maintained regular contact with Soviet Ambassador Yuri Andropov, initiating the withdrawal of Soviet troops first from Budapest, then from the entire territory of Hungary during their consultations. The Soviet government's October 30, 1956, declaration regarding the restoration of the principle of equality in inter-state relations, respect for state sovereignty and social-historical individuality, and non-interference in the internal affairs of states within the Soviet Union's sphere of interest appeared to heighten the prospect of Soviet troops leaving the country. Moreover, the document indicated in a separate passage that "The Soviet government is prepared to undertake negotiations with the government of the People's Republic of Hungary and the governments of other states participating in the Warsaw Pact regarding the stationing of Soviet troops in Hungary."[45] This was encouraging news following a week of atrocities, armed clashes, innocent victims, bloodbaths and political mud wrestling. On the day following the Soviet statement, radio commentators in Hungary alluded to the "final outcome of the uplifting struggle" and the government declaration "from the heart of the people."

However, during the final two days of October, a continual succession of Soviet military units that had not previously been stationed in Hungary streamed into the country from Sub-Carpathian Ukraine.[46] Dire reports of the troop movements arrived in Parliament one after another on October 30 and 31, indicating that instead of withdrawing from Hungary, regular Soviet troops had crossed the country's eastern frontier at the Záhony–Csap (Chop, Ukraine) border crossing and were proceeding towards Budapest, encircling airports and military barracks *en route*. Prime Minister Nagy, either personally or through his minister of foreign affairs, appealed to Andropov for information regarding the reported military advance, although the Soviet ambassador claimed to know nothing about it. Nagy himself assumed the duties of minister of foreign affairs on November 1, convening a series of cabinet meetings to discuss the increasingly ominous news. Eventually, the government adopted a resolution calling for the publication of official statements aimed at counterbalancing the indefinite threat through statements intended to create diplomatic pressure. On the final day of October, Nagy delivered a speech before the Parliament building in which he announced that he had initiated negotiations with the Soviet Union regarding not only the departure of Soviet troops from Hungary, but the country's withdrawal from the Warsaw Pact as well. On November 1, the prime minister made a statement on the radio declaring Hungary's neutrality, while later that day he dispatched a communiqué to United Nations Secretary-General Dag Hammarskjöld regarding the recent developments and "requesting assistance from the four Great Powers."[47]

Shortly after Prime Minister Nagy's November 1 radio statement, listeners heard a speech from János Kádár. Those who were attuned to the nuances of political dialog immediately perceived that although Kádár had praised "the glorious uprising of our people… [which] secured its freedom" and called for cooperation among the "newly formed democratic parties," he alluded neither to the issue of neutrality nor to that of withdrawal from the Warsaw Pact. Radio listeners were unaware that Kádár's speech was a taped transmission. Not even his fellow ministers yet realized that Kádár had already left Budapest. Subsequent attempts to locate the Hungarian Socialist Workers' Party leader and state minister revealed that he had departed from the Parliament building with Minister of the Interior Ferenc Münnich in the direction of the Soviet Embassy, although in response to Imre Nagy's inquiries Ambassador Andropov denied having any information regarding their whereabouts.

3. Khrushchev: "If We Were to Withdraw from Hungary, It Would Be Perceived as a Sign of Our Weakness."

Events continued to proceed at a stunning pace. Their chronology is important, because to this day it is a commonly held belief that the Nagy government incited the second Soviet military intervention in Hungary through its unilateral withdrawal from the Warsaw Pact and declaration of the country's neutrality. This is not true. On October 31, one day after the seemingly propitious Soviet government statement cited above, the Presidium of the CPSU Central Committee decided in favor of military intervention. Here we may cite a lengthy quote from Khrushchev: "The [previous] assessment must be reexamined, we will not withdraw troops from Hungary and Budapest, we will take the initiative to restore order in Hungary. If we pull out of Hungary, it will encourage the English and French imperialists. They would interpret this as weakness and go on the attack. [Through withdrawal] we would demonstrate the weakness of our positions. In this case our party would not understand us. *In addition to Egypt, we would give them Hungary as well.'*"[48] Most of Khrushchev's statement speaks for itself, although the underscored reference to the Suez crisis that had erupted two days previously merits comment. CPSU leaders could not have known at this time that superpower opposition would compel the retreat of Anglo-French invasion forces that were to attack Egypt in response to the crisis. They were therefore concerned that the Soviet Union might be obliged to relinquish its recently acquired bridgehead in North Africa, although they were also aware that it would not be permissible to fail on "two fronts" simultaneously. Moreover, Soviet party leaders recognized that "restoring order" in Hungary entailed no real global political risks. The conjuncture of the two crises in this way virtually ensured that Hungary would emerge from the situation as the aggrieved party. Ambassador of Austria to the Soviet Union Norbert Bischoff aptly described the state of affairs in a November 12, 1956, communiqué: "Khrushchev, Bulganin and the other Soviet leaders who issued the command to bloodily suppress the Hungarian popular uprising might expect an expression of gratitude from those responsible for the attack on Egypt. Without the Hungarian catastrophe, they undoubtedly would have had to pay a much greater price for their adventure."[49]

Therefore the CPSU leadership's decision to intervene took place before Imre Nagy announced the unilateral withdrawal of Hungary from the Warsaw Pact and declared the country's neutrality. Imre Nagy's national government reacted to the news of cross-border Soviet troop movements conducted in preparation for the attack by issuing political and diplomatic declarations. In retrospect, it thus became clear why Ambassador Andropov had avoided responding to previous Hungarian inquiries regarding the preventative actions. After having been placed in command of all Soviet military forces stationed in Hungary as well as those that were just being deployed to the country, Marshal I. S. Konev arrived with his staff at the military base near Szolnok on October 31, the day on which the decision to intervene was made.[50] On November 1, Soviet leader Nikita Khrushchev met with Władysław Gomułka and other Polish leaders in Brest, where the CPSU leader informed them of the impending military intervention in Hungary. From here, Khrushchev flew to Bucharest in order to notify leaders of other socialist countries of the impending assault on Budapest, and then proceeded immediately to the island of Brioni, where on November 2 the CPSU general secretary gained Tito's approval for the intervention as well. It was in the course of the latter talks that Tito convinced Khrushchev to place János Kádár rather than Ferenc Münnich, both of whom had fled to Moscow after defecting from Imre Nagy's cabinet, at the head of the Communist restoration that the impending Soviet military intervention was designed to precipitate.

Signs of consolidation began to emerge in Hungary during the first days of November in which the covert preparations for the second Soviet intervention described above took place. Supplies of donated food had begun to arrive regularly in Budapest from throughout Hungary. Shipments of medicine, medical dressings, blood and blood plasma arrived one after another in Hungary from various countries via the Vienna–Budapest and Warsaw–Budapest "air bridges," partially under the auspices of the International Red Cross. Even more importantly, those revolutionary organizations that had gained recognition following their direct meetings with the prime minister expressed their support for the Nagy government. The Budapest University Revolutionary Student Committee (*Egyetemi Forradalmi Diákbizottság*), the Revolutionary Committee of the Hungarian Intelligentsia (*Magyar Értelmiség Forradalmi Bizottsága*) and the transformed trade union alliance MSZOSZ also offered public backing for the prime minister and his multi-party coalition cabinet, as did the Győr national council representing the region of Transdanubia, workers' councils from the former city as well as Csepel Island (Budapest), the largest working-class district in Hungary, and revolutionary organizations from the industrial city of Miskolc. Furthermore, the workers' councils decided on Saturday, November 3, to resume work at plants and factories throughout Hungary on the following Monday.[51] The new local forums that had emerged during the Revolution, many of which had originally been regarded and aptly designated as "provisional," began to reelect officials and consolidate their operations.

The Nagy government formed delegations, including one to be sent to the United Nations, for the purpose of conducting international negotiations, while the prime minister issued a series of protests regarding the reported influx of Soviet troops. News of the Suez crisis that erupted on October 29 pushed that regarding the Hungarian Revolution from the front pages of newspapers around the world. Hungarian–Soviet negotiations regarding details of the stipulated withdrawal of Soviet troops from Hungary began in Parliament on the morning of November 3. Following the consultations, the two sides decided to reconvene for a second round of talks that evening at the Soviet military headquarters in Tököl, about 20 kilometers south of Budapest. The appointed Hungarian government delegation arrived at the specified location for the scheduled negotiations late on the evening of November 3. However, as it turned out, the Soviets had something else in mind: KGB Chairman General Ivan Serov unceremoniously took every member of the Hungarian deputation into custody. An ÁVH detachment under the command of the former minister of the interior László Piros assisted in this operation.

Due to the staggering number of events that were taking place during these days, a November 3 appeal from Archbishop of Esztergom József Mindszenty, who had regained his freedom just a few days previously after eight years of captivity, was largely without consequence:

> Work and production must be resumed in all places: this is in the interests of our nation and necessary in order for the life of the nation to continue—urgently... The lawful administration of justice through impartial tribunals must begin at all levels. The motive of personal revenge must be avoided and eliminated. The heirs and associates of the failed system bear a particular responsibility for their actions, failures, delay and improper measures. We cannot append a single statement to their confessions, because this would hinder the continuation of work and production throughout the country. If the outcome of the situation transpires honorably in accord with stated promises, this cannot be our duty.[52]

There was, however, no opportunity for an outcome to the situation. Just more than seven hours following the broadcast of Mindszenty's appeal on the radio, in the early morning hours of November 4 (Sunday), Soviet forces launched their attack. Moscow had mobilized a force of such overwhelming size and firepower that even coordinated resistance on the part of the entire Hungarian army could have at most slowed the Soviet advance at the cost of incalculable losses. The objective of the Marshal Konev-led military units that took part in the offensive, dubbed Operation Cyclone, was to suppress any potential armed resistance. Since the Soviets had already "pacified"[53] regular Hungarian military forces through the publication of a counterfeit order in the name of the previously seized Minister of Defense Pál Maléter, they counted on resistance mainly from armed revolutionaries and National Guard units. The General Serov-led KGB units participating in the operation had received the mission of apprehending the leaders of the various revolutionary organizations (revolutionary committees and workers' councils) and, if possible, deporting them to Sub-Carpathian Ukraine.

One hour after the start of the Soviet attack, at 5 a.m. on the morning of November 4, a radio station in Ungvár (Uzhhorod, Ukraine), began to broadcast an appeal from a János Kádár-led counter-government. (This announcement "drifted" onto the frequency of Budapest's Kossuth Radio that morning as well, although the identity and location of those addressing them was not initially clear to listeners. The high-power "pro-Kádár" station began to dominate the Kossuth Radio frequency only after 8 a.m.) The declaration stated that Antal Apró, János Kádár, István Kossa and Ferenc Münnich had left the Nagy government on November 1 and formed a Hungarian Revolutionary Worker–Peasant Government under Kádár's leadership. "We decided to fight with all our might against reaction, fascist danger and the murderous gangs." The announcement specified György Marosán, Imre Horváth, Imre Dögei and Sándor Rónai as members of the newly formed government as well.[54]

Imre Nagy was awakened at daybreak to the news of the undeclared war launched against Hungary. Based on the ominous Soviet troop movements of the previous days, it was hardly open to doubt what was taking place. In a statement broadcast over the radio at 5:30 a.m. on the morning of November 4, the prime minister informed "the people of the country and world public opinion: at dawn this morning, Soviet troops launched an attack on our capital city with the obvious intention of overthrowing the lawful Hungarian democratic government." Before Soviet units heading towards Hungary's Parliament reached their destination, Nagy and many members of his entourage, taking advantage of an offer from Tito's diplomats made on the previous evening, fled to the Yugoslav Embassy in Budapest. State Minister István Bibó was the only member of the Nagy government to remain in the Parliament building over the next two days. Bibó issued the following concise statement to both his compatriots and the international community:

> I appeal to the Hungarian people to regard neither the occupation force nor the puppet government that it establishes as lawful authority and to utilize against them all the weapons of passive resistance with the exception of those involving public provision and utilities in Budapest. It is not within my power to order armed resistance… it would be irresponsible of me to place the precious blood of Hungarian youth at my disposal. The people of Hungary have already rendered enough blood to demonstrate to the world their devotion to freedom and justice. It is now up to the world powers to demonstrate the power of the principles contained in the UN Charter and that of the freedom-loving peoples of the world. I appeal to the Great Powers and the UN to reach a wise and courageous decision on behalf of my subjugated people.[55]

To quote the November 4 entry in the journal of Pius Zimándi, the previously mentioned chronicler of the everyday events that took place during the Revolution,

> In the meantime, we learned from the radio that János Kádár had formed a new government. He personally introduced its program. It is, in fact, Imre Nagy's program: anathematizing the Rákosi–Gerő clique, abolishing compulsory deliveries, small-scale industry, retail trade, the freedom of collectivization for peasants, pulling out of the Warsaw Pact, withdrawal of Soviet troops, independence, sovereignty, non-interference in internal affairs. In this tragic hour, one doesn't know whether to laugh or seethe at this cynical program that contradicts the true facts. The non-interference contained in the program and the actual intervention of Soviet troops; the sovereignty and independence contained in the program and the actual foreign military subjugation of the country. Furthermore, if—with the exception of free elections—it is the same

> program as Imre Nagy's, then why was it necessary to drive Imre Nagy so brutally away, to destroy and spill so much blood? Or are they afraid of free elections? *Difficile est satiram non scribere* [It is difficult not to write satire].[56]

Rather than Juvenal, it would have been just as appropriate for Zimándi to have quoted another Classical poet, Ovid, in his journal entry: *Difficile est crimen non prodere vultu* (It is difficult for our faces to disguise our misdeeds).

Although this bloody Sunday in November 1956 has come to represent the beginning of the Kádár era in historical chronology, the Revolution, although placed on the defensive, did not end on this day. In fact, it may be regarded as the beginning of the third and longest phase of the Revolution even in spite of the fact that overwhelming Soviet military power succeeded in forcing armed resistance to its knees in just over two weeks. Revolutionaries equipped with only small arms and a few National Guard units were virtually the only obstacles standing in the way of the Soviet armored units that were streaming into Budapest. The freedom fighters held out for several days at strategic points throughout the city, suffering a considerable number of casualties in their struggle against Soviet forces that were vastly superior in terms of both numerical strength and firepower. On November 7, the military commander of the Soviet "armada" in Budapest, Major General Grebennik, had a notice printed claiming that "we have eliminated the main concentrations of resistance." In fact, revolutionaries in the workers' metropolis of Csepel repelled Soviet attacks for a complete week, shooting down an airplane in the process, while the National Guard general headquarters held out until November 11. Armed resistance came to an end in the city of Sztálinváros and the vicinity of Pécs on around this same date.

The increasingly isolated revolutionary groups lost an average of 400 people per day during the one week of organized resistance, while armed combat claimed a total of approximately 2,700 direct casualties. The Soviet military suffered 670 dead and 1,500 wounded. The inner districts on the Pest side of the capital city suffered as much damage as they had twelve years earlier during the siege of Budapest at the end of World War II. Some armed resistance fighters who fell into Soviet captivity—and left alive—were sent, along with regular civilians, to prisons in Sub-Carpathian Ukraine. In a communiqué to Khrushchev, General Serov reported that 4,700 people had been taken into custody, while data from Georgy Malenkov one week later indicated that in the course of mopping-up operations that started in parallel to the military attack, 7,250 people had been detained, of whom 860 had been transported to the Soviet Union.[57]

For three full days, János Kádár's counter-government essentially existed as a mere virtual phantom, perceptible only in its statements mediated via radio. The members of this government had been transferred incognito from Moscow via Ungvár to the Soviet military base near Szolnok. Then, on November 7, they were hidden in tanks and smuggled into the Parliament building in Budapest, where they and a few other members of the new government took their oaths of office before Presidential Council Chairman István Dobi. This act placed Hungary in the legal dilemma of having two governments. Realizing this, the Kádár government unilaterally declared the Nagy cabinet to be void on November 11.

Although János Kádár's government had occupied the Parliament building, it continued to operate in a political vacuum. On the one hand, this vacuum stemmed from the fact that the Kádár government lacked its own political base and network of connections through which it could establish contact with Hungarian society. (Although it did have the support of the Soviet military, the latter could only be utilized as an *ultima ratio* as a means of intimidation.) On the other, a large majority of Hungarian society rejected the new, self-proclaimed government, continuing to regard the revolutionary organizations as their own. The disappearance of Imre Nagy and the members of his cabinet, initially presumed to be in Soviet custody, and the brutal suppression of armed resistance did not entail the paralysis and collapse of institutions born during the Revolution. On the contrary: the process of coordinating the activities of these bodies and integrating them at a local and regional level began in parallel to the Soviet military intervention. In the course of the month of November, the focal point of revolutionary and social self-defense shifted to the workers' councils. The Soviet armed intrusion could only delay, not prevent the organizational consolidation of the workers' councils. The Greater Budapest Central Workers' Council (*Nagy-Budapesti Központi Munkástanács*) formed on November 15. The Kádár government was forced to recognize the necessity of coming to accord with this representative social organization. Talks between the Kádár government and the newly formed Greater Budapest Central Workers' Council began on the evening of November 15, although the government's insistence that the council submit unconditionally and declare an immediate resumption of work precluded the possibility of an agreement. Preparations were then begun for the establishment of the National Workers' Council, whose founding session was scheduled to take place on November 21.

Kádár, who in the course of closed consultations was forced to admit that he stood at the head of a puppet government, fell into multiple legitimacy traps. The workers' councils maintained the same November 1 platform that Kádár himself had approved before he quit the Nagy government and departed for Moscow. It had become obvious that the "workers' power" that formed the regime's ideological cornerstone had come into complete opposition with its own reference base—the working class—and its freely elected representative organizations. The unsettled status of Imre Nagy and those who had fled with him to the Yugoslav Embassy also presented János Kádár with a major predicament. Kádár had made a signed pledge to permit Nagy and those in his entourage to return home unmolested. At the same time, the leader of the Hungarian Revolutionary Worker–Peasant Government declared the following:

> If Imre Nagy leaves the Yugoslav Embassy, it will make it possible for him to negotiate and come to an understanding with us... We will relinquish the party's monopoly—we want pure, decent elections. We know that this will not be simple, because it is possible to shoot down workers' power

> not only with the bullet, but with the ballot as well. We have reckoned with the fact that they may thoroughly beat us in elections, if we accept the electoral fight, because the Communist Party will have the strength to again gain the confidence of the working masses.[58]

In fact, of the seven-member Hungarian Socialist Workers' Party Executive Committee formed just a few days previously, Nagy, Ferenc Donáth, Géza Losonczy, György Lukács and Zoltán Szántó were under lock and key in the protective custody of the Yugoslav Embassy, while Sándor Kopácsi had already fallen into Soviet custody. Only Kádár himself was still at liberty.

The November 21 formation of the National Workers' Council and the departure one day later of Imre Nagy and his followers from diplomatic asylum pursuant to an agreement with the Yugoslav deputy minister of foreign affairs could have served to create a collective sociopolitical center of power against which the Kádár cabinet would have had little chance of survival. Within the existing domestic political force field, only Soviet military power could counterbalance this losing position—and its deployment was not long in coming: Soviet armored units surrounded the location at which the founding session of the National Workers' Council was taking place, taking several worker representatives prisoner. On November 22, following preliminary consultations with Kádár, Soviet security forces took Imre Nagy and his entourage into custody after they renounced their right to asylum and left the Yugoslav Embassy, taking them first to a Soviet military base, from which they were deported to Romania.

From the end of November, all of that which over the previous month the Kossuth Coat-of-Arms and, to a lesser degree, the so-called "flag with the hole" had come to symbolize either gradually weakened or was destroyed. The political stalemate in which the power of the workers' councils managed to counterbalance that of the Kádár government began to shift in favor of the latter. Even the heroism of the participants in the 1956 Hungarian Revolution was incapable of altering the Cold War status quo that the superpowers had created and worked in collusion to preserve—or rather by that time to "stabilize." The restoration of the collapsed Communist dictatorship began under the auspices of the János Kádár-led Hungarian Socialist Workers' Party with the support of the Soviets. Nearly 200,000 people fled abroad to escape the expected—and soon initiated—reprisals, choosing to spend the rest of their lives in exile. In a dismal symptom of world political amnesia, the US weekly magazine *Time* selected "The Hungarian Freedom Fighter" as its Man of the Year in 1957 and the person responsible for crushing the Revolution, Nikita Khrushchev, as its Man of the Year in 1958.

***

The 1956 Hungarian Revolution had several longer-term domestic and foreign political consequences. The Revolution also produced a direct result in spite of its defeat—or more precisely its brutal crushing. Although it has now passed into obscurity, following World War II Hungary—which had remained in the Axis alliance until the end of the war under the madness of Szálasi's exhortation to fortitude—was cast under the stereotype of "Hitler's final satellite." Communist Party leaders, primarily Rákosi and József Révai, occasionally played this card in an attempt to maintain and arouse collective guilt. The events that took place in Hungary during the autumn of 1956 contributed greatly to the disappearance of this stigma. Following the Revolution, international public opinion began to associate Hungarians with the term "freedom fighter."

Historical composition naturally differs from literary composition. The historian, maintaining the requisite detachment, describes the contradiction that emerged following Stalin's death: "The empire needs reform in order to survive, although reform jeopardizes the empire's existence."[59] The 1956 Hungarian Revolution fell victim to this intractable dilemma, among other things. French author and philosopher Albert Camus reasoned against the crushing of the Revolution with the emotion and moral self-examination essential to his profession:

> [The Kádár] regime of terror has as much right to call itself socialist as the executioners of the Inquisition had to call themselves Christians... Hungary conquered and in chains has done more for freedom and justice than any people for twenty years. But for this lesson to get through and convince those in the West who shut their eyes and ears, it was necessary, and it can be no comfort to us for the people of Hungary to shed so much blood, which is already drying in our memories. In Europe's isolation today, we have only one way to be true to Hungary, and that is never to betray, among ourselves and everywhere, what the Hungarian heroes died for, never to condone, among ourselves and everywhere, even indirectly, those who killed them.[60]

More than half a century has passed since the Revolution. And although the professional maxim states that one can never know what the *past* will bring, for the time being it appears that *the 1956 Revolution was the most outstanding collective national achievement in Hungary's twentieth-century history.*

Notes

1 Lajos Izsák, *A Magyar Dolgozók Pártja határozatai, 1948–1956* [Resolutions of the Hungarian Workers' Party, 1948–1956] (Budapest, 1998), pp. 466–467.

2 From the minutes of the Petőfi Circle debates. *VI. Pedagógusvita* [Sixth Teachers' Debate] (Budapest, 1992).

3 János Kornai, *A szocialista rendszer* [The Socialist System] (Budapest, 1993), pp. 592–594.

4 Pius Zimándi, *A forradalom éve. Krónika 1956-ról* [The Year of Revolution. Chronicle from 1956] (Budapest, 1992). Zimándi was originally a Premonstratensian monk. Following the dissolution of Hungary's religious orders, Zimándi was among the lucky few to make a smooth transition to the civil sphere, using his knowledge of literature and languages to gain employment as a dictionary editor at the Hungarian Academy of Sciences Institute of Philology. Zimándi's precisely dated journal entries represent a virtual "data

bank" documenting the events and public discourse in Hungary during the period.

5 Gyula Háy, "Miért nem szeretem [Kucsera elvtársat]?" [Why Don't I Like (Comrade Kucsera)?], *Irodalmi Újság*, October 6, 1956.

6 October 6 has been a national day of mourning in Hungary for over 100 years, since Emperor Franz Joseph had 13 Hungarian generals and high-ranking officers as well as the revolutionary prime minister Lajos Batthyány executed on that date in 1849.

7 Béla Szász, *Minden kényszer nélkül* [With No Compulsion] (Budapest, 1989), p. 343.

8 János Kornai, *A gondolat erejével. Rendhagyó önéletrajz* [With the Power of Thought. An Exceptional Autobiography] (Budapest, 2005), p. 111.

9 Tibor Beck and Pál Germuska, *Forradalom a bölcsészkaron* [Revolution at the Faculty of Arts] (Budapest, 1997), pp. 44–48.

10 Attila Szakolczai, "Győr-Sopron megye" [Győr-Sopron County], in idem, ed., *A vidék forradalma, 1956* [Revolution in the Provinces, 1956], vol. 2 (Budapest, 2006), pp. 143–210.

11 The Pilvax café was the Budapest meeting place for the group of young law students and writers who later became known as the "March youth" that set the stage for the Revolution of 1848. For more information regarding these organizations, see Attila Szakolczai and László Á. Varga, eds., *A vidék forradalma, 1956* [Revolution in the Provinces, 1956] vols. 1–2 (Budapest, 2003 and 2006).

12 István Vida, ed., *Diák és ifjúsági mozgalmak, 1956–1958. Forradalom—ellenállás—megtorlás* [Student and Youth Movements, 1956–1958. Revolution—Resistance—Reprisal] (Budapest, 2007).

13 *Ibid.*, p. 74. See also Csaba Farkas, "Csongrád megye" [Csongrád County], in Attila Szakolczai and László Á. Varga, eds., *A vidék forradalma, 1956* [Revolution in the Provinces, 1956], vol. 1 (Budapest, 2003), pp. 199–323, and Tamás Kis, *Magyar Egyetemisták és Főiskolások Szövetsége, 1956* [The Alliance of Hungarian University and College Students, 1956] (Szeged, 2002).

14 Attila Szakolczai, *Az 1956-os forradalom és szabadságharc* [The 1956 Revolution and Fight for Freedom] (Budapest, 2001), p. 23.

15 For a discussion of issues related to revolutionary theory and the 1956 Hungarian Revolution, see Péter Kende, *Eltékozolt forradalom?* [Wasted Revolution?] (Budapest, 2006), particularly pp. 88–120.

16 Vida, ed., *Diák és ifjúsági mozgalmak, 1956–1958*, pp. 75–76. This list continues with demands related to local city politics and university educational and curricular policy.

17 Many students at various institutions of higher education in Hungary were acquainted with one another from their high school days, which facilitated the establishment of contacts between them. Moreover, the Communist youth organization DISZ had mobilized university and college students from throughout the country to participate in relief efforts following the devastating Danube flood in the summer of 1956, creating the opportunity for them to establish inter-institutional contacts, which the Unified Alliance of Hungarian University and College Students used to its advantage in the dissemination of the organization's proclamation during the autumn of 1956.

18 "Az MDP Központi Vezetősége Párt és Tömegszervezeti osztályának tájékoztatója a funkcionáriusokról és a lakosság hangulatáról" [HWP Central Directorate Party and Mass Organizational Department Report on Functionaries and the Mood of the Population], in Lajos Gecsényi and Gábor Máthé, *Sub clausula, 1956* (Budapest, 2006), p. 467.

19 See Szakolczai, *Az 1956-os forradalom és szabadságharc*, pp. 124–126, and Vida, ed., *Diák és ifjúsági mozgalmak, 1956–1958*, pp. 110–112. The Technical University proclamation differed from the other lists of student demands, such as those published at the universities of Debrecen, Miskolc and Veszprém, as well as the Keszthely agricultural academy, in one regard: it lacked the stipulation that the Hungarian government initiate contact with neighboring Danubian states, including Austria, regarding the establishment of a central European confederation. See György Gyarmati, *Március hatalma – a hatalom márciusa. Fejezetek március 15. ünneplésének történetéből* [The Power of March—the March of Power. Chapters from the History of March 15 Celebrations] (Budapest, 1998), pp. 144–149.

20 György Gyarmati, "Kossuth-címeres forradalom" [Kossuth Coat-of-Arms Revolution], in Gábor Gyáni and János M. Rainer, eds., *Ezerkilencszázötvenhat az újabb történeti irodalomban* [Nineteen Fifty-Six in Modern Historical Literature] (Budapest, 2007), pp. 254–274.

21 Miklós Horváth, *1956 hadikrónikája* [1956 Military Chronicle] (Budapest, 2003).

22 Tibor Valuch, "Hajdú-Bihar megye" [Hajdú-Bihar County], in Szakolczai and Á. Varga, eds., *A vidék forradalma, 1956*, vol. 1, pp. 236–265.

23 János Gyurgyák, *A forradalom hangja. Magyarországi rádióadások, 1956* [The Voice of the Revolution. Radio Broadcasts in Hungary, October 23–November 9, 1956] (Budapest, 1989), pp. 29–39.

24 Gecsényi and Máthé, *Sub clausula, 1956*, p. 616.

25 Hanna Szalay, ed., *Napról napra. 1956 sajtója, október 23. – november 4.* [From Day to Day. The 1956 Press, October 23–November 4] (Budapest, 1989), pp. 59–60, and Gyurgyák, *A forradalom hangja*, pp. 82–88.

26 Vida, ed., *Diák és ifjúsági mozgalmak, 1956–1958*. pp. 201–203.

27 Gyurgyák, *A forradalom hangja*, p. 76.

28 János M. Rainer, *Nagy Imre II. 1953–1958* [Imre Nagy, Vol. 2: 1953–1958] (Budapest, 1999) pp. 261, 263, and Zoltán Ripp, "A pártvezetés végnapjai" [The Final Days of the Party Leadership], in Julianna Horváth and Zoltán Ripp, eds., *Ötvenhat októbere és a hatalom* [October of Fifty-Six and the Political Power] (Budapest, 1997), pp. 165–210.

29 Gyurgyák, *A forradalom hangja*, pp. 131–132.

30 András B. Hegedűs, ed., *1956 kézikönyve. Kronológia* [1956 Handbook. Chronology] (Budapest, 1996), p. 129.

31 György Kövér, *Losonczy Géza, 1917–1957* [Géza Losonczy, 1917–1957] (Budapest, 1998), p. 261.

32 Nagy's biographer aptly describes his pre-Revolution outlook with regard to the possibility of reappointment to the office of prime minister as "confident anticipation." Rainer, *Nagy Imre II. 1953–1958*, pp. 220–233.

33 Imre Nagy, *A magyar nép védelmében* [In Defense of the Hungarian People] (Brussels, 1957), p. 23. The writings of Imre Nagy appeared outside Hungary in deceptive bindings of several types following the Revolution. In order to disguise them for smuggling back into the country, Nagy's works were published in various cover jackets, chapter layouts and "pocket calendar" sizes. The cited passage appears on page 51 of one such version of Nagy's writings, entitled *Problèmes de la bombe H.* Other false titles include *L'agression Franco-Britannique contre L'Egypte, 1956*, *Les troubles du grand sympathique*, and *La concezione materialistica della storia.*

34 See Charles Gati, *Vesztett illúziók. Moszkva, Washington, Budapest és az 1956-os magyar forradalom* [Failed Illusions: Moscow, Washington, Budapest, and the 1956 Hungarian Revolt] (Budapest, 2008), particularly pp. 73–99, 165–173, 197–200, 215–217.

35 The author does not view the "Hungarian policy" of the United States of America as one of these factors, since it was essentially a non-policy. Washington's response to the Revolution permitted Moscow to handle the Hungarian question as it saw fit in the form of an "internal affair of the Communist empire."

36 "Minutes from the HWP Political Committee's October 28, 1956, Meeting," in Gecsényi and Máthé, *Sub clausula, 1956*, pp. 572–585.

37 This is a summary of the information contained in Szakolczai and Á. Varga, eds., *A vidék forradalma, 1956*, vol. 1 and Szakolczai, ed. *A vidék forradalma, 1956*, vol. 2.

38 László Eörsi, *Corvinisták* [Corvinists] (Budapest, 2001), and idem, *A Széna tériek, 1956* [Széna Squarers, 1956] (Budapest, 2006); Gyula Kozák, "Szent csőcselék" [Holy Rabble], in Éva Standeisky and János M. Rainer, eds., *Magyarország a jelenkorban. Évkönyv, 1999* [Hungary in Modern Times. Yearbook, 1999] (Budapest, 2000), pp. 255–281.

39 Rainer, *Nagy Imre II. 1953–1958*, pp. 244–249.

40 János M. Rainer and Judit Topits, eds., "Ötvenhat az ötvenediken. Kritikai szemle a magyar forradalom félévszázados évfordulóján megjelent művekből" [Fifty Six on the Fiftieth. Critical Review of the Works Appearing on the Semicentennial of the Hungarian Revolution] (www.rev.hu/reviews).

41 It must be noted that the present assessment of Imre Nagy's actions during these days differs in some regards from that contained in Charles Gati's previously cited work: Gati, *Vesztett illúziók. Moszkva, Washington, Budapest és az 1956-os magyar forradalom*, particularly pp. 149–162 and 212–214.

42 István Vida, ed., *1956 és a politika pártok. 1956. október 23.–november 4.* [1956 and the Political Parties. October 23–November 4] (Budapest, 1998), pp. 144–145.

43 Gecsényi and Máthé, *Sub clausula, 1956*, pp. 646–647, and Béla Király, *Honvédségből néphadsereg. Személyes visszaemlékezések, 1944–1956* [From National Army into People's Army. Personal Reminiscences, 1944–1956] (Paris and New Brunswick, NJ, 1986), pp. 251–253.

44 It was primarily for this reason that following the Revolution the Kádár regime wanted to prosecute Béla Király as part of the main trial of Imre Nagy and his associates. Alajos Dornback, Péter Kende, János M. Rainer and Katalin Somlai, eds., *A per. Nagy Imre és társai. 1958, 1989* [The Trial. Imre Nagy and His Associates. 1958, 1989] (Budapest, 2008), pp. 145, 159, 154–156.

45 Éva Gál, András B. Hegedűs, György Litván and János M. Rainer, eds., *A Jelcin-dosszié. Szovjet dokumentumok 1956-ról* [The Yeltsin Dossier. Soviet Documents about 1956] (Budapest, 1993), pp. 64–67.

46 Jenő Györkei and Miklós Horváth, *Szovjet katonai intervenció, 1956* [Soviet Military Intervention, 1956] (Budapest, 1996), pp. 199–200, and Horváth, *1956 hadikrónikája*, pp. 250–251.

47 Gecsényi and Máthé, *Sub clausula, 1956*, pp. 638–639, 644–645, 655–658, 666–667.

48 Ignác Romsics, ed., *Magyar történeti szöveggyűjtemény. 1919—1999* [Hungarian Historical Texts, 1919–1999] vol. 2 (Budapest, 2000), pp. 118–119.

49 Gecsényi and Máthé, *Sub clausula, 1956*, p. 716.

50 Horváth, *1956 hadikrónikája*, p. 389.

51 Szakolczai, *Az 1956-os forradalom és szabadságharc*, pp. 68, 190, 293, and Lajos Izsák, *Krónika, 1956* [Chronicle, 1956] (Budapest, 2006), pp. 158–159.

52 "Mindszenty József rádióbeszéde" [József Mindszenty's Radio Address], in Tamás G. Korányi, *Egy népfelkelés dokumentumai, 1956* [Documents from a Popular Uprising] (Budapest, 1989), pp. 107–109.

53 Szakolczai, *Az 1956-os forradalom és szabadságharc*, pp. 73, 300–301.

54 See Gyurgyák, *A forradalom hangja*, p. 489, and Korányi, *Egy népfelkelés dokumentumai, 1956*, pp. 313–315.

55 István Bibó, *Életút dokumentumokban* [A Life Path in Documents], ed. Tibor Huszár and Gábor Hanák (Budapest, 1995), pp. 448–450.

56 Zimándi, *A forradalom éve. Krónika 1956-ról*, p. 233.

57 Vjacseszlav Szereda and Alekszandr Sztikalin, eds., *Hiányzó lapok 1956 történetéből* [Missing Pages from the History of 1956] (Budapest, 1993), pp. 161–174.

58 *Népszabadság*, November 15, 1956. See Korányi, *Egy népfelkelés dokumentumai, 1956*, pp. 148–151.

59 Zoltán Szász, "A nemzeti kérdés a kelet-közép-európai rendszerváltásban" [The Nationality Question in the Central and Eastern European System Change], in Mariann Nagy, ed., *Híd a századok felett. Tanulmányok Katus László 70. születésnapjára* [Bridge Above the Centuries. Studies for the 70th Birthday of László Katus] (Pécs, 1997), p. 503.

60 Albert Camus, "A magyarok vére" [The Blood of the Hungarians], in Tibor Tollas, ed., *Gloria victis* (Vienna and Munich, 1986), pp. 5–6.

VII. AFTER THE REVOLUTION (1956–1963) PACIFICATION, RETRIBUTION, STABILIZATION[1]

1. Domestic Politics

In the last days of October 1956, the Revolution seemed to have been successful, and the fate of Hungary seemed to have been solved. However, out of the two assessments, only one was proved to be correct, since the Soviet leadership made their final decision—right at that moment, in those days that were still holding out a promise of hope for the Hungarians—to eliminate the Revolution by means of armed force. Indeed Hungary's fate was decided, and for long decades.

Soviet forces launched a concerted attack at dawn on November 4, 1956. Within hours, they had seized public institutions and other locations of strategic importance throughout Hungary, disarmed Hungarian military units, occupied major towns and cities, and begun to quell armed resistance.[2] The Hungarian military, with the exception of a few minor units, did not oppose the occupying forces. The newly formed Hungarian Revolutionary Worker–Peasant Government broadcast a summons from the studios of Radio Szolnok announcing the formation of a new, János Kádár-led cabinet[3] and declaring that an escalation of the counterrevolutionary threat had necessitated the Soviet armed intervention. The Worker–Peasant Government then enjoined the Hungarian people to discontinue its armed resistance to Soviet forces and to preserve the achievements of socialism. Around the same time, at 5:20 a.m., Radio Free Kossuth interrupted its programming to broadcast a statement from Imre Nagy in which the prime minister announced that Soviet forces had launched an attack on Budapest with the intention of overthrowing Hungary's democratic government. Although Nagy did not call for armed resistance, he did declare the following: "Our forces are engaged in battle. The government remains in place."[4] During the chaotic morning hours of November 4, Imre Nagy and several of his followers accepted an invitation from the ambassador of Yugoslavia to take refuge at the Yugoslav Embassy in order to avert capture at the hands of the Soviets. Nagy and his associates were not aware that the ambassador's offer was a product of previous Soviet–Yugoslav negotiations regarding the Hungarian crisis. Cardinal József Mindszenty, who had been released from house arrest during the Revolution, did likewise, taking refuge at the US Embassy in Budapest, where he was to stay for the next 15 years. Among the members of Imre Nagy's final cabinet, only István Bibó remained at the Parliament, from which he issued a declaration[5] asserting that the entire Hungarian people had risen against tyranny in October, and that the Soviet intervention was unlawful and would provoke further conflict, finally calling for passive resistance and an urgent UN response. Over subsequent days, Bibó composed a memorandum in which he summarized the conditions for a possible resolution to the conflict, which included the restoration of Hungary's sovereignty, the introduction of parliamentary democracy, the calling of free elections and the establishment of a social system based on respect for private property, although barring exploitation.

The armed conflict that reignited in November was concentrated primarily in Budapest,[6] the Mecsek Hills near Pécs, and Dunapentele, where clashes of varying intensity took place between revolutionaries and militarily superior Soviet forces for a period of several days. The Soviets encountered stiff resistance at the Budapest revolutionary strongholds of Corvin Alley, Baross Square, Tűzoltó Street, Tompa Street, Széna Square, Móricz Zsigmond Circus, Pesterzsébet, Újpest and Csepel, extinguishing organized armed resistance at these locations by November 11 only at the cost of significant casualties. In the end, Soviet troops numbering in the hundreds of thousands defeated armed revolutionary groups consisting of a total of 10,000–15,000 combatants. A total of 2,700 Hungarians were killed and approximately 19,000 were wounded in the course of the armed conflict, while the Soviet army sustained losses of 669 dead, 1,500 wounded and 51 missing in action.[7] Following the end of armed conflict, a total of 200,000 people fled Hungary for fear of reprisal and restoration of the Stalinist system. There was no sign of the help from the West that had been promised so often in October. The leaders of Western European countries and the United States did not want to risk changing the status quo that had emerged between the Great Powers in Europe following World War II, focusing instead on the provision of humanitarian aid, support for Hungarian refugees and attainment of Hungary's political isolation.

Following their return from Moscow, János Kádár[8] and his entourage met on November 5 in Szolnok with those members of his cabinet—István Kossa and Antal Apró—who had learned of their appointment to the Hungarian Revolutionary Worker–Peasant Government from the previously mentioned radio summons. On the night of November 6–7 a Soviet armored unit transported Kádár and the members of his government to Budapest, where they took their oaths of office in front of Presidential Council Chairman István Dobi at 2 p.m. the following afternoon, thus ensuring that the Soviet puppet government would be invested with the appearance of legitimacy. However, the situation was, in fact, more complicated: since Imre Nagy had not resigned even after taking refuge at the Yugoslav Embassy, the country in effect had two prime ministers. The newly inducted government attempted to resolve this constitutional predicament by formally appointing János Kádár to the post of prime minister and announcing Imre Nagy's dismissal, to be considered as applying retroactively from November 4.

After taking political control of Hungary following the second Soviet military intervention on November 4, János Kádár found himself to be operating in a vacuum. The majority of Hungarian society pointedly rejected his policies, a repudiation that post-Revolution political rearguard actions lasting until January 1957 served to reinforce.[9] For a period of several months, the large number of Soviet troops stationed in Hungary represented the Kádár government's most important source of political support. Hungarian Workers' Party membership shrank to a fraction of its pre-Revolution size in the autumn of 1956, increasing significantly again only in the spring of 1957. Moreover, most of those who had remained in the party were dogmatic communists who viewed Kádár as insufficiently committed to the doctrinaire notion of proletarian dictatorship. After in January 1957 becoming the only member of the Rákosi era's inner party leadership to return to Hungary, József Révai used the support of these hard-line communists and the Stalinist members of the CPSU Presidium to launch an attack on Kádár and attempt to vindicate the pre-1956 HWP leadership to which he himself had belonged. Révai, however, failed on both accounts.

The Kádár government's most important task was to reorganize its political and institutional system, thus establishing its own armed force, reconstituting the political police and restoring the functional capacity of the state administration. This process progressed very slowly, concluding only in the summer of 1957.

Following the formation of the Hungarian Revolutionary Worker–Peasant Government, the party initiated the process of reorganization, establishing the Hungarian Socialist Workers' Party (HSWP) Interim Executive Committee on November 7 and its Provisional Central Committee four days later. This took place under both strict Soviet political supervision and the peculiar circumstance that Imre Nagy and the other members of the HSWP organizing committee instituted in the place of the Hungarian Workers' Party on November 1 were "enjoying" the seemingly "boundless" hospitality of the Yugoslav Embassy in Budapest.

The Soviet army instituted military administration in Hungary as a substitute for the administrative and police organizational system that had collapsed in October. In order to fulfill his government's objective of establishing its own armed force, János Kádár initiated the rearming of two battalions of the Hungarian army on November 8, a measure that the CPSU Central Committee authorized on the following day, although it took several weeks to implement. Meanwhile, the internal security forces of KGB Chairman General Ivan Aleksandrovich Serov assisted the Soviet army in its supervision over Hungary from November 1956 until the spring of 1957. Along with the establishment of its occupational system, Soviet military and security forces began to take suspected revolutionaries into custody, transporting several thousand Hungarian citizens to the Soviet Union in the days after November 4. Kádár, who feared that these arrests would serve to further increase his political isolation, quickly convinced the Soviets to halt the deportations and to permit some of those taken out of the country to return. In mid-November high-ranking Soviet party leaders Malenkov, Suslov and Aristov arrived in Hungary, where they exercised practical control over the process of political restoration in the country for the next month. The extensive authority with which the three Soviet party officials had been invested enabled them to essentially govern Hungary until their departure from the country at the end of 1956.

In addition to the reorganization of the political system, the exceptionally frail Kádár government was forced to manage a continual stream of daily political issues, receiving delegations from throughout Hungary and attempting to check resistance to its policies in accordance with Soviet instructions. From the middle of November, workers' councils, which had begun to coordinate their activities at both a local and a national level, became the most important focal points of social self-defense. These councils demanded the immediate withdrawal of Soviet military forces, the reinstatement of the Nagy government, freedom of the press, the declaration of Hungary's neutrality, and worker supervision over factories and institutions. The workers' councils called a national strike to accentuate these demands, although they temporarily suspended the work stoppage in the second half of November while reaffirming the right to strike at a subsequent date.

A dual political system had essentially been established in Hungary, with one pole centered on the Sándor Bali- and Sándor Rácz-led Greater Budapest Central Workers' Council and the local revolutionary committees that operated in numerous locations until January 1957 and the other on the Soviet-supported Kádár government. The primary points of contention that emerged between the workers' councils and the Kádár government in negotiations that took place between them in November 1956 were the restoration of Hungary's sovereignty, withdrawal of Soviet troops, establishment of democratic political conditions, the calling of free elections and the guarantee of the right to strike. The councils and the government were unable to reach a consensus on these issues during the talks, while Kádár, with the support of Soviet military forces, prevented the National Workers' Council from forming in Budapest on November 21. Many workers' council leaders had, in fact, already been taken into custody by this time.

In order to solidify its political position, the Kádár government, again with the support of the Soviet military, sought to resolve another urgent issue, that of what to do with Imre Nagy and his associates—Ferenc Donáth, György Lukács, Géza Losonczy, Miklós Vásárhelyi, Sándor Haraszti, Gábor Tánczos, Szilárd Újhelyi, Zoltán Szántó, József Szilágyi and Zoltán Vas—who had taken refuge at the Yugoslav Embassy in Budapest. During preliminary Hungarian–Yugoslav negotiations, Kádár had issued a written promise to permit all those who had sought asylum at the Embassy to return home freely under no threat of retribution. However, the Hungarian Socialist Workers' Party leader quickly came to support a Soviet decision pursuant to which a KGB detachment abducted Imre Nagy, his political colleagues and their family members as they attempted to return home from the Yugoslav Embassy on November 22. During interrogations held prior to his deportation to Romania, the Soviets and their Hungarian collaborators urged Nagy to resign as prime minister, although he refused to do so.

These actions, whose chief objective was to prevent the reestablishment of a political counter-pole, on the one hand served to increase János Kádár's unpopularity, and on the other foreshadowed the probable future direction of politics in the country. Although Kádár continued to conduct negotiations with the workers' councils and representatives from various parties until the end of November, even alluding to the prospect of a communist-dominated multi-party system, the Hungarian Socialist Workers' Party leader abandoned his centrist political notions at the beginning of December, instead voicing unambiguous support for the Soviet concept of a rapid rebuilding of the proletarian dictatorship's institutional system. Following this unequivocal shift to the left, the HSWP Provisional Central Committee adopted a resolution at its session held on December 2, 3 and 5 that explicitly referred to the October events as a counterrevolution. Furthermore, the resolution blamed the October upheaval not primarily on the dogmatic policies of Rákosi and Gerő, but on the activities of the Imre Nagy-led revisionist group. The ideologically resolute document also denounced representatives of "the reactionary Horthy system" and international imperialism for having played a role in triggering the October events.

In November and December 1956, the majority of Hungarian society strongly rejected the Kádár government and the prospect of political restoration. A few days after summoning Hungarians to return to work, the workers' councils called another strike at major factories for November 21 and 22, while the streets of Budapest emptied for a silent demonstration between 2 p.m. and 3 p.m. on the afternoon of November 23, and several thousand participants took part in a women's demonstration held on Heroes' Square in Budapest on December 4. The general strike that paralyzed the country on December 11 and 12 provides a clear indication of the significant degree of support that the workers' councils commanded in Hungary following the Revolution. In order to subdue the workers' council-led resistance to his government, Kádár declared martial law,[10] while punitive measures including arrests and mass internments were also initiated. Additionally, authorities imposed an evening curfew, which was suspended only for Christmas before being lifted permanently in April 1957. Gunfire was used to disperse anti-government demonstrations in Miskolc, Eger, Tatabánya, Salgótarján, Gyula and Kecskemét at the beginning of December 1956, claiming the lives of hundreds of people. The Kádár government was clearly attempting to permanently quash resistance and social solidarity.

Two well-known leaders of armed revolutionary groups that had operated in Budapest in the autumn of 1956, József Dudás and János Szabó, were condemned to death in a summary procedure and executed in January 1957. Beginning in the middle of the latter month, newly constituted people's tribunals conducted expedited political trials in which the accused were not granted the right to defense, appeal or other forms of legal redress. Mass political resistance had come to an end by January 1957. On January 11 the Kádár government used the Soviet military to disperse a Csepel workers' strike. The armed intervention claimed even more victims. Sporadic, mostly silent, commemorations of the October events took place on January 23, although they did not generate broad-scale demonstrations. With the active assistance of Soviet internal security and military forces, the Kádár government managed to suppress essentially all legal and illegal resistance organizations by the end of January 1957. The government ordered the dissolution of both the Writers' Union, which had played an important role in post-Revolution political rearguard actions, and the Journalists' Union. The slogan "We will start again in March!" emerged at the time of the March 15 national holiday, although a renewal of political resistance had become impossible by this time. The Kádár government made a demonstration of its power on the eve of the holiday, deploying the freshly organized Workers' Militia and police units to carry out a massive number of preemptive arrests and internments.

By December 1956, newly established police forces had begun to gradually assume control over law enforcement duties from the Soviet army, launching a nationwide campaign of terror in the name of restoring order. Although the State Protection Authority was not reconstituted following its October dissolution, a significant number of the members of the new political police were veterans of the former coercive organization. Under the close supervision of party leaders and with the active participation of Soviet advisors, the reorganization of the political police was completed rather quickly, becoming the main vehicle for the implementation of the government's retaliatory measures. In addition to the procedures against revolutionaries, rebuilding of the system of total supervision began as well, with the resurrection of informant networks and an increase in the number of people kept under surveillance. Prior to 1956, the police had kept files on 1.5 million people, or every fifth citizen of Hungary over the age of 15. This number had declined to 550,000 by the autumn of 1956 before rising back to 650,000 by October 1957, when the police maintained records on "only" every tenth citizen over the age of 15.[11]

The reorganization of the army began in December 1956 and was completed about a year and a half later. Members of the military who had taken part in the Revolution were put on trial, while the officer corps was subjected to a thorough review and only those who consented to swear an oath of allegiance to the government in the form of a "officer's declaration" were allowed to retain their rank. Only four fifths of the commissioned and non-commissioned officers from the pre-revolutionary period elected to take the oath, while the remaining one fifth left the military. At the beginning of 1959, Hungary's armed forces included 84,000 personnel, just two thirds of the number on active duty before 1956. This number was supplemented by 60,000–70,000 Soviet troops stationed in Hungary temporarily in accordance with an inter-state pact signed on May 27, 1957. The issue of the withdrawal of Soviet forces from Hungary never emerged during the period in which the socialist system held sway.

By the early spring of 1957, it had become clear to members of various social groups that both active and passive political resistance had become futile. The Kádár government resorted to the very same means of coercion utilized during the Rákosi era, while also making minor social concessions. During the first few months of 1957, the government attempted to solidify its power through mass retribution against those who took part in the Revolution, sending special police referred to popularly as "pufajkás" due to their Russian-style quilted "pufajka" jackets to intimidate villagers through the frequently fatal physical assault of local revolutionary leaders. Several thousand people were imprisoned and subjected to police and legal procedures as a result. A great deal of publicity was initially accorded to subsequent show trials[12] (such as the trials of those who had participated in the resistance group that had operated at the Sándor Péterffy Street hospital, and the cases of revolutionary commander István Angyal and the writer István Eörsi), procedures whose objective was to punish politically active groups and people, provide a display of the government's power, and intimidate a broad section of Hungarian society. Later such bogus legal proceedings were conducted in private, although investigators, prosecutors and judges continued to utilize every means at their disposal to prove that the accused had participated in counterrevolutionary activities aimed at overthrowing the people's republic. There were nevertheless very few people among the accused who had shown demonstrable support for the pre-1945 system or could otherwise be qualified as what contemporary terminology referred to as a "reactionary class alien." The large majority of those put on trial were, in fact, students, young workers and intellectuals who had been socialized amid the new environment that arose in Hungary following the end of World War II.

In the spring of 1957, Hungarian and Soviet officials decided to initiate legal procedures against Imre Nagy and his associates,[13] who were shortly thereafter transported from their captivity in Snagov, Romania, to Budapest. Both Kádár and his fellow party leaders believed that they must use every means at their disposal to prevent the formation of a political counter-pole led by Imre Nagy and his allies. To quote temporary documents, the latter effort required "giving free rein to the organs of justice," which in essence connoted that the Imre Nagy trial would be politically guided and result in the imposition of capital punishment. The Hungarian Socialist Workers' Party Political Committee and Central Committee discussed the criminal procedures against Imre Nagy and his associates on several occasions, expressing agreement with János Kádár's argument in favor of severe sentences. The trial of former Prime Minister Imre Nagy[14] and his associates that took place in the spring and early summer of 1958 became one of the key elements in the process of retribution directed at those who had been involved in revolutionary activity. Of those accused at the trial, Imre Nagy, Pál Maléter and Miklós Gimes were sentenced to death and executed on June 16, 1958, while József Szilágyi was executed in April and Géza Losonczy died in prison during forced feeding at the end of 1957. Among the other defendants, Ferenc Donáth, Zoltán Tildy and Miklós Vásárhelyi were sentenced to twelve, six and five years in prison respectively, while other noted personalities who had taken an active role in resistance during and/or after the Revolution, such as Árpád Göncz, István Bibó, Domokos Kosáry, Ferenc Mérei, Tibor Déry, László Mensáros and György Litván, were also imprisoned for shorter or longer periods of time.

The mass retribution that followed the Revolution came to a close at the end of 1958, after which time the number of newly initiated legal procedures against alleged participants in the Revolution underwent a continuous decline (although death sentences were pronounced and carried out as late as 1961). A total of 229 people were executed for their participation in the 1956 Revolution, most of them leaders and members of armed revolutionary groups and those who had engaged in political resistance following the suppression of the Revolution beginning on November 4.[15] A further 20,000 people were imprisoned for a longer or shorter period of time, while 13,000 others were interned for between six months and a year and a half between 1957 and 1959, and tens of thousands were placed under police observation. For the lack of precise data, the number of people dismissed from their jobs can be estimated to have been in the tens of thousands. The Kádár regime continued to punish its enemies even following their deaths, burying those executed following the 1956 Revolution in unmarked graves whose location was revealed to their next of kin only at the time of the system change in 1989–1990.

In 1958–1959, the Ministry of the Interior conducted so-called "mapping" in which it identified an average of 5,000–6,000 people who had taken part in the events of 1956 in each of Hungary's counties, which, including those counted in Budapest, resulted in a total of at least 110,000–130,000 "counterrevolutionaries" throughout the country. It was "much easier" to acquire a dossier in secret police files than it was to escape the heightened attention of the "organ." The Ministry of the Interior's infamous III/III internal security division kept a significant proportion of those who had played a role in the 1956 Revolution under surveillance until the collapse of the socialist regime.

During the period of pacification from 1957 to 1961, the Hungarian Socialist Workers' Party leadership made broad use of the instruments of reprisal in an attempt to either incapacitate or force into exile those who had engaged in conspicuous political activity during the days of the Revolution. This effort focused on neutralizing those "seminal figures" who would have been capable of organizing and directing dissident political activities. In this sense, retribution for participation in the Revolution was systematic, albeit frequently capricious in that some people who had played prominent roles in the events of 1956 escaped punishment, while their revolutionary associates were imprisoned or even executed. The feeling of defenselessness in the face of political authority and of discouragement following the suppression of the Revolution had a significant tangible impact on the behavior of certain individuals and social groups in the period following the 1956 Revolution.

Throughout this period of pacification following the Revolution, the Kádár government employed every means at its disposal to restore political control over the press and institutions of mass communication.[16] The regime had already seized the positions of power within Hungary's media by November 1956, taking quick and decisive action to subdue any trace of resistance among journalists. The Hungarian Socialist Workers' Party launched *Népszabadság* to replace *Szabad Nép* as its most important daily newspaper, serving as the party's official party organ for the next three and a half decades. In addition to the central HSWP newspaper(s),[17] county party committee dailies continued to play an important political role as well. The press structure that was to exist in Hungary with only minor modifications throughout the Kádár era was essentially put in place during the years 1957–1958. It should be noted, however, that the newspapers published during this period—with the exception of the dailies—gradually become more readable and digestible in terms of content.

Following the Revolution, the Kádár regime did not reinstate publication of *Irodalmi Újság*, the periodical that had served as the most important political forum prior to 1956, launching in its place *Élet és Irodalom*, whose staff of editors and journalists was composed of party loyalists. Hungary's most influential authors maintained voluntary silence at this time, refraining from public expression of opinion in spite of various forms of political pressure that had been placed on them in 1958–1959 to advocate the interests of the party. A compromise between writers and the regime began to emerge in 1959–1960 with the reorganization of the Writers' Union in November 1959 and the renewed publication of works from proscribed or voluntarily silent authors.[18]

The introduction of modern electronic communications media, primarily television, represented a significant change. In 1953 a decision was made to establish the State Television Company, which began weekly trial transmissions of an hour and a half to two hours in length beginning in 1958. Regular programming was launched in 1958 with three or four hours of scheduled broadcasts per week. Lengthy debates took place at this time regarding the new medium's potential value as a means to propagate party propaganda, although direct use of television for this purpose diminished gradually even during its initial years of operation. The number of television subscribers in Hungary rose from 16,000 in 1958 to more than 100,000 in 1960.

Following his initial period of weakness, János Kádár's political position began to become stronger continuously both within the Hungarian Socialist Workers' Party and in the country in general beginning in the late spring of 1957. The Kádár government's effort to gain the allegiance of the essentially passive majority of society, which had been somewhat supportive of the active post-revolutionary opposition, certainly played a role in strengthening the Hungarian Socialist Workers' Party leader's political standing. In order to mollify the populace, the government raised wages, temporarily reduced taxes imposed on merchants and craftsmen, annulled the tax on childless couples, removed restrictions on the free choice of employment and agricultural activity, permitted limited land sales, settled the issue of pensions that had been unlawfully revoked after 1948, legalized abortion, and declared Christmas and Easter to be public holidays (although the March 15 national holiday commemorating the outbreak of the 1848 Revolution was only partially reinstated in the form of an exclusively school holiday). The positive popular response to these measures was reflected in the more or less willing participation of hundreds of thousands of people in the May 1 parade on Budapest's Heroes' Square in 1957. The aforementioned initiatives represented a pragmatic supplement to the Kádár government's pacification program, not completely new policies.

Following sharp debate, the Hungarian Socialist Workers' Party officially adopted the Kádár government's policies at the party's national conference in June 1957, while both the József Révai-led ideological dogmatists and the party's reform advocates were pushed into the background. As a result of the latter, reform proposals formulated under the guidance of economics professor István Varga were permanently removed from the HSWP's agenda at the end of the summer. At the beginning of 1957, the Kádár government had commissioned a group of economists to conduct an analysis of the socialist planned economic system and submit proposals aimed at increasing its efficiency. The economists presented their recommendations to the party in June 1957,[19] urging a decrease in centralization, an increase in company autonomy and the total elimination of plan-based production commands. Kádár reshuffled the HSWP leadership at the party conference, promoting domestic communists who had been marginalized after 1949, although they had not compromised themselves in 1956—Gyula Kállai, Lajos Fehér and Jenő Fock—to important positions within the party.

In an important step towards making Hungary's system of political institutions functional again, Parliament convened for the first time following a prolonged pause in May 1957, reconfirming János Kádár's appointment to the post of prime minister, a position that the Hungarian Socialist Workers' Party leader held until 1958. During the 1956–1957 restoration period, the government made not even so much as a pretense of observing such constitutional formalities.

Cabinet members carried out their duties for months on end without any valid authority, while the Presidential Council simply renewed the mandates of parliamentary representatives when they expired in the spring of 1957 without calling new elections. The Presidential Council assumed legislative duties in its capacity as a collective presidency, issuing decrees that carried the same authority as laws. In the spring of 1957 the Communist Youth Alliance (KISZ) was founded to serve as the successor to the party's pre-1956 youth organization, DISZ. The alliance's main function was to popularize Hungarian Socialist Workers' Party policies among Hungary's youth, to generate a steady supply of new party cadres and, not least importantly, to provide institutional supervision over young people. Among national party organizations, the political functions of the Patriotic People's Front, whose official purpose was to serve as a representative body for non-party members who were nevertheless committed to "people's power," were essentially limited to nominating candidates to run for the position of parliamentary representative and to organize and carry out elections. The party maintained strict control over trade unions, whose interest-advocacy prerogatives were confined to expression of accord with party policies and whose basic objectives included "promoting production." The party never even considered the notion of providing unions with the right to strike, declaring that a workers' strike directed against a workers' state represented a violation of the principles of socialism. The reorganization of the party continued to proceed as well. By the summer of 1957, HSWP membership had risen to approximately 350,000. While this number represented just 40 percent of the party's pre-1956 membership, more than four fifths of these 350,000 people had been members of the Hungarian Workers' Party before the Revolution and thus maintained a personal interest in restoring the political conditions that had prevailed in the country prior to 1956. In addition to the aforementioned trial of Imre Nagy and his associates, the main political events that took place in Hungary during the year 1958 were the holding of postponed parliamentary elections, Khrushchev's visit to Budapest, during which the CPSU leader reconfirmed his support for János Kádár's political course and the government's decision to collectivize agriculture. Implementation of this socially turbulent transformation determined the course of domestic politics in Hungary at the beginning of the 1960s. (See the subsequent sections of this chapter.)

The parliamentary and council elections that had been postponed in 1957 until 1958 as a result of the political uncertainty that predominated in Hungary following the 1956 Revolution were of some political significance. (Nearly one tenth of the country's parliamentary representatives had been forced to resign in the spring of 1957 as a result of their political activities in 1956.) By 1958, the Revolutionary Worker–Peasant Government, then under the leadership of Prime Minister Ferenc Münnich, was prepared for a "political contest," which in fact represented nothing more than securing a manifestation of society's loyalty. This took place with the anticipated degree of success in the autumn of 1958, when 98 percent of eligible voters took part in the national elections, which according to official records produced an average of only 0.5–0.6 percent of either invalid ballots or votes against the party. This election essentially completed the restoration of the political regime, although 1956 revolutionaries were put to death as late as 1961 and the "struggle against hostile elements" continued to play a central role in politics between 1960 and 1962. The party's campaign against the Church also continued during this period, resulting in several trials of greater or lesser importance.

The frequency of the regime's open use of force to achieve its objectives subsequently began to decline. The gradual change in the regime's political bearing is reflected in its release of the majority of those imprisoned for their conduct during the 1956 Revolution in two small-scale amnesties in 1959 and 1960 and a comprehensive amnesty in 1963. These amnesties did not, however, apply to those who had been convicted of treason or criminal attempted murder for their roles in the armed clashes that took place during the Revolution. The more than 4,000 political detainees released from prison pursuant to the amnesties faced great difficulty in their effort to reintegrate into society, often remaining under police surveillance until the end of their lives. It took the majority of these former political prisoners five to ten years to overcome the stigma associated with their convictions and to escape the marginalized circumstances that the regime had established and maintained for them.

The political changes that took place in Hungary at the beginning of the 1960s show that Kádár had permanently split with the Rákosi system and its most prominent political representatives as well as with the Rákosi era's lower-ranking officials who had played a decisive role in the process of pacification and restoration following the Revolution. In the years after the suppression of the Revolution, the Hungarian Socialist Workers' Party general secretary ensured in the course of his negotiations with Soviet party leaders that Rákosi would be denied even the possibility of regaining an influence over Hungarian politics. The former Hungarian Workers' Party leader, who had on several occasions indicated that he wished to return to Hungary, spent the initial period of his forced exile in Moscow, from which location the CPSU central committee subsequently compelled him to move to Gorky. The party resolution that the HSWP central committee adopted in August 1962 pertaining to the errors committed during the era of the cult of personality both mandated the expulsion of former dogmatic communist leaders such as Rákosi and Ernő Gerő from the party and established the ideological premise for the HSWP to distance itself from the radically dictatorial methods utilized during the Rákosi era without severing the necessary continuity with the period, in accordance with the principle that "socialism was being built then as well." Also in 1962, the Central Committee divested György Marosán, who had assumed a dominant political role within the party following the 1956 Revolution, of all his offices, relegating him to the status of rank-and-file HSWP member as punishment for allegedly spreading discord within the party. These measures signified an end to the process of stabilizing the political power of both János Kádár personally and the regime as a whole, as well as that of pacification and consolidation of post-revolutionary Hungarian society. In November 1962 the HSWP's seventh congress announced, among other things, that the laying of Hungary's socialist foundations had been completed with the socialist reorganization of the agricultural system. The regime's social policies underwent a commensurate transformation at this time, as a result of what documents from the period claimed was the fact that "there are no longer any segments of people in the country whose interests are contrary to those of socialism." The stabilization of the political situation in Hungary entailed a gradual decrease in "hand-controlled" Soviet supervision as well as the enactment of policies intended to promote consolidation, most important among them the application of the "he who is not against socialism is with us" principle, the elimination of social origin as a factor to be taken into consideration in the evaluation of applications for university admission and removal of restrictions regarding the appointment of non-party members to leadership positions.

Another critical element in the process of political stabilization was the restructuring of relations between the state and Church.[20] During the period of the 1956 Revolution, Hungary's Churches attempted to increase their scope of action, which had been severely curtailed at the beginning of the 1950s. Most denominations initiated leadership changes at this time, replacing prelates, priests and pastors who had maintained excessively close relations with the Rákosi regime with ecclesiastical and secular leaders advocating more autonomous Church policies. Among these changes, Protestant religious leaders Reformed bishops Albert Bereczky and János Péter and Lutheran bishops Lajos Vető and László Dezséry were forced to resign in 1957. Following this temporary period of conciliation, the Kádár government restored the anti-Church policies of the early 1950s towards the end of 1958, appointing people to leading ecclesiastical offices who were prepared to cooperate with party authorities. The struggle against "clerical reaction" and the religious worldview was relaunched at the same time, and party functionaries, Ministry of the Interior employees, soldiers and their families were forbidden to participate in religious events and rituals, with the exception of funerals, weddings and baptisms. Municipal and village councils were instructed to take measures to curb clerical influence and to reduce the number of students receiving religious instruction. Attempts were also made at this time to make relations between the Church and state more productive: the Catholic Committee of the National Peace Council was established in May 1957, while in the autumn of 1957 the Hungarian Bishops' Council condemned the United Nations Special Committee on the Problem of Hungary report on the Hungarian Revolution, and the Hungarian Socialist Workers' Party Political Committee issued a resolution in the summer of 1958 stating that the struggle against the religious worldview should be rooted in persuasion rather than compulsion. The latter principle was not, however, fully observed for a period of many years. Leaders of Hungary's still widely supported Churches essentially abandoned their former policy of non-engagement in the autumn of 1958 and began to obliquely encourage their faithful to vote for party candidates standing in elections under the auspices of the Patriotic People's Front. This indirect support was undoubtedly one of the factors that facilitated the conclusion of an agreement in 1959 that stipulated state subsidies for the Churches, permitted religious instruction to be held at schools outside regular teaching hours, and provided preliminary state approval for the Vatican to appoint new Catholic bishops in Hungary for the first time since 1951. These bishops swore an oath of allegiance to the constitution along with President of the Hungarian Catholic Bishops' Conference

President József Grősz, who had assumed leadership over the Catholic Church after József Mindszenty took sanctuary at the US Embassy in Budapest. Endre Hamvas took over as president of the Hungarian Catholic Bishops' Conference following Bishop Grősz's death in 1961. Bishop Hamvas was a firm advocate of further conciliation, although even this occasionally proved to be insufficient at the beginning of the 1960s, when the government again started pursuing strongly anti-Church and anti-religious policies. Approximately 300 ecclesiastical and secular officials were arrested and imprisoned for greater and longer periods of time in the course of a new wave of persecution aimed particularly at the Catholic Church. The Kádár administration reserved the right to veto appointments to even the most minor ecclesiastical offices, mandating that all Church officials swear an oath of allegiance before assuming their posts. Many long years were to pass before the emergence of more pragmatic policies *vis-à-vis* the Church.

The intensity of Hungarian society's rejection of the communist regime began to diminish perceptibly beginning in the middle of the 1960s. Convinced that political circumstances would not and could not change in the foreseeable future, the majority of Hungarians chose to accept the political hegemony of the Hungarian Socialist Workers' Party, contenting themselves with the minor liberties that were permitted within the confines of the regime.

2. Foreign Policy[21]

Hungary essentially had no autonomous foreign policy in the middle of the 1950s. The Kádár government was internationally isolated in the period following the Revolution: the Western powers refused to recognize the new regime, while the Soviet-controlled Hungarian government was compelled to reject UN demands calling for the withdrawal of Soviet forces from Hungary, the holding of free elections and permission for international observers to enter the country.[22] As a result, the Kádár government's international relations were for a long time confined to other countries in the socialist camp. However, Hungary occupied a subordinate role even within this system of "fraternal socialist countries," the majority of whose leaders placed various forms of pressure on the Kádár government late in 1956 and early in 1957 to accelerate the pace of restoration. At the beginning of January 1957, Communist Party leaders from Bulgaria, Romania and Czechoslovakia accompanied a Khrushchev-led Soviet party and government delegation to Budapest, where they held talks with their Hungarian Socialist Workers' Party and Kádár government counterparts regarding the situation in Hungary. Then in the middle of January, Zhou Enlai led a Communist Party of China delegation to Hungary, where the Chinese premier and minister of foreign affairs personally urged Hungarian leaders to restore the proletarian dictatorship and severely punish those who had taken part in the Revolution. HSWP and government officials attempted to more or less satisfy the counsel of these visiting leaders in the hope that maintaining good relations with fellow socialist countries, particularly those bordering Hungary, would serve to ease the country's international isolation. The Kádár government viewed intensification of its diplomatic contacts in the Third World as another possible means of putting an end to Hungary's international isolation, conducting high-level negotiations with India, Indonesia, Egypt and Syria at the end of the 1950s aimed at strengthening political and economic relations with these countries.

Bilateral Soviet–Hungarian negotiations took place frequently in the years after 1956, particularly in 1957 and 1958, when leaders from the two countries convened essentially every other month at meetings whose basic purpose was to provide the Hungarian Socialist Workers' Party leadership with an occasion to outline the prevailing state of affairs in Hungary and to receive Soviet instructions. The Soviet–Hungarian bilateral agreement signed in the spring of 1957 formally authorizing the Soviet Union to station its military forces in Hungary was both prepared and adopted within the framework of these bimonthly talks. Following the initial period of uncertainty, Kádár's efforts to restore order in Hungary managed to win the confidence of the CPSU leadership, notably Khrushchev, with whom the HSWP general secretary had cultivated warm personal relations. Kádár became one of Khrushchev's most loyal and committed allies, satisfying the Soviet party leader's expectations in terms of both foreign and domestic politics. At the November 1957 conference of Communist and Workers' Parties in Moscow, Kádár retroactively justified the need for Soviet intervention in 1956, while in the spring of 1958 the HSWP general secretary temporarily suspended the trial of Imre Nagy and his associates at Khrushchev's request. Moreover, Kádár was among the first leaders to publicly condemn Chinese communist policy following the deterioration of relations between the Soviet Union and China. Khrushchev traveled frequently to Hungary in the late 1950s and early 1960s, awarding the HSWP leader a Hero of the Soviet Union decoration during his final visit to the country in the spring of 1964.

The wave of retribution that followed the 1956 Revolution, including the Nagy trial, served to further increase Hungary's international isolation and ensure that the Western powers would continue to view the Kádár government as an unsuitable diplomatic partner. The Hungarian question remained on the agenda of the United Nations for many years, while in the autumn of 1957 the organization's General Assembly adopted a report from the Special Committee on the Problem of Hungary concluding that a popular uprising had taken place in Hungary during the autumn of 1956 and that the Kádár government had come to power as a result of unlawful Soviet intervention. Representatives from Hungary were not permitted to take part in UN proceedings until 1961, fundamentally signifying that the country was not a fully fledged member of the international community. It was for this reason that János Kádár's first official visit to the West in the autumn of 1960 took him to New York, where the Hungarian Socialist Workers' Party general secretary addressed the UN General Assembly.

From the beginning of the 1960s, the Kádár government made an increasing effort to break Hungary's international isolation, conducting secret negotiations with the United States[23] that produced an agreement according to which an amnesty would be proclaimed in Hungary for those imprisoned for their activities during the 1956 Revolution, while US representatives would submit a proposal at the United Nations to terminate the organization's examination of the Hungarian question. As a result, the UN removed the question from its agenda at the end of 1962 and accepted the credentials of Hungarian delegates in January 1963, while UN Secretary-General U Thant made an official visit to Hungary during the summer of 1963. The Kádár government introduced other measures in the first half of the 1960s aimed at improving Hungary's international relations, easing restrictions on travel abroad, making it easier to obtain a visa, and taking steps to promote tourism. The Hungarian leadership nevertheless acted in total compliance with Soviet interests in the sphere of East–West relations both at this time and for many years thereafter, a circumstance reflected clearly in Hungary's diplomatic pronouncements blaming US imperialism for the outbreak of the Berlin and Cuban crises.

The Kádár government's declaration of a general amnesty in the spring of 1963 represented an important step in the normalization of US–Hungarian relations, while Hungary's diplomatic affairs also become increasingly amicable with other Western countries such as the United Kingdom, France and Canada, which beginning in 1963–1964 gradually raised their bilateral contacts with Hungary to ambassadorial status.

Minority issues played almost no role in Hungary's relations with its socialist neighbors at this time, in spite of the fact that a total of more than three million Hungarians lived in Czechoslovakia, Romania, Yugoslavia and the Soviet Union.[24] In conformity with the precepts of proletarian internationalism, the leaders of both Hungary and the latter countries considered the question of national minorities to represent a strictly internal affair. Thus Hungary did not raise minority issues in the course of its inter-party and inter-state contacts with neighboring socialist states, even though authorities from Czechoslovakia, Romania and the Soviet Union often employed aggressive assimilatory measures, primarily with regard to education, mother-tongue use and culture, against the Hungarian minorities living in their countries. Taken within the historical context of Central and Eastern Europe, the Kádár government's clear indication to Romanian and Czechoslovak leaders in 1957–1958 that it harbored no demands whatsoever on territory in their countries was exceptionally important.

3. The Economy[25]

The 1956 Revolution served to temporarily hamper the performance of Hungary's economy. Continual recurring strikes paralyzed economic production from the end of October until the middle of December. It took months to restore economic production to its pre-revolutionary level and revive the normal functions of Hungary's centrally planned economy. This economic disruption caused Hungary's GDP to decline by 20 percent in 1956. Emergency relief aid and a preferential loan of nearly 1.5 million rubles in cash and commodities from the Soviet Union and other socialist countries undeniably played an important role in moderating Hungary's economic difficulties, while Western assistance also helped to quickly restore the system of public provision, although authorities did not highlight this fact at the time. The Government Restitution Commission and Government Public Provision Commission were established in November 1956 in order to organize reconstruction and public provision efforts. The government also raised wages, introduced profit-sharing and lifted restrictions on private economic activities in order to revive the economy.

The 1956 Revolution brought a temporary easing of Stalinist agricultural and peasant policies. During the Revolution, the main demands articulated within Hungary's rural society were the elimination of compulsory deliveries, a reduction in tax burdens, redress for the illegalities committed under the guise of land consolidation, removal of restrictions on the free trade of land, and authorization to leave and in certain instances disband the agricultural cooperatives.[26] Among these desiderata, only that of abolishing compulsory deliveries was fully satisfied—twice, first in a decree issued by the Nagy government at the end of October 1956 and again in another issued by the Kádár government following the crushing of the Revolution in November. The cancellation of obligatory produce deliveries, the granting of permission to leave the cooperatives, the moderate liberalization of land-sale regulations and the announcement of sector neutrality with regard to agricultural production served to stimulate production incentives for peasants in Hungary. The reestablishment of continuity in food production and the functionality of economic organizations also facilitated this. The ownership and production structure of the agricultural system again underwent a significant change following the Revolution, when a large proportion of the agricultural cooperatives that had been established by force between 1948 and 1956 disintegrated, almost three quarters of arable land reverted to private ownership, and smallholders generated four fifths of Hungary's agricultural production.

In an economic sense, the greatest lesson that Hungary's communist leaders learned from the 1956 Revolution was that it was essential for them to avoid intensifying social tension. Certain groups of Hungarian Workers' Party and/or Hungarian Socialist Workers' Party officials conducted an analysis of both the political and the social tensions that had erupted in late October, determining that further such conflicts were avoidable if personal consumption as a proportion of national income were increased and the standard of living palpably raised, even at the expense of industrial investment. This change in approach prevailed to a greater or lesser degree in terms of both economic policy and administration beginning at the end of the 1950s. However, only a few political leaders, those who were later to serve as the primary advocates of reform (such as Lajos Fehér and Rezső Nyers), perceived at the beginning of the 1960s the other significant economic lesson to be learned from the 1956 Revolution—the fact that the planned economic system[27] in its *original, rigorously centralized command form* essentially did not work. Implementation of the Varga committee's economic reform proposals formulated at the beginning of 1957 was removed from the agenda following the consolidation of the Kádár government in the middle of the year. The most important among the ideological justifications for rescinding the reform program was the claim that it represented nothing less than an economic variant of Imre Nagy-style revisionism preparing the ground for a restoration of capitalism. The Kádár government introduced only a few elements of the Varga committee's proposals aimed at a moderate rationalization of the economy, such as reducing the number of centrally stipulated command quotas and relaxing the strict centralization of labor production.

Thus, as in the political sphere, only minor adjustments were made to the primary functional and structural attributes of the Hungarian economy after 1956. This is clearly reflected in the targets contained in the three-year economic plan launched in 1958, which entailed a reduction in the proportion of national income allocated to investment and a modification of sector distribution stipulating an increase in expenditures for agricultural development. Although Hungary's economy remained focused on industrial development, beginning in the 1970s the government began to apportion more resources to the service sector, although infrastructural investments, particularly with regard to telecommunications, continued to significantly lag behind those required.

At the end of the 1950s and beginning of the 1960s, command-based three- to five-year plans and the principle of forced growth continued to dictate the operations of Hungary's economic system. Following the Soviet paradigm, Hungary contrived "overarching" economic concepts aimed at reaching and exceeding the level of economic development in more advanced industrialized countries based on the premise that socialist states would more or less concurrently complete the process of "socialist construction" by the end of the 1970s, fulfilling the social, economic, technical and cultural conditions necessary for the establishment of a "communist society." Political officials in the socialist countries of Europe, including those in Hungary, believed at the beginning of the 1960s that it would be possible to prove the viability of the state-socialist structure by surpassing the economic capacity of Western countries. In Hungary, the collectivization of agriculture and the completion of heavy industrial and energy investments, such as the Danube Ironworks, that had been postponed or left unfinished during the Rákosi era were designed to foster an "acceleration in the building of socialism." The excessive elevation of production targets continued to be a standard economic practice in Hungary at the end of the 1950s and in the first half of the 1960s. In the spring of 1959, for example, the Hungarian Socialist Workers' Party Central Committee issued an appeal calling for workers to reach the targets contained in the three-year plan launched in 1958 in just two years. Hungary's leaders believed that they could utilize internal reserves—such as increasing labor efficiency, improving economic administration and reorganizing socialist work competitions—to generate economic growth. Prevailing economic policies maintained the system of quantity-based targets, resulting in an increase in the production of raw materials that far surpassed the true needs of the economy. Just as in the early 1950s, nearly four fifths of Hungary's investment resources were directed towards mining, metallurgy, the chemical and construction materials industries and electricity production between the years 1961 and 1965. At the planning level, the only new element at this time was a 40 to 50 percent increase in production targets for consumer goods, including precise numerical targets for main products. Officials attempted in this way to moderate the degree of social tension stemming from shortages of such goods.

Disorganization, low productivity, operation and in many instances expansion of factories that made inefficient use of raw materials and energy, lack of incentive, and inadequate wages resulted in a decline in industrial production. As a consequence, targets contained in the 1961–1965 economic plan, with the exception of those pertaining to investment expenditure, were not met and the rate of national income growth declined from 4.6 percent in 1961 to 0.1 percent in 1965. This in itself indicated that the centrally planned economic system was not functioning smoothly in the first half of the

1960s. At the same time, the stock of unmarketable goods increased significantly, while in 1961 Hungary had to pay off the loans that it had taken to expedite the post-revolutionary stabilization process in 1957, inaugurating a period in which the country's debt towards both socialist and capitalist states began to rise. The rearmament of Warsaw Pact armies in the first half of the 1960s represented another significant burden on the Hungarian economy.

Officials paid increasing attention to the sources of economic tension in part because they believed that the process of political consolidation was in jeopardy in both domestic and foreign terms. They first attempted to bring these difficulties under control through a structural transformation of industry, abolishing the industrial directorates that functioned at an intermediary level between government ministries and industrial companies and consolidating production companies within certain sectors. The number of industrial companies had declined from 1,138 to 840 as a result of the centralization process. However, since this did not produce the expected increase in productivity, a total review of the system of economic administration and a determination of the possible direction of changes soon surfaced at the top of the agenda.[28]

As a result of the greater and lesser degree of modification to the "classical *kolkhoz* model" in Hungary, the country's "establishment of socialist agriculture" entailed somewhat less conflict than the formation of agricultural cooperatives had done in the first half of the 1950s. The process of post-revolutionary political stabilization having progressed to a sufficient degree, the Kádár government decided at the end of 1958 to decree the total collectivization of Hungarian agriculture in accordance with the expectations of the socialist camp, accomplishing the announced objective in three concentrated campaigns that took place between 1958 and 1961. Contrary to that which had occurred during previous attempts to restructure the agricultural system, the government's well-organized collectivization campaign was suspended during the spring–autumn growing season. As part of this collectivization effort, "agitation teams" consisting of urban workers, teachers and party activists were dispatched to rural communities in an attempt to convince their inhabitants that it would be to their advantage to join agricultural cooperatives. The government used every means at its disposal to promote the cause of collectivization, including, in addition to press propaganda and personal persuasion, tax penalties and forgiveness—or, conversely, more rigorous collection—of back taxes. Although less physical compulsion was employed in the course of this collectivization campaign than had occurred in previous such efforts, authorities resorted to practically every possible method of psychological pressure and inducement in their attempt to persuade people to join cooperatives, including the prospect of appointment to leadership positions, family blackmail and the threat of existential ruin. Attempts were made to gain the support of the leading local personalities—people whose personal decisions officials believed could serve to influence others. In another contrast to pre-1956 collectivization, the declared kulaks, Hungary's agricultural elite, were permitted to become cooperative directors. The collectivization process progressed in the form of a well-organized and efficient campaign. Authorities focused particular attention on the most powerful peasants and farmers within a given community, since their "voluntary" decision to join the local cooperative frequently served to convey the message that further resistance to collectivization was futile. Furthermore, officials made it possible for various segments of village society to separately join cooperatives. Newly formed agricultural cooperatives began regular operations only slowly and with great difficulty in spite of these concessions, in part because the process of establishing new labor organizations entailed many difficulties. Moreover, the cooperatives did not offer sufficient material incentive for their members, who during the first half of the 1960s did not earn regular cash wages, receiving their pay in the form of so-called work units[29] that they could redeem for cash at the end of the year. Finally, the state began providing the cooperatives with the degree of state support necessary for development beginning only in the second half of the 1960s. The level of agricultural production reached the average recorded in the years 1958 and 1959 only in the half a decade following the completion of collective restructuring. The majority of agricultural cooperatives were for many years unable to provide their members or other citizens of Hungary with evidence of the superiority of large-scale production. Most cooperatives became increasingly productive beginning in the middle of the 1960s, to a significant degree as a result of the government's authorization of household farming,[30] yield-based compensation and the introduction of regular cash wages. Another factor promoting the increased stability of agricultural cooperatives was the decision to abolish the separate organizational network of machine and equipment depots and permit the cooperatives to buy and operate their own machinery.

However, the restructuring of agriculture that took place in the first half of the 1960s, contrary to political expectations, resulted in a chronic shortage of goods and an insufficient level of food supplies. Statistical data indicate that domestic consumption of milk, flour, potatoes, legumes, vegetables and so on did not regain the level recorded in 1960 for more than half a decade, until 1967. Officials attempted to eliminate these shortages through extensive food imports and the continual elevation of the consumer prices in order to moderate demand.

The rising import requirement and the need to subsidize the operations of newly established agricultural cooperatives saddled Hungary's government budget with tens of millions of forints in extra expenditure in the 1960s. At the same time, the agricultural investment ratio began to grow significantly only at the end of the decade. It is only a slight simplification to state that the collectivization process resulted in the nationalization of farmland, and broke the established chain of production, while under the prevailing conditions the cooperatives were unable to provide their members with incomes necessary for subsistence. This is why it was necessary to help cooperative members to become self-sufficient through access to household farmland. The production role of these household parcels increased as incomes derived from agricultural cooperatives became larger and more regular. During the first half of the 1960s, cooperative members regularly generated more income from their household farming operations than they did from their collective undertakings.

Although average income and consumption remained low in Hungary, a modest improvement was perceptible in both domains as compared to the pre-1956 period. The average monthly wage in 1960 was more than 1,500 forints,[31] an increase of 35 percent compared to the average wage in 1955. Real wages also increased as a result of low inflation. There was a significant disparity in wages between the various economic sectors in Hungary. Miners and heavy industrial workers were among those earning the highest monthly pay, while those engaged in agriculture were among those earning the lowest. The most highly paid social categories earned between four and five times more income than those in the lowest-paid social categories at the end of the 1950s. Although the supply of consumer goods became more stable, shortages remained a part of everyday life in Hungary, albeit to a lesser degree than before.

Industrial production rose by an average of between 8 and 8.5 percent in the decade after 1956. This rise in production stemmed primarily from an immense expansion of the active workforce and a continual increase in capacity. The structure of the industrial sector underwent a transformation in which the proportion of national income derived from the food and textile industries declined by nearly half, while that stemming from heavy industry rose by a commensurate 50 percent. Within the latter sector, the machine industry developed to a particularly great magnitude at this time. Production of industrial implements (machine tools and heavy trucks) as well as consumer appliances (washing machines, refrigerators and televisions) increased gradually from the beginning of the 1960s. As a result of the division of production within the Council for Mutual Economic Assistance (Comecon), Hungary manufactured buses, but no passenger cars. The Comecon production system also stipulated that Hungary cease its longstanding manufacture of motorcycles, telecommunications instruments, agricultural machinery and other goods, a circumstance that entailed the loss of a considerable store of professional and technological capital. The increasing weight of heavy industry within the economy served to increase domestic demand for raw materials and energy, much of which Hungary imported from the Soviet Union, thus heightening the country's dependence on the USSR.

In 1957, Hungary's political and economic leaders still believed that it would be possible to generate dynamic and balanced growth through more prudent planning and production-management without making any fundamental changes to the system. However, economic developments during the first half of the 1960s clearly demonstrated that rigid central planning produced an inherent set of problems that it was by its nature unable to resolve. Widespread recognition of this defect prompted the Hungarian Socialist Workers' Party Central Committee to adopt a resolution in December 1964 calling for a reassessment of the command-based economic system and proposals aimed at improving the efficiency of the economy.

4. Society[32]

One of the initial and most far-reaching social consequences of the 1956 Revolution was the exodus of refugees that lasted from the suppression of the uprising until the spring of 1957. Nearly 200,000 people,[33] the majority of them male university students, educated professionals or skilled workers under the age of 25, decided to leave Hungary in order to make a new beginning in Western Europe or North America. Thus most of the refugees who fled Hungary following the Revolution possessed the skills and education necessary to facilitate the reestablishment of their livelihoods abroad. The revolutionary events spurred legal emigration from Hungary as well. During the first five months of 1957, the Ministry of the Interior permitted a total of 12,345 people to leave the country legally. The majority of both the legal and the illegal emigrants settled in the United States, Great Britain, Canada, Germany, Switzerland and France. The exodus of refugees altered Hungary's demographic balance as well, reducing the proportion of people in younger age groups, increasing the female majority within the population and transforming employment distribution. The demographic attributes of Hungarian society would have changed even without the mass emigration that followed the Revolution: the number of births declined following the repeal of the ban on abortions, thus reducing the rate of natural population increase. The average number of children per family decreased slightly. The number of women among active wage earners in Hungary increased.

The following elements continued to guide the transformation of Hungary's social structure between 1956 and 1963: highly idealistic communist ideology and frequently arbitrary policies aimed at its practical application; a disproportionate appreciation in the role of political capital of the realignment of social groups and the attainment of personal position; the expropriation of private property; a moderation of disparities in the distribution of income; a separation of earnings from the true value of production. A transformation in the circumstances surrounding potentially revenue-generating private property was a primary factor governing the social processes that predominated during the socialist era. With the exception of a short transitory period, the divestment of property continued for three quarters of a decade following the Revolution. The proletarization of Hungarian society dragged on until the third quarter of the 1960s, although private property and the small ownership class had not been totally eliminated even by this time. It is nevertheless certain that Hungary's private sector, consisting primarily of tradesmen and retail merchants, had shrunk to its smallest size ever at the beginning of the 1960s. Moreover, in 1962, the government officially announced that the building of Hungary's socialist foundations had been completed, which in practical terms meant that the comprehensive nationalization of society had essentially been concluded, thus placing a significant majority of the population in a position of direct existential dependence on the state. A total of 95 percent of active wage earners worked at state-run institutions, factories and plants, creating a situation in which the following was the case: "Control and regulation over everyday subsistence placed all of society in a subordinate role. Those who did not rebel against their subservience to state socialism were allowed to seek prosperity, although the state largely determined the possible degree of this as well."[34]

The demographic changes that took place in Hungary in the 1950s and 1960s were primarily the result of external and political factors that had little or no relation to the country's established social structure. Beginning in the 1950s, politics had taken almost complete control over every sphere of social existence. Channels of mobility were subordinated to the social objectives of the new communist system. Both individual and collective repression were utilized to regulate the process of social mobility. Boundaries between various social groups either shifted or came into existence, such as those that developed between private farmers and members of agricultural cooperatives and between the old and the new socialist intelligentsia.

The two most extensive changes to Hungary's social structure during the era under discussion were a drastic decrease in the number of independent, landowning peasants and a dynamic increase in the number of urban industrial workers. The former structure of peasant society existed in its fundamental form until 1960–1961, when the majority of the independent landowning peasantry became "cooperative peasants," essentially transforming them into wage workers. Peasant society and village society underwent a permanent split at this time, as an increasing number of those living in villages abandoned agriculture for the industrial sector.

Cooperative chairmen represented a new group, along with agronomists, agriculturalists and production managers. The ideologically and politically preferred heavy industrial workforce was characterized by continual growth and transitivity. The influx of people engaged in agriculture was equal to the outflux from the sector as a result of an increase in cadre personnel. The approximately 180,000–190,000-strong force of skilled workers was one of the most significant bases for measuring the latter. In terms of mobility, Hungary became more open in the second half of the 1950s and the early part of the 1960s than it had been during the Horthy era. It should be noted, however, that the country's degree of social mobility did not surpass that prevalent in Western Europe. Another significant difference with regard to Western Europe was the fact that the great degree of mobility that characterized Hungarian society at this time lacked organic foundations and was almost exclusively politically stimulated.[35] That is, many among the large number of people who switched jobs, addresses and social classes in Hungary did not do so voluntarily, but because political changes had rendered their former occupations and lifestyles impracticable. This process contributed significantly to a weakening of Hungarian society's former class affiliations and to the emergence of a widespread moral and identity crisis. The opening up of new avenues and directions of social mobility coincided with the narrowing and marginalization of traditional channels.

The Hungarian Socialist Workers' Party in fact, represented an independent channel of mobility in itself: those who displayed an adequate degree of loyalty and allegiance, who unconditionally accepted the "mameluk mentality" that predominated within the organization and managed to find sponsorship at a higher level, were almost certain to gain advancement in their careers. The two possible routes of promotion to offices of authority underwent a divergence. For a long period of time, greater importance was placed on immediate appointment to leadership positions than on the traditional means of career progression through education, training and "official" advancement. It is, however, also true that the number of leadership positions involving direct management of production was on average twice as high as that existing at the ministerial level.

This politically induced movement triggered a far-reaching social realignment in which occupational mobility and status mobility underwent a separation, while forced intra-generational mobility supplanted more traditional and organic forms of intergenerational mobility. Thus, with regard to the period of classical socialism that ended in the first half of the 1960s, the premise that the feudal character of Hungarian society did not disappear after World War II, although the factors influencing this feudalistic social structure changed radically, while it is a simplification, does not seem to be totally groundless. The most important formative factor became political capital and power. Social status was largely contingent upon the amount of political capital that a given individual had at his or her disposal. From a structural standpoint, the neo-feudal approach is much simpler, since it contains just two estates: the political order and the non-political order. At the same time, it is undeniably true that party membership remained the fundamental requirement for attaining political capital and social influence at this time and for decades to come. It must be noted that from the middle of the 1960s, a greater number of those who possessed political capital attempted to utilize it to compensate for their former lack of cultural capital. According to another interpretation of the social transformation that occurred in Hungary at this time, the classical socialist system nationalized the society, economy, living circumstances and means of subsistence of the 1930s and 1940s that it had inherited following World War II, in conformity with its own objectives and functional logic. This nationalization fundamentally transformed the system of relationships and cooperation within the important institutions of social reproduction—state, family, school and workplace. With the nationalization of family resources such as shops and land, modes of subsistence and the forms connected to mobility and transmission of social status decreased in value, shifting largely to the school system. The realignment processes begun in the 1950s remained steady and pervasive in the 1960s. Political objectives undoubtedly served as the dominant factor steering this realignment, while the independent mobility of society was of little importance.

The proportion of urban workers, those who earned their livelihoods through physical labor, within Hungarian society grew rapidly as a result of forced industrialization. State-run industry employed a significant share of these industrial workers, whose number rose by between two and two and a half times from 1950 until 1970. The fact that the process of forced industrialization underpinned this increase in the size of Hungary's industrial workforce in the 1950s and 1960s represented a significant structural change. The skills and qualifications of workers also underwent a major transformation during this period. In the 1950s, the unskilled workforce expanded substantially, while in the 1960s the number of skilled and semi-skilled workers rose at a relatively rapid rate. The social composition of the industrial workforce began to change significantly in the 1950s, when women were first extensively employed in industry and the majority of fresh industrial workers emerged from the ranks of the peasantry—agricultural and day laborers, new smallholders and landowning peasants who had been forced to either temporarily or semi-permanently abandon their farming activities. These newcomers frequently had difficulty adapting to industrial work and orienting themselves within the existing plant hierarchy, especially amid the decidedly hectic political and social environment that prevailed in the era. The peasant-to-worker transformation was not a novel phenomenon in the history of twentieth-century Hungary, although the massive scale on which this took place beginning in the 1950s was unprecedented. Transience became one of the main characteristics of Hungary's industrial workforce in the 1960s, a condition that stemmed equally from the disintegration and transformation of the traditional working-class lifestyle and the mass migration of peasants to the industrial sector. The lives of those who remained within a single social stratum, either the peasantry or the working class, were very different from those of people who relocated from one stratum to another. The complexity of these changes is reflected clearly in data stemming from a 1962–1964 survey of social stratification[36] indicating that 36 percent of skilled workers, 60 percent of semi-skilled workers and 68 percent of unskilled workers were of peasant origin. Extrapolation of these data indicates that in the 1950s the majority of Hungary's skilled labor force descended from the traditional working class.

Although the comprehensive social realignment that took place in Hungary in the 1950s and 1960s generated a dynamic increase in the number of industrial workers, it simultaneously prevented the development of a loyal, performance-oriented, skilled and easily trained working class around which an industrial-worker society could be built. The process of industrial development produced a large number of new workplaces that served to sustain the urban proletarian livelihoods of unskilled and uneducated itinerant workers.

> The transformation of peasants into workers represented one of the most strenuous tasks. Adaptation to urban life and industrial work represented a particularly great burden. The fact that some kind of community or association existed in every workplace and that newcomers did not understand the established modes of social intercourse and agreement that existed between long-acquainted workers made acclimatization to industrial labor more difficult. Veteran workers thought it natural that novices should do the hardest work amid the most unfavorable conditions and derive the least benefit from their labor. Aversion towards newcomers was even stronger if the new workers came from a rural background and thus not only had difficulty comprehending customary workplace practices, but were also unaware of standard urban signals and connotations, making them appear to be slow-witted. The loss of former bonds and customs and the consequent loneliness and insecurity contributed to this. The peasant who moves to the city is deprived of his kindred and neighborly relationships and requires a great deal of time in order to establish new human contacts in the city.[37]

The peasantry also underwent a significant transformation during this period. The process of "limited repeasantification" that took place in 1957–1958 initially engendered the prospect of establishing and maintaining an autonomous existence, although this was removed from the agenda permanently during the 1958–1961 collectivization campaign. The question of how authorities convinced peasants in the late 1950s and early 1960s to relinquish the autonomy that they had acquired in 1945, 1953 and 1956 and leave the land that had provided their lives with meaning is an important issue in the social history of Hungary. What social, economic, political and psychological factors lay in the background? In searching for possible answers to this question, one must take into consideration the fact that after 1956 nobody harbored the illusion that the regime would change within the foreseeable future, a condition that in itself the weakened the prospect of resistance. Following the suppression of the Revolution, the Kádár government utilized its "erratically systematic" methods of reprisal to provide a demonstration of its power in the villages as well, dispensing various forms of punishment to politically active individuals that rendered the organization of engaged people into groups impossible. This served to fortify the "feeling of failure" that predominated in Hungarian society following the suppression of the 1956 Revolution. The government gradually withdrew the economic concessions that it had made after 1956, increasing the tax burdens of individual farmers. It became obvious that agricultural cooperatives would continue to enjoy significant practical advantages over the private agricultural sector. The conditions surrounding individual farming deteriorated continually as the collectivization campaign progressed, again dashing the peasantry's prospects for earning and for an independent livelihood. Chronic existential uncertainty and acute political and psychological pressure prompted an increasing number of farmers to conclude that resistance to collectivization was futile. It must be noted that in the late 1950s the peasantry was the only stratum of Hungarian society to retain a substantial amount of private property, thus providing it with a relatively high degree of personal and economic autonomy. This circumstance was not, however, sustainable within a socialist system that aimed to effectuate a complete centralization of resources and gain total supervision over society.

The realignment that took place in Hungary's villages between 1959 and 1962 was the most intensive transformation to take place during this period. The magnitude of this change is demonstrated clearly in data showing that private farmers composed 79 percent of those engaged in the agricultural sector in 1958, while in 1962 a total of 75 percent of those engaged in the sector were cooperative members. In numerical terms, there were 1.2 million cooperative members in Hungary at the end of 1962, compared to 169,000 at the end of 1958.[38]

Distribution of those engaged in agricultural according to social sector, 1959–1963

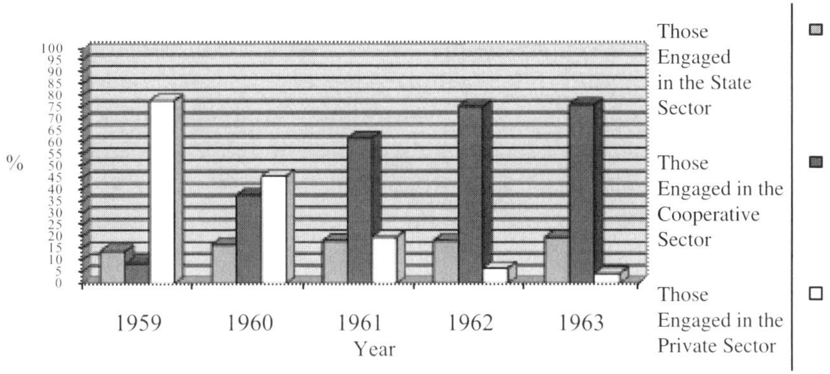

Very few people were left out of the collectivization campaign. Statistics indicate that there were 145,000 individual farmers in 1962, a figure that had declined to 80,000 by 1968. The number of those engaged in private agriculture decreased continually in the 1960s, remaining in the mere tens of thousands throughout the following decades. During the 1950s and 1960s, nearly one million people, a fifth to a quarter of all active wage earners in Hungary, abandoned agriculture to seek a livelihood in another sector of the economy. The prestige of agricultural work diminished continually and remained low, thus losing its appeal as a potential career for young people growing up in the villages.

Hungary's system of collectivized agriculture attained long-term viability primarily because it underwent a gradual departure from the requisites contained in the established "*kolkhoz* model."

The concept that the restructuring of agriculture represented an element of class struggle was abandoned at the beginning of the 1960s, when principles of economic rationalism and practices aimed at ensuring the viability of cooperatives gradually came to predominate. The payment in work units was first curtailed, and then eliminated altogether in favor of incentive-generating yield-based compensation and regular cash wages. Benefits connected to household agricultural activities were also expanded in order to further motivate cooperative members. The introduction of the new organizational order exercised a decisive impact on the internal structure and stature of agricultural society both during and after the period of collectivization. Most of those appointed to the most important positions within the new mass-scale labor organization[39] possessed an understanding of production processes, a circumstance that provided those who had previously been engaged in larger-scale private agricultural operations with an implicit advantage in terms of occupational promotion. Agricultural workplaces associated with those possessing a background in hired agricultural and proletarian labor developed mainly in the domain of livestock farming. The majority of horse drivers, horticultural and crop production supervisors and brigade leaders were former private farmers, while their children and relatives became tractor drivers, granary and warehouse foremen, gristmill operators, payroll accountants and cashiers, and worked in other jobs involving production and personnel tasks. Two thirds of cooperative chairmen belonged to this category. Workers were divided into crop labor and tillage labor groups of two types—one composed of people from families of former private farmers and another of members of proletarian families who also worked as day laborers and thus earned dual incomes when the agricultural cooperatives had been formed. The system of family relationships was an important element in the formation of internal structure and distribution of roles based on informal stratification factors in the years following the launching of agricultural cooperatives: most of those who exercised the greatest degree of influence on the opinion of members were work supervisors who belonged to families that had attained leading positions within the new agricultural cooperatives. Traditional internal stratification persisted more or less intact until the late 1960s, when technical innovations, extensive mechanization and the introduction of the industrial production system supplanted longstanding farming methods and transformed the established structure of agriculture. The value of traditional peasant labor and related proficiency underwent a continual depreciation within the agricultural cooperatives, while increasing emphasis was placed on professional expertise and the knowledge necessary for the operation of "industrial agriculture." At the same time, cooperative members gradually assumed the *de facto* status of wage workers.

The forced "modernization" that took place in Hungary in the 1950s and 1960s resulted in an intensification of individualization, atomization and secularization, thus producing a new model of social integration. Pre-war behavioral norms played a decreasing role in this model, while, contrary to expectation, new modes of conduct stemming from those in power—the Hungarian Socialist Workers' Party cadre elite—exercised a disintegrative effect on society.

Notes

1 See the following: György Litván, ed., *The Hungarian Revolution of 1956* (New York, 1996); Lee Congdon, Béla K. Király and Károly Nagy, eds., *1956 The Hungarian Revolution and War of Independence* (Highland Lakes, NJ, 2006), p. 956; Charles Gati, *Failed Illusions. Moscow, Washington, Budapest and the Hungarian Revolution* (Washington, DC – Stanford, CA, 2006), p. 264. For a historical summary of the entire era, including the period discussed in the present chapter, see Ignác Romsics, *Hungary in the Twentieth Century* (Budapest, 1999).

2 For a history of the armed conflict, see Miklós Horváth, *1956 hadikrónikája* [1956 Military Chronicle] (Budapest, 2003), p. 482.

3 The text of this summons is published in the following work: Tamás G. Korányi, ed., *Egy népfelkelés dokumentumai* [Documents of a Popular Uprising] (Budapest, 1989), pp. 114–116.

4 *Ibid.*, p. 112.
5 *Ibid.*, pp. 112–113.
6 For a systematic history of armed revolutionary groups in Budapest, see László Eörsi, *Corvinisták 1956 (A VIII. kerület fegyveres csoportjai)* [Corvinists 1956 (Armed Groups of the Eighth District)] (Budapest, 2001), p. 648, and idem, *Széna tériek 1956* [Széna Squarers 1956] (Budapest, 2004), p. 369.
7 For the number of Hungarian casualties, see the common report (without authorial attribution) "Az (1956.) október 23-i és az azt követő eseményekkel kapcsolatos sérülések és halálozások" [Injuries and Deaths Connected to Events that Took Place on and after October 23 (1956)], *Statisztikai Szemle* 10 (1990): 797–816. For the number of Soviet casualties, see Éva Gál, András B. Hegedűs, György Litván and János M. Rainer, eds., *Jelcin-dosszié. Szovjet dokumentumok 1956-ról* [Yeltsin Dossier. Soviet Documents about 1956] (Budapest, 1993), p. 103.
8 János Kádár's political career is given a detailed description in Tibor Huszár's two-volume biography of the Hungarian communist leader. For Kádár's post-1956 political biography, see the following work: Tibor Huszár, *Kádár János politikai életrajza 1956. november – 1989. június* [János Kádár's Political Biography, November 1956–June 1989] (Budapest, 2003).
9 A detailed summary of armed and political resistance after November 4, 1956, is contained in the following work: Attila Szakolczai, *Az 1956-os magyar forradalom és szabadságharc* [The 1956 Hungarian Revolution and Fight for Freedom] (Budapest, 2001), pp. 73–83.
10 Detailed prescriptions connected to the implementation of martial law are contained in government resolution A6/1956 (XII.1), to be found in *Törvények és rendeletek tára, 1956* [Law and Regulation Repository, 1956].
11 These data are contained in the following work: János Kenedi, *Kis állambiztonsági olvasókönyv* [Little State Security Reader] (Budapest, 1996).
12 During political trials staged following the 1956 Revolution, facts were grouped in order to support the charge of attempted overthrow of the socialist system.
13 For documents and analysis related to the subsequent trial, see the following work: Alajos Dornbach, Péter Kende, János M. Rainer and Katalin Somlai, eds., *A per. Nagy Imre és társai. 1958, 1989* [The

Trial. Imre Nagy and His Associates. 1958, 2008] (Budapest, 2008), p. 430.

14 János M. Rainer, *The Leader and Martyr of the Hungarian Revolution of 1956* (Budapest, 2006) (Bulletins on 1956, No. 1), p. 68.

15 See Litván, ed., *The Hungarian Revolution of 1956*, and Szakolczai, *Az 1956-os magyar forradalom és szabadságharc*.

16 The following work contains a summary of this issue as well as relevant documents: Gergő Bendegúz Cseh, Melinda Kalmár and Edit Por, *Zárt, bizalmas, számozott. Tájékoztatáspolitika és cenzúra 1956–1963* [Closed, Confidential, Numbered. Information Policy and Censorship 1953–1963] (Budapest, 1998).

17 Three other daily newspapers were published in Hungary in addition to *Népszabadság* during the Kádár era: the Patriotic People's Front's *Magyar Nemzet*, the National Council of Trade Unions' *Népszava* and the Hungarian government's *Magyar Hírlap*.

18 Éva Standeisky, *Az írók és a hatalom 1956–1963* [Writers and the Regime 1956–1963] (Budapest, 1996).

19 The document outlining these proposals is contained in the following work: László Szamuely, ed., *A magyar közgazdasági gondolat fejlődése 1954–1978* [Development of Hungarian Economic Thought 1954–1978] (Budapest, 1986).

20 Jenő Gergely, József Kardos and Ferenc Rottler, *Az egyházak Magyarországon* [The Churches in Hungary] (Budapest, 1997).

21 For the history of foreign policy, see the following work: László Borhi, *Vasfüggöny mögött –Magyarország nagyhatalmi erőtérben 1945–1968* [Behind the Iron Curtain—Hungary in the Great Power Arena 1945–1968] (Budapest, 2000).

22 This issue is considered in detail in the following work: Csaba Békés, *Az 1956-os magyar forradalom a világpolitikában* [The 1956 Hungarian Revolution in World Politics] (Budapest, 2006), p. 391.

23 László Borhi, *A magyar–amerikai viszony változásai, 1957–1978* [Transformations in Hungarian–American Relations, 1957–1978] (Budapest, 2004).

24 For an historical overview of Hungarian minority issues, see Nándor Bárdi, Csilla Fedinecz and László Szarka, *Kisebbségi magyar közösségek a XX. században* [Hungarian Minority Communities in the 20th Century] (Budapest, 2008).

25 The present historical synopsis of Hungary's economy between the years 1956 and 1963 is based primarily on the following monograph:

Iván Pető and Sándor Szakács, *A hazai gazdaság négy évtizedének története I* [Four Decades of Domestic Economic History I] (Budapest, 1985). Also see Iván Berend T., *Terelőúton. Szocialista modernizációs kísérlet Közép- és Kelet-Európában 1944–1990* [Detour. Socialist Modernization Attempt in Central and Eastern Europe, 1944–1990] (Budapest, 1999), and Iván Berend T., *Gazdasági útkeresés 1956–1965* [Economic Reorientation, 1956–1965] (Budapest, 1983).

26 Tibor Valuch, "Agrárkérdések és a magyar falu 1956–57-ben" [Agricultural Issues and the Hungarian Village in 1956–1957], in *Évkönyv 2000* (Budapest, 2000), pp. 286–302.

27 For a history of the economic history of the period, see János Kornai, *The Socialist System: The Political Economy of Communism* (Oxford, 1992), pp. xxvii, 644.

28 For a detailed account of this matter, see Zsuzsanna Varga, "Questioning the Soviet Economic Model in the 1960s," in György Péteri and János M. Rainer, eds., *Muddling Through in the Long 1960s. Ideas and Everyday Life in High Politics and the Lower Classes of Communist Hungary* (Trondheim, 2005) (Trondheim Studies on East European Cultures & Societies, No. 16), pp. 109–134.

29 A certain number of work units were allotted for each given task at agricultural cooperatives. These units could only be exchanged for cash at the end of the year, a fact that deterred many people from engaging in collective labor.

30 Parcels consigned to new cooperative members for cultivation, garden plots connected to private residences, and necessary agricultural equipment and tools were included under the rubric "household farming." Household farmland was generally just over half a hectare (1 *kataszterális hold*) in size. Livestock corresponding to two fully grown animals was permitted to remain on household farm holdings at the time of joining agricultural cooperatives. Income derived from the sale of produce grown on household farm plots could be disposed of freely. With regard to yield-based compensation, cooperative members were offered the option of receiving a certain proportion—usually one quarter to one half—of the yield produced on a given agricultural territory in addition to earning work units.

31 These data are contained in the following work: Mihály Zafír, ed., *Életszínvonal 1960–1980* [Standard of Living 1960–1980] (Budapest, 1981), pp. 79–86.

32 For a thorough examination of the social repercussions of the Revolution, see Tibor Valuch, *Magyarország társadalomtörténete a XX. század második felében* [The Social History of Hungary in the Second Half of the 20th Century] (Budapest, 2001).

33 According to data from an unpublished Central Statistics Office survey of emigration following the 1956 Revolution (Budapest, 1991), pp. 174–211.

34 György Gyarmati, "Politika és társadalom 1945–1989 között" [Politics and Society between 1945 and 1989], in István Kollega Tarsoly, ed., *Magyarország a XX. században* [Hungary in the 20th Century] (Szekszárd, 1996), p. 228.

35 The following article contains a detailed analysis of this issue: Antal Örkény, "A társadalmi mobilitás történelmi perspektívái" [The Historical Perspectives of Social Mobility], *Valóság* 4 (1989): 20–33.

36 Mrs. Sándor Ferge, István Kemény, Mrs. György Láng and Mrs. Aladár Mód, *Társadalmi rétegződés Magyarországon* [Social Stratification in Hungary] (Budapest, 1966).

37 István Kemény, "A magyar munkásosztály rétegződése" [Stratification of the Hungarian Working Class], *Szociológia* 1 (1972): 36–48.

38 These data are contained in the following work: Iván Oros, ed., *A falu és a mezőgazdaság főbb társadalmi és gazdasági jelzőszámai* [The Primary Social and Economic Data of Villages and Agriculture] (Budapest, 1994).

39 Pál Juhász, "Adatok és hipotézisek a mezőgazdasági szövetkezetek dolgozóinak rétegződéséről" [Data and Hypotheses regarding the Stratification of Agricultural Cooperative Workers], *Társadalomtudományi Közlemények* 2 (1979): 62–81.

VIII. THE KÁDÁR CONSOLIDATION (1963–1978)[1]

1. Domestic Politics[2]

Those 1956 revolutionaries released from prison as part of the 1963 general amnesty returned to a transformed country, one in which the 1956 Revolution and the freedom experienced during the uprising had become taboo subjects. Within Hungary's broader social milieu, there was no longer much, if any, solidarity with either the 1956 Revolution or those who had made great sacrifices for the cause of the uprising. The majority of Hungarian citizens did not consider those who had been imprisoned for their activities during the Revolution to be heroes, but at best victims, at worst dupes.[3] This was partially a consequence of the greater social acceptance of the Kádár government's policies. Following the establishment of stable political circumstances, the primary domestic political objective during the era of Kádár consolidation was to depoliticize and neutralize society as much as possible. Communist leaders, having learned from previous mistakes, attempted to restore and ensure the greatest possible degree of sovereignty in private life, hoping that this would facilitate the process of gaining and maintaining the loyalty of society. In practical terms, this entailed, among other things, a reduction of the political and ideological pressure exercised on non-party members. Compulsory half-hour discussions of headline articles in the Hungarian Socialist Workers' Party's central party newspaper were no longer held at the beginning of the working day as they had been before 1956, and party members were no longer automatically subjected to party disciplinary measures in the event of marital infidelity. "It was even possible to express disinterest in politics. Although this attitude continued to result in the insertion of the comment 'apolitical, does not participate in community life' in the identification card of the person in question, it seldom occasioned open provocation or exposure on what by this time had become a merely imaginary workplace table of glory and shame."[4] Politics did, however, remain present in communal domains such as schools, workplaces and public institutions, where ideological expectations and considerations still prevailed, although to a diminishing magnitude.

To this day, a portion of Hungarian historiography is inclined to emphasize in general terms the discontinuity between the Rákosi and Kádár eras. Interpretation of this question requires a refined approach with regard to both time and content. An analysis of the two periods from the standpoint of the concepts, principles and fundamental ideology upon which the systems were established and operated reveals that there were essentially no substantial differences between the two.[5] For a long period of time, there existed no significant incongruities in the fundamental structure of the two political regimes (party configuration, public life and the practical absence of separation between the various branches of government), although the functioning of their political mechanism did gradually undergo a significant transformation. It is an unquestionable fact that beginning in the second half of the 1960s, the political practices associated with the Kádár consolidation gradually diverged from those characteristic of "the long decade of the 1950s" in which the loss of security in everyday life was one of the organic corollaries of "the building of socialism." The degree of uncertainty and fear of what the following day would bring slowly subsided, although fundamental conditions did not change significantly. The defenselessness of certain individuals and social groups *vis-à-vis* the dictatorial regime and potentially unlimited state supervision continued to characterize the relationship between the government and society. The issue of political rights and their exercise emerged neither at this time nor later. It is characteristic of the era that the single-party system left nothing to chance. During a meeting of the HSWP Central Committee held on February 15, 1967, to discuss preparations for the impending March elections, HSWP General Secretary János Kádár said the following:

> The outcome looks promising for us. However, I hope that you won't misunderstand me if I point out that we falsified the results of the last elections a bit here at the headquarters and ask that we don't win this way again! When the results were tallied, it turned out that we had won by a margin of 102 percent. We plainly and simply changed this number, reducing it by some 6 percent, a fact that I ask should remain just between you and me.[6]

Beginning in the middle of the 1960s, the process of political consolidation no longer entailed spectacular show trials, while the total intimidation of a broad segment of society no longer represented the predominant political objective and the methods of exercising power became more subtle. The number of political trials decreased continuously during the period, stabilizing in the vicinity of 150 to 200 per year from the beginning of the 1970s. The majority of these cases involved the allegation of political incitement, such as the preparation and distribution of leaflets. No considerable anti-government organization occurred at this time. The criminal proceedings stemming from the spontaneous demonstrations that took place in Budapest in 1972 and 1973 represented the exception to this rule. By the end of the 1970s, the number of people who came into open political conflict with the regime had decreased to no more than a few dozen per year. The aforementioned demonstrates that there existed no significant domestic resistance or hostility to the prevailing circumstances in Hungary, while there were no groups active within society that were either willing or able to advocate an opposition perspective. The political police continued, however, to serve as a state within a state.[7] The large number of people kept under surveillance and the substantial network of informants reflected the tight supervision and dictatorial conditions that prevailed in the country. And while the "doorbell fright" characteristic of the 1950s was not part of everyday life during this period, limits to the freedom of movement within the "happiest barracks" of the socialist camp were nevertheless clearly defined.

Beginning at the end of the 1960s, the Kádár regime offered Hungarian society the pragmatic prospect of an increase in available consumer goods and the possibility of material improvement, while history, historical consciousness and any values unrelated to consumption or subsistence were relegated to the background. Within the logic of this system, only those routine acts associated with practical livelihood and attainable material goods proved to be important.[8] The natural desire to improve one's living conditions made it possible for many people to forget where they were actually living. The greater availability of bread and meat, the more comfortable and slightly bigger apartment, the summer home and weekend garden plot, the Trabant, Wartburg or Lada automobiles and the restricted, although existing, liberty to travel abroad made life within the freedom-deficient regime more tolerable. There came about a social psychology in which certain groups of people recognized the uniformity of their prospects for prosperity, and understood that while their opportunities were limited within the confines of the regime, respect for the existing political and historical taboos made it possible to establish "pretty acceptable" living conditions. This contributed in large part to the development of a consciousness of relative social equality in spite of the fact that both the greater and lesser community acknowledged success stemming from individual effort. Friends, relatives, acquaintances and colleagues did not dispute the validity of heightened social status or living conditions obtained in this way, often expressing esteem for those people who were "clever" enough to adapt to the often enigmatic conditions of the era and utilize them to their own advantage.

Beginning in the mid-1960s, the importance of the standard of living in political practice and propaganda rose to a substantial degree.

> Promising a 'better life' can be a suitable means of creating social consensus and promoting the acceptance of the existing structure. At long last there emerged a common point, which, albeit under the influence of propaganda,

> nevertheless engendered the realistic prospect of establishing unity and a common platform of consumption upon which popular support in its broadest sense might be built, thus serving to a certain extent as a substitute for political consensus.[9]

Cadre policies underwent a transformation as well, abandoning the former practice of appointment based exclusively on political factors in favor of increased emphasis on competence and proficiency. From the end of the 1960s, non-party members were considered to be eligible for appointment to practically all leading positions with the exception of party functions. Political dependability temporarily reemerged as the most important qualification for attaining office during the anti-reform period in the early and mid-1970s. These transformations in practice and approach exercised a positive impact on popular sentiment and opinion, laying the foundations for the long-term social acceptance of the communist regime. The notion of economic reform resurfaced within this positive political and social-psychological environment, primarily as the result of an abatement in forced economic growth. It was, however, characteristic of both the era and the regime that political, economic and social circumstances became increasingly obscure at the same time. With the exception of the clearly defined political and ideological taboos that continued to exist during this era, clear and unambiguous regulation was lacking in practically every domain of life.

At the beginning of the 1960s, János Kádár not only served as the general secretary of the Hungarian Socialist Workers' Party, but filled the post of prime minister from September 1961 until June 1965 as well, the second time that he had occupied this office in a relatively short period of time. This concentration of power reflected Kádár's strengthened political position as well as a stabilization of the political base within the party, since during the Kádár era a large portion of the prime minister's duties involved direction of the state apparatus.[10] This shift in emphasis obviously constituted an element of policies aimed at promoting political consolidation. The handling of everyday tasks related to state administration compelled the most powerful man in Hungary to confront the difficulties and tensions that existed within the system and to face the fact that the gradually increasing degree of political stability in the country could be maintained either by force or through a more or less continual increase in wages. Although this did not prompt Kádár to delve into a thorough investigation of economic affairs, the HSWP general secretary did after a period of time arrive at the conclusion that changes were unavoidable within the established confines of the system. As a result of this recognition, the political environment that prevailed in Hungary during the years 1964–1971 was basically favorable for the formulation and implementation of economic reform. This factor, along with Brezhnev's succession of Khrushchev as the head of the Communist Party of the Soviet Union, prompted Kádár to again separate the offices of prime minister and party general secretary and to propose organizational and personnel changes to the HSWP leadership in the spring and early summer of 1965. Kádár loyalist Gyula Kállai became Hungary's new prime minister, while the HSWP general secretary again focused "only" on the direction and supervision of politics.

During the second half of the 1960s, the initiators and supporters of reform such as Lajos Fehér and Rezső Nyers gained a dominant position within the leadership of the Hungarian Socialist Workers' Party, while those who opposed reform—HSWP Central Committee member and former Minister of the Interior Béla Biszku, National Council of Trade Unions Chairman Sándor Gáspár and Communist Youth Alliance leader Zoltán Komócsin—filled offices that curtailed their room for political maneuver until the beginning of the 1970s. The political foundations for economic reform solidified further in the spring of 1967, when Kállai ceded his post as the head of the government to his pro-reform deputy Jenő Fock, who as prime minister named specialists such as Mátyás Tímár, Péter Vályi and Imre Dimény to serve in his cabinet in place of politically appointed cadres.

The gradual modification of the political mechanism did not entail a significant transformation of political institutions. A 1966 amendment of the electoral law established the individual voting districts that delegated an average of 345 deputies to Parliament in elections held between 1967 and 1980. Furthermore, in 1970 individual citizens or groups of citizens were granted the right to nominate candidates to stand in parliamentary elections in addition to the Patriotic People's Front, although such candidates were "naturally" compelled to accept the People's Front program. These legal changes did not, however, produce a significant transformation in Hungary's system of "sham parliamentarianism." All but a few districts continued to nominate only a single candidate, whose subsequent election was certain. The only change that took place to punctuate the monotony of parliamentary and local elections was the extension of the electoral cycle from four to five years in 1975.

The Hungarian Socialist Workers' Party Political and Central Committees continued to serve as the setting for genuine political debate, while the role of Parliament, which convened for only four sessions of six to eight days per year, was restricted to approving submitted bills and legislation without material deliberation. The amendment of the constitution that took place in 1972 was an important event from a political standpoint. Contrary to its predecessor, the modified constitution was not simply a replica of the Soviet model, declaring the People's Republic of Hungary to be a socialist state in which the working people exercised total political power and formally guaranteeing fundamental human rights as well.

Official Church policy also underwent a slow transformation during the period of Kádár consolidation. Although the significant majority of those who claimed religious affiliation in Hungary continued to belong to either the Roman Catholic or Reformed Church, the social role and status of religion changed significantly during this period. The atheism stemming from socialist ideology served to accelerate the trend towards secularization that was prevalent throughout Europe in general. Since the Churches were neither willing nor able to function in opposition to the regime and rapidly lost their capacity for community organization, the number of active worshippers and the social prestige of the Church both declined sharply during the era of consolidation. The radical change that took place in the domain of religion is reflected in data showing that while 46 percent of Hungary's population claimed to be religious in 1972, this number had fallen to 36.6 percent by 1978. A steady decrease in the number of children who participated in Bible studies from 40 percent of all elementary school students in 1955 to 10 percent in 1965 and 6 percent in 1975 probably contributed to the decline in religious faith. The proportion of those born between the early 1960s and the mid-1970s whose religious belief was either weak or non-existent grew significantly. The number of people raised in a secular environment grew, while the number of people who received an explicitly religious upbringing declined. The impact of militant secularization materialized in somewhat delayed form at a time when the socialist system began to take on a permanent character and more and more people concluded that a religious education would prove to be an impediment within the prevailing social and political context.[11]

During the period of Kádár consolidation, the communist government attempted to utilize the Churches in order to increase its popular approval. By this time, the regime had contented itself with the exercise of more or less non-violent forms of pressure, maintaining its rigorous supervision over the various religious denominations active in Hungary through the State Office for Church Affairs, the political police and the cooperation of the generally compliant Church prelates. A peculiar situation developed in Hungary's Churches at this time in which the lower-ranking clergy and a substantial number of the church-going public came into conflict with the Church leadership and administration. Prelates often did anything within their power to avoid political conflict, obstructing those standard pastoral activities that invited the disapproval of the regime and supporting the controversial peace priest movement. Beginning in the 1970s, the Churches expanded their charitable and cultural institutions and activities as much as possible within the narrowly defined limits that the regime had established for them. In exchange for these concessions, the clergy remained more or less loyal from a political standpoint, declining to openly challenge the validity of the socialist system in their sermons and occasionally even taking an active part in political campaigns on behalf of the regime. In the year 1977, six Church leaders also served in the capacity of parliamentary representative. Bishop László Lékai was appointed as Archbishop of Esztergom in 1976, thus rounding out the Catholic Church hierarchy that had been incomplete since József Mindszenty's departure from Hungary in 1971.

One of the most important political steps taken during the period of Kádár consolidation was the introduction of an economic reform program known as the New Economic Mechanism in January 1968. Following a year- to a year-and-a-half-long interval of political and technical preparation and debate, a decision was made in May 1966 to scrap the command economy in favor of a less centralized and flexible system based on company autonomy and at least a limited regard for market conditions. The planned reforms were confined exclusively to the economy and did not pertain to the political system in any way whatsoever. In 1968 and 1969 János Kádár emphatically supported a continuation of the reforms, attempting to neutralize the adverse impact of the events in Czechoslovakia. At the same time, ideas connected to politics that had emerged along with the plans for economic reform were removed from the agenda indefinitely as a result of the change in circumstances stemming from the intervention in Czechoslovakia. The party leadership continued to organize and govern Hungary's political life according to "Leninist norms." Uninitiated outsiders could have hardly noticed the separation of pro- and anti-reform partisans into more distinct camps at this time. Even those observers who were capable of deciphering the more subtle messages transmitted via Hungary's tightly controlled media could have at most detected a shift in the emphasis placed on the statements of various officials. The fact that in the period following the Prague Spring the Soviet party leadership viewed Hungary's liberalization as an increasing threat to the imperial unity of the USSR, going so far as to contemplate replacing János Kádár with a member of the anti-reform camp[12] that had been criticizing the New Economic Mechanism from a classically socialist ideological perspective, further complicated the domestic political situation at the beginning of the 1970s. The political conflict between the pro- and anti-reform factions culminated in 1971–1972. In February 1972 János Kádár traveled to Moscow, where the Soviet Politburo, above all Brezhnev, reprimanded the Hungarian Socialist Workers' Party general secretary for his somewhat more cautious and reserved bearing towards the Brezhnev-led Soviet party leadership since 1964 and for what the Soviets claimed was an upsurge in political tension, lagging economic development, an increasingly pointed departure from the *kolkhoz* cooperative model and rising debt stemming from the economic reforms introduced in 1968. Kádár's talks with Soviet party leaders in Moscow convinced him that his anti-reform critics within the HSWP had essentially been serving as mediators for Soviet criticism of the New Economic Mechanism, prompting the general secretary to call a halt to the process of economic reform at a November 1972 meeting of the HSWP Central Committee. One of the most important stakes in the political struggle that was taking place within the HSWP was the post of party leader. Kádár, however, managed to emerge from the conflict with his power intact after having withdrawn his support for the economic reforms, tendered his resignation as general secretary—an extremely rare gesture in the Soviet bloc—and provided a demonstration of the unity of the Hungarian Socialist Workers' Party leadership while more or less mollifying the inter-party opposition through anti-reform concessions. The success of Kádár's strategy is illustrated in the fact that, in addition to the HSWP Central Committee, the Soviet party leadership also expressed public confidence in the general secretary, thus informally reconfirming his position as party chief. Following this brief power struggle, nobody seriously called Kádár's hold on leadership over the HSWP into question again until the mid-1980s. A long road still lay ahead, however, until that time.

A modification of both domestic and economic politics was the heavy price to be paid for János Kádár's triumph. This change in political course was manifested in personnel changes that took place in the middle of the 1970s. During the initial phase of this reshuffle of party officials, prominent proponents of reform—Rezső Nyers, Lajos Fehér, György Aczél and Jenő Fock—were dismissed from their leading political positions, while the anti-reform faction gained a slight increase in power at the 1975 party congress. Many members of the latter camp were subsequently forced into retirement between 1976 and 1978. The typical civil servant cadre György Lázár replaced Fock as prime minister in 1975.

The anti-reform about-face described above resulted in an intensification of cultural-political and ideological rigor during the first half of the 1970s. Between 1973 and 1975, social scientists such as István Kemény, Iván Szelényi and András Hegedüs, philosophers such as Ágnes Heller, György Márkus, János Kis and György Bencze, and writers such as Miklós Haraszti and György Konrád were censured for holding anti-Marxist and/or anti-socialist viewpoints. The Hungarian Socialist Workers' Party members among them were expelled from the party and were often dismissed from their jobs and prohibited from publication just as non-party members. Several of these people accepted the regime's offer to provide them with an emigration passport and left the country.

The balance of power in Hungarian domestic politics more or less reached a state of equilibrium during the final years of the Kádár consolidation, a condition substantiated in the reappointment of nearly all 127 members of the Central Committee at the era-ending 1980 party congress. The aging of the Hungarian Socialist Workers' Party leadership and the repeated delay of its planned rejuvenation became an increasingly serious problem. Although the issue of János Kádár's eventual successor as party general secretary had not yet arisen, an increasing number of potential candidates, self-proclaimed and otherwise, emerged, beginning in the late 1970s.

The mentality of the 25,000–30,000 leading party officials[13] in Hungary also changed somewhat during the period. More and more members of the *nomenklatura* ceased to regard themselves as professional revolutionaries on a mission to "make the people happy," transforming gradually into civil servants operating the system. The shifting of positions within the party underwent a corresponding decline, while the number of educated and professionally trained cadres increased. This slow process of professionalization was only partially evident to the Hungarian public, as a result of the social distance that separated the average citizen from those filling political office and the absence of normal communication between the two groups.

The functions of the press and other channels of public communication remained essentially unchanged during the period of Kádár consolidation, although they displayed an increasing departure in style and tone from those characteristic of the pre-1956 era and the years following the Revolution. The use of militant terminology diminished, articles were less imbued with the ideological outlook of class struggle, and the previous role of the press as an everyday tool for mobilization of the public changed. There emerged at this time a peculiar balance based on self-censorship in which the press and other forms of media attempted to convey the message that everything was running smoothly in the country, that there was no conflict, tension or scandal. Reports in the printed press as well as the increasingly influential media of radio and television described the wage disputes and strikes of workers in Western Europe and "the American imperialists' merciless war in Vietnam," and issued a terse communiqué in 1968 announcing that "The armies of the socialist countries have extended Soviet-led fraternal assistance to Czechoslovakia in its struggle against forces of counterrevolution." Meanwhile, domestic news coverage focused on the opening of new factories, kindergartens and schools, and other everyday events connected to Hungary's peaceful development, only occasionally citing the presence of some minor difficulties that had to be overcome.

The palpable rise in the social acceptance of the socialist regime during the period of Kádár consolidation from the middle of the

1960s until the end of the 1970s was founded upon a tangible increase in the standard of living, the end of political uncertainty, and the establishment of a social security network that ensured somewhat more than minimal subsistence to a broad segment of society. A continual expansion of the possible sources of supplementary income—household farming, legal second jobs and black market employment[14]—served to further fortify society's acceptance of the regime. The legitimacy of the Hungarian Socialist Workers' Party leadership remained unchallenged as long as it proved capable of maintaining the conditions described above. Not even such symbolic events as the spontaneous demonstrations that broke out on March 15 in both 1972 and 1973 caused the government to waver. These demonstrations involving a few thousand people served primarily to indicate that a generation had come of age for whom the memory of the suppressed 1956 Revolution and subsequent reprisals did not represent a total encumbrance and who no longer gauged their living circumstances, future prospects and rights against those of the Rákosi era, but against the prevailing standards in Western Europe. This generation had been socialized within the context of the subculture and rock music of the 1960s and rejected the conformist thinking and behavior of their predecessors, although it required nearly another decade for the members of this generation to establish the various forms and institutions of political opposition. It became clear only at the end of the 1970s—in 1978 to be precise—that the arrest and containment of the 1968 reforms and the response to the global economic situation stemming from the oil crisis would have unavoidable domestic political consequences. The drastic and thereafter continual rise in consumer prices and decline in incomes undermined political stability and the Kádár consolidation policy of providing the population with a steady increase in the standard of living, thus eroding the regime's social acceptance. This necessitated political changes aimed at gradual restoration of the economic reforms.

2. Foreign Affairs[15]

Hungarian–Soviet relations,[16] which had become increasingly cordial beginning in 1957–1958, also underwent a moderate change during the period of Kádár consolidation, primarily the result of the CPSU Central Committee's coup-like dismissal of Nikita Sergeyevich Khrushchev as party general secretary and his replacement with Leonid Ilyich Brezhnev on October 14, 1964. János Kádár learned of the loss of his primary supporter within the Soviet party leadership while on a visit to Poland, making the uncharacteristic gesture for a leader of an Eastern Bloc country of articulating his incomprehension and disappointment at Khrushchev's removal and his acclaim for the former CPSU general secretary's achievements in a speech following his return to Hungary. A subsequent letter from the Hungarian party leadership to the Soviets voiced a slightly modified version of this viewpoint. Kádár continued to express praise and best wishes for Khrushchev whenever the opportunity arose. These acts, although by no means signifying opposition to Brezhnev, did serve to somewhat cool relations between the most powerful groups within the Hungarian and Soviet party leadership, particularly those between János Kádár and the newly appointed general secretary of the CPSU.[17] As a consequence, the room for Hungary to maneuver in its relations with the Soviet Union diminished to a fluctuating degree during the Brezhnev era.

From the middle of the 1960s, diplomatic efforts intensified to improve and normalize relations between Hungary and the West, initially Austria and Germany, then France, the United States and the Vatican. The Vietnam War temporarily weakened the dynamic of rapprochement with the United States, although US–Hungarian diplomatic contacts were nevertheless elevated to an ambassadorial level in 1967.[18] Then, following a period of extensive negotiations, Hungary and the United States reached an agreement in 1973 regarding compensation for US assets nationalized after World War II that obliged the Hungarian state to remit a sum of 19 million dollars over a period of 20 years.

Hungary's foreign policy, although conceived in the unremitting shadow of the Soviet Union, was nevertheless capable of undertaking occasional independent initiative during this period, a condition that produced a unique duality: on the one hand Hungarian diplomacy was always compelled to espouse those positions incumbent upon it as a socialist bloc country—to "condemn imperialist aggression"—while on the other hand it utilized the standard means of negotiation in an attempt to exploit the possibilities engendered in the process of détente that had commenced following the conclusion of the Cold War period. The slow expansion of Hungary's cultural and scientific contacts with Western Europe and the United States stemming from this diplomatic opening served to further encourage this process. The Soviets attempted to restrain Hungary's rapprochement with the West, although the success of this endeavor proved to be only temporary. Hungarian political leaders continued to provide unqualified support for Soviet policies with regard to the global political conflicts of the late 1960s such as the Vietnam War and the 1967 Six Day War, in response to which Hungary severed its diplomatic relations with Israel.

Between 1966 and 1968, Soviet–Hungarian diplomatic relations focused on Hungary's increasingly autonomous foreign policy, economic reform and other general economic and commercial issues. In September 1967 János Kádár persuaded Brezhnev to accept the reintroduction of economic reform in Hungary, albeit within an atmosphere of moderate skepticism. The Hungarian Socialist Workers' Party general secretary justified the need to transform the economic system on the premise that it would be impossible to resolve the existing economic stress in Hungary without such change. At the same time, however, intense Soviet misgivings compelled Hungarian officials to first curtail, then suspend altogether, their financial and membership negotiations with the World Bank and the International Monetary Fund. The diversion of the CPSU leadership's attention at the time of the 1968 Prague Spring proved to be a short-term benefit to Hungary in terms of its renewed program of economic reform. However, over the longer term, the events in Czechoslovakia served to strengthen the more dogmatic orientation within the Soviet leadership that advocated preserving the unity of the socialist camp at all costs.

The Hungarian Socialist Workers' Party leadership adopted an ambiguous stance with regard to the political changes that took place in Czechoslovakia in 1968, when János Kádár initially exhibited a supportive posture towards Alexander Dubček and his policies, but then, partially in acquiescence to Soviet pressure and partially in defense of domestic economic reform, agreed with some reluctance to dispatch Hungarian military forces to participate in the August 21, 1968, invasion of Czechoslovakia. However, not even participation in the Soviet-led suppression of the Prague Spring in 1968 and the 1972–1973 anti-reform policy shift were enough to totally erase the varying degree of mutual suspicion that had characterized relations between Soviet and Hungarian leaders since the middle of the 1960s. This mistrust remained intact until Brezhnev's death in 1982, although it must be noted that the Soviet party leader's illness and gradual intellectual and physical decline played a certain role in this circumstance.

Relations between the various countries in the socialist bloc were strikingly diverse in quality during the 1970s. Party leaders in Berlin and Prague were wary of Hungary's reform endeavors and liberalization, while Nicolae Ceauşescu's maverick personality and the nationality question began to exercise a more evident impact on Hungarian–Romanian relations beginning in the 1970s.

However, under the given geopolitical circumstances, Hungarian foreign policy could be regarded as successful in the 1970s in terms of building relations with Western Europe and the United States. Hungary's relations with Austria and Finland were normalized at the end of the 1970s, when Hungarian leaders conducted high-level negotiations with their counterparts from these countries. After a long period of preliminary talks, Hungary and the Federal Republic of Germany established official diplomatic relations in December 1973.[19] West Germany's *Ostpolitik*, aimed at improving relations with countries in Eastern Europe, played an important role in the rapprochement between West Germany and Hungary, although both Soviet and more dogmatic Hungarian leaders attempted to impede this process. Secret negotiations between Hungary, the Vatican and the United States resulted in a 1971 agreement that made it possible for József Mindszenty, who had been staying at the US Embassy in Budapest since taking refuge there on November 4, 1956, to leave the country. Pope Paul VI subsequently stripped Mindszenty of his post as Primate of Hungary, appointing László Lékai to serve as Archbishop of Esztergom in 1976. Resolution of the Mindszenty question accelerated the effort to rebuild diplomatic contacts between Hungary and the Vatican, and served to improve Hungarian–US relations as well. This process culminated in János Kádár's visit to the Vatican in 1977, when the Hungarian Socialist Workers' Party leader became the first communist leader from Eastern Europe to meet with Pope Paul VI while in office.

The return in 1978 of the Holy Crown to Hungary from the United States, where it had been taken following World War II, was also an important symbolic gesture. During this same year, an agreement was signed in the course of US–Hungarian negotiations granting most favored nation (MFN) trade status to Hungary. Hungary's bilateral relations with West Germany, France and Great Britain improved steadily at this time, an amelioration that the Kádár government's rising foreign financing requirement made all the more necessary. Hungarian foreign policy placed great emphasis on developing and maintaining European diplomatic contacts and promoting the process of détente.[20] Hungary signed the Helsinki Accords, including the articles pertaining to human rights. János Kádár spoke at the Helsinki Conference, declaring the inviolability of European borders and raising the issue of national minorities at a European political forum for the first time after a long period of silence with regard to this question. Recognition of the principle of peaceful coexistence became a cornerstone of Hungarian foreign policy during the decade of the 1970s. Hungary continued to espouse this principle even after the reescalation in tension between the Great Powers at the end of the 1970s, intensifying its high-level foreign diplomatic activity with the West during this period, when János Kádár met for talks with the leaders of numerous European countries, including Austria, Italy, West Germany and France.

Hungary's opening towards the outside world entailed an increase in tourism beginning in the mid-1960s. Whereas at the beginning of the 1960s only 300,000 Hungarian citizens were permitted to travel abroad each year, primarily to neighboring countries, this number had risen to more than one million per year by 1970 and to five million per year by 1980. This increase in tourism took place in spite of Hungary's preservation of rigid foreign travel restrictions, which were nevertheless moderate in comparison to those imposed in other Eastern Bloc countries. Hungarian citizens received a red passport for "Eastward" visits to other socialist countries, while they were permitted to request a 50-dollar exit permit for travel to the West with a blue passport every two years in order to visit family members and every three years for touristic purposes. The number of foreign guests visiting Hungary rose to a similar degree during this period, when an increasing number of commercial tourists from the Soviet Union, Poland, Romania and Czechoslovakia accounted for much of the boost in domestic tourism. More and more Hungarian citizens traveled to neighboring countries, notably Austria, for commercial reasons, beginning in the middle of the 1960s, as well.

Although the issue of Hungarian minorities living in surrounding countries still did not represent a primary factor guiding Hungary's foreign policy during the consolidation era, by 1970 Hungarian diplomats were beginning to express indirect criticism of their socialist neighbors, particularly Romania, with regard to their minority policies. Raising the question of national minorities was no longer viewed automatically as a manifestation of "bourgeois nationalism." The taboo surrounding this issue had diminished to such a degree that the Hungarian press even began to publish sporadic reports regarding the assimilatory policies practiced in some of the neighboring socialist countries, voicing specific objection to the retrenchment of Hungarian-language education. Members of the Hungarian minority living in the Sub-Carpathian region of the Ukrainian Soviet Socialist Republic faced many of the same problems as their fellows in Romania and Czechoslovakia, although this issue remained off limits under the prevailing political conditions.

Hungarian minorities lived amid more favorable conditions in Yugoslavia than they did in other socialist successor states in the 1960s and 1970s. Although the Hungarian minority did not enjoy full territorial autonomy in Yugoslavia either, four fifths of Hungarian children living in the Socialist Autonomous Province of Voivodina had access to native-language education, independent Hungarian-language departments operated at the University of Novi Sad (Újvidék) and the Subotica (Szabadka) teacher training college, and the right to mother-tongue use and the operation of Hungarian-language cultural institutions were guaranteed. Although various degrees of conflict involving Hungarian minorities took place in Yugoslavia as well, such disputes were rarely so serious as to merit reference in the course of Hungarian–Yugoslav inter-state and inter-party negotiations.

Although the Kádár government's policies with regard to Hungarian national minorities continued to be rooted in the ideology of "proletarian internationalism," they did undergo an incremental transformation beginning in the late 1960s. In spite of the assimilatory pressure that weighed on Hungarians living in Czechoslovakia, for example, János Kádár declared during a visit to Prague in 1967 that as a result of a resolution of earlier difficulties, the country's Hungarian minority had attained satisfactory living circumstances in terms of exercise of their national identity; however, by 1968, the government had established a committee under the auspices of the Patriotic People's Front to examine issues related to Hungarian minorities, while the Mother Tongue Conference, an organization whose primary objective was to preserve the cultural traditions of Hungarians living outside the borders of Hungary and to provide a demonstration of national unity, held its first meeting in 1970.

János Kádár's speech at the 1975 Helsinki Conference was one of the cardinal events signaling the transformation of Hungary's political position and practice with regard to nationality and national issues. During his address, the Hungarian Socialist Workers' Party general secretary referred to the fact that Hungary had lost two thirds of its territory and population as a result of the Treaty of Trianon following World War I and to the country's subsequent losses in World War II, citing the long-term consequences related to the incorporation of a large number of Hungarians into post-war successor states, where they were entitled to the same rights as the majority nationalities. Participants in the Helsinki Conference agreed to refrain from the threat or use of force against the territorial integrity or political independence of any state, a stipulation that pleased countries neighboring Hungary. The Helsinki Final Act called upon signatories to ensure the free flow of information and the comprehensive recognition of human rights, which won approval among people in socialist countries. All in all, the Helsinki Accords served to strengthen Hungary's legal grounds for taking more decisive political action in support of Hungarian minorities, which Hungarian diplomats, in fact, attempted to do at the so-called Helsinki follow-up meetings held in Belgrade in 1977, in Madrid in 1980 and in Ottawa in 1983. However, under the given circumstances, the Kádár government's modest intervention on behalf of Hungarian minorities at these follow-up conferences hardly had any effect.

The Kádár government's policies towards national minorities living in Hungary—Germans, Slovaks and South Slavs—also changed significantly starting in the 1970s. It is only a slight exaggeration to state that beginning at this time these minorities benefited from positive discrimination in terms of education, culture and political representation, the objective of which was to provide neighboring states with a positive example that might encourage them to abandon their assimilatory policies *vis-à-vis* Hungarian national minorities. This endeavor had little impact. In the 1970s Romania launched its so-called "national homogenization" program aimed at the total assimilation of national minorities and the establishment of a homogeneous Romanian nation state. Hungarian political officials, including János Kádár, urged Romanian leader Nicolae Ceauşescu to halt discriminatory minority practices during meetings held in Debrecen, Hungary, and Oradea (Nagyvárad), Romania, in 1977, although Romanian authorities ignored these appeals. Kádár declined to engage in further bilateral negotiations with Ceaușescu following the failure of the 1977 talks, thereafter meeting the Romanian party and state leader exclusively at meetings of Comecon or the Warsaw Pact. The events that took place in Czechoslovakia in 1968 offered hope that the era of forced assimilation may have come to an end in that country, although the Gustáv Husák-led regime that came to power following the suppression of the Prague Spring routinely played the Hungarian card and resumed policies aimed at curtailing Hungarian-language education throughout the 1970s.

The gradual moderation of travel restrictions facilitated cross-border contacts to a significant degree, although customs officials in Ceaușescu's Romania exercised increasing cultural censorship at frontier crossings beginning in the 1970s, when they regularly confiscated Hungarian-language books, newspapers and periodicals.

3. The Economy[21]

Principles of economic rationalism began to play a more significant role in the function and output of the Hungarian economy beginning in the second half of the 1960s, although political considerations remained an extremely important economic factor as well. Hungary's national income grew by an annual average of 3.5 to 4 percent in the first half of the 1960s, 7 percent in the second half of the 1960s and 6.5 percent in the first half of the 1970s. A turning point took place in this domain during the second half of the 1970s, when national income growth began to decline steadily. The Hungarian economy grew at an average rate in comparison to other socialist countries and at an even higher pace than the global average during the 1960s and 1970s, although this expansion was not enough to significantly decrease Hungary's legacy of underdevelopment. The structure of the economy underwent a gradual transformation during this period, when the role of industry in generating gross national product rose steadily, while that of agriculture declined and the service sector remained insignificant in this regard. Hungary's industrial output increased by an average rate of 6 to 7 percent a year beginning in the latter half of the 1960s, growth that stemmed primarily from the employment of a massive number of new workers in the industrial sector and a continual increase in production capacity, not an improvement in efficiency. The Coordinating Committee for Multilateral Export Controls (CoCom) established in 1947 to limit Western exports to Eastern Bloc countries restricted Hungary's access to advanced industrial technology, thus impeding its technological development. The process of specialization that took place within the Council for Mutual Economic Assistance at this time resulted in the termination of parallel production in member states. With regard to Hungary, this entailed the halt of essentially all vehicle production in the country, with the exception of buses.

Agricultural production rose by an annual average of 2.5 percent during the 1960s, rising in the second half of the decade as compared to the first. Contrary to growth in the industrial sector, the agricultural output rose primarily as the result of a rapid increase in efficiency, since both the number of people employed in agriculture and the area of land under cultivation declined steadily from the beginning of the 1960s. Small-scale agricultural production units established as part of household farming operations, most of which produced labor-intensive commodities, played an important role in the rise in agricultural output in Hungary. The country's agricultural output continued to increase in the 1970s, growing by an average of 4 to 5 percent during the decade. Organizational and technological innovations introducing the industrial production model[22] in the agricultural sector served to consolidate large-scale production units specializing in extensive farming and the aforementioned small-scale production units involved in intensive farming[23] Hungary's agricultural production yields either equaled or surpassed those in the rest of Europe during this period. This process of transformation was rooted in the widespread recognition that collectivized agriculture could only be productive if it departed completely from the Soviet *kolkhoz* model, generating an incentive for cooperative members and providing sufficient capital for agricultural development. As a result of measures taken in the second half of the 1960s, a unique organizational structure emerged in Hungary's agricultural sector, one that was founded upon collective ownership, incentive-based growth and large-scale farming. As a consequence of these changes, food supplies grew steadily in Hungary, while rising profitability finally convinced the country's rural peasant community to accept the situation that had emerged as a result of collectivization. The rise in agricultural production stemming from the improved efficiency of the system also helped to boost overall economic growth.

Hungary's investment ratios underwent a fundamental transformation during the second half of the 1960s, when the proportion of the government budget allocated towards agricultural development began to rise significantly for the first time since the period following the communist takeover, remaining relatively high throughout the subsequent years. A distinction was made between productive and non-productive activities in the course of establishing economic priorities both before and after 1968. As a result, funding for commerce, the various branches of the service sector, telecommunications and transport was below that required to maintain the status quo for several decades on end, thereby compounding Hungary's infrastructural underdevelopment and all of the disadvantages that this entailed.[24]

In principle, the economic and institutional reforms that took place in 1968 should have served to promote Hungary's development and counteract the effects of the voluntaristic growth policies that had foundered in the mid-1960s, although in fact their primary objective was to sustain the viability of the socialist system. In order to achieve this goal, bureaucracy related to economic planning and management was streamlined, company production and investment autonomy was increased, a comprehensive price reform was carried out and the system of wage and income regulation was modified.[25] Following these reforms, the assessment of companies depended—in theory—on the amount of profit generated from the sale of their products. Propagation of the profit motive was intended to increase the efficiency of Hungary's economy.

At the same time, the introduction of quasi-market elements, an increased emphasis on consumption, the authorization of industrial operations (auxiliary production branches) at agricultural cooperatives and the heightening of incentive through a more tolerant handling of both legal and semi-legal economic activities, represented an attempt to promote economic rationalism. Following the steps initiated at the beginning of 1968, further reform measures were devised over the following two years focusing on the establishment of a unified currency exchange rate and issues related to investment decisions and finance. However, subsequent political developments delayed implementation of these measures.

The difficulty with which Hungary's macroeconomic system adapted to the new conditions hampered the practical application of the economic reforms. The system of contractually fixed trade prices continued to govern commerce between Comecon member states, thus preventing a portion of Hungary's major enterprises from introducing the incentive principle and perpetuating unprofitable production.

Hungary's 1968 reforms instituted a unique economic system in which central planning and social and cooperative ownership of production continued to predominate, although genuine market and quasi-market factors and economic activities falling outside the control of the state were also permitted to play an increasing role in the operation of the economy. The Kádár government attempted to curtail the influence of independent market forces in the economy as part of its halt of the reform process at the beginning of the 1970s, although this effort was only temporarily successful. Restrictions imposed on household farming and other forms of agricultural activity reduced production incentive, leading to a temporary shortage of fruits and vegetables. Although it was not possible to completely restore the economic conditions that had existed in Hungary prior to 1968, the reinstatement of centralized administration curtailed the autonomy of enterprises. A modification to the system of profit withdrawal at this time resulted in the removal of resources from profitable companies in proportion to their earnings for transfer to unprofitable companies.

Hungary's political and economic leaders misjudged the global economic consequences of the first oil crisis in the mid-1970s, concluding that the rise in oil and raw material prices would not have a major impact on the Hungarian economy, partially as the result of the Comecon price regulation system. Therefore Hungarian officials, contrary to those in the majority of Western countries, failed to recognize the need for urgent structural changes to the economy, continuing the development of raw material- and energy-intensive industrial sectors. Moreover, Hungarian leaders considered the crisis to represent a merely temporary downturn that they could overcome through borrowing. The extremely questionable results of this measure are manifested in the fact that domestic consumption basically continued to rise steadily throughout the rest of the 1970s. This occurred despite the inherent incapacity of the ideologically and politically encumbered socialist economic system to satisfy rising consumer demand. As a matter of course, the regime preserved certain areas of the economy in which it had not only broadly renounced supervision over economic activity, but had incorporated the output of services and labor falling outside the system of state redistribution into its own production.

According to the results of a representative opinion poll taken in Hungary during the autumn of 1981, a total of 56 percent of people surveyed viewed the notion of holding a second job as positive, while 74 percent stated that it would be worthwhile to start a private enterprise and 70 percent said that supplies and provisions would improve if there were more such enterprises. Within the socialist shortage economy, private and secondary economic activities often generated a significant degree of supplementary income from which people could finance the accumulation of consumer goods and capital. The value of personal connections and the propensity for corruption increased among those private entrepreneurs operating on the periphery of the scarcity-driven system, since the acquisition of goods and materials often required the payment of a bribe, while the inclination to conceal income also grew at this time. These changes in practice and outlook expanded the room for economic maneuver within Hungary's system of "goulash communism," making it possible to "rise above" Eastern European norms.[26] The fragility of the private economy is illustrated clearly in the changes that took place in the mid-1970s, when a retrenchment of reform and temporary restrictions on both legal and illicit private economic activity stemming from a partial restoration of former economic policies triggered the beginning of another economic collapse beginning in the late 1970s. All of this coincided with a fundamental change in global economic conditions that triggered a continual deterioration in Hungary's economy. In the years after 1973, the prices of Hungarian exports rose by 60 to 70 percent, while the prices of Hungarian imports increased by only 30 to 40 percent. A significant proportion of this imbalance stemmed from Soviet energy imports, the cost of which was calculated according to global energy prices following the oil crisis in the mid-1970s rather than the previously utilized five-year average price base. In practical terms, this meant that Hungary had to export six to eight times more products for each unit of imported energy that it had five years previously. By the end of the 1970s, it had become clear that the rise in living standards and economic growth financed through foreign loans was not sustainable, a condition that signaled the collapse of the "economic foundation" underpinning the Kádár consolidation. However, generation of continual growth in the economy and the standard of living continued to serve as the primary goals of Hungary's economic policies even after the Hungarian economy had lost its capacity to furnish the resources needed to finance these objectives in the late 1970s. This situation naturally resulted in a rise in Hungary's debt, which grew from just 800 million dollars in 1970 to 3.1 billion dollars in 1975 and 9.1 billion dollars in 1980. This increase in debt would have required urgent measures to restructure the economy and gradually legalize the unofficial private sector, although these steps were taken only at the beginning of the 1980s.

The years from 1965 until 1978 produced a palpable improvement in the income conditions and material circumstances of the Hungarian population. It is, of course, questionable whether this improvement stemmed primarily from genuine political initiative or from social necessity and exertion. And the magnitude of their social costs is also debatable. Official statistics do, however, demonstrate that the national income underwent an essentially continual increase and real wages more than doubled during this period. Hungary's real wage index rose from 168 in 1965 to 234 in 1975, while its real income index increased from 181 to 306 during the decade. Among the various components of household income, social cash benefits rose to the greatest degree, growing tenfold between 1960 and 1980. This sharp rise was primarily the result of an increase in the number of pensioners and average pension benefits, an expansion of the family allowance and the introduction of childcare assistance.[27] In a survey of 4,000 families that the Central Statistics Office conducted at the beginning of the period of Kádár consolidation in 1965 to measure changes in their living conditions, nearly half of all worker-employee and so-called dual-income-peasant households reported that their standard of living had remained unchanged in the years 1962–1964, while one sixth of them said that their standard of living had deteriorated to various degrees during the period. Fewer than one third of worker-employee families and just one quarter of peasant families participating in the Central Statistics Office survey reported that their standard of living had improved somewhat between 1962 and 1964, while only 6–7 percent of both groups said that their standard of living had improved significantly during the period.

Assessment of changes in living standards between 1964 and 1976

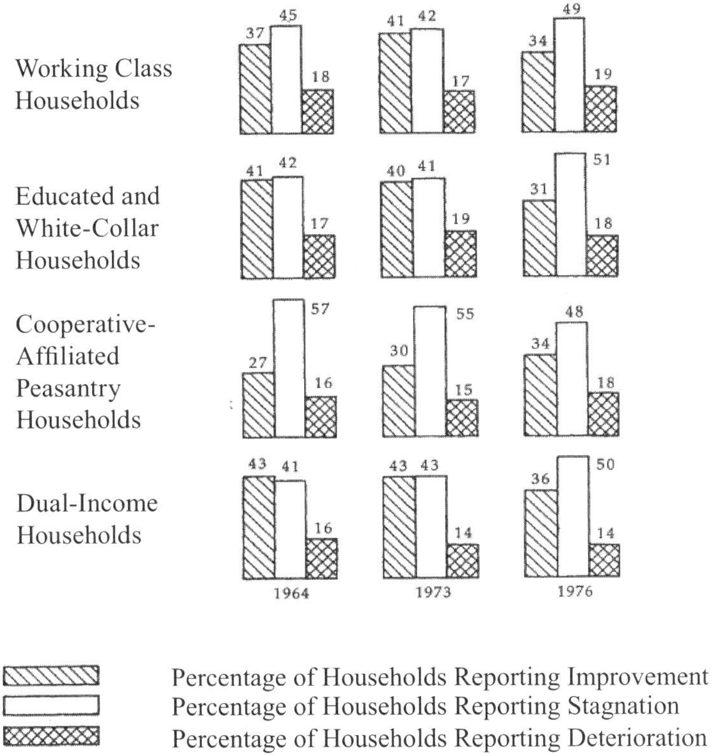

Source: *Életszínvonal II. Az életszínvonal alakulásának lakossági megítélése* [Living Standards II. The Popular Assessment of Changes in the Standard of Living] (Budapest, 1978).

The results of similar surveys that the Central Statistics Office conducted in 1973 and 1976 provide a clear demonstration of the "ascendant" phase and differentiation that lasted until the middle of the 1970s. While in 1973 a significant majority of households reported that their standard of living and income conditions had improved, by 1976 almost all households, with the exception of those belonging to the "agricultural cooperative-affiliated peasantry" category, reported that their standard of living and income conditions had deteriorated. Data from surveys conducted between 1964 and 1976 indicate that among the four established types of household, the percentage of those that reported rising living standards rose continually only within the category affiliated with agricultural cooperatives. Nearly 50 percent of households in all categories consistently reported that their living standards had stagnated, while a similarly steady 16–17 percent reported that their living circumstances had deteriorated. The fact that all (state) employees either received or were eligible to receive non-wage benefits and allowances regardless of their work performance served to somewhat distort the income data. Hungary's pricing system, which often separated the cost of products and services from their true value, thus benefiting those with lower earnings, also had an impact on income conditions during the period. Although the negligible inflation rate recorded in Hungary throughout the 1960s and the first half of the 1970s contributed to a general improvement in income conditions in the country, the artificial price regulation that underpinned low inflation also served to exacerbate economic tension. The peculiarity of the Kádár government's pricing policies is reflected clearly in the fact that Hungary's average annual inflation rate more than doubled from 2.8 percent in the first half of the 1970s to 6.3 percent in the second half of the decade. During the socialist era, the acquisition and accumulation of wealth were not among the activities supported by the regime. This was primarily the result of ideological factors, since the accumulation of private property and assets for other than personal use, that is, for the purpose of accumulation, contradicted the concept of public property that prevailed within the socialist system, as well as the Marxist-Leninist principles aimed at establishing social equality, preventing the generation of profit without work and eliminating exploitation. An excerpt from a speech that János Kádár made in the early 1970s gives clear expression to the official viewpoint regarding the acquisition of wealth:

> We approve of the idea of somebody saving money earned through honest work in order to buy a television, a refrigerator, a motorbike or a car, to travel or to build a family house. However, we do not approve when somebody's outlook becomes so distorted that honest work is no longer a source of common human joy and the honor of doing such work no longer provides life with meaning, when acquisition and stockpiling like a squirrel becomes the most important thing.[28]

The process of divesting Hungarian citizens of their private property had been completed by the early 1960s, while that of their "reacquisition of wealth" began in the middle and final years of the decade. Data regarding the composite value of the Hungarian population's bank deposits and consumption of durable consumer goods substantiate the latter process. The rise in the number of families in possession of what by Hungarian standards represented a significant amount of property and assets rose steadily even within the changing income conditions of the 1970s and 1980s. Two of the several factors that underpinned this phenomenon were a relatively dynamic rise in real wages in the 1960s and 1970s, which established the financial foundations for accumulating wealth, and a recognition on the part of a broad segment of the population that the state, with its system of centralized redistribution, was unable to satisfy even its most basic needs, such as that for housing. Hungary's market for tenement housing remained small as a result of ownership restrictions, while even construction of state-owned housing, heralded as a triumph of socialism, did not come close to resolving Hungary's chronic housing shortage. Home building evolved into the most common form of wealth acquisition (as well) during the period in question. It is also clear that, with the exception of the most disadvantaged groups in Hungarian society, wealth acquisition was largely unconnected to social status. Families both with and without means could be found within all segments of society. The factors of capacity for income generation, circumstances of employment and inherited material background naturally exercised a fundamental impact on a given individual's potential for acquiring wealth. A family composed of two wage earners and two dependents that owned its living accommodation and was able to generate a supplementary income from the second economy obviously had a much better chance of accumulating wealth than a family composed of a single wage earner and four dependents that lived in rental housing.

During the socialist era, the savings account was the only legal form of financial savings in Hungary. The country's composite value of retail savings accounts rose from 5.5 billion forints in 1960 to 42.7 billion forints in 1970 and 81.2 billion forints in 1975, a considerable increase even if the effects of inflation and low real interest rates are taken into account. The fact that retail interest—that which applied to the purchase of commodities and housing—was also relatively low, thus making indebtedness towards the state worthwhile, represented the other side of this equation. The tenfold rise in the composite stock of retail loans between 1960 and 1980 reflects a widespread awareness of this benefit. Data showing that there were 339,000 active savings accounts in Hungary containing more than 50,000 forints in 1975 provide indirect evidence of the accumulation of wealth that was taking place in the country. The composite value of these savings accounts was 32.1 million forints, which suggests that more prosperous Hungarians maintained an average of 100,000 forints in their savings accounts, corresponding to nearly three years' worth of an average wage. If only this factor is taken into consideration, one could say that based on the value of their savings accounts, the number of millionaires in Hungary rose approximately ten times during the decade of the 1970s. Moreover, those who had managed to accumulate this amount of money in their savings accounts amid the circumstances that prevailed in Hungary at the time almost certainly possessed real estate and personal property of a significant value as well.

In addition to cash savings, real estate—houses, apartments, holiday homes and garden plots—made up another common form of private property. Statutes in effect until the 1980s restricted one family or individual to ownership of one piece of residential real estate and a single holiday home. However, these regulations were often circumvented through such devices as purchases conducted in the name of a family member who had not yet reached legal age or after a nominal divorce. The rental of residential real estate began to strengthen Hungary's housing rental and subleasing sector beginning in the 1970s.

Personal property was the third form of wealth accumulation in Hungary. Ownership of the means of production was of negligible significance due to restrictions that remained in force until the 1980s, while possession of precious metals was also subject to regulation until 1974. The fact that these restrictions were unenforceable and thus routinely violated is another matter. Among the various types of personal property, ownership of durable consumer goods, such as cars[29] and inherited valuables, grew to a relatively substantial degree. The state naturally commanded a monopoly over the official trade of precious metals and valuables.

At the end of the 1970s, Zsuzsa Ferge estimated the number of wealthy families in Hungary, defined as those whose composite wealth surpassed 3–4 million forints, to be in the several thousands—10,000 at most.[30] (In 1978, an average Škoda automobile cost 84,000 forints and a 54-square-meter apartment in a housing estate cost between 400,000 and 500,000 forints, while Hungary's *per capita* average monthly wage was 3,687 forints.) This estimate suggests that 250,000–350,000 people belonged to this "upper 10,000" by the late 1970s or early 1980s. The number of prosperous families whose cash savings amounted to between a year and a half's to two years' worth of average wages was 20 to 25 times this number, totaling a minimum of 750,000–900,000 people.

Material gain required a great deal of effort from the population during this period. Although the average number of hours that Hungarians spent working at their primary places of employment declined between the 1960s and the 1980s, the amount of time that they devoted to small-scale agricultural production and to their endeavors connected to the second economy in general rose during this period, particularly among men. The significant amount of time dedicated to income acquisition in Hungary indicates that the majority of families in the country changed their earnings strategy at this time, taking advantage of the increasingly broad opportunities for obtaining secondary income. Scarcity was another factor that served to bear and sustain the household-farming and supplementary economies. Profit derived from these endeavors manifested itself most apparently in the rise in retail consumption.

Shortages of various degrees of gravity plagued centrally planned socialist economies throughout their existence. The change in economic conditions is reflected in the transformation in the type of goods that were subject to scarcity: by the 1970s, it was no longer basic food staples and clothing that were in chronic short supply, but modern and expensive consumer items. This shortage was one of the main factors influencing society's mentality and conduct.

The material gain ensured as part of the Kádár consolidation is manifested in data showing that the value of the household stock of durable goods in Hungary rose from 73.3 million forints in 1960 to 180 million forints in 1974, an increase of over two and a half times. The standard of living and consumption of a significant proportion of rural families underwent a major change in the 1960s and 1970s. Successful strategies of adapting to new economic conditions, such as the establishment of mixed households and intensive engagement in household farming and activities related to the supplementary economy, played an important role in this transformation. It is an indisputable fact that these adaptation strategies represented a significant burden on rural society, although they did make it possible for the village population to improve their social conditions, sometimes in spite of political impediments to this process.

Consumer behavior changed continuously during this period, when the list of the most popular goods in the country fluctuated periodically. Differences in living conditions, type of employment, household work structure and place of residence naturally exercised an impact over consumption, determining spending priorities such as whether to purchase tools and equipment or durable consumer goods aimed at raising the level of household comfort. Disparities in consumer behavior and income among the various segments of Hungarian society are reflected in the statistics from the year 1976 showing 37 passenger vehicles for every 100 households whose wage earners were involved in intellectual and white-collar occupations, compared to 17 passenger vehicles for every 100 working-class households and 12.5 passenger vehicles for every 100 peasant households. (It must also be noted that these data show that Hungary lagged behind other countries in both Eastern and Western Europe with regard to *per capita* vehicle ownership at this time.)

4. Society[31]

The demographic characteristics of Hungarian society changed to only a minor degree between the mid-1960s and the end of the 1970s. The number of births underwent a continual decline, although they still exceeded the number of deaths. As a consequence, Hungary's population continued to grow, although at a decreased rate, reaching 10.7 million in 1980. Mortality, conversely, began to rise in the mid-1960s, primarily as the result of a significant increase in the death rate among middle-aged men, eventually stabilizing at between 13 and 14 per 1,000 inhabitants. Family structure also underwent a transformation in Hungary during this period, when the frequency of the extended family diminished, while that of the nuclear family grew. The average number of children per family declined continually, falling to just above that needed for natural replacement of the population. The number of unmarried couples living together in long-term relationships increased sharply beginning in the early 1970s, while the marriage rate declined. The average age and the average life expectancy within certain age categories also increased as a result of an improvement in living circumstances and medical care. The age distribution of the population also changed at this time, when the number of children and young people decreased steadily, while the number of people within the older age groups underwent a corresponding increase.

Hungarian society was extremely homogeneous from an ethnic perspective. Only 3–4 percent of the population belonged to Hungary's German, Slovak, Romanian or South Slav national minority groups. There were also some 100,000 Jews and 300,000 to 400,000 Gypsies within the population. Questions related to Hungary's Jewish minority were considered to be taboo throughout the socialist era, while efforts were made from time to time to integrate the Gypsy population into society. The regime attempted to eliminate segregated Gypsy settlements beginning in the middle of the 1960s, but this initiative produced only partial success. The low level of education and vocational skills among Hungary's Gypsies[32] severely hampered attempts to improve their social status, while the great contrast between Gypsy customs and traditions and those of the majority population served to sustain the strong degree of prejudice against them.

Trends active within Hungary's vocational structure in the 1950s remained prevalent during the period presently under discussion, when the number of industrial workers continued to rise, primarily as a result of migration from the agricultural sector. The number of people employed in the service, transport and commercial sectors of the economy began to rise significantly only in the early 1970s. In terms of territorial distribution, Hungary's population continued to gravitate away from the countryside towards the cities, particularly Budapest, and other centers of industry and government administration. Budapest's population growth stemmed almost exclusively from rural migration in the 1960s and 1970s.

Emigration decreased with the slow consolidation that took place in Hungary following the mass exodus of refugees in 1956. From the middle of the 1960s until the end of the 1970s, an average of 3,500–4,000 people emigrated each year, both legally and illegally. Hungary's penal code continued to define the act of leaving the country without official permission as a criminal offense punishable by imprisonment of between one and three years. Since the border between Austria and Hungary was fortified with mines and barbed wire, most emigrants chose to leave the country with tourist passports and simply not return home rather than risk crossing the "green border." As punishment for unauthorized emigration, the relatives of these so-called "defectors" were denied passports for years on end, while the state confiscated both the real estate and personal property of people who had settled abroad illegally, if they had not already sold it before they left the country. More than half of those Hungarians who emigrated in the 1970s were between 21 and 30 years old and one fifth were under the age of 20, while most of them were educated skilled, technical or clerical employees, and relatively few of them were unskilled or agricultural laborers.[33] The majority of those who left Hungary during this period received refugee status abroad, although most of them had not, in fact, suffered direct political persecution at home, but had emigrated in search of better economic opportunities.

By the beginning of the 1970s, channels of social mobility founded upon the traditional factors of education and vocational skill gradually began to reemerge in place of those based on mass relocation.[34] An examination of the role of various forms of capital (cash-property, political-social connection, educational-cultural) in social stratification between the middle of the 1960s and the end of the following decade reveals that the supremacy of political capital began to decline slowly beginning in the 1970s, while the role of knowledge and education, as well as that of money and what was humbly referred to as "personal property," started to increase.

The emergence of a quasi-middle class, differentiation based on property and income, and a gradual reduction in mobility were among the processes that contributed significantly to the changes in Hungary's social structure that took place in the 1970s. During this period, there was a general social trend towards the middle that took place irrespective of occupational—and to a certain extent financial—status: this centripetal force acted upon a broad segment of society, from well-paid skilled workers, through agricultural cooperative members who maintained intensive household farming operations, or office administrators who undertook freelance typing work, to high school teachers and military officers. At the same time, data from studies conducted at the end of the 1970s reveal that there was an increase in differentiation within Hungarian society during this period, when the contrasts between the highly educated leadership and intellectual strata and other social groups widened. After being deprived of their property, Hungary's "old," pre-World War II bourgeoisie began to view education, family reputation and inherited cultural capital as the primary criteria for membership of the middle class. At the same time, status mobility generated an expansive and educated new middle class. In the 1970s and 1980s, the "middle class"[35] consisted primarily of those whose education, knowledge and skills had enabled them to obtain a better than average position on the labor market.

During the Kádár era, the lifestyle of the middle class essentially followed the traditional pattern. The value placed on occupational prestige, consumption and the quality of one's home and its furnishings rose continually during this period, while the role of property signifying social status (apartment, house, vacation home, parcel of land, or car) and the acquisition and maintenance of a high income also grew to a significant degree. Techniques of concealing property and investing accumulated capital to preserve its value arose as a means of circumventing imposed restrictions. Personal ability reemerged as a factor in differentiation. Disparities in wealth and income increased not only between the most prosperous and downcast segments of society, but within the "center," between the elite and the middle class as well.

Following the nationalization of farmland and disruption of the production chain that took place as part of the collectivization process, the agricultural cooperatives essentially proved unable to generate even a subsistence income for their members until the end of the 1960s. This is why it was necessary to provide them with a means of self-sufficiency in the form of household agricultural plots, which, following the regularization and increase of cooperative wages, assumed a greater role in production. In accordance with the new survival strategies that emerged following the end of the collectivization process, members of Hungary's younger age groups who had left the agricultural sector to become urban industrial workers retained their connections to the peasantry,[36] returning home after work to help their family members to cultivate household farmland. During the period presently under examination, one quarter of annual agricultural production stemmed from household agricultural activities, thus generating a considerable amount of secondary income. These played a decisive role in the process of stratification within rural society in the 1970s.

Primary and secondary economies functioned in unison not only in the agricultural sector, but in the industrial and service sectors as well. The quasi-market secondary economic sector took advantage of opportunities rooted in the condition of scarcity to mitigate economic difficulties stemming from the anarchy of central planning and the inefficiency of the primary economy. The term secondary economy applied to all forms of income generation, from tips and gratuities, to moonlighting and the illegal private sector, that were not part of the gainful economic activities that took place within the state sector. Beginning at this time, the transformation in economic mentality, individualization, the aspiration for autonomy, the change in lifestyle and the expansion of "civil" forms of behavior exercised a heavy impact on the structure of Hungarian society.

The complexity of stratification factors active in Hungary during the 1970s makes it impossible to identify unified classes or macrosocial strata based on criteria of any sort. Skilled workers descended from third- or fourth-generation working-class families could obviously not be classified within the same social group as peasants who following collectivization had taken jobs as unskilled or semi-skilled laborers. Daily commuters who continued to reside in the villages even after joining the urban industrial workforce, returning home from the factory every evening to perform three or four hours of agricultural labor with their family members, constituted a distinct group within the working class. Collectivized peasants who had previously worked as agricultural laborers could not be classified in the same social category as the descendants of the former agricultural elite, while cooperative members who made entrepreneurial use of household farming opportunities composed yet another autonomous group within rural society. The social status of an educated intellectual holding either fixed or freelance employment was completely different from that of a company secretary or office employee, even though all of them were classified as intellectual workers.

Hungary's private sector was composed primarily of retail merchants and tradesmen, whose number rebounded to an average of between 80,000 and 110,000 in the 1960s and 1970s after having undergone a drastic decline in the first half of the 1950s. The number of retail traders—tobacconists, market vendors and caterers—fluctuated between 10,000 and 12,000 between 1960 and 1980, while the number of people engaged in freelance intellectual occupations, the third component of the private sector, varied between 15,000 and 20,000. Significant changes took place within these groups only during the decade of the 1980s, when the number of independently employed and full-time wage earners increased dynamically within the private sector (see the following chapter for further details). Any attempt to calculate the size of Hungary's legal private sector at this time must not disregard the average of 30,000 to 40,000 people who worked for independently managed enterprises. Even when calculated with an average family size of three, the number of people and their dependents who subsisted on income earned in the private sector was at least between 500,000 and 700,000, or 5–7 percent of Hungary's total population, in the decades between 1960 and 1980.

An examination of social stratification in terms of occupation reveals that consolidation took place within this domain as well in the 1970s. The rise in the number of active wage earners declined during this decade, when growth in the labor force stemmed primarily from the employment of former homemakers. The number of economically inactive people generating income also underwent a rapid increase during this period as a result of an expansion of social benefits, particularly pensions and childcare allowances. Although the socialist policy of full employment permitted no official joblessness, one tenth of active wage earners, or approximately 400,000 to 500,000 people, belonged to the ranks of the hidden, or so-called "in-house" unemployed as a consequence of overemployment.

Distribution of active wage earners according to social stratum 1960–1980 (in percentages)

Social Stratum	*1960*	*1970*	*1980*
Managers and Intellectuals	3.0	5.1	7.8
Mid-Level White-Collar	13.7	20.7	22.5
Autonomous Retail Merchants	2.4	1.6	1.5
Skilled Laborers	15.5	19.5	23.2
Semi-Skilled Laborers	13.1	16.6	20.8
Unskilled Laborers	14.0	13.0	7.7
Autonomous Farmers	19.9	1.6	0.6
Agricultural Laborers	18.4	21.9	15.8
Total	100.0	100.0	100.0
Number of Actively Employed	4,759,616	4,988,840	5,068,157

Source: Rudolf Andorka, *Bevezetés a szociológiába* [Introduction to Sociology] (Budapest, 1997), p. 177.

Mass social movement within the various branches of the economy essentially ended around 1970. The number of people engaged in the urban industrial workforce grew at a slower rate in the 1970s, while the outflux from the agricultural sector also diminished during this decade as a result of the increasing stability of agricultural cooperatives. (There was even a minor rise in the number of people employed in the latter sector during the first half of the 1970s). The proportion of active wage earners employed in the service sector underwent a slow and steady increase beginning in the early 1970s. Another significant process that took place within Hungary's social structure during the era of Kádár consolidation was the closing of mobility channels, a circumstance that signaled an end to the mass changes in social status and heightened the inclination towards internal regeneration within various social groups. The proportion and number of skilled workers within the urban industrial workforce began to increase during the decade of the 1970s, while the number of unskilled ones declined to a moderate degree. Members of the agrarian intelligentsia, engineers and economists played a more prominent role within the segment of Hungarian society engaged in intellectual occupations during this period.

The process of individualization accelerated in Hungarian society during the 1960s and 1970s. With social self-organization unable to develop normally under the prevailing political system, the role of the family as a basic social institution grew. At the same time, the importance of private life and informal relations with family and friends increased, playing a significant role in improving the quality of everyday existence. The role of the family in promoting social stability and moderating the impact of inequality probably stood at the root of this increased emphasis on family life, while the significance of the family work unit, which was a crucial factor in the generation of material prosperity, must not be overlooked.

The socialist system by its very nature strengthened the attitude of subservience towards the state within Hungarian society, while at the same time preventing the growth of the democratic outlook and the development of civil autonomy and behavioral norms. During this period, social institutions (schools, mass communication and the formal social environment) and the private sphere (family, friends and localities) often promoted parallel and in many cases contradictory value systems. For example, while official institutions portrayed social equality as the fundamental principle governing Hungarian social conditions in the 1970s, mechanisms of socialization active in the private sphere, although they did not completely reject the notion of equality, placed increasing emphasis on personal achievement, consumption and values related to material prosperity that obviously contravened the precept of equality. This dual system of values was present in all realms of existence, exercising an influence over everything from modes of behavior to historical consciousness.

The type of fundamental life objectives that were attainable within the socialist system must be viewed as a basic problem. How did the system's political and ideological "excesses" influence the quality of life? According to surveys conducted at the end of the 1970s, family life and material well-being were the most significant factors in the attainment of fundamental objectives. At the same time, nearly half of the representative sample of Hungary's adult population polled as part of these inquiries reported that they had failed to reach their basic educational and occupational goals.

The aspiration to achieve material prosperity had become one of the predominant objectives within Hungarian society by the end of the 1970s, an attribute that stemmed from a moderation of the material and political impediments of the previous decades and a continual improvement in the conditions necessary to reach such goals following the conclusion of a protracted period of scarcity.

An assessment of private and public life in Hungary during the 1960s and 1970s reveals the existence of significant disparities. Policies in effect during the period of Kádár consolidation presumably contributed to the emergence and preservation of these disparities in that they renounced regulation over private life and abandoned the aspiration of politicizing the lives of individual members of society. For the majority of Hungarians, with the exception of believers and careerists, public events and functions as well as individual public activity became formal and essentially worthless, since one could gain as much through non-participation in public life as through participation, that is, the possibility of attaining individual/group political influence. This circumstance exercised a negative impact on the mentality of Hungarian society, whose majority regarded the notion of community as a mere empty slogan. Most Hungarians declined to participate in community affairs, an indifferent outlook that became one of the primary characteristics of the Hungarian public disposition over subsequent decades.

Notes

1 The period of consolidation began with the 1963 general amnesty, which, in addition to the release of imprisoned 1956 revolutionaries, contained the symbolic message that the communist government was prepared for conciliation and no longer automatically considered the considerable number of people who did not agree with its views to be hostile, as long as they did not openly express their antipathy. The year 1978 can be regarded as the end of the Kádár consolidation, primarily because it represents the point in time from which the communist government was no longer able to elevate real wages and the standard of living, the cornerstones of its domestic policy during the period.

2 For information regarding the political history of the period, see the following works: Tibor Huszár, *Kádár János politikai életrajza* [Political Biography of János Kádár], vols. 1–2 (Budapest, 2001 and 2003); Rudolf L. Tőkés, *Hungary's Negotiated Revolution—Economic Reform, Social Change and Political Succession, 1957–1990* (London and New York, 1996); Ignác Romsics, *Hungary in the Twentieth Century* (Budapest, 1999) János M. Rainer, "The Sixties in Hungary—Some Historical and Political Approaches," in György Péteri and János M. Rainer, eds., *Muddling Through in the Long 1960s. Ideas and Everyday Life in High Politics and the Lower Classes of Communist Hungary* (Trondheim, 2005) (Trondheim Studies on East European Cultures & Societies, No. 16), pp. 4–26.

3 The "56ers" released from prison almost without exception felt these changes in the comportment of the (external) world and Hungarian society as well as the strengthening of depoliticization. See István Eörsi, *Emlékezés a régi szép időkre* [Memory of the Good Old Days] (Budapest, 1989), and Tibor Valuch, *"Ötvenhatosok"* ["56ers"] (Debrecen, 1996).

4 György Gyarmati, "Politika és társadalom 1945–1989 között" [Politics and Society between 1945 and 1989], in István Kollega Tarsoly, ed., *Magyarország a XX. században* [Hungary in the 20th Century] (Szekszárd, 1996), p. 232.

5 For a detailed examination of this issue, see János M. Rainer's 2005 work listed above.

6 István Feitl, "1999," in György Földes and László Hubai, eds., *Parlamenti képviselőválasztások 1920–1998* [Parliamentary Elections 1920–1998] (Budapest, 1998).

7 For more information, see Gábor Tabajdi and Krisztián Ungváry, *Elhallgatott múlt. A pártállam és a belügy. A politikai rendőrség működése Magyarországon 1956–1990* [Concealed Past. The Party State and Internal Affairs. The Operations of the Political Police in Hungary 1956–1990] (Budapest, 2008).

8 See Miklós Szabó, "A magyar társadalmi és nemzettudat az elmúlt harminc évben" [Hungarian Social and National Consciousness over the Past Thirty Years], in Júlia Szalai, ed., *Arat a magyar* [The Hungarian Reaps] (Budapest, 1988).

9 László Reisz, *Gazdasági és társadalmi koncepciók a politikai propagandában 1962–1980* [Economic and Social Concepts in Political Propaganda 1962–1980] (Budapest, 1988), p. 107.

10 For a detailed analysis of János Kádár's political career, see Huszár, *Kádár János politikai életrajza.*

11 János Szántó, *Vallásosság egy szekularizált társadalomban* [Religious Faith in a Secularized Society] (Budapest, 1997).

12 Sándor Gáspár, Béla Biszku and Zoltán Komócsin were among the most prominent figures in what technical terminology refers to as the "workers' opposition." Members of this anti-reform faction contended that the reforms would benefit agricultural-cooperative workers to the detriment of the heavy industrial workforce, a circumstance that they regarded as unacceptable in a "workers' state."

13 See the following: István Vida, *Az állami politikai vezetőréteg összetétele az 1980-as évek elején* [The Composition of the State Political Leadership Stratum at the Beginning of the 1980s] (Budapest, 1992), p. 35; György T. Varga and István Szakadát, "Íme, a nómenklatúrák!" [Here Are the *Nomenklaturas*!], *Társadalmi Szemle* 3 (1992): 73–95; András Nyírő, ed., *Segédkönyv a Politikai Bizottság tanulmányozásához* [Handbook for Study of the Political Committee] (Budapest, 1989).

14 The term "household farming" designated the intensive, income-generating utilization of land left in the possession of agricultural cooperative members, while black market labor included a broad range of economic activities, from unregistered and temporary employment to the provision of transport and other services without a relevant permit and private work done at plants and factories. Second

jobs consisted of legal employment undertaken outside regular working hours for the purpose of earning supplementary income.

15 For more information on issues related to foreign policy, see the following: Csaba Békés, *Európából Európába. Magyarország konfliktusok kereszttüzében, 1945–1990* [From Europe to Europe. Hungary in the Crossfire of Conflict, 1945–1990] (Budapest, 2004), p. 350; György Földes, *Magyarország, Románia és a nemzeti kérdés 1956–1989* [Hungary, Romania and the Nationality Question 1956–1989] (Budapest, 2007), p. 526; Ignác Romsics, *Magyarország története a XX. században* [History of Hungary in the 20th Century] (Budapest, 1999).

16 Magdolna Baráth, "Magyarország és a Szovjetunió" [Hungary and the Soviet Union], in János M. Rainer, ed., *"Hatvanas évek" Magyarországon. Tanulmányok* ["The 1960s" in Hungary. Essays] (Budapest, 2004), pp. 31–62.

17 Magdolna Baráth, "Kádár, Hruscsov, Brezsnyev. Szovjet külügyi dokumentumok a magyar pártvezetés reakciójáról Ny. Sz. Hruscsov leváltására" [Kádár, Khrushchev, Brezhnev. Soviet Ministry of Foreign Affairs Documents Regarding the Hungarian Party Leadership's Reaction to N. S. Khrushchev's Dismissal], *Történelmi Szemle* 3–4 (2003): 331–349.

18 See László Borhi, "A magyar–amerikai viszony változásai, 1957–1978" [Changes in Hungarian–American Relations, 1957–1978], in László J. Kiss and Ferenc Gazdag, eds., *Magyar külpolitika a huszadik században* [Hungarian Foreign Relations in the Twentieth Century] (Budapest, 2004).

19 István Németh and István Horváth, *És a falak leomlanak. Magyarország és a német egység 1945–1990* [And the Walls Came Down. Hungary and German Unity 1945–1990] (Budapest, 1999).

20 Mihály Fülöp and Péter Sipos, *Magyarország külpolitikája a XX. században* [Hungary's Foreign Policy in the 20th Century] (Budapest, 1998).

21 Ivan T. Berend, *Hungarian Economic Reforms 1953–1988* (Cambridge, 1990).

22 In practice, this signified the use of production technologies based on large-scale, intensive monoculture and use of chemical fertilizers and pesticides.

23 Imre Kovách, *Termelők és vállalkozók* [Farmers and Entrepreneurs] (Budapest, 1988).

24 Construction of roads and highways lagged as a result of an economically motivated delay in motorization, while Hungary was in the lowest third of all countries in Europe in terms of telephones *per capita.*

25 János Kornai, *The Socialist System: The Political Economy of Communism* (Oxford, 1992) pp. xxvii, 644.

26 Sándor Szakács, "A gulyáskommunizmustól a csődig" [From Goulash Communism to Bankruptcy], in Béla Király and Lee. W. Congdon, eds., *A magyar forradalom eszméi. Eltiprásuk és győzelmük 1956–1999* [The Ideas of the Hungarian Revolution. Their Suppression and Triumph 1956–1999] (Budapest, 2001).

27 The family allowance was a fixed-sum, non-wage social benefit for actively employed workers and employees. The sum of this benefit for families with two children was 37.5 forints in 1960, 150 forints in 1970 and 490 forints in 1980. See *Életszínvonal 1960–1980* [Living Standards, 1960–1980] (Budapest, 1981), p. 108. Childcare assistance was a form of social subsidy designed to help women to compensate for any loss of income stemming from the need to provide care for their children.

28 János Kádár's address at the 7th congress of the Communist Youth Alliance (KISZ), in János Kádár, *Hazafiság és internacionalizmus* [Patriotism and Internationalism] (Budapest, 1968).

29 There were one million privately owned passenger vehicles in Hungary in 1980.

30 Zsuzsa Ferge, *Társadalmi újratermelés és társadalompolitika* [Social Reproduction and Social Policy] (Budapest, 1982), p. 380.

31 For details, see Tibor Valuch, "Changes in the Structure and the Lifestyle of the Hungarian Society in the Second Half of the XXth Century," in Gábor Gyáni, György Kövér and Tibor Valuch, *Social History of Hungary from the Reform Era to the End of the Twentieth Century* (Highland Lakes, NJ, 2004).

32 István Kemény, "A magyarországi cigányok helyzete" [Circumstances Surrounding Gypsies in Hungary], in idem, *Beszámoló a magyarországi cigányságról* [Report on the Gypsy Population in Hungary] (Budapest, 1976), pp. 7–67.

33 Ferenc Szászi, "A magyar kivándorlás történetéhez 1945–1989" [Data Regarding the History of Hungarian Emigration 1945–1989], *Történelmi Szemle* 35 (1993) 3–4: 313–338.

34 Rudolf Andorka, "Társadalmi változások és társadalmi problémák 1941–1990" [Social Changes and Social Problems 1941–1990], *Statisztikai Szemle* 4–5 (1992): 301–323.

35 Tibor Gáti and Ágota Horváth, "A háború előtti középosztály utótörténete" [Epilogue of the Pre-War Middle Class], *Szociológiai Szemle* 1 (1992): 81–97.

36 István Márkus, "Az utóparasztság arcképéhez" [Portrait of the Post-Peasantry], *Szociológia* 1 (1973): 56–67.

IX. THE KÁDÁR SYSTEM IN CRISIS (1978–1985)

1. Domestic Politics[1]

One of the major underlying issues in domestic policy in the period 1978–1985 was the question of how the regime could get the better of the emerging economic crisis without eliciting an acute political crisis and widespread social discontent. In other words, the Hungarian Socialist Workers' Party was anxious not to lose the relative legitimacy and social acceptance gained during the Kádárite consolidation by raising and maintaining the standard of living, or the loyalty typical of relatively broad swaths of society. Similarly important was a second issue: whether the inescapable reforms and alterations could still be confined to the economy, without changing the political system, jeopardizing its operability, or questioning the monopoly of power held by the HSWP. A third issue was a personal one that became urgent only at the beginning of the 1980s: how could the succession to János Kádár be carried out smoothly? Could the policy associated with him be kept up indefinitely without him? Most of the country's communist politicians did not think these issues through. In line with their practice hitherto, most of them focused on resolving immediate problems, seeing the difficulties as exclusively economic ones, even ones that they would solve themselves in time. This stance contributed significantly to deepening the economic problems and producing a crisis in the system.

By the end of the 1970s and beginning of the 1980s, politics had become to average Hungarian citizens a boring and uninteresting routine to be kept at arm's length as far as possible. There were domestic political cycles from one party congress to the next. Party leaders went on factory visits from time to time, while the top man, János Kádár, paid visits of varying frequency to the counties and cities of the country, meeting there with workers, local leaders and intellectuals. Meanwhile, the Central Committee of the Hungarian Socialist Workers' Party met every two or three months, publishing scarcely intelligible several-page communiqués on its decisions in the central party daily newspaper, *Népszabadság*. New institutions and factories would be opened. There were parliamentary and local council elections every five years, up to 1995 almost always with a single candidate standing. On the state holidays on April 4, May 1, August 20 and November 7, there would be customary ceremonies and processions. Major anniversaries were marked by socialist work competitions. By this time people were not greatly concerned by this. They accepted that they lived in such a country under political conditions where repeated events provided a framework for daily life and there was little real chance of having a voice in matters. Far more excitement was caused by announcement of centrally determined price increases in staple foods, energy sources and housing rents, which became increasingly common after 1976–1977.[2] These moves certainly caused a measure of tension in Hungarian society at the time, and the political leadership waited nervously for any political reactions on the following day, but there were scarcely any. The Hungarian population, unlike the Poles, did not go out onto the streets to demand the withdrawal of electricity price increases, and although confidence in the leadership was waning, the need for political change had not been essentially raised by that time. Explanations worth emphasizing are the fact that the memory of the defeat in 1956 was too fresh, and the fact that the mechanisms of the Kádárite policy to keep society politically neutral were still effective and operable. The deterioration of living conditions had not reached a level sufficient to cause tensions to break out. The majority still felt that it had some regained freedoms to lose, along with personal wealth and possessions, and better living conditions gained by great effort.[3]

The situation was different within the country's political leadership, where the stalemate after the halting of the reforms was over. Previously defeated reformers and politicians with ties to them gradually came to the fore again, while the opponents of reforms were relegated to the sidelines. Debates on the reforms and the possible lines of change broke out again in the political and specialist press. Part of the reason was the fact that János Kádár himself was coming by the end of the 1970s to see that the political stability of earlier decades was in peril, and the economic problems were worse than expected. Although the changes might be postponed, they could not be ignored indefinitely, or law and order—a key policy element at the time—would be endangered. Kádár felt that parts of the system had to be corrected from time to time to ensure its operability, but without changing its underlying values or constituents. In other words, he was committed to a policy of small steps. His way of thinking in this period was becoming slower and more conservative, due to his age.[4] On the whole he would support only the changes deemed to be necessary to maintain the system. This was essentially the message of his 1982 speech in reply to the congratulations that he received on his seventieth birthday.

Kádár, of course, was not the only one to age. The same applied to the whole political leadership. Of the 120 members of the Central Committee at the end of the 1970s, 25 were over 60, 73 between 51 and 60, and only 12 under 50. In terms of occupation, the majority were members of the party or state apparatus. In neither regard did the Central Committee's structure change in the next, 1980–1985 political (party congress) cycle either. The most influential section of the country's political elite was steadily ageing. That in itself influenced strongly domestic political relations, and the responses, solutions and experiments elicited by the new foreign policy, foreign economic and social policy challenges. (Another important factor beside the immutability of the upper level of leadership was the fact that there was a process of change in the lower levels of leadership in the 1970s. This had lost the Hungarian Socialist Workers' Party its agitator character,[5] turning it into a party of officials concerned with furthering their own official careers.) Among the typical political personalities of the Kádár period for various periods of time were György Aczél, Antal Apró, János Berecz, Béla Biszku, Róbert Burgert, Lajos Czinege, Lajos Fehér, György Fejti, Jenő Fock,

Sándor Gáspár, Károly Grósz, Ferenc Havasi, Ede Horváth, Mihály Korom, Zoltán Komócsin, György Marosán, László Maróthy, Rezső Nyers, Károly Németh, János Pap, Imre Pozsgay and Frigyes Puja.

In 1976 came a decision by the Politburo of the Hungarian Socialist Workers' Party requiring the collection of uniform statistical data on state and cooperative leaders. This was repeated in 1978 and every two years thereafter. The social structure of the 33,140-strong leading stratum of so-called "cadre bureaucracy"—recorded institution by institution and covering the party apparatus, the mass organizations, the trade unions, the Communist Youth League, the armed forces, and state, economic and cooperative leaders—was examined sociologically in retrospect. The stratum in decisive decision-making positions in 1983 numbered 5,793, of whom more than four fifths were men. About two thirds of the cadre staff belonged to the 41–50 or 51–60 age cohorts, the average age being 44. The average age was far higher in higher levels of political leadership, but there was a significant proportion from younger age groups in the official apparatus of the HSWP. This resulted partly from a conscious effort to bring younger, better-educated and qualified cadres forward, and partly from major changes in the way in which people were recruited. In 1983, 72.3 percent of the "cadre bureaucracy" had a university or college degree, 25.5 percent had only completed high school, and just 2.2 percent only the eight years of elementary school. There is no way of scientifically analyzing the social or family background of those in leading positions as the surveys only asked respondents whether *they* considered themselves to be of worker–peasant, intellectual, clerical or other background. There was strong pressure on respondents to meet official expectations by ticking the worker–peasant box. This is what three quarters of the 33,140 people in leading posts did, while one tenth called their background intellectual and one sixth clerical.

A decisive majority of the 1983 cadre stratum had joined it in the Kádár period; hardly a tenth had been in such a position before 1956 as well. In fact more than half had attained their position since 1971. According to original occupation, 43.5 percent of cadres had been workers or peasants, 29.3 percent intellectuals, and 27 percent clerical employees. In 1983, 84.4 percent were Hungarian Socialist Workers' Party members. This supports the general view that political reliability played a big part in selection.

The average monthly pay of cadres in 1983 was 9,100 forints, but the pay of a third exceeded 10,000 forints—far higher than the national average. The best pay went to state, economic and cooperative leaders.[6] One favorite pastime of theirs was shooting game, which also helped them to build up their personal connections and assert their interests informally.

At the pinnacle of power were those whose appointment had required the prior approval of the Hungarian Socialist Workers' Party Central Committee. In 1983, the upper stratum of the *nomenklatura* numbered 979, of whom 552 were senior party workers, 373 state leaders, and 52 leaders of mass organizations. The decisive majority was male, with an average age of 55—seven years older than the full cadre group. Of those at the top in 1983, 94.5 percent had a higher education, most of them having been teachers, economists or party instructors. There was strong elite circulation among them, meaning that more than two thirds had previously held other leading posts; this is confirmed by examining their individual careers.

The leadership managed to postpone the inescapable economic measures[7] (described later in more detail) for so long that it brought about an economic crisis, but to recover from the crisis would have entailed winding up loss-making industries, accepting a radical cut in living standards, seeing forced growth replaced with stagnation and mounting inflation, allowing hidden unemployment to come out into the open, and enhancing welfare provisions for impoverished victims. Essentially it would have meant jettisoning all the benefits to which people had grown used over the 15 years of Kádárite consolidation: improved supplies of goods, slowly but surely rising pay and living standards, full employment, and a concomitant general sense of relative security. This reversal of the "achievements of developed socialism," as they were referred to officially, was something that neither Kádár nor most others in leading positions would contemplate. There remained the possibility of emergency measures that became almost incessant. The party leaders decided to spare no energy or money to protect the "achievements of socialism." Politics became increasingly enmeshed by the economy.

Hungary's politics (and economic policy) in 1977–1978 faced a situation in which some changes could be postponed no longer. It was essential to curb economic growth and slow mounting indebtedness largely attributable to the cost of maintaining the standard of living, or the country would become insolvent. To prevent that from happening, the country's political leaders made contact again with the international financial agencies, and despite Soviet rejection of the idea, preparations began to join the International Monetary Fund and the World Bank. The question came up again in 1979 during talks between Kádár and Brezhnev.[8] The Hungarian party leader argued that it was fundamentally important to safeguard public supplies and increase real incomes, and for that Hungary needed more financial leeway, but the Soviets rejected the idea of this move, as they had done a decade earlier. The subject was next on the agenda at talks between the Hungarian and Soviet party leaders in the summer of 1981. There the Soviets, although still against the idea, did not reject it out of hand, mainly because they could not comply with Hungarian requests to increase oil supplies: indeed, they had to reduce them in the summer. Nor could they offer appreciable financial help with restoring stability to the balance of the Hungarian economy. Hungary, meanwhile, had an immediate need for more room for financial maneuver, and in the autumn of 1981, after long preparations, the minister of foreign affairs requested Hungary's admission to the two organizations, without giving appreciable advance warning to the Soviet leaders. IMF and World Bank consent was obtained at general assemblies in 1982.

As the economic problems came to the fore in the early 1980s, the leeway in domestic policy was still set by a basic stance in defense of the socialist system taken by a less than healthy Kádár. It could be sensed in the debates over the 1983–1984 plans for reform that he was becoming trapped in his own concept of socialism. His influence over the innermost power elite was lessening perceptibly, although he was not yet opposed openly. He abandoned, steadily and finally, his earlier centrist political position of waging a struggle on two fronts. In other words, he sought to prevent the collapse of the system associated with his name and in doing so shifted a little to the left, but the results in personal terms were less pronounced by then, and it impinged on Hungarian domestic policy mainly as an old-fashioned, more conservative intellectual and political stance.

The political currents in the Hungarian Socialist Workers' Party did not alter substantially in the early 1980s. There largely remained two groups, whose struggles of varying intensity determined the course at any one time. The emblematic figures among the reformers were Rezső Nyers and also Imre Pozsgay. On the other side was a looser grouping of those arguing for moderate changes or even no change at all, with Károly Grósz and János Berecz as the ones whose opinions came over the strongest. Their position was seen to strengthen in 1984 when they both joined the upper leadership: Grósz the Politburo and Berecz the Central Committee Secretariat. At the same time, others were losing their position in the top sphere of power, including György Aczél, responsible for decades for directing cultural affairs and a close ally of Kádár tending to support cautious change. Ground was lost for a time by Pozsgay, who had close contacts in the intelligentsia, notably with followers of the populist tradition in literature,[9] and did not rule out political reforms on some scale.

The political leadership still operated according to a political routine developed over several decades. The one serious alteration in the political system came with the Electoral Act passed in 1983. To further "socialist democratism," it would be compulsory at the 1985 parliamentary elections to have two candidates. This in itself lent those elections greater political significance, along with the fact that the crisis within the system was becoming more open. Dual candidacy in itself was not an essential change, but it did mean that candidates favored by the communist political leadership might lose seats to less well-known candidates, although both still had to endorse the electoral program put forward on behalf of the regime by the Patriotic People's Front. At the same time, the country's most important political figures and leaders were "tactfully" spared the prospect of electoral defeat, as they were placed on a national list that could not be opposed. In the event, there were some surprising results, with nationally known politicians losing to locally known candidates; altogether 41 independent, spontaneously chosen candidates, not nominated by the Hungarian Socialist Workers' Party, entered the new Parliament. But there was no need to fear that Parliament would take on a political life of its own, as the decisive majority of members were still members of the HSWP.

For the first time since 1947, there were attempts by opposition groups to stand for election, but their candidates were challenged by the Hungarian Socialist Workers' Party before they got onto the ballot paper.[10] There would be five more years to wait before voters faced real political alternatives again.

The political leadership still viewed turnout as an issue of confidence and legitimacy. As Kádár put it in a speech in Csepel a few days before the June 1985 elections, they "have their own very great significance. Of course there are no criminal-law sanctions against those who fail to vote… Voting constitutes a position, a stand in favor of our policy, our system, our people's power, socialism, peace and programs of construction." In the event, there was a 94 percent turnout to elect the 387 representatives, two thirds of whom had not been members of the previous Parliament.[11]

The political leaders of the late Kádár period, drifting into economic crisis, also faced another quite new and unusual problem. There appeared sporadic opposition after 1968, mainly in the cultural sphere, but in the final third of the 1970s taking a more organized, decidedly political shape. There were domestic reasons for this, but an important part was played by international events: the Polish crisis, which worsened in the 1970s and became open by the end of the decade with the formation of the Solidarity movement, the Charter 77 opposition movement in Czechoslovakia, and the emphasis gained by human rights in US foreign policy.

One of the earliest acts of Hungary's opposition groups[12] was to issue a statement of solidarity with the persecuted Czech opposition activists. By the end of the 1970s, these groups had become stronger and more organized. Their political spectrum reflected in practice a longstanding politico-ideological division expressible by the home country/progress pair of concepts. The liberal democratic opposition attached prime importance to establishing democratic conditions and safeguarding human rights to the full, as that would ensure the country's development and resolve its political and social problems, which the socialist period had failed to do. Another grouping, known as *népi-nemzeti* ("popular/national" or "people's/national"), gave precedence to resolving problems to do with the so-called national question—the position of Hungarians living as a minority in neighboring countries, and strengthening national awareness. A third group, consisting of former '56-ers, was concerned mainly for the ideas that the Revolution had represented, the creation of an independent, democratic Hungary, a change in the official evaluation of the Revolution, and rehabilitation of the reprisal victims.

At the center of the democratic opposition's activity stood the establishment of independent institutions, and free and uncensored newspapers, periodicals and books. One initiative carried out in 1979–1980 had been a memorial *festschrift* for István Bibó, in which most of Hungary's leading intellectual personalities expressed their ideas about the work of Bibó as an outstanding democratic political thinker, and about its currency. This made the works of Bibó an intellectual and ideological source for the oppositionism that was taking shape at the time.

The democratic opposition went on in the late 1970s to organize "flying universities," where well-known experts and scholars lectured in private homes on matters of political history, principally on questions that the regime was treating as taboo, such as 1956, the minority Hungarians, the dictated Treaty of Trianon, and present-day poverty and inequalities. At about the same time, there appeared the first charitable organization, the Szegényeket Támogató Alap (Fund for Support of the Poor), which sought to raise money for relief.

In the autumn of 1981 there appeared the first issue of the one of the major illegal periodicals, *Beszélő*,[13] just as tensions between Solidarity and the Polish authorities were heightening, while in Hungary the approaching twenty-fifth anniversary of the 1956 Revolution was being marked with a grand campaign of state propaganda in support of the official interpretation of it.[14] *Beszélő* appeared quarterly thereafter. Thenceforth, the democratic opposition likewise presented the 1956 Revolution as a decisive point of reference.

The early 1980s saw the beginning of a parallel, "second" institutional system of publicity, devoted to all the questions that the communist-supervised Hungarian press had to ignore: the Polish situation, the position of Hungarian minorities, human rights matters, and poverty. Other important *samizdat* papers besides *Beszélő* were *Hírmondó* (Messenger), *Demokrata* (Democrat), and *Égtájak között* (Between Climes). Unsanctioned, private publication of books also became frequent. These initiatives had undoubted effects on officially controlled, "first" publicity as well, extending the bounds of what it was permissible to discuss and shrinking the area that was taboo.

The opposition grouping associated with the tradition of the *népi* ("popular" or "people's") writers and the "popular/national" or "people's/national" sphere of ideas worked during this period in the border area between legality and illegality, but illegal activity and organization were not thought to be expedient. Efforts were made to avoid exclusion from "first" publicity; literary papers and journals remained important fields for the group to express its views. Members criticized the measures of the Hungarian government in minority matters as ineffective and called for stronger political moves. Efforts to restore freedom of speech and eliminate restrictions on it included repeatedly unsuccessful efforts to have their periodicals officially sanctioned and legally published.

Relations between the infant opposition groups and the general public in the early 1980s were affected by the fact that Hungarian society in the decades after 1956 had adopted an indifferent, loyal form of political behavior, with most people trying to avoid politics altogether. Public support for the groups of a few hundred illegally operating activists that formed at the turn of the decade was still meager, despite the falling living conditions. Their social and political significance lay mainly in their attempt to exercise in practice the rights that the communist system ensured formally by producing an uncensored press, whose effect was increased by regular reviews of it broadcast on Radio Free Europe and other Western stations. The important side in the founding period was less direct political action than setting an example by repeatedly questioning the regime's political and historical taboos: 1956, the Soviet occupation, or the Hungarian Socialist Workers' Party's monopoly of political power. This was a new situation in which Hungarian society had been joined by a group that was trying to break the monopoly of political opinion-forming. The communist authorities, of course, had their methods of keeping opposition initiatives under surveillance, mainly through the political police. From time to time, independent periodicals would be raided and manuscripts and copiers confiscated, but violence was used only to a limited extent. The commonest methods were telephone tapping, regular police harassment, loss of employment, and bans on publication and travel, with the aim of marginalizing and undermining the livelihood of certain people. The Hungarian government had signed the 1975 Helsinki Accords, so that use of open force against the opposition would have questioned Hungary's credibility. In addition, it would have threatened the financing of the Hungarian economy and its access to Western markets—dependence on those was one obstacle to a full assault on the opposition.

Spontaneous public protests were not typical of the Kádár period before 1987–1988. Industrial action arising out of conflicts in the workplace remained rare, and the public usually learned nothing about them. They remained within the factory gates and in general did not take on any political character. The unofficial commemorations on March 15—spontaneous demonstrations of a few thousand people in the streets—became regular after 1982.

Also in the early 1980s, the techniques of crowd dispersal developed in Poland began to be used, for instance armored crowd-dispersal vehicles, along with training courses in how to use them. That was when the Hungarian police acquired their first water cannon and other equipment for coercion.[15]

Opposition political activity and spontaneous organization in society gained an added environmental dimension in the early 1980s. This was precipitated by joint Hungarian–Czechoslovak plans for a huge hydroelectric barrage scheme on the Danube between Gabčikovo and Nagymaros, which was vocally opposed in 1983–1984 by a protest movement that became known as the Danube Circle. The movement organized several protests, including a petition and a living chain, and won an alternative environmental Nobel Prize in 1985.[16]

Beside the open opposition there arose circles, clubs and occasional publications that occupied an intermediate position between "first" and "second" publicity. Participants helped to extend the bounds of what could be expressed, but without losing their place in the first sphere or sinking into illegality. Among them were the Rakpart Club, university periodicals such as *Századvég*, various university debating clubs and specialist colleges, and organizations of young writers and artists.

The independent social endeavors and rebirth of democratic public life were much assisted by the Soros Foundation, set up in 1984. This also supported scientific research and health service development.

Church–state relations in the early 1980s were free of obvious conflict. By then the Churches were largely willing to confine themselves to the sphere that politicians assigned to them, which had changed little since the turn of the 1970s and 1980s. Pope John Paul II, as a Pole, was aware of the conditions in Eastern Europe. The longstanding Churches in Hungary, including the Roman Catholics, did not follow the Polish example and distanced themselves from the expressions of opposition. Church leaders were concerned primarily to preserve and make use of the institutional system allowed to them.

Church influence and strict political surveillance were provided by the State Office for Church Affairs and the political police.

A new stage in secularization was reached in the latter half of the 1970s, as the generations socialized in a secular society became a decisive majority. About two thirds of those growing up at that time were raised in a secular atmosphere devoid of religion. A decisive factor behind the change was the fact that a high proportion of parents had been raised with a secular outlook in the 1960s, a period of "delayed secularization," while the number of religious grandparents was falling fast. The trend was then reversed, with the number who considered themselves to be religious showing a steady rise to 51 percent by 1990. A similar process was seen among those who practiced their religion "according to the teachings of the Church." They accounted for 8 percent of the population in 1978, but 16 percent twelve years later. One marked feature of the reviving interest in religion was a slow revival based on small communities, although these were seldom more than tolerated by leaders of the various Churches in the 1970s and 1980s. In 1982, György Bulányi, leader of the Bokor Basis Community,[17] was stripped by the Bench of Bishops of his right to celebrate mass, preach, or distribute the sacraments. This served to define the limits of organization or self-organization within the Churches. Most Churches began at the end of the 1960s to be short of clergy. The Catholic Church had 3,128 priests in 1984, of whom 2,517 were active. The Reformed Church had 1,200–1,300 clergy at the end of the 1980s. Estimates of the number of Evangelical (Lutheran) clergy at that time range from 370 to 430.[18]

The crisis in the Kádár system deepened economically, politically and socially in 1985. Most of the reports to the 13th Congress of the Hungarian Socialist Workers' Party held in that year still spoke of successes and there was no substantive debate among delegates about the signs of crisis. The lead of the party chiefs was followed in seeing artificial stimulation of the economy as the key to solving the situation, and decisions were made to take steps to do so. From a power point of view, there continued to be attempts to argue in domestic policy and before the public that "there are difficulties, but there is no crisis; we are defending the socialist achievements." An attempt to lay bare the true situation in the country and explore possible routes out of the crisis was made in the summer of 1985, not by the HSWP leadership—although the latter thought that it alone was called upon to lead society—but by the "illegal" Monor Meeting.[19] All strands of the opposition and the reforming intelligentsia were represented at the debates, which questioned the sustainability of the whole socialist system and outlined the possibilities for political action and opposition cohesion. But that all marked the end of one period and the beginning of a new one whose end would be uncertain.

2. Foreign Affairs[20]

The system of conditions for international relations began to be affected strongly in the last third of the 1970s by some heightening of Soviet–US antagonism and tensions. The subject of human rights came to the fore in American policy under the Carter administration. Then in the early 1980s the arms race speeded up again. The Soviets found it harder and harder to keep up with technical and technological development under the Reagan administration, which put this on a military level with its concept of a "Star Wars" defense. Tension increased further in 1979, as the Soviets began an Afghan War designed to strengthen the Soviet presence in Asia. Then came the Polish crisis in August 1980, which again questioned the sustainability of the Soviet empire. Hungary's policy in this situation was to try as far as possible to present the country as an independent international player. Even as Great Power relations deteriorated, Hungary still pressed consistently for peaceful coexistence between the two world systems and for control of the arms race.

The sense of failure engendered by none-too-successful management of the domestic political crisis was relieved for leading politicians by the way in which Hungary's role and significance in Eastern and Western European relations gained greater appreciation.

Among the causes were the less pragmatic domestic and foreign policies pursued at the time in Bulgaria, Czechoslovakia and East Germany, which left them with only an assisting role in international politics, as unconditional supporters of the Soviet Union. Earlier Romania had tried to detach itself from the Soviet line, but its increasingly aggressive, anti-minority, nationalistic communism had lost the country its ties with Western Europe. Poland had dropped off the diplomatic map with the deepening of its crisis in 1980–1981 and the declaration of a state of emergency. In Hungary, on the other hand, the policy of opening up continued and the country became increasingly important in international tourism.[21] The number of visitors to the country from Eastern and Western Europe increased steadily—Balaton became a favored meeting place for East and West German relatives and friends unable to cross into the other half of their own country. Increasing numbers of Hungarians also traveled to Western Europe and overseas, although foreign exchange controls meant that they could only do so every three years. One development that pointed beyond tourism occurred in 1979, when Austria became the first Western country to lift the visa requirement for Hungarian travelers.

Hungary was an increasingly popular destination not only for tourists but also for Western European leaders, while Hungarian politicians, headed by János Kádár, became frequent visitors to Western Europe. The success of these stronger relations and greater autonomy in Hungary's foreign policy is clear: Budapest was visited in 1977–1984 by the French prime minister, the West German chancellor, the cardinal secretary of state at the Vatican, the US vice-president, and the British prime minister. Kádár-led delegations were received in return at the highest level in Britain, West Germany, Italy, France, Austria, and elsewhere. This diplomatic activity was not just intended to develop Hungary's international relations. Another big factor was the need for Western political support for resolving Hungary's economic problems, obtaining foreign loans, and increasing trade and other foreign economic links. All this was clearest in Hungarian–West German ties, which became ever more cordial and increasingly valuable economically.[22]

Hungary was far from vital to American foreign policy as such, and served only as an exemplification of a country with a different approach from the classic Soviet model to East–West relations, US foreign policy in Eastern Europe, and domestic, foreign and economic relations. Bilateral relations were much enhanced when US Secretary of State Cyrus Vance and a delegation arrived on January 6, 1978, after long preparations and negotiations, to return the symbolically important Holy Crown of St. Stephen and coronation regalia, taken as spoils of war by US forces at the end of World War II. Also of importance was American support for Hungary's accession to the IMF and World Bank. In 1982 there was a visit by an American delegation headed by Vice-President George Bush, offering a chance for the highest level of negotiations for several decades during an occasion hitherto unprecedented in Eastern Europe. The mounting recognition for Hungary meant that Budapest was chosen in 1985 to host the European Cultural Forum and Counter-Forum—under the close surveillance of the political police, of course, as conditions at the time demanded.[23]

However, Hungary's relations with the other Eastern Bloc countries varied considerably. Multilaterally, they were conducted through the Political Consultative Council of the Warsaw Treaty Organization, where common stands were taken on the international situation, the foreign policy line to follow, and occasionally specific US or Western European initiatives and measures and counter-measures to them, under full Soviet dominance. Also taken there were political and economic decisions on the military activity of the Warsaw Pact. The other sphere of cooperation was the Council of Mutual Economic Assistance—Comecon—which discussed the system and operation of economic cooperation.

The intensity of bilateral relations varied from country to country. The importance of them could always be gauged accurately by comparing the ranks of those leading the fraternal party delegations to congresses, or the frequency of bilateral talks between any two countries. Relations were cooling with Bulgaria, East Germany and Czechoslovakia, which clung to the Soviet line more closely and looked askance at Hungary's version of a socialist system. Yugoslav–Hungarian relations were even until the death of Tito in May 1980, but top-level meetings then became rarer, partly because of domestic problems in Yugoslavia. Bilateral relations with Czechoslovakia and Romania were sullied by strongly assimilatory policies towards their Hungarian minorities.[24] Both were stepping up the pressure on local Hungarians to assimilate in the 1970s and 1980s. Those in Slovakia had their scope for education in their native language curtailed at all levels. Local government borders were gerrymandered to prevent Hungarian control, and Slovaks were given incentives to settle in Hungarian communities. The Defense Committee for Czechoslovak Hungarian Minority Rights was an illegal organization dedicated to combating the infringement of rights, its best-known figure being Miklós Duray, but it was ceaselessly harassed and activists were regularly imprisoned.

Romania developed its version of national communism in the second half of the 1970s. Important features of it were the drive to present the Hungarian and other minority communities as enemies and the attempt to assimilate them forcibly. This policy of ethnic homogenizing was carried out under the most extreme form of communist dictatorship. The official Romanian position was that there were no minorities living in the country, but simply Romanian citizens with a non-Romanian native language. One settlement policy devised became notorious as the village demolition campaign, under which traditional village settlements (especially if non-Romanian) were to be replaced by new settlements of prefabricated apartment buildings. This would have driven the rural Hungarians from their homes. There were efforts to alter the ethnic consistency of cities with a Hungarian majority, by resettling there Romanians still living beyond the Carpathians. Use of the Hungarian language in educational and cultural institutions was curtailed and the notorious political police (*Securitate*) were especially keen to observe and intimidate the Hungarians of Transylvania, especially the intellectuals with influence over public opinion. Yet there were attempts at the beginning of the 1980s to organize minority rights protection and create an uncensored press. For instance, the Transylvanian Hungarian News Agency and its periodical *Kiáltó Szó* were active for a few years, one of the best-known organizers of them being Géza Szőcs. The violent pressure to assimilate caused a wave of emigration from Transylvania to Hungary in 1985–1986. In general, the anti-Hungarian policies of the Romanian authorities were a source of tension in relations between the two countries.

Very little had changed for the 150,000 Hungarians of Sub-Carpathia living under Soviet rule. They had schooling in their own language and chances to use and pursue cultural activities in it. The conditions in the Soviet empire being what they were, Hungary would not in any case have been able to influence policy in any important regard.

Official Hungarian policy in the first half of the 1980s was to treat minority issues as an internal affair, but there were regular unpublicized attempts by the Hungarian side at inter-party and diplomatic talks to raise problems to do with education and native-language culture.[25] One policy approach was to persuade neighboring countries by positive example to reduce assimilatory pressure on minority Hungarians. In practice this meant that great attention was paid to the problems of national minorities in Hungary, who made up 2–3 percent of the population, and to providing them with educational and cultural rights. There were also moves against cases of "excessive nationalism." The well-known author Sándor Csoóri, for instance, was subjected to a campaign of denigration in the official press after contributing a foreword to a New York publication by Miklós Duray, describing the history and situation of the Hungarians in Slovakia.

Hungarian–Soviet relations at the turn of the 1970s and 1980s changed little. Kádár, in adapting to Soviet expectations in the first half of the 1970s, had placed relations with Soviet leaders on an even footing, although he found it harder to follow changes in the Soviet Communist Party after the death of Brezhnev in November 1982, who was succeeded first by Yuri Andropov and then by Konstantin Chernenko. Andropov's rise to power seemed at first to favor Kádár, who had known him personally since his time as ambassador in Budapest before and during the 1956 Revolution, but Hungarian–Soviet relations did not alter appreciably during the year and a half when Andropov headed the Soviet Communist Party.

Although most people in 1984–1985 saw Gorbachev as the potential successor to the ailing Chernenko, it was not a foregone conclusion as preparations were made for the 13th Congress of the Hungarian Socialist Workers' Party in March 1985. Chernenko died on March 10, and Grigory Romanov, the left-winger, seemed to have almost as much chance of winning the post of general secretary of the CPSU Central Committee as Gorbachev, the candidate willing to make some changes in order to maintain the Soviet empire. Kádár paid two visits to Moscow in 1985, as head of the delegation attending Chernenko's funeral, and in September for his first substantive talks with Gorbachev.[26] In line with the customary agenda for a summit meeting, the two sides briefed each other on the situation in their countries, then the Soviet party leader reviewed the international situation, and then the questions of bilateral relations and other agenda points could be covered. The talks were successful for the Hungarian side in economic terms: the Soviet leadership agreed to reschedule a due debt of 600 million rubles. But they were darkened when Gorbachev politely and diplomatically remarked that it was time for Kádár to be thinking of the succession. This idea the top man in the HSWP dismissed at that time.

The early 1980s brought uncertainties in Hungarian–Soviet relations, notably after Brezhnev's death, but foreign policy was still guided by Soviet expectations. Hungary joined, for example, in boycotting the 1984 Olympics.

3. The Economy[27]

It was clear by the turn of the 1970s and 1980s that it had been a grave error to halt the economic reforms a few years before. It had wrecked the chances of the Hungarian economy of adapting to changed conditions in the world economy. The treatment of crisis events brought brief improvements, but then further declines. Economic performance fell and the main economic indicators worsened almost continuously. By 1981 Hungary faced a prospect of insolvency, averted only by rescheduling debt and raising further loans.

Adaptation to changed conditions was cited when restrictions on the private farming undertaken by cooperative members introduced a few years earlier were removed, and those members could take long leases on cooperative lands. This gave a new boost to small-scale farm production. Taxes on operators in the private sector were reduced at the end of the 1970s and a start was made to altering the price system. Set official prices remained for basic products, but other product prices were freed. Other moves to increase room for economic maneuver were to decentralize big enterprises, end tied labor, and extend enterprise rights to trade abroad in their own right, made in the early 1980s.

To prepare for further changes, the Economic Policy Commission, with Politburo approval, convened in the autumn of 1982 a Consultative Body of reform economists, charged with devising a comprehensive reform of the economic structure. The resulting debates raised numerous concepts, which shared in most cases belief in the need for ownership independence of enterprises, a greater role for the market and market prices, a change to a two-tier system of banking, alteration in income controls and the system of incentives, and modernization of domestic and foreign trade institutions. The political debates on the reforms took place in 1983–1984. As a result, reform of the price system was introduced progressively, the state's ownership rights in enterprises were curtailed, the role of central economic management was reduced, the institution of enterprise councils (boards) was introduced to exercise ownership rights, and a decision was made to transform the banking system. After the debates, the Central Committee of the Hungarian Socialist Workers' Party decided on continuing the economic reforms, setting as a goal the creation of a guided market economic system based on state, cooperative and private ownership.

The position that János Kádár took in these debates was increasingly one of guarding a fundamentalist image of socialism whose basic elements were unconditional preservation of the socialist character of the system (by which he presumably meant the dominance of state ownership), retention of state and party rights of management, and preservation of job security.

In 1982, as the economic crisis deepened and the search for solutions continued, the leadership began to substantially liberalize the regulations on the operation of the private sector. It became possible to start small business associations that were not treated as legal entities—general partnerships, deposit partnerships, business associations (GMKs) and small cooperatives—while the rules for licensing artisans and retail traders were simplified. For the first time, private entrepreneurs were allowed legally to transport passengers and goods and buy commercial vehicles for the purpose. The regulations restricting the fields in which private artisans could work were set aside. In practice, obtaining an operating license became a civil right, and the authorities lost the power to adjudicate on cases individually, as long as formal requirements were met. The ceiling for the number working in an artisan's workshop was raised from five to thirty in 1987. Under the new regulations, existing artisans also could form GMKs from January 1982, although this did not prove popular, and only about 500 did so between 1982 and 1984, and most GMK members retained their individual operating license, along with their own clientele. The more favorable terms of operation brought about a steady increase in the number of artisans and their employees in the 1980s. The mounting spirit of enterprise and willingness to take risks, along with the direction of social change in the 1980s, showed that market participation was increasing rapidly in the Hungarian economy and society. The number of artisans grew by a third between 1982 and 1988. If the various other forms of business operation are included, the number working in the private sector exceeded half a million by the end of 1988, which was more than 10 percent of all active earners.

The intention behind these steps to put life into private enterprise again was to improve the performance and efficiency of the Hungarian economy. They had important effects, of course, on the social structure as well as the economy. They legalized part of the black economy, and the forms of small business introduced allowed people to amass property and enrich themselves, which involved processes of social restratification.

There was also a revival in the 1970s and 1980s of private trading, which for decades had accounted for only about 1 percent of national retail turnover. A start was made at the end of the 1970s to renting out state-owned stores and catering establishments, and by the mid-1980s there were 10,000–12,000 such leases in operation. The number of proprietors and employees in the private retail sector was 16,462 in 1981, but by 1989 it had reached 51,217 persons, even discounting the tenants. The rapidity of the increase is obvious from the fact that the private sector accounted for 11.5 percent of domestic retail trading by 1988.

The rate of increase in national income slowed down sharply at the turn of the 1970s and 1980s, averaging only 1.5 percent a year in 1981–1985. Hungary's reaction to the rising prices of fuels and raw materials was not to run down energy-intensive industries or take saving measures, but to raise new loans. The main goal was to keep the system operable. But the measures to liven up the economy endorsed at the 1985 party congress had no effect. On the contrary, they speeded up the country's indebtedness.[28] Hungary fell into a debt trap that repeatedly brought it to the brink of collapse.

Meanwhile, the contribution of the hidden economy to the real economy continued to grow. Various estimates suggest that the gray or black economy was contributing 20–30 percent of the national product in the mid-1980s. Members of some social groups made very strong efforts to keep up their standard of living under the deteriorating economic conditions.

The alterations at the end of the 1970s also changed income relations. The economic policy of curbing incomes was achieved through the rise in inflation that began in 1979. That was how the authorities intended to restore the balance of the economy lost since 1973. This reduction in real wages affected large sections of the population. The reduction in real wages in 1979–1987 was still less (0.6–0.8 percent a year) than it would be at the turn of the 1980s and 1990s, as some of the loss could still be offset against earnings in GMKs and other extra work. The early 1980s brought a period when accumulated private capital could be put to use in production as well, thanks to the more liberal political approach to private enterprise. Almost three quarters of families in the 1970s and 1980s were involved in the second economy in some form. Wages were accounting for only 56 percent of the income of actively earning households in 1987: scarcely more than half the average family income was being earned in ordinary working hours. The inequalities of income, incidentally, came mainly from the other earnings, not from wages. This was a period when a desire to conceal income became a basic feature of the economic behavior of Hungarian families.

In 1982, a subsistence calculation was introduced by a decision of the Politburo, and thereafter it became possible to more realistically measure the numbers living below subsistence level. However, it must be added that this statistic measured little more than income from the "socialist sector" of the economy, not income from the hidden economy. Furthermore, the data referred essentially to those in regular employment; casual workers were only included sporadically. The subsistence level per head was calculated in 1982 at 1,900 forints a month. At the beginning of the 1990s, there were 72,000 dwellings consisting of a room of 6–12 square meters and a kitchen, and 12,000 dwellings without any facilities and no full-sized room at all.[29] Calculating on an average household size of four, there were 320,000–340,000 people living in such accommodation, without heating, running water or electricity. They obviously made up Hungary's poorest stratum. However, it can also be seen in the period that the poverty threshold and the level of facilities increased in parallel to some extent, but the essential aspect of a day-to-day struggle for livelihood remained.

Average monthly pay, nominal average earnings, consumer price index and real pay between 1975 and 1990

Year	Gross average monthly pay or earnings per earner (HUF)	Net nominal average earnings per earner	Consumer price index	Real pay per earner
1975	3,018	466	199	234
1980	4,098	655	270	243
1985	5,961	873	374	233
1990	13,446	1,639	749	219

Source: *Magyarország népessége és gazdasága – múlt és jelen* [Hungary's Population and Economy, Past and Present] (Budapest, 1996), p. 195.
Note: Indices: 1950 = 100

4. Society[30]

The population of Hungary ceased to increase at the turn of 1980–1981; the number of inhabitants in post-Trianon Hungary peaked at 10.7 million. The natural increase of previous decades became a natural decrease, as the number of live births eased and the death rate stabilized at 13–14 per thousand. Initially the annual decrease was a few thousand, but it was in the tens of thousands by mid-decade. The willingness to have children decreased despite the introduction in the mid-1970s of forms of support for acquiring a first home and in the mid-1980s of additional childcare allowances related to historical earnings. The average number of children per family sank below two, which was insufficient for the population to reproduce itself.

The 1980 number of almost 5 million active earners began to decline slowly, and there was less demand for unskilled labor. The number of inactive earners continued to increase, mainly because state old age pensions almost became a civil right after 1975, if minimal conditions were met and flat-rate childcare allowances became available to mothers at home with small children. One fifth of the country's population (2.2 million) was made up of pensioners in 1983. Non-manual work was gaining ground, accounting for one third of the active earners by 1980, as opposed to a quarter in 1970. The branch structure of employment continued to alter, with manufacturing and agriculture slowly losing ground to the services, transport and trade.

The characteristics of the social structure in the late 1970s and early 1980s clearly resulted from processes that had begun at the end of the 1960s. Within politically determined frames and conditions, the second economy became widespread, initially in agriculture and later in industry and the services. This became an increasingly important stratifying factor, as did participation from the early 1980s in the new legal forms of small business activity. Those conclusions are backed up by various public opinion polls and sociological surveys taken in the second half of the 1980s, showing that four fifths of Hungarian society thought that the small businesses were useful. This means at the same time that possession of political capital became less and less important to stratification after the turn of the 1970s and 1980s; Hungarian Socialist Workers' Party membership remained a requirement only for promotion to special leading posts and positions in the *nomenklatura*. Although there were no surveys taken on the subject, it can be inferred from historical writings and memoirs that the prestige of communist politicians and party secretaries, having climbed rapidly in the post-war years, went into steady decline, with few exceptions.

There was only partial overlap in estimations of social status by the formal and informal segments of public opinion in the Kádár period. The formal segment attributed high status to professional politicians and party officials, while the informal segment attributed little or none to them. The social estimation of doctors, lawyers and other highly trained intellectuals stayed high. This was expressed in daily social life. It was almost unknown for a doctor or lawyer to be referred to as "comrade" in private contact.

The real social changes taking place in public thinking can be traced in the findings of status surveys carried out by the Central Statistics Office. In 1983, social positions and occupations were being judged by their earnings potential, the knowledge required for them, the power that they possessed, and their social usefulness. That order had changed little in 1988. The estimation of knowledge, independence and money increased in the 1980s. The survey shows an increase in the social estimation of occupations where the factors mentioned were prominent. They include medical practitioners, lawyers, artisans, retail traders and journalists. The occupations whose status was declining were county party secretaries, miners, police, army officers and unskilled factory workers.[31] These approaches include subjective elements and are obviously confined to showing the direction of social changes. But the research recorded the tendencies in which informal public estimations began to dominate over formal ones.

Closing of mobility relations could be discerned primarily in a stronger self-reproducing propensity in various social groups. This applied as much to the intelligentsia descended from managers and professionals trained in the 1950s as to stronger inheritance positions among the children of manual/urban workers. The sociological analysis of this shows strong differentiation beginning in the 1980s among generations of skilled workers under the age of 30. Essentially, a smaller proportion bettered their chances of attaining a higher social position, while the majority were "unable even to maintain the social position of their parents and slid down into the more backward strata," in other words becoming semi-skilled, skilled or casual workers.[32]

A new occurrence in the early 1980s was the emergence of a small business stratum and rapid rises in the numbers of artisans and small traders. Mobility surveys show that the skilled working class was the main recruiting ground for small business. This means not that the traditional *petite bourgeoisie* was reborn, but that a new small business stratum was developing. Inheritance of a trade was more important with artisans.[33]

The crisis of morality and values deepened in society during the period. The vast majority of Hungarians in the 1970s and 1980s felt that they were able only in part to get where they wanted; their lives depended not on personal will, but on the often mysterious intentions of the authorities. In other words, feelings of helplessness had increased. The mentality of fulfilling financial obligations to the state and being a "good taxpaying citizen" was unattractive in a situation full of uncertainties. Social orientations hardly displayed signs of change; Hungarian society proved extremely creative in avoiding tax, concealing income, and finding legal loopholes, both then and in subsequent decades. The shortage economy tended to perpetuate the system of personal connections, rather than performance. The mechanisms of counter-selection, protection and corruption remained rife, which ultimately exacerbated the demoralization of society, and lessened the chance of general social norms developing and applying. Official institutions in the 1970s and 1980s still strove to instill the idea of equality as a basic virtue under social conditions. Although the socialization mechanisms did not lead to total rejection of the idea of equality, such concepts as individual achievement, consumption and values connected with material prosperity came increasingly to the fore, which worked against equality. Comparing survey data for 1977 and 1981, using Max Weber's triple scoring system (secularization/rationalization/individualization), it can be said that the value system of Hungarian society was becoming more secular, more worldly, than the American one, although the criteria of rationality and individualization left the picture more complex. The American value system is more rational and practical, giving greater scope to autonomous personalities, and thus more individualized than the Hungarian one. At the same time, the traditional communal values are stronger in American society than they are in the Hungarian one. One reason for that is inconsistency in the modernization processes. Hungarian society at the end of the 1970s can be said to have shown a very strong demand for material prosperity, which can be explained by the removal of the material and political constraints of earlier decades. After the long period of penury ended in the 1970s, conditions for fulfilling plans and ambitions steadily improved.[34]

Problems apparent in human relations worsened in the 1980s. Toleration clearly decreased, as did solidarity, respect for others and acceptance of otherness. In a sociological survey of values made in 1982–1983, fewer than a third of respondents placed toleration among the five most important values.[35] Intolerance results from the absence of civil society and inconsistent social modernization; in fact in this case it was a question of a "negative modernization" that emphasized some materialistic modernization elements, destroyed existing small communities, and strove to reorganize or eliminate the system of informal social contacts. The prime target of prejudices in Hungarian society in recent decades was the Gypsy community of some 400,000.[36]

Hungary society and its mentality in the mid-1980s were marked by a further inconsistency. Its openness to new initiatives and values—enterprise and risk-taking, for instance—was accompanied by a desire to cling on to the conditions of the Kádár period, which had come to offer political and social security.

Notes

1 On domestic political history, see the following: Rudolf L. Tőkés, *Hungary's Negotiated Revolution. Economic Reform, Social Change and Political Succession, 1957–1990* (London, 1966); Ignác Romsics, *Hungary in the Twentieth Century* (Budapest, 1999); György Gyarmati, "Politika és társadalom 1945–1989 között" [Politics and Society between 1945 and 1989], in István Kollega Tarsoly, ed., *Magyarország a XX. században* [Hungary in the 20th Century] (Szekszárd, 1996).

2 Compared with the relative price stability of earlier periods, it was unusual and shocking to have official prices of staple foods (such as meat, bread and sugar) rise by 20–50 percent year after year, along with energy and service prices. Reactions were not wholly predictable, and there was no freedom of expression: politicians rightly feared that moves that made daily life harder might elicit spontaneous mass protest.

3 Gyarmati, "Politika és társadalom 1945–1989 között," p. 248.

4 János Kádár's political position and cast of mind are analyzed in detail in Tibor Huszár, *Kádár János politikai életrajza* [Political Biography of János Kádár], vols. 1–2 (Budapest, 2001 and 2003).

5 Most of the party leadership no longer saw themselves as professional revolutionaries or agitators, but as officials; so their thinking and behavior assumed features typical of expert bureaucrats.

6 Huszár, *Kádár János politikai életrajza.*

7 László Csaba, "Változó erőtérben – változó egyensúlyozás. Adalék Magyarország háború utáni gazdaságtörténetéhez" [Variable Field—Variable Balance. Contributions to the Post-War Economic History of Hungary], in György Majtényi and Csaba Szabó, eds., *Rendszerváltás és a Kádár-korszak* [System Change and the Kádár Period] (Budapest, 2008), pp. 199–218.

8 Huszár, *Kádár János politikai életrajza.*

9 There arose in interwar Hungary a school of literature whose main aim was to present the social conditions and situation of the people as truthfully as possible. An important part of its work consisted of "sociographic" depictions of society, portraying the social relations and living conditions of a particular village or district using a mixture of sociological and literary techniques. Among the main exponents were Gyula Illyés, Zoltán Szabó, Imre Kovács, Géza Féja and Péter Veres.

10 Gyula Kozák, ed., *Választási almanach* [Electoral Almanac] (Budapest, 1985).

11 István Kukorelli, *Így választottunk* [How We Elected] (Budapest, 1988).

12 Ervin Csizmadia, *A magyar demokratikus ellenzék* [The Hungarian Democratic Opposition], vols. I–III (Budapest, 1998).

13 The word denotes speaker, commentator or interlocutor, but also prison visiting hours.

14 The Communist Party (in all its forms), in line with the position that it had formulated in December 1956 and for obvious reasons to do with its legitimacy, insisted up to February 1989 on classing the events of 1956 as a counterrevolution. The only concession had been in the mid-1970s, when they were sometimes referred to as the unfortunate events of October 1956. The official propaganda campaigns of 1981 and 1986 did not accomplish their original purpose of reinforcing that official view, but public interest was aroused by the detailed accounts that appeared in the press and media.

15 Máté Szabó, "Tüntetések a Kádár-rendszerben: történeti vázlat" [Protests under the Kádár System: a Historical Outline], in Máté Szabó and Dominique Wisler, eds., *Tüntetés, rendőrség, demokrácia* [Protests, Police, Democracy] (Budapest, 1999), pp. 131–154.

16 Gyarmati, "Politika és társadalom 1945–1989 között," p. 253.

17 The Catholic Bokor Basis Community was started in 1945 by the Piarist teacher György Bulányi, at the instigation of a Croatian Jesuit. Its prime aim was to preserve Christian belief, thinking and practice through communist dictatorship and persecution. It gained and developed a more distinct image after its founder was released from prison. It became clear to many members in the late 1970s that the teachings of Jesus could not be reconciled with taking life—murder—and they began to refuse to do military service, receiving prison sentences of 1–3 years instead.

18 Jenő Gergely, József Kardos and Ferenc Rottler, *Az egyházak Magyarországon* [Churches in Hungary] (Budapest, 1997).

19 The minutes appeared in *samizdat* form and were later republished: János M. Rainer, ed., *A monori tanácskozás 1985. június 14–16.* [The Monor Meeting, June 14–16, 1985] (Budapest, 2005).

20 On this, see the following: Ignác Romsics, ed., *Magyarország és a nagyhatalmak a XX. században* [Hungary and the Great Powers in the 20th Century] (Budapest, 1995), pp. 185–278; Charles Gati, *Magyarország a Kreml árnyékában* [Hungary in the Shadow of the Kremlin] (Budapest, 1990); Romsics, *Hungary in the Twentieth Century.*

21 The number of tourist visits to Hungary in 1980 approached 9.5 million, a large number even if multiple entries and exits are discounted. *Magyar Statisztikai évkönyv, 1980* [Hungarian Statistical Yearbook, 1980] (Budapest, 1981).

22 István Németh and István Horváth, *És a falak leomlanak. Magyarország és a német egység 1945–1990* [And the Walls Fall Down. Hungary and German Unity, 1945–1990] (Budapest, 1999).

23 See Rolf Müller, ed., *Európai kulturális fórum és ellenfórum* [European Cultural Forum and Counter-Forum] (Budapest, 2005).

24 Nándor Bárdi, Csilla Fedinecz and László Szarka, *Kisebbségi magyar közösségek a XX. században* [Minority Hungarian Communities in the 20th Century] (Budapest, 2007).

25 Nándor Bárdi, *Tény és való – a budapesti kormányzatok és a határon túli magyarság kapcsolattörténete* [Undeniable—The

History of Relations between Budapest Governments and Hungarian Communities outside the Country] (Pozsony, 2004).

26 The documentation has appeared: János M. Rainer and Magdolna Baráth, eds., *Gorbacsov tárgyalásai a magyar vezetőkkel. Dokumentumok az egykori SZKP és MSZMP archívumaiból* [Gorbachev's Talks with Hungarian Leaders. Documents from the Archives of the Former CPSU and HSWP] (Budapest, 2000).

27 László Csaba, "Economics in Hungary (1945–2001)," in M. Kaase, V. Sparsbuch and A. Weninger, eds., *Handbook on Three Social Sciences in Central and Eastern Europe: Economics, Political Science and Sociology* (Budapest, 2002), pp. 83–101.

28 György Földes, *Az eladósodás politikatörténete* [The Political History of Indebtedness] (Budapest, 1998).

29 For details, see *Az 1980-as népszámlálás lakásstatisztikai adatai* [Housing Statistics from the 1980 Census] (Budapest, 1984).

30 Elemér Hankiss, *East European Alternatives* (Oxford, 1990); Tibor Valuch, "Changes in the Structure and the Lifestyle of Hungarian Society in the Second Half of the XXth Century," in Gábor Gyáni, György Kövér and Tibor Valuch, *Social History of Hungary from the Reform Era to the End of the Twentieth Century* (Highland Lakes, NJ, 2004).

31 Rózsa Kulcsár and János Kisdi, *Foglalkozások presztízse* [Occupational Prestige] (Budapest, 1990).

32 Erzsébet Bukodi, "A nemzedékek közötti társadalmi mobilitás főbb jellemzői" [The Main Features of Social Mobility between Generations], *Statisztikai Szemle* 4–5 (1995): 324–339.

33 Rudolf Andorka, "A társadalmi mobilitás változásai 1973-tól 1992-ig" [The Changes in Social Mobility from 1973 to 1992], *Statisztikai Szemle* 2 (1995): 101–120.

34 Elemér Hankiss, Róbert Manchin, László Füstös and Árpád Szakolczai, *Kényszerpályán? A magyar társadalom értékrendszerének alakulása 1930 és 1981 között* [Forced Path? The Evolution of the Value System of Hungarian Society between 1930 and 1981] (Budapest, 1982).

35 Péter Heltai and Árpád Szakolczai, "Erőltetett modernizáció és elhanyagolt tolerancia" [Forced Modernization and Neglected Toleration], *Valóság* 4 (1989): 35–47.

36 Árpád Szakolczai, "A cigányság értékrendjének változásai" [Changes in the Value System of the Gypsy Community], *Szociológia* 4 (1982): 521–533.

X. COLLAPSE—PATH TO THE SYSTEM CHANGE (1985–1989)

1. Domestic Politics[1]

The events that took place in 1985–1986 demonstrate that the era of "feverish inactivity," ostensible acts and formal political routine had come to an end. The "genie" of reform had escaped from the bottle in spite of the political leadership's effort to prevent it from doing so: no longer was debate regarding unavoidable economic and, by now, political change confined to a narrow group of economic and political officials. Discussion regarding the future course of action in Hungary and János Kádár's possible successor as the leader of the country had become animated not only within the various civil organizations that were forming at the time, but within the Hungarian Socialist Workers' Party as well.

Kádár's opinion with regard to the issue of his succession continued to predominate at this time. Although the Hungarian Socialist Workers' Party general secretary's health had begun to fail at the beginning of the 1980s, when an array of ailments increasingly curtailed his capacity to handle leadership duties, he nevertheless continued to ignore the question of his eventual replacement as the head of the party in the middle of the 1980s. Not only did Kádár reject overtures in this regard from CPSU leader Mikhail Gorbachev, but he did not even introduce the issue of succession as part of debate within the HSWP leadership. At the same time, Kádár's personal politics grew increasingly muddled and capricious during the 1980s, making it harder and harder to discern clear political considerations in the party leader's personal proposals. Kádár was obviously more or less aware that a process of decomposition-fermentation had begun within the party as well as the political system at large, although even as late as 1987 he continued to publicly reject the notion that any kind of crisis was taking place in Hungary. In the middle of the 1980s, the HSWP general secretary promoted officials holding ideologically rigid political views to positions of power, justifying the appointment of Károly Grósz as prime minister on the grounds that decisive personalities were needed during times of difficulty. Three distinct factions emerged within the HSWP at this time with regard to the issue of Hungary's future political direction: the first espoused a neo-leftist course in which the socialist system would be strengthened through a return to its "true" values; the second also supported preservation of the existing system, although through innovative changes aimed at improving its efficiency; meanwhile, the third group advocated comprehensive economic, political and social reform that in some regards transcended the boundaries of the socialist system.

The rising uncertainty that predominated within the high-level Hungarian Socialist Workers' Party leadership[2] is reflected in the increasingly frequent reshuffling that took place inside both the state and the party apparatus, personnel changes whose political antecedents and message were in many instances no longer clear. In 1987, for example, Károly Németh was appointed to replace Pál Losonczi as chairman of the Presidential Council following the retirement of the latter, while the ambitious, moderately pro-reform leftist and lifelong member of the party apparatus Károly Grósz replaced György Lázár as prime minister. Grósz conducted his duties as prime minister with great energy and enthusiasm, probably viewing his position at the head of the government as a station on the path towards the pinnacle of power at the head of the party. Although Grósz was, in fact, appointed to serve as HSWP general secretary in 1988, by this time the post of party leader no longer entailed unlimited political power. (Grósz was, nevertheless, one of the most influential political figures in Hungary during the final half-decade of the Kádár regime.)

Doubt and indecision were among the primary characteristics of the Hungarian Socialist Workers' Party during this half-decade. The pronounced aging[3] of the party leadership exacerbated this condition, while the middle generation of HSWP officials who had thus been molded exclusively within the environment of the party apparatus had never been exposed to the rigors of true political competition and conflict. It is probably for this reason that the HSWP's standard method of managing political challenge during this period was to issue stern initial pronouncements and statements, then to gradually retreat from these hard-line positions in an attempt to resolve the conflict through compromise and concession. The party, of course, always acted with the implicit support of the police, workers' militia and army, which, although of uneven strength, had all nevertheless retained a basic capacity to maintain public and social order. The political police took a particularly active role in providing the regime with support during this period. The regular police, obviously on orders from above, rarely utilized open force against members of the opposition or participants in the increasing number of spontaneous demonstrations that took place at this time, dispersing such protests only on March 15, 1986, June 16, 1988, and October 23 of the same year. Although the regime mobilized highly equipped units of the riot police to control larger demonstrations, such as that which took place when Imre Nagy and his fellow martyrs were reburied in 1989, these forces were never called into action.

A characteristic aspect of this era was the fact that politics routinely lagged behind the spontaneous social and economic changes that were occurring at this time. Thus the political system often merely adopted and legitimized economic and social innovations that were already in widespread use among the general population. Those affected were naturally not always entirely pleased with this situation, since it rendered them more transparent as well.

The crisis that was taking place within Hungary's socialist system deepened between the years 1985 and 1989. Attempts on the part of the Hungarian Socialist Workers' Party leadership to resolve economic problems were not very successful, thus causing the government debt to rise and severely curtailing its room for economic maneuver. There was no longer any doubt that Hungary's standard of living would decrease—only the magnitude of this decline remained in question.

The party leadership still believed that it could employ artificial measures to stimulate the economy, although such steps quickly proved to be counterproductive. This served to further accelerate the decline in the Kádár regime's legitimacy, although this phenomenon did not manifest itself in widespread social discontent. Although a large number of Hungarian citizens faced increasing economic hardship in the middle of the 1980s, they sought solutions to their material difficulties not primarily through demonstrations and political organization, but via greater exploitation of opportunities contained in the second economy and other forms of activity aimed at generating supplementary income. Deeply ingrained mechanisms of political indifference stemming from decades of depoliticization proved stronger, at least temporarily, than social constraint. This is reflected clearly in the fact that social support for opposition demonstrations, such as those that took place on the March 15 national holiday and with connection to the construction of the Gabčíkovo (Bős)–Nagymaros hydroelectric dam, began to grow considerably beginning only in 1987. The two-day Pécs mineworkers' strike in August 1988, the first successful major work stoppage in Hungary since 1956, substantiated this gradual change in outlook.

The gradual weakening of the Kádár regime and the marked rise in autonomous sociopolitical organization were the principal characteristics of Hungarian domestic politics beginning in 1985–1986. This unofficial activity took place primarily within certain groups of intellectuals and university students that gathered to examine various aspects of "Hungary's unexplored past," discuss current affairs and investigate possible future courses of action. In the spirit of collaboration that had emerged as the result of the Monor consultations, the opposition organized an academic conference to mark the thirtieth anniversary of the 1956 Revolution. The regime chose not to ban the two-day conference, which was held at the home of the well-known writer István Eörsi, who had himself been an active participant in the Revolution.[4] By the mere fact of its existence, the conference touched upon the taboo theme of the Kádár regime's legitimacy.[5]

The November general assembly of the Writers' Federation turned out to be the other major political event in Hungary during the year 1986. Not only did those present at the gathering voice open criticism of the political regime, but, contrary to the wishes of the party leadership, they also voted all of those members of the federation's directorate who espoused support for the Kádár government's cultural policies out of office in organizational elections. The events described above, although they took place within a relatively narrow segment of society, nevertheless provided a clear indication of the rising importance of domestic politics, a transformation in the nature of the public domain and an expansion in the boundaries of open expression. Although the latter did not by any means entail a restoration of freedom of the press, the political processes that were taking place in Hungary during this period suggested that the Hungarian Socialist Workers' Party would sooner or later be compelled to relinquish its total supervision and control over public activity, admitting expression of contrary opinions and viewpoints into the "primary public sphere" as well. During the summer of 1986, for example, the literary periodical *Tiszatáj* published Gáspár Nagy's poem "From a Boy's Diary" (*Fiú naplójából*), which dealt with the 1956 Revolution and also the issue of responsibility for the post-Revolution reprisals. In response, the regime temporarily suspended the periodical's publication rights, while the HSWP leadership discussed the affair on several occasions, obviously due to János Kádár's personal implication in the matter.[6] Punitive measures such as these could not, however, prevent a gradual expansion in the freedom of expression. By 1988, *samizdat* publications were often sold openly, while the first issue of the popular-nationalist democratic opposition periodical *Hitel* was published in the autumn of that year and programs on state-run television and radio devoted an increasing amount of broadcast time to open debate regarding Hungary's history, current political circumstances and necessary changes.

The organization of Hungary's opposition political forces into what were initially viewed as "proto-parties" prior to their transformation into genuine political parties became more dynamic during the years 1986–1987, when these newly constituted formations exercised a decisive impact on the direction of public discourse and domestic politics. The process became truly explicit when these fledgling parties began to publish comprehensive programs detailing possible measures to be taken to alleviate the crisis into which Hungary had fallen. A special edition of the periodical *Beszélő* published in the early summer of 1987 outlined the democratic opposition's viewpoint with regard to this matter in a treatise entitled "Social Contract," which asserted that the economic crisis had brought an end to the era of public consensus rooted in a tacit understanding of the system's benefits. The authors of the piece declared that an increasing number of Hungarians considered the Hungarian Socialist Workers' Party leadership to be incapable of resolving the difficulties that had emerged in Hungary, holding János Kádár personally responsible for the country's failures.

> The general secretary's popularity is depreciating faster than the value of the forint. There is one thing upon which everybody from the worker to the party cadre agrees: Kádár must go! … Although Kádár's resignation would not in itself solve anything… It is necessary to move from the disintegrated tacit public consensus to open negotiation. The social contract instead of the mobilizing dictatorship or the demobilizing dictatorship. Those interested take part in the establishment of compromise. There will be no national revival without the social contract.[7]

This program drew a mixed reception, with some of the newly formed opposition groups holding it to be too radical. For Hungarian Socialist Workers' Party officials, the *Beszélő* article probably served as an indication that the process of opposition political organization had accelerated, which was certainly not a cause for unmitigated joy among them. Moreover, the piece had broken a taboo in its open call for Kádár's removal, although even the HSWP leadership had become aware by this time that the replacement of the long-time party leader was unavoidable and could not be postponed for much longer.

At this time, a group of economists published another important article, called "Turning Point and Reform" (*Fordulat és reform*),[8] which presented proposals for stemming the increase in Hungary's government debt and set forth an economic reform program advocating the introduction of free-market conditions and in essence totally ignoring the political and ideological requisites of the socialist planned economy.

All of the other significant political programs formulated during this period, such as Mihály Bihari's "Reform and Democracy" (*Reform és demokrácia*), called for an end to the single-party system, endorsing the internal reform of the Hungarian Socialist Workers' Party and the introduction of a multi-party parliamentary system. All of these programs were calculated upon the *realpolitik* consideration of a long-term presence of this Communist Party, showing caution with regard to the restoration of Hungary's state sovereignty as a result of the powerful Soviet presence that had continued to prevail in the central and eastern European region.

The process of organizational restructuring began to occur within Hungary's political sphere at the time of the formulation and publication of these programs. On September 27, 1987, the Hungarian Democratic Forum (HDF) became the first opposition political formation to be established in Hungary. According to the HDF's charter, "Imbued with a sense of obligation towards the country and the Hungarian nation, those gathered felt it to be both necessary and opportune to found an organizational framework that would enable members of society to participate as true partners in the establishment of public consensus… It is for this reason that they have proposed the formation of a Hungarian democratic forum to serve as an arena for continual public dialog…"[9] The foundation of the HDF following the consultations held in the village of Lakitelek not only represented a nullification of the opposition unity that had been established at the Monor Meetings two years earlier, but also served as evidence of an increasingly broad demand for a swift termination of the Hungarian Socialist Workers' Party's monopoly over power. Representatives of Hungary's popular-nationalist democratic opposition played a decisive role in the foundation of the HDF, which thereafter attempted to forge its own political identity under the benevolent shadow of the Imre Pozsgay-led reform communists as neither an opposition nor a pro-government political formation. The pace of political organization and initiative became increasingly intense during the subsequent period lasting until the late autumn of 1988. The democratic opposition that had been built upon a foundation of liberal doctrine and respect for human rights did not completely abandon the ideal of opposition unity even after the establishment of the HDF, playing a predominant role in the May 1988 formation of the Network of Free Initiative (*Szabad Kezdeményezések Hálózata*), which was in theory designed to serve as an umbrella organization for all of Hungary's newly founded political and social organizations. However, this undertaking proved to be unsuccessful, prompting representatives of the democratic opposition to form an autonomous, liberal political coalition, the Alliance of Free Democrats, in November 1988.

The wave of political organization in Hungary escalated beginning in the spring of 1988. Fidesz, at the time an age-based liberal political formation, was founded in March of that year, while the first independent trade union since 1949, the Democratic Union of Scholarly Workers (*Tudományos Dolgozók Demokratikus Szakszervezete*), was also established during that month. The Committee for Historical Justice (*Történelmi Igazságtétel Bizottsága*) was instituted in the late autumn of 1988 in order to promote the rehabilitation of those executed or imprisoned for their roles in the 1956 Revolution. The reorganization of the post-World War II coalition parties also began at this time. The Hungarian Socialist Workers' Party, meanwhile, continued to adhere rigidly to the notion of preserving the single-party political system, a persuasion that the party based on the "convincing premise" that the emergence of single-party control in Hungary had been the outcome of an organic historical process. Because the laws still in effect at this time banned the formation of political parties, a significant majority of those organizations established during the first half of the year 1988 defined themselves as independent public bodies, thus denying the party state system the legal grounds for taking action against them. The emergence of these new organizations presented both the leadership and the rank-and-file membership of the HSWP with a completely fresh set of circumstances that (would have) required adaptation to political conditions based on competing political programs, freedom of expression and democracy, although the majority of both party leaders and members proved to be unable to maintain pace with the flow of events and make this adjustment. Some within the HSWP leadership occasionally voiced support for political measures aimed at putting a stop to the changes that were taking place and preserving the hegemony of the HSWP itself, attempting for a time to portray the multi-party system, free parliamentary elections and the market economy as being incompatible with the socialist system. However, following this initial period of resistance, the state party's ruling faction yielded on basically every one of the essential issues in question during this period. The lengthy process of replacing János Kádár as general secretary of the HSWP and political infighting between the party's various platforms served to heighten the sense of confusion and discord among communist officials. The disarray that prevailed within the HSWP leadership is reflected in the fact that on November 25, 1988, HSWP Political Committee member Imre Pozsgay announced that the party would initiate negotiations with opposition organizations, while just four days later Károly Grósz, who had succeeded Kádár as party general secretary that spring, delivered an address at an assembly in Budapest in which he spoke of urgent measures required to safeguard the single-party system and counteract the "threatening white terror."

In the years preceding the political transformation, institutions that had previously functioned under strict party supervision gradually became more autonomous, receiving fewer instructions from above and making a greater number of independent decisions. "Although the party continued to govern in a procedural sense, it ruled to a lesser and lesser degree."[10] In the meantime, the option of direct political intervention had ceased to exist as a result of the policies of *perestroika* and *glasnost* that CPSU General Secretary Mikhail Gorbachev had introduced in the Soviet Union.

The Hungarian Socialist Workers' Party conference held in May 1988 fundamentally transformed the party leadership, which had remained more or less intact following the 1985 party congress that had served to prolong the stalemate between party reformers and dogmatists. In the course of preparatory deliberations held prior to the conference, the increasingly infirm János Kádár had agreed to resign from his post as party general secretary, consulting just minutes before the start of the conference via telephone with Gorbachev, who ardently supported the move.[11] Delegates attending the HSWP conference essentially adopted all proposed personnel changes without debate, relieving Kádár of his duties as party general secretary and electing him to the honorary post of party president. Moreover, several of the Kádár era's most prominent political officials—György Aczél, Sándor Gáspár, György Lázár and Károly Németh—were dismissed from the HSWP Political Committee, thus divesting them of their leadership power within the party. Among party hardliners, Károly Grósz and János Berecz gained accession to the Political Committee during the conference, while among party reformers, Miklós Németh, Rezső Nyers and Imre Pozsgay likewise fortified their positions within the HSWP through appointment to the powerful body. In the year following the HSWP conference, the latter advocates of socialist reform came to exert an increasing influence over party policies, while the hardliners gradually faded into the background. These reformers attempted to distance themselves as much as possible from the legacies of the Kádár era and to preserve the political strength of the party over which they had gained predominant control.

One of the primary manifestations of the attempt on the part of reformers to separate themselves from the Kádár era was

Imre Pozsgay's January 1989 declaration redefining the events that had taken place in 1956 as a popular uprising rather than a counterrevolution. Miklós Németh's replacement of Károly Grósz at the head of the government provided a further indication of the pro-reform faction's growing ascendancy. During the early months of 1989, Hungary's Parliament adopted a law regarding the right of association that stipulated the freedom to establish political parties. The Hungarian Socialist Workers' Party Central Committee officially confirmed this right as well, thus signifying the party's recognition that it would thereafter be forced to compete for political support with other participants in Hungary's evolving multi-party system. János Kádár's dismissal from his honorary post as HSWP president in May 1989 represented another significant milestone in the party's transformation. Three weeks earlier, the rapidly failing Kádár had made an unexpected appearance at a meeting of the HSWP leadership, making a confused speech in which he attempted to clarify his role in the Rajk trial, the suppression of the 1956 Revolution and execution of Imre Nagy.[12] Meanwhile, the HSWP leadership assented to the exhumation and ceremonial reburial of Imre Nagy and other 1956 revolutionaries.

The process of pre-party formation accelerated at the beginning of 1989. In March that year, the officially designated "alternative social organizations" established the Opposition Roundtable (*Ellenzéki Kerekasztal*) in order to coordinate and promote opposition political platforms.[13] In the middle of June 1989, the Opposition Roundtable initiated trilateral negotiations with the Hungarian Socialist Workers' Party and social organizations close to the HSWP in order to forge consensus on issues related to the impending political transformation, concluding the talks in September of that year with agreement regarding most of the relevant primary political and legal matters, such as amendment of the constitution, the holding of free elections, the function of political parties and the establishment of the Constitutional Court.[14]

Political behavior underwent a significant change in Hungary during the period of negotiated revolution, when the previous indifference of Hungarian society towards politics subsided and the general level of political interest and activity rose. An increasing number of people began to attend opposition demonstrations, most of which were held for one of the following three reasons: to "force" the implementation of change and voice support for democratic initiatives, to express opposition to the planned Gabčíkovo (Bős)–Nagymaros dam, and to demand that neighboring countries, particularly Romania, cease pursuing policies aimed at the forced assimilation of Hungarian minorities. A steady increase in freedom of the press represented another of the major changes that took place in Hungary during the years 1988–1989, when major daily newspapers and periodicals began to write about previously taboo issues that had formerly fallen within the exclusive domain of the unauthorized, illegally published press. After many long decades of silence, it had by this time become possible to freely discuss sensitive questions related to events that had taken place in the more and less recent past. These changes all served as important factors in the psychological liberation of Hungarian society. The year 1989 was one of particular social catharsis in Hungary. That spring, the remains of Imre Nagy, his political associates and other revolutionaries executed between 1957 and 1961 were identified and exhumed from unmarked graves, and preparations were made for their formal reinterment. The ceremonial reburial of Imre Nagy and his associates took place on the thirty-first anniversary of their execution on June 16, 1989, which was formally declared a national day of mourning for both them and all other victims of the reprisals that took place following the 1956 Revolution. Approximately a quarter of a million people attended the memorial service, which took place without incident. The formal reburial of those whom the communist regime had officially regarded as enemies marked the definitive end of the Kádár era.

János Kádár lived long enough to witness all of these events, although his physical and mental infirmity may well have prevented him from fully understanding what was taking place.[15] Kádár died three weeks following the ceremonial reburial of his former adversaries, precisely on the day when Hungary's Supreme Court rehabilitated Imre Nagy and his associates, ruling that their death sentences had been unlawful. The fact that a large number of people also visited Kádár's catafalque to pay final tribute to the former Hungarian Socialist Workers' Party general secretary also represented a symbolic expression of farewell to the era named after him.

Hungary's domestic political circumstances were in a state of constant flux throughout this period. By the autumn of 1989, the number of registered political parties and organizations had reached nearly 100. Support for the primary opposition forces rose steadily, while that of the Hungarian Socialist Workers' Party eroded at an accelerating pace. The reform faction of the HSWP gained increasing control over the party, while reform communist leader Imre Pozsgay became one of the most popular political figures in Hungary. Beginning in the summer of 1988, Pozsgay's political background and stature made the prospect of his leaving the HSWP to form a new social democratic party seem very conceivable, although he did not take advantage of this opportunity.

Political conditions were changing continually throughout (Eastern) Europe as well at this time, when it became obvious that communist leaders could no longer count on Soviet support to subdue political upheaval and opposition. This condition naturally served to alter the balance of political power in Hungary, significantly undermining the authority of the disintegrating Hungarian Socialist Workers' Party and indirectly strengthening that of the opposition. It was for this reason that the more radical opposition parties Fidesz and the Alliance of Free Democrats refused to sign the agreement that had emerged from the roundtable negotiations, instead initiating a national referendum aimed at preventing presidential balloting from taking place prior to parliamentary elections, an arrangement that they believed provided the communists with a means of preserving their political power.

Meanwhile, the transformation of the political structure also continued. During the Hungarian Socialist Workers' Party conference held at the beginning of October 1989, the party's pro-reform faction seceded in order to form the Hungarian Socialist Party (HSP), while the minority of party members who continued to espouse conventional communist dogma remained in the reconstituted HSWP. This split signaled a permanent end to the state party that had ruled Hungary for four decades. The HSP maintained more influence and support than the new version of the HSWP, although it found the tasks of distancing itself from the Kádár era and establishing new party organization to be difficult. This, of course, did not in the least imply that the HSP had totally forfeited the benefits and connections stemming from the party's former political hegemony.

The refusal of Fidesz and the Alliance of Free Democrats to sign the roundtable agreement caused a rift within the opposition camp. The parties then initiated a national referendum that passed by a narrow majority in the autumn of 1989 with regard to several issues that they considered to be of primary importance, such as the method of electing the president of the republic and the disbanding of the workers' militia. Meanwhile, in October 1989, the single-party Parliament adopted legislation regarding voting rights, the democratic institutional system and the form of state that were relevant to the roundtable agreement on political transition, subsequently passing a series of laws restoring the freedoms of religion and the press and ensuring fundamental human and democratic rights. On October 23, 1989, interim President Mátyás Szűrös proclaimed the establishment of the Third Hungarian Republic.

During the year 1989, serious debate took place within all of Hungary's major opposition groups regarding the advantages and disadvantages of party formation, more specifically, whether it would be more beneficial to function as a political party or a social movement. The referendum campaign that took place in the autumn of 1989 presented these groups with both the obligation to make a decision regarding whether or not to form political parties and the opportunity to gauge their strength and support without risk of serious political failure.

In contrast to Poland, the Churches played only a marginal role in the collapse of the socialist system and the democratic transition in Hungary, where their autonomy had been restored only at the very end of the 1980s. In 1989, the State Office for Church Affairs was abolished, regulations stipulating prior state authorization of appointments for Church offices were annulled, monastic orders were permitted to function freely again, the amount of broadcast time devoted to religious programming was increased in state-run media, and preliminary censorship of Church press publications was ended. Moreover, Churches were permitted to either reclaim or seek restitution for property that had been subjected to unlawful seizure during the socialist era, while Church–state agreements concluded between the years 1948 and 1950 were abrogated and Parliament adopted legislation guaranteeing the freedom of religious expression as a fundamental human right and declared the separation of Church and state.

2. Foreign Affairs[16]

The external environment shaping Hungary's foreign policy underwent a fundamental transformation during the second half of the 1980s. Following Mikhail Gorbachev's rise to power as general secretary of the CPSU in 1985, the intensity of strategic arms reduction talks and overall bilateral relations between the Soviet Union and the United States increased, while the USSR also heightened its diplomatic activity in Western Europe as well. At the same time, the CPSU leadership conducted a thorough review of Soviet policy with regard to Eastern Europe, fundamentally transforming its relations with other socialist countries. By 1988, CPSU leaders had essentially reached the conclusion that they must be prepared to relinquish Soviet hegemony over Eastern Europe, thus signaling a nullification of the Brezhnev Doctrine.

Although Hungarian–Soviet relations, which frequent changes in the CPSU leadership had rendered somewhat uncertain during the first half of the 1980s, became much more balanced following

Mikhail Gorbachev's rise to power, János Kádár's advanced age and deteriorating health made it increasingly difficult for him to understand the implications of the policy changes that the much younger and more dynamic Soviet leader was making. Gorbachev's praise for Kádár during their first face-to-face encounter in the autumn of 1985 seemed to provide the Hungarian Socialist Workers' Party general secretary with a personal guarantee of continued firm relations between Hungary and the Soviet Union, although the new CPSU leader noted during the meeting that the issue of succession to leadership of the Hungarian party needed to be resolved as quickly as possible. Gorbachev's relaxation of the Soviet Union's imperialistic foreign affairs network and the increasing "impracticability" of the CPSU leader's reform policies determined the course of Hungarian–Soviet relations during this period. By 1988, Soviet diplomats had begun to conduct high-level negotiations, regarding the management of economic difficulties and the rapidly changing political circumstances both at home and abroad, with Károly Grósz, the Kremlin's preferred successor to Kádár.[17]

The most significant foreign policy move that Hungary took at this time was its opening of the Iron Curtain. Already in August 1989, participants in the "Pan-European Picnic" held on the border between Austria and Hungary called for the removal of the fortifications situated along the frontier, while on September 11, 1989, the Hungarian government opened the border and permitted East German tourists residing temporarily in the country to depart freely to the West, in effect signifying an end to four decades of geopolitical division in Europe. Tens of thousands of East German citizens took advantage of Hungary's opening of the frontier to escape to West Germany via Austria, a mass exodus for which Communist Party leaders in East Berlin sharply rebuked the Hungarian government, although the latter lacked the political power and means to contain it. By this time, not even the Soviet party leadership, which was preoccupied with domestic difficulties inside the USSR, would have supported measures aimed at stemming the flow of East German refugees towards the West. Authorities in West Germany voiced wholehearted support for the Hungarian government's decision to open the Iron Curtain, which in its overturning of Europe's post-war geopolitical status quo entailed the prospect of German reunification.

By the middle of the 1980s, Hungarian foreign policy had attained a great degree of autonomy in terms of relations with Western Europe, advocating a renewal of the process of détente and dialog between the superpowers. Hungarian political officials made frequent visits to countries throughout Europe, while in 1988 Károly Grósz became the first incumbent Hungarian prime minister in decades to make an official visit to the United States, where he met not only with leading US statesmen, but with Hungarian emigrant leaders as well. Hungary had fully consolidated its economic and diplomatic contacts with states in Western Europe by the end of the 1980s, when the country maintained particularly fruitful relations with the Federal Republic of Germany, which in the autumn of 1987 provided Hungary with one million deutschmarks in unrestricted credit to finance investments to aid industrial modernization. Diplomatic relations between Hungary and the United States also became more active at this time. United States Ambassador Mark Palmer provided energetic support for the process of democratic transformation after becoming the top US diplomat in Hungary late in 1986, while President George Bush made an official trip to the country in 1989, meeting with both Hungarian Socialist Workers' Party and opposition leaders during his visit. Hungary's increasingly robust foreign policy also resulted in the initiation of negotiations with Israel in the autumn of 1987 regarding the restoration of diplomatic relations severed following the Six Day War in 1967 and the beginning of preparations aimed at the establishment of bilateral contacts with South Korea, which took place at the beginning of 1989.

Relations between Hungary and other countries in the socialist camp did not change significantly during the final years of the Eastern Bloc's existence. Hungary's diplomatic contacts with

Poland remained smooth during this period, while those with Bulgaria were routinely sluggish, those with Yugoslavia became less active as a result of the intensifying South Slav conflict, and those with East Germany, Czechoslovakia and Romania deteriorated. Leaders of the East German Communist Party had long frowned upon the "suspicious" reform measures taking place in Hungary, while the country's admission and subsequent release to the West of an immense number of East German tourists in 1989 resulted in serious bilateral diplomatic conflict with the GDR. Czechoslovakia's assimilatory policies towards its Hungarian minority and Hungary's unilateral suspension of work on the Gabčíkovo (Bős)–Nagymaros hydroelectric dam hampered Hungarian–Czechoslovak relations. Hungary's relations with Romania sank to an all-time low during this period, when the Ceauşescu regime's homogenization and systematization policies, particularly its rural resettlement program, prompted thousands of Hungarians to flee from their native land. The wave of Hungarian refugees from Romania to Hungary increased sharply beginning in the middle of the 1980s.[18] After initially attempting to ignore the problem, the Hungarian government began to openly address the refugee issue, establishing the temporary housing and institutional system necessary to accommodate the influx of Hungarian refugees from Romania and signing the UN Convention Relating to the Status of Refugees. The issue of Hungarian minorities living in neighboring countries became part of public political discourse and a topic of increasing popular interest in Hungary during the late 1980s. On June 27, 1988, more than 100,000 people attended an opposition-organized peaceful demonstration on Heroes' Square in Budapest to protest against the Ceauşescu regime's rural resettlement program, the largest spontaneously coordinated demonstration to take place in Hungary since 1956. Romania declared that this demonstration represented interference in its internal affairs.

The changed circumstances prompted the leadership of the Hungarian Socialist Workers' Party to revise its policies with regard to Hungarian minorities. Two young foreign affairs specialists,

Csaba Tabajdi and Imre Szokai, devised the fundamental elements of the government's new program to provide Hungarians living in neighboring states with open support. In August 1988, the high-level HSWP leadership made its first attempt in a long time to mitigate the tension that had emerged in Hungary's relations with Romania, although negotiations held in Arad, Romania, between the new party general secretary Károly Grósz and Romanian party and state leader Nicolae Ceauşescu concluded in failure. Hungarian–Romanian relations improved only following the Romanian revolution in December 1989, when hundreds of spontaneously organized relief transports were sent from Hungary to Romania to help people of both Hungarian and Romanian nationality living in that country.

Hungary had become the most open country in the Eastern Bloc and a popular tourist destination by the end of the 1980s. It also became much easier for Hungarian tourists to travel abroad during this period, particularly following Hungary's introduction in the autumn of 1987 of a universal passport valid for travel throughout the world.

3. The Economy[19]

Delegates at the Hungarian Socialist Workers' Party Eighth Congress in 1985 adopted a resolution[20] declaring that measures must be taken to stimulate economic growth in Hungary in order to restore the balance of the country's economy. However, neither internal nor external conditions were conducive to meeting this objective, and thus the HSWP's initiative collapsed within one year, while incentive to increase inefficient production continued to impair Hungary's economy. The poor performance of the Hungarian economy in the second half of the 1980s is reflected clearly in data showing that Hungary's national income rose by an annual rate of just 0.3 percent between 1986 and 1990, while the decline in real wages accelerated to between 3.0 and 3.5 percent per year and consumption dropped by an average of 4.5 percent per year beginning in 1988. Hungary's economic system slipped into a state of deeper and deeper structural and functional crisis, and the country's debt continued to grow, reaching 18 million US dollars by the end of 1988. Inflation, meanwhile, rose to above 15 percent annually. The standard of living decreased throughout all segments of Hungarian society: only those who were able to generate significant supplementary income through auxiliary employment, personal connections and/or previously accumulated wealth managed to either prevent or moderate this decline. During the 1980s, the growing level of economic deficiency and the removal of restrictions on travel abroad spurred a sharp increase in Hungarian commercial tourism: in 1988, for example, the number of Hungarians who traveled to Western Europe, primarily Austria, to purchase popular durable consumer goods such as color televisions, VCRs and computers rose by 50 percent compared to the previous year, while the private import of used Western-made vehicles also rose sharply. In 1987, families in Hungary derived nearly 40 percent of their composite annual income from supplementary economic activities conducted outside regular working hours.[21]

Income disparities grew at an increasing rate during the second half of the 1980s. According to official statistics, those in the highest income category in Hungary earned 5.8 times as much as those in the country's lowest income category in 1988. The 1–2 percent of the Hungarian population classified in the highest income category was made up of those who were able to adapt to the changing economic conditions, those who made successful use of the increasing opportunities in the private sector, and those who held positions of authority. A total of 19 percent of Hungary's population was classified in the category of those earning between one and a half and two times the average income. A significantly larger proportion of the country's population fell within the impoverished income categories: 11 percent of Hungarian citizens earned less than the minimal subsistence income of 3,400 forints per month, while a further 18 percent earned only between 3,400 and 4,500 per month, compared to an average monthly income of 6,900 forints during this period. According to data from the year 1987, people living in urban multi-child households whose active wage earners were classified as minimally skilled or unskilled workers composed the majority of those classified within the lowest income categories in Hungary, while both urban and rural pensioners also constituted a significant proportion of the country's poor. With regard to the direction and characteristics of the economic changes that were taking place in Hungary at this time, the following could be said:

> If the poor in the late 1960s and early 1970s were mostly elderly rural residents who had already stopped working, the poor of the 1980s and 1990s were primarily actively employed city dwellers between the ages of 30 and 40 and their children… These were the people who had strung their lives together at the bidding of the now vanished socialist system: they learned a "large-scale industrial" trade or during their period of apprenticeship acquired vocational skills that were gradually becoming useless and moved to the city, often relinquishing the possibility of earning extra income through supplementary economic activity.[22]

Both rural and urban poverty increased significantly in Hungary at the end of the 1980s.

The Soviet Union was increasingly immersed in efforts to contain its own domestic crisis, and thus Hungary could no longer expect to receive significant economic support from that direction. The increasing intensity of Hungary's economic problems compelled Hungarian Socialist Workers' Party officials to introduce economic reforms, such as their establishment in 1985 of company councils aimed at providing workers with representation and supervision and the adoption in 1986 of insolvency legislation designed to make the liquidation of unprofitable companies possible. However, rapidly changing conditions soon deprived the company councils of their purpose, while the state continued to provide subsidies to foundries, machine factories and mines employing between 5,000 and 15,000 workers that had been sustaining financial losses for years, thus mitigating the impact of the bankruptcy law. In the course of the nearly year-and-a-half-long period in 1987–1988 during which Károly Grósz served as prime minister of Hungary, the government sharply reduced state consumer price subsidies and gradually decreased financial support for unprofitable companies, although not even these measures could stem the progression of the adverse economic processes that were taking place in the country. The HSWP Central Committee adopted a resolution in July 1988 calling for the devaluation of the forint, the renunciation of the principle of full employment, the termination of central wage and price regulation, and the sanction of income-generating private property and its associated economic forms. As a consequence, the transformation of Hungary's system of economic institutions became more dynamic at the end of the 1980s, when the dual banking structure and revised tax system were introduced and, in 1988, regulations regarding the foundation and operation of companies were amended so as to increase the maximum number of employees permitted to work at privately owned enterprises to 500. It is important to note that Hungary became the first country in Eastern Europe to enact such free-market economic reform at a time when the process of democratic political transformation had just begun to unfold.

The spontaneous privatization of state-owned companies began to take place in Hungary during the final third of the 1980s.[23] This procedure often entailed the company management's acquisition of ownership rights over the most efficient production units within state companies, which they transferred to privately owned business entities before initiating the liquidation of the remaining segments of the dismantled and frequently insolvent state enterprise. The establishment of a company or other type of business association utilizing foreign capital to acquire a majority stake in state-owned companies represented another common form of spontaneous privatization.[24]

In June 1989, Hungary's Parliament adopted the so-called transformation law, which required state-owned companies to organize themselves into a business entity of some type. As a result of this legislation, the number of registered limited liability companies and joint stock companies underwent a steady increase, while the number of sole proprietorships also rose significantly, reaching more than 300,000 in 1989 and 400,000 a year and a half later. The State Asset Management Agency (*Állami Vagyonügynökség*) was established to supervise and direct privatization under parliamentary supervision.[25] This transformation towards private company ownership is reflected in statistics showing that the proportion of Hungary's GDP generated within the private sector rose from 15 percent in 1985 to 30 percent by the end of 1989.[26]

4. Society

Hungary's predominant demographic trends remained negative during the second half of the 1980s.[27] The number of births dropped, while mortality stagnated at a high rate, producing an average annual population decline of 20,000 by the end of the decade. The consequent aging of Hungary's populace resulted in a decrease in the proportion of citizens who were under the age of 15 and an increase in the proportion of citizens who were above the age of 60. In terms of occupational structure, the number of people employed in the industrial and agricultural sectors underwent a steady fall, while the number of people employed in the service sector rose. The number of active wage earners in Hungary declined considerably as a result of the transformation that was taking place within the country's economic structure, while the number of unemployed officially exceeded 50,000 by 1989. Many people chose to take early or disability retirement rather than join the growing ranks of the unemployed, thus contributing to a rapid increase in the number of economically inactive citizens.

The principles and practices that governed the organization and direction of Hungarian society underwent a significant change during the period of political transition in the late 1980s and early 1990s, when a new social construction based on law, liberty, autonomy and democracy superseded the previous centralistic, authoritarian order. During the more than five-year-long period of transformation, the value of education, occupational skills and professional know-how, particularly those applicable within a market economy, grew continuously, while the significance of the various forms of symbolic capital—social connections, creativity, entrepreneurial impulse and adaptability—also increased sharply. Property ownership again became a decisive stratification factor during this period, when the quantity of previously accumulated capital exercised a great impact on the social standing of both groups and individuals. Disparities in wealth and income grew at an accelerating pace throughout the decade. In another significant change, status within the primary and secondary economies frequently became unified, for the most part through the elimination of jobs in the primary economy or the transformation of activities in the secondary economy into personal or group enterprises.

The restratification of Hungarian society manifested itself most apparently in a spectacular growth in income disparity. By the end of the 1980s, consumption and lifestyle increasingly joined occupation and income as the primary stratification factors active in Hungary. The emergence of true alternatives in the choice of economic activity, the open exercise of previously hidden entrepreneurial undertakings, the strengthening of the legal private sector, the weakening of the state sector, a relaxation of state supervision and the total "muddling" of the system provided the background for these changes.

The gradual official recognition of previously hidden unemployment began during the final third of the 1980s, culminating in the government's introduction of jobless assistance in 1988. Similarly, formal acknowledgement of the problem of homelessness occurred only in 1989. The number of homeless people in Hungary increased significantly during this period as a result of the rapid rise in social inequality. Impoverishment, growing expenses related to home maintenance and long-term unemployment contributed, both individually and in unison, to the increase in homelessness. Many young people released from state guardianship, uneducated rural citizens who had migrated to the city in search of employment, and a significant number of people who had fallen from higher social strata became homeless in the late 1980s. Hungary's homeless population consisted primarily of the following groups of people at the end of the 1980s: young people who had run away from home or escaped from state custody, young and middle-aged drug addicts, alcoholics, the mentally ill, elderly and infirm vagrants, ex-convicts, vagabonds by choice, members of the underworld, casual laborers, former commuters and inhabitants of workers' dormitories, divorced people, and those evicted from their homes.[28]

Hungary's small and medium-sized business sector also began to form at this time.[29] The number of small-scale tradesmen also began to rise sharply beginning in the late 1980s, reaching 187,586 by March 1990. All of this reflected the increasingly dynamic process of restratification and differentiation that was taking place in Hungary.

Changes in the number of enterprises according to type between 1985 and 1988

Type of Enterprise	*1985*	*1988*
Company Economic Collectives	19,169	15,428
Industrial and Service Cooperative Specialized Groups	2,613	1,530
Economic Collectives	9,312	10,889
Civil Legal Companies	2,181	3,507
Small-Scale Tradesmen	154,611	162,217
Small-Scale Merchants	31,827	34,541

Source: *Market Participants in the Hungarian Economy, 1982–1989* (Budapest, 1990).

In 1988, a total of 178,018 people worked in company economic collectives, while 72,199 people participated in non-company economic collectives, 47,828 people worked in specialized groups, and 14,817 people were involved in enterprises of other types. As a result of this sharp growth, the number of people employed in the private sector had already surpassed the half-million mark by the end of the 1980s. Including their dependents, between 1.5 million and 1.8 million people, or 15 to 17 percent of Hungary's total population, derived their subsistence from the private sector at this time. A significant majority of those employed in the private sector were between 30 and 50 years of age and highly educated. Those originating from families with a background in the private sector were much more likely to become independent entrepreneurs during the System Change period than those with no such family background in the private sector.[30] Cultural capital and connections enabled many people to overcome financial or material impediments to their progress in Hungary's emerging market economy. Economic and social experience gained as part of small-scale industrial operations conducted within Hungary's previously legal private sector played a major role among economic players of the new era.

A significant degree of transformation and restructuring took place within Hungary's elite and powerful social groups as well at the end of the 1980s. A large majority of the older members of the Kádár era's political leadership retired at this time, while a significant number of the more highly qualified and well-educated members of the younger age groups changed careers, either returning to their original professions or utilizing the social capital that they had acquired in the course of their pre-1989 political activities to gain economic benefit as participants in the emerging private sector. Among leading economic officials, those belonging to the older generation often chose to retire, while most younger and middle-aged economic leaders managed to successfully adapt to the new market environment as either owners or managers. There was, however, only minor movement within the cultural and intellectual sphere in the late 1980s, when essentially only those who had offered conspicuous support for the socialist system during the Kádár era were forced to withdraw into the background, while former dissidents regained the positions that they had lost as a result of their political opposition. At the beginning of the 1990s, every elite segment of Hungarian society became younger, better educated and more highly qualified. The social status of Hungary's new elite groups was reflected clearly in their lifestyles and living conditions, although social representation, not the establishment of civil paradigms, doubtlessly represented the dominant motive in this regard.

A transformation in public outlook attended the political, social and economic changes cited above. The communist ideological system weakened to such a degree in Hungary during the first half of the 1980s that by the final third of the decade it had ceased to play any social role in the country, thus creating a partial vacuum that, with the exception of a few general political-ideological values, was left unfilled. Beginning at the end of the 1970s, the following was the case:

> Intellectual values became dominant in the hierarchy of instrumental values, occasionally exceeding ethical values, while at the same time gaining an almost exclusive role in determining aspirations arising within the structure of the value system. Although thanks to the Hungarian Socialist Workers' Party the process of individualization, atomization and intellectualization had accelerated, this process remained autonomous even after the collapse of the regime… There are many indications suggesting that the year 1990 signaled not only the death of the former regime and system, but the birth of a new, healthier society as well.[31]

Public acceptance of social inequality represented one of the most significant problems in Hungary at this time. The continuously rising degree of inequality that had characterized Hungarian society during the Kádár era had been obscured in a shroud of equality propaganda, many of whose cognitive elements persisted after political transformation had begun, while recognition of a further narrowing of opportunity and changes in economic and social conditions was also a protracted process. Consequently, Hungarian society was slow to accept the fact that new social conditions would generate a greater measure of social inequality than that which had existed during the Kádár era. Meanwhile, material success became the main objective of a significant segment of society, while people who attained wealth were the object of distinct jealousy and the notion of dishonesty became tightly linked to that of financial and material gain. Within the given circumstances, a major portion of Hungarian society concluded that it was necessary to violate certain regulations, laws and social norms in order to attain material success, thus making the revival of civil attitudes and behavior that had been eradicated from economic and social life a long and difficult process.

Notes

1 For a history of the era, see András Bozóki *et al.*, eds., *A rendszerváltás forgatókönyve. Kerekasztal-tárgyalások 1989-ben. Tanulmányok* [Script for the System Change. Roundtable Negotiations in 1989] (Budapest, 2000), and Ignác Romsics, *Volt egyszer egy rendszerváltás* [Once Upon a Time There Was a System Change] (Budapest, 2003).

2 For more information on this matter, see György Schöpflin, Rudolf Tőkés and Iván Völgyes, "Leadership Change and Crisis in Hungary," *Problems of Communism* (September–October 1988): 23–46.

3 Ignác Romsics, *Hungary in the Twentieth Century* (Budapest, 1999), p. 512, and András Nyírő, ed., *Politikai szociológiai tanulmányok a kommunista bürokrácia vezérkaráról* [Political and Sociological Studies Regarding the Leadership of the Communist Bureaucracy] (Budapest, 1989).

4 Ervin Csizmadia, *A magyar demokratikus ellenzék* [The Hungarian Democratic Opposition], vols. 1–3 (Budapest, 1998).

5 György Gyarmati, "Politika és társadalom 1945–1989 között" [Politics and Society between 1945 and 1989], in István Kollega Tarsoly, ed., *Magyarország a XX. században* [Hungary in the 20th Century] (Szekszárd, 1996), pp. 252–253.

6 See Gyarmati, "Politika és társadalom 1945–1989 között," and Tibor Huszár, *Kádár János politikai életrajza* [Political Biography of János Kádár], vols. 1–2 (Budapest, 2001 and 2003).

7 János Kis, "Társadalmi Szerződés" [Social Contract], in idem *et al.*, eds., *Beszélő összkiadás* [The Complete *Beszélő*] (Budapest, 1992).

8 This article was published in the periodical *Medvetánc*, 1987, no. 2.

9 The text of the Hungarian Democratic Forum's founding charter is contained in the following work: Sándor Agócs and Endre Medvigy, eds., *Lakitelek, 1987. A magyarság esélyei* [Lakitelek, 1987. The Prospects of the Hungarian Nation] (Budapest–Lakitelek, 1991), pp. 177–178.

10 Gyarmati, "Politika és társadalom 1945–1989 között," p. 256.

11 See Tibor Huszár, *Kádár János politikai életrajza* [Political Biography of János Kádár], vol. 2 (Budapest, 2003).

12 *Ibid.*

13 Among the founders of the Opposition Roundtable were the Hungarian Democratic Forum, the Alliance of Free Democrats, the Hungarian Social Democratic Party, the Independent Smallholders, Agrarian Workers and Civic Party, the Christian Democratic Party and several smaller organizations.

14 For more detail on the negotiations, see Ignác Romsics, *From Dictatorship to Democracy. The Birth of the Third Hungarian Republic 1988–2001* (Highland Lakes, NJ, 2007), p. 471.

15 Huszár, *Kádár János politikai életrajza.*

16 For more information on questions related to foreign affairs, see János M. Rainer and Magdolna Baráth, eds., *Gorbacsov tárgyalásai a magyar vezetőkkel. Dokumentumok az egykori SZKP és MSZMP archívumaiból* [Gorbachev's Negotiations with Hungarian Leaders. Documents from the CPSU and HSWP Archives] (Budapest, 2000), and Csaba Békés, "Vissza Európába: a magyarországi rendszerváltás nemzetközi háttere" [Back to Europe: the International Background of Hungary's System Change], in András Bozóki, Márta Elbert, Melinda Kalmár, Béla Révész, Erzsébet Ripp and Zoltán Ripp, eds., *A rendszerváltás forgatókönyve. Kerekasztal-tárgyalások 1989-ben. 7. kötet. Tanulmányok* [The Script of the System Change. Roundtable Negotiations in 1989. Volume 7. Studies] (Budapest, 2000), pp. 792–825.

17 For more information regarding this issue, see Csaba Békés, "Magyar külpolitika a szovjet szövetségi rendszerben" [Hungarian Soviet Policy in the Soviet Alliance System], in Ferenc Gazdag and László J. Kiss, eds., *Nemzeti érdek és kontinuitás* [National Interest and Continuity] (Budapest, 2004).

18 Endre Sík, "Erdélyi menekültek Magyarországon" [Transylvanian Refugees in Hungary], in Rudolf Andorka, Tamás Kolosi and György Vukovich, eds., *Társadalmi Riport, 1990* [Social Report, 1990] (Budapest, 1990), pp. 516–533.

19 László Csaba, "Economics in Hungary (1945–2001)," in M. Kaase, V. Sparsbuch and A. Weninger, eds., *Handbook on Three Social Sciences in Central and Eastern Europe: Economics, Political Science and Sociology* (Budapest, 2002), pp. 83–101.

20 For the text of this resolution, see *A Magyar Szocialista Munkáspárt XIII. kongresszusának jegyzőkönyve* [Minutes of the 8th Congress of the Hungarian Socialist Workers' Party] (Budapest, 1985).

21 János Árvay and András Vértes, *A magánszektor és a rejtett gazdaság súlya. Magyarországon (1980–1992)* [The Significance of the Private Sector and the Hidden Economy in Hungary (1980–1992)] (Budapest, 1994).

22 Júlia Szalai, "Néhány gondolat a szegénységről és a létminimumról" [Some Ideas about Poverty and the Subsistence Level], in Andorka, Kolosi and Vukovich, eds., *Társadalmi Riport, 1990*, pp. 418–429.

23 Péter Mihályi, *A magyar privatizáció krónikája 1989–1997* [Chronicle of Hungarian Privatization 1989–1997] (Budapest, 1998).

24 David Stark, "Privatization in Hungary: From Plan to Market or from Plan to Clan?" *East European Politics and Societies.* 4 (1990) 3: 351–392.

25 For an economic history of privatization in Hungary, see Péter Mihályi, *A magyar privatizáció krónikája 1989–1997* [Chronicle of Hungarian Privatization 1989–1997] (Budapest, 1998).

26 János Kornai, "Szocializmusból a kapitalizmusba" [From Socialism to Capitalism], in Sándor Kurtán, Péter Sándor and László Vass, eds., *Magyarország évtizedkönyve (1988–1998) – A rendszerváltás I–II* [Hungary's Decade Book (1988–1998)—The System Change I–II], vol. 1 (Budapest, 1998), pp. 21–41.

27 Tamás Katona, "Magyarország társadalmi és gazdasági fejlődése" [Hungary's Social and Economic Development], in József Kovacsics, ed., *Magyarország történeti demográfiája (896–1995)* [The Historical Demography of Hungary] (Budapest, 1997), pp. 271–292.

28 Péter Győri, "Gyorsjelentés a hajléktalanságról, Magyarországon, 1990" [Flash Report on Homelessness in Hungary, 1990], in Andorka, Kolosi and Vukovich, eds., *Társadalmi Riport, 1990*, pp. 430–446.

29 Teréz Laky and László Neumann, "A nyolcvanas évek kisvállalkozói" [Small Businessmen in the 1980s], in Andorka, Kolosi and Vukovich, eds., *Társadalmi Riport, 1990*, pp. 272–287.

30 Tibor Kuczi and Ágnes Vajda, "A kisvállalkozók társadalmi összetétele" [The Social Composition of the Small Business Sector], *Közgazdasági Szemle* 1 (1991): 83–97.

31 László Füstös and Árpád Szakolczai, "Az értékek változásai Magyarországon 1978–1993" [Value Transformations in Hungary 1978–1993], *Szociológiai Szemle* 1 (1994): 57–90.

XI. CULTURE, EDUCATION AND SCIENCE[1]

1. Cultural Policy and Culturization

The dominant tradition-based European cultural tradition prevalent in Hungary was replaced in 1948–1949 by a system of cultural organization and values taking after the Soviet pattern and modeled upon it. That rigid system persisted and proved more or less viable until the early 1960s. Thereafter Hungarian culture was marked, for a decade and a half beginning in the mid-1960s, by relaxation and progressive openness. The shackles of doctrinaire Marxism-Leninism were gradually loosened and the country's cultural and scientific isolation was mitigated, opening it up to new intellectual achievements and initiatives, mass communications that increasingly shaped daily life, towards adaptation of the developing global culture of information and the latest artistic and scientific directions and findings. It was the period when cultural policy adopted the "three Ts" approach—*tiltás* (prohibition), *tűrés* (toleration) and *támogatás* (support). Initially, prohibition and support tended to predominate, but the category of creators, creations and cultural and artistic initiatives viewed with toleration steadily grew.

As for the developments in the final decade of Hungary's socialist period, they can be described as a "linking-up" culture, in which barriers were increasingly removed to increasing ties and cooperation between the Hungarian and European workshops of culture, science and art, along with stronger personal and institutional relations. The bounds of tolerance in cultural policy steadily broadened. Many Hungarian intellectuals (provided that they did not indulge expressly in political opposition) moved from the prohibited to the tolerated or the tolerated to the supported category. Cultural policy-makers no longer sought to retain a monopoly on socialist ideas; a steadily less conspicuous hegemony was enough.

The decades after World War II brought marked changes in modes and means of cultural transmission and the habitual culture consumption of various social groups. The same applied in relation to communications. The survival of traditional, communal forms of culture, entertainment and recreation was clearly not helped by the rapid spread of television viewing.

The image and ideal of being educated that was created and transmitted by schools, teaching and propaganda in the early 1950s differed sharply from the hitherto typical humanistic and democratic outlook or the ideal picture of national culture. Some of the change was just formal—the attribute "socialist" was added to all concepts belonging to the sphere of erudition. Then mention could only be made of *socialist* culture, education, literature, drama or cinema. But the essential side of the change was its standardization and reduction of content. Placed to the fore were everyday political and ideological elements, while the image of erudition and the syllabus to be taught were purged of everything that cast the slightest doubt on the ideas of socialism as a dogma. The "socialist cultural revolution" was cited when "culture houses" were established, based on a network of existing institutions under the aegis of the Free Education Directorate. There were 433 such institutions in operation in 1950; most Hungarian communities gained such an institution of communal and cultural life in the following years. The number of culture houses run by local government or trade unions reached 2,770 in 1960 and 3,634 in 1971.[2] They ran the libraries that replaced the reading circles. They put on the cultural contests, the ballroom dancing events, the balls, and the village weddings, which became bigger than ever in the 1960s. The culture houses of the Kádár period eschewed the direct cultural agitation of the 1950s, in favor of public education, entertainment and comprehensive cultural services.

Personal spending on books multiplied eight and a half times between 1951 and 1966—a big increase even allowing for inflation. Sociological surveys of reading habits made in the mid-1960s found that 60 percent of Hungarians read books and 24 percent described themselves as regular readers. Among the most popular authors were Mór Jókai, Zsigmond Móricz, Kálmán Mikszáth, Géza Gárdonyi, Victor Hugo, Leo Tolstoy, András Berkesi, Jenő Rejtő, László Passuth, Lajos Szilvási, Ernest Hemingway and Magda Szabó. This list changed little in the 1970s but was joined by Erich Maria Remarque, Norman Mailer, Alberto Moravia, László Németh and Eric Knight. The fashionable reading of the time before the war became unacceptable after the communist takeover. The books of Jenő Rejtő and the detective stories of Nick Carter were withdrawn from bookshops and libraries, but so were many masterpieces of classic literature. In 1954 the Olcsó Könyvtár (Cheap Library) appeared, making a wide range of Hungarian and foreign classics and contemporary works available in a simple low-cost edition. The state subsidy to publishing meant that works of literature appeared in editions of several tens of thousands, in the same way as the light novels did, when they reappeared in the 1960s.

Privately or locally owned museums were nationalized and county museum directorates were put in place in the early 1950s. The number of museums and other exhibition areas increased rapidly from 72 in 1950 to 183 in 1970 and 754 in 1990. The number of museum visits per hundred people rose from 13 in 1950 to 71 in 1970 and 139 in 1990.

There were 2,486 public libraries in the country in 1949, but the number rose steeply, stabilizing at just over 9,000 in the mid-1960s, then declining slightly, only to recover in the mid-1970s, so that the number of public libraries operating in 1980 was 10,498. It then declined rapidly to 6,585 in 1990. The stock of books in the country's libraries rose from 2.2 million in 1950 to 51.6 million in 1990.

Some indicators of cultural consumption, 1950–1990

Year	Books published		Library stock	Registered borrowers	Cinema-goers	Theater-goers	Museum visitors
	Titles	Copies	(t h o u s a n d s)				
1950	1,880	20.1	2,246	403	47,069	2,961	1,308
1960	2,972	34.7	11,115	1,627	140,060	6,429	3,640
1970	4,793	46.9	24,716	2,225	79,571	5,591	7,153
1980	8,241	94.7	40,654	2,222	60,718	5,635	16,217
1990	7,464	113.1	51,608	1,856	36,220	4,991	13,977

Source: *Magyarország népessége és gazdasága – múlt és jelen* [Hungary's Population and Economy—Past and Present] (Budapest, 1996).

The numbers of titles published (and of copies printed) rose continually, if at varying speed, in the decades after World War II: 1,880 titles (20.1 million copies) in 1950, 4,793 (46.9 million) in 1970 and 7,464 (113.1 million) in 1990. The figures certainly indicate qualitative changes in book publishing. A rather similar tendency appears in the figures for the number of copies of dailies, weeklies and periodicals per head of population. Concurrently, the average daily time spent reading was increasing up to the early 1960s (42 minutes in 1963) but then decreased until 1986 (36 minutes in 1977, but 45 minutes in 1986).[3]

Meanwhile, the relation of cultural policy to mass culture underwent continual changes, as official ideological and moral expectations became more pragmatic and even showed sporadic willingness to accept products of Western mass culture, in an attempt to respond to the public mood. That tended to boost individualization, not the strength of the community as originally intended. For the mass culture of the 1970s and 1980s played, with the spread of modern techniques of mass communications, a significant part in preparing for acceptance in Hungary of a global worldview. Books, radio, cinema and theater were among the most important cultural media in the 1950s and 1960s, but began to decline steadily in importance in the 1970s with the rapid spread of television. This correlates closely with the numbers of regular cinema- and theater-goers. The movies were still very popular in 1960, when there were approximately 4,500 places in the country where they were shown and 1,401 movie theater visits per 100 people. The second figure fell to 772 in 1970, 567 in 1980 and 440 in 1989, while the number of movie theaters declined to 3,813 in 1970 and 1,960 in 1990. The 17 live theaters in the country in 1950 became 32 in 1960, 34 in 1970, 33 in 1980 and 43 in 1990. Theater attendance more than doubled between 1950 and 1960, declined in the 1960s, and stabilized in the 1970s (56 visits per 100 people), and then declined by 10 percent towards the end of the 1980s.

The mass media—television viewing and radio listening—became a major component in the time budget of Hungarian society.

Television viewing, from the early 1960s, not only altered the way in which people spent their free time, but also changed the rhythm of life and the manner in which homes were furnished. It meant that masses of people did the same thing at the same time—relaxing, socializing and performing the repeated actions of daily life. Television became for many the one opportunity to inform and educate themselves. It played a major part in gathering of information and orientation of values, by displaying specific behavior patterns in society that provided intellectual and behavioral stereotypes, although the extent of television's reciprocal effect on reality is questionable. The watching of videos at home began to spread in the early 1980s, as did the ownership and use of personal computers at the end of the decade. The latter can be said to have brought about a more marked change than television on every aspect of daily life. The rapid increase in educational means and activities typically occurred up to the mid-1970s, after which it began to slow or reverse, along with the time spent on such activity.

2. Reorganization of the Education System[4]

The starting point for radical alteration of the education system was Act XXXIII/1948 on the nationalization of schools, passed on June 16, 1948. All but a handful of church schools and all private schools ended as approximately 6,500 educational institutions passed into state hands in the autumn of 1948, 85 percent of them elementary schools and 15 percent secondary schools and teacher training colleges. The youth and children's movements were abolished in favor of the Pioneer Federation and the Association of Democratic Youth (DISZ), which became the Association of Communist Youth (KISZ) in 1957. The act also placed kindergartens under state control. Following the scheme already mooted in Act XX/1940, the four-year elementary school was replaced by eight years and the eight-year secondary school system by four years. It became the fundamental task of the education system to meet the needs of the political system by raising the younger generation exclusively in a materialist/atheist spirit. Russian became a compulsory subject in the autumn of 1949 and the teaching of other foreign languages was sharply reduced. As for religious education, it formally became optional but actually became almost impossible to continue. The system of grading schoolwork out of seven introduced in 1948 was replaced in 1950 by a system of grading out of five.

An agreement with the Bench of Catholic Bishops left two *gymnasia* (academically oriented high schools) each in the hands of the Benedictine, Franciscan, Piarist and Poor School Sister[5] orders. Initially the Reformed Church was allowed to run four *gymnasia* and the Evangelical (Lutheran) Church and Jewish congregation one each, but in 1952, the Evangelical *gymnasium* was closed and only one school left to the Reformed Church.

The system of higher education was reformed in line with the ideas of the new political system in 1948–1949.[6] The purpose was to place higher education "in the service of the people, to match the operation of the universities to the needs of people's democracy." The other aim was to open the universities to young people of worker or peasant background. There was continual screening of the teaching staff, which meant that many professors of European repute—István Bibó, István Hajnal, Sándor Domanovszky, Farkas Heller, Simon Papp, Elemér Mályusz, Ákos Navratil and Gyula Prinz, for example—were deprived of their chairs, posts, academic titles, or Academy membership. The economics faculty of Budapest Technical University was hived off as the University of Economic Sciences and named after Karl Marx in 1953. In 1950–1951 specialist technical universities were established for the metallurgy and engineering industries in Miskolc and the chemical industry in Veszprém. The arts and natural science faculties were separated. The theology faculties of the Catholic, Reformed and Evangelical Churches were split off from the universities of Budapest, Pécs and Debrecen, and the denominational law academies were closed. Budapest's Péter Pázmány University of Sciences was named after Loránd Eötvös instead and a separate department of Marxism-Leninism was added in the autumn of 1950. At the beginning of

1951, the medical schools were hived off from the universities of sciences and continued as the University of Medical Studies. The Forestry Engineering College was founded in Sopron in 1952. The system of degrees and titles was altered to comply with the Soviet system, with new grades of Candidate of Sciences and Doctor of Sciences introduced under the control of a National Scientific Qualifications Council attached to the Hungarian Academy of Sciences. Another indication of the Sovietization of the universities was the appearance of 175 new university textbooks in 1950–1952, of which 86 were Hungarian translations of Soviet works.

Ideological control over the school system relaxed for a while after the 1956 Hungarian Revolution. Languages other than Russian could be chosen, and religious education became an optional subject. These moves were reversed in the first half of 1957 as the Kádár regime consolidated. The reprisals affected large numbers of teachers in elementary, secondary and tertiary education, who were disciplined or spent various periods in prison. The scope in the pacification period was defined by "Principles of Education Policy" passed by the Politburo in 1958. These defined the prime task in education and culture as contributing "by raising the cultural level of working people" to "reinforcement of the socialist mentality and the spread of Marxist-Leninist ideas." Ideological commitment continued to be a prominent factor in the system of scientific qualifications. Academy degrees could only be gained by those conversant with the theory of Marxism-Leninism and active "in the building of socialism." Practical steps included the restoration of university-awarded doctorates ("little doctorates") in 1958, and reorganization of the Scientific Qualifications Committee in 1959.

The autumn of 1957 saw the introduction of evening university courses in Marxism-Leninism, in the capital and the county seats, mainly to offer training and extension training for party cadres. In 1968 the central party school was named the Political College and given university rank. Under a policy of limited opening up, the Hungarian Academy in Rome, closed in 1948, was reopened in 1959 as a state institution that provided facilities for Hungarian researchers and students in Italy. Collegium Hungaricum in Vienna, likewise closed in 1948, reopened in 1953.

A further wave of reorganization occurred in the early 1960s. The main goal of the school reform covered by the 1961 education act was to link study with the acquisition of practical knowledge. Most of the secondary-level technical colleges became tertiary instead. The *gymnasia* were obliged to offer preliminary training in some vocational field; their students were to spend one of the six weekly schooldays on practical work. A new type of tertiary institution known as higher trade schools appeared in the fields of commerce and catering, foreign trade, finance and accounting. Continuity was apparent in the 1965 introductory document to the new *gymnasium* syllabuses: "The most comprehensive element in all the *gymnasium* subjects is the effort to instill the foundations of a Marxist worldview. The syllabuses of the individual subjects… contribute their bricks [*sic*] to the school's task of shaping communist man."[7]

There were signs of consolidation when the ruling Hungarian Socialist Workers' Party declared in a 1962 resolution that political criteria for access to education would be gradually eliminated. Applicants of worker or peasant background would lose their priority for admission to universities and colleges. Development of higher education in the early Kádár period was founded on "Guidelines for Further Development of Our Education System," published in the autumn of 1960. The aim in transforming the structure and content of higher education was a higher-standard "communist training of experts" to be provided "in close connection with practical life."[8] In 1978 there were 57 separate institutions of higher education in the country.

Some of the tertiary technical schools founded a few years before were closed in the second half of the 1960s, while others were converted into full technical colleges. By the early 1970s, the 48 schools had given rise to 13 colleges, 12 college departments, and two detached departments. Thereafter the education structure did not change much, except that *gymnasium* vocational sections became optional courses preparing students for further study. There was marked modernization of the teaching materials and textbooks for most school subjects.

The process of change also slowed down in higher education, with agricultural and technical subjects mainly affected. The Pécs section of the Karl Marx University of Economic Studies became a faculty of the University of Pécs. A college of state administration was founded in Budapest to expand the teaching of law and administration. Teacher training institutes in Debrecen, Kaposvár and Szombathely became full colleges of education. By the early 1970s, some Hungarian teaching staff, researchers and undergraduates were able to make funded study trips to foreign universities, at first in Eastern and later in Western Europe.

There were only minor organizational changes in education in the 1980s. The Education Act of 1985, in line with the times, increased the scope for pedagogical initiative within the central determined national curriculum. Detailed applications had to be made for directors' posts and approved by the teaching staff. The act retained the requirements "of principle" for education and compulsory elementary schooling up to the age of 16. In September 1987 14 *gymnasia* with two languages of instruction opened.

The situation in institutes of higher education began to deteriorate in the mid-1980s, along with the country's general economic condition. This applied to expenditure on personnel and funds for maintenance, research and the purchase of materials and instruments. Their scope was affected not only by the economic difficulties, but also by some stipulations of the 1985 Education Act, whereby all colleges offering university-type courses became universities and all other institutes of higher education full colleges. This effectively gave sanction to developments that were already occurring. Pécs College of Education, for instance, had been merged into the University of Pécs at the beginning of the 1980s, later becoming its arts faculty. The same period saw the beginning of law training at Miskolc University. Higher education in Hungary became more diverse in the 1980s: some would say fragmented. By the end of the decade, almost four fifths of Hungarian cities had some institute or section of an institute of higher education.

The state monopoly of founding and maintaining schools came to an end in the spring of 1990. A minister of education's order allowed free choice of the foreign language to be learnt. It also wound up the Hungarian Socialist Workers' Party's Political College, which had latterly ranked as a university, and abolished the compulsory teaching of Marxist ideology. University ideology sections were turned into institutes of social theory or political science, with many of their faculty unchanged, which was not always to the benefit of research and instruction in the social sciences.

Also in the spring of 1990, the Budapest theological colleges run by the Catholic, Reformed, Evangelical and Jewish denominations were raised to university rank. All the main ("historical") Christian denominations went on to found universities or colleges, in the case of the Péter Pázmány Catholic University and the Gáspár Károli Reformed University with several secular faculties alongside that of theology.

3. Changes in Educational Achievement in Hungarian Society[9]

The earlier inequalities in access to education eased in the decades after World War II, especially at elementary level. The proportions of successive cohorts of pupils completing the eight compulsory years of schooling and going on to secondary and higher education all steadily increased. There was also a sharp reduction in the sex difference in educational achievement, to a point where the disadvantage for girls was more or less eliminated. But it was also noticeable that the general increase in the level of schooling and qualifications in the population did not automatically end inequality; rather, the level of selection was raised. The dividing line no longer ran at entry level, but at the level of access to secondary and higher education. The question of overcoming inequalities remained one of the major issues in the cultural sphere, including education. Children's chances of further education were still influenced in various ways by the social status of their parents, with social advantage translating into essential educational advantage. The effect of politically motivated positive and negative discrimination had become minimal by the end of the 1970s, along with its secondary effect on equality of opportunity. Research into the relation between schooling and social mobility showed that "even in the period of administrative measures, the children of intelligentsia families had better chances of a higher education than young people of worker or peasant origin did."[10]

Changes in educational achievement, 1950–1990, in thousands

Year	Eight grades of elementary schooling		Trade certificate	Trade school certificate	Secondary school certificate		Higher education degree	
	All	Full-time			All	Full-time	All	Full-time
1950	70	70	79	N/A	16	14	4	N/A
1960	120	107	60	N/A	32	26	6	4
1970	173	166	81	N/A	62	45	18	12
1980	130	120	67	3	72	43	27	15
1990	168	165	58	3	68	53	24	16

Source: *Magyarország népessége és gazdasága – múlt és jelen* [Hungary's Population and Economy—Past and Present] (Budapest, 1996).

Regardless of parents' social status, chances of further study were affected by place of residence. Those in villages were at a disadvantage. Those in cities, especially the capital, were at a relative advantage. In other words, an essential contribution to perpetuating and reproducing social differences was made by the degree of settlement urbanization.

Education contributed to easing educational inequalities by reducing illiteracy and raising the numbers with vocational or higher educational qualifications. This relative equalization is statistically clear: four fifths of those over 15 in 1949 had completed fewer than eight grades of schooling, while four fifths in 1994 had completed more than eight grades of schooling. In 1980 92.8 percent of those under 16 had completed eight grades, while from the early 1970s onwards 90 percent of those completing the eight grades went on to secondary education. On the other hand, it became characteristic in the 1980s that 3–4 percent of the 20–29 age cohort lacked the eight grades, which meant that a group of 30,000–40,000 with a very low level of educational achievement was still reproducing.

The main change in Hungarian higher education in the post-war decades was quantitative. One positive aspect was the fact that it became accessible to groups previously excluded from it. Comparing 1938 with the end of the 1980s, there were more than five times as many students in full-time higher education. The number of university and college graduates increased sixfold between 1949 and 1985, while the number teaching in higher education rose in the four decades after 1945 to nine times the figure in 1938. There was an important change in the subject structure as well. Law, once the dominant subject, fell back, but technical and agricultural subjects and teacher training gained rapidly. Higher education policy in the period meant that quality was neglected in favor of an abiding trend of leveling downward. This was reinforced by the burgeoning of evening and correspondence courses, especially in the 1960s and 1970s. However, the increasing number of institutes of higher education produced 400,000 graduates of full-time courses and another 300,000 from evening and correspondence courses between

1950 and 1990. In 1949 5.5 percent of the population had been secondary school graduates, but the proportion rose to 16.5 percent in 1960 and 23.6 percent in 1990. There was a similar increase in the number of higher education graduates. Nevertheless, Hungary at the end of the 1980s still had fewer university and college students per hundred thousand people than most other European countries.

Numbers in education, 1950–1990, in thousands

Year	At kinder-garten	Receiving elementary schooling	At full-time elementary	At trade school	At trade secondary	**At secondary school**		In higher education	
						All	Full-time	All	Full-time
1950	106	1,268	1,238	57	-	108	96	33	27
1960	184	1,509	1,433	125	-	241	156	45	29
1970	227	1,166	1,154	223	-	347	233	81	54
1980	478	1,221	1,200	154	9	334	203	101	64
1990	392	1,179	1,167	209	15	360	292	102	77

Source: *Magyarország népessége és gazdasága—múlt és jelen* [Hungary's Population and Economy—Past and Present] (Budapest, 1996).

4. Scientific and Scholarly Institutions and Results

Scientific institutions lost their autonomy with the change of political system in 1947–1949. The Hungarian Academy of Sciences changed from a self-governing public body into one that was funded and run by the state.[11] The universities were shorn of their research-related role and assignments, which were transferred in the early 1950s to a network of new Academy-controlled scientific institutions. This period and the wave of emigration after the 1956 Revolution caused the country untold losses of intellectual capacity. One of those who left, in 1948, was the leading biochemist, academician and Nobel Prize winner Albert Szent-Györgyi. He was the president of the Hungarian Academy of Sciences from 1945 to 1948. The following president was the well-known physicist Zoltán Bay. He left Hungary in 1949 too.

It became clear that structural and organizational change was inevitable when the Hungarian Scientific Council in 1948 was established in 1948.[12] This immediately robbed the Hungarian Academy of Sciences of its autonomy, as the Council was invested with all the rights to organize and direct science that the Academy had exercised. In 1949 the Academy accepted new statutes based on the Soviet example, which remained in force until the early 1990s. They included a sharp reduction in the number of academicians, from 257 to 128. Almost everybody who failed to meet strict ideological criteria was dropped, including Szent-Györgyi, Bay, Gyula Moór, Tivadar Thinemann, Simon Papp, Sándor Márai, Dezső Laky and András Alföldi. The new president of the Hungarian Academy of Sciences was a medic, Professor István Rusznyák, who remained in office until 1970 and was followed by the chemist Tibor Erdey-Grúz (1970–1976), the anatomist János Szentágothai (1976–1985) and the historian Iván T. Berend (1985–1990).

Important changes were also made in the system of scientific qualifications. When the universities lost the right to bestow doctorates, honorary lectureships, and so on, they also lost control over their own staff appointments. A three-year "aspirant's" course was introduced with the degrees of candidate and doctor of sciences. This gave the party state another opportunity to screen scientists and scholars thoroughly. Only 148 were awarded a doctorate and 757 a candidacy, out of 2,447 applicants for reassignment. The political and personnel changes meant that Hungarian science and scholarship were almost excluded from international scientific life in the early 1950s. Contacts only began to revive again in the early 1960s. Research and teaching in the fields of sociology and psychology were formally ended in Hungary at the turn of the 1940s and 1950s.

By 1957, Hungary had 114 research institutes employing almost 10,000 people, of whom 3,665 were researchers. Rather fewer than a third of these operated under the auspices of the Hungarian Academy of Sciences, the rest being run by branch ministries. Around 500 million forints a year were being spent on research. At the same time, a Scientific and Higher Education Council was set up to harmonize research and higher educational work. Some of the university research stations came under Academy control at the end of the 1950s, and new institutes were established from time to time. Clearer division of research tasks among the Academy and university institutes came in the 1970s. The number of research institutes and stations was 1,071 in 1970, 1,442 in 1980 and 1,256 in 1990, with 64,419, 85,356 and 59,723 employees respectively, including 23,721, 38,705 and 30,256 respectively involved in research. Expenditure on research amounted to 2.79 percent of GDP in 1970, 3.75 percent in 1980 and 1.61 percent in 1990.

The number of R and D personnel with scientific degrees was 2,266 in 1961, 4,329 in 1970, 7,066 in 1980 and 9,885 in 1990. The Academy had 157 members in 1961, 184 in 1970, 204 in 1980 and 280 in 1990.

A system of institutions for psychology and sociology, previously banned on ideological grounds, began to reemerge in the early 1960s. The Academy set up a Psychology Committee in 1958 to encourage psychological research, and a similar Sociology Committee in 1961. The Academy's separate Sociology Research Group began to operate in 1963. The Academy set up a Biological Sciences Department to further research in 1962. Other bodies founded in the 1960s were the Institute of Musicology, the Ethnological Research Group, the Archaeological Research Institute, and the Art History Research Group.

The National Technical Development Commission, an important body for preparation, organization and development, was founded in 1961. Its position of subordination to the Hungarian Academy of Sciences and its operation as a national authority were largely unchanged through the 1970s and 1980s. The network of institutions answerable to it was modernized continually, as the research institutes and research stations became less centralized and gradually came to cover all the branches of science. The management of scientific research and scope for researchers were defined by the Hungarian Socialist Workers' Party in its 1969 "Guidelines for Scientific Policy." It became possible in the latter half of the 1960s for some scientists and researchers prosecuted after the 1956 Revolution—for example Ferenc Mérei and Domokos Kosáry—to return to their professions. By 1969, the Hungarian Academy of Sciences had a network of 43 research institutes.

Direct management of "scientific policy" steadily lost force and efficiency during the 1970s and 1980s. The ideological offensive that came as the economic reforms were halted in 1972–1973 meant that publicity was denied not only to the philosophers associated with György Lukács, but also to the sociologist Iván Szelényi and some members of the school of sociology associated with István Kemény. However, the moves to curb such research groups and lines of exploration helped indirectly to harden the critical attitudes of some academics, especially in the social sciences. The prestige and influence of the Hungarian Academy of Sciences increased in the 1980s. It became more important than it had been in previous decades to rank people according to their real worth, so that formal and informal prestige converged, with the latter becoming the decisive factor. The political influence of science and culture mainly assumed indirect forms, to such a degree that an increasing contribution to funding them came from private foundations, including the new Hungarian Academy of Sciences–Soros Foundation (later the Soros Foundation) and the Gábor Bethlen Foundation.

The least durable scholarly achievements by groups and individuals in the socialist period proved to be ones where the ideological element dominated and real scientific effort was lacking. A number of encyclopedic works were compiled in the period between the 1960s and the 1980s, including the definitive seven-volume *Dictionary of the Hungarian Language*, the *Atlas of Hungarian Dialects*, the *Corpus of Hungarian Folksong* embodying the Bartók tradition, the six-volume *History of Hungarian Literature*, most of the ten-volume *History of Hungary*, the *Charter Archive of the Sigismund Period*, the *Hungarian Ethnographic Atlas*, the *Hungarian Ethnographic Lexicon*, the *Topography of Hungarian Archeology*, the three-volume *History of Transylvania*, much of the *Lexicon of World Literature*, and the *History of Hungarian Art*.[13]

Some of those in the national (and later the international) research forefront were Tibor Szele, Pál Turán, Alfréd Rényi, Béla Szőkefalvi-Nagy, György Hajós, Pál Erdős and László Kalmár in mathematics, Károly Novobátzky, Pál Gombás, Imre Fényes, Sándor Szalay, Zoltán Gyulai, Géza Györgyi and Tibor Neugebauer in physics, Simon Papp, Ferenc Pávai Vajna, László Egyed and Gyula Prinz in geographical studies, László Erdey and Elemér Schulek in chemistry, and László Forgó, László Heller and László Gillemot in engineering. The foreign-based Hungarian scientists to win a Nobel Prize were George Békésy for medicine in 1961, Eugene Wigner and Dennis Gábor for physics in 1963 and 1971 respectively, John C. Polányi and George Oláh for chemistry in 1986 and 1994 respectively, and John Harsányi for economics in 1994.

In May 1989 the Presidency of the Hungarian Academy of Sciences revoked the 1949 decision to exclude several excellent Hungarian scientists from membership. In May 1990 came full rehabilitation of the cultural and scientific figures who suffered legal injuries under the communists: Domokos Kosáry, Iván Szelényi, István Borzsák, István Kemény, Béni Ferenczy, György Jendrassik, Albert Szent-Györgyi, and many others.

Notes

1 On this, see Tibor Valuch, "Cultural and Social History of Hungary 1948–1990," in László Kósa, ed., *Cultural History of Hungary in the Nineteenth and Twentieth Century* (Budapest, 2000).

2 József Kovalcsik, *A kultúra csarnokai* [Halls of Culture], vols. I–III (Budapest, 1986).

3 Béla Falussy, ed., *A magyar társadalom életmódjának változásai az 1976–77. évi, az 1986–87. évi és az 1993. évi életmód-időmérleg alaján. I. A társadalmi idő felhasználása* [Lifestyle Changes in Hungarian Society Based on Lifestyle Time Budgets for 1976–1977, 1986–1987 and 1993. Vol. I. Utilization of Social Time] (Budapest, 1994).

4 István Mészáros, *A magyar nevelés- és iskolatörténet kronológiája 996–1996* [Chronology of Hungarian Educational and School History 996–1996] (Budapest, 1996).

5 Known in the United States as the School Sisters of Notre Dame.

6 József Kardos, Elemér Kelemen and László Szögi, *A magyar felsőoktatás évszázadai* [Centuries of Hungarian Higher Education] (Budapest, 2000).

7 Mészáros, *A magyar nevelés- és iskolatörténet kronológiája 996–1996.*

8 *Az MSZMP határozatai és dokumentumai 1960–1965* [Resolutions and Documents of the Hungarian Socialist Workers' Party, 1960–1965] (Budapest, 1967).

9 On this, see Ferenc Gazsó, *Iskolarendszer és társadalmi mobilitás* [School System and Social Mobility] (Budapest, 1976).

10 Rudolf Andorka and Albert Simkus, "Az iskolai végzettség és a szülői család társadalmi helyzete" [Educational Achievement and Social Position of the Parental Family], *Statisztikai Szemle* 6 (1983): 592–611.

11 Judit Bíró and Mária Székelyi, "A tudomány újjáépítése, 1945–1950" [The Rebuilding of Science, 1945–1950], *Szociológiai Szemle* 3–4 (1996): 82–104.

12 Tibor Huszár, *A hatalom rejtett dimenziói – Magyar Tudományos Tanács 1948–1949* [Concealed Dimensions of Power—The Hungarian Scientific Council 1948–1949] (Budapest, 1995).

13 *A magyar nyelv értelmező szótára*, *Magyar nyelvjárások atlasza*, *Magyar népzene tára*, *Magyar irodalomtörténet*, *Magyarország története*, *Zsigmond-kori Oklevéltár*, *Magyar néprajzi atlasz*, *Magyar néprajzi lexikon*, *Magyar régészeti topográfia*, *Erdély története*, *Világirodalmi lexikon*, and *Magyarországi művészet története*, respectively.

XII. EVERYDAY LIFE

1. The Transformation of Lifestyle and Everyday Activities

Following the Communist takeover in Hungary, lifestyle, consumption patterns and norms of social behavior and communication underwent what András Kovács has referred to as "negative" homogenization as a result of proletarianization and a general downward leveling of society. The reemergence of divergences in lifestyle corresponding to the norms of a quasi-consumer society at the end of the 1960s thus began at a higher level.

An examination of the attributes and transformation of lifestyle in Hungary during this period must address the issue of the relationship between rural and urban lifestyle and culture. Although changes in Hungary's social structure undeniably produced a certain trend towards uniformity, those living in the countryside tended to preserve traditional customs and modes of life to a greater degree than those living in the city.

> Temporal differences as well as many similarities are thus apparent with regard to life in both types of community. As a result of strong community supervision and the very ecological nature and community structure of villages—house, land, courtyard and garden—the predominant rural lifestyle has retained more differences with regard to that in the city than it has developed commonalities. It is for this reason that village culture does not disappear.[1]

The character and chronology of the transformation in lifestyle that occurred in Hungary are reflected in data from surveys that the Central Statistics Office conducted in 1963, 1977 and 1986. Among the changes that took place with regard to the usage of time, the most significant was a decrease in the amount of time spent on income-generating and production work and an increase in the amount of leisure time. However, the amount of time spent engaging in activities designed to generate supplementary income underwent a general increase from the early 1960s until the end of the 1980s, although time spent satisfying physiological needs did not change significantly. The average amount of time that Hungary's economically active male population spent on income-generating activities decreased from 450 minutes per day in 1963 to 378 minutes per day in 1977, primarily as a result of a decline in regular working hours. The average amount of time that Hungary's economically active female population spent on income-generating activities, however, increased from 204 minutes per day in 1963 to 245 minutes per day in 1977, primarily as a result of a rise in the number of women participating in the workforce. The average amount of time that women spent on domestic duties declined from 336 minutes per day to 260 minutes per day between 1963 and 1977, when increased household mechanization and expansion of the public utilities network (water and gas) reduced the amount of time needed for cooking, washing, heating and carrying water.

The average amount of time that Hungary's economically active population spent working decreased by 10 to 15 minutes per day between 1977 and 1986 in the case of both males and females. However, the amount of time that the economically active male population spent on activities related to the generation of supplementary income increased significantly during this period, a phenomenon that is also reflected in an expansion of opportunities to earn income aimed at either preserving or raising living standards in the 1970s and 1980s. The amount of time that women spent on household duties continued to decline during this period.

During the first half of the 1960s, women spent an average of four times as many hours working on household duties as men did, mostly as a consequence of the fact that women continued to play traditional domestic roles and had not yet joined the workforce in great numbers. The amount of time that men devoted to housework remained low before beginning to rise steadily during the 1970s, although the amount of time that women spent on housework did not decrease during this decade. Hungarians did the greatest amount of housework on Saturday, particularly after the introduction of the two-day weekend at the beginning of the 1980s. Among leisure activities, the time spent watching television increased at the greatest rate.[2] As a result, the amount of time spent reading, listening to music and socializing underwent a continuous decline, while the amount of leisure time spent on active intellectual and physical recreation stagnated before beginning to decrease in the middle of the 1980s. Data regarding the usage of time suggest that the division of labor between the sexes did not change significantly in Hungary, where men continued to spend most of their working time engaged in income-generating activities, while women continued to spend a greater proportion of their working hours involved in activities related to the family and household. The data also indicate that Hungarian society was work-centric during the second half of the twentieth century. The improvement in living conditions in Hungary during the 1960s and 1970s played a major role in this general social focus on work, which is illustrated clearly in data from 1976–1977 showing that Hungarian males spent approximately 150 million hours working on home construction during these years, when a total of 48,000 new houses were built using private resources.

2. Housing Conditions

The quality of housing underwent a significant transformation in Hungary during the second half of the twentieth century, when homes became bigger and more comfortable. The number of dwellings grew sharply between 1960 and 1990 after having decreased between 1949 and 1960. From 1960 until the early 1980s, an average of 9.0 new homes was built per 1,000 inhabitants each year—a *per capita* ratio that translates into a total of 80,000 and 100,000 new homes annually. Hungary's peak year for new home construction in the post-war period was 1975, when 9.4 new homes were built per 1,000 inhabitants. New home construction began to decline beginning in the first third of the 1980s as a result of deteriorating economic conditions, falling to just 3.9 new homes per 1,000 inhabitants in 1990.

Number of dwellings between 1949 and 1990

Year	1949	1960	1970	1980	1990
Number of Dwellings	2,466,514	2,757,625	3,122,164	3,542,418	3,853,228

Source: *Census Data, Microcensus 1996. Homes and Their Inhabitants* (Budapest, 1996).

One of the primary characteristics of this period in terms of housing construction was the fact that with very few exceptions the number of new homes built per year using private resources exceeded that of homes built using state funds. The new structure placed housing within the category of social allocations, while housing management was centralized and the mechanism of redistribution created a significant degree of inequality. Housing policies diverged significantly in terms of practice and principle in Hungary during the socialist era, when the state theoretically provided all citizens with equal housing opportunities, although in fact it furnished only urban housing construction with a significant degree of support, to the detriment of rural housing. Moreover, beyond child-based, so-called sociopolitical allowances, access to private housing construction loans was much more limited for those living in villages than it was for those living in cities. "Centralized housing policy had no bearing on nearly half of the country's population."[3] A total of 87 percent of villagers who changed residence in the year 1981 moved into homes that they had either purchased, built themselves or inherited. Although house construction was a significant financial burden, for a long period of time it represented the only legal and profitable means of investing accumulated capital. In cities, leading officials and those engaged in intellectual occupations tended to move from large housing estates into owner-occupied apartments or family houses. The issue of who lived where and under what conditions depended to a great degree upon the level of education and occupational skill, the market situation of the workforce and family background. Housing conditions obviously served as an indication of social status as well. During the 1960s, citizens belonging to the most influential social strata had the greatest access to state-owned apartments, while beginning in the 1970s, unskilled and semi-skilled workers and large families were added to the list of those receiving preferences for state housing.

Fewer and fewer new homes were built with adobe at this time, while use of brick and, beginning in 1960, pre-cast concrete panels increased in urban housing construction. The comfort level of housing increased to a significant degree in the decades following World War II, while the average size of dwellings also grew substantially during this period. Just 10 percent of apartments built in Hungary before 1960 were larger than 100 square meters in area, while in 1990 a total of 47 percent of new apartments were at least this size. In 1949, more than one third of apartments in Hungary had one room and only 4.9 percent of apartments had three or more rooms, while in 1990 fewer than one sixth of apartments had one room and 40.5 percent had three or more rooms.

Apartment utilities 1949–1990 (in percentages)

Utility	1949	1960	1970	1980	1990
Water	17.0	22.5	35.6	64.0	83.3
Gas	-	-	16.2	25.5	40.2
Public Utilities	-	-	27.0	37.0	43.8
Toilet	12.6	16.0	27.0	52.5	74.1
Bathroom	10.1	17.5	31.6	59.7	81.2
Central Heating	-	-	9,0	19,1	41.2
Electricity	46.0	73.8	91.7	98.1	99.0

Source: *Statistical Yearbooks, 1960, 1970, 1980, 1990.*

The furnishings and utilities of apartments also improved significantly during the period. Access to electricity became nearly universal, while more than four fifths of apartments had running water, a bathroom and a toilet by the middle of the 1990s. Connection to public utilities was the only area in which housing conditions improved at an inferior rate in Hungary during this period. There were significant regional differences with regard to the furnishings and utilities of housing. The proportion of fully equipped homes and apartments was greater in cities with a population of over 100,000 than it was in small villages. It should be noted that temporary housing, and cave dwellings, sheds and other non-residential buildings used as homes were part of everyday life in Hungary during the fifty-year period in question. The government launched occasional campaigns to eliminate such substandard housing, although these routinely failed to achieve significant results. (For statistical purposes, homes had to have at least one room of at least six square meters in area, at least one window or glass-paned door, heating, water and a toilet or access to an outhouse to qualify as temporary housing.) Other types of buildings used as dwellings were defined as "a premises or group of premises used for residential purposes that does not qualify as temporary housing and that consists of a single space of at least four square meters in area or more than one space of which one is used as a room whose area is between four and six square meters..."[4]

The architecture of rural and village housing underwent a significant transformation during the period under examination. Until the middle of the 1960s, new village homes were built in the traditional architectural style, with three main rooms, including an interior kitchen and situated parallel to the street. Following the changes that had taken place in the first half of the century, kitchens with an independent chimney were no longer characteristic of housing built after World War II. Houses were planned and built so that more rooms, pantries or sheds could be added to them later. Although there were certain regional differences in housing architecture, most rural and village dwellings shared the characteristics described above. During the second half of the twentieth century, traditional forms of architecture became increasingly rare, while the materials used to build homes also changed considerably. Brick was increasingly used instead of mud and adobe to build walls, while tile roofs generally replaced traditional reed or straw thatched roofs.

The appearance of villages changed substantially beginning in the 1960s. Architectural uniformity practically eliminated previous regional differences in design. In deference to the fashion of building cube-shaped houses, many villagers added a room to the extended street-front facade of their homes, placing a pyramidal roof on the addition, while others demolished their houses completely in order to build completely new cube-shaped dwellings. During this period of architectural transition, new rural and village houses were frequently built without sheds and other agricultural buildings, although such structures were added later as a result of the increase in household and small-scale production farming. Thus the square form of rural and village dwellings gradually assumed an "L" form. Beginning in the 1970s, mezzanines were often added to cube-shaped houses, a construction process that typically entailed building rooms at the head of a staircase of ten to twelve steps as well as sinking the ground-floor rooms. This left room to add more rooms below, such as sheds, workshops and kitchens. Traditional lower- and upper-floor (summer and winter) kitchens were often built in these houses. The size of such homes was typically between 150 and 170 square meters, with between 75 and 90 square meters of space on each two- to three-room floor. A growing number of multi-floor houses with alpine roofs were built in Hungarian villages beginning in the 1970s, while the number of rectangular-shaped homes also increased. Many of these houses included lofts and a living room. These houses were not infrequently 200 square meters in area.

In addition to building new houses, a lot of time and a lot of energy were devoted to the modernization of existing rural and village houses. Almost all kitchens' independent chimneys disappeared as part of this process in the early 1960s, when kitchen stoves used for both food preparation and heating were dismantled and replaced with tile, iron and, beginning in the 1970s, gas-powered stoves. An important aspect of house remodeling was the addition of running water, which became a general feature of homes built in the 1970s. Due to the irregularity of infrastructural development in the villages, many houses were equipped for running water before they were actually connected to the public utility network. Moreover, those who lived in the villages were obliged to take a much greater part in the development of the water, sewage and gas networks than those who lived in the city. The new and remodeled village houses had large windows installed facing the street. Attic space was no longer used for storage of agricultural produce. Courtyards, however, largely preserved their traditional agricultural function, although they likewise underwent a significant transformation in which garages often replaced stables and sheds were converted into workshops. The remaining stables, animal shelters and agricultural implements remained an inseparable part of the employee-small-scale producer and employee-entrepreneur forms of life.

According to research carried out by Annamária Lammel, a total of 70 houses were built in the village of Atkár between 1960 and 1980. These dwellings were of two basic types: cube-shaped houses of between 80 and 130 square meters in size with pyramid roofs, two or three rooms, an entry hall, kitchen and bath, and multi-floor houses of more than 150 square meters in size built on the urban model. Both types of house used predominantly oil heating. "Residents of dwellings built on the urban model consciously distinguish their family homes from the 'tiny' city apartments, expressing pride at the spaciousness of their homes, although in terms of comfort they strive to imitate urban residences."[5]

One of the characteristics of Hungarian urban architecture at this time was the fact that multi-floor residential buildings were built primarily in major cities, whereas in smaller cities buildings of more than four floors were exceptionally rare even in the downtown area. Most downtown structures were between two and four floors in height, while apartments in these buildings were for the most part regarded as prestigious living quarters. There were four major types of residential district in Hungary during this period: downtown luxury apartment districts, inner-city tenement/housing estate districts, suburban family house or owner-occupied apartment districts, and urban slums. The mass construction of housing estates beginning in the 1960s fundamentally changed the appearance of cities in Hungary. With rare exceptions, these housing estates were built in the city, exercising a profound impact on the urban lifestyle. Housing-estate apartments were characteristically small to medium-sized, while 65 percent of such apartments were built from pre-fabricated reinforced concrete components and were located in buildings classified in either the medium-tall or tall category. According to a 1970 article in the periodical *Lakáskultúra* (Home Culture), "in many cities, the Győr-type apartments produced under the Soviet system for more than a year have been built with salutary speed by the hundreds and thousands." Eight different types of apartments were constructed in the buildings of between five and ten floors. The interior configuration of these dwellings

> determined that the apartments would be built from primary components of 3.6 meters in width and 5.4 meters in length. With a wall width of 15 centimeters, room dimension was thus 3.45 meters by 5.25 meters… The entryway of these apartments contained ceiling-height, built-in closets. The interiors of the bathroom and toilet are completely pre-fabricated and have built-in furnishings. Kitchens also have built-in furnishings and appliances (cupboard, sink, table and gas stove) and a pantry. There is also room for a refrigerator. One-and-a-half-room small apartments contain a pipe-ventilated interior cooking cabin. The rooms have rubber-lined fixed parquet flooring, while the other spaces have foam-lined plastic flooring. The walls are wallpapered, while the kitchen and bathroom interior surfaces are covered with plastic tiles. The ceilings are whitewashed. The apartments are connected to district heating and have continual centrally heated water.[6]

The construction of housing estates was designed to satisfy the sharp need for housing as well as to accelerate the process of social leveling through a linking of necessity, technology and ideology. These housing estates, which typically accommodated between 20,000 and 40,000 residents, were initially built on the outskirts of cities, although they gradually tended to be located closer to their inner districts. Historical urban areas frequently fell victim to this "modernization." The inner cities of Óbuda, Debrecen and Kecskemét, among others, essentially lost their historical character as part of this process. Neither city officials nor construction authorities paid sufficient attention to making an organic connection between the new and old urban areas. Urban residential districts built in the 1960s and 1970s were generally overly uniform in character and located too close to industrial sectors, thus exposing them to pollution (Kazincbarcika, Komló, Tatabánya, Ajka and Dunaújváros). The building of housing estates often led to a significant reduction in the amount of urban space available for recreation, while planners regularly neglected to take elementary quality-of-life factors, city structural attributes and transport into consideration in their selection in their selection of sites for new residential districts. Housing estates built in Hungary during the 1960s, 1970s and 1980s were visually uninteresting and functionally barren. Most of the residential buildings in the housing estates constructed during this era were either four-floor horizontally oriented or ten-floor vertically oriented prism-shaped structures containing modest apartments whose average size was 54 square meters. There were so few objects located in the physical environment of housing estates, and the number of architectural forms used in their design was so limited, that these new residential districts contained no conventional visual order. The function of these new spaces had been reduced to the minimum necessary for biological subsistence and was mostly unsuitable for any kind of community activity. With few exceptions, the comfort level of housing estates built during this period was low. According to 1985 data, a total of 1.6 million people lived in 518,000 apartments on 408 housing estates in Hungary. Although it had proven temporarily possible to establish nearly identical living conditions for people of various social status, a process of differentiation began in the 1970s, accelerating steadily in proportion to the rise in social inequality in the following decade.

3. Furnishings, Use of Residential Space

The changes in housing architecture and layout naturally resulted in a transformation in home furnishings and the use of residential space. The previous focus on the kitchen diminished gradually in worker and peasant houses during this period, when an increase in the number of rooms made it possible to physically separate various domestic activities. The large degree of residential and social movement that took place in Hungary beginning in the 1950s also exercised a considerable impact on housing practices. Those who moved from the village to the city changed not only their residence, but their lifestyle as well. The living conditions of those who moved from village to city environments also underwent a fundamental transformation. These people often left their possessions behind, furnishing their new urban apartments in accordance with the norms of their new surroundings. A radical shift in consumer goods took place in village households as well in the 1970s, when those who built cube-shaped houses often acquired new domestic goods and appliances for their newly constructed homes. The contradiction between tradition and innovation in this regard is reflected in the fact that village houses built in the 1970s often included a conventional parlor room (*tiszta szoba*), sometimes in somewhat modified form. The emergence of the new minimal urban standard of "two rooms with all the amenities" exercised the most significant influence on home furnishings and the use of residential space in Hungary at this time.[7]

A significant transformation in the type of domestic appliances and furnishings used in village homes took place in parallel to the change in the design and configuration of village houses. The establishment of new customs, however, often required a longer time. "The bathroom was often an untouched sight (perhaps because it was unheated during the winter, for example), while in spite of the new dining room and kitchenette, life continued to center around the old kitchen and maybe even the porch, where guests were received, children did their homework and the young women engaged in home-industry activities kept their sewing machines. Objects placed in the home often filled a function contrary to that intended or were purchased merely for prestige purposes. Thus new cupboards and chairs often remained untouched."[8]

What could be regarded in a modern sense as kitchen appliances and furniture became widespread in village households only in the decades following World War II. People bathed in the kitchen until the introduction of separate bathrooms. Until the late 1950s and early 1960s, the most important furniture in the homes of more well-to-do peasants involved the arrangement of two wardrobes, two night tables, two beds, a mirror, chairs and a table placed in either a symmetrical or a central configuration. In the symmetrical configuration, the beds were placed next to the walls, with the two wardrobes at the foot of the beds and the table and chairs in the middle. In the central configuration, the two beds were situated side by side in the middle of the room, while the table and chairs were placed at the foot of the beds and the wardrobes alongside the walls. During the initial half of the period under examination, there was also a third, so-called angled interior configuration, in which a table or corner seat was situated in the corner of the room opposite the street front next to the stove or ceramic heater, while the wardrobe or chest of drawers was placed behind the table or corner seat and the beds were positioned alongside the opposite wall.

All inhabitants of village homes generally lived in one room, even if several generations resided together in one house. Only more prosperous families living in dwellings of at least four spaces, including an independent bedroom, occasionally reserved a separate place for the youngest couple residing in the house to sleep, usually in an unheated room.

> Until the 1970s, it was standard for couples to use the furniture that they had received at the time of their wedding or during the early years of their marriage for their entire lives. For couples who had been married after 1950, this custom began to change beginning in the 1970s. That is, a married couple could purchase several sets of furniture, changing the objects in their environment several times.[9]

The interior arrangement of village homes underwent its first significant transformation during the second half of the 1960s. The new types of furniture introduced during this period, much of which was factory-made, often appeared in the homes of the newly married. For the most part, these new home furnishings consisted of a twin, fold-out couch, two wardrobes, a polished table and four upholstered chairs. Beginning in the mid-1970s, the side-by-side standing closet configuration, which generally consisted of two armchairs, two chairs, a coffee table, twin couch beds and a four- or five-section row of standing closets, became common in village households. This new wave of modernization entailed the introduction of double beds, separate dining areas and novel uses of residential space corresponding to the increase in the number of rooms. Whereas the majority of space in the earlier cube-shaped homes had served merely representative purposes and only the kitchen and one other room were used for everyday activities, new houses, an increasing number of which were multi-floor, frequently contained rooms for each generation, including separate bedrooms for the parents and children, while their biggest room was typically a combination living room/guest room/parlor in which the television was located. In multi-floor houses, everyday activities typically took place on the lower floor, while the upper floor contained bedrooms and, beginning in the 1980s, often an upstairs bathroom. The ground floor played an important economic role, often serving as the location for the garage, storage rooms, pantries and second kitchens, which generally had two entries—one from the street front via the entry hall and the other from the courtyard, thus establishing a direct connection with the garden.[10]

In terms of interior decoration, needlework, sheepskin shepherd's cloaks (*suba*) and tapestries often replaced the previously standard sacred images and family photographs. For a long time, wrought iron decorative objects, such as lamps, flowers and candlesticks, were very popular. Ornaments such as bottles were often used in the 1970s and 1980s to break the monotony of side-by-side standing closets. Overuse of "decorative objects" was characteristic of both village and urban homes in the 1970s and 1980s. The choice of new furniture and interior decoration was sometimes based primarily on their ornamental and prestige value. "Villagers take much greater care of their durable consumer items than urbanites do. The television occupies a central location in Atkár homes and is surrounded by decorative objects and covered with an embroidered cloth. Villagers also placed emphasis on what type and size of refrigerator they were able to purchase."[11]

In the decades following World War II, primarily between 1945 and 1965, urban working-class housing was generally located in tenements built at the turn of the century. The amenities in these apartments, which typically consisted of a kitchen and one or, more rarely, two rooms, were confined to a kitchen wall faucet and, perhaps, electricity. The notion of including a bath or toilet in such housing did not even arise during its construction, while installation of such conveniences during subsequent modernization projects was difficult due to a lack of space. As a result of the architectural design of these apartments, the lives of their inhabitants became closely intertwined.[12] A portion of the "new workers" who streamed into the cities during the 1950s settled in former middle-class homes, while beginning in the middle of the 1960s the large majority of those who moved to the city took up residence in the newly built housing estates. Most of the working-class apartments built in the second half of the 1940s and throughout the 1950s were located in three- or four-floor buildings, were 45 to 60 square meters in size and had running water and a toilet, sometimes even all the up-to-date amenities. The idea of establishing colonies of family houses for workers surfaced after 1945, although it was rejected as an "anti-community" solution to the problem of working-class housing following the Communist takeover, which signaled the beginning of mass-scale housing construction based on standardized design.

> Apartments built according to 1948 designs generally consisted of a living room, a sleeping niche, kitchen, entry hall, bathroom and lavatory, and were around 50 square meters in area. By 1949, a reduction in the size of the entry hall and kitchen, an integration of the lavatory and bathroom, and, finally, an elimination of the larder made it possible to increase the size of the "sleeping niche," thus transforming them into two-room apartments.[13]

Purely traditional peasant, worker or lower middle-class interior decoration became increasingly rare in the decades following World War II, when furnishings became an eclectic mix of different worlds and conventions. Urban working-class apartments tended to be arranged according to styles that emerged in the 1920s and 1930s: among the standard furnishings in such housing, which usually consisted of one room and a kitchen or one and a half or two rooms, were a twin bed, a dark-colored, usually two-door, wardrobe, and an all-purpose closet that could be used for storage of consumer and decorative items. "Those who moved from their village environment to the city for work brought with them their middle-class-peasant housing model, which they followed in part, although they also attempted to imitate the lower middle-class style of apartment furnishing."[14]

The inhabitants of both one-room and two-room working-class apartments had to make maximal use of their modest amount of living space in order to make it accommodate essentially all their daily human activities (sleeping, eating, relaxing, bathing and recreation). According to a survey of people living in newly built apartment buildings at the end of the 1940s,

> The number of people living in the apartments was between two and fourteen people and averaged between four and seven people… In apartments with eight to ten residents, the men slept in one room and the women slept in another… Family life continued to take place primarily in the kitchen, where residents cooked, ate and bathed; about one third of residents spent the daytime hours in the room as well: children played and studied there, parents listened to the radio there, and some people even ate there.[15]

Even in the 1960s and 1970s, the number of people living in working-class apartments exceeded the number of sleeping places.

Lower middle-class—neither peasant nor middle-class—interior decoration was less connected to a certain type of residential architecture, appearing in both housing estates and suburban family houses of two or two and a half rooms. The primary status symbol in lower middle-class homes was the living room, which also served as a dining room, parlor and study. The spatial functions of rooms within small housing estate apartments became mixed during this period, when studies were often used as dining rooms during the day and playrooms as bedrooms at night.

In the 1960s and 1970s, china cabinets, pull-out beds with built-in illumination and a coffee table with large, upholstered chairs were also typical pieces of furniture in lower middle-class homes, whose residents often attempted to put their economic and material status on display through an accumulation of consumer and decorative objects. Just as in some village houses, the television was placed in a central location in lower middle-class homes and was often covered with a lace cloth or other type of fabric and decorated with ornamental items. Although the term "lower middle-class" was used less and less to designate a specific social group in the decades following World War II, it continued to represent a specific lifestyle and outlook.

The extremely limited supply of consumer goods in Hungary during the 1950s and 1960s restricted the possible degree of change with regard to interior decoration practices and the modernization of home appliances. Domestic demand for consumer and decorative goods was satisfied beginning in the 1970s. In spite of difficult procurement conditions and limited supply, a significant number of Hungarian citizens felt that they were able to freely transform their personal environment, generate prosperity, consume food and drink beyond that needed to meet their biological needs, and purchase property (parcels of land, weekend houses and automobiles). It is interesting to follow the process by which products regarded as status symbols in the 1970s, such as brand-name beverages and gift items, became everyday consumer goods during the 1980s.

Interior decoration intended as a symbol of social status became less common in urban homes during the 1950s and 1960s. Hungary's housing culture was characterized by a relatively low number of rooms, thus making it difficult to separate various activities and individuals into distinct spaces. The latter situation began to change only in the 1980s. With regard to the spatial arrangement of their homes, people most often followed the patterns that others of similar lifestyle and social background had already established. "Within the confines of the state-socialist system, people adapted to the customs of twentieth-century consumer society, attempting to furnish and arrange their personal space according to a consumer-centric, pleasure-focused outlook. They did not follow the puritan, practical, thrifty civil housing model, but the modern consumer society's pattern of material accumulation."[16] The transformation that took place with regard to Hungarian interior decoration during this period indicates a shift in cultural custom and tradition. The increasing prevalence in Hungary of a lifestyle focused on the private sphere reflected a desire to identify with consumer societies in Western Europe.

4. Dress, Apparel, Fashion

Shortages of clothing and apparel gradually diminished in Hungary in the years following World War II. Big fashion houses began to operate again following the rebuilding of factories destroyed during the war. Within a short period of time, urban fashion again became diverse and colorful, following European fashion trends. Urban dress had attempted to keep pace with the rapidly changing fashions until 1948, a pursuit in which such women's magazines as *Asszonyok* (Ladies), which appeared between 1946 and 1949, and its successor, *Nők Lapja* (Women's Journal), which began publication in 1949, played an important role. The program for the Union of Hungarian Fashion Design Artists' fashion show held at the end of 1947 reflected the change in outlook that had already begun in Hungary when it asserted that "the working woman naturally needs different everyday clothing from the 'decorative' woman. It is the mission… of the modern design artist… to design pretty and practical clothing for millions and millions of women, clothing that will meet the needs of millions and millions of working women at home and work as well as for sports and holiday festivities."[17] After 1948–1949, it was no longer necessary to provide "working women" with fashion salons, singularity and conspicuous beauty in order to meet their needs. The era of more or less uniform dress in the name of puritan workers' morality had begun. Any article of clothing that contradicted the ideal of practicality and expediency (sometimes even including neckties) was deemed to be unnecessary. Fashion magazines published at the time praised the mass-produced ready-to-wear products manufactured at state-run clothing factories, not individual taste. Shoppers, however, did not show great enthusiasm for such uniformly fashioned clothing. By 1950, not only had "self-serving trendiness" become the object of official disapproval, but hats, neckties, frilled women's clothing, low necklines, lipstick and nail polish had also become qualified as "rejected, *petit-bourgeois* style." Working men and women were portrayed as the ideal. Working girls often walked down the catwalk at fashion shows instead of models. "Healthy-bodied young working girls and women presented the clothing, not the slimmed-down, shriveled models bred specifically for this purpose."[18] Clothing selection became narrower at the beginning of the 1950s. Urban men attempted to look like workers in their dress. Among typical garments worn during this period were green and grey loden coats and berets for men and military clothing or skirts and flannel blouses for women.

Only the so-called "swanker" fashion (drainpipe pants, thick-soled shoes and tight skirts) managed to break the monotony of overalls and loden coats to some degree. In 1950, the Clothing Industry Design Company (later the Hungarian Fashion Institute) replaced the design salons that had determined the direction of Hungarian fashion. Hungary's evolving ready-to-wear state clothing industry attempted to totally eliminate demand for individually tailored garments. Although fashion shows were still held to display the new ready-to-wear products, portraits of Rákosi, Lenin and Stalin were placed above the catwalk. However, relatively high prices, inadequate selection and poor quality often disappointed those who decided to purchase the clothing presented at the shows.

Forced fashion puritanism and the monotony of the loden coat and beret began to subside only during the second half of the 1950s, when femininity and individuality in attire were no longer viewed as political issues. Following the 1956 Revolution, the ideological boundaries placed on fashion started to dissipate, while the issue of dress decreasingly lost its political character and puritanism began to lose its status as a compulsory ideal. Because Hungarian industry had proven incapable of satisfying the domestic demand for clothing, high-quality and fashionable apparel, such as nylon stockings and blouses and trench coats, were smuggled into the country. Media reports about Parisian fashion shows began appearing in 1957. Beginning in the 1960s, it was not only the party that expressed disapproval of new fashion trends, but social and political conservatives as well. It took many years before the elements of fashion subculture connected to rock music, such as blue jeans, and long hair for men, gained acceptance in Hungary. Both the party and society became more tolerant of such expression of diversity and individuality during the 1970s as a result of a decrease in the significance of ideology and the emergence of a "more or less middle-class" system of values.

The increasingly conspicuous forms of urban clothing and fashion subculture in Hungary that emerged in the 1970s gave rise to cultural youth groups such as the *digó* ("dagos," very well-dressed young Hungarians who followed the Italian style of fashion and listened to disco music) and the *csöves* ("pipes," a special type of Hungarian rockers). Fashion trends had an increasing influence on urban dress in Hungary during the 1970s and 1980s. At the beginning of the 1980s, there emerged in Hungary a "boutique cult," which essentially made it possible for people who were willing to pay several times more for "cool duds" than for clothing available at state-operated stores in order to keep up with the latest fashion trends.

The expanding influence of consumerism in Hungarian society exercised a significant impact on both clothing culture and fashion. Within Hungary's economy of scarcity, domestic industry was slow to adapt to the shifting demand for clothing, although beginning in the 1980s it made gradual progress in this domain. The selection of ready-to-wear clothing increased steadily, while production of blue jeans (*Trapper-farmer*) and licensed production of global brands began in the second half of the 1970s. The variety of clothing shops and the apparel available at them underwent a continual increase at this time. Exclusive retail clothing-store chains such as S-modell and the expanding private sector moderated the lack of clothing selection in Hungary in the 1980s. Sales at clothing stores in the Váci Street shopping district, one of the most elegant in Budapest, underwent a sharp and steady increase during this decade. The long lines of people waiting to get into the only Adidas brand-name store in Hungary were certainly not indicative of the country's generally deteriorating living conditions. Beginning in the 1970s, magazines such as *Nők Lapja* (Women's Journal) and *Ez a divat* (This is Fashion) kept Hungarian women up to date on the latest fashions. The role of dress and clothing in signaling social status declined significantly in Hungary in the 1960s and 1970s as compared to the first half of the century before beginning to increase again in the 1980s and 1990s.

Self-sufficiency in terms of clothing temporarily increased in Hungary following World War II, when homemade linen again became one of the basic materials used for making garments. During the World War II era, the middle generations in Hungary did not frequently abandon their traditional garments, for the most part wearing standard festive and everyday clothing for their age group. Among members of younger generations, however, people increasingly tended to shun traditional forms of dress, preserving custom mainly with regard to their choice of color and the wearing of headscarves. Until the middle of the 1950s, village dress preserved its "local community-marking function" (to use the words of Péter Szuhay). Clothing served as an indication of local patriotism, true or desired economic status, age group and often religion. There was a significant difference between everyday and holiday clothing, which often played a role in the preservation of values. Women's clothing was much more elaborate than men's clothing. Women wore shirts, bodices, vests, blouses, chemises, skirts, underskirts and aprons. The other prevalent form of dress reflected only a larger regional character and played no role in the preservation of values. Tradition was weaker, innovation was stronger, clothing was less layered, and only everyday and holiday garments remained distinct. The clothing of village men was much simpler. Flannel pants replaced the knee-breeches that had become common by the middle of the twentieth century, while homemade shirts, vests, overcoats and, in colder weather, jackets were also frequently worn clothing items. For the most part, village men wore boots, while the cap was an indispensable part of their attire.

The government's anti-peasant policies of the 1950s probably played a role in the rising tendency to abandon customary forms of peasant dress that occurred in Hungary at this time. Peasants increasingly discarded the external manifestations of their peasant affiliations in order to defend themselves from the negative effects of these policies. Moreover, materials used to make clothing became scarce and the production of homemade clothing materials also diminished. Traditional peasant clothing began to disappear at an increasing rate during the second half of the 1950s, when, almost without exception, members of the younger generation wore ready-to-wear clothing, and girls, contrary to custom, did their own hair. Older people soon followed this trend as well, while only the generation of peasants born before World War I continued to totally or partially adhere to traditional forms of dress. During the late 1960s and early 1970s, it became acceptable for village women to wear pants, while the frequency of headscarves declined significantly. It often took some time for urban women's fashion trends to appear in the village. "Beginning in the late 1950s, there was a clear tendency for the village population to integrate to a greater and lesser degree with the urban population in terms of clothing. During the first phase of this process, villages integrated with one another in terms of clothing—in the course of which inhabitants of 'dressed up' villages abandoned their traditional clothing—while in the second phase the village population began to integrate with society as a whole."[19] This process of adaptation and standardization was composed of several phases, each of which varied according to the latest fashion trends. It often took several years for these new clothing styles to become established in the villages. The specific clothing items that distinguished the various fashion "eras" during this period were, among others, the leather jacket, the trench coat, artificial fur, the dressing gown, leisure wear and the sweat suit. Clothing made from synthetic textiles became widespread in the villages in the 1970s. The "salesgirl" clothing fashion remained popular in many places. Among traditional clothing items, the kerchief and the apron remained common. With regard to men's clothing, the declining prevalence of knee-breeches and boots signaled the beginning of the integration phase in the transformation of village dress. During the second half of the 1970s, village men began to wear work clothing on an everyday basis. The gradual process of abandoning traditional village clothing culminated in the 1960s, primarily as a result of changes in lifestyle and the large-scale integration of women into the labor force. "The decomposition of peasant culture had become unstoppable by this time. During the 1960s, not only did villagers find it desirable to dispense with the external appearance of their peasant existence, but a great number of them left the peasantry altogether, bearing all the consequences of mobilization."[20] Very often, those who initiated changes in village dress belonged to the poorest segment of rural society, which was frequently forced to seek work elsewhere and was thus exposed to new styles and fashions. Pragmatism remained the determining factor in the selection of everyday clothing in the villages. Urban clothing fashions supplanted the multi-layered skirt. The body posture, movement and gait of villagers often changed along with the transformation in clothing style. By the 1960s, those who had not adopted the new forms of dress were regarded as backward. Beginning at the end of the 1960s, radio and television commercials presenting non-traditional living patterns exercised a significant impact on the village lifestyle in Hungary. Forced collectivization and excessive industrialization led to the disappearance of the convention-bound middle peasantry, thus breaking up the traditional village community, which became incapable of either incorporating into its culture or rejecting the great number of changes that were taking place at the time.[21] Beginning in the 1970s, a revival of certain forms of traditional village dress occurred in some rural regions of Hungary, partially as the result of external interest in folk costume. The desire to preserve tradition promoted a resurrection of obsolete village clothing, although mostly in terms of weekend and holiday dress.

Dress in general became much simpler during the second half of the twentieth century, when the demand for utility exercised an increasing influence over clothing production and styles. The design and selection of clothing became dependent on everyday activities and work, although distinctive holiday dress did endure. The difference in dress and clothing between various social strata underwent a gradual decrease. Occupational dress standards and regulations became more rigorous again beginning only at the end of the 1980s.

5. Nutrition and Dietary Habits

There were widespread food shortages in Hungary during the reconstruction period following World War II, when the majority of the country's population suffered from inadequate nutrition, particularly in Budapest and other major cities. Alimentation often remained substandard and invariable until the middle of the 1950s. During the 1960s and 1970s, food supplies stabilized, the selection of food gradually increased, and *per capita* consumption of food grew. Food consumption began to increase spectacularly at the beginning of the 1960s, reaching its post-war pinnacle in both quantity and quality during the middle of the 1980s. In 1987, *per capita* meat consumption was close to 80 kilograms a year, while annual *per capita* consumption of milk and dairy products was 170 kilograms.[22] Consumption of high-calorie foods was rooted in Hungarian culinary tradition, while the previously slow transformation in food consumption accelerated during the second half of the 1980s. The political opening that took place in Hungary during the 1980s and 1990s helped to modernize the country's dietary culture, prompting a transformation in Hungarian cuisine. Pork consumption decreased in proportion to other meats, while that of poultry grew. At the same time, consumption of animal fats underwent a sharp decline, while that of vegetable fats and oil gradually increased. The spread of modern dietary culture was, however, only partial.

Consumption of purchased food rose steadily in Hungary in the decades following World War II, particularly from the second half of the 1960s, while that of food produced at home underwent a commensurate decline. The following concrete example serves as an illustration of this transformation: between 1968 and 1979, retail grocery sales in the village of Atkár in northeastern Hungary rose by 275 percent.[23] It must be noted, however, that although the majority of food was acquired through retail trade, the function of self-sufficiency never disappeared completely, particularly with regard to vegetables, fruits and meat.

Per capita food and nutrient consumption between 1950 and 1990

Year	Meat, Meat Products and Fish	Milk and Dairy Products	Eggs, no./yr.	Fats	Flour and Rice	Sugar	Potatoes	Nutrients, kj/day
	kg/year			kg/year				
1950	34.9	99.0	85	18.7	142.1	16.3	108.7	11,317
1960	49.1	114.0	160	23.5	136.2	26.6	97.6	12,301
1970	60.4	109.6	247	27.7	128.2	33.5	75.1	12,971
1980	73.9	166.2	317	30.5	115.2	37.9	61.2	13,486
1990	75.8	169.9	389	38.6	110.4	38.2	61.0	14,164

Source: *Magyarország népessége és gazdasága – múlt és jelen* [Hungary's Population and Economy—Past and Present] (Budapest, 1996).

Workplace dining also became increasingly common in Hungary following World War II, when practically every major factory in the country established its own kitchen and provided its workers with lunch. At the same time, development of retail catering declined during the 1950s. Only the number of people's snack bars aimed at "ensuring that workers have access to a broad range of inexpensive provisions" increased dynamically during this period.[24] Self-service restaurants also became much more prevalent beginning in the late 1960s and early 1970s. The slow strengthening of the private sector beginning in the late 1970s produced a significant transformation in this domain. In accordance with the accelerating pace of life, American-style fast-food restaurant chains began to expand into Hungary beginning in the late 1980s.

Eating and dietary habits changed to a significant degree in Hungary during the second half of the twentieth century. Scarcity was characteristic of the 15 to 20 years following the end of World War II in this respect. Traditional eating and dietary patterns remained intact within the majority of rural families, while they underwent the most radical transformation among previously *petit-bourgeois* or middle-class families as a result of changes in living circumstances and conditions. It was, however, apparent that those who had joined the "new elite" attempted to follow these traditions. According to observers at the end of the 1950s, working-class households had begun to follow a pre-war bourgeois dietary regimen at this time. Beginning in the mid-1960s, even those segments of the population that had previously been subject to dietary privation became acquainted with the feeling of satiation. Thus quantitative food scarcity slowly diminished within the confines of Hungary's shortage economy, while qualitative changes became widespread only in the 1970s.

Disparities in income and discrepancies in dietary practices more or less persisted. Those earning lower incomes spent less on provisions, tending to purchase inexpensive and high-calorie foods that could be obtained in large quantities, while higher-income households were more disposed towards dietary innovation.

Preference for foods regarded as traditional Hungarian cuisine was prevalent in Hungary in the 1940s and 1950s regardless of social status. Rationality, not diversity, governed the formation of dietary practice and regimen at this time, when the nature and seasonality of the family breadwinner's employment largely determined the timing and content of meals. This circumstance applied especially to peasant households. Social changes, notably the increasing participation of women in the active workforce beginning in the 1950s, served to accelerate the transformation in lifestyle and dietary habits. As a consequence of these changes, the amount of time available for domestic duties decreased. It was partially for this reason that labor-intensive and time-consuming household tasks subsided into the background. According to an analysis from the early 1960s, "almost exclusively those families that received in-kind allowances of grain or flour continued to bake bread at home."[25]

Around 1960, it was still common in Hungary to consume large quantities of only one or two different types of food at each meal. Beginning in the late 1960s, the amount of food prepared and consumed underwent a significant increase. As a result of a decline in the active practice of religion and the increasing secularization of Hungarian society, sectarian dietary prescriptions, such as those connected to Lent, decreased in significance. Social and regional disparities in food consumption decreased, while urban and rural dietary customs merged in many respects. Pre-war differences in food consumption between various strata of rural society also began to fade at this time. Inter-generational discrepancies, however, persisted in the 1970s and 1980s, when older people continued to show a greater inclination to preserve traditional dietary customs than younger people did. Culinary practices connected to family celebrations retained their importance throughout all strata of Hungarian society. Festive meals served to distinguish the given holiday from any other day, while also performing a prestige function, even among those living under the most unfavorable income conditions.[26] Culinary and dietary traditions connected to various festive occasions, particularly weddings, also underwent a significant change. Foods that had previously been consumed only on weekends, holidays or other festive occasions were gradually incorporated into the weekday dietary regimen. Within the changed circumstances, dinner increasingly supplanted lunch as the main meal of the day.

The rapid expansion of technical innovations also contributed to these changes. There was a time lag between urban and rural households in their adoption of new kitchen technology during the 1960s and 1970s. A large number of peasant households continued to use iron stoves of various types, while many city households had begun to use gas or electric stoves. With the reconstruction of village homes, traditional kitchen chimneys were gradually phased out of use, disappearing almost completely by the 1970s. Whereas ice boxes were used to keep food cold in bourgeois/urban homes in the 1940s and 1950s, use of electric refrigerators became increasingly prevalent in the 1960s, expanding to include half of the households in Hungary by 1970. Freezers became more popular in Hungary beginning in the early 1980s. A similar transformation occurred during this period with regard to other kitchen appliances and technology: metal ovenware gradually replaced earthenware, while electric coffeemakers superseded stove-top coffee pots, among many other changes. Electric kitchen appliances became increasingly common in Hungary beginning in the early 1980s. These devices produced a significant change in the methods of preparing food and generally reduced the amount of time spent on cooking and other kitchen duties. The appearance and continual expansion in the selection of canned and frozen foods likewise served to facilitate kitchen work. At the same time, home canning became somewhat less common, particularly in urban households.

New items rarely appeared on grocery shelves in Hungary until the 1980s, while formerly common foods such as barley, millet and hominy began to disappear. The baking of bread at home essentially ended during the second half of the twentieth century. By the 1970s, homemade bread had become rare even in village households.[27] However, there were some "traditions," such as the "pig slaughtering custom," that remained part of everyday life in spite of the changing circumstances. During the 1970s and 1980s, even small kitchens in urban households were transformed into "butcher's shops." If this was not possible, rural relatives provided the space and ingredients. Meat-processing practices changed with the rapid spread of cooling and freezing at this time, when the use of smoking as a means of preservation decreased steadily.

For two decades following the end of World War II, income conditions and limited access to food prompted village residents to seek self-sufficiency in terms of provision. Until the end of the 1960s, peasant families followed established nutritional norms and customs. The seasonal fluctuations in the routine of rural labor dictated the pattern of daily life, including alimentation, within Hungary's traditional peasant society, which existed until the late 1960s. Peasants typically ate two meals per day during the winter and four meals per day during the summer. During the weeks preceding the start of spring agricultural labor, peasants usually began eating three abundant meals per day in order to fortify themselves in preparation for the hard work that lay ahead. Peasant meals were generally more nutritional and higher in calories during periods of heavy labor such as the planting and harvest seasons. The number of peasant meals then declined back to three per day during the autumn, with the exception of the grape harvest. "Food and drink served not only as sustenance to provide strength for work, but as a source of pleasure. There thus existed a distinction not only between substantial and insubstantial foods, but between those whose consumption provided a greater or lesser degree of pleasure."[28] In certain households, the production of food for private consumption was its primary undertaking. Grain, lard, bacon, meat, corn meal and vegetables were among the main foodstuffs produced in order to attain nutritional self-sufficiency in rural Hungary. As late as the 1950s, many peasants used the grain that they had grown to bake loaves of bread that were generally around 5 kilograms in weight. The most sumptuous meals were often served at weddings. According a study that Edit Fél and Tamás Hofer conducted in the village of Átány, a total of 30 houses, or around 120 people, were usually invited to wedding feasts. Feeding this number of people required meat from three sheep or a 100-kilogram calf and 30 chickens, four hectoliters of wine and eight loaves of bread each five to six kilograms in weight. A wedding feast typically consisted of chicken soup, mutton stew, corn meal mush with meat, or milk and pastries.

The rural custom of eating meals from a single bowl ended in the 1950s, when peasants generally began to use plates and forks. Aside from the latter, peasant dietary and nutritional practices essentially continued to follow the established patterns until the second half of the 1960s, when significant changes began to take place in this regard. The consumption of three meals per day gradually became standard in peasant households at this time. Cereals, potatoes and corn remained the staples of the peasant diet.[29] The calorie content of peasant food began to rise beginning in the 1960s, when increasing material prosperity made it possible for rural inhabitants to eat meals that were both more abundant and higher in fat. This transformation in dietary customs was most conspicuous at wedding feasts, where foods common in middle-class kitchens gradually supplanted traditional peasant fare.

Changes in social structure and lifestyle stood at the root of this departure from traditional dietary and nutritional customs. Work schedules at plants and factories operating in the agricultural sector differed greatly from traditional patterns of peasant labor, while a large number of those who had undertaken employment in factories began to eat at plant cafeterias. As a consequence, the rhythmic variation of meat, meatless, pasta and vegetable dishes diminished. Until the late 1960s, peasants customarily ate meat on two or three days per week, typically on Tuesday, Thursday and Sunday. The frequency of this practice decreased with the rise in meat consumption in the 1970s. The increasing prevalence of refrigerators prompted a transformation in the traditional modes of meat production and processing—the pig slaughter, salting and smoking—at the beginning of the 1980s, when peasants began to process only a small part of the meat derived from the two or three slaughters per year, freezing the rest. The custom of bartering finished products continues to this day in rural Hungary. Poultry farming practices, however, underwent a change in the middle and late 1960s. Whereas the initial slaughter of chickens had previously taken place during harvest season, the rising availability of hatchery-raised chicks during this period entailed an increase in the regularity of chicken consumption.

Beginning in the 1970s, "a merging process took place with regard to meat preparation. As a result, the highly spiced, fatty foods that had previously been characteristic of the Great Hungarian Plain, such as stews, goulash soup and pan-fried meats, became common throughout Hungary." Other dishes, such as pork or veal cutlets and fried meats, also became more popular at this time. The consumption of meat continued to reach its peak during holidays, when meals for guests typically consisted of three to six courses, all of them including meat, depending on the importance of the occasion and the number of guests.[30]

The baking of homemade bread had essentially ended throughout Hungary by 1970, thus freeing up half a day to a full day of labor that this task had required for other activities. The role of raised and baked dough in the village diet underwent a significant decrease. The consumption of brioche and tarts first began to decline at wedding feasts in favor of cakes, and then started to fall gradually on an everyday basis as well.

With regard to consumption of alcoholic beverages, wine and *pálinka* (fruit brandy) retained their leading position until the early 1970s, when beer consumption, which had been rising steadily since the end of World War II, also became significant, replacing the former drinks as those consumed on festive occasions such as weddings and during communal work.

Beginning in the 1970s, the level of retail provision underwent a continuous improvement, while the network of retail grocery stores expanded. However, the role of self-sufficiency in terms of provision remained significant in villages located in underdeveloped regions of Hungary where no such stores were built until the 1970s and 1980s.

Household data from the post-World War II period reflect changes in food consumption and dietary customs. A study conducted late in 1958 and early in 1959 recorded and compared urban and rural nutritional practices, classifying households according to whether their primary wage earners were worker-employees or peasants. The breakfasts of a large proportion of households in the worker-employee category consisted of liquids only, while those of every fifth peasant household contained no liquids at all. Fewer than 50 percent of households in both categories consumed complex breakfasts. Of those households from both categories that consumed liquids for breakfast, a total of 41 percent of worker-employee households and 53 percent of peasant households drank coffee with milk. The second-most commonly consumed breakfast beverage in urban households was tea, while that in village households was milk, although tea had started to become a more popular breakfast beverage in the latter type of household as well. At the end of the 1950s, high-calorie foods such bacon, fats and potatoes remained the primary elements in the breakfasts of peasant families, while butter, cheese and other dairy products played an equally prominent role in those of worker and employee families.[31] Lunch represented the principal meal in households within both categories. These freshly prepared, hot midday meals typically consisted of two courses—soup or stew and meat or boiled pasta. Urban households customarily consumed meat or dishes containing meat every other day, while those in villages ate such foods every third day. Meat consumed as a primary course in main meals was usually stewed or sliced and served with potatoes or dumplings. In village households, meat was most often served as a main course on Sundays, while among urban households meat was most often served as a main course on weekdays. Worker-employee households consumed stews as a second course every third day on average, slightly more often than peasant households. Both urban and rural households typically consumed pasta dishes every fourth day.

The importance and composition of the evening meal displayed relatively marked differences in both groups. More than half of worker-employee households ate cold dinners, while one third ate leftovers from lunch and only one tenth consumed freshly prepared hot meals. Among peasant households, one fifth ate freshly prepared dinners, while two fifths ate cold dinners and almost one third consumed leftovers from lunch.[32] The rhythm of agricultural work continued to determine the timing and composition of meals among peasant families even in the late 1950s, when cold lunches and hot dinners were most common during periods of more intensive labor such as the planting and harvest seasons.

In both groups, those with higher incomes ate more diverse and abundant meals than those with lower incomes did. Families with higher incomes consumed more meat, butter and cheese than those with lower incomes, whose diets were high in inexpensive fats, did. Poor families satisfied their calorie requirements through consumption of bread with lard and sugar or bread dipped in tea, milk or cocoa. There were significant contrasts between weekday, Sunday and festive meals in terms of both content and the number of courses. Sunday lunch usually consisted of a first course of meat soup, followed by one or several meat dishes and pastries.[33]

6. Customs and Leisure Time

Established customs with regard to social life, communal interactions and leisure time activities endured to a greater and lesser degree for a short time following World War II. Beginning in the second half of the 1940s, the Communist-controlled Ministry of the Interior continually "thinned out" the number of groups, clubs and associations operating in cities, towns and villages throughout Hungary, thus depriving them of the institutions necessary to run a community. By the beginning of the 1950s, the largely self-governing institutional system that had emerged during the first half of the century had essentially been abolished. From this time onwards, authorities took a dim view of participation in "events that were not centrally organized."

Farmers' associations and book clubs operated libraries, saloons and meeting halls in villages throughout Hungary in the middle of the twentieth century, providing rural society with a vehicle for exchanging opinions and pursuing self-education. The cultural centers established in their place served other purposes and principles. The institution of the Sunday promenade persisted until the 1960s. "Young people from the village strolled up and down the center of the village, while children played playground games. This custom endured in the Northern-Middle Hill Country [*Északi-Középhegység*]."[34] Taverns lost their broader social function during the 1950s, becoming simple drinking establishments. The complex, community-building institution of communal work persisted in essentially unchanged form until the end of collectivization in the 1960s and 1970s, when the type of labor performed during such joint undertakings shifted in relative proportion from agricultural tasks to house construction. Moreover, collective recreation and entertainment following the completion of communal work became less frequent. Inhabitants of both cities and villages spent an increasing amount of their leisure time with their families. (The policies of the Kádár era reinforced this trend to a significant degree.) The celebration of holidays underwent a significant change before 1956, when religious festivals such as Christmas, Easter and Pentecost were declared work days as part of the regime's effort to diminish their importance. Christmas and Easter were reinstated as public holidays during the Kádár era. Events connected to the economic year and social institutions, such as schools, were transformed significantly during this period. Politically and ideologically motivated intervention achieved the least impact with regard to family-based ceremonies and events signifying major turning points in life, such as births, baptisms and deaths. As a result of political pressure, an increasing percentage of weddings included no religious ritual. State "naming ceremonies" gradually began to supplant traditional baptisms, although to a lesser degree in rural areas than in the city. However, "social farewells" never gained widespread popularity as an alternative to Church funerals.

Among the customs connected to birth, providing mothers of newborn children with help, particularly during the first month after giving birth, remained prevalent in both urban and, to an even greater degree, rural areas. Close relatives helped mothers of newborn infants with housework and care for older children, while in villages they were often provided with food as well. Baptisms and, less frequently, the aforementioned naming holidays were also regarded as important events. Baptisms traditionally took place following Sunday religious services. The parents of the baptized child generally hosted a lunch for their relatives following the ceremony. Family ceremonies held in connection to a child's first Communion, confirmation and—until 1989 party-sponsored—school graduation were of similar importance. The farewell ceremony for high school graduates (*ballagás*) became the most significant of these events. Typically this ceremony "is followed by a lunch consisting of several courses, and giving the graduating student a significant gift has practically become obligatory. (In terms of the value of gifts, the *ballagás* has assumed second place behind weddings.) The importance of the *ballagás* ceremony reflects an increase in value placed on education."[35]

Social ethnographers remarked a significant change in wedding customs in Hungary during the second half of the twentieth century. Beginning in the late 1960s and early 1970s, the endogamous character of marriage began to diminish in most places, while the practice of choosing a partner from within the same socioeconomic, religious and nationality group also subsided. Following World War II, dances replaced traditional social events as the primary vehicle for prospective couples to meet. In the 1950s three or four young men visited unmarried young women, while beginning in the 1960s only suitors did so.

The primary functions of the wedding ceremony remained the introduction of the young couple to the community and the celebration of the beginning of their communal life, although it increasingly attained an economic function of providing the newlyweds with material support as well. Customs with regard to wedding gifts and endowments changed during this period, when in the village of Nógrádsipek, for example, furniture became a common dowry following World War II.[36] At the beginning of the 1970s, a total of 20,000 to 30,000 forints was collected during dances with the bride in Nógrádsipek. In addition to a steadily rising amount of money, wedding presents came to include valuable durable consumer items such as washing machines, vacuum cleaners, gas stoves and refrigerators, occasionally even cars or houses as well. Prior to 1945, family gifts and dowry constituted the major share of the marriage endowment, while wedding guests provided newlyweds with only smaller tokens of their best wishes. In the decades following World War II, the value of wedding gifts and the role of the dance with the bride rose steadily. The revenue-generating function of the latter began to grow in the 1960s, rising from 2,000–5,000 forints at the beginning of the decade to 20,000–50,000 forints by the mid-1970s.[37] Weddings were celebrations of abundance. Wedding hospitality was almost always bountiful regardless of social status. Wedding dinners typically consisted of four to six courses.

As a result of changes in lifestyle, weddings began to take place on weekends and became shorter beginning in the 1950s, when traditional games were eliminated from the ceremony. The parents of the bride and groom bore the expense of the wedding. The social function of wedding ceremonies also changed at this time, when families began to view them as a means of demonstrating their income and social status.

Traditional village weddings persisted in every major region of Hungary. In certain parts of the Northern-Middle Hill Country, for example, wedding festivities including several hundred guests were held at the homes of both the bride and the groom. Wedding preparations—erecting tents, cooking and baking—usually required seven to ten days.

> Wedding entertainment began with the taking of presents to the newlyweds on Thursday and Friday. Only witnesses took part in civil wedding ceremonies, which took place on Saturday morning. A delegation from the groom's house

> went to that of the bride that afternoon to collect the bride. After the guests were provided with hospitality, the bride bade farewell to her parents and proceeded to the church with the groom's delegation. The subsequent religious ceremony signified the true union of the young couple. Following the church ceremony, the bride went to the groom's house, while her relatives visited the house of her parents. Both parties received a multi-course dinner in the evening. At midnight, wedding guests reunited at the groom's house for the dance with the bride. In most instances, guests paid to dance with the bride. The value of the wedding gifts and money collected at the midnight dance with the bride exceeded the cost of the wedding to a significant magnitude. Guests viewed their gifts and contributions as an investment that they would recoup when their children were married.[38]

Society's relationship with death changed in Hungary as well during the second half of the twentieth century. As a result of changes in lifestyle and outlook, an improvement in health care and secularization, the "only certain thing in life" gradually receded into the hidden regions of consciousness. Particularly in the city, the act of death moved from the private domain to hospitals. Funeral customs also underwent a transformation at this time, when formal cemetery burials gradually replaced the home wakes that were common until the middle of the century. More impersonal, mechanical rituals aimed at stifling emotions connected with death replaced traditional death rituals. According to Edit Fél and Tamás Hofer, close and distant relatives, friends and colleagues visited the terminally ill daily or every other day. Following death, a close male relative of the deceased dressed in formal clothing reported the fact to both secular and religious officials.

> Even in the twentieth century, the toll of church bells informed local residents of the death of a community member in most Hungarian-speaking regions. The number of bell rings indicated the gender and age (adult or child) and occasionally even the social status of the person who

> had died. Following the ringing of the bells, neighbors and all of those who knew the deceased were obliged to go to the house of mourning that very same day to pay their final respects. [...] The knell of church bells summoned people to the funeral as well. In most villages, a wagon transported the coffin through the village to the cemetery, while the funeral procession followed behind on foot. The relatives and friends of the deceased generally dug the grave. [...] In funeral processions in Hungary, family members proceeded behind the coffin, followed by relatives, friends and neighbors. [...] The requiem took place a certain amount of time following the funeral.[39]

Among the ceremonies marking less significant turning points in life, the celebration of name days and birthdays remained an active custom and tradition, creating the opportunity for close relatives as well as a broader circle of acquaintances to meet and providing a means for strengthening and maintaining relations with friends and family.

Leisure time activities also changed along with transformations in lifestyle. A work-centric outlook did, however, continue to predominate in Hungary throughout the period. Thus "passing the time idly" continued to be frowned upon, particularly in peasant/village society. Even in the 1970s and 1980s, the urban notion of leisure time had not yet taken root in the villages.

* * *

The history of Hungary in the second half of the twentieth century was determined by the fact that after the end of World War II the country fell into the sphere of influence of the Soviet Union and it remained within this until the 1989–1990 change of regime. This meant not only that the sovereignty of the country remained limited, but also that the Communist Party, which had become dominant in 1948–1949, aimed for the Sovietization of the country's political, economic and social relations. The totalitarian policy of the Rákosi era was geared towards applying the Soviet system to Hungarian society, by indiscriminate means. However, the outbreak of the Revolution and War of Independence of 1956 strongly indicated the failure of this policy. Hungary was prevented only by the preponderance of Soviet weapons from seceding from among the countries of the Eastern bloc and striking out on its own path. János Kádár rose to power through the support of the Soviets who beat down the Revolution of 1956. The Communist Party and government, led by him, had managed to reconcile the Hungarian society to this situation, by applying severe retaliatory measures, by the 1960s. He made it clear that the only realistic possibility for the country was the acceptance of the Soviet political, economic and social model. It is significant in this that during the period of consolidation—from the middle of the 1960s until the end of the 1970s—the application of overt violence lessened, living conditions gradually improved, and the practice of total control over Hungarian society became less operable. The economy and society of Hungary modernized, but the human price to be paid for this was greater than necessary.

From the turn of the 1970s and 1980s, the socialist system—first in the economic and later on in the social sphere—fell into an increasingly deepening crisis. The desire for the change of the previously more or less accepted state socialist system was emerging among growing groups within Hungarian society. This desire led to the restoration of the democratic status and the sovereignty of the country, and the reintroduction of a market economy, by the end of the 1980s. In the 1990s Hungary—after a long detour and a lot of sacrifice—got back on the road that it should have traveled in the decades following 1945.

Notes

1 Péter Szuhay, "Az életmód változása a magyarországi falvakban" [Village Lifestyle Changes in Hungary], in István Orosz, Lajos Für and Pál Romány, eds., *Magyarország agrártörténete* [Hungary's Agrarian History] (Budapest, 1996), pp. 705–720.
2 Béla Falussy and György Vukovich, "Az idő mérlegén (1963–1993)" [Time on Its Balance], in Rudolf Andorka, Tamás Kolosi and György Vukovich, eds., *Társadalmi Riport, 1996* [Social Report, 1996] (Budapest, 1996).
3 Ágnes Vajda, "Nagyvárosi és falusi lakásformák" [Forms of Housing in the Big City and Village], *Statisztikai Szemle* 8–9 (1986): 852–863.
4 Central Statistics Office, *Mikrocenzus, 1996. A népesség és a lakások jellemzői* [Microcensus, 1996. Characteristics of the Population and Housing] (Budapest, 1997), p. 372.
5 Annamária Lammel, "Kontinuitás, átrétegződés, akkulturáció (Atkár 1920–1980)" [Continuity, Restratification and Acculturation (Atkár 1920–1980)], in Mihály Hoppál and Tamás Szecskő, eds., *Életmód: modellek és minták* [Lifestyle: Models and Patterns] (Budapest, 1984), pp. 310–345.
6 *Lakáskultúra* 4 (1970).
7 Katalin S. Nagy, *Lakberendezési szokások* [Interior Design Practices] (Budapest, 1987).
8 Lammel, "Kontinuitás, átrétegződés, akkulturáció," p. 335.
9 Szuhay, "Az életmód változása a magyarországi falvakban."
10 *Ibid.*
11 Lammel, "Kontinuitás, átrétegződés, akkulturáció," p. 338.
12 Péter Ambrus, *Dzsumbuj* [Tenement] (Budapest, 1988).
13 Sándor Horváth, "A magyar társadalom életmódjának változásai a fordulat éveiben 1945–1949" [Lifestyle Changes in Hungarian Society during the Years of Transition 1945–1949], in István Feitl, Lajos Izsák and Gábor Székely, eds., *Fordulat a világban és Magyarországon* [Transition in the World and in Hungary] (Budapest, 2000), pp. 347–367.
14 Nagy, *Lakberendezési szokások.*

15 Horváth, "A magyar társadalom életmódjának változásai a fordulat éveiben 1945–1949," p. 351.
16 Nagy, *Lakberendezési szokások.*
17 Katalin F. Dózsa, "Magyar divattörténet I–II. 1945–1958" [Hungarian Fashion History I–II. 1945–1958], *História* 4 (1991): 22–24 and *História* 5–6 (1991): 50–51.
18 *Ibid.*, p. 22.
19 Szuhay, "Az életmód változása a magyarországi falvakban," p. 714.
20 Ágnes Fülemile, "Megfigyelések a paraszti női viselet változásaihoz Magyarországon az első világháborútól napjainkig" [Observations Regarding the Changes in Dress among Peasant Women in Hungary from the First World War to the Present Day], *Ethnographia* 1–2 (1991): 50–78.
21 Judit Stefany, "Paraszti öltözködés Nógrád megye, 1960-as évek" [Peasant Dress in Nógrád County during the 1960s], *História* 5–6 (1986): 32–33.
22 *Élelmiszermérlegek 1970–1997* [Food Balance 1970–1997] (Budapest, 1998).
23 Lammel, "Kontinuitás, átrétegződés, akkulturáció," p. 336.
24 Imre Gundel and Judit Harmath, *A vendéglátás emlékei* [Memories of Hospitality] (Budapest, 1979).
25 István Makkay, *A bérből és fizetésből élő családok élelmiszerfogyasztásának néhány jellegzetessége* [Some Characteristics Regarding the Food Consumption of Families Living on Pay and Wages] (Budapest, 1962).
26 Ambrus, *Dzsumbuj.*
27 Eszter Kisbán, "Táplálkozáskultúra" [Nutritional Culture], in Iván Balassa, ed., *Magyar Néprajz IV. Életmód* [Hungarian Ethnology IV. Lifestyle] (Budapest, 1997), pp. 417–581.
28 Edit Fél and Tamás Hofer, *Arányok és mértékek a paraszti gazdálkodásban* [Degree and Proportion in Peasant Agriculture] (Budapest, 1997).
29 Kisbán, "Táplálkozáskultúra."
30 Szuhay, "Az életmód változása a magyarországi falvakban," p. 711.
31 *Étrendi Szokások* [Nutritional Habits] (Budapest, 1960).
32 *Ibid.*
33 *Ibid.*
34 Szuhay, "Az életmód változása a magyarországi falvakban," p. 715.

35 *Ibid.*, p. 719.
36 Zsuzsa Tátrai, "A lakodalmi szokások változás" [Changes in Wedding Custom], in Ágnes Szemerkényi, ed., *Nógrádsipek – tanulmányok egy észak-magyarországi falu folklórjáról* [Nógrádsipek—Studies on the Folklore of a Village in Northern Hungary] (Budapest, 1980).
37 Mihály Sárkány, "A lakodalom funkciójának megváltozása falun," *Ethnographia* (1983): 279–285.
38 Szuhay, "Az életmód változása a magyarországi falvakban," p. 719.
39 Attila Paládi-Kovács, ed., *Magyar néprajz VIII. – A társadalom* [Hungarian Ethnography VIII—Society] (Budapest, 2000).

BIOGRAPHIES OF KEY PERSONALITIES

Aczél, György (1917–1991)

Originally a building worker, he joined the Communist Party of Hungary [KMP] in 1935. He rescued several hundred Jews under the German occupation and Arrow Cross government of 1944. In 1946 he became Communist Party secretary in Zemplén County and then Baranya County. A National Assembly member in 1947–1949, he was arrested on July 6, 1949, and sentenced to life imprisonment in a trial subsidiary to the Rajk show trial, but released and rehabilitated in August 1954. He was a deputy minister of culture from April 1957 to February 1958, then first deputy minister of culture until April 1967, devising the "three Ts"—*tiltás* (prohibition), *tűrés* (toleration) and *támogatás* (support)—program of cultural policy. In April 1967 he was elected as Communist Party Central Committee secretary of the Science, Education and Culture Department. He joined the Politburo at the Tenth Congress of the Communist Party in November 1970. In 1974 he was relieved of all Central Committee positions, but retained his Politburo membership and became deputy prime minister, a post that he held until 1976 and again in 1980–1982. He was then made cultural secretary again at the June 1982 Central Committee meeting, but was dismissed in 1985. Finally, he became a National Assembly member for the third time in 1985–1990.

Andropov, Yuri Vladimirovich (1914–1984)

Soviet politician. A member of the Communist Party from 1939, he participated in the partisan movement in Karelia during World War II. He joined the administrative apparatus of the Central Committee of the Communist Party of the Soviet Union [CPSU] in 1951; he served as a diplomat at the Soviet Embassy in Budapest from 1953, and he was the ambassador of the Soviet

Union in Hungary from July 1954 to March 1957. He was head of the KGB from May 1967 to May 1982. He served as secretary of the Central Committee of the Communist Party from May 1982 and became its general secretary in November 1982; beginning in June 1983, in addition to his post as general secretary, he was also president of the Supreme Council of the Soviet Union.

Antall, József (1932–1993)

The prime minister in the first freely elected Parliament after the change of system was a teacher, librarian, museum curator and politician. After school, he obtained a teaching degree from the arts faculty of Budapest University along with a degree in librarianship and museum studies. He went to work in the National Library and then the Scientific Institute of Pedagogy. In 1955 he began to teach at József Eötvös Gymnasium (high school), heading the revolutionary committee there in the 1956 Revolution. He moved to Ferenc Toldy Gymnasium in 1957, but was banned from teaching on political grounds in 1959. After two years as a librarian, he joined the Semmelweis Museum, Library and Archives of Medical History when it opened in 1964, as a research fellow, then deputy director, and from 1974 director. He was delegated by the Hungarian Democratic Forum [MDF] to the Opposition Roundtable, which opened on March 22, 1989. He was elected overwhelmingly on October 21 that year to be MDF president and its candidate for prime minister. When his party won the 1990 general elections, he formed a coalition government with the Smallholders' and Christian Democratic groups on May 23, 1990. Although suffering from cancer by then, he was instrumental in establishing the political, economic and diplomatic conditions for the change of system. His government put through the requisite legislation and set the economy on a path of recovery. He died in office on December 13, 1993.

Apró, Antal (1913–1994)

Politician, originally a construction worker and house painter. He became a member of the Central Committee of the illegal

Hungarian Communist Party; as a member of the party apparatus, he directed labor union activities. Not much later he joined the highest organs of the Communist Party of Hungary [KMP], when he became a member of the Politburo and the Organizational Committee; between 1948 and 1952 he served as the general secretary of the National Committee of Labor Unions [SZOT], and then became minister of the construction materials industry. After the upheaval of June 1953 he lost his membership in the highest party organs; four months later, however, he returned to the Politburo and in November 1953 he was appointed as deputy chairman of the Council of Ministers. He attempted to go along with Imre Nagy's political direction but did not compromise his standing with Rákosi and his allies. From the end of 1954 until June 1956 he served as the president of the National Council of the Patriotic Popular Front [HNF], and on October 26, 1956, he was entrusted with the leadership of the Military Committee. In this capacity he favored a military *Putsch* and the reintroduction of dictatorship. On the same day he also became a member of the Directory of the Extraordinary Committee [Directorium], and he served as deputy president in Imre Nagy's government from October 27 to November 3. On November 2 he went to Tököl and then to Szolnok and took part in the formation of the Kádár government; he served as a member of the Provisional Executive Committee and became deputy president of the Council of Ministers when the new government was organized in May 1957. In 1971 he was elected as president of the Hungarian Parliament and for all practical purposes lost his political power; in 1980 he was left out of the Politburo and in 1984 he gave up his post as president of the Parliament; on March 8, 1989, he resigned his parliamentary mandate.

Badalik, Bertalan (1890–1965)

Catholic priest and diocesan bishop. He was consecrated as a priest in 1914; from 1929 he served as the parish priest of the St. Martin church parish in Szombathely; after 1946 he served as the national president of Actio Catholica, and the national leader of the Credo; from 1949 onwards he was Bishop of Veszprém. In 1957 he was interned at Hejce and allowed to return from there to Budapest only in 1964.

Balogh, István (1894–1976)
Roman Catholic priest and politician. From 1945 to 1947 he served as political state secretary in the Prime Minister's Office; in March 1947 he was elected as general secretary of the Independent Smallholders' Party [FKGP]; in June he left the Smallholders and founded the Independent Hungarian Democratic Party [FMDP]; in 1949 he became a member of the National Council and the Executive Committee of the Hungarian Popular Front for Independence; in 1950 he participated in the organization of the clerical peace movement; between 1949 and 1951 he was a member of the Hungarian Presidential Council; afterwards he withdrew from political public life.

Bán, Antal (1903–1951)
Social Democrat politician, originally an ironworker. Until 1943 he participated in the Social Democratic movement in Yugoslavia; between 1945 and 1948 he was a part of the leadership of the Social Democratic Party [SZDP] and a member of the Politburo; from 1945 to 1947 he was a deputy general secretary of the party; from June 1, 1945, to February 26, 1948, he was minister of industry. Then he was forced to leave the country and not allowed to return; he settled in Switzerland. His ashes were returned home in 1988.

Barankovics, István (1906–1974)
Journalist and Catholic politician. From 1943 he was the editor-in-chief of *Magyar Nemzet*; from 1945 he served as the general secretary of the Hungarian Popular Democratic Party [DNP] and was an editor of *Hazánk*; he became a representative in the Parliament after the elections of August 31, 1947; he emigrated on February 2, 1949, and settled in the United States.

Bata, István (1910–1982)
Military officer and politician. He attended military academy in Moscow from 1949 to 1950; from 1950 he was the chief of

staff of the Hungarian People's Army; from 1953 to 1956 he was minister of defense; also from 1953 to 1956 he served as a deputy member of the Politburo of the Hungarian Workers' Party [MDP]. At the end of October 1956 he fled to the Soviet Union; he returned to Hungary in September 1958 and became an executive with the Budapest Transport Company [BKV].

Berecz, János (b. 1930)

A party functionary, he gained a candidacy degree from the Soviet Communist Party's Academy of Social Studies in 1966, for a thesis on the 1956 Hungarian "Counterrevolution." He became deputy head of the Foreign Affairs Department of the Hungarian Communist Party Central Committee in 1972, its head in 1974, a Central Committee member in 1980, and editor-in-chief of *Népszabadság*, the party's central daily newspaper, in 1982. He became ideological secretary of the Central Committee in 1985, then chair of the Agitprop Committee, and a Politburo member in 1987. He withdrew from politics in June 1989 and went into business.

Beria, Lavrentiy Pavlovich (1899–1953)

Soviet politician from Georgia. A member of the Soviet Communist Party from 1917. From 1931 he was the first secretary of the Communist Party of Georgia and the Trans-Caucasian Territorial Commission of the Soviet Communist Party; from 1939 he served as an alternate member of the Soviet Communist Party's Political Office and its Executive Committee; from 1938 to 1953 he served as people's commissar for, and was later minister of, state security; from 1941 he was deputy president of the Council of People's Commissars. He was arrested and executed in 1953 as one of the arbiters of "criminal activities against the Party and the State."

Belkin, Mihail Ilyich (Fyodor) (1901–?)

Soviet lieutenant general. He was a member of the People's Commissariat for State Security [NKGB] and the Ministry of State Security [MGB]; he was already known by the Hungarian political police in Budapest in March 1945 as a member of the Allied Control Commission [SZEB]: Bielkin directed counterintelligence, which controlled the center at Baden bei Wien and the Kőhida Prison of Sopron. He arrived in Budapest with his state security "advisory" associates at the request of Rákosi at the beginning of July 1949. Along with several associates, Belkin was supposedly arrested before November 7, 1952; several versions exist of his subsequent fate but none has been officially confirmed (and consequently his execution has not been confirmed either).

Bibó, István (1911–1979)

Born in Budapest, he obtained a law degree at Szeged University, where he became close to Ferenc Erdei. He studied on state scholarships in Vienna in 1933–1934 and Geneva in 1934–1935. During the 1944 German occupation, he used his position as a ministry official to assist many Jews with safe-conduct passes. In February 1945 he was invited by Ferenc Erdei to take up the post of minister of the interior in the provisional government. He was a professor at Szeged University from July 1946 to 1950, becoming a member of the Hungarian Academy of Sciences in July 1946, as well as a professor and then director in 1946–1949 of the Central European Scientific Institute. In 1950 he was relieved of all posts and went to work as a librarian in the Szeged University Library. He took part in reviving the National Peasants' Party on October 31, 1956, and, as his party's nominee, joined Imre Nagy's coalition government as minister of state on November 3. On November 4 he and Zoltán Tildy held talks with Soviet forces occupying Parliament, drawing up a proclamation on that day as representative of the lawful government. On November 6 he wrote a study entitled "Draft for a Compromise Solution to the Hungarian Question" and left the Parliament building. Early in December he held talks with Indian Ambassador K. P. S. Menon and handed him a statement entitled "The Basic Principles of Hungary's State, Social and Political System and the Road to Political Development," formulated with Ferenc Farkas, Árpád Göncz, István Varga, Géza Féja and Áron Tamási. Early in 1957 he wrote a study called

"Hungary and the World Situation," which he managed to send to London, where it appeared. He was arrested on May 23, 1957, and sentenced by the Supreme Court on August 2, 1958, to life imprisonment. On his release under the 1963 amnesty, he went to work for the library of the Central Statistics Office. During his retirement, he organized his writings, made translations, and had some shorter work published. He died in Budapest on May 10, 1979. His funeral marked one of the first occasions when the various strands of the opposition appeared in public.

Biszku, Béla (b. 1921)

Turner's apprentice, party functionary, minister of the interior and Communist Party Central Committee secretary. He was appointed as minister of the interior on February 28, 1957, and was the main person responsible for carrying out the reprisals after the 1956 Revolution. As administrative Central Committee secretary from 1962, he oversaw all the armed forces and the judicial service. However, he was dismissed from all posts for his intrigues against Kádár in 1978, and worked as president of the audit committee of the trade union federation SZOT until his retirement.

Bulganin, Nikolay Aleksandrovich (1895–1975)

Soviet politician. He was minister of defense of the Soviet Union between 1953 and 1955, and served as prime minister from 1955 to 1958.

Churchill, Winston Spencer (1874–1965)

British politician, statesman and author. First lord of the Admiralty from 1911, he was minister of war and the air between 1918 and 1921, he served as chancellor of the exchequer from 1924 to 1929, and was again first lord of the Admiralty from September 3, 1939. He was the world's most persistent opponent of Hitler. From May 10, 1940, to July 28, 1945, he was prime minister and minister of defense. He was elected as prime minister of Great Britain once again after World War II, serving from 1951 to 1955. At the same time he received the Nobel Prize for Literature in 1953 for his historical works, above all for his six-volume study *The Second World War.*

Csornoky, Viktor (1919–1948)
Lawyer and diplomat; descended from a wealthy banking family, he was also the brother-in-law of Zoltán Tildy. A member of the Independent Smallholders' Party [FKGP] from 1942 onwards, after 1945 he was the secretary of the party in Budapest and a representative in the Parliament; at the start of 1946 he was named counselor to the Embassy in Washington and from the autumn of 1947 he was the Hungarian ambassador to Cairo. On November 15, 1948, he was sentenced to death and executed. Later the Executive Committee of the Supreme Court absolved him of the charge of any crime against the people, due to the lack of any evidence of a crime having been committed.

Czakó, Kálmán (1919–1985)
Jurist. From February 2, 1952, he was first deputy to the minister of justice; on July 4, 1953, the Parliament elected him as chief public prosecutor; he filled this post until August 4, 1955. According to *Magyar Közlöny* (the Hungarian official gazette) 1955: 83, Czakó was relieved of his duties as chief public prosecutor by the Presidential Council of the Hungarian People's Republic [NET]. Later he served in several capacities, including executive and legal positions, in the confectionary industry.

Czapik, Gyula (1887–1956)
Catholic prelate. Consecrated as a priest in 1910, he was Diocesan Bishop of Veszprém from 1939, and Bishop of Eger from 1943 to 1956. He served as a negotiator in Rome in 1948 after the nationalization of the Catholic schools; he was a member of the Peace Council and the leadership of the Patriotic Popular Front [HNF].

Déry, Tibor (1894–1977)
Writer and political figure. Member of the Communist Party of Hungary [KMP] in 1919. He joined the Hungarian Communist Party [MKP] in 1945. In 1952 József Révai severely criticized him for his novel *Felelet* [Answer]. After the dismissal of Imre Nagy as prime minister, Déry participated in the activities of

the writers' opposition movement: at the end of 1955 he was disciplined by the party, and after his participation in the press debate of the Petőfi Circle in June 1956 he was expelled from the party. He was an active participant in the October Revolution of 1956, and was sentenced to nine years in prison at a show trial in 1957, but was freed by an amnesty in 1960.

Dimitrov, Georgi Mikhaylov (1882–1949)

Bulgarian peasant politician. Until January 20, 1945, he served as the general secretary of the Bulgarian Popular Agricultural Alliance. In order to avoid arrest, he escaped abroad with American help and later settled in the United States.

Dinnyés, Lajos (1901–1961)

Independent Smallholders' Party [FKGP] politician. Minister of defense from May 14, 1947, to September 24, 1947, and also head of government from May 31, 1947, to December 10, 1948.

Dobi, István (1898–1968)

Smallholder, later Communist, politician. He was a member of the Independent Smallholders' Party [FKGP] from 1937, its managing director from 1943, and president of the party from May 1947. From 1945 to 1948 he was minister of state and minister of agriculture, and from 1949 to 1952 president of the Council of Ministers. From 1952 to 1967 he was president of the Executive Committee; from 1959 to 1968 he served as a member of the Central Committee of the Hungarian Socialist Workers' Party [MSZMP].

Donáth, Ferenc (1913–1986)

Born in Jászárokszállás, he entered Budapest University as a law student in 1930 and joined the illegal Communist Party in 1934. In 1937 he took part in organizing the March Front. He worked briefly in early 1945 for the newspaper *Szabadság*, before becoming in February a member of the land reform preparatory committee headed by Imre Nagy. He became a political state secretary of the Ministry of Agriculture and a member of the Hungarian Communist Party Central Committee. He was arrested on February 15, 1951, and sentenced to 15 years' imprisonment after a closed trial, but released in July 1954. He only became active again as deputy director of the Economics Institute in the late spring of 1956, becoming on November 1 a member of the Provisional Executive of the reconstituted Communist Party, the Hungarian Socialist Workers' Party. On November 4 he was one of those who fled to the Yugoslav Embassy and were later interned in Romania. He was the second accused in the Imre Nagy trial in June 1958, being sentenced to 12 years' imprisonment and then released under an individual act of clemency in April 1960. Thereafter he dealt with issues of agrarian history and economics. In 1977 he was among the first to declare solidarity with Charta '77. He also agreed to chair the editorial committee for the *Festschrift* in honour of István Bibó and supported efforts to create an independent press. He played a decisive role in facilitating dialog among variously oriented opposition groups critical of the system. His greatest contribution in this integrative role was made with the Monor Meeting on June 14–16, 1985. He died in Budapest in 1986.

Eörsi, István (1931–2005)

A Kossuth and Attila József prizewinning author, poet, translator and commentator, he espoused Marxist views early in life, even writing memorial verses on Stalin's death. By 1953 he was a reformer in his thinking and a follower of Imre Nagy. He was active in the 1956 Revolution mainly as a journalist. He was sentenced in December 1956 to eight years' imprisonment, but amnestied on August 20, 1960. Thereafter he became a freelance writer, living mainly by translations. In 1977–1982 he was a script writer with the Gergely Csiky Theater in Kaposvár, but was then dismissed for his opposition stance. He lived in West Berlin in 1983–1986, but returned to Kaposvár in 1989. After the change of system he was a member of the Alliance of Free Democrats until 2004, when he resigned on political grounds. He was a regular contributor to literary and political publications such as *Élet és Irodalom*, *Beszélő* and *Magyar Narancs*.

Erdei, Ferenc (1910–1971)

Writer, member of the Peasant Party, and later Communist politician. After completing his legal studies at the University of Szeged, he joined the movement to carry out research in the villages; he was one of the founders of the National Peasant Party [NPP], and its general secretary and president in 1945–1946; he was minister of the interior in the Provisional National Government, and then minister of state in 1948–1949. He was also minister of agriculture until 1953 and again in 1954–1955, and minister of justice in 1953–1954. From 1955 to 1956 he served as deputy chairman of the Council of Ministers, after 1957 he was director of the Institute for Agricultural Research, and from 1962 he was president of the Cooperative Scientific Council. From 1957 to 1964, as well as from 1970 to 1971, he served as the general secretary of the Hungarian Academy of Sciences [MTA] and from 1964 to 1970 as its vice-president.

Faragho, Gábor (1896–1953)

Military officer, officer on the General Staff and minister. From 1940 to 1941 he served as military attaché with the rank of general in Moscow; from November 1942 he was supervisor of the constabulary; in 1943 he was promoted to vice-field marshal; in 1944 he was a part of the delegation that Horthy sent to Moscow to negotiate an armistice; then he served as the minister of food in the Provisional National Government until June 21, 1945, after which he was sent into retirement.

Farkas, Mihály (1904–1965)

Born in Abaújszántó, he took part in the Spanish Civil War in 1936–1937 and then became a second secretary of the Communist Youth International in Moscow. He arrived in Szeged from Moscow on November 5, 1944, with Ernő Gerő, József Révai and Imre Nagy, to set up the Central Committee of the Hungarian Communist Party, becoming a Central Committee secretary on May 11, 1945, and later a member of the Politburo, with duties that included supervising the army and police. In 1948 he became a member of the Joint Executive

Committee of the Party of Hungarian Communists and the Social Democratic Party. As minister of defense from 1948, he directed the forced development of the Hungarian armed forces. In April 1951 he headed the Politburo investigation against János Kádár, Gyula Kállai and Gábor Péter. However, he was removed from all his positions in July 1953. In March 1956 a Central Leadership investigation of him began. He was then excluded from the party in June for the part that he had played in illegal acts, and demoted from the army rank of field marshal to that of private. On October 13, 1956, he was arrested along with his son Vladimir. He was sentenced on March 23, 1957, to six years' imprisonment, but a retrial on April 19 led to the sentence being increased to 16 years. He was freed under an individual act of clemency on April 5, 1960, and died in Budapest on December 5, 1965.

Fehér, Lajos (1917–1981)

Born at Szeghalom, he became a politician and journalist. He was active in the March Front and wrote for the newspaper *Szabad Szó*, joining the Hungarian Communist Party in 1942. In 1944–1945 he was an organizer of partisan groups in Budapest. In 1945–1947 he was deputy head of the political department at Budapest police headquarters, then an editor of the newspaper *Szabad Föld* in 1947–1954. He was an editor of the central party daily newspaper *Népszabadság* from 1956 to 1959, having played an important part in reorganizing the Communist Party as the Hungarian Socialist Workers' Party in 1956. He then held party positions and served as deputy prime minister in 1962–1974. He remained a Politburo member from 1957 to 1975, and was president of the Hungarian Partisans' Association from 1959 until his death.

Field, Noel Haviland (1904–1970)

American Communist. On May 11, 1949, he was hauled from Prague to Budapest; although his name appeared several times at the Rajk trial and in later trials in the surrounding countries, he was never formally charged; on October 11 he was transferred to the Conti Street Prison, from which he was freed in November 1954, and in December the same year he was granted Hungarian citizenship.

Fischer, József (1901–1995)

Architect. After World War II he was the president of the Budapest Council of Public Works. He participated in the Aster Revolution of 1918 and joined the Red Army during the time of the Hungarian Soviet Republic; in 1932 he came into contact with several members of the Hungarian Social Democratic Party [MSZDP] and joined the party. For incitement against social classes, he was sentenced to a one-month suspended sentence. After regaining his freedom, he continued his association with the Social Democrats and ran as a candidate of the party in the parliamentary elections of 1939; at this time he was also elected as president of an architectural association, which had been established at the initiative of the Hungarian Social Democratic Party. From January 1946 he was government commissioner for reconstruction and later he served as the president of the Council for Reconstruction of the Capital until 1948; after that year he was excluded from public life. During the Revolution of 1956 his home hosted the meetings of the Social Democrat politicians, and he was elected to be one of the leaders of the newly reconstituted Social Democratic Party [SZDP]. From November 2 he was a minister of state in Imre Nagy's government. In 1965 he emigrated to the United States and settled in New York; he returned permanently to Hungary in 1978.

Fock, Jenő (1916–2001)

He began work as a technician at the Ganz Wagon Factory in 1930 and joined the Communist Party in 1932. On January 27, 1951, he was appointed as deputy minister of foundries and engineering. He completed the course at the Economic and Technical Academy. In 1955 he became a secretary of the Central Council of Trade Unions and in July 1956 an alternate member of the Communist Party Central Leadership. In November 1956 he became a member of the Provisional Executive of the

Hungarian Socialist Workers' Party, and in February 1957 the Central Committee secretary for economic policy. In June that year he joined the Politburo and remained a member until 1980. In September 1961 he was relieved of his post as a Central Committee secretary and was appointed as deputy prime minister. He played an active part in introducing the New Economic Mechanism. He was retired on May 15, 1975, but remained a Politburo member until 1980 and a Central Committee member until 1989. He was a member of Parliament in 1945–1947, 1958–1967 and 1971–1985. At the May 1988 plenary of the Central Committee, it was he who proposed that János Kádár should retire as general secretary and become party president instead. After 1989, he lived in retirement until his death.

Gerő, Ernő (1898–1980)

Born Ernő Singer in Terbegec (Trebušovce), he joined the Hungarian Communist Party in 1918. In the 1920s and 1930s he found his way onto the Executive Committee of the Communist International and did party work in France, Belgium, Spain and Portugal. He took part in the talks with the Hungarian armistice delegation that visited Moscow on November 11, 1944. Then he, Mihály Farkas, József Révai and Imre Nagy moved to Szeged, where they set up the Central Leadership of the Hungarian Communist Party. In December 1944 he was elected as a member of the National Supreme Council and in May 1945 he took the commerce and transport portfolio, becoming minister of transport after the elections. In December 1948 he was made minister of finance and in June 1949 president of the People's Economic Council. Following the arrest of László Rajk, he, Rákosi and Farkas formed a secret supreme "troika." On November 14, 1952, he became deputy prime minister, but after the June 1953 conference of parties in Moscow, he was dismissed as deputy general secretary of the Central Leadership, although he was voted onto the Politburo. He was then deputy prime minister and minister of the interior in the first Imre Nagy government. The plenary of the Central Leadership in July 1956 elected him as first secretary – it was he who requested armed Soviet intervention from Khrushchev on October 23, 1956. Two days later he was dismissed by the Central Leadership on the proposal of Mikoyan and Suslov, the Soviet envoys who had arrived in Budapest, and on October 29 he and his family were taken to Moscow. The Central Committee moved in February 1957 that Gerő should never return to Hungary, but in March his exile was reduced to a term of one year. He actually returned in 1960, and lived as a pensioner by doing translations. He died in Budapest on March 12, 1980.

Gimes, Miklós (1917–1958)

Born in Budapest, he was called up for labor service in World War II but escaped in the summer of 1944 and joined Tito's partisans in Yugoslavia. Back in Budapest in January 1945, he joined the Communist Party and worked for the communist daily newspaper *Szabad Nép*. After 1953, he backed Imre Nagy's reform policy. Speaking at a party meeting in May 1955, he called for reopening of the Rajk and other show trials, for which he was expelled from the party and dismissed from his job. He returned to *Szabad Nép* in October 1956, and produced with friends a daily paper, *Magyar Szabadság*, during the 1956 Revolution. He became a leading figure in the intellectual opposition after November 4, editing an illegal paper called *Október Huszonharmadika* and organizing an opposition Hungarian Democratic Independence Movement. He was arrested by the Soviets in Budapest on December 5, 1956. At the Imre Nagy trial, the People's Judicial Council of the Supreme Court chaired by Ferenc Vida sentenced him to death on June 15, 1958, for organizing and leading espionage, without possibility of appeal. The sentence was carried out at dawn on June 16.

Gomułka, Wladislaw (1905–1982)

Polish politician. Deputy prime minister from 1943 to 1948; general secretary of the Polish Workers' Party and the Unified Polish Workers' Party [LEMP] from 1956 to 1970; he was also the first secretary of the Unified Polish Workers' Party.

Gordon, Ferenc (1893–1972)
Businessman and politician. A member of the Independent Smallholders' Party [FKGP] from 1934; a representative in the National Assembly from November 1945; minister of finance from 1945 to 1946; ambassador to Bern from 1946 to 1947; he resigned in June 1947 and did not return to Hungary.

Grebennik, Kuzma Evdokimovich (1900–1974)
Russian officer, originally a miner. He fought in the civil war, and participated in the Battle of Hassan Lake between the Soviet Union and Japan; his journal on these events was published in 1978 in Vladivostok under the title *Hassan Dnevnik*. During World War II he commanded the 37th Rifle Regiment of the Second Byelorussian Front as a brigadier general; for his actions during World War II he received the decoration "Hero of the Soviet Union." He commanded the Soviet troops occupying Budapest beginning on November 4, 1956, by then as a brigadier general of the guards. In 1961 he retired as a major general. He is buried in the Baykovo Cemetery in Kiev.

Grósz, Károly (1930–1996)
Born in Miskolc, he joined the Communist Party in 1945 and became Borsod County secretary of the National Association of Hungarian Youth in 1948. He became a political staffer of the Central Leadership in 1950, but was called up in the same year for military service, where he completed the course at the Petőfi Academy for Political Officers. On his demobilization in 1954, he went to work for the Borsod County Party Committee. On October 26, 1956, he forbade journalists to report on the events in the 1956 Revolution, and on October 28 had the Kossuth coat-of-arms removed from the banner of the local daily newspaper *Észak-Magyarország*. On November 4 he became a member of the County Revolutionary Worker–Peasant Committee and head of the party apparatus in Borsod County. He became secretary of the Party Committee of Hungarian Radio and Television in 1962. He held various other party offices in 1973–1987, including membership of the Central Committee

(1980–1989) and the Politburo and Political Control Committee (1985–1989). He became prime minister on June 25, 1987, and also general secretary of the Communist Party in May 1988. He was a member of the party Presidium in June–October 1989, and from December 1989 a Central Committee member of the reorganized Hungarian Socialist Workers' Party.

Groza, Petru (1884–1958)

Romanian statesman. He was a member of the Transylvanian governing council from 1918 to 1919; he served in the Romanian Parliament from 1920 to 1927; he was a minister between 1921 and 1922 and between 1926 and 1927; he became Romanian president in March 1945, and he was president of the Executive of the Great National Assembly from 1952 to 1958.

Grősz, József (1887–1961)

Catholic priest and archbishop. A bishop from 1929, the apostolic governor of the Bishopric of Szombathely from 1936, and a member of the Upper House beginning in 1939, he became Archbishop of Kalocsa in 1943. In 1950 he signed the agreement between the state and the Catholic Church. He was imprisoned based on false charges from 1951 to 1955. From 1957 he served as the president of Opus Pacis, a Catholic peace organization, and was a member of the National Peace Council and the National Council of the Patriotic Popular Front [HNF].

Gyöngyösi, János (1893–1951)

Smallholder politician. From 1944 to 1951 he was also a high school teacher, bookseller in Békéscsaba and newspaper editor. From December 22, 1944, to 1947 he served as minister of foreign affairs; in 1946–1947 he was part of the Hungarian delegation to the Paris Peace Conference; from September 1947 he was the national general secretary of the Independent Smallholders' Party [FKGP]; from 1947 to 1951 he was president of the Center for Monetary Institutions.

Hammarskjöld, Dag (1905–1961)

Swedish diplomat. He obtained humanities, business and legal degrees at the University of Uppsala, served as a secretary in the Swedish National Bank, and was later an administrative state secretary in the Ministry of Finance and at the same time from 1941 to 1948 president of the Swedish National Bank. From the beginning of 1945 he was an economic and financial adviser to the government: he coordinated the government's programs designed to alleviate the economic problems in the post-war period. He joined the Ministry of Foreign Affairs in 1947, where he was responsible for financial matters; in 1949 he was named general secretary of the Ministry of Finance; in 1951 he joined the government as minister without portfolio, but in reality he was the deputy minister of foreign affairs. In 1949 and again between 1951 to 1953 he represented Sweden at the United Nations; from 1953 until his death he served as the secretary-general of the United Nations. On the night of September 18, 1961, in South Africa he was the victim of an airplane accident under circumstances that remain unclarified to this day; after his death he was awarded the Nobel Peace Prize in 1961.

Hamvas, Endre (1890–1970)

Catholic priest. After serving in several ecclesiastical capacities he became diocesan Bishop of Csanád, and was Archbishop of Kalocsa from 1964 to 1970.

Haraszti, Sándor (1897–1982)

Journalist. He served in the Red Army during the Hungarian Soviet Republic of 1919, lived abroad during the 1920s and returned home in 1929, after which he took part in the illegal Communist movement and spent time in jail. From 1945 to 1948 he edited the daily newspaper *Szabadság* and was later the deputy chief of the Communist Party's Department of Agitation and Propaganda; beginning in 1949 he was the editor of the Athenaeum Publishing House. He was arrested in 1950 and sentenced to death at a show trial in 1951; however, the sentence was commuted to life imprisonment. He was freed from imprisonment during the summer of 1954, and became one of the leaders of the opposition group within the party that clustered around Imre Nagy. In the autumn of 1956 he became acting president of the National Organization of Hungarian Journalists [MÚOSZ]; after the formation of the Hungarian Socialist Workers' Party [MSZMP], he became a member of the Administrative Committee [Intéző Bizottság] and received the position of editor-in-chief of *Népszabadság*. On November 4 he fled with Imre Nagy to the Yugoslav Embassy and was later deported to Romania with the Nagy entourage. On August 9, 1958, he was sentenced to six years in prison, although he was freed by an amnesty in April 1960. Until 1980 he worked in the editorial office of the Lexicons of the Akadémiai Kiadó (the publishing house of the Hungarian Academy of Sciences).

Házi, Árpád (1908–1970)

Politician. In 1945 he became the vice-lord lieutenant of Pest County. From 1946 to 1956 he was a member of the Hungarian Communist Party [MKP], then the Hungarian Workers' Party [MDP] and the Central Leadership. He was president of the State Center for Supervision [ÁEK] from 1949–1951; he served as minister of the interior from 1951 to 1952 and deputy prime minister until July 1953, at which time he once again became president of the ÁEK. From 1955 to 1956 he was minister of state supervision. From 1951 to 1953 he was an alternate member of the Politburo; from the beginning of 1957 to 1963 he was a leader of a department in the Hungarian Socialist Workers' Party [MSZMP] of Pest County Commission.

Hegedüs, András (1922–1999)

Politician and sociologist. From 1945 to 1947 he was the national secretary of the Hungarian Democratic Youth Organization [MADISZ], from 1948 to 1950 leader of the Agricultural and Labor Union Policy Department of the Central Leadership of the Hungarian Workers' Party [MDP], from 1951 to 1956 a member of the Central Leadership of the MDP and the Politburo, from 1951 to 1953 secretary of the Central Leadership, from 1952 to 1953 minister of the state farms, from 1953 to 1955 the first deputy president of the Council of Ministers, and also during 1953 and

1954 minister of agriculture, from April 18, 1955, to October 24, 1956, president of the Council of Ministers, and until October 27, 1956, first deputy prime minister. From October 28, 1956, to September 1958 he stayed in the Soviet Union; after his return home he returned to professional activities: from 1958 to 1961 he was a senior member of the Institute for Economic Studies of the Hungarian Academy of Sciences [MTA], from 1961 to 1963 deputy president of the Central Statistics Office [KSH], from 1963 to 1968 director of the Committee on Research of the MTA, and from 1968 to 1973 a senior member of the Research Committee of Industrial Economy. He was expelled from the Hungarian Socialist Workers' Party [MSZMP] in 1973. In 1982 he was allowed to teach at the Economics University.

Hitler, Adolf (1889–1945)

German politician and dictator, originally from Austria. Leader of the German National Socialist Workers' Party from 1920 to 1945; chancellor in 1933–1934; commander-in-chief of the Defense Forces from 1938 to 1945; "leader" [Führer] and again chancellor from 1934 to 1945.

Horthy, Miklós (Nagybányai) (1868–1957)

Vice-admiral and head of state. From 1909 to 1914 he was *aide-de-camp* to King and Emperor Francis Joseph; in 1918 he was the last commander-in-chief of the Austro-Hungarian fleet; in the spring of 1919 he was minister of war in the opposition's government in Szeged and commander-in-chief of the National Army. From March 1, 1920, to October 16, 1944, he was Regent of Hungary. After the failure of Hungary's attempt to drop out of the war and the seizure of power by the Arrow Cross, he lived under house arrest in Germany and fell into American captivity at the end of the war, and thus was a witness at the Nürnberg trials. After his release he lived in Estori, Portugal, until his death; his ashes were returned to Hungary and buried at Kenderes on September 4, 1993.

Illyés, Gyula (1902–1983)

Writer, poet and editor. He was the most highly respected of the popular writers; in 1945–1946 he was one of the leaders of the National Peasant Party [NPP]. With the exception of the days surrounding the Revolution of 1956, from 1948 to the 1960s he lived removed from public life.

Janza, Károly (1914–2001)

Union leader and politician, originally an ironworker. In 1932 he joined the illegal Communist Party; in 1945 he became the provisional president of the Trade Union Committee of the Ganz Shipyard and became the first worker director of the yard after it was nationalized in 1948. He became a soldier and reached the rank of brigadier general, but then resigned from the military. In January 1951 he was named deputy minister of defense, and on October 27, 1956, he became minister of defense; he served in this capacity until November 3, 1956.

Justus, Pál (1905–1965)

Poet and politician. From 1945 he was a member of the leadership of the Social Democratic Party and director of the party's propaganda department; he was also one of the editors of the periodical *Szocializmus*, a member of the Central Leadership of the Hungarian Workers' Party from 1948 to 1949, and vice-president of Hungarian Radio from 1948 to 1949. He was condemned to life imprisonment during the Rajk show trials; after his release in 1955 he became a translator and an editor of the Corvina Publishing House.

Kádár, János (1912–1989)

He was born János Csermanek in Fiume (Rijeka), but his mother, dismissed as a domestic servant, took him to her parents' home in Kapoly, Somogy County, before moving in 1918 to Budapest, where he did eight years of elementary and civil school. He finished his apprenticeship as a typewriter mechanic in 1930 and joined the Communist Party in 1931. He was arrested in November 1931; although he was released for lack of evidence, he was placed under police surveillance. Rearrested in

1933, he was sentenced in October to two years' imprisonment for communist agitation. He worked as a laborer after his release and joined the work of the Social Democratic Party. He became a member of the Budapest Committee of the Communist Party in the spring of 1941 and of its Central Committee in May 1942, a Central Committee secretary in December 1942, and leading secretary in February 1943. After dissolution of the Communist International, the Hungarian Communist Party was dissolved, reemerging as the Peace Party. He was elected as a Central Leadership secretary of the Communist Party in April 1945, and a Politburo member in May. In 1946 he was appointed as deputy general secretary. Instrumental as minister of the interior from 1948 to June 1950 in preparing the Rajk trial, he was himself arrested by the secret police in the spring of 1951 and stripped of all positions. The Supreme Court sentenced him in December 1952 to life imprisonment, but he was rehabilitated and freed in July 1954. He rejoined the Central Leadership at the July 1956 plenary, where he was elected as a Politburo member and later second secretary of the Central Leadership. On October 25, 1956, he was elected as first secretary of the Hungarian Workers' Party Central Leadership and on October 26 took a seat on the Directory, which replaced the Politburo. On October 28 he became a member of the Hungarian Workers' Party Presidium formed on that day. On October 31 he became a member of the Executive of the successor Hungarian Socialist Workers' Party, but on November 1 he and Ferenc Münnich went over to the Soviets and left Hungary. He then took part in meetings of the Soviet Communist Party Presidium in Moscow on November 2–4, was charged by the Soviet leaders with the task of forming a Hungarian Revolutionary Worker–Peasant Government, and was flown back on the same day by military plane to Szolnok. On November 7 he was taken by the Soviet army to Budapest, where head of state István Dobi named him prime minister. On February 26, 1957, he was chosen as president of the Provisional Central Committee of the Hungarian Socialist Workers' Party.

The national party conference in June 1957 elected him as Central Committee first secretary and a Politburo member. He resigned as prime minister on January 28, 1958, and became minister of state, but returned as premier from September 13, 1961, to June 30, 1965. He remained first secretary and then general secretary of the Communist Party Central Committee until the national party conference in May 1988, when he was also dropped from the Politburo, but elected as president of the party. He was relieved of his Central Committee membership and the presidency on health grounds at the May 1989 Central Committee meeting. He died on July 6, 1989, after a long illness.

Kállai, Gyula (1910–1996)

Communist politician. One of the organizers of the March Front and the Commission for Historical Remembrance. During the German occupation he represented the Communist Party in the Executive Committee of the Hungarian Front. In 1945 he became an undersecretary in the Prime Minister's Office, then until 1947 he served as an undersecretary for communication; from 1946 to 1948 he led the Cultural Department of the Central Leadership of the Hungarian Communist Party and then from 1948 to 1949 the Office of the President of the Republic; then he served as minister of foreign affairs from 1949 to 1951. Arrested in 1951 under false charges, he was freed in 1954 and became leader of the Main Directory of Publishers. Later he became deputy minister of people's education, and from 1957 minister of education and later state secretary; from 1960 to 1964 he served as the deputy president of the Council of Ministers, and then until 1967 was its president.

Kállay, Miklós (1887–1967)

Politician and landowner in Nagykálló. From 1929 to 1931 he served as political state secretary in the Ministry of Commerce; from 1931 he was a representative in the Parliament; in 1935 he followed Bethlen and left the Unity Party; in 1937 he became a member of the Upper House. From March 9, 1942, to March

19, 1944, he served as Hungary's prime minister, and in the meantime was also minister of foreign affairs from May 1942 to July 1943. Instead of pursuing a one-sided pro-German policy, he attempted to find accommodation with the Anglo-Saxon powers. After the war he settled first in Italy and then from 1954 in the United States.

Kardos, László (1918–1980)
Ethnographer. As a ministerial commissioner he participated in the land reform of 1945; he was director of the István Györffy College and from 1946 to 1948 the general secretary of the National Association of People's Colleges [NÉKOSZ]. After October 23, 1956, he was one of the leaders of the Revolutionary Committee of the Hungarian Intellectuals. In 1957 he helped to transmit Imre Nagy's writings to the West and was arrested during that year; in 1958 he was condemned to life imprisonment at a show trial, but was freed under amnesty in 1963.

Kelemen, Gyula (1897–1973)
Social Democrat politician and state secretary. He was active in the Újpest organization between the two world wars; from 1939 to 1940 he was a member of the national executive committee of the Social Democratic Party [SZDP]; after 1945 he again became a member of the national party leadership; he was the municipal representative of Újpest and Pest County; from 1945 to 1948 he served as a representative in the National Assembly, then in the Parliament, and became state secretary for industrial affairs. In January 1948 he was arrested on trumped-up charges and sentenced to life imprisonment, but was freed under amnesty in 1956. On October 31, 1956, he was elected as general secretary of the newly reconstituted SZDP; On November 4–5, 1956, he was a minister of state; this led to his being was arrested again. He was rehabilitated in the 1963 amnesty.

Kertész, István (1904–1987)
Jurist, diplomat and diplomatic representative. Even during the war he worked on the preparations for peace; after 1945 he was leader of the section in the Ministry of Foreign Affairs charged with drawing up the peace agreement. From 1946 he was the

general secretary of the Hungarian peace delegation in Paris, and in 1947 the Hungarian ambassador to Rome. On September 12, 1947, he left his post and settled in the United States.

Kéthly, Anna (1889–1976)

Social Democrat politician, and employee in a private firm. From 1922 to February 1948, when she was expelled from the party, she was a member of the party's national leadership and its representative in the Parliament. She was also the editor-in-chief of *Világosság* and president of the National Committee for the Organization of Women. In 1950 she was illegally jailed, and later, from 1954 to the summer of 1956, she was held under house arrest. She became president of the newly reconstituted Social Democratic Party [SZDP] on October 31 and state secretary on November 3, 1956. However, she was forced to emigrate in November 1956.

Khrushchev, Nikita Sergeyevich (1894–1971)

Soviet politician. A member of the Communist Party from 1918; general secretary of the Central Committee of the Ukrainian Communist Party and the party committees for Kiev County and the city of Kiev from 1938 to 1947; president of the Council of the People's Commissars for the Ukrainian Socialist Soviet Republic from August 1944 to December 1949 (also president of the Council of Ministers from March 1946). From December 1949 until March 1953 he was secretary of the Central Committee of the Communist Party of the Soviet Union [CPSU] and at the same time the general secretary of the party's Moscow municipal commission; from March 1953 he was the general secretary of the Central Committee of the CPSU, and simultaneously and until October 1964 the president of the Council of Ministers of the Soviet Union. The October 1964 meeting of the Central Committee of the CPSU stripped him of his posts as general secretary and president of the Council of Ministers.

Király, Béla (b. 1912)

Military officer and historian. He graduated from the Ludovika Military Academy, and served as a professional military officer from 1935 onwards; in early 1946 he joined the newly organized army and became a lieutenant colonel; from 1950 he was commander of the Academy of National Defense, with the rank of major general. He was arrested in 1951 and sentenced to death on trumped-up charges; however, on appeal a high court reduced his sentence to life imprisonment, and he was freed from prison in early September 1956. On October 30, 1956, he became the chairman of the Revolutionary Military Committee; on October 31 he was named as commander of the troops in Budapest and the commander-in-chief of the National Guard. On November 10 his troops were still engaging the Russians at Nagykovácsi. From 1958 he was the president of the Alliance of Hungarian Freedom Fighters. He left Hungary, settled in the United States and carried out research in military history, becoming a university professor. He returned to Hungary in 1989 and served as a representative in the Parliament from 1990 to 1994. Today he is a retired colonel general.

Kiselyov, Yevgeny Dimitrievich (1908–1963)

Soviet diplomat. From 1949 to 1954 he was the Soviet ambassador to Hungary, from 1954 to 1955 and from 1959 to 1962 he was departmental leader in the Ministry of Foreign Affairs, from 1955 to 1959 he was ambassador to Egypt, and from 1962 to 1963 he served as deputy secretary-general of the UN.

Kodály, Zoltán (1882–1967)

Born in Kecskemét, he arrived in Budapest in September 1900 to study Hungarian and German at university, while also studying composition at the Academy of Music, where he wrote his doctoral dissertation in 1906 on the strophic structure of Hungarian folksongs. There he examined the phonographic recording collection of Béla Vikár, which decided him on taking up folksong collection in Hungarian villages. While researching, he met Béla Bartók, who remained a lifelong friend. The two composers jointly published in 1906 a collection of ten folksongs each, arranged with piano accompaniment. He was appointed as Academy professor of musical theory in 1907 and composition in 1908. In August 1910 he married Emma Sándor.

In just two months in 1923 he composed *Psalmus Hungaricus* to mark the fiftieth anniversary of the merger of Pest, Buda and Óbuda as Budapest. This made him a leading Hungarian composer overnight, marked by the award of a Corvin Wreath in 1930. Alongside his orchestral compositions in the 1930s, he managed to bring Hungarian folksong onto the concert and opera stage. He retired in 1942 but continued to teach folksong at the Academy of Music. The Hungarian Academy of Sciences elected him as a corresponding member in 1943 and a full member in 1945. He worked in 1944–1945 to help Jews to escape. After his first wife's death in 1958, he married the young musician Sarolta Péczely on December 18, 1959. Meanwhile he played a decisive part in the country's postwar musical and public life. He chaired the Hungarian Arts Council and the Free Union of Musicians, sat in Parliament, and was appointed as president of the executive council of the Academy of Music. He died in Budapest on March 6, 1967.

Komócsin, Zoltán (1923–1974)

On leaving school in Szeged he worked as a casual laborer, domestic servant and commercial clerk up to the autumn of 1944, when he became an organizer for the Hungarian League of Democratic Youth, then its district secretary. He was then Szeged city secretary of the Hungarian Communist Party in 1945–1948, Vas County Party Committee secretary in 1948, and head of the agitprop department of the Hungarian Workers' Party Central Leadership in 1949–1950 and in 1953. In 1950–1953 he studied journalism at the Moscow school run by the Central Committee of the Soviet Communist Party. In the spring of 1957 he took a lead in reorganizing the communist youth movement as the League of Communist Youth, acting as first secretary of its Central Committee in 1957–1961. In February 1957 he became a member of the Provisional Central Committee of the Hungarian Socialist Workers' Party. He was editor-in-chief of the party daily newspaper *Népszabadság* from September 1961 to June 1965. As a Central Committee secretary from

June 1965 to 1974, he dealt mainly with international affairs. He became a member of Parliament in 1949, serving on its Defense Committee from 1958 and chairing its Foreign Affairs Committee from 1967. He was appointed to head *Népszabadság* again in 1974, but a sudden worsening of his health prevented him from taking up the post.

Konev, Ivan Stepanovich (1897–1973)

Soviet military officer. He served in the Red Army in various capacities. During the civil war he was in turn the commander of an armored train, a brigade and an army corps; in 1921 he helped to suppress the rebellion at Kronstadt; during World War II he first commanded the nineteenth army and then fought on various fronts, including the Western, the Kalinin, the Northwestern, the Second Ukrainian and the First Ukrainian; he participated in the Battles of Moscow and Kursk, the liberation of the Ukraine, and the capture of Berlin and Prague. In 1945–1946 he was the commander-in-chief of the Central Army Group and the high commissioner of Austria; from 1946 to 1950 he was the commander-in-chief of the land army forces and the deputy minister of the Armed Forces of the Soviet Union; in 1950–1951 he was chief inspector of the Soviet Army; from 1951 to 1955 he was commander-in-chief of the Cis-Carpathian Military District; from 1955 to 1958 he was first deputy minister of defense and at the same time the commander of the unified Warsaw Pact forces; in 1961–1962 he was commander-in-chief of the Soviet military group in Germany. Based on the decision of the Central Committee of the Communist Party of the Soviet Union [CPSU], he directed the Soviet military maneuvers in Hungary beginning in the first days of November 1956.

Kopácsi, Sándor (1922–2001)

Police official. During World War II he participated in the resistance at Miskolc; after 1945 he served in the police and became a department head in the Ministry of the Interior in 1950; from 1952 to November 5, 1956, he was the chief of police in Budapest. During the time of the Revolution, he attempted to dampen the conflicts with the revolutionaries and tried wherever possible to avoid bloodshed. On October 31, 1956, he became a member of the Revolutionary Committee for the Defense of the Homeland, and then became deputy commander-in-chief of the National Guard; also on October 31 he was elected to serve on the seven-member Executive Committee of the newly formed Hungarian Socialist Workers' Party . He was arrested by the KGB on November 5, 1956, and during the proceedings against Imre Nagy and his associates he was sentenced to life imprisonment; however, he regained his freedom with the amnesty of 1963, emigrated to Canada in 1975 and returned to Hungary in 1989. After 1994 he lived as a retired police brigadier general.

Korom, Mihály (b. 1927)

Originally a day laborer, he became a detective sub-lieutenant of police in 1945. In 1954 he was made a secretary of the Communist Party Central Leadership, joining its staff in December 1958 and later moving to head the Investigation Department of the Ministry of the Interior. He became commander of the Border Guard in July 1960, a Central Committee member in 1962, administrative secretary to the supervisor of armed forces in 1963, minister of justice in December 1966, and a Politburo member in 1980. He was recalled from all positions in 1985, but was a member of Parliament in 1986–1989.

Kosáry, Domokos (1913–2007)

A historian and university professor born in Selmecbánya (Banská Štiavnica), the turning points in his life coincided with those of twentieth-century history. During his childhood, his family (his mother was the bestselling author Lola Réz) moved to Budapest, after their home town had been incorporated into Czechoslovakia under the Treaty of Trianon. There he studied history and Latin at university and was a pupil of Gyula Szekfű, one of the foremost historians of the period. Unlike many of his contemporaries, he won scholarships to study in England and France, rather than Germany, encountering in France the Annales school of history. He was soon appointed as deputy director of the History Institute within the Pál Teleki Institute of Science. He continued his university teaching after the war until mounting attacks by Marxist historians led to his dismissal. In 1956 he chaired the Revolutionary Council at the Institute of History, for which he received a two-year prison sentence. He then worked for Pest County Library for a while, before being readmitted to the Institute of History. This was a productive period in which he contributed several important works on modern Hungarian and European history, although he was kept out of positions of responsibility in the Kádár period. He became a corresponding member of the Hungarian Academy of Sciences in 1982, a full member in 1985, and its president in 1990–1996.

Kossa, István (1904–1965)

Born in Balatonlelle, he joined the Communist Party Central Leadership and the Politburo in May 1945 and was a member of Parliament from November 4, 1945, until his death. He held economic ministerial posts in 1948–1954. On December 30, 1954, he became vice-president of the Central Planning Bureau. Although minister of finance in Imre Nagy's government from October 27 from November 3, 1956, he was appointed on November 4 to head financial affairs in the Revolutionary Worker–Peasant Government. He was minister of transport and posts from May 9, 1957, until his retirement in 1963.

Kovács, Béla (1908–1959)

Smallholder politician, originally a peasant with a medium-sized land holding. He became a member of the Independent Smallholders' Party [FKGP] in 1933. From 1939 he was its deputy general secretary and a friend of Ferenc Nagy, from 1941 the general secretary of the Hungarian Peasant Alliance, from December 23, 1944, to November 15, 1945, state secretary in the Ministry of the Interior, and from November 15, 1945, to February 23, 1946, minister of agriculture. From August 20, 1945, he was also the general secretary of the FKGP. He was arrested by the Soviet authorities in Hungary on February 25, 1947, and without trial was sentenced to twenty years in prison in the Soviet Union. He was released early and returned to Hungary in 1955; he was allowed to return to his family on April 2, 1956. He served as a representative in the Parliament from November 1958 until his death.

Kovács, Imre (1913–1980)

Writer, journalist and politician in the Peasant Party. One of the founders of the March Forum, editor of *Szabad Szó* from 1938; one of the founders of the National Peasant Party [NPP] in 1939. He participated in the resistance movement led by Endre Bajcsy-Zsilinszky. After his release from Russian captivity in April 1945 he became a member of the Provisional National Assembly and the general secretary of his party, and later its vice-president; from November 4 he was a representative in the National Assembly; on February 25, 1947, he left the National Peasant Party and on August 31 that year he joined the Independent Hungarian Democratic Party [FMDP] and again became a representative in the Parliament. However, he was increasingly forced into the background in public life and emigrated in November 1947.

Kovács, István (b. 1913)

Communist politician, originally an assistant carpet layer. From 1945 he was the leader of the Organizational Department of the Hungarian Communist Party and later the Central Leadership of the Hungarian Workers' Party; later he was secretary of the Central Leadership until 1953, and a member of the Central Leadership from 1945 to 1956. From 1949 to 1950 and from 1954 to 1956 he served as the general secretary of the Budapest Committee of the Hungarian Workers' Party. From October 31, 1956, to September 1958 he lived in the Soviet Union; after his return he became a department head in the Ministry of Light Industry.

Kuczka, Péter (1923–1999)

Poet and editor. His first book of verse, which received the Baumgarten Prize, appeared in 1949; he became a contributor to *Irodalmi Újság* and actively participated in the social and political movements of the Literary Association; thus, for example, he went to Szabolcs-Szatmár County as a Communist writer in the autumn of 1953, working as a contemporary researcher of the village and trying to understand the socialist way of village life, together with his fellow writers, who also visited other parts of the country with the same goal. In October, in so-called village evaluation meetings, they provided demoralizing accounts of their experiences. On the eve of the Revolution of 1956 he wanted to dissuade the students from demonstrating, but despite this on the next day did everything possible to intervene with the authorities so that there would be no clashes between the authorities and the demonstrators. He became a member of the Hungarian Intellectuals' Revolutionary Committee and the Revolutionary Council, which survived beyond the Revolution; after the arrival of the new government, however, his efforts were foiled. In the 1970s he became an editor at the Móra Ferenc Publishing House.

Lénárd, Ödön (1911–2003)

Teacher from the Piarist Order. In the spring of 1945 he became the national cultural secretary of the Actio Catholica: the various threads of the protests against the nationalization of the Church schools came together in his hands, and therefore he was arrested in 1948 and sentenced to six years in prison for incitement. However, he was freed by an amnesty in 1953. Arrested again in 1961, this time for taking the lead in organizing to topple the democratic people's system of government, he received a sentence of seven and a half years in prison, but was freed again by an amnesty in 1963. Arrested for the third time in 1966, he was freed in 1977 but did not go abroad. In 2001 he became the pastor of the women's Cistercian cloister of the House of Our Blessed Lady in Kismaros, which he had founded in 1955.

Losonczy, Géza (1917–1957)

Journalist and Communist politician. Born in Érsekcsanád, he studied Hungarian and French at Debrecen University, during which time he became involved in the March Front. Completing his studies in Budapest in 1941, he took part there in the illegal communist movement. In March 1945 he became a senior staffer at the communist daily newspaper *Szabad Nép* and in 1946 an alternate member of the Communist Party Central Leadership. He entered Parliament in 1947 and became state secretary to the Prime Minister's Office in December 1948 and political state secretary at the Ministry of Education in 1949–1951. He was then tried on fabricated charges and sentenced to 15 years' imprisonment, but released due to severe illness in the summer of 1954. Rehabilitated in April 1955, he became a leading figure in the party opposition group surrounding Imre Nagy. He addressed the 1956 press debate of the Petőfi Circle. At the Communist Party Central Leadership meeting on October 26 that year, he demanded that the party cease calling the events an uprising and negotiate on the main demands of the revolutionaries. On October 30 he became a minister of state in the government of Imre Nagy, responsible for press and propaganda matters. Like Nagy and others, he fled on November 4 to the Yugoslav Embassy, only to be exiled to Romania, where he was arrested in Snagov on April 11, 1957. He became the second accused in the Imre Nagy trial, but died under unexplained circumstances on December 21, 1957, while awaiting trial.

Lukács, György (1885–1971)

He studied law in Budapest and then studied further in Berlin in 1906–1907, receiving a doctorate there in 1909. (He was awarded a second doctorate in 1942 for a monograph, *The Young Hegel*.) Despite publishing in major Hungarian journals such as *Nyugat* and *Huszadik Század*, he lived mainly in Berlin until 1911 and then in Heidelberg until November 1917, when he returned to Budapest, joining the Communist Party in December 1918. In February 1919 he became a member of the still-illegal Central Committee and on March 1 an editor of the communist newspaper *Vörös Újság*. When the Hungarian Soviet Republic was declared on March 21, he became education commissar, then on April 3 people's commissar, and in May and June political commissar for the armed division of the Red Army. When the republic fell in August, he remained in the country to organize the illegal Communist Party, but soon had to flee. In 1929 the Second Congress of the Hungarian Communist Party rejected the draft program known as the Blum Theses, which he had prepared. In 1930 he was awarded a scholarship to study in Moscow, where he joined the staff of the Marx/Engels/Lenin Institute. In the summer of 1931 he went to live in Berlin again, but returned to Moscow in March 1933, and worked there as a researcher for scientific institutes. He arrived back in Budapest on August 1, 1945, and became a professor at Budapest University. He was made an honorary member of the Hungarian Academy of Sciences in 1948 and later a full member and member of its Presidium. He returned to political life in the spring of 1956, delivering an address in the Petőfi Circle. During the 1956 Revolution, he was elected as a member of the Central Leadership of the Hungarian Workers' Party at its meeting on October 23–24, 1956, and was appointed as minister of education on October 26. He joined the Provisional Organizing Committee for the successor party, the Hungarian Socialist Workers' Party, on October 30. On November 4 he took refuge in the Yugoslav Embassy. He was then arrested by the Soviets and taken to Romania, whence he returned home on April 11, 1957, with his wife, with no judicial proceedings being taken against him. He was sent into retirement in 1958 and from then until 1965 acted as an internal exile, publishing only in the West. He became a member of the Hungarian Socialist Workers' Party in 1967, but the 1968 events in Czechoslovakia prompted him to submit a study to the Central Committee in which he said that the real alternative to Stalinism was social democracy. From the second half of the 1960s until his death in 1971 he was working on his book *Towards the Ontology of Social Being.*

Malenkov, Georgy Maximilianovich (1902–1988)

Soviet Communist politician. Member of the Central Leadership of the Soviet Communist Party from 1930, then one of the leaders of the Moscow party committee until 1934. Member of the Defense Committee between 1941 and 1945, that of the Politburo of the Central Committee of the Communist Party of the Soviet Union [CPSU] and deputy prime minister from 1946. President of the Council of Ministers between 1953 and 1955. In 1961, he was expelled from the Communist Party and exiled within the Soviet Union.

Maléter, Pál (1917–1958)

Born in Eperjes (Prešov), he began to study medicine at Prague University. Although he continued the course in Budapest, he was unable to qualify for financial reasons. He then volunteered for military service as a way of gaining Hungarian citizenship. He was admitted to the Ludovika Academy in the autumn of 1940. Once commissioned, he served in Kassa (Košice) before being sent to the Eastern Front, where he was taken prisoner. He then volunteered to join the fight against the Germans, which he and his unit did in the autumn of 1944 in Transylvania. In January 1945 he took command of the brigade guarding the Provisional Government. He served in the People's Army until the 1956 Revolution broke out, by which time he was a colonel. On October 25, 1956, he was ordered by the chief of staff to assist, with five tanks and officer cadets accompanying him, one of the units in the Kilián Barracks in Budapest. He took part in the surrender talks in Corvin Köz. Imre Nagy appointed him as first deputy minister of defense on November 1 and minister of defense on November 3, when he was a member of the team negotiating with the Soviet army command in Parliament. When the team arrived on that evening at the Soviet base at Tököl to continue the talks, several of them were arrested, on the orders of General Serov, the KGB chief. On June 15, 1958, he was sentenced to death by the People's Council of the Supreme Court chaired by Ferenc Vida on charges of initiating and leading a conspiracy, rebellion and treason, without possibility of appeal. The sentence was carried out on June 16.

Maniu, Iuliu (1873–1953)

Romanian politician from Transylvania. He studied law in Kolozsvár, Budapest and Vienna. In 1897 he became a member of the leadership committee of the Romanian National Party in Transylvania and after 1904 the vice-president of the party. From 1906 to 1910 he represented Alvinc in the Hungarian Parliament. He was the leader of the Romanians in their negotiations with István Tisza from 1910 to 1914; he declared the intention to separate Transylvania from Hungary at the Romanian–Hungarian negotiations in Arad on November 15–16, 1918; after the general Romanian meeting at Gyulafehérvár on December 1, 1918, he became the president of the Romanian governing council in Transylvania and was also responsible for matters relating to the interior. The National Party led by him united with the Peasant Party of the old Romanian kingdom in 1926 and so the National Peasant Party became the largest political power in Romania. He served as Romanian prime minister from December 12, 1928, to October 1, 1930, and from October 19, 1932, to January 12, 1933. In the Crown Council he opposed the Second Viennese Decision, the acceptance of the return to Hungary of Northern Transylvania: he protested publicly by writing open letters of protest to Hitler and Mussolini, and he became the president of the Pro-Transylvania mass organization. During World War II he was the leader of the opposition to the Antonescu regime and the director of the effort to negotiate a separate peace with the Western allies; after Romania suddenly abandoned the war he became minister without portfolio. He was a determined enemy of Communist expansion; as the leader of the largest opposition group and of a Western orientation, he was sentenced in the spring of 1947 to life imprisonment in a show trial: he died in prison. He was rehabilitated in 1998.

Márai, Sándor (1900–1989)

A writer and journalist born in Kassa (Košice), he traveled extensively in his youth, learning German and becoming a correspondent of the *Frankfurter Zeitung* newspaper in the 1920s. But he reverted to his native Hungarian and developed a precise, spare style that won him fame. He was elected as a member of the Hungarian Academy of Sciences in 1945. He took a critical, distant approach to the Horthy system, the nationalists and the communists, and in 1948 decided that he had better leave Hungary. After a spell in Switzerland, he lived in Italy and then moved to New York. He continued to write in Hungarian, but his works were not published until the end of the Cold War. In 1952–1967 he joined Radio Free Europe. He returned to Salerno, Italy, in 1968 before moving to San Diego, California. He became increasingly reclusive after the death of his wife and took his own life in San Diego in 1989.

Marosán, György (1908–1992)

Born at Hosszúpályi, he worked as a baker's assistant. He joined the Social Democratic Party in 1927, becoming national secretary in August 1945 and in February 1947 its deputy general secretary. He was one of the main advocates of the merger between the Social Democrats and the Hungarian Communist Party, becoming on March 10, 1948, deputy president of the joint Politburo and a member of the joint Steering Committee. He entered the Provisional National Assembly in 1945 and remained a member of Parliament until 1963. Arrested in July 1950, he was sentenced to death, but this was altered administratively to life imprisonment. He was freed on March 29, 1956, then rehabilitated and restored to Politburo membership at the Communist Party Central Leadership meeting on July 18–21 and appointed as deputy prime minister a week later. Speaking in the Politburo on October 23, 1956, he spoke of the danger of counterrevolution and pressed for orders to fire on demonstrators. On November 7, 1956, he joined the Hungarian Socialist Workers' Party Provisional Executive and the Soviet-installed Revolutionary Worker–Peasant Government. At the Central Committee meeting in February 1957, he was appointed as administrative Central Committee secretary and deputy to János Kádár. He served as minister of state from May 9, 1957, to January 15, 1960. However, he addressed a letter of criticism of policy to the Central Committee, which responded at its meeting on October 11–12, 1962, by recalling him from the Politburo and his Central Committee secretary post and expelling him from the Central Committee. He resigned from the Communist Party in 1965 but later rejoined. He died in Budapest in 1992.

Mező, Imre (1905–1956)

Party functionary. From 1948 to 1950 he was the leader of the Budapest Party Committee's Organizational Department, and from 1950 to 1956, with brief interruptions, its secretary; from July 1956 he was a member of the Central Leadership. On October 30, 1956, he received a fatal wound while helping to defend the Party Headquarters in Budapest.

Mićunović, Veljko (b. 1916)

Yugoslav diplomat. From 1956 to 1958 he was the Yugoslav ambassador to Moscow.

Miklós, Béla (Dálnoki) (1890–1948)

Military officer. He began his military career in 1910; from 1933 to 1936 he was a military attaché in Berlin. He served actively in the military, and participated in the actions against Yugoslavia and the Soviet Union from November 1942. He was Horthy's main assistant for military affairs and the director of his military office. On October 17, 1944, he defected to the Soviets and participated in the negotiations for the forming of a new government in November; from December 22, 1944, to November 15, 1945, he was the president of the Provisional National Government.

Mikołajczyk, Stanisław (1901–1966)

Polish politician. Head of state in exile, and deputy prime minister, he emigrated to the West after the elections of January 1947.

Mikoyan, Anastas Ivanovich (1895–1978)

Soviet politician. From 1955 to 1964 he was the first deputy minister of the Council of Ministers of the Soviet Union, and from 1964 to 1965 head of state.

Mindszenty (Pehm), József (1892–1975)

Catholic priest and cardinal. From March 4, 1944, he was Bishop of Veszprém; from August 16, 1945, he was Archbishop of Esztergom; from February 21, 1946, he was Cardinal of Hungary. He was arrested on December 26, 1948, and in a show trial of 1949 the People's Tribunal sentenced him to life imprisonment; he was freed on October 30, 1956, and from this time until February 2, 1974, he retained his position as the head of the Catholic Church in Hungary. From November 4, 1956, to September 28, 1971, he lived in the United States Embassy in Budapest, and then departed for Rome. He lived the last years of his life in the Pazmaneum in Vienna. He was reburied at Esztergom in 1992.

Molnár, Erik (1894–1966)
Historian and Communist politician. From 1924 to 1944 he was an attorney in Kecskemét, in 1944 deputy mayor of Kecskemét, from December 22, 1944, to 1947 minister of welfare, and from 1947 to 1948 minister of foreign affairs. Later he was ambassador to Moscow. He was also director of the Institute for Historical Studies of the Hungarian Academy of Sciences [MTA] in 1949–1950 and again in 1957–1966. He was minister of justice in 1950–1952 and minister of foreign affairs in 1952–1953. Then he became president of the Supreme Court, and minister of justice again in 1954–1956.

Molotov, Vyacheslav Mikhailovich (1890–1986)
Soviet politician. President of the Council of People's Commissars, and also people's commissar for foreign affairs after 1939; he was relieved of his duties in 1949, but he became minister of foreign affairs again from 1953 to 1956. The Central Committee of the Communist Party of the Soviet Union [CPSU] excluded him from all leading organs at the June plenary session in 1957. From 1957 to 1960 he was ambassador to Mongolia and later represented the Soviet Union on the International Atomic Energy Commission.

Münnich, Ferenc (1886–1967)
Communist politician. After the fall of the Hungarian Soviet Republic he lived first in Vienna and then in Berlin; he went to the Soviet Union in 1922. He fought in Spain and after the

fall of the Spanish Republic he was interned, but was freed at the intervention of the Soviet Union in 1940. For a while he led the Hungarian edition of Radio Moscow. He returned to Hungary in 1945, and served as a police captain in Budapest from 1946 to 1949. In 1950 he became a diplomat. From October 27, 1956, to November 3 he was the minister of the interior in the government of Imre Nagy; in the Hungarian Revolutionary Worker–Peasant Government he served as minister of armed forces and public security and deputy prime minister; he was prime minister from 1958 to 1961, minister of state from 1961 to 1965, a member of the Central Committee of the Hungarian Socialist Workers' Party [MSZMP] from 1956 to 1967, and a member of the Politburo until 1966.

Nagy, Ferenc (1903–1979)

Prime minister, originally a farmer. In 1930 with Zoltán Tildy and others he founded the Independent Smallholders' Party [FKGP], of which he remained a leader until the end of May 1947. He was elected as a parliamentary representative in 1939. He was a founder of the Peasant Alliance and later its president; he was minister of reconstruction from May 1945, a parliamentary representative from April 1945, and then Hungary's prime minister from February 4, 1946, to June 2, 1947. At that time, while he was on holiday in Switzerland, a putsch was implemented against him under the leadership of Mátyás Rákosi. He arrived in the United States at the end of June 1947 and became one of the leaders of the Hungarian emigrant community there; he was a founding member of the Hungarian National Committee. At the end of 1956 he tried to return to Hungary but the Austrian government, invoking its neutrality, prevented this. On November 2, 1956, he called Zoltán Tildy, a minister of state and his former political colleague, and offered his services. He was a member of many international organizations and lectured on the situation in Hungary and Eastern Europe at more than 400 colleges and universities; in 1977 he urged the United States to return to Hungary the Crown of St. Stephen and the coronation symbols that had been seized by the Arrow Cross. He is buried in Herndon, Virginia.

Nagy, Imre (1896–1958)

Born into a poor Reformed peasant family in Kaposvár, he quit school there in 1912 and became an apprentice turner. He served on the Russian front in 1916–1918 and was taken prisoner. At the beginning of the Russian Civil War, he joined the Red Army and the Bolshevik party. He returned to Hungary in 1921 and joined the largely communist-controlled Hungarian Socialist Workers' Party in 1925. Between early 1921 and 1927 he spent a total of three years in prison for political offenses. He lived in the Soviet Union from 1930 to November 1944, working for the International Agrarian Institute, an offshoot of the Communist International, until he was expelled from the Communist Party and dismissed in 1936. In 1941 he rejoined the Red Army but did not see active service. In the autumn of 1944 he drafted a plan for general land reform in Hungary, where he returned in November with the first group of Muscovite Hungarian communists to become a member of the Central Leadership, and in December, the Provisional National Assembly, as well as minister of agriculture in the provisional government. As such he issued the land reform government order on March 15, 1945. On September 16, 1947, he became speaker of Parliament until June 1949. In August 1949 he was dismissed from the Politburo for "opportunist, anti-collectivization views." He then became rector of Gödöllő Agricultural University. He was elected as a full member of the Hungarian Academy of Sciences in 1953 for his agricultural work. After Stalin's death, he was appointed as prime minister on Soviet instigation on July 4, 1953, and proclaimed a New Course in his inaugural speech in Parliament. Reconsideration of earlier show trials began in 1954, leading to the release, for instance, of János Kádár. In April 1955 he was dismissed when Rákosi's power temporarily strengthened, was dropped from the Central Leadership, and on December 3 was expelled from the party. He was encouraged by many to reactivate himself in the summer of 1956, as the center of an "Imre Nagy Circle." He was readmitted into the Communist Party on October 13. One of the demands of the protesting students on October 23 was his return to power. He gave a speech before the Parliament building that night and was named prime minister early on the following day. Much influenced by the arguments of Ferenc Donáth and Géza Losonczy, he came out on October 28 in favor of the 1956 Revolution and introduction of a multiparty system. He announced the dissolution of the State Protection Office (secret police) and an end to compulsory crop sales. On October 31 he became a member of the Provisional Steering Committee of the Hungarian Socialist Workers' Party, formed in place of the old Communist Party. On November 1 his government announced withdrawal from the Warsaw Pact and declared Hungary's neutrality, and turned to the United Nations for assistance. At dawn on November 4 he announced in a dramatic radio broadcast the second Soviet intervention and then sought asylum with his group in the Yugoslav Embassy. On November 21 a prior agreement with the Yugoslavs was broken when he was kidnapped on his return home and flown with his family to Snagov in Romania. He was brought back to Hungary in April 1957. After a closed trial on June 9–15, 1959, he was sentenced to death and executed on the following day. (The sentence had been endorsed in advance by the Politburo of the Hungarian Socialist Workers' Party.) His ashes were exhumed in 1989 and reburied ceremoniously on June 16. He was officially rehabilitated by the Supreme Court on July 6 that year.

Németh, Károly (1922–2008)

A politician, he joined the Communist Party in 1945 and became in 1954 first secretary of its Csongrád County Party Committee. He became an alternate member of the Central Committee after the 1956 Revolution, then a full member until 1988. He sat in Parliament from 1958 to 1988. A Central Committee secretary in 1962–1965, secretary of the Budapest Committee in 1965–1974, and Central Committee secretary again in 1974–1985, he was a Politburo member from 1970 to 1989 and deputy general secretary of the Communist Party under János Kádár. In 1987 he was chosen to succeed Pál Losonczi as president of the Presidential Council (head of state). He retained this post until June 1988, when he withdrew from politics.

Németh, Miklós (b. 1948)

An economist and politician born into a peasant family in Monok, he was Hungary's last prime minister before the change of system. He graduated from the Karl Marx University of Economics in 1971 and studied at Harvard on a scholarship in 1974–1975. He became a deputy department head at the National Planning Bureau in 1977, having joined the Communist Party in 1976. He moved to the party's economic policy department in 1981 and was appointed as economic policy secretary to the Central Committee in 1987. He joined the Politburo after the dismissal of János Kádár in 1988 and remained there until the dissolution of the Hungarian Socialist Workers' Party in October 1989. He formed a government on November 24, 1988: this stayed in office until May 23, 1990. In this period, Parliament passed the cardinal legislation required for a peaceful and relatively smooth change of system. He issued a remembrance statement for Imre Nagy and all victims of the 1956 Revolution, on July 14, before the reburial of Imre Nagy.

Nógrádi, Sándor (1894–1971)

Communist politician. In 1923 he went into political exile in Berlin and soon moved on to Moscow; for longer and shorter periods he worked in Austria, Romania, Czechoslovakia, Germany and Spain. After the outbreak of World War II he lived again in Moscow and worked for the Communist International; he joined the Hungarian Communist Party at that time. At first he worked as an editor of Moscow's Kossuth Radio and later as the commander of the school for partisans in Kiev. He was a member of the Provisional National Assembly; from November 1945 he was a state secretary for the Ministry of Industry;

in October 1946 he became the leader of the Department of Agitation and Propaganda of the Central Leadership of the Hungarian Communist Party [MKP]; after the election of 1956 he was a political state secretary of the Prime Minister's Office; from 1948 to 1955 he was the leader of the Hungarian People's Army's Chief Group Command; from 1957 to 1960 he was Hungary's ambassador to Peking and Hanoi.

Nyers, Rezső (b. 1923)

Born in Budapest, he became a printer in 1942. He joined the Social Democratic Party in 1940, acting as deputy secretary of the Kispest branch in 1945–1946, and deputy secretary, later secretary for Pest and Pest District in 1947–1948. After the merger with the Communist Party, he was an alternate Central Leadership member until 1954, then a full member. He also sat in Parliament in 1948–1953. He was minister of the food industry from August 1 to November 3, 1956. Then on November 12, 1956, he was appointed by the Kádár government to head the Government Public Supplies Commission. He played an active part in introducing the New Economic Mechanism in 1968. He chaired the government's Consultative Commission on Economic Management. In 1974 he was relieved of all his political posts and became director of the Economics Institute of the Hungarian Academy of Sciences in 1974, continuing as an adviser there in 1981. In 1988 he became a founder and the president of the New March Front. He again became a member of the Communist Party Politburo in 1988–1989, also serving as the president of the party and a member of the Political Executive and the Presidium from June 24 to October 7, 1989. In 1989 he became president of the successor Hungarian Socialist Party, and returned to Parliament in 1990–1998.

Ognyenovics, Milán (1916–1980)

National secretary of the South Slav Democratic Alliance in Hungary, and later its deputy general secretary. He was arrested on July 5, 1949, and sentenced to nine years in prison during the proceedings against László Rajk and his associates; however, he was released on January 6, 1956, and on July 24 he was absolved of all charges and rehabilitated on appeal.

Ordass, Lajos (1901–1978)

Lutheran bishop. Consecrated as pastor in 1924, he served as an assistant pastor in Harta, Mezőség, Soltvadkert and Budapest, studied in Sweden in 1927–1928, and became a pastor in Czegléd in 1931, was a dean from 1937 to 1941, and finally became the Lutheran Bishop of the Bánya Ecclesiastical District. He resisted the nationalization of the Church schools and for this was sentenced to two years in prison in 1948; after regaining his freedom in 1950 he was stripped of his position as bishop by the Separate Disciplinary Committee of the Hungarian Lutheran Church, but he was rehabilitated both by the Church and by the state in 1956. He lived in seclusion in Budapest until his death.

Pálffy, György (1909–1949)

Professional military officer. He resigned his commission in 1939, and joined the Communist Party in 1942; after 1945 he was the head of the military policy department of the Ministry of Defense; in 1946 he became the secretary of the Military Committee of the Hungarian Communist Party [MKP]; in 1948 he was named chief inspector of the army. In 1949 he was condemned on false charges and executed. In 1956 he was rehabilitated.

Papp, Simon (1886–1970)

Geologist; the first Hungarian to research the geology of oil. He earned an international reputation for his work on natural gas: he helped to establish drilling for oil in Hungary, and was made professor in the Department of Oil Research and Production, which had been established at Sopron. His scientific research was further acknowledged when in 1946 he was elected as a regular member of the Hungarian Academy of Sciences [MTA]. During the 1910s he participated in the exploration of the oil and natural gas fields in Slovakia and Transylvania; from 1933 to 1947 he led the effort to discover oil and natural gas in Transdanubia; in 1938 he became the chief geologist of the Hungarian American Oil Industry Corporation [MAORT] and later its director. In

1944, by using his personal connections, he was able to prevent German seizure of MAORT's plants; he later played a key role in restarting the wells after World War II. He repeatedly, but unsuccessfully, warned that overproduction would eventually have drastic consequences, but when the sudden drop in production that he had forecast arrived in 1948, he was charged with sabotage and arrested on August 12, 1948. In the following year, as a part of the so-called MAORT proceedings, he was condemned as the leader of crimes against the state and the democratic system and sentenced to life imprisonment; also as a result of the proceedings the government was able to seize the company, which had previously been partially owned by Americans. He was freed from prison due to an amnesty on June 4, 1955, and then worked in the oil trust until his retirement in 1962.

Péter, Gábor (1906–1993)

Communist politician. He joined the workers' movement in the 1920s, and was a member of the Communist Party of Hungary [KMP] from 1931 onwards. In 1943 he became a member of the leadership of the Peace Party; after 1945 he was the head of the political police and until 1953 the head of the Office of State Security [ÁVH]; he was also a member of the Hungarian Communist Party [MKP] from 1945 and of the Central Leadership of the Hungarian Workers' Party [MDP] to 1952. In 1954 he was sentenced to life imprisonment; on appeal in 1957 his sentence was reduced to 14 years, and he was freed in 1962.

Petkov, Nikola Dimitrov (1893–1947)

Bulgarian peasant politician. Minister, and general secretary of the Bulgarian Popular Agricultural Alliance from January 20, 1945. He was condemned to death on trumped-up charges and executed on August 16, 1947.

Peyer, Károly (1881–1956)

Social Democrat politician. Minister of welfare and labor in the Huszár government from November 24, 1919, to January 16, 1920; after resigning he emigrated to Vienna and returned to Hungary in 1921; he signed the agreement between the

Social Democrats and the Bethlen government that has become known as the Bethlen–Peyer Pact; he was a representative in the Parliament from 1922 to March 19, 1944. The Germans hauled him off to the concentration camp at Mauthausen, from which he returned home in May 1945. In June 1945 he was made a delegate in the Provisional National Assembly; he worked in the Ministry of Foreign Affairs during 1946; he left the Social Democratic Party and in 1947 won a seat in the Parliament as a member of the Hungarian Radical Party [MRP]. However, he left Hungary on November 20, 1947.

Pfeiffer, Zoltán (1900–1981)

Lawyer and Smallholder politician. A member of the Independent Smallholders' Party [FKGP] from 1931 onwards, and a representative in the National Assembly from 1945. He was state secretary of the Ministry of Justice from November 22, 1945, to December 31, 1946. In connection with the Hungarian Community (a secret irredentist association) affair, which led to the attack from the left against his party on March 10, 1947, at the request of Ferenc Nagy he resigned from the FKGP; during the summer he founded and became the president of the oppositional Hungarian Independence Party [MFP]. He emigrated in November 1947.

Piros, László (1917–2006)

Communist politician, originally an assistant butcher. Representative in the Parliament from 1945 to 1957; at first he filled leading positions in the labor union movement; from 1948 he was a member of the Central Leadership of the Hungarian Workers' Party [MDP], and in 1955–1956 he was a member of the Politburo; from 1950 he was the commander of the Border Guards of the Office of State Security. From June 1953 as deputy minister of the interior he was in charge of state security. He was minister of the interior from 1954 to 1956. He left the country for the Soviet Union on October 28, 1956, and could return only in August 1958. He was the director of the Szeged Salami Factory between 1969 and 1977.

Pozsgay, Imre (b. 1933)

Born in Kóny, he joined the Communist Party in 1950 and then the successor Hungarian Socialist Workers' Party in 1956. In 1957 he graduated from the Lenin Institute in Budapest. From then until 1965 he held various positions with the Communist Party's Bács-Kiskun County Party Committee. His first government appointment came in 1975, as deputy minister of culture, then minister of culture in 1976. In 1980 he also became a member of the party Central Committee. In 1982 he was transferred to the position of general secretary of the Patriotic People's Front National Council. He entered Parliament in 1980. In 1988 he became a member of the Communist Party Politburo and returned to the government, acting as minister of state under Károly Grósz and then Miklós Németh. He was the member of the governing party who first referred to the 1956 Revolution as a people's uprising. In 1989 he became a founder member and Presidium member of the new Hungarian Socialist Party, and his party's candidate for president of the republic. After a brief period as vice-president of the Hungarian Socialist Party in 1990, he left the party to continue as an independent member of Parliament. In the following year, he and Zoltán Bíró, who had been first president of the Hungarian Democratic Forum, founded the National Democratic Association, of which he was executive secretary and then president, but the organization dissolved itself in 1996. In 1997 he became an adviser to the Hungarian Democratic Forum and a parliamentary candidate for it in 1998. He reappeared on the political scene in 2005, as a member of the National Consultative Body headed by Viktor Orbán. Meanwhile he had become a professor of political science at Debrecen University in 1991 and at the Gáspár Károli Reformed University in 2003.

Puja, Frigyes (b. 1921)

Born in Battonya, he was district Communist Party secretary there in 1945–1946, then secretary of its Csanád County Party Committee from 1949. He was a Ministry of Foreign Affairs department head in 1951–1953, then Hungarian envoy in Stockholm, Oslo, Copenhagen and Vienna in 1953–1959, deputy minister of foreign affairs from August 14, 1959, to December 7, 1963, then for five years head of the Communist Party foreign affairs department, before becoming first deputy minister of foreign affairs (1968–1973) and minister of foreign affairs (up to 1983). He was in Parliament from 1975 until the change of system. He served on the Central Committee of the reorganized Hungarian Socialist Party in 1989–1992.

Puskin, Georgi Maximovich (1909–1963)

Soviet diplomat. He joined the Soviet Ministry of Foreign Affairs in 1939; he was chief consul in China from 1942 to 1944, a Soviet commissioner assigned to work with the Allied Control Commission [SZEB] from 1945 onwards, then the ambassador of the Soviet Union in Hungary until 1948, and led the Soviet diplomatic delegation in the German Democratic Republic from 1948 to 1952.

Rajk, László (1909–1949)

A member of the Communist Party from 1931, he was arrested several times for political activity. In 1937 he went to fight in the Spanish Civil War, fleeing in 1939 to France, where he was then interned. He was again arrested and interned on his return to Hungary in 1941. On his release in September 1944, he became a secretary of the Communist Party Central Committee and one of the main resistance organizers. He was arrested by the Arrow Cross in December 1944 and taken off to Sopronkőhida and then Germany, whence he returned on May 13, 1945. He then became a member of the leading bodies of the Communist Party and of the Provisional National Assembly and the legislature. He was minister of the interior from March 1946 to August 1948, but in August he was moved to the foreign affairs portfolio. On May 30, 1949, he was arrested on fabricated charges. He was sentenced to death by the People's Court on September 24 and executed on October 15. He was rehabilitated in 1955 and reburied on October 6, 1956.

Rákosi, Mátyás (1892–1971)

Born in Ada, he gained a commercial diploma in 1912, having joined the Social Democratic Party in 1910. He returned to Ada in 1914 and volunteered for military service. He was taken prisoner by the Russians in April 1915, but escaped early in 1918 and returned to Hungary. In November 1918 he became a founder member of the Hungarian Communist Party. When the Hungarian Soviet Republic was proclaimed in March 1919, he became a member of the Revolutionary Governing Soviet. After the collapse, he fled to Vienna, where he was interned with other communist émigrés. He moved to the Soviet Union in 1920 and began to work for the Executive of the Communist International, becoming a secretary of the organization in 1921. Returning to Hungary illegally in 1924, he was arrested in September 1925 and sentenced in August 1926 to eight and a half years' imprisonment for rebellion and common crime. When the sentence expired, he was again prosecuted for his activity under the Hungarian Soviet Republic and sentenced to life imprisonment in February 1935. He was released in 1940 on condition that he left immediately for the Soviet Union. Once in Moscow, he became a leading figure in the exiled Hungarian Communist Party. He returned to Hungary on January 30, 1945. On February 22, 1945, he became general secretary of the combined Debrecen and Budapest Central Leadership. After the 1947 elections, he became deputy prime minister and minister of state. On June 12, 1948, he became general secretary of the combined communist/social democratic Hungarian Workers' Party, and in August 1952 he became prime minister. This gave him total political sway to impose Stalinist socialism until he was dismissed as prime minister in June 1953, but after Kremlin criticism of the government of Imre Nagy, he became the country's real leader again in January 1955. At the July 18–21, 1956, meeting of the Communist Party Central Leadership, he was relieved of his leadership on health grounds and immediately left for Moscow for treatment. There he stayed during the 1956 Revolution. The Soviet Communist Party Presidium decided on November 5, 1956, to remove him permanently from power, and the Provisional Executive of the newly constituted Hungarian Socialist Workers' Party decided in February 1957 that he should not return to Hungary for five years. He left Moscow in June 1957 for Krasnodar, then Tokmak (Kirghizia), and finally Gorky. On May 5, 1957, he was removed from his seat in Parliament, and on November 1, 1960, the Politburo expelled him from the Communist Party. In April 1970 the Politburo was prepared to allow him back into the country against a written undertaking to eschew politics, but he refused to give this. He died in Gorky on February 5, 1971. His ashes were returned in secret to Hungary on February 16.

Ravasz, László (1882–1975)

Reformed bishop. In 1904 he passed his pastoral examinations and became a relatively young professor at the Reformed Theological Academy at Kolozsvár. In 1921 he was invited to become pastor of the Reformed Church community on Kálvin tér in Budapest, and during the same year he was elected as Bishop of the Duna Region Reformed District. He was a member of the Upper House from 1927 to 1941, and also a member of the Hungarian Academy of Sciences [MTA] from 1925 to 1949: from 1931 to 1940 he was a vice-president of the Academy. The Rákosi clique forced him to resign from his bishop's office, and he retired from his position as pastor in 1953. The National Executive Committee of the Hungarian Reformed Church, which had been formed on November 1, 1956, removed the leadership that had been collaborating with the Communist authorities and recalled Ravasz to lead the Church. After the suppression of the Revolution in April 1957 the State Office for Ecclesiastical Affairs again removed him from his office, and he retired to his home in Leányfalu.

Révai, József (1898–1959)

Born into a *petit-bourgeois* Budapest family, he graduated from university and went to work in a bank. In November

1918 he took part in the founding the Hungarian Communist Party and joined the newspaper *Vörös Újság*. He was on the Central Workers' and Soldiers' Soviet under the Hungarian Soviet Republic, fleeing to Vienna in the autumn of 1919. He was appointed as head of the Secretariat at the Vienna First Congress of the Hungarian Communist Party in 1925. On December 31, 1930, he was arrested in Hungary and sentenced to three and a half years' imprisonment. He left for the Soviet Union in January 1934. On his return on November 7, 1944, he headed the communist group in the National Assembly. He was editor-in-chief of the communist daily newspaper *Szabad Nép* from March 1945 to 1950. From June 1949 to July 4, 1953, he was minister of education, but in June 1953 he was dropped from the Politburo. From July 3, 1953, to November 26, 1958, he was vice-president of the Presidential Council (deputy head of state). He reentered the Communist Party Politburo at the July 1956 Central Leadership meeting, but fled to Moscow in October. From there he sent back in early 1957 a long article about the Soviet Union entitled "Ideological Cleanliness," calling criticism of the earlier leadership in Hungary exaggerated. In February he was the one old leader in Moscow to be recalled, as an advisor to the Provisional Executive of the Hungarian Socialist Workers' Party. He returned in March 1957 to join the Provisional Central Committee. His article led to a debate in the columns of the party daily newspaper *Népszabadság* and the party ideological journal *Társadalmi Szemle*. Révai argued that there was "no need to follow a new policy, just apply the old one well." This continued as a struggle between the followers of Kádár and those of Révai at the Communist Party national meeting in July 1957, where Révai was defeated. He then "accepted the majority view" and was reelected to the Central Committee. He was a member of the Presidential Council from November 1958 until his death. In his final years, he was doing research on the poet Attila József.

Ries, István (1885–1950)
Lawyer and Social Democrat politician. A member of the leadership of the Hungarian Social Democratic Party [MSZDP] from 1934 to 1935 and the Social Democratic Party [SZDP] after 1939; he was a member of the Political Committee of the Social Democratic Party from August 20, 1945, and minister of justice from July 21, 1945, to July 17, 1950. Arrested in 1950 on trumped-up charges, he was beaten to death in jail.

Rokossovsky, Konstantin Konstantinovich (1896–1968)
Soviet marshal of Polish origins. During World War II he served as commander of an army and later of a front; from 1949 to 1956 he was Polish minister of defense and deputy prime minister; from 1958 to 1962 he was the deputy minister of defense of the Soviet Union.

Rónai, Sándor (1892–1965)
Social Democrat, later Communist, politician, originally a construction worker. After 1945 he was a member of the national leadership of the Social Democratic Party; at the congress that united the two workers' parties in June 1948 he was elected to be a part of the Central Leadership of the Hungarian Workers' Party [MDP]. From July 1945 until 1950 he filled several ministerial posts: Public Supply, Commerce, Labor Union Affairs and Foreign Commerce. From 1950 to 1952 he was president of the Presidential Council, and until 1962 the president of the Parliament; until his death he was a member of the Central Committee and the Politburo of the Hungarian Socialist Workers' Party [MSZMP].

Serov, Ivan Aleksandrovich (1905–1990)
Soviet politician. A student at the Frunze Military Academy, 1935–1939, from February 1939 he was director of the headquarters of the Worker–Peasant Militia of the NKVD, from July 1939 deputy director of the headquarters for state security of the NKVD, and director of the secret political section, and from September 1939 the people's commissar for the interior in the Ukrainian Soviet Socialist Republic. In 1941 he became deputy

commissar for State Security of the Soviet Union, from 1941 to 1947 deputy people's commissar (and after March 1946 deputy minister) for the interior of the Soviet Union, while at the same time, from April to July 1945, he was the deputy commander of the First Byelorussian Front. From July 1945 to November 1946 he was the deputy commander-in-chief for civil matters of the Soviet Military Command in Germany, from 1947 first deputy minister of the interior for the Soviet Union, and from March 1954 to 1958 head of the KGB. In October and November 1956 he directed the operations of state security in Hungary. From 1946 to 1962 he was a member of the Supreme Council of the Soviet Union, but in 1965 he was expelled from the party.

Shvoy, Lajos (1879–1968)
Catholic diocesan bishop. He taught religion, and then became director of the Regnum Marianum Society and the St. Cecilia Society. In 1944 the Arrow Cross hauled him off to the Kőhida Prison in Sopron. He was Bishop of Székesfehérvár from 1927 to 1968 and also a papal throne guard.

Slachta, Margit (1884–1974)
Police chief, legitimist politician and member of the Christian National Unity Party [KNEP]. In 1920 she became the first female member of the Hungarian Parliament; she organized her own movement, the Christian Women's Camp. She was a founder of the Society of Social Brothers and also its director from 1923 to 1949. During World War II she protested against racial hatred and racial persecution and saved people from being persecuted. She ran as a Smallholder during the municipal elections in Budapest held on October 7, 1945, but was elected to the National Assembly as a member of the Civic Democratic Party [PDP] on November 4, 1945. In 1947 she represented the Christian Women's Camp. She left Hungary in 1949 and settled in the United States.

Stalin, Joseph (Joseph Vissarionovich Djugashvili) (1879–1953)
Soviet politician and dictator, originally from Georgia. A member of the Communist Party from 1898, he was a professional revolutionary from 1900 onwards: the Tsarist

authorities arrested him several times for his revolutionary activities. After the February Revolution of 1917 he became a member of the party's Office of the Central Committee and the editorial board of *Pravda*; from October 1917 he was also a member of the Revolutionary Military Council of Petrograd; from October 1917 to July 1923 he was the people's commissar for national minorities of the Russian Soviet Socialist Republic; in 1918 he was the president of the Military Council of the Northern Caucasus Military District, and also a member of the Revolutionary Military Council of the Southern Front; from April 1922 he was the secretary of the party's Central Committee, later its general secretary; he was also president of the Council of People's Commissars and from March 1946 the president of the Council of Ministers; at the same time he was the president of the Committee for State Security and its supreme commander from June 1941 to September 1945.

Sulyok, Dezső (1897–1965)

Lawyer; pro-government, and later Smallholder, politician. In 1935 he was a representative of the National Unity Party [NEP], but in 1937 he changed over to the Independent Smallholders' Party [FKGP]; he was a representative from June 24, 1945 onwards. He was also president of the Center for Monetary Institutions after 1945. Along with twenty colleagues he was expelled from the FKGP on March 12, 1945; he then became president of the Hungarian Freedom Party [MSZP], which he himself had founded. He resigned his mandate on July 22, 1947, and left the country, later settling in the United States.

Suslov, Mikhail Andreyevich (1902–1982)

Soviet politician. From 1931 onwards, he filled various party functions: director of the Agitation and Propaganda Department of the Soviet Communist Party from 1947 to 1948, and director of its foreign affairs department from 1948 to 1949; editor-in-chief of *Pravda* from 1949 to 1951; a member of the Central Committee of the Soviet Communist Party from 1941; a member of the Central Committee's Politburo and its Executive Committee from 1952 to 1953 and July 1955 to his death. From

1947 until his death he was a secretary of the Central Committee of the Communist Party of the Soviet Union [CPSU] from 1952 and oversaw propaganda, ideology and cultural life. He visited Budapest during the first few days of July 1956 in order to try to solve the internal crisis of the Hungarian Workers' Party [MDP], and strengthened the position of Mátyás Rákosi at that time; he was sent to Budapest with Anastas Mikoyan on October 23, 1956, to deliver the Soviet intention to intervene, was recalled to report on the situation on October 28, 1956, and returned again to Budapest on November 11 in order to consult with Kádár on what was to be done. During the time of the Hungarian Revolution he was considered to be a "hard-liner" among the leadership of the Central Committee of the CPSU.

Sviridov, Vladimir Petrovich (1897–1963)
Soviet general. Between 1945 and 1947 he was the managing vice-president of the Allied Control Commission [SZEB].

Szakasits, Árpád (1888–1965)
Social Democrat politician. A member of the leadership of the Social Democratic Party [SZDP] from 1925, and general secretary of the party from 1938 to August 1942. He became editor-in-chief of *Népszava* in 1940. Then he became minister of state, and later deputy prime minister from 1945 onwards. He was minister of industry in 1948, and president of the Republic in 1948–1949, and also president of the Council of Ministers. From 1948 he was a member of the Central Committee and Politburo of the Hungarian Workers' Party [MDP], and the president of the party. He was arrested and condemned to life imprisonment in 1950 on false charges, but was rehabilitated later that year. From 1958 he was the president of the National Organization of Hungarian Journalists [MÚOSZ], and later of the World Federation of Hungarians and the National Peace Council.

Szalai, András (1917–1949)
Politician, originally a metalworker. He became a member of the Young Hungarian Communist Workers' Organization [KIMSZ] at Pécs. He was sentenced to prison for his political

activities; after regaining his freedom he joined the work of the KIMSZ at Budapest, the Red Assistance and the National Youth Committee, but was rearrested in 1942 and sentenced by the court to two and a half years in prison. Beginning in 1945 he worked in the Hungarian Communist Party's [MKP's] Fourth District organization in Budapest; from 1947 to 1949 he was a deputy department head in the Central Leadership of the MKP and later the Hungarian Workers' Party. [MDP] He was arrested on May 18, 1949, and formally accused as a part of the proceedings against László Rajk: he was then condemned and executed on those trumped-up charges. He was rehabilitated in 1956.

Szalai, Béla (1922–2008)

Economist. Director of the Office of the Council of Ministers in 1952–1953; president of the National Planning Office in 1953–1954; minister of light industry in 1954–1955. From 1952 to 1956 he was one of Mátyás Rákosi's closest collaborators. He was a member of the Central Leadership of the Hungarian Workers' Party [MDP] from 1953 to 1956, and secretary of the Central Leadership from 1955 to 1956.

Szálasi, Ferenc (1887–1946)

Major on the General Staff and politician. Imprisoned from 1938 to 1940 for organizing radical right-wing political groups, he was the founder and leader of the Arrow Cross Party; as such, from October 16, 1944, to March 28, 1945, he was head of state and head of government, the "leader of the nation," and supported the German occupation with complete military and economic mobilization. For his war crimes the People's Court sentenced him to death by hanging on March 1, 1946.

Szeder, Ferenc (1881–1952)

Social Democrat politician, originally an agricultural worker, and one of the leaders of the agricultural movement. He was three times elected to Parliament between the two world wars. He was general secretary of the Hungarian Social Democratic Party from 1942 to 1943, and its deputy general secretary after

1945. He was expelled from the party in February 1948 and arrested under false charges in 1950: he died in captivity.

Szegedy-Maszák, Aladár (1903–1988)

Diplomat. He worked in the Ministry of Foreign Affairs from 1928, and led the political section of the Ministry of Foreign Affairs from the summer of 1943 until the German occupation; he was ambassador to Washington from the end of 1945 to the summer of 1947. In protest against Ferenc Nagy being forced into exile, he resigned his position and remained in the United States.

Szélig, Imre (1903–1968)

Social Democrat politician, originally a locksmith. After 1945 he was a part of the National Leadership of the Social Democratic Party and one of the secretaries of the Political Committee, also head of the party organization in the area around Pest, and the leader of the Organizational Department. He was expelled from the party in February 1948, after which he left Hungary, lived for a while in Sweden, and then settled in England. He became the secretary of the Social Democratic Party in exile.

Szentágothai, János (1912–1994)

Born into a Budapest medical family, he began his career in the Anatomy Institute of Budapest University, where he remained for ten years after qualifying as a doctor. In 1946, at the age of 34, he was appointed as head of the Anatomy Institute in Pécs. He received a Kossuth Prize for his research in 1950. While in Pécs, he became chairman of the city's Revolutionary Intellectual Committee during the 1956 Revolution and signed the October declaration calling for immediate withdrawal of Soviet occupation forces. He returned to Budapest in 1963 as head of department at the Anatomy Institute. He was made a member of the Hungarian Academy of Sciences at the age of 36 and received several more high state awards. He became a nationally known, respected and appreciated man with a very large number of state functions and an active part to play in research. He was president of the Hungarian Academy of

Sciences in 1976–1985. He was active during the change of system, playing a big part in the debates between May 1989 and March 1990, which led the leaders of the Hungarian Democratic Forum to place him on their list in the 1990 elections.

Szent-Györgyi, Albert (1893–1986)

Born in Budapest, he qualified as a medical doctor in 1917. He then did a doctorate in chemistry at Cambridge and spent a year working in the United States. He was called back by Minister of Education Kuno Klebelsberg and was a professor of medical chemistry at Szeged University in 1931–1945. In 1937 he won the Nobel Prize for Medicine "for his discoveries in the field of Vitamin C and the role of fumaric acid as a catalyst." In 1945–1947 he was professor of biochemistry in the medical school of Budapest University. He was made a corresponding member of the Hungarian Academy of Sciences in 1935, a full member in 1938, and an honorary member on May 30, 1945. He left the country at the end of 1947 and settled at Woods Hole near Boston, Massachusetts, where he headed the Marine Biological Laboratory in 1947–1962. In 1962–1971 he was a professor at Dartmouth University. He kept up contacts with Hungary and began to visit regularly in the 1960s.

Szilágyi, József (1917–1958)

He was born in Debrecen, where he obtained a law degree in 1939. By then he was already active in the March Front and had joined the illegal Communist Party in 1938. At the end of 1944 he became chief of police in Debrecen and was then charged by the Communist Party with organizing the national police. In 1948 he became a member of the Central Control Committee of the combined communist/social democrat Hungarian Workers' Party, but he was relieved of his posts after questioning the truth of the charges against László Rajk and his associates in 1949. He joined Imre Nagy's circle after 1953 and was expelled from the Communist Party early in 1956. He spoke at the rally at Budapest Technical University on October 22, 1956. On October 28 he and Jenő Széll set up the prime ministerial secretariat. He and his family took refuge in the Yugoslav Embassy on November 4 and were interned in Romania after November 22. He was arrested in Snagov on March 27, 1957. He refused all cooperation with the judiciary, which is why he was tried separately from Imre Nagy and his other associates. He was sentenced to death by the People's Judicial Council of the Supreme Court chaired by Ferenc Vida on April 22, 1958, without possibility of appeal, and executed two days later.

Szirmai, István (1906–1969)

Born in Zilah (Zilău), he studied law at university in Paris and Kolozsvár (Cluj-Napoca), and joined the Romanian Communist Party in 1929. In October 1944 he became deputy secretary, then secretary of the Hungarian Communist Party's South Hungary District Committee, based in Szeged, and at the end of 1945 a staff member for the Central Leadership. He entered Parliament in November 1945. He was appointed as president of Hungarian Radio in September 1949. In January 1953 he was arrested in connection with the planned Zionist trial and deprived of his seat in Parliament and alternate membership of the Central Leadership, but was released without charge in 1954. In December 1956 he was appointed as president of the government's new Information Bureau for controlling the press. He became a Communist Party Central Committee member in June 1957, and from July 1957 to December 1959 was head of the Central Committee's Agitprop Department. He became a member of Parliament again in 1958. At the Seventh Congress of the party in 1959, he became an alternate member of the Politburo and a Central Committee secretary, in charge of culture and ideology. In 1962 he became a full member of the Politburo. Although he was retired for health reasons in the spring of 1969, he remained a member of the Politburo until his death.

Szőnyi, Tibor (1903–1949)

Communist politician. In 1936 he was active for the party in Vienna and afterwards in Czechoslovakia; later he worked in Switzerland. After 1945 he was the instructor of the

Organizational Department of the Hungarian Communist Party [MKP], later its deputy director; in 1946–1947 he was director of the Office of the Organizational Committee; later he led the Cadre Department of the Central Leadership and was a member of the Central Leadership and the Organizational Committee. He was arrested and executed on trumped-up charges in 1949.

Sztójay, Döme (1883–1946)

Military officer and politician. Military attaché in Berlin from 1927 to 1933; then director of the Executive Department of the Ministry of Defense until 1936, the Hungarian ambassador to Berlin from the end of 1935 to March 1944, and prime minister and minister of foreign affairs from March 22 to August 29, 1944. He was executed as a war criminal.

Szurdi, István (1911–1987)

Social Democrat, later Communist, politician. He worked at the headquarters of the Social Democratic Party from 1945 to 1948, and was a senior member of the Organizational Department of the Central Leadership of the Hungarian Workers' Party [MDP] from 1948 to 1950, and a member of the Central Leadership of the MDP from 1948 to 1951. Between 1950 and 1957 he was a department head and deputy department director in the Ministry of Light Industry; after 1957 he was director of the Department of Industry and Transport of the Hungarian Socialist Workers' Party [MSZMP]. He was a secretary of the Central Committee of the MSZMP from 1963 to 1966, a member of this Central Committee from February 26, 1957, to 1980, and minister of internal commerce from 1966 to 1976.

Szűcs, Ernő (1908–1950)

Communist, state security specialist, originally a textile technician, who returned from the Soviet Union. Between the two world wars he was imprisoned several times; between 1931 and 1933 he studied at the University for Westerners in the Soviet Union; he returned home and was imprisoned; in June 1941 the Soviet Embassy in Budapest provided him with a repatriation passport, and he left on June 6 that year; he came back from the

Soviet Union (where he worked for the NKDV) on August 28, 1946, and became the deputy of Gábor Péter and a colonel in state security. On September 23, 1950, he was arrested on trumped-up charges (like Rajk and his associates) and beaten to death.

Szűrös, Mátyás (b. 1933)

Born in Püspökladány, he studied at the Institute of International Relations in Moscow and at the Miklós Zrínyi Military Academy. He became a third secretary at the East Berlin Embassy in 1962. He joined the staff of the Foreign Affairs Department of the Communist Party Central Committee in 1965 and became its deputy head in 1974. He was ambassador in East Berlin and Moscow in 1975–1982, then head of the Central Committee Foreign Affairs Department in 1983. He had joined the Central Committee of the Communist Party in 1978 as ambassador to Moscow, and in 1983–1989 he was a Central Committee secretary. He belonged with Imre Pozsgay and Miklós Németh to the reform wing of the Communist Party. He entered Parliament in 1985. In March 1989 he was elected as speaker of Parliament. On declaring the Republic of Hungary on October 23, 1989, in Parliament he became president *ad interim* from November 3, 1989, to May 1, 1990. In 1989 he joined the successor party to the communists, the Hungarian Socialist Party, and he was its only candidate to gain a constituency seat in Parliament in 1990. He left the party in 2002 and stood again for the New Left Wing, but the party gained only 0.1 percent of the vote in the general elections. In 2003 he joined the "historical" Social Democratic Party and was elected as its president, but resigned in 2005.

Tánczos, Gábor (1928–1979)

Teacher and Communist politician. In 1945 in his home town of Baja he participated in the organization of the people's college and the Hungarian Democratic Youth Organization [MADISZ], and then joined the Communist Party. He became a victim of the great purges that followed the Rajk trial, and he was driven away from the political apparatus. He received his university degree in 1953 and he became a student assistant in the philosophy department of Loránd Eötvös University [ELTE]. He was a follower of Imre Nagy's reform policies. At the beginning of 1955 the Union of Working Youth entrusted him with the leadership of the so-called Petőfi Circle, an intellectual debating organization in Budapest; he had a decisive role in later turning this debating circle into one of the main forums for supporting the policies of Imre Nagy, and did not change his position even after the decision of the party to condemn the activities of the Petőfi Circle in July 1956: he still openly supported the politics of Imre Nagy. In the days after October 23, 1956, he tried to mediate and establish connections between Imre Nagy and the events in the country far from the party center. He became a member of the group that sought the protection of the Yugoslav Embassy, and on November 22 he was also taken to Romania: he was arrested on March 17, 1957, in Snagov. In August 1958 he was sentenced to fifteen years in prison, but was freed by an amnesty in the spring of 1962.

Teleki, Géza, Count (1911–1983)

Professor and Conservative politician. Beginning in 1936 he worked as a geologist at the Hungarian Geological Institute in Budapest; from 1940 he was a professor at the University of Kolozsvár and director of the Institute for Geographical Economy and Geology. He was the minister of religion and education in the Provisional National Government from December 22, 1944, to November 15, 1945.

Teleki, Pál, Count (1879–1941)

Jurist, geographer and politician. Prime minister and minister of foreign affairs in 1920–1921, minister of religion and education in 1938–1939, and again prime minister in 1939–1941. He was also minister of foreign affairs from the end of 1940. In protest over Hungary's participation in the attack on Yugoslavia, he committed suicide.

Tildy, Zoltán (1889–1961)

Reformed pastor and Smallholder politician. He was a founding member of the Independent Smallholders' Party [FKGP], and its managing vice-president from 1930 onwards; he was also a representative in the Parliament from 1936 to 1944. Then he participated in the resistance movement. He was prime minister from November 15, 1945, to February 1, 1946, and then president of the Republic until August 3, 1948. He lived under house arrest from 1949 to 1956. He was a minister of state in the government of Imre Nagy from October 27 to November 4, 1956. In 1958 he was condemned to six years in prison, but was freed in 1959.

Tito, Josip Broz (1892–1980)

Yugoslav political leader. He joined the Social Democratic Party of Croatia and Slovenia in 1910. During World War I he fell into Russian captivity on the Eastern Front, and became a member of the Russian Communist Party during the spring of 1918. Then in 1920 he became a member of the Yugoslav Communist Party; in 1934 he was coopted into the Central Committee and also elected as a member of the Politburo. He assumed the name Tito at this time. He played an important role in transporting volunteers to Spain during the time of the Civil War. He was sent to Yugoslavia in 1936 in order to execute the purges in the Yugoslav Communist Party. From 1937 to 1966 he was the general secretary of the Yugoslav Communist Party and the Yugoslav Communist Alliance, and after 1966 he became the president of the party. In 1941 he was elected as head of the Military Committee; he was the commander-in-chief of the Yugoslav partisan movement during World War II, and the decisive personality in the Yugoslav People's Liberation Anti-Fascist Council; at the second meeting of the Council Tito was elected as president and marshal of Yugoslavia. From 1953 until his death he was the president of the Yugoslav Republic, and one of the leaders of the non-aligned movement.

Újhelyi, Szilárd (1915–1996)

Jurist, politician and member of the Imre Nagy group. He obtained his legal degree in Debrecen in 1937; in the same year he was one of the initiators of the March Front; he edited the periodical *Tovább* and after 1940 became a part of the illegal Communist Party, and participated in the resistance movement. From 1945 he was a state secretary in the Ministry of Welfare, and from 1948 the general secretary of the Institute for Cultural Exchanges; from the end of 1949 he was deputy director of Hungarian Radio. He was arrested in March 1951 and received a sentence of eight years in prison on trumped-up charges, but was freed during the summer of 1954. In 1955 he joined the interparty opposition that developed around Imre Nagy, and during the days of the Revolution of 1956 he was one of Imre Nagy's circle of advisers. He also sought the protection of the Yugoslav Embassy on November 4, and was hauled off to Romania on November 23; however, he was one of the few who were not formally charged and tried: he was allowed to return to Hungary in the autumn of 1958 after the trial of Imre Nagy. After his return to Hungary he worked first at the Institute for History of the Hungarian Academy of Sciences and later was also employed by the Ministry of Education. In 1988 he was one of the founding members of the New March Front; later he was one of the founders and later president of the Committee for Historical Justice. He was also a vice-president of the Mihály Károlyi Society.

Varga, Béla (1903–1995)

Catholic priest and Smallholder politician. A parish priest in Balatonboglár from 1929 to 1947, he was one of the founders of the Independent Smallholders' Party [FKGP], and its vice-president after 1937, and a representative in the Parliament from 1939. During the war he actively participated in helping Polish refugees. From February 1945 he was the president of the party organization in Budapest; from August 20, 1945, he was the managing vice-president of the party; from April 1945 he was a member of the Provisional National Assembly; from December 7, 1945, to mid-January 1946, he was a member of the National High Council; from February 7, 1946, he was president of the National Assembly. After the resignation of Prime Minister

Ferenc Nagy he emigrated on June 2, 1947, and returned permanently to Hungary only on July 2, 1991.

Vas, Zoltán (1903–1983)

Journalist and Communist politician. He was arrested in 1921 for participating in Communist organizing of young workers; he went to the Soviet Union as part of an exchange of prisoners, and after returning to Hungary served as government commissioner for food in Budapest; later until 1949 he was the secretary of the High Council for the Economy; then he became president of the National Planning Office until 1953, director of the Mine Trust of Komló in 1953–1954, head of the Council of Ministers from August 1954 to January 1955, and also deputy minister of foreign trade; from 1945 to 1956 he was a member of the Central Leadership of the Hungarian Communist Party [MKP] and then the Hungarian Workers' Party [MDP], and from 1948 to 1953 an alternate member of the Politburo. In October 1956 he was the commissioner for public provisioning in Imre Nagy's government. On November 4, 1956, he also sought protection in the Yugoslav Embassy, and on November 23 he was interned in Romania; in 1958 he returned home. In the 1970s he was accused again because of his memoirs.

Vásárhelyi, Miklós (1917–2001)

Journalist. During the 1930s he studied law in Rome and at the University of Debrecen; he joined the illegal Communist Party in 1938 and participated in the resistance. After 1945 he was a contributor to first *Szabadság* and then *Szabad Nép*; in the 1950s he was director of Hungarian Radio; after 1951 he was an editor of *Művelt Nép*; from 1952 to 1954 he was the editor of *Hungary-Vengrija*. After 1953 he belonged to the inner circle of the opposition group that grew up around Imre Nagy; in May 1954 he was appointed as deputy president of the Communications Office of the Council of Ministers, a position that he held until the end of Imre Nagy's premiership. In 1955 he was expelled from the party due to his involvement with the opposition; afterwards he worked as a librarian. At the time of the Revolution of 1956 he became Imre Nagy's press chief on November 1; he received sanctuary in the home of a Yugoslav diplomat on November 4, but on November 22 he was deported with the rest of Imre Nagy's group to Romania, where he was arrested on April 17, 1957; on June 14, 1958, during the Imre Nagy trial he was sentenced to five years in prison; however, he was freed by an amnesty in April 1960. From 1965 he was a contributor to *Élet és Irodalom* and from 1972 to 1990 a research associate of the Institute for Literature of the Hungarian Academy of Sciences [MTA], and one of the founding members of the Committee for Historical Justice and its president until 1992. He gave a speech at the reburial of Imre Nagy and his associates on June 16, 1989. He was one of the founders of the Alliance of Free Democrats [SZDSZ], and after 1990 a member of the party's National Council, and a representative in the Parliament from 1990 to 1994.

Veres, Péter (1897–1970)

Farmer, writer, publicist and politician of the Peasant Party. He was one of the founders of the National Peasant Party [NPP]; in early 1945 he was elected as president of the party in Debrecen; from April 1945 until his death he was a representative. He accepted appointment as minister twice: minister of reconstruction and public work from March to September 1947, and minister of defense from September 1947 to November 1948. From 1954 he was the president of the Hungarian Writers' Union. At the meeting where the Petőfi Party was founded he resigned from all previous party positions. He remained active as a writer until his death.

Voroshilov, Kliment Yefremovich (1911–1969)

Soviet politician. He was a member of the Central Committee of the Soviet Communist Party from 1921 (later of the Communist Party of the Soviet Union [CPSU]) to 1961, and a member of the Politburo from 1926 to 1961. He was commissar for military, naval and defense matters from 1925 to 1940; he served in Hungary as president of the Allied Control Commission [SZEB] from 1945 to 1947; he was vice-president of the Council of Ministers of the Soviet Union from 1946 to 1953. Later he became a member of the Executive of the Supreme Council and then its president.

Vyshinsky, Andrey Januaryevich (1883–1954)

Soviet politician and jurist. Public prosecutor of the Soviet Union from 1933 to 1935; vice-president of the Council of People's Commissars of the Soviet Union from 1939 to 1944. From 1940 onwards he held several leading positions relating to foreign relations; after 1949 he was minister of foreign affairs.

Zöld, Sándor (1913–1951)

Physician and politician. During his years in Debrecen he became a member of the Communist Party of Hungary [KMP], and took part in the organization of the March Front. From December 1944 to July 1945 he was a state secretary in the Ministry of the Interior of the Provisional National Government; from July 1948 he was an alternate, later regular, member of the Central Leadership of the Hungarian Workers' Party [MDP]; from May 1950 he was a member of the Politburo; between October 1948 and June 1950 he was the administrative state secretary of the Ministry of the Interior, later becoming minister of the interior. On April 19, 1951, Rákosi launched a personal attack on him at the meeting of the Politburo; the next day he was found dead, together with his entire family.

Zsedényi, Béla (1894–1955)

Lawyer and president of the Provisional National Assembly. He was arrested on October 16, 1950, and sentenced to life imprisonment by the Budapest Criminal Court on November 27, 1950, as a part of the proceedings against József Kővágó and his associates. The decision was reversed on June 27, 1957, and the prosecution was ended by the Budapest Capital Court due to the fact that he could no longer be punished, due to his death in prison. In 1962 the Public Prosecutorial Office proposed to renew the prosecution, and the Supreme Court on December 9, 1963, dropped the prosecution of Zsedényi, now deceased. But the fact was told to his family only in 1989.

SELECTED BIBLIOGRAPHY

Az 1980-as népszámlálás lakásstatisztikai adatai [Housing Statistics from the 1980 Census]. Budapest: KSH, 1984.

A. Sajti, Enikő. *Impériumváltások, revízió, kisebbség. Magyarok a Délvidéken, 1918–1947* [Exchanging Empires, Revision, Minority. Hungarians in the Southern Region, 1918–1947]. Budapest: Napvilág, 2004.

Agócs, Sándor, and Endre Medvigy, eds. *Lakitelek, 1987. A magyarság esélyei* [Lakitelek, 1987. The Prospects of the Hungarian Nation]. Budapest: Püski, and Lakitelek: Antológia, 1991.

Ambrus, Péter. *Dzsumbuj* [Tenement]. Budapest: Magvető, 1988.

Andorka, Rudolf. *Bevezetés a szociológiába* [Introduction to Sociology]. Budapest: Osiris, 1997.

Andorka, Rudolf, Tamás Kolosi, and György Vukovich, eds. *Társadalmi Riport, 1990* [Social Report, 1990]. Budapest: TÁRKI, 1990.

Andorka, Rudolf, Tamás Kolosi and György Vukovich, eds. *Társadalmi Riport, 1996* [Social Report, 1996]. Budapest: TÁRKI, 1996.

Árvay, János, and András Vértes. *A magánszektor és a rejtett gazdaság súlya Magyarországon (1980–1992)* [The Significance of the Private Sector and the Hidden Economy in Hungary (1980–1992)]. Budapest: Gazdaságkutató Rt., 1994.

Balassa, Iván, ed. *Magyar Néprajz IV. Életmód* [Hungarian Ethnology IV. Lifestyle]. Budapest: Akadémiai, 1997.

Balogh, Margit. *Mindszenty József, 1892–1975* [József Mindszenty, 1892–1975]. Budapest: Elektra, 2002.

Balogh, Margit, and Jenő Gergely, eds. *Állam, egyház, vallásgyakorlás Magyarországon, 1790–2005* [State, Church and

Religious Practice in Hungary, 1790–2005]. Vol. 2. Budapest: MTA Történettudományi Intézete, 2005.

Bánkuti, Gábor. *A Rend és a Szerv, 1948–1956. A jezsuita rend "átfogásának" kísérlete* [The Order and the Organ, 1948–1956. The Attempt to "Seize" the Jesuit Order]. (Ph.D. dissertation. Pécs, 2009.)

Baráth, Magdolna, ed. *Szovjet nagyköveti iratok Magyarországról, 1953–1956. Kiszeljov és Andropov titkos jelentései* [The Papers of the Soviet Ambassadors on Hungary, 1953–1956. The Secret Dispatches of Kiszeljov and Andropov]. Budapest: Napvilág, 2002.

Bárdi, Nándor. *Tény és való – a budapesti kormányzatok és a határon túli magyarság kapcsolattörténete* [Undeniable—The History of Relations between Budapest Governments and Hungarian Communities outside the Country]. Pozsony: Kalligram, 2004.

Bárdi, Nándor, Csilla Fedinecz and László Szarka, eds. *Kisebbségi magyar közösségek a XX. században* [Hungarian Minority Communities in the 20th Century]. Budapest: Gondolat – MTA Etnikai-Nemzeti Kisebbségkutató Intézet, 2008.

Barth, Berndt-Rainer, and Werner Schweizer. *Der Fall Noel Field. Schlüsselfigur der Schauprozesse in Osteuropa.* Vols. 1–2. Berlin: BasisDruck, 2005–2007.

Beck, Tibor, and Pál Germuska. *Forradalom a bölcsészkaron* [Revolution at the Faculty of Arts]. Budapest: 1956-os Intézet, 1997.

Békés, Csaba. *Az 1956-os magyar forradalom a világpolitikában* [The 1956 Hungarian Revolution in World Politics]. Budapest: 1956-os Intézet, 2006.

Békés, Csaba. *Európából Európába. Magyarország konfliktusok kereszttüzében, 1945–1990* [From Europe to Europe. Hungary in the Crossfire of Conflict, 1945–1990]. Budapest: Gondolat, 2004.

Berend T., Iván. *Gazdasági útkeresés 1956–1965* [Economic Reorientation, 1956–1965]. Budapest: Magvető, 1983.

Berend T., Iván. *Hungarian Economic Reforms 1953–1988.* Cambridge: Cambridge University Press, 1990.

Berend T., Iván. *Terelőúton. Szocialista modernizációs kísérlet Közép- és Kelet-Európában 1944–1990* [Detour. Socialist Modernization Attempt in Central and Eastern Europe, 1944–1990]. Budapest: Vince, 1999.

Bölöni, József, ed. *Magyarország kormányai, 1848–1992* [Hungary's Governments, 1848–1992]. Budapest: Akadémiai, 1992.

Borhi, László. *A magyar–amerikai viszony változásai, 1957–1978* [Transformations in Hungarian–American Relations, 1957–1978]. Budapest: Zrínyi, 2004.

Borhi, László. *Magyarország a hidegháborúban. A Szovjetunió és az Egyesült Államok között, 1945–1956* [Hungary in the Cold War. Between the Soviet Union and the United States, 1945–1956]. Budapest: Corvina, 2005.

Borhi, László. *Vasfüggöny mögött – Magyarország nagyhatalmi erőtérben 1945–1968* [Behind the Iron Curtain—Hungary in the Great Power Arena 1945–1968]. Budapest: Ister, 2000.

Botos, János, György Gyarmati, Mihály Korom and Tibor Zinner. *Magyar hétköznapok Rákosi Mátyás két emigrációja között* [Everyday Life in Hungary between the Two Emigrations of Mátyás Rákosi]. Budapest: Minerva, 1988.

Bozóki, András, Márta Elbert, Melinda Kalmár, Béla Révész, Erzsébet Ripp and Zoltán Ripp, eds. *A rendszerváltás forgatókönyve. Kerekasztal-tárgyalások 1989-ben. 7. kötet. Tanulmányok* [The Script of the System Change. Roundtable Negotiations in 1989. Volume 7. Studies]. Budapest: Új Mandátum, 2000.

Census Data, Microcensus 1996. Homes and Their Inhabitants. Budapest: KSH, 1996.

Congdon, Lee, Béla K. Király and Károly Nagy, eds. *1956. The Hungarian Revolution and War of Independence.* Highland Lakes, NJ: ARP, 2006.

Cseh, Gergő Bendegúz, Melinda Kalmár and Edit Por. *Zárt, bizalmas, számozott. Tájékoztatáspolitika és cenzúra 1956–1963* [Closed, Confidential, Numbered. Information Policy and Censorship 1953–1963]. Budapest: Osiris, 1998.

Csicsery-Rónay, István, Géza Cserenyei and Mária Palasik. *Koncepciós per a Független Kisgazdapárt szétzúzására* [Show Trial for the Destruction of the Independent Smallholders' Party]. Budapest: 1956-os Intézet, 1998.

Csizmadia, Ervin. *A magyar demokratikus ellenzék* [The Hungarian Democratic Opposition]. Vols. 1–3. Budapest: T-Twins, 1998.

Donáth, Ferenc. *A Márciusi Fronttól Monorig* [From the March Front to Monor]. Budapest: Századvég – MTA KGI., 1992.

Dornbach, Alajos, Péter Kende, János M. Rainer and Katalin Somlai. *A per. Nagy Imre és társai. 1958, 1989* [The Trial. Imre Nagy and His Associates, 1958, 1989]. Budapest: 1956-os Intézet – Nagy Imre Alapítvány, 2008.

Élelmiszermérlegek 1970–1997 [Food Balance 1970–1997]. Budapest: KSH, 1998.

Életszínvonal 1960–1980 [Living Standards 1960–1980]. Budapest: KSH, 1981.

Életszínvonal II. Az életszínvonal alakulásának lakossági megítélése [Living Standards II. The Popular Assessment of Changes in the Standard of Living]. Budapest: KSH, 1978.

Eörsi, István. *Emlékezés a régi szép időkre* [Memory of the Good Old Days]. Budapest: Napraforgó, 1989.

Eörsi, László. *Corvinisták 1956 (A VIII. kerület fegyveres csoportjai)* [Corvinists 1956 (Armed Groups of the Eighth District)]. Budapest: 1956-os Intézet, 2001.

Eörsi, László. *Széna tériek 1956* [The Freedom Fighters of Széna Tér, 1956]. Budapest: 1956-os Intézet – ÁBTL, 2004.

Erdmann, Gyula. *Begyűjtés, beszolgáltatás Magyarországon, 1945–1956* [Harvest and Compulsory Delivery to the State in Hungary, 1945–1956]. Gyula: Békés Megyei Levéltár, n.d.

Étrendi Szokások [Nutritional Habits]. Budapest: KSH, 1960.

Évkönyv 2000. Budapest: 1956-os Intézet, 2000.

Falussy, Béla, ed. *A magyar társadalom életmódjának változásai az 1976–77. évi, az 1986–87. évi és az 1993. évi életmód-időmérleg alapján. I. A társadalmi idő felhasználása* [Lifestyle Changes in

Hungarian Society Based on Lifestyle Time Budgets for 1976–1977, 1986–1987 and 1993. Vol. I. Utilization of Social Time]. Budapest: KSH, 1994.
Feitl, István. *Az Ideiglenes Nemzetgyűlés és az Ideiglenes Nemzeti Kormány* [The Provisional National Assembly and the Provisional National Government]. Budapest: Politikatörténeti Alapítvány, 1995.
Feitl, István, Márta Lázár Gelleriné and János Kende, eds. *Demokratikus köztársaságok Magyarországon, 1918–1989* [Democratic Republics in Hungary, 1918–1989]. Budapest: Napvilág, 2007.
Feitl, István, Lajos Izsák and Gábor Székely, eds. *Fordulat a világban és Magyarországon, 1947–1949* [Revolution in the World and in Hungary, 1947–1949]. Budapest: Napvilág, 2000.
Fél, Edit, and Tamás Hofer. *Arányok és mértékek a paraszti gazdálkodásban* [Degree and Proportion in Peasant Agriculture]. Budapest: Balassi, 1997.
Ferge, Sándor, Mrs., István Kemény, Mrs. György Láng and Mrs. Aladár Mód. *Társadalmi rétegződés Magyarországon* [Social Stratification in Hungary]. Budapest: KSH, 1966.
Ferge, Zsuzsa. *Társadalmi újratermelés és társadalompolitika* [Social Reproduction and Social Policy]. Budapest: KjK, 1982.
Fischer, Ferenc. *A megosztott világ, 1941–1991* [The Divided World, 1941–1991]. Budapest and Pécs: Dialóg Campus, 2001.
Földes, György. *Az eladósodás politikatörténete* [The Political History of Indebtedness]. Budapest: Maecenas, 1998.
Földes, György. *Magyarország, Románia és a nemzeti kérdés 1956–1989* [Hungary, Romania and the Nationality Question 1956–1989]. Budapest: Napvilág, 2007.
Földes, György, and László Hubai, eds. *Parlamenti képviselőválasztások 1920–1998* [Parliamentary Elections 1920–1998]. Budapest: Politikatörténeti Alapítvány, 1994.
Földes, György, and László Hubai, eds. *Parlamenti választások Magyarországon, 1920–1998* [Parliamentary Elections in Hungary, 1949–1998]. Budapest: Napvilág, 1998.

Font, Márta, and István Kajtár, eds. *A magyar államiság első ezer éve* [The First Thousand Years of the Hungarian State]. Pécs: Pécsi Tudományegyetem, 2000.

Fülöp, Mihály. *A befejezetlen béke. A Külügyminiszterek Tanácsa és a magyar békeszerződés* [The Unfinished Peace Agreement. The Foreign Ministers' Council and the Hungarian Peace Treaty]. Budapest: Héttorony, n.d.

Fülöp, Mihály, and Péter Sipos. *Magyarország külpolitikája a XX. században* [Hungary's Foreign Policy in the 20th Century]. Budapest: Aula, 1998.

G. Vass, István, ed. *Dinnyés Lajos első kormányának minisztertanácsi jegyzőkönyvei, 1947. június – szeptember* [The Minutes of the Meetings of the Council of Ministers of Lajos Dinnyés's First Government, June to September 1947]. Budapest: MOL, 2005.

G. Vass, István, ed. *Tildy Zoltán kormányának minisztertanácsi jegyzőkönyvei, 1945. november – 1946. február* [The Minutes of the Meetings of the Zoltán Tildy Government's Council of Ministers, November 1945 to February 1946]. Budapest: MOL, 2005.

Gál, Éva, András B. Hegedűs, György Litván and János M. Rainer, eds. *Jelcin-dosszié. Szovjet dokumentumok 1956-ról* [The Yeltsin Dossier. Soviet Documents about 1956]. Budapest: Századvég – 1956-os Intézet, 1993.

Gati, Charles. *Failed Illusions. Moscow, Washington, Budapest and the Hungarian Revolution.* Washington, DC: Woodrow Wilson Center, and Stanford, CA: Stanford University Press, 2006.

Gati, Charles. *Magyarország a Kreml árnyékában* [Hungary in the Shadow of the Kremlin]. Budapest: Századvég, 1990.

Gati, Charles. *Vesztett illúziók. Moszkva, Washington, Budapest és az 1956-os magyar forradalom* [Lost Illusions. Moscow, Washington, Budapest and the Hungarian Revolution of 1956]. Budapest: Osiris, 2008.

Gazdag, Ferenc, and László J. Kiss, eds. *Nemzeti érdek és kontinuitás* [National Interest and Continuity]. Budapest: Zrínyi, 2004.

Gazsó, Ferenc. *Iskolarendszer és társadalmi mobilitás* [School System and Social Mobility]. Budapest: Kossuth, 1976.

Gecsényi, Lajos, and Gábor Máthé, eds. *Sub clausula, 1956.* Budapest, Közlöny Kiadó: 2006.

Gergely, Jenő. *Az 1950-es egyezmény és a szerzetesrendek feloszlatása Magyarországon* [The Agreement of 1950 and the Disbanding of the Religious Orders in Hungary]. Budapest: Vigília, 1950.

Gergely, Jenő, József Kardos and Ferenc Rottler. *Az egyházak Magyarországon* [The Churches in Hungary]. Budapest: Korona, 1997.

Gundel, Imre, and Judit Harmath. *A vendéglátás emlékei* [Memories of Hospitality]. Budapest: KjK, 1979.

Gyáni, Gábor, György Kövér and Tibor Valuch. *Social History of Hungary from the Reform Era to the End of the Twentieth Century.* Highland Lakes, NJ: ARP, 2004.

Gyáni, Gábor, and János M. Rainer, eds. *Ezerkilencszázötvenhat az újabb történeti irodalomban* [Nineteen-Fifty-Six in Recent Historical Writing]. Budapest: 1956-os Intézet, 2007.

Gyarmati, György. *Március hatalma – a hatalom Márciusa. Fejezetek március 15. ünneplésének történetéből* [The Power of March, the March of Power. Chapters from the Celebrations of March 15]. Budapest: Paginarum, 1998.

Gyarmati, György. *A politika rendőrsége Magyarországon a Rákosi-korszakban* [The Political Police in Hungary during the Rákosi Era]. Habilitációs Füzetek 1. Pécs: Pécsi Tudományegyetem, 2002.

Gyarmati, György, ed. *Államvédelem a Rákosi-korszakban* [Defending the State during the Rákosi Era]. Budapest: Történeti Hivatal, 2000.

Gyarmati, György, ed. *Trezor 1. A Történeti Hivatal évkönyve, 1999* [Trezor 1. The Yearbook of the History Office, 1999]. Budapest: Történeti Hivatal, 1999.

Gyarmati, György, ed. *Trezor 2. A Történeti Hivatal évkönyve 2000–2001* [Trezor 2. The Yearbook of the History Office, 2000–2001]. Budapest: Történeti Hivatal, 2002.

Gyarmati, György, Erzsébet Kajári and Katalin S. Varga, eds. *A Belügyminisztérium Kollégiumának ülései, 1953–1956* [Meetings of the Ministry of the Interior Council, 1953–1956]. Vols. 1–3. Budapest: ÁBTL, 2001–2006.

Györkei, Jenő, and Miklós Horváth, eds. *Szovjet katonai intervenció, 1956* [The Soviet Military Intervention, 1956]. Budapest: Argumentum, 1996.

Gyurgyák, János, ed. *A forradalom hangja. Magyarországi rádióadások, 1956. október 23. – november 9.* [The Voice of the Revolution. Hungarian Radio Transmissions, October 23 – November 9]. Budapest: Századvég. 1989.

Hajdú, Zoltán. *A magyar közigazgatás földrajza* [The Geography of Hungarian Public Administration]. Pécs: Dialóg Campus, 2001.

Halas, Lajos. *Az R[endező] Gárdától a Munkásőrségig* [From the O[rganizing] Guard to the Workers' Militia]. Budapest: Zrínyi, 1986.

Hankiss, Elemér. *East European Alternatives.* Oxford: Calderon, 1990.

Hankiss, Elemér, Róbert Manchin, László Füstös and Árpád Szakolczai. *Kényszerpályán? A magyar társadalom értékrendszerének alakulása 1930 és 1981 között* [Forced Path? The Evolution of the Value System of Hungarian Society between 1930 and 1981]. Budapest: MTA Szociológiai Kutató Intézete, 1982.

Hantó, Zsuzsa, and Miklós Füzes, eds. *Kitaszítottak* [Expelled]. Vols. 1–3. Budapest: Alterra, 2001–2006.

Hegedűs B., András, ed. *1956 kézikönyve. Kronológia* [1956 Handbook. Chronology]. Budapest: 1956-os Intézet, 1996.

Hegedűs B., András, and János M. Rainer, eds., *A Petőfi Kör vitái* [The Debates of the Petőfi Circle]. Vol. 1. Budapest: Kelenföld Kiadó – ELTE ÁJK, 1989.

Hetényi Varga, Károly. *Papi sorsok a horogkereszt és a vörös csillag árnyékában* [Clerical Destinies in the Shadow of the Swastika and the Red Star]. Vols. 1–4. Abaliget: Lámpás, 1992–1998.

Hetényi Varga, Károly. *Szerzetesek a horogkereszt és a vörös csillag árnyékában* [The Members of Religious Orders in the Shadow of the Swastika and the Red Star]. Vols. 1–3. Abaliget: Lámpás, 1999–2003.

Hoppál, Mihály, and Tamás Szecskő, eds. *Életmód: modellek és minták* [Lifestyle: Models and Patterns]. Budapest: Tömegkommunikációs Kutatóközpont, 1984.

Horváth, Ibolya, Pál Solt, *et al.*, eds. *Iratok az igazságszolgáltatás történetéhez* [Documents on the History of Justice]. Vol. 1. Budapest: KjK, 1992.

Horváth, Julianna, and Zoltán Ripp, eds. *Ötvenhat októbere és a hatalom* [October of Fifty-Six and the Political Power]. Budapest: Napvilág, 1997.

Horváth, Julianna, Éva Szabó, László Szűcs and Katalin Zalai, eds. *Pártközi értekezletek. Politikai érdekegyeztetés és politikai konfrontáció, 1944–1948* [Discussions among the Parties. Political Discussions and Political Confrontations, 1944–1948]. Budapest: Napvilág, 2003.

Horváth, Miklós. *1956 hadikrónikája* [The Military Chronicle of 1956]. Budapest: Akadémiai, 2003.

Horváth, Sándor, ed. *Mindennapok Rákosi és Kádár korában* [Everyday Life in the Rákosi and Kádár Era]. Budapest: Nyitott Könyvműhely, 2008.

Huszár, Tibor. *Az elittől a nómenklatúráig. Az intézményesített káderpolitika kialakulása Magyarországon, 1945–1989* [From the Elite to the Nomenklatura. The Formation of Institutionalized Cadre Policy in Hungary 1945–1989]. Budapest: Corvina, 2007.

Huszár, Tibor. *A hatalom rejtett dimenziói – Magyar Tudományos Tanács 1948–1949* [Concealed Dimensions of Power—The Hungarian Scientific Council 1948–1949]. Budapest: Akadémiai, 1995.

Huszár, Tibor. *Kádár János politikai életrajza* [The Political Biography of János Kádár]. Vols. 1–2. Budapest: Szabad Tér – Kossuth, 2001 and 2003.

Huszár, Tibor, and Gábor Hanák, eds. *Bibó István: Életút dokumentumokban* [István Bibó: a Biography in Documents]. Budapest: 1956-os Intézet, Osiris, Századvég, 1995.

Izsák, Lajos. *A polgári ellenzéki pártok Magyarországon, 1944–1949* [The Opposition Civic Parties in Hungary, 1944–1949]. Budapest: Kossuth, 1983.

Izsák, Lajos, ed. *Krónika, 1956* [Chronicle, 1956]. Budapest: Kossuth, 2006.

Izsák, Lajos, ed. *A Magyar Dolgozók Pártja határozatai, 1948–1956* [The Decrees of the Hungarian Workers' Party, 1948–1956]. Budapest: Napvilág, 1998.

Izsák, Lajos, and Miklós Kun, eds. *Moszkvának jelentjük... Titkos dokumentumok, 1944–1948* [We Report to Moscow... Secret Documents, 1944–1948]. Budapest: Századvég, 1994.

Kaase, Max, Vera Sparsbuch and Agnieszka Wenninger, eds. *Handbook on Three Social Sciences in Central and Eastern Europe: Economics, Political Science and Sociology*. Budapest: Collegium Budapest, and Berlin: Social Science Information Centre, 2002.

Kádár, János. *Hazafiság és internacionalizmus* [Patriotism and Internationalism]. Budapest: Kossuth, 1968.

Kardos, József, Elemér Kelemen and László Szögi. *A magyar felsőoktatás évszázadai* [Centuries of Hungarian Higher Education]. Budapest: Nemzeti Tankönyvkiadó, 2000.

Kardos, László, ed. *Sej, a mi lobogónkat fényes szelek fújják... Népi Kollégiumok, 1939–1949* [Ho, Radiant Winds Blow Our Banner... Peoples' Colleges, 1939–1949]. Budapest: Akadémiai, 1977.

Kelety, Géza. *Szeretetből élni* [Living on Love]. Budapest: Márton Áron, 1997.

Kemény, István. *Beszámoló a magyarországi cigányságról* [Report on the Gypsy Population in Hungary]. Budapest: MTA, 1976.

Kende, Péter. *Eltékozolt forradalom?* [Wasted Revolution?]. Budapest: Új Mandátum, 2006.

Kenedi, János. *Kis állambiztonsági olvasókönyv* [Little State Security Reader]. Budapest: Magvető, 1996.

Király, Béla. *Honvédségből néphadsereg. Személyes visszaemlékezések, 1944–1956* [From National Army into People's Army. Personal Reminiscences, 1944–1956]. Paris and New Brunswick, NJ: Magyar Füzetek – Magyar Öregdiákok Szövetsége, 1986.

Király, Béla, and Lee. W. Congdon, eds. *A magyar forradalom eszméi. Eltiprásuk és győzelmük 1956–1999* [The Ideas of the Hungarian Revolution. Their Suppression and Triumph 1956–1999]. Budapest: Atlanti Kutató és Kiadó, 2001.

Kis, János, *et al.*, eds. *Beszélő összkiadás* [The Complete *Beszélő*]. Budapest: Stencil Kulturális Alapítvány, 1992.

Kiss J., László, and Ferenc Gazdag, eds. *Magyar külpolitika a huszadik században* [Hungarian Foreign Relations in the Twentieth Century]. Budapest: Zrínyi, 2004.

Kiss, Tamás. *Magyar Egyetemisták és Főiskolások Szövetsége, 1956 – Szeged* [The Alliance of Hungarian College and University Students. 1956 – Szeged]. Szeged: Belvedere Meridionale, 2002.

Köbel, Szilvia. *"Oszd meg és uralkodj!" Az állam és az egyházak politikai, jogi és igazgatási kapcsolatai Magyarországon 1945–1989 között* ["Divide and Conquer!" The Political, Legal and Administrative Relations of the State and the Churches in Hungary between 1945 and 1989]. Budapest: Rejtjel, 2005.

Kollega Tarsoly, István, ed. *Magyarország a XX. században* [Hungary in the 20th Century]. Szekszárd: Babits, 1996.

Koltay, Gábor, and Péter Bródy, eds. *El nem égett dokumentumok* [Unburned Documents]. Budapest: Szabad Tér, 1990.

Korányi G., Tamás, ed. *Egy népfelkelés dokumentumai* [Documents of a Popular Uprising]. Budapest: Tudósítások, 1989.

Kornai, János. *A gondolat erejével. Rendhagyó önéletrajz* [The Power of Ideas. An Unorthodox Autobiography]. Budapest: Osiris, 2005.

Kornai, János. *A hiány* [The Absence]. Budapest: KjK, 1980.

Kornai, János. *The Socialist System: The Political Economy of Communism*. Oxford: Clarendon Press, 1992.
Kornai, János. *A szocialista rendszer* [The Socialist System]. Budapest: HVG, 1993.
Kőrösi, Zsuzsanna, and Pál Péter Tóth, eds. *Pártok, 1956* [Parties, 1956]. Budapest: 1956-os Intézet, 1997.
Kósa, László, ed. *Cultural History of Hungary in the Nineteenth and Twentieth Century*. Budapest: Corvina – Osiris, 2000.
Kovách, Imre. *Termelők és vállalkozók* [Farmers and Entrepreneurs]. Budapest: MTA Társadalomtudományi Intézet, 1988.
Kovács, Lajos Péter, and József Sipos, eds. *A Nagy Imre vonal* [The Imre Nagy Line]. Budapest: Reform, 1989.
Kovacsics, József, ed. *Magyarország történeti demográfiája (896–1995)* [The Historical Demography of Hungary (896–1995)]. Budapest: KSH, 1997.
Kovalcsik, József. *A kultúra csarnokai* [Halls of Culture]. Vols. 1–3. Budapest: Művelődéskutató Intézet, 1986.
Kövér, György. *Losonczy Géza, 1917–1957* [Géza Losonczy, 1917–1957]. Budapest: 1956-os Intézet, 1988.
Kozák, Gyula, ed. *Választási almanach* [Electoral Almanac]. Budapest: ABC Független, 1985.
KSH [Central Statistics Office]. *Mikrocenzus, 1996. A népesség és a lakások jellemzői* [Microcensus, 1996. Characteristics of the Population and Housing]. Budapest: KSH, 1997.
Kukorelli, István. *Így választottunk* [How We Elected]. Budapest: ELTE ÁJTK, 1988.
Kulcsár, Rózsa, and János Kisdi. *Foglalkozások presztízse* [Occupational Prestige]. Budapest: KSH, 1990.
Kurtán, Sándor, Péter Sándor and László Vass, eds. *Magyarország évtizedkönyve (1988–1998). A rendszerváltás I–II* [Hungary's Decade Book (1988–1998). The System Change I–II]. Vol. 1. Budapest: Demokrácia Kutatások Magyar Központja Alapítvány, 1998.
Ladányi, Andor. *Felsőoktatási politika, 1949–1956* [Higher Education Policy, 1949–1956]. Budapest: Kossuth, 1986.

Litván, György, ed. *The Hungarian Revolution of 1956*. New York: Longman, 1996.

A Magyar Dolgozók Pártja III. kongresszusának jegyzőkönyve [The Minutes of the Third Congress of the Hungarian Workers' Party]. Budapest: Szikra, 1954.

A Magyar Népköztársaság Alkotmánya [The Constitution of the Hungarian People's Republic]. Budapest: KjK, 1956.

A Magyar Népköztársaság Alkotmánya [The Constitution of the Hungarian People's Republic]. Budapest: Kossuth, 1972.

Magyar statisztikai évkönyv, 1980 [Hungarian Statistical Yearbook, 1980]. Budapest: KSH, 1981.

A Magyar Szocialista Munkáspárt XIII. kongresszusának jegyzőkönyve [Minutes of the 13th Congress of the Hungarian Socialist Workers' Party]. Budapest: Kossuth, 1985.

Magyarország népessége és gazdasága – múlt és jelen [Hungary's Population and Economy—Past and Present]. Budapest: KSH, 1996.

Majtényi, György, and Csaba Szabó, eds. *Rendszerváltás és a Kádár-korszak* [System Change and the Kádár Period]. Budapest: ÁBTL – Kossuth, 2008.

Makkay, István. *A bérből és fizetésből élő családok élelmiszer-fogyasztásának néhány jellegzetessége* [Some Characteristics Regarding the Food Consumption of Families Living on Pay and Wages]. Budapest: Belkereskedelmi Kutató Intézet, 1962.

Market Participants in the Hungarian Economy, 1982–1989. Budapest: KSH, 1990.

Medvegyev, Roy. *Hruscsov. Politikai életrajz* [Khrushchev. A Political Biography]. Budapest: Laude, 1989.

Mészáros, István. *A magyar nevelés- és iskolatörténet kronológiája 996–1996* [Chronology of Hungarian Educational and School History 996–1996]. Budapest: Nemzeti Tankönyvkiadó, 1996.

Mićunović, Veljko. *Tito követe voltam. Moszkva, 1956–1968* [I Was Tito's Envoy. Moscow, 1956–1968]. Budapest: Interart, 1990.

Mihályi, Péter. *A magyar privatizáció krónikája 1989–1997* [Chronicle of Hungarian Privatization 1989–1997]. Budapest: KjK, 1998.

Molnár, Miklós. *Egy vereség diadala* [The Triumph of a Defeat]. Paris and New Brunswick, NJ: Magyar Füzetek, 1988.

Az MSZMP határozatai és dokumentumai 1960–1965 [Resolutions and Documents of the Hungarian Socialist Workers' Party, 1960–1965]. Budapest: Kossuth, 1967.

Müller, Rolf, ed. *Európai kulturális fórum és ellenfórum* [European Cultural Forum and Counter-Forum]. Budapest: ÁBTL, 2005.

Nagy, Ferenc. *Küzdelem a vasfüggöny mögött* [The Struggle behind the Iron Curtain]. Vols. 1–2. Budapest: Európa – História, 1990.

Nagy, Imre. *Egy évtized. Válogatott beszédek és írások, 1948–1954* [One Decade. Selected Speeches and Writings, 1948–1954]. Vols. 1–2. Budapest: Szikra, 1954.

Nagy Imre: A magyar nép védelmében [Imre Nagy: In the Defense of Hungary's People]. [Brussels]: Forradalmi Tanács, 1957.

Nagy, Mariann, ed. *Híd a századok felett. Tanulmányok Katus László 70. születésnapjára* [Bridge over the Centuries. Studies in Honor of László Katus's Seventieth Birthday]. Pécs: University Press, 1997.

Németh, István, and István Horváth. *És a falak leomlanak. Magyarország és a német egység 1945–1990* [And the Walls Came Down. Hungary and German Unity 1945–1990]. Budapest: Magvető, 1999.

Nyírő, András, ed. *Politikai szociológiai tanulmányok a kommunista bürokrácia vezérkaráról* [Political and Sociological Studies Regarding the Leadership of the Communist Bureaucracy]. Budapest: Interart, 1989.

Nyírő, András, ed. *Segédkönyv a Politikai Bizottság tanulmányozásához* [Handbook for Study of the Political Committee]. Budapest: Interart, 1989.

Okváth, Imre. *Bástya a béke frontján. Magyar haderő és katonapolitika, 1945–1956* [A Bastion on the Peace Front. Hungarian Military Power and Military Policy, 1945–1956]. Budapest: Aquila, 1988.

Okváth, Imre, ed. *ÁVH – politika – 1956* [ÁVH – Politics – 1956]. Budapest: ÁBTL, 2007.

Orbán, József Gyula. *Katolikus papok békemozgalma Magyarországon, 1950–1956* [The Peace Movement of the Catholic Clergy in Hungary, 1950–1956]. Budapest: Magyar Egyháztörténeti Enciklopédia Munkaközösség (METMK), 2001.

Ormos, Mária. *Magyarország a két világháború korszakában, 1914–1945* [Hungary during the Age of the Two World Wars, 1914–1945]. Debrecen: Csokonai, 1998.

Oros, Iván, ed. *A falu és a mezőgazdaság főbb társadalmi és gazdasági jelzőszámai* [The Primary Social and Economic Data of Villages and Agriculture]. Budapest: KSH, 1994.

Orosz, István, Lajos Für and Pál Romány, eds. *Magyarország agrártörténete* [Hungary's Agrarian History]. Budapest: Mezőgazda, 1996.

Paládi-Kovács, Attila, ed. *Magyar néprajz VIII. A társadalom* [Hungarian Ethnography, vol. VIII. Society]. Budapest: Akadémiai, 2000.

Palasik, Mária. *Kovács Béla, 1908–1959* [Béla Kovács, 1908–1959]. Budapest: Occidental Press, 2002.

Papp, István. *A népi kollégiumi mozgalom története, 1944-ig* [The History of the Movement of Popular Boarding Schools until 1944]. Budapest: Napvilág, 2008.

Papp, László. *Tíz év és ami utána következett, 1945–1963. Adalékok a Magyarországi Református Egyház XX. századi történetéhez* [Ten Years and What Followed Afterwards 1945–1963. Contributions to the History of the Reformed Church in Hungary in the Twentieth Century]. Bern: Európai Protestáns Magyar Szabadegyetem, [1992].

Péteri, György, and János M. Rainer, eds. *Muddling Through in the Long 1960s. Ideas and Everyday Life in High Politics and the Lower Classes of Communist Hungary.* Trondheim: Norwegian University of Science and Technology, and Budapest: 1956-os Intézet, 2005.

Pető, Iván, and Sándor Szakács. *A hazai gazdaság négy évtizedének története. I. 1945–1968* [Four Decades of Domestic Economic History. Vol. I. 1945–1968]. Budapest: KjK, 1985.

Pfitzner, Rudolf, Kamil Kárpáti, Tibor Tollas and Bálint Tóth, eds. *Füveskert, 1954–1995* [Herb Garden, 1954–1995]. Budapest: Stádium, 1995.

Pünkösti, Árpád. *Rákosi bukása, száműzetése és halála* [The Fall, Exile and Death of Rákosi]. Budapest: Európa, 2001.

Rainer M., János. *Imre Nagy. The Leader and Martyr of the Hungarian Revolution of 1956.* Budapest: Atlanti Kutató és Kiadó, 2006.

Rainer M., János. *Az író helye. Viták a magyar irodalmi sajtóban, 1953–1956* [The Writer's Place. Debates in the Hungarian Literary Press, 1953–1956]. Budapest: Magvető, 1990.

Rainer M., János. *Nagy Imre, 1953–1958. Politikai életrajz* [Imre Nagy, 1953–1958. A Political Biography]. Vols. 1–2. Budapest: 1956-os Intézet, 1996–1999.

Rainer M., János, ed. *"Hatvanas évek" Magyarországon. Tanulmányok* ["The 1960s" in Hungary. Essays]. Budapest: 1956-os Intézet, 2004.

Rainer M., János. ed. *A monori tanácskozás 1985. június 14–16.* [The Monor Meeting, June 14–16, 1985]. Budapest: 1956-os Intézet, 2005.

Rainer M., János, and Magdolna Baráth, eds. *Gorbacsov tárgyalásai a magyar vezetőkkel. Dokumentumok az egykori SZKP és MSZMP archívumaiból* [Gorbachev's Negotiations with Hungarian Leaders. Documents from the Archives of the Former CPSU and HSWP]. Budapest: 1956-os Intézet, 2000.

Rajk László és társai a népbíróság előtt [László Rajk and His Associates in Front of the People's Court]. (Reprint) Budapest: Magyar Eszperantó Szövetség, 1989.

Rákosi, Mátyás. *Válogatott beszédek és cikkek* [Selected Speeches and Articles]. Budapest: Szikra, 1955.

Rákosi, Mátyás. *Visszaemlékezések, 1945–1960* [Memories, 1945–1960]. Vols. 1–2. Budapest: Napvilág, 1997.

Reisz, László. *Gazdasági és társadalmi koncepciók a politikai propagandában 1962–1980* [Economic and Social Concepts in Political Propaganda 1962–1980]. Budapest: KSH, 1988.
Romsics, Ignác. *Az 1947-es párizsi békeszerződés* [The Paris Peace Agreement of 1947]. Budapest: Osiris, 2006.
Romsics, Ignác. *From Dictatorship to Democracy. The Birth of the Third Hungarian Republic 1988–2001.* Highland Lakes, NJ: ARP, 2007.
Romsics, Ignác. *Hungary in the Twentieth Century.* Budapest: Corvina – Osiris, 1999.
Romsics, Ignác. *Magyarország története a XX. században* [History of Hungary in the 20th Century]. Budapest: Osiris, 1999.
Romsics, Ignác. *Volt egyszer egy rendszerváltás* [Once Upon a Time There Was a System Change]. Budapest: Rubicon, 2003.
Romsics, Ignác, ed. *Amerikai béketervek a háború utáni Magyarországról. Az Egyesült Államok Külügyminisztériumának titkos iratai, 1942–1944* [American Peace Plans for Hungary after the War. The Secret Documents of the United States' Department of State, 1942–1944]. Gödöllő: Typovent, 1992.
Romsics, Ignác, ed. *Magyar történeti szöveggyűjtemény, 1914–1999* [Hungarian Historical Documents, 1914–1999]. Vols. 1–2. Budapest: Osiris, 2000.
Romsics, Ignác, ed. *Magyarország és a nagyhatalmak a XX. században* [Hungary and the Great Powers in the 20th Century]. Budapest: Teleki László Alapítvány, 1995.
S. Nagy, Katalin. *Lakberendezési szokások* [Interior Design Practices]. Budapest: Magvető, 1987.
Saád, József, ed. *Telepessors* [The Fate of the Villagers]. Budapest: Gondolat, 2005.
Srágli, Lajos. *A MAORT* [The Hungarian–American Oil Industry Company]. Budapest: Útmutató, 1998.
Standeisky, Éva. *Gúzsba kötve. A kulturális elit és a hatalom* [Hamstrung. The Cultural Elite and the Political Power]. Budapest: 1956-os Intézet, 2005.

Standeisky, Éva. *Az írók és a hatalom 1956–1963* [Writers and the Regime 1956–1963]. Budapest: 1956-os Intézet, 1996.

Standeisky, Éva, ed. *Írók lázadása. 1956-os írószövetségi jegyzőkönyvek* [The Writers' Rebellion. Minutes of the 1956 Meetings of the Writers' Union]. Budapest: MTA Irodalomtudományi Intézete, 1990.

Standeisky, Éva, Gyula Kozák, Gábor Pataki and János M. Rainer, eds. *A fordulat évei, 1947–1949* [The Decisive Years, 1947–1949]. Budapest: 1956-os Intézet, 1988.

Standeisky, Éva, and János M. Rainer, eds., *Magyarország a jelenkorban. Évkönyv, 1999* [Hungary in Contemporary Times. Yearbook, 1999]. Budapest: 1956-os Intézet, 2000.

Sz. Varga, Lajos. *Szakszervezetek a diktatúrában, 1948–1953* [Labor Unions under the Dictatorship, 1948–1953]. Pécs, 1995. (Published by the author.)

Szabó, Bálint. *Az "ötvenes évek"* [The "Fifties"]. Budapest: Kossuth, 1986.

Szabó, Bálint, ed. *A szocializmus útján. A népi demokratikus átalakulás és a szocializmus építésének kronológiája, 1944–1980* [On the Path towards Socialism. Chronology of the People's Democratic Transformation and the Building of Socialism, 1944–1980]. Budapest: Akadémiai Kiadó, 1982.

Szabó, Csaba. *A Grősz-per előkészítése, 1951* [The Preparations for the Grősz Trial, 1951]. Budapest: Osiris, 2001.

Szabó, Csaba, ed. *Egyházügyi hangulatjelentések, 1951–1953* [Reports on the Mood of the Churches, 1951–1953]. Budapest: Osiris, 2000.

Szabó, Máté, and Dominique Wisler, eds. *Tüntetés, rendőrség, demokrácia* [Protests, Police, Democracy]. Budapest: Villányi úti könyvek, 1999.

Szakács, Sándor. *A népi demokratikus agrárfejlődés kezdetei Magyarországon, 1945–1948* [The Beginnings of the People's Democratic Agricultural Development in Hungary, 1945–1948]. Budapest: Akadémiai, 1971.

Szakolczai, Attila. *Az 1956-os forradalom és szabadságharc* [The 1956 Revolution and Fight for Freedom]. Budapest: 1956-os Intézet. 2001.

Szakolczai, Attila, ed., *A vidék forradalma, 1956* [The Revolution in the Countryside, 1956]. Vol. 2. Budapest: 1956-os Intézet – Budapest Fővárosi Levéltára, 2006.

Szakolczai, Attila, and László Á. Varga, eds., *A vidék forradalma, 1956* [The Revolution in the Countryside, 1956]. Vol. 1. Budapest: 1956-os Intézet – Budapest Főváros Levéltára, 2003.

Szalai, Júlia, ed. *Arat a magyar* [The Hungarian Reaps]. Budapest: MTA Szociológiai Kutató Intézete, 1988.

Szalay, Hanna, ed. *Napról napra. 1956 sajtója, október 23. – november 4.* [Day by Day. The Press in 1956, October 23 to November 4]. Budapest: Magyar Krónika, 1989.

Szamuely, László, ed. *A magyar közgazdasági gondolat fejlődése 1954–1978* [Development of Hungarian Economic Thought 1954–1978]. Budapest: KjK, 1986.

Szántó, János. *Vallásosság egy szekularizált társadalomban* [Religious Faith in a Secularized Society]. Budapest: Új Mandátum, 1997.

Szász, Béla. *Minden kényszer nélkül* [Without Any Compulsion]. Budapest: Európa – História, 1989.

Szemerkényi, Ágnes, ed. *Nógrádsipek – tanulmányok egy észak-magyarországi falu folklórjáról* [Nógrádsipek—Studies on the Folklore of a Village in Northern Hungary]. Budapest: Akadémiai, 1980.

Szereda, Vjacseszlav, and Alexandr Sztikalin, eds. *Hiányzó lapok 1956 történetéből. Dokumentumok a volt SZKP KB levéltárából* [Missing Pages from the History of 1956. Documents from the Former Archives of the CPSU Central Committee]. Budapest: Móra, 1993.

Szűcs, László, ed. *Nagy Ferenc első kormányának minisztertanácsi jegyzőkönyvei, 1946. február – november* [The Minutes of the Meetings of Ferenc Nagy's First Government's Council of Ministers, February to November 1946]. Vols. 1–2. Budapest: MOL, 2003.

Tabajdi, Gábor, and Krisztián Ungváry. *Elhallgatott múlt. A pártállam és a belügy. A politikai rendőrség működése*

Magyarországon 1956–1990 [Concealed Past. The Party State and Internal Affairs. The Operations of the Political Police in Hungary 1956–1990]. Budapest: Corvina – 1956-os Intézet, 2008.

Tőkés, Rudolf L. *Hungary's Negotiated Revolution. Economic Reform, Social Change and Political Succession, 1957–1990.* London: Cambridge University Press, 1996.

Tollas, Tibor, ed. *Gloria victis.* Vienna and Munich: Nemzetőr, 1986.

Valuch, Tibor. *Magyarország társadalomtörténete a XX. század második felében* [The Social History of Hungary in the Second Half of the 20th Century]. Budapest: Osiris, 2001.

Valuch, Tibor. *"Ötvenhatosok"* ["56ers"]. Debrecen: Civis, 1996.

Vida, István. *Az állami politikai vezetőréteg összetétele az 1980-as évek elején* [The Composition of the State Political Leadership Stratum at the Beginning of the 1980s]. Budapest: MTA TTI, 1992.

Vida, István, ed. *1956 és a politikai pártok. 1956. október 23.–november* [1956 and the Political Parties. October 23–November 1956]. Budapest: MTA, 1998.

Vida, István, ed. *Diák és ifjúsági mozgalmak, 1956–1958. Forradalom – ellenállás – megtorlás* [Student and Youth Movements, 1956–1958. Revolution – Resistance – Retribution]. Budapest: Gondolat – Nagy Imre Alapítvány, 2007.

Vonyó, József, ed., *Az ötvenes évek Magyarországa játékfilmeken* [Hungary during the Fifties in Film]. Pécs: Asoka Bt., 2004.

Zafir, Mihály, ed. *Életszínvonal 1960–1980* [Standard of Living 1960–1980]. Budapest: KSH, 1981.

Zimándi, Pius. *A forradalom éve. Krónika 1956-ról* [The Year of the Revolution. A Chronicle of 1956]. Budapest: Századvég – 1956-os Intézet, 1992.

THE AUTHORS

GYÖRGY GYARMATI (b. 1951)

He graduated (history and geography) from the Lajos Kossuth University of Debrecen in 1976. In 1981, he defended his doctoral thesis. He became an academic candidate in 1996 and he received his habilitation in 2002. He worked at the Institute of History of the Hungarian Academy of Sciences from 1976 until 1990, when he became a professor at the Faculty of Law and Political Sciences at Loránd Eötvös University (Budapest). He has been working at the Historical Archives of Hungarian State Security since 1997. Between 1997 and 2003, he also held the position of Academic Department Director. He has been the Director-General since 2003. In 1977, he also became involved in university education, teaching courses at Loránd Eötvös University's Faculty of Law and Political Sciences until 2002. In 1990, he became professor of the Institute for History of the Faculty of Arts at the University of Pécs. His current status is Habilitated Associate Professor. His major field of research is the Hungarian political and social history of the twentieth century. He has authored and edited several books, including *A politika rendőrsége Magyarországon a Rákosi-korszakban. Die Polizei der Politik in der Rákosi-Ära in Ungarn* (2002).

TIBOR VALUCH (b. 1963)

He got his university degree as a secondary school teacher of history and geography at Lajos Kossuth University, Debrecen. He has been working as a senior research fellow at the Institute for the History of 1956, the Hungarian Academy of Sciences.

He is an associate professor at the Department of Historical Sociology, Loránd Eötvös University, Budapest. His main fields of research are the contemporary history of Hungary and the Hungarian social and cultural history of the period after World War II. He has also authored and edited several books, including: *A Cultural History of Hungary* (1998, Co-author) and *Social History of Hungary from the Reform Era to the End of the Twentieth Century* (2004, Co-author).

Name Index

Place Index

All places are located in present-day Hungary unless otherwise stated.
A – Austria, AU – Australia, B – Bulgaria, C – Croatia, CD – Canada, CH – China, CR – Czech Republic, E – Egypt, F – France, FL – Finnland, G – Germany, GB – Great Britain, I – Italy, IL – Israel, P – Poland, R – Romania, RU – Russia, S – Serbia, SK – Slovakia, SL – Slovenia, SP – Spain, SW – Switzerland, U – Ukraine, USA – United States of America

Volumes Published in "Atlantic Studies on Society in Change"

No. 1* T 1	*Tolerance and Movements of Religious Dissent in Eastern Europe*. Edited by Béla K. Király. 1977.
No. 2	*The Habsburg Empire in World War I*. Edited by R. A. Kann. 1978.
No. 3 T 2	*The Mutual Effects of the Islamic and Judeo-Christian Worlds: The East European Pattern*. Edited by A. Ascher, T. Halasi-Kun and B. K. Király. 1979.
No. 4	*Before Watergate: Problems of Corruption in American Society*. Edited by A. S. Eisenstadt, A. Hoogenboom, H. L. Trefousse. 1979.
No. 5	*East Central European Perceptions of Early America*. Edited by B. K. Király and G. Barány. 1977.
No. 6	*The Hungarian Revolution of 1956 in Retrospect*. Edited by B. K. Király and Paul Jonas. 1978.
No. 7	*Brooklyn U.S.A.: Fourth Largest City in America*. Edited by Rita S. Miller. 1979.
No. 8	*Prime Minister Gyula Andrássy's Influence on Habsburg Foreign Policy*. János Decsy. 1979.
No. 9	*The Great Impeacher: A Political Biography of James M. Ashley*. Robert F. Horowitz. 1979.
No. 10 W I**	*Special Topics and Generalizations on the Eighteenth and Nineteenth Century*. Edited by Béla K. Király and Gunther E. Rothenberg. 1979.
No. 11 W II	*East Central European Society and War in the Pre-Revolutionary 18th Century*. Edited by Gunther E. Rothenberg, Béla K. Király and Peter F. Sugar. 1982.
No. 12 W III	*From Hunyadi to Rákóczi: War and Society in Late Medieval and Early Modern Hungary*. Edited by János M. Bak and Béla K. Király. 1982.

* Vols. T 1 through 17 refer to the series *Tolerance and Discrimination in the Danubian Region*

** Vols. W I through XLI refer to the series *War and Society in East Central Europe*

No. 13 W IV — *East Central European Society and War in the Era of Revolutions: 1775-1856.* Edited by B. K. Király. 1984.

No. 14 W V — *Essays on World War I: Origins and Prisoners of War.* Edited by Samuel R. Williamson, Jr., and Peter Pastor. 1983.

No. 15 W VI — *Essays on World War I: Total War and Peacemaking, A Case Study on Trianon.* Edited by B. K. Király, Peter Pastor and Ivan Sanders. 1982.

No. 16 W VII — *Army, Aristocracy, Monarchy: War, Society and Government in Austria, 1618-1780.* Edited by Thomas M. Barker. 1982.

No. 17 W VIII — *The First Serbian Uprising 1804-1813.* Edited by Wayne S. Vucinich. 1982.

No. 18 W IX, T 3 — *Czechoslovak Policy and the Hungarian Minority 1945-1948. Kálmán Janics.* Edited by Stephen Borsody. 1982.

No. 19 W X — *At the Brink of War and Peace: The Tito-Stalin Split in a Historic Perspective.* Edited by Wayne S. Vucinich. 1982.

No. 20 — *Inflation Through the Ages: Economic, Social, Psychological and Historical Aspects.* Edited by Edward Marcus and Nathan Schmuckler. 1981.

No. 21 — *Germany and America: Essays on Problems of International Relations and Immigration.* Edited by Hans L. Trefousse. 1980.

No. 22 — *Brooklyn College: The First Half Century.* Murray M. Horowitz. 1981.

No. 23 — *A New Deal for the World: Eleanor Roosevelt and American Foreign Policy.* Jason Berger. 1981.

No. 24 T 4 — *The Legacy of Jewish Migration: 1881 and Its Impact.* Edited by David Berger. 1982.

No. 25 — *The Road to Bellapais: Cypriot Exodus to Northern Cyprus.* Pierre Oberling. 1982.

No. 26 — *New Hungarian Peasants: An East Central European Experience with Collectivization.* Edited by Marida Hollos and Béla C. Maday. 1983.

No. 27 — *Germans in America: Aspects of German-American Relations in the Nineteenth Century.* Edited by Allen McCormick. 1983.

No. 28 — *A Question of Empire: Leopold I and the War of Spanish Succession, 1701-1705.* Linda and Marsha Frey. 1983.

No. 29 *The Beginning of Cyrillic Printing—Cracow, 1491. From the Orthodox Past in Poland. Szczepan K. Zimmer.* Edited by Ludwik Krzyżanowski and Irene Nagurski. 1983.

No. 29a *A Grand Ecole for the Grand Corps: The Recruitment and Training of the French Administration.* Thomas R. Osborne. 1983.

No. 30 W XI *The First War between Socialist States: The Hungarian Revolution of 1956 and Its Impact.* Edited by Béla K. Király, Barbara Lotze, Nandor Dreisziger. 1984.

No. 31 W XII *The Effects of World War I, The Uprooted: Hungarian Refugees and Their Impact on Hungary's Domestic Politics.* István Mócsy. 1983.

No. 32 W XIII *The Effects of World War I: The Class War after the Great War: The Rise of Communist Parties in East Central Europe, 1918-1921.* Edited by Ivo Banac. 1983.

No. 33 W XIV *The Crucial Decade: East Central European Society and National Defense, 1859-1870.* Edited by Béla K. Király. 1984.

No. 35 W XVI *Effects of World War I: War Communism in Hungary, 1919.* György Péteri. 1984.

No. 36 W XVII *Insurrections, Wars, and the Eastern Crisis in the 1870s.* Edited by B. K. Király and Gale Stokes. 1985.

No. 37 W XVIII *East Central European Society and the Balkan Wars, 1912-1913.* Edited by B. K. Király and Dimitrije Djordjevic. 1986.

No. 38 W XIX *East Central European Society in World War I.* Edited by B. K. Király and N. F. Dreisziger, Assistant Editor Albert A. Nofi. 1985.

No. 39 W XX *Revolutions and Interventions in Hungary and Its Neighbor States, 1918-1919.* Edited by Peter Pastor. 1988.

No. 41 W XXII *Essays on East Central European Society and War, 1740-1920.* Edited by Stephen Fischer-Galati and Béla K. Király. 1988.

No. 42 W XXIII *East Central European Maritime Commerce and Naval Policies, 1789-1913.* Edited by Apostolos E. Vacalopoulos, Constantinos D. Svolopoulos and Béla K. Király. 1988.

No. 43 W XXIV *Selections, Social Origins, Education and Training of East Central European Officers Corps.* Edited by Béla K. Király and Walter Scott Dillard. 1988.

No. 44 W XXV *East Central European War Leaders: Civilian and Military.* Edited by Béla K. Király and Albert Nofi. 1988.

No. 46 *Germany's International Monetary Policy and the European Monetary System.* Hugo Kaufmann. 1985.

No. 47 *Iran Since the Revolution—Internal Dynamics, Regional Conflicts and the Superpowers.* Edited by Barry M. Rosen. 1985.

No. 48 W XXVII *The Press During the Hungarian Revolution of 1848-1849.* Domokos Kosáry. 1986.

No. 49 *The Spanish Inquisition and the Inquisitional Mind.* Edited by Angel Alcala. 1987.

No. 50 *Catholics, the State and the European Radical Right, 1919-1945.* Edited by Richard Wolff and Jorg K. Hoensch. 1987.

No. 51 W XXVIII *The Boer War and Military Reforms.* Jay Stone and Erwin A. Schmidl. 1987.

No. 52 *Baron Joseph Eötvös, A Literary Biography.* Steven B. Várdy. 1987.

No. 53 *Towards the Renaissance of Puerto Rican Studies: Ethnic and Area Studies in University Education.* Maria Sanchez and Antonio M. Stevens. 1987.

No. 54 *The Brazilian Diamonds in Contracts, Contraband and Capital.* Harry Bernstein. 1987.

No. 55 T 5 *Christians, Jews and Other Worlds: Patterns of Conflict and Accommodation.* Edited by Philip F. Gallagher. 1988.

No. 56 W XXVI *The Fall of the Medieval Kingdom of Hungary: Mohács 1526, Buda 1541.* Géza Perjés. 1989.

No. 57 *The Lord Mayor of Lisbon: The Portuguese Tribune of the People and His 24 Guilds.* Harry Bernstein. 1989.

No. 58 *Hungarian Statesmen of Destiny: 1860-1960.* Edited by Paul Bödy. 1989.

No. 59 *For China: The Memoirs of T. G. Li, Former Major General in the Chinese Nationalist Army.* T. G. Li. Written in collaboration with Roman Rome. 1989.

No. 60 *Politics in Hungary: For A Democratic Alternative.* János Kis, with an Introduction by Timothy Garton Ash. 1989.

No. 61 *Hungarian Worker's Councils in 1956.* Edited by Bill Lomax. 1990.

No. 95 W XXXVI	*Through the Prism of the Habsburg Monarchy: Hungary in American Diplomacy and Public Opinion during World War I.* Tibor Glant. 1998.
No. 96	*Appeal of Sovereignty in Hungary, Austria and Russia.* Edited by Csaba Gombár, Elemér Hankiss, László Lengyel and Györgyi Várnai. 1997.
No. 97 T 11	*Geopolitics in the Danube Region. Hungarian Reconciliation Efforts, 1848-1998.* Edited by Ignác Romsics and Béla K. Király. 1998.
No. 98	*Hungarian Agrarian Society from the Emancipation of Serfs (1848) to Re-privatization of Land (1998).* Edited by Péter Gunst. 1999.
No. 99 T 12	*"The Jewish Question" in Europe. The Case of Hungary.* Tamás Ungvári. 2000.
No. 100	*Soviet Military Intervention in Hungary, 1956.* Edited by Jenő Györkei and Miklós Horváth. 1999.
No. 101, T 13	*Jewish Budapest.* Edited by Géza Komoróczy. 1999.
No. 102	*Evolution of Hungarian Economy, 1848-1998. Vol. I. One and a Half Centuries of Semi-Successful Modernization, 1848-1989.* Edited by Iván T. Berend and Tamás Csató. 2001.
No. 103	*Evolution of Hungarian Economy, 1848-1998. Vol. II. Paying the Bill for Goulash-Communism.* János Kornai. 2000.
No. 104	*Evolution of Hungarian Economy, 1848-2000. Vol. III. Hungary: from Transition to Integration.* Edited by György Csáki and Gábor Karsai. 2002.
No. 105	*From Habsburg Agent to Victorian Scholar: G. G. Zerffi (1820-1892).* Tibor Frank. 2000.
No. 106	*A History of Transylvania from the Beginning to 1919. Vol. I.* Edited by Zoltán Szász and Béla Köpeczi. 2000.
No. 107	*A History of Transylvania from the Beginning to 1919. Vol. II.* Edited by Zoltán Szász and Béla Köpeczi. 2002.
No. 108	*A History of Transylvania from the Beginning to 1919. Vol. III.* Edited by Zoltán Szász and Béla Köpeczi. 2002.
No. 109	*Hungary: Governments and Politics, 1848–2000.* Edited by Mária Ormos and Béla K. Király. 2001.
No. 110 T 14	*Hungarians in the Voivodina, 1918–1947.* Enikő A. Sajti. 2003.

No. 111 *Hungarian Arts and Sciences, 1848–2000.* (Hungarian Nobel prize winners, innovators, film makers, Olympic champions, etc.) Edited by László Somlyódy and Nóra Somlyódy. 2003.

No. 112 *Hungary and International Politics in 1848–1849.* Domokos Kosáry. 2003.

No. 113 *Social History of Hungary from the Reform Era to the End of the Twentieth Century.* Edited by Gábor Gyáni, György Kövér and Tibor Valuch. 2004.

No. 114 *A Millennium of Hungarian Military History.* Edited by
W XXXVII László Veszprémy and Béla K. Király. 2002.

No. 115 *Hungarian Relics. A History of the War Banners of the Hungarian Revolution and War of Independence, 1848-49.* Jenő Györkei and Györgyi Cs. Kottra. 2000.

No. 116 *From Totalitarian to Democratic Hungary. Evolution and Transformation, 1990-2000.* Edited by Mária Schmidt and László Gy. Tóth. 2001.

No. 117 *A History of Eastern Europe since the Middle Ages.* Emil Niederhauser. 2003.

No. 118 *The Ideas of the Hungarian Revolution, Suppressed and Victorious, 1956–1999.* Edited by Lee W. Congdon and Béla K. Király. 2002.

No. 119 *The Emancipation of the Serfs in East and East-Central Europe.* Emil Niederhauser. 2004.

No. 120 *Béla K. Király: Art of Survival. Hungarian National Defense and Society in Modern Times.* Edited by Piroska Balogh and Tamás Vitek. 2003.

No. 121 *Army and Politics in Hungary, 1938–1944.* Lóránd
W XXXVIII Dombrády. Edited by Gyula Rázsó. 2005.

No. 122 *Hungary and the Hungarian Minorities (Trends in the Past*
T 15 *and in Our Time).* Edited by László Szarka. 2004.

No. 123, T 16 *Roma of Hungary.* Edited by István Kemény. 2005.

No. 124 *National and Ethnic Minorities in Hungary, 1920–2001.*
T 17 Edited by Ágnes Tóth. 2005.

No. 126 *The Occupation of Bosnia and Herzegovina in 1878.* László
W XXXIX Bencze. 2005.

No. 127	*Wars, Revolutions and Regime Changes in Hungary, 1912–2004. Reminiscences of an Eyewitness.* Béla K. Király. Edited by Piroska Balogh, Andrea T. Kulcsár and Tamás Vitek. 2005.
No. 128 W XL	*1956: The Hungarian Revolution and War for Independence.* Edited by Lee W. Congdon, Béla K. Király and Károly Nagy. 2006.
No. 129 W XLI	*The History of the Hungarian Military Higher Education, 1947–1956.* Miklós M. Szabó. 2006.
No. 130	*Reform and Revolution, 1830–1848.* András Gergely. 2009.
No. 131	*From Habsburg Neo-Absolutism to the Compromise, 1849–1867.* Ágnes Deák. 2008.
No. 132	*Hungary in the Dual Monarchy, 1867–1914.* László Katus. 2008.
No. 133	*Hungary in the Age of the Two World Wars, 1914–1945.* Mária Ormos. 2007.
No. 134	*Hungary under Soviet Domination, 1944–1989.* György Gyarmati and Tibor Valuch. 2009.
No. 135	*From Dictatorship to Democracy. The Birth of the Third Hungarian Republic, 1988–2001.* Ignác Romsics. 2007.